EVER CLOSER UNION

THIRD EDITION

EVER CLOSER UNION

An Introduction to European Integration

Desmond Dinan

LYNNE
RIENNER
PUBLISHERS

BOULDER
LONDON

Published in the United States of America in 2005 by
Lynne Rienner Publishers, Inc.
1800 30th Street, Boulder, Colorado 80301
www.rienner.com

Library of Congress Cataloging-in-Publication Data
Dinan, Desmond, 1957–
    Ever closer union : an introduction to European integration / by Desmond Dinan.— 3rd ed.
        p. cm.
    Includes bibliographical references and index.
    ISBN 1-58826-234-0 (alk. paper) — ISBN 1-58826-208-1 (pbk. : alk. paper)
    1. European Economic Community.   2. European federation.   I. Title.
    HC241.2.D476 2005
    337.1'42—dc22

                                                           2005010768

Printed and bound in the United States of America

The paper used in this publication meets the requirements
of the American National Standard for Permanence of
Paper for Printed Library Materials Z39.48-1992.

    5 4 3 2 1

To Wendy
and the kids—Conor, Cian, and Cliona—
in Ottawa

Contents

Illustrations

Preface

W ill the European Union forever be in flux? I often asked myself that question as I prepared this new edition of *Ever Closer Union.*

Even as this book goes to press, member states are grappling with the process of ratifying the constitutional treaty, a major step forward politically for the EU. The French and Dutch rejections of the treaty, in referendums in spring 2005, as well as the UK decision to postpone a vote, make it unlikely that the treaty will be accepted in its present form. Certainly the EU will continue to muddle through on the basis of existing treaties; nevertheless, the failure of two of its founding member states to ratify the new treaty raises serious questions about public alienation from the EU and prospects for further political integration.

Despite the ratification setbacks, the Convention on the Future of Europe and the intergovernmental conference that paved the way for the constitutional treaty were important undertakings in the history of the EU. Accordingly, they are covered in Part 1 of this book. Moreover, the treaty portends institutional and policy changes that will probably come to pass in the not-too-distant future, even though the current round of ratification has not been successful. Regardless of the outcome of the entire ratification process, it seemed reasonable to incorporate the treaty's provisions into Parts 2 (institutions) and 3 (policies).

Although this is a big book, it does not include every policy area or noteworthy EU event. Nevertheless, it seeks to provide comprehensive coverage of the EU for students and others interested in learning about the process of European integration, one of the most interesting and important developments—not only regionally but also globally—since the end of World War II. Readers wanting to supplement or update their knowledge of the EU might like to use *Europa,* the EU's official website (www.europa.eu.int), from which I drew heavily while writing this new edition. *Europa* contains a wealth of summaries, speeches, and other documents on every aspect of the EU. Although difficult to navigate, it is well worth a visit.

—Desmond Dinan

The European Union, 2004

Introduction

A first-time visitor to Europe would soon realize that something called the European Union (EU) exists but might not understand exactly what it is. Signs at the airport in an EU member state (by far the majority of European states) would direct the visitor into the "Non-EU" line for inspection by national immigration officers (there are no EU immigration officers). Once finished with border formalities, the visitor would need to change money. In twelve of the EU's twenty-five member states the visitor would receive euro notes and coins but in the other member states would receive national currency.

Traveling around the country, the visitor would see the distinctive EU flag (a circle of twelve gold stars set against a deep blue background) prominently displayed. In the EU's poorer regions, the visitor would notice signs adorned with the EU flag, proudly proclaiming that various infrastructural projects were being funded in part by the EU. Staying within the territory of the EU, the visitor would be able to travel unimpeded across some, but not all, national borders.

A curious and discerning visitor would discover that national political systems are alive and well in the EU, but that there is a complementary political system centered on Brussels, meaning in this case not the political capital of Belgium but the locus of EU policymaking. National governments, parliaments, courts, and other bodies participate in the EU system, as do separate EU institutions such as the European Commission and the European Parliament. Further inquiry would reveal that a complex system of EU governance produces rules and regulations covering a host of policy areas ranging from agriculture to antitrust, the environment, immigration, and international development. The visitor would soon realize that there is considerable variation in the applicability and implementation of EU policy among the member states.

Why, the visitor might ask, does such an elaborate system exist? The answer, quite simply, is that it developed in response to national governments' efforts to increase their countries' security and economic well-being in an increasingly interdependent and competitive global environment. Europe has a history of instability and war; tying countries together politically and economically is a way to consolidate democracy and resolve the traditional causes of conflict. No European country is bigger than a midsized global power; close political and economic collaboration helps European countries maximize their global influence and potential. As Wim Kok, a former prime minister of the Netherlands, put it in a recent report on the state of the European economy, "The principle underpinning the European Union is well established: Europeans better hang together or [most assuredly] they will hang separately."[1]

Six countries (France, Germany, Italy, Belgium, the Netherlands, and Luxembourg) therefore came together and signed a treaty in 1951 to establish the European Coal and Steel Community and another treaty in 1957 to establish the European Economic Community. The Coal and Steel Community had a narrow economic focus but an ambitious political goal: to achieve a peace settlement primarily between France and Germany. The treaty establishing the European Economic Community was more ambitious in its economic objectives but no less significant politically. It sought to establish a common or single market in which goods, capital, services, and people could move freely within the European Community (as the European Economic Community came to be called). It also envisioned an "ever closer union" among the states and peoples of the European Community (hence the title of this book).

In order to go beyond a customs union and take the steps necessary to eradicate nontariff, behind-the-border barriers to the free movement of capital, services, and people, member states agreed to share sovereignty or national authority in certain policy areas. Only by doing so could they lock themselves into a long-term process of market integration based on treaty obligations, shared sovereignty, and the rule of a new form of international law. Governments were not enthusiastic about sharing sovereignty but appreciated that it was in their national interests to do so. Far from handing over authority in certain policy areas unreservedly to the supranational European Commission, they retained considerable national control through the Council of Ministers, a key EU decisionmaking body. They also agreed to establish a parliament to enhance the democratic legitimacy of the Community.

Tension between intergovernmentalism (traditional state-to-state relations) and supranationality (the sharing of national sovereignty) has pervaded the EU since the beginning. Yet intergovernmentalism and supranationality are not irreconcilable; they complement rather than conflict with each other in the day-to-day operations of the EU. Nor has the relationship between intergovernmentalism and supranationality remained static over time. The Commission has acquired additional supranational authority through the years, but its influence in the EU system has waxed and waned (currently it is waning).

In most policy areas government ministers are willing to be outvoted in the Council, but EU legislation is rarely enacted in the face of strong national reservations, especially on the part of big member states. The European Council, a distinct entity consisting of national leaders and the Commission president, is the most powerful body in the EU today. The European Parliament is more and more influential, yet its members are motivated by national as well as supranational considerations.

The membership and the policy scope of the EU have increased dramatically since the 1950s due to changing political and economic circumstances in Europe and beyond (Table 0.1). Sometimes the increase in policy scope has been incremental; at other times member states negotiated treaty changes in order to revitalize European integration or extend the remit of the EU into new policy areas. Whenever they changed the treaties to broaden the policy scope of the EU, member states also altered the EU's institutional arrangements in an effort to improve efficiency and democratic legitimacy (two objectives that are often difficult to reconcile).

Clearly, "deepening" (in functional terms) and "widening" (in membership) are not contradictory processes. Sometimes deepening has attracted new

Table 0.1   The Ever Deeper Union

1951	Treaty of Paris establishes the European Coal and Steel Community
1957	Treaties of Rome establish the European Economic Community and the European Atomic Energy Community
1962	Launch of the Common Agricultural Policy
1968	Completion of the customs union
1970	Launch of European Political Cooperation (foreign policy coordination)
1975	Launch of the European Council
1979	Launch of the European Monetary System
1986	The Single European Act launches the single-market program and extends Community competence in the fields of environmental policy, economic and social cohesion, research and technology policy, and social policy
1989	Extension of Commission responsibility for competition policy
1992	The Treaty on European Union sets the EU on the road to economic and monetary union, transforms European Political Cooperation into the Common Foreign and Security Policy, and launches intergovernmental cooperation on justice and home affairs
1997	The Treaty of Amsterdam extends Community competence over certain aspects of justice and home affairs and sets a target date for completion of "an area of freedom, security, and justice"
1999	Launch of a common monetary policy and a single currency (the euro)
2001	The Nice Treaty reforms the EU's institutions and decisionmaking procedures
2002	The Convention on the Future of Europe begins
2003	The Convention submits a draft Constitutional Treaty
2004	EU leaders agree on and later sign the Constitutional Treaty

members; for example, completion of the single market in the late 1980s and early 1990s had a powerful magnetic effect on Austria, Finland, Norway, Sweden, and Switzerland, which applied to join the EU (three of them eventually did so). Sometimes impending enlargement has impelled the EU to deepen; for example, the imminent accession of the Central and Eastern European countries in the early 2000s spurred member states to intensify integration in the area of justice and home affairs (immigration and internal security).

Between 1973 and 2004 the EU grew from six to twenty-five member states (Table 0.2). Not all of the new entrants shared the founding member states' commitment to political integration. Some, like Denmark, Britain, and Sweden, were openly skeptical of political integration and averse to sharing more than the minimum amount of sovereignty necessary to achieve common economic goals. The accession of so many new member states, with so many more interests, perspectives, and preferences, further complicated the process of European integration. It also brought more policy differentiation to the EU, one of the most striking examples being the decisions by Denmark, Britain, and Sweden not to adopt the euro.

Major treaty changes in the history of the EU, such as the Single European Act of 1986 or the Maastricht Treaty of 1992, encapsulate the symbiotic nature of deepening and widening. This is especially true of the Constitutional Treaty, signed by national leaders in October 2004. The Constitutional Treaty originated in a desire to enhance the legitimacy and efficacy of the EU, not least because of the imminent accession of at least ten new member states. The Constitutional Treaty is not the last word in treaty reform, but it streamlines the EU's existing treaties and "pillar" structure (see Box 0.1), improves decisionmaking procedures, and emphasizes the EU's political character.

The EU has now reached the point where it touches upon almost every aspect of public policy and includes almost every European country. Iceland,

Table 0.2   The Ever Wider Union

Original Member States (1958)	First Enlargement (1973)	Second Enlargement (1981)	Third Enlargement (1986)	Fourth Enlargement (1995)	Fifth Enlargement (2004)
Belgium	Britain	Greece	Spain	Austria	Czech Republic
France	Denmark		Portugal	Finland	Cyprus
Germany	Ireland			Sweden	Estonia
Italy					Hungary
Luxembourg					Latvia
Netherlands					Lithuania
					Malta
					Poland
					Slovakia
					Slovenia

Box 0.1   The EU's Treaties and "Pillars"

The EU rests on two treaties and three pillars.
The two treaties are:
Treaty Establishing the European Community: This is the original Rome
    Treaty, amended by the Single European Act (1986), Maastricht Treaty
    (1991), Amsterdam Treaty (1997), and Nice Treaty (2001).
Treaty on European Union: This is the original Maastricht Treaty (1991),
    amended by the Amsterdam Treaty (1997) and Nice Treaty (2001).
The three pillars are:
First Pillar: the European Community (covering most of the policy areas en-
    compassed by the EU)
Second Pillar: the Common Foreign and Security Policy, including the Euro-
    pean Security and Defense Policy
Third Pillar: police and judicial cooperation

   Decisionmaking in the first pillar is supranational (it involves all of the
EU's institutions); decisionmaking in the other two pillars is intergovernmental (national governments are mostly in control). The *Constitutional Treaty* replaces the two treaties and the three pillars with a single legal and institutional
arrangement.

Norway, and Switzerland are the only unequivocally European countries that
are neither members nor aspiring members of the EU. The use of the adjective "unequivocally" in the previous sentence points to one of the greatest difficulties facing the EU today: the difficulty of defining which countries on the
EU's eastern borders are "European" and therefore eligible to join the EU
(presuming that they meet the political and economic criteria for membership). The EU has accepted Turkey's "Europeanness," despite widespread
concerns in many of the existing member states about the cultural as well as
economic impact of Turkey's membership. But the fundamental question remains: Where do the geographical limits of the EU lie?

   The all-encompassing nature of the EU poses a formidable hurdle for
prospective member states. Indeed, the so-called chapters that applicant states
must now negotiate in order to join the EU give a good idea of the EU's extensive policy remit (see Table 0.3).

   Despite (or perhaps because of) the relatively rapid increase in its policy
and geographical scope, all is not well in the EU. Apart from concerns about
sluggish economic performance, international terrorism, and the assimilation
of ethnic minorities, and apart also from the usual complaints about politics
and politicians, Europeans are ill at ease with the EU. A few are outright hostile, wishing that their countries would leave or that the EU would cease to
exist. Others are "Euroskeptical" to some extent, meaning that they strongly
resent the perceived intrusion of the EU into what a British government minister described in the early 1990s as "every nook and cranny of daily life."[2]

Table 0.3   Joining the EU: What Needs to Be Negotiated

Chapter 1:	Free Movement of Goods
Chapter 2:	Free Movement for Persons
Chapter 3:	Freedom to Provide Services
Chapter 4:	Free Movement of Capital
Chapter 5:	Company Law
Chapter 6:	Competition Policy
Chapter 7:	Agriculture
Chapter 8:	Fisheries
Chapter 9:	Transport Policy
Chapter 10:	Taxation
Chapter 11:	Economic and Monetary Union
Chapter 12:	Statistics
Chapter 13:	Social Policy
Chapter 14:	Energy
Chapter 15:	Industrial Policy
Chapter 16:	Small and Medium-Sized Enterprises
Chapter 17:	Science and Research
Chapter 18:	Education and Training
Chapter 19:	Telecommunications and Information
Chapter 20:	Culture and Audiovisual Policy
Chapter 21:	Regional Policy and Coordination
Chapter 22:	Environment
Chapter 23:	Consumers and Health Protection
Chapter 24:	Justice and Home Affairs
Chapter 25:	Customs Union
Chapter 26:	External Relations
Chapter 27:	Common Foreign and Security Policy
Chapter 28:	Financial Control
Chapter 29:	Finance and Budgetary Provisions
Chapter 30:	Institutions
Chapter 31:	Other

For the most part, Europeans find the EU's political pretentiousness mildly irritating and would like the EU to deliver more (especially in terms of jobs, economic growth, internal security, and external stability) and pontificate less.

The EU is a complex political system, difficult even for interested Europeans to understand. It is both pervasive (in its impact) and remote (in its policymaking). There is a surfeit of information on the EU but a deficit of knowledge. EU leaders are keenly aware of the need to make a better connection between the EU's citizens and its institutions. People in the EU grumble about a democratic deficit, yet they turn out for direct elections to the European Parliament in record low numbers. They also complain about lack of transparency in Brussels, although EU politicians and officials have taken huge strides toward making the system more open and accessible.

The problem lies partly in the novelty and scale of European integration. People are familiar with their regional and national governments, which have been around forever (or so it seems). People in a national political system speak the same language, read the same newspapers, and see the same television programs. By contrast, the EU is distant, impersonal, and operates in twenty official languages; there is no European "people," only European "peoples"; there is no common language or media. But the problem also lies in the politics of European integration. National politicians like to take the credit when things are going well in the EU and blame "Brussels" when things are going badly.

Opinion polls constantly show that most Europeans appreciate the underlying advantages of European integration but are uneasy about certain EU policies and developments. Many Europeans either do not know or have forgotten how far Europe has come in the past fifty years. Regardless of the past or of people's understanding of it, some Europeans would argue that the EU has outlived its usefulness (if it ever had any). Without doubt, some EU policies and programs are dispensable or superfluous. However, European integration seems more essential than ever at a time of rapid globalization and widespread global uncertainty. The same yearning for security and economic well-being that animated the founders of the European Community underpins the EU today, though the regional and global circumstances are radically different (Box 0.2).

By now our visitor may have had heard enough about the EU. But someone so curious and discerning would surely want to learn more. What should our visitor do? Read this book, of course. It provides a thorough introduction to European integration, covering the history, institutions, and policies of the EU. It is comprehensive but not all-encompassing, focusing on key players, institutions, and policies. For reasons of space the book does not examine every EU policy area, but it mentions most of them. Nor is it in any way theoretical. Instead, *Ever Closer Union* describes and analyzes the EU's extraordinary growth from an association of six member states in the immediate af-

---

Box 0.2   EC Versus EU

The European Union came into existence in May 1993, following implementation of the Treaty on European Union, better known as the Maastricht Treaty. Nevertheless, the European Community continued to exist as an integral part of the EU. Strictly speaking, policies such as agriculture and antitrust were EC rather than EU activities. I generally use "EC" when referring to developments before 1993 and "EU" when referring to developments thereafter, although I also refer generally to "EU history," meaning the history of European integration since the launch of the original communities. At the risk of sacrificing accuracy for narrative flow, I refer to "European Union" policy and "European Union" decisionmaking even when the policies and decisions in question are, strictly speaking, "European Community" policies and decisions.

termath of World War II to a union of twenty-five member states (and rising) in the early twenty-first century. While critical of certain aspects of the EU, its underlying premise is that European integration is a fascinating phenomenon that anyone interested in contemporary history, politics, and economics needs (and deserves) to study.

▩ Notes

1. Wim Kok et al., *Facing the Challenge: The Lisbon Strategy for Growth and Enlargement: Report of the High Level Group* (Brussels: European Commission, 2004), p. 17.

2. The minister was Douglas Hurd, quoted in the *Financial Times,* January 10, 1992, p. 1.

Part 1

History

1

Reconstruction, Reconciliation, and Integration, 1945–1957

A famous poster commemorating the birth of European integration depicts two men, Jean Monnet and Robert Schuman, standing together "at the beginning of the European Community (9 May 1950)." The date is the day on which Schuman, then foreign minister of France, announced an unprecedented plan to place "the whole of Franco-German coal and steel production under a common High Authority, within the framework of an organization open to the participation of the other countries of Europe."[1] Monnet, a senior French official, was the brains behind the initiative.

It is difficult to appreciate today the boldness and prescience of Schuman's proposal. The intervening decades have virtually obliterated our awareness not only of the depth of distrust toward Germany in the immediate postwar years but also of the importance of coal and steel for European prosperity at that time. Schuman's short, simple statement outlined a strategy to reconcile German economic recovery and French national security. By accepting the recently established Federal Republic of Germany as an economic equal and handing over responsibility for both countries' coal and steel industries to a supranational authority, the Schuman Plan gave substance to the hitherto vague notion of European integration. Fleshing out the Schuman Declaration resulted first in the European Coal and Steel Community and later in the European Atomic Energy Community and the European Economic Community (EEC)—later known as the European Community (EC). Schuman Day is celebrated annually on May 9 in Brussels, Luxembourg, and Strasbourg as the birthday of what is now known as the European Union (Table 1.1).

Celebration of Schuman Day and solemnization of the Schuman Plan bolster what can be called the "official history" of European integration, which depicts Monnet and Schuman as visionaries soaring above the squalor and squabbles of postwar Europe, pointing the way to the promised land of peace and prosperity along the prudent path of economic and political integration. Without doubt, Monnet and Schuman *were* men of vision who sin-

Table 1.1   Chronology, 1945–1957

1945	May	End of World War II in Europe
1946	September	Churchill's "United States of Europe" speech
1947	March	Truman Doctrine announced; Britain and France sign Dunkirk Treaty (defensive alliance)
	June	Marshall Plan announced
	July	Committee for European Economic Cooperation established in Paris
	October	General Agreement on Tariffs and Trade (GATT) launched
	December	International Committee of the Movements for European Unity established in Paris
1948	January	Benelux customs union launched
	March	Brussels Treaty (defensive alliance of France, Britain, and Benelux) signed
	April	Organization for European Economic Cooperation (OEEC) established in Paris
	May	Congress of Europe held in The Hague
	June	Berlin blockade begins
1949	April	North Atlantic Treaty signed in Washington, D.C.; International Ruhr Authority established; Federal Republic of Germany (West Germany) established
	May	Council of Europe launched; end of Berlin blockade
1950	May	Schuman Declaration
	June	Negotiations begin to establish the European Coal and Steel Community (ECSC)
	October	Pleven Plan for a European Defense Community (EDC)
	November	European Convention for the Protection of Human Rights and Fundamental Freedoms signed in Rome
1951	April	Treaty establishing the ECSC signed in Paris
1952	May	Treaty establishing the EDC signed in Paris
	August	ECSC launched in Luxembourg
	September	ECSC Assembly holds first session in Strasbourg
1954	August	French National Assembly rejects EDC treaty
	October	Brussels Treaty amended to establish the Western European Union
1955	May	Germany joins the North Atlantic Treaty Organization (NATO)
	June	Messina Conference to relaunch European integration; Spaak Committee meets for first time
1956	May	Venice Conference: Spaak Committee recommends a European Economic Community (EEC) and a European Atomic Energy Community (Euratom)
	June	Intergovernmental conference to negotiate EEC and ECSC treaties opens in Brussels
	October–November	Suez crisis
1957	January	The Saar rejoins Germany
	March	Treaties of Rome (establishing the EEC and Euratom) signed

cerely believed in the virtues of integration and the necessity of European unity. But the declaration of May 9 owed as much to narrowly defined national interest as to broadly based international altruism and was rooted as much in the experience of the interwar years as in the special circumstances of the postwar world. Just as the Schuman Declaration was itself the product of clever political calculation, the institutions to which it ultimately gave rise were the result of intense intergovernmental bargaining.

▦ Jean Monnet and the European Movement

At the time of the Schuman Declaration, Monnet was director of the French Modernization Plan. As its name implies, the plan was designed to overhaul the French economy, which had shown signs of serious sickness well before World War II. General Charles de Gaulle, leader of the provisional government formed immediately after the liberation, realized that France could never become great again barring a radical economic revitalization. Without improving its performance and competitiveness, France would be unable to satisfy the domestic demands for economic growth on which the postwar political consensus rested, nor would it be able to play a leading role in the emerging international order. Keenly aware of the need to increase national production, improve productivity, boost foreign trade, maximize employment, and raise living standards, de Gaulle charged Monnet with achieving these objectives at the head of the newly established economic planning office.[2]

Despite his unconventional background, Monnet was an ideal choice. Then in his late fifties, he had spent a lifetime working in the private and public sectors in France and abroad. Monnet's experience as a senior Allied administrator during both world wars convinced him of the potential of peacetime economic planning. Nor was he encumbered by political baggage. Atypically for a Frenchman who had lived through the intensely ideological 1920s and 1930s, Monnet had no party affiliation. Inasmuch as he was politically motivated, it was by the remorseless ideology of efficiency.[3]

Monnet concluded during World War II that economic integration was the only means by which conflict in Europe could be avoided. In a note in August 1943 to the French Committee of National Liberation in Algiers, Monnet argued that there would be no peace in Europe "if States reestablished themselves on the basis of national sovereignty with all that this implies by way of prestige politics and economic protectionism." Instead, Monnet argued, "the States of Europe must form a federation or a 'European entity,' which will make them a single economic entity."[4]

Although such sentiments seem radical in retrospect, they were by no means unusual at the time. On the contrary, during and immediately after the war public figures and political pundits on both sides of the Atlantic outdid themselves in their advocacy of European integration. Repugnance at the slaughter of two European civil wars in as many generations and the economic depression and political extremism of the intervening years fueled popular support for a reorganization of the international system. Words such as "integration," "union," and even "supranationalism" were bandied about as panaceas for Europe's ills. The popular and political mood gave rise in the late 1940s to the European movement, a loose collection of individuals and interest groups ranging across the political spectrum, from the noncommunist left to the discredited far right, that shared advocacy of European unity.[5]

The intellectual ancestry of the European movement may have stretched into antiquity, but its immediate roots lay in the interwar years. In 1923 an Austro-Hungarian aristocrat, Count Richard Coudenhove-Kalergi, buoyed by the success over the previous year of his book *Pan-Europa,* launched an organization of the same name. Inspired as much by the devastation of the Great War as by the emergence during it of a powerful United States and a fledgling Soviet Union, Pan-Europa quickly acquired an ardent following, not least among influential politicians. The zenith of the pan-European movement was a stirring speech by French foreign minister Aristide Briand at the League of Nations in 1929. But the lofty ideals of European unity were soon swept aside by the flood tide of fascism in the 1930s. It took the bitter experience of defeat and occupation in 1939 and 1940 for pan-European ideas to revive and flourish in European minds.[6]

The resistance movement, a loose collection of individuals and groups opposed to Axis occupation, took up the cause of European unity as one plank of a proposed radical reorganization of postwar politics, economics, and society. Resistance literature, secretly circulated in occupied Europe, espoused the goal of international cooperation and integration as a basis for future peace and prosperity. Altiero Spinelli, a fervent federalist and a leading player in what eventually became the European Community, drafted a manifesto in 1940 and 1941 for a "free and united Europe" while imprisoned on the Italian island of Ventotene. Following his release after Mussolini's ouster, Spinelli traveled secretly to Switzerland for a meeting of European resistance representatives. Out of that meeting, held in Geneva in June and July 1944, came the "Draft Declaration of the European Resistance," which included a call for a "Federal Union among the European peoples."[7]

Support for European Unity

The legacy of the prewar Pan-Europa and the wartime resistance movements generated a groundswell of support for European unity in the early postwar years. Politicians of all persuasions espoused the cause of economic and political integration. One above all others came to personify the European movement: Winston Churchill, then Europe's best-known and most respected statesman. Renowned especially for his inspiring oratory, which had boosted British spirits during the dark days of 1940 and 1941, Churchill raised European morale by calling for a "United States of Europe" in a speech in Zurich in September 1946.[8]

Churchill advocated a far more limited and cautious form of European integration than did many of his continental colleagues. The United Europe Movement, which Churchill launched in May 1947, promoted what became known as the "unionist" position, as distinguished from the more radical "federalist" position of Spinelli and his Union of European Federalists. Differences between the unionists and federalists, based on political, geographical, and cultural considerations, came to the fore at the Congress of Europe, a glittering gathering of over 600 influential Europeans from sixteen countries held in The Hague in May 1948. Both sides agreed only on the desirability of European unity and on the need to institutionalize it by establishing an international organization with a parliamentary body. For the unionists, that body would be merely a consultative assembly bound to defer to a committee of government ministers. For the federalists, by contrast, it would be a constituent assembly charged with drafting a constitution for the United States of Europe.

What emerged from the acrimonious Hague congress and from follow-up negotiations had the appearance of a compromise but was in fact a capitulation to the unionist position. The ensuing Council of Europe was a far cry from what the federalists wanted. Although pledged "to achieve a closer union between its members in order to protect and promote the ideals and principles which constitute their common heritage and to further their economic and social progress," the Council of Europe did little more than exchange ideas and information on social, legal, and cultural matters.[9] Only in one important area, that of human rights, did the Council of Europe stand out. Its Court of Human Rights, often confused with the EU's Court of Justice, became a bulwark for the protection of civil liberties throughout Europe. More broadly, the Council of Europe enjoyed a brief resurgence in 1989 during the revolution in Central and Eastern Europe when public attention once again focused, as it had forty years earlier, on the possibility of establishing pan-European institutions.

The Council of Europe had a marginal but tangible impact on the future EC. Its member states wanted to locate the Council of Europe away from a national capital to symbolize European reconciliation, and they settled on Strasbourg, a frequently fought-over city on the border between France and Germany. Later the EC's member states placed the European Parliament there also. As the EC revived and flourished in the 1980s, many members of the European Parliament regretted the choice of Strasbourg, nearly 300 miles from the European Commission and the Council secretariat in Brussels. For them, Strasbourg came to symbolize not Franco-German reconciliation but the obscurity and relative unimportance of their own institution.

Almost alone among influential Europeans at the time, Monnet stood aloof from the European movement and from the Council of Europe that emerged from it. Monnet's detachment was due not to doubts about European unity but to disdain for the populism of the movement and its constituent parts. Monnet was an elitist and a pragmatist. His road to European unity would follow the unglamorous path of functional integration. Close cooperation between countries in specific economic sectors, Monnet believed, held the key to overcoming national divisions and ultimately achieving European federation. Decisions to implement functional economic cooperation would be taken not by 600 delegates at the Congress of Europe but by powerful politicians in the privacy of their government ministries.

Monnet loved aphorisms. "Nothing is possible without men; nothing is lasting without institutions" was one of his favorites. Another one—"People only accept change when they are faced with necessity, and only recognize necessity when a crisis is upon them"—offers a clue to how Monnet operated.[10] At a decisive moment early in World War II, Monnet saw an opportunity to act. With France on the verge of military defeat and political capitulation in June 1940, Monnet proposed to Churchill an "indissoluble union" between both countries. By offering common citizenship, forming a joint government, and pursuing a single war strategy, Monnet hoped to strengthen the French government's flagging position, encourage French forces in North Africa to continue the war alongside Britain, and lay the foundation for future European union.[11]

Despite the failure of this extraordinary initiative, Monnet remained convinced that only great crises move politicians to act against their cautious instincts, and that only a future crisis would provide the necessary push for European integration. It also taught Monnet something about Churchill. Although he had brought the offer to the British cabinet's attention, the prime minister had been skeptical, if not hostile, from the outset. It must have irritated Monnet to see Churchill emerge after the war as the mouthpiece of the European movement. That alone might have convinced Monnet to find other ways to pursue his cherished goal of European integration.

Uninvolved in the federalist or unionist movement, Monnet devoted his considerable energy to drafting the French modernization plan. Given his conviction that Europe could not be united unless France was resurgent, the plan was an indispensable component of Monnet's strategy for European integration. Monnet toiled with a troupe of young disciples to transform the ailing French economy. Based on lengthy consultations with employers, workers, and consumers, Monnet's team set production targets, foreign trade goals, and employment objectives. Few were ever met, but the plan instilled badly needed confidence that helped France achieve an enviable economic recovery (although not by later German standards).

No catalytic crisis had occurred so far to allow Monnet to take a bold initiative on the European stage, although two ominous developments greatly alarmed European governments and boosted the European movement. The first was the state of the European economy after six years of invasion and occupation, blitzkrieg and aerial bombardment. World War II was the most costly conflict in modern history, and its destructiveness has been well documented. Perhaps the most surprising aspect of the war, however—precisely because of the technological and strategic innovations unleashed during it—was that six years of incessant fighting had not caused even greater destruction. The war's major material impact was less on industrial plants than on infrastructure, compounded by shortages of raw materials and skilled labor. Both Monnet and his assistant Robert Marjolin mentioned in their memoirs that there was less material destruction in France in 1945 than either had expected to find on their return from exile.[12] Wartime demolition of roads, bridges, canals, dikes, and docks posed a more formidable challenge to postwar planners than did the destruction of factories.

The task of economic recovery was doubtless daunting, but it could be undertaken without challenging the authority of the nation-state. Although the unprecedented extent of material destruction during the war was certainly a factor in the growth of the postwar movement for European integration, it was not, Monnet realized, serious enough to trigger the kind of political reaction that would cause European countries to pool their sovereignty in a unique, supranational entity. Nor were the collapse of the wartime alliance against Germany and the emergence of the Cold War sufficient in themselves to produce the desired result.

Onset of the Cold War

Like the destructiveness of World War II, the origins and development of the Cold War are well-known. As hostility between the erstwhile allies intensified, Western European governments grew increasingly alarmed, not as much about the prospect of direct Soviet attack as about the more realistic prospect of internal communist subversion. Communist parties were popular in Western Europe immediately after the war and fared well in early postwar elections, especially in Italy and France. They owed their popularity to the corresponding unpopularity of capitalism—a reaction against the economic depression and the outbreak of war at either end of the 1930s. More important, communist parties reaped the electoral rewards of their participation in, and often leadership of, wartime resistance movements. They also benefited from wartime admiration in Europe and the United States of the Soviet Union's heroic stand against Nazi Germany, a struggle led by the indomitable "Uncle Joe" Stalin.

In 1946 and 1947, the French Communist Party shared power with the Christian Democrats and the Socialists, and the Italian Community Party seemed on the verge of an outright election victory. As relations between the Soviet Union and the Western powers deteriorated, relations between communist parties and their noncommunist counterparts in Western Europe degenerated. In May 1947 Paul Remadier, the French premier, ousted the Communists from government; in Italy, U.S. money and Christian Democratic scaremongering helped keep the Communists in opposition. Although communism remained popular with large numbers of people, electoral support waned as the Cold War intensified, notably after the February 1948 Communist coup in Czechoslovakia and during the Berlin blockade of 1948–1949. Nevertheless, the economic consequences of the war, exacerbated by a summer drought in 1946 and an icebound winter in 1947, seemed to offer ideal conditions for communist parties to exploit.

The emergence of the Cold War and its domestic political repercussions contributed to the growth of the European movement, whose rhetoric stressed the need for the countries of Europe, once at the center of the international system, to join together to assert their position in an increasingly rigid bipolar world. As the Cold War intensified and the Iron Curtain descended abruptly to divide the continent, integration became a means by which Western Europe could defend itself, in close collaboration with the United States, against external Soviet aggression and internal Communist subversion. Western Europe's presumed economic weakness and supposed political vulnerability drew the United States deeper into the continent's affairs and turned Washington into a zealous champion of European integration.

▇ The Marshall Plan and European Integration

Probably the best-known U.S. international initiative ever, the Marshall Plan was the main instrument used by the United States to encourage European integration.[13] But the Marshall Plan—or the European Recovery Program, as it was formally called—had many origins and objectives, all of them interconnected. One was humanitarian. Indeed, reports of privation in occupied Germany contributed directly to General George Marshall's Harvard commencement speech of June 1947, in which the U.S. secretary of state pledged wholehearted U.S. support for European postwar reconstruction.[14]

Healthy economic and political self-interest also guided the U.S. undertaking. Fear of an imminent economic recession, similar to that which had followed the cessation of hostilities in 1918, was one such motivation. Without economic growth in Europe, U.S. exports would stagnate and decline, and the United States itself would follow Europe into depression. However, the U.S. economy depended much less on exports to Europe in the late 1940s than it does today, so the export argument alone would not have sufficed to convince a skeptical Congress to give substance to Marshall's speech in the form of massive financial assistance.

A less immediate but nonetheless palpable concern about economic security, coupled with powerful political and strategic arguments, finally made the difference. Twice in the previous thirty years the United States had become directly involved in Europe's wars, and hundreds of thousands of American lives had been lost. Despite its strong emotional appeal, isolationism had patently failed. Apart from the emerging consensus that postwar U.S. security depended on increasing international involvement, the onset of the Cold War provided a powerful incentive for the United States to play a leading part in European affairs. A future resurgent Germany, however unlikely in 1947, might have posed a serious threat to U.S. security, but the immediate danger seemed to come from the Red Army in the East and local communist parties in the West.

Americans and Europeans agreed about the problem and the prescription. The direct Soviet threat could best be countered by immediate U.S. intervention (as in Greece in 1947) and military alliance building and leadership (as in the case of the North Atlantic Treaty Organization two years later). The indirect communist danger, by contrast, could best be defused by restoring Western Europe to sound economic health. The United States would play the role of pharmacist, dispensing large doses of drugs in the form of badly needed dollars. On both sides of the Atlantic, the prescription emphasized the importance of integration for future peace and prosperity in Europe.

The lessons of the interwar years had led U.S. officials and policymakers, like their European counterparts, to endorse postwar integration. A small number of influential Americans had been swayed by the teaching and writing of Coudenhove-Kalergi, who had spent the war at New York University.[15] Others, who would play a pivotal role in the formulation and implementation of U.S. policy toward Western Europe in the late 1940s and early 1950s, had become close friends of Monnet when he worked in Washington, D.C., in the early 1940s. With Monnet, "the eminence grise of the Wise Men of American foreign policy," they discussed the limits of national sovereignty and advantages of supranationality.[16] Also, they applied the lessons of modern U.S. history to war-torn Europe. Just as the United States had grown strong and prosperous by promoting interstate commerce and establishing a single market, so, too, could Europe. In that simple, straightforward way, European integration became an essential part "of a grand design for remaking the Old World in the likeness of the New."[17]

The Marshall Plan occupies a special place in the historiography of the Cold War. Some revisionist historians see in it an effort by the United States to acquire an empire in Europe by design; others argue that Europe's economic weakness allowed the United States to acquire an empire by default. Many contemporary Europeans were well aware of the dangers of relying too much on U.S. economic largesse and military protection and perceived European integration as a means of asserting the continent's independence. Similarly, perhaps paradoxically, many contemporary Americans looked to European integration, which the Marshall Plan aimed to enhance, as a way of obviating future U.S. intervention in the Old World.

Disputes about the significance of the Marshall Plan for postwar U.S. foreign policy are related to an equally important question: What part did the

Marshall Plan play in fostering European integration? The accepted view is that the Marshall Plan failed to break down national barriers. Neither Marshall's stricture that aid recipients had to act together and present a common recovery program nor the enormous influence and wealth of the United States could overcome the reluctance of European governments to cooperate closely, let alone share sovereignty. By effectively excluding the Soviet Union and its satellite countries in Eastern Europe, the Marshall Plan at least ensured that integration would be confined to Western Europe. But the degree of integration attained was far from what U.S. planners had sought.[18]

For all their platitudes about integration, European governments were unwilling to turn rhetoric into reality. To meet the prerequisite for Marshall Plan assistance they established the Organization for European Economic Cooperation (OEEC), an umbrella body to solicit U.S. funds. But the OEEC was too large and diverse to act as an institutional instrument of integration. Its eighteen members varied greatly in size, population, and economic well-being. Perhaps more important, widely differing political cultures and wartime experiences made the prospect of agreement on integration extremely remote. Thus, the OEEC failed to live up to its foster parents' expectations. Instead, shortly after the EEC began functioning in 1958, the OEEC turned into the Organization for Economic Cooperation and Development (OECD), the Paris-based body for international economic research and analysis.[19]

French Fear of Germany

Like the contemporaneous Congress of Europe, the OEEC triggered debate on European integration, but it produced a paucity of tangible results. For all their interest in integration and European unity, governments were unwilling to take concrete steps to surrender some of their sovereignty. Yet the Marshall Plan indirectly caused the cataclysmic crisis that Monnet knew was necessary to prompt the French government to act. Because it involved the reconstruction of West Germany as part of the reconstruction of Western Europe, the Marshall Plan set the stage for a series of diplomatic decisions that would gradually rehabilitate the former enemy, much to the consternation of Germany's neighbor to the west. The threat to France's own economic recovery and security was immense. Here was a situation that Monnet could exploit to the full.

Even as the United States and Britain revised their harsh policies toward Germany, France stuck stubbornly to a number of severe strictures. Germany would be demilitarized, decentralized, and deindustrialized. France had suffered grievously from German militarism and expansionism, far more than either Britain or the United States. The humiliation and horror of World War II—defeat and occupation, deportation and enslavement, pillage and destruction—would not quickly be forgotten. France had salvaged some of its honor

through the resistance movement and by raising an army in 1944 that participated in the final stages of the national liberation and the subsequent invasion
of Germany. Denied a place at the negotiating table in Yalta and Potsdam,
where the "Big Three" (Britain, the Soviet Union, and the United States) decided the fate of the world, France at least won the right to occupy a small part
of the vanquished Third Reich. The gradual softening of British and U.S. occupation policy served only to strengthen French determination to stick to a
rigid course. Not surprisingly, France refused to merge its occupation zone
into the newly established Anglo-American "Bizonia" in May 1947.[20]

For all his remonstrations about integration and reconciliation, even
Monnet was not unaffected by the rampant Germanophobia that swept France
at the time. After all, Monnet had predicated his plan for French economic
modernization upon a punitive policy toward Germany. Coal and steel, the
two key industrial sectors in mid-twentieth-century Europe, lay at the heart of
the plan. Postwar French policy toward Germany sought to win control over
the coal-rich Saar, which France then occupied, and to prevent the economic
recovery of the Ruhr. Not only had the Ruhr become a synonym for the evil
German military-industrial complex, but also its resuscitation would threaten
France's own economic revival. Monnet based his economic planning
squarely on the assumption that Ruhr coal would be available to fuel French
steel mills, whose increased output would find buyers in displaced German
markets. German economic rehabilitation, if it came before full implementation of the Monnet Plan, would greatly imperil France's economic fortunes
and, by extension, France's international stature.

As long as the Soviet Union was somehow involved in formulating Allied policy toward Germany, France had a good chance of thwarting Britain's
and the United States' increasingly benign approach. Although there had
never truly been four-power cooperation on Germany, the Western Allies were
reluctant to break openly with the Soviet Union, hoping perhaps to avert an
irrevocable collapse of the wartime alliance. To try to negotiate a postwar settlement, or at least to maintain the fiction of Allied unity, the foreign ministers of Britain, France, the United States, and the Soviet Union met periodically. The breakdown of the Moscow meeting of foreign ministers in March
1947 proved decisive. Thereafter, the Anglo-Americans increasingly acted
unilaterally in the West while the Soviet Union pursued its own policy in the
East.

Control of the Ruhr

French difficulty in adhering to a repressive policy came to a head in early
1948. The Ruhr lay within the British zone of occupation, and France was not
party to Anglo-American planning in Germany. As long as France remained
outside Bizonia, officials in Paris could only watch angrily as those in Lon-

don and Washington gradually loosened the Ruhr's economic shackles. Prag-matism briefly triumphed when France agreed to cooperate with Bizonia in an effort to influence Anglo-American policy from within. During the subse-quent London Conference of the Western Allies, which led eventually to the merging of the French zone and Bizonia into the Federal Republic of Ger-many, France supported the establishment of the International Ruhr Authority as a vehicle of controlling industrial production there.

The Federal Republic of Germany, conceived in the Western Allies' con-ference and born in September 1949, lacked many attributes of sovereignty. Apart from accepting limits on foreign policy and a complete absence of de-fense policy, the new German state had to acquiesce in the existence and oper-ation of the International Ruhr Authority. But French hopes that the authority would serve French interests by maintaining strict controls on Ruhr production soon proved unrealistic. Realizing that the Ruhr was the industrial heartland (or, to use the metaphor current at the time, the "spark plug") of Europe,[21] the United States pushed more and more for German industrial recovery as a pre-requisite for European economic recovery. By the same token, the United States appreciated the implications for France and understood the need to in-volve France fully in bringing about a durable European settlement. Accord-ingly, officials in Washington and London pressed their counterparts in Paris to devise a mutually acceptable solution to the Ruhr problem and to take the ini-tiative in proposing a new Allied policy toward the Federal Republic.

By the end of 1949, therefore, France faced the failure of its restrictive Ruhr policy. The International Ruhr Authority, a body intended to perpetuate French control over the area under the guise of Allied cooperation with the Federal Republic, had made little headway. French officials quickly grasped the fact that policy toward Germany would have to be revised, not least in order to salvage the all-important and closely related Monnet Plan. Thus, in the following months they searched for a strategy that would satisfy their country's overriding concern with security, meet its industrial demands for ad-equate supplies of coal and markets for steel, and relieve U.S. pressure for a policy that would accommodate Germany's rapid economic recovery.[22]

Monnet himself had the most to gain—and the most to lose—from this challenge. After all, the modernization plan, now at risk, was his. Apart from a vested personal interest in the plan's success, Monnet bore primary respon-sibility in the French civil service for efforts to overcome exacting economic obstacles. The particular set of problems facing France in 1949 and 1950 of-fered Monnet a welcome opportunity to act. Capitalizing on the growing sen-timent in official French circles that policy toward Germany should in future be based on economic association rather than antagonism, he approached Schuman with the imaginative idea of a supranational coal and steel commu-nity. Thus, the lifting of Allied restrictions on German steel production and the prospect of renewed Franco-German tension provided the crisis that, Monnet was certain, would force his government to take a dramatic step on the road to Franco-German reconciliation and European integration.

■ The Schuman Plan

In his memoirs, Monnet described the melodrama surrounding the Schuman Declaration.[23] Monnet sent his proposal for a coal and steel community to both René Pleven, the French prime minister, and Schuman. Pleven failed to act immediately, thus allowing Schuman to take the initiative that subsequently bore his name. Schuman's background lent poignancy to the coal and steel proposal. Coming from the disputed province of Lorraine, where he had suffered personally from the incessant conflict between France and Germany, Schuman sought above all else to promote reconciliation between the two countries.[24] As a Christian Democrat, Schuman held political principles that reinforced his personal convictions. Constrained by the climate of retribution toward Germany that pervaded postwar France and by a natural reserve and inhibition, Schuman had hitherto refrained from taking any conciliatory steps in the direction of the erstwhile enemy. Now, emboldened by Monnet's suggestion and by the swing in official French opinion toward economic accord with Germany, Schuman floated the fateful proposal with secrecy and speed.

Before the proposal could be made public, Monnet and Schuman needed the approval of three key parties: the French, German, and U.S. governments. On May 9, 1950, Schuman simultaneously placed the proposal before his own cabinet in Paris and brought it to Chancellor Konrad Adenauer's attention in Bonn. The German leader responded enthusiastically. Like Schuman, Adenauer had a strong personal yearning for Franco-German reconciliation. Moreover, keenly aware of the depth of French distrust toward the new Federal Republic, Adenauer realized that shared sovereignty pointed the way to Germany's international rehabilitation. Only by integrating closely with neighboring countries could Germany hope to remove the remaining controls on its domestic and foreign policies. Three months previously, Adenauer had taken the initiative by floating the idea of a full Franco-German union. Although Adenauer's trial balloon had alarmed nervous French officials, it clearly indicated the chancellor's receptiveness to a proposal for integration of any kind.[25]

Alerting the Americans

Monnet had earlier alerted U.S. officials to the French initiative. Secretary of State Dean Acheson had arrived in Paris on May 7, en route to London for a meeting of British, French, and U.S. foreign ministers to discuss German economic issues. Taking advantage of Acheson's presence, Monnet and Schuman quickly took him into their confidence. Acheson, they knew, strongly supported not only European integration but also the necessity of French efforts to bring it about. The previous October, Acheson had shared with Schuman his belief that "our policy in Germany, and the development of a German Government which can take its place in Western Europe, depends on the assumption by your country of leadership in Europe on these problems."[26]

Not surprisingly, Acheson endorsed the Schuman Plan and drafted a statement of support for President Harry Truman to release once the plan became public. Yet Acheson's immediate reaction was cautious and pointed to what would become a persistent source of tension between the United States and the European Union. At first Acheson feared that the Schuman Plan was a clever cover for "a gigantic European cartel." Acheson drafted the presidential statement of support partly to allay his "apprehension that upon receiving partial information, the Antitrust Division in the Department of Justice might stimulate some critical comments, which would have been damaging at that stage."[27] U.S. suspicion of the European Union's commitment to international economic competition would deepen in the years ahead, and the Department of Justice would lose none of its misgivings.

The happenstance of Acheson's presence in Paris suggests that Monnet and Schuman would not otherwise have advised the U.S. secretary of state in advance of their coal and steel proposal. But U.S. support was too important to have been jeopardized by their waiting to inform Washington until after a public announcement. In the event, Monnet's assiduous and prolonged cultivation of the U.S. establishment bore fruit as he astutely lined up support by drawing on close friendships with key U.S. policymakers. Within a month the United States set up the special working group on the Schuman Proposal in its Paris embassy. The working group soon became "a hotbed of Monnet enthusiasts [with] the thinking of Monnet and the young American integrationists . . . often so similar as to be indistinguishable."[28]

Buoyed by Acheson's endorsement and Adenauer's approval, Schuman easily convinced his cabinet colleagues to support the scheme. A public announcement immediately followed at a hastily convened press conference in the French foreign ministry. The result was "a public relations coup of heroic proportions."[29] Although French officials had been moving in the direction of Franco-German economic association for some time, the Schuman Declaration had all the appearance of a dramatic reversal of policy. Instead of trying to keep the traditional enemy down, France would build a new Europe on the basis of equality with Germany. Coal and steel, the two key sectors of industrial production and war-making potential, would be removed from national control and placed under a single, supranational authority. As Monnet put it, "If . . . the victors and the vanquished agreed to exercise joint sovereignty over part of their joint resources . . . then a solid link would be forged between them, the way would be wide open for further collective action, and a great example would be given to the other nations of Europe."[30]

How Many Members?

Schuman's offer to open the proposed organization "to the participation of the other countries of Europe" was not as generous as it seemed. For one thing, the countries of Eastern Europe were automatically excluded by the onset of the Cold War. For another, the Scandinavian countries had shown, during the Congress of Europe and subsequently in the Council of Europe, their skepticism about supranationalism. For Schuman and Monnet, European integration meant, essentially, Franco-German integration. Germany was the traditional enemy, the economic powerhouse of Europe, and the country that posed the greatest threat to France. Franco-German reconciliation, by means of "European" integration, apparently offered the only opportunity to avoid a repetition of the disastrous conflict that had characterized the first five decades of the twentieth century. Schuman's image of "the other countries of Europe" meant, in reality, the neighboring countries of Belgium, the Netherlands, and Luxembourg (known as the Benelux countries) to the north and Italy to the south.

Britain was most conspicuous by its absence from the French view of this "new" Europe. After all, as France's traditional twentieth-century ally, Britain was surely the first country to which France would look for support of an international initiative to come to terms with postwar Germany. Indeed, Monnet's first proposal for European integration, the dramatic offer of Anglo-French union, had centered on Britain. Similarly, during the war itself, Robert Marjolin, Monnet's deputy, had stated his "profound conviction" that "the key to any politico-economic reorganization in continental Europe has to be sought in Franco-British relations."[31] Even as late as 1948, "Western European integration without Britain was unacceptable in Washington," where the ultimate decision about Europe's future would be made.[32] By 1950, however, both France and the United States had dropped Britain from their plans for European integration. Britain's obvious reluctance to involve itself in European integration, despite Churchill's memorable endorsement of a United States of Europe, convinced officials in Washington and Paris that progress would have to be made without British support.

Britain preferred to remain aloof because of a political culture that emphasized national sovereignty and abhorred supranationality, a long history of only occasional direct involvement in continental European affairs, and the special wartime experience of having escaped invasion. In addition, Britain saw itself as an intermediary between the United States and continental Europe, an aspect of the Anglo-American "special relationship" that officials in

London feared would be endangered by participation in European integration despite their U.S. counterparts' assertions to the contrary. British officials also thought that too close an involvement in the process of European integration would jeopardize Britain's strong political and economic orientation toward the declining empire and emerging Commonwealth.[33]

Schuman's decision to give the British government no more than a few hours' notice of his groundbreaking declaration vividly illustrates French indifference to British involvement in the future coal and steel community. British foreign minister Ernest Bevin was furious, doubly so when he discovered that Acheson had known all about the impending declaration when he had arrived in London the day before Schuman's press conference.[34] Any French embarrassment at slighting Bevin rapidly dissipated when the British government belittled the plan.

Yet the French government held open the door to British participation in the coal and steel negotiations. Other prospective member states, especially the Benelux countries, hoped that Britain would take the decisive step. But in order to cross the threshold, all participants had to accept the principle of shared sovereignty, whatever that would turn out to mean in practice. Monnet stuck to the position that if the principle of supranationality itself was debatable, the proposed organization would soon go the way of the ineffectual OEEC. Following a series of cabinet meetings and diplomatic exchanges with France, the British government reached a predictable but discouraging conclusion. At the definitive cabinet meeting, "there seems to have been a general, resentful agreement to give a negative answer [to France]."[35]

■ The ECSC and the EDC

With understandable artistic license, Theodore White wrote in retrospect that "Monnet's prestige in French politics was akin to that of George Marshall in American politics. . . . Watching Monnet thread his suggestion [the Schuman Declaration] through the bureaucracies and foreign ministries of Europe was to take delight in his political art."[36] Monnet's standing may indeed have been high, but his proposal for a coal and steel community by no means sailed easily through the relevant government departments of the negotiating states: France, Germany, Italy, Belgium, the Netherlands, and Luxembourg (thereafter known collectively as "the Six").

John Gillingham, author of an authoritative history of the Schuman Plan, titled his chapter on the coal and steel negotiations "From Summit to Swamp."[37] The summit was the high point of the declaration itself, made in the glare of publicity and self-congratulation; the swamp was the low point of intergovernmental squabbling as each country jockeyed for advantage in pursuit of its own interests. Monnet thought the negotiations, which began in

June 1950, would be over by the end of the summer, but they did not begin in earnest until August 1950 and did not end until April 1951. Ratification by the member states' parliaments took nearly another year. The European Coal and Steel Community (ECSC) finally began operating in August 1952.

Negotiating New Treaties

Monnet negotiated for France and prevailed upon Adenauer to appoint Walter Hallstein, a law professor, state secretary in the foreign office and later the Commission's first president, as Germany's representative. The main agenda items were the proposed community's competence, institutions, and decision-making procedures. Based on a French document, the negotiators gradually gave substance and shape to the new organization. What emerged was a supra-national High Authority, the institutional depository of shared national sovereignty over the coal and steel sectors. The High Authority would be responsible for formulating a common market in coal and steel and for supervising such related issues as pricing, wages, investment, and competition. As Monnet saw it, the purpose of the community was not "to substitute the High Authority for private enterprise, but . . . to make possible real competition throughout a vast market, from which producers, workers and consumers would all gain."[38] Sensitive especially to U.S. concerns, doubly so in view of Acheson's first reaction, Monnet also wove into the treaty a number of antitrust provisions.

Because of the High Authority's small size, national bureaucracies would have to cooperate closely with it to implement community legislation. A separate institution, the Court of Justice, would adjudicate disputes and ensure member states' compliance with the terms of the treaty. The other negotiators forced Monnet to accept the Council of Ministers in the institutional framework. Initially intended to be advisory and intermediary, as the embodiment of the member states' interests, the Council would increasingly act as a brake on supranationalism within the community. Finally, a Common Assembly consisting of delegates of the national parliaments would give the ECSC the appearance of democratic accountability.

A contemporaneous controversy over German remilitarization initially imperiled the coal and steel negotiations. Faced with U.S. demands for German rearmament following the outbreak of the Korean War, French prime minister Pleven announced in October 1950 a plan for German remilitarization under the aegis of a European defense community, just as Schuman had earlier proposed German reindustrialization under the aegis of a coal and steel community. Monnet was the architect of both ideas. His advocacy of the European Defense Community (EDC) grew directly out of his championing of the Schuman Plan.

Fierce French hostility toward German remilitarization, even in the face of Anglo-American pressure and the seriousness of the Cold War, caused Adenauer to doubt France's commitment to Franco-German reconciliation and European integration. If shared sovereignty was good enough for German industry, Adenauer asked, why was it not also acceptable for German rearmament? Faced with possible German recalcitrance in the coal and steel talks, Monnet pressed Pleven to pursue the parallel idea of a supranational organization for European defense.[39]

Negotiations to form the EDC, in which German units would be integrated into a European army, began in February 1951. Five of the six nations negotiating a treaty to establish the European Coal and Steel Community simultaneously participated in the defense discussions (the Netherlands, the odd country out, delayed taking part until October 1951). Although Monnet was not directly involved in the EDC talks, he again used his influence behind the scenes to win powerful U.S. support for the Pleven Plan. Based on a deep distrust of supranationalism, Britain resisted U.S. entreaties to enter the EDC talks. Despite British aloofness the Six persevered in their negotiations. After complex and hard bargaining, they signed the EDC treaty in May 1952, in Paris.

The EDC negotiations spawned another initiative that raised federalists' hopes for the future of European integration. Article 38 of the Paris Treaty called for the establishment of a supranational political authority to direct the EDC. Deferring to domestic parliamentary opinion, in September 1952 the foreign ministers of the Six acted on a resolution passed by the Council of Europe's Assembly calling on them to entrust a parliamentary body with the task of implementing Article 38 by drafting the statute for the proposed European Political Community. Reflecting, perhaps, the six governments' indifference toward the initiative and doubts that it would ever come to anything, the foreign ministers asked a special committee of the newly established ECSC Common Assembly to draft the additional treaty.[40]

The so-called constitutional committee lost little time in drawing up plans for a political community that would not only encompass the EDC and ECSC but also embrace foreign, economic, and monetary policy coordination. Even in the heated climate of the early 1950s, however, with the Korean War and the attendant acceptance of German rearmament acting as a spur to greater European integration, the Six balked at the constitutional committee's extravagant recommendations. At a series of intergovernmental meetings in 1953 and early in 1954, the Six successfully diluted the more far-reaching clauses of the draft treaty establishing the political community. Much to the member states' relief, the proposed community soon withered away, a casualty of its stillborn sibling, the EDC.

Having survived the penultimate negotiating stage, the EDC foundered on the rock of ratification. Gaullist hostility toward sharing sovereignty over sacrosanct national defense policy, coupled with implacable communist opposition to German rearmament, resulted in August 1954 in defeat of the EDC treaty in the French parliament. It was paradoxical that the EDC failed in

France, where the original initiative had been taken in 1950 and the treaty had been signed in 1952. In the interim, Stalin's death and the end of hostilities in Korea had lessened Cold War tensions and made the issue of German remilitarization less urgent. Moreover, in the early 1950s France had become increasingly preoccupied with the dissipating colonial conflict in Indochina (later Vietnam).[41]

But the genie of German rearmament could not be stuffed back in the bottle. With the collapse of the EDC, Anthony Eden, Britain's prime minister, proposed instead that Germany join with Britain, France, Italy, and the Benelux countries in the Western European Union (WEU), a new defense organization intended to facilitate German entry into the North Atlantic Treaty Organization (NATO). Mollified by Britain's membership in the intergovernmental WEU, France reluctantly endorsed the initiative. In a fitting finale to the EDC debacle, France thereby acquiesced in Germany's entry into NATO in May 1955, a prospect that five years previously had filled it with fright.

The EDC left an interesting legacy. Having marked the high point of European federalist aspirations, the failed proposal quickly acquired the aura of a great opportunity lost. As the EC struggled through the political setbacks of the 1960s, the economic difficulties of the 1970s, and a belated revival in the 1980s, supporters of supranationalism harked back to the early 1950s as the European movement's golden age. If only the EDC and related political community had been ratified, the argument went, European integration would have reached a level considered unattainable in later years. Yet the collapse of both proposals and the failure of subsequent initiatives along similar lines clearly indicated the limits on European integration in the 1950s and beyond. It was no accident that the EDC fell at the final hurdle of French ratification or that the political community languished in the wings. Only with great reluctance had the Six confronted the question of a defense community and the equally daunting challenge of a supranational political community. The outcome of both issues allowed them to concentrate instead on the kind of integration politically possible in the 1950s and for many years thereafter: functional economic cooperation.

Launching the ECSC

As the epitome of functionalism, the ECSC survived the wreckage of the EDC. Together with lofty references to world peace and a "contribution . . . to civilization," the preamble of the ECSC treaty explicitly stated the organization's functionalist mission. By referring to the ECSC's role in rebuilding Europe, the preamble set the seal on Monnet's tendency to blur the distinction between Europe and Western Europe and to confine the geopolitical scope of the ECSC (and later the EC) to a core group of countries centered on the Rhine.

Concerned about the possible consequences of the EDC controversy for the Schuman Plan, Monnet pushed for early ratification of the ECSC treaty. In each prospective member state, the ratification debate was lively: producer associations complained about the High Authority's ability to interfere in their affairs, labor groups fretted about the impact of keener competition, and nationalist politicians railed against the supposed onslaught of supranationalism. However, the ongoing EDC debacle channeled criticism of shared sovereignty away from the contemporaneous ECSC debate. While the EDC issue raged, the ECSC treaty was ratified in national parliaments with relatively little fanfare.

One of the issues still to be worked out was the site of the institutions themselves. Despite Monnet's hope that a special area analogous to the District of Columbia would be set aside in the community, national governments eventually settled on Luxembourg as the site of the High Authority. It was there, in the capital of the small, sleepy Grand Duchy, that the ECSC began to function in August 1952.

The ECSC disappointed European federalists both in its conceptual framework and in its actual operation. It was an unglamorous organization that inadequately symbolized the high hopes of supranationality in Europe. Yet the ECSC served a vital purpose in the postwar world in terms of Franco-German reconciliation and the related goal of European integration. To quote John Gillingham at some length:

> A supranational authority had been created, a potential nucleus for a European federal system. It would serve in lieu of a peace treaty concluding hostilities between Germany and Western Europe. This was no grand settlement in the manner of Westphalia or Versailles. The agreement to create a heavy industry pool changed no borders, created no new alliances, and reduced only a few commercial and financial barriers. It did not even end the occupation of the Federal Republic. . . . By resolving the coal and steel conflicts that had stood between France and Germany since the Second World War, it did, however, remove the main obstacle to an economic partnership between the two nations.[42]

These were by no means inconsiderable achievements.

◼ The EEC and Euratom

A favorite metaphor of European federalists depicts the EU as a fragile, delicate craft constantly running aground on the treacherous shoals of national sovereignty and self-interest. With each repair and relaunch the ship gets stronger, while navigational hazards are charted and exposed. Eventually, one supposes, the United States of Europe will resemble a supranational supertanker plying stormy economic, political, and security seas, invulnerable to the perils lurking beneath the surface.

The first relaunch of the community concept took place immediately after the EDC foundered in 1954, but there was nothing inevitable or inexorable about the revival of European integration at that time. Certainly the ECSC continued to operate unabated, but it was not a striking success. The High Authority struggled in vain to formulate and implement effective pricing and competition policies and managed only with difficulty to regulate other aspects of the coal and steel sectors. Yet the political lessons of functional integration were not lost on the member states. Despite the bitterness engendered by the EDC debate, a willingness persisted to maintain, or even extend, functional economic cooperation for the sake of Franco-German cooperation and European integration.

A specific idea for economic integration, floated by the Dutch as part of the moribund European political community proposal, survived the defeat of the EDC. It called for the Six to abolish quotas and tariffs on trade among themselves, establish a joint external tariff, unify trade policy toward the rest of the world, devise common policies for a range of socioeconomic sectors, and organize a single internal market. Monnet thought this idea too ambitious. Enamored as always of narrower and more definite proposals, he continued to advocate the functional approach of sectoral integration. Even while the ECSC treaty was being negotiated, Monnet knew that coal was rapidly losing its position as the basis of industrial power and, by extension, military might. Atomic energy had already revolutionized strategic doctrine and seemed poised to replace coal and oil as the elixir of the future. Not surprisingly, Monnet now proposed a European atomic energy community, to be structured along the lines of the ECSC, in order both to achieve the immediate objectives of the ECSC itself and to promote the distant goal of European federation.

In November 1954, disappointed with the Coal and Steel Community's progress, concerned about the consequences of the EDC's failure, and impatient to play a more active and aggressive role in advocating European unity, Monnet announced his intention to resign from the High Authority. As he explained to the ECSC Common Assembly in Strasbourg, "It is for Parliaments and Governments to decide on the transfer of new powers to the European institutions. The impulse must therefore come from without. [By resigning from the High Authority,] I shall be able to join in the efforts of all those who are working to continue and enlarge what has been begun."[43] Monnet's vehicle for influencing "Parliaments and Governments . . . from without" would be the Action Committee for a United States of Europe, a small, "private supranational organization" of political party and trade union leaders.[44] Monnet envisioned the committee as a powerful pressure group that would lobby for implementation of his new initiative.

Monnet's decision to resign took national governments by surprise. At a meeting in Messina in June 1955, ECSC foreign ministers discussed not only Monnet's replacement but also the future of European integration. Paul-Henri Spaak, Belgium's foreign minister, had prepared a memorandum on behalf of the Benelux countries suggesting further integration along the lines of Monnet's idea for an atomic energy community and the rival proposal for a common market. The foreign ministers asked Spaak to form a committee and write a report on future options. In later years, the Messina meeting came to be seen as a pivotal point for European integration.

Spaak was well suited by temperament and conviction to draft the necessary report. His enthusiasm for integration had already won him the nickname "Mr. Europe." As chairman of the conference that opened in Brussels later in 1955, Spaak steered the work of the various committees and subcommittees that drafted specific sections. The final report, presented to his fellow foreign ministers at a meeting in Venice in May 1956, proposed that the two objectives of sectoral (atomic energy) integration and wider economic integration (a common market) be realized in separate organizations with separate treaties. The Venice foreign ministers' meeting marked the opening of an intergovernmental conference that culminated in the establishment of the European Atomic Energy Community (Euratom) and the European Economic Community (EEC).

Foreign Adventures and Domestic Interests

The October–November 1956 Suez debacle—in which an Anglo-French military intervention ended in political disaster—turned the French government's attention squarely back to the continent and made the prospect of a wider economic agreement with neighboring countries seem more important than before. As it was, Guy Mollet, the French prime minister, was staunchly in favor of integrating Europe. Until the Suez crisis cleared the air, however, Mollet refrained from pushing renewed efforts to do so, largely because of the bitter EDC legacy. French political opinion seemed well disposed toward Euratom, which offered an opportunity to share the exorbitant costs of atomic energy research and development while enjoying all the benefits. U.S. president Dwight Eisenhower's recent Atoms for Peace initiative increased Euratom's attraction. Not only was the United States willing to share nuclear technology for peaceful purposes, but also the State Department recognized that "the most hopeful avenue for relaunching the movement toward European integration now appears to be the creation of a European common authority, along the lines of the Schuman Plan, to be responsible for the development of atomic energy for peaceful purposes."[45]

By contrast, reaction in France to the possible establishment of a common market was almost uniformly hostile. Robert Marjolin, who advised the French government on European affairs and subsequently participated in the Euratom and EEC negotiations, noted in his memoirs, "*the hostility of almost the whole of French opinion to the removal, even gradual, of the protection which French industry enjoyed*" (original emphasis). That hostility led to intense confrontations between the negotiators in Brussels on the one hand and recalcitrant ministers and bureaucrats in Paris on the other. In addition to fighting for France in the intergovernmental conference, Marjolin found himself waging a rearguard action that he called the "Battle of Paris."[46]

Marjolin and others argued the case for a customs union and common market on its own merits but bolstered their position with the assertion that France could not have the desirable atomic energy community without the undesirable economic community. With the exception of Britain, which participated in the EEC negotiations until November 1955, France's partners in the intergovernmental conference eagerly sought a common market in Europe. The advantage of a single market in industrial goods was obvious to Germany, although Ludwig Erhard, the economics minister, objected to the proposed community on the grounds that it would be protectionist and therefore would distort world trade. As for Euratom, the other countries in the negotiations did not share France's enthusiasm and doubted that the French government would exploit atomic energy only for civil projects.

A vote in the French parliament in July 1956 on whether to continue the Euratom negotiations resulted in an easy government victory. A similar vote on the EEC negotiations, in January 1957, proved far more contentious. A vague desire to improve the country's image after the negative EDC vote of August 1954, a reaction against the French Communist Party in the wake of the Soviet invasion of Hungary in October 1956, the legacy of Suez, and a concern that France might be left permanently behind its more economically advanced neighbors undoubtedly contributed to the government's success. Yet the outcome was close. Only by guaranteeing clauses in the EEC treaty that favored France's overseas possessions and promising to include agriculture in the proposed common market did the government carry the day.

Negotiation and Ratification

Having accepted these conditions during the parliamentary debate, the French government had to convince its partners to incorporate them into the draft treaty. The other countries agreed to do so in part because of the benefits that would accrue to all from a common agricultural policy and in part because Belgium and the Netherlands would benefit as well from extending EEC privileges to member states' overseas possessions. But the main reason for the other nations' acquiescence was the importance of including France in the community. An EEC without Britain was possible; an EEC without France was impracticable. As Franco-German rapprochement lay at the core of the EEC, and the EEC was the key to Germany's postwar rehabilitation, Adenauer would pay almost any price to placate the government in Paris.

The conference came to an end in a series of high-level meetings in February 1957. The outcome was two treaties, one for Euratom and the other for the EEC. Both were signed at an elaborate ceremony in Rome in March. Although officially both are called the Rome Treaties, in practice only the treaty establishing the EEC is known today as the Rome Treaty.

Only in France was there a serious problem with ratification, posed this time not by concerted Gaullist and communist opposition but by the fall of Mollet's government during the early summer. Here Monnet's Action Committee was instrumental, if not decisive, in ensuring swift and successful ratification. First the committee pressed for early ratification in the German parliament. The committee's influence helped win the support of the Social Democratic Party, which had previously opposed both the ECSC and the EDC. With German ratification secure, the Action Committee turned its attention to the French parliament, where a comfortable majority endorsed the treaties in July 1957.[47] By the end of the year, the Six had ratified the two treaties, allowing the two new communities to begin operating in January 1958.

On an ancillary issue, Monnet did not prevail. As he had done in the early 1950s during the launching of the ECSC, Monnet championed the cause of a special "European District" to house the new EEC institutions. Still dealing with an influx of ECSC officials and associated personnel into the Grand Duchy, the Luxembourg government declined to accept any more. Almost by default, Brussels, site of the conference that gave birth to the new communities, became their home.

By the time of the Brussels negotiations, held in the aftermath of the EDC debacle, "supranationality" was a term from which even the most ardent federalists recoiled. As Marjolin noted, "Nowhere did it appear in the documents drafted during the negotiations; no one so much as mentioned the word."[48] The preamble of the EEC treaty was far less flamboyant than its ECSC counterpart, referring only to the signatories' determination "to lay the foundations of an ever closer union among the peoples of Europe." The treaty itself outlined the essential principles of the common market: the free movement of goods, persons, services, and capital; a customs union and common external tariffs; and various community policies. The new communities' institutional architecture emulated that of the ECSC but included a stronger Council and a correspondingly weaker Commission (because of the odium attached to "supranationalism" in the wake of the EDC debacle, the name "Commission" replaced the more pretentious "High Authority" in the Treaty of Rome). In effect, "an institutional system was set up [in the communities] with the aim of doing justice to both the intergovernmental and supranational concepts."[49]

At first the EEC seemed an even greater disappointment than the ECSC. Neither organization realized the high hopes of advocates of European integration in the postwar period. The EEC's importance was nonetheless profound, politically as well as economically. In his memoirs, Robert Marjolin, who had fought hard in Brussels and Paris to make the EEC possible, described the significance of the Rome Treaty in the following way: "I do not believe it is an exaggeration to say that this date [March 25, 1957] represents one of the greatest moments of Europe's history. Who would have thought during the 1930s, and even during the ten years that followed the war, that European states which had been tearing one another apart for so many centuries and some of which, like France and Italy, still had very closed economies, would form a common market intended eventually to become an economic area that could be linked to one great dynamic market?"[50]

■ Notes

1. Pascal Fontaine, *Europe, a Fresh Start: The Schuman Declaration, 1950–90* (Luxembourg: Office for Official Publications of the European Communities, 1990), p. 44.

2. Jean Monnet, *Memoirs* (Garden City, NY: Doubleday, 1978), p. 239.

3. On Monnet's life and career, see ibid.; Douglas Brinkley and Clifford Hackett, eds., *Jean Monnet: The Path to European Unity* (New York: St. Martin's Press, 1991); and François Duchêne, *Jean Monnet: The First Statesman of Interdependence* (New York: W. W. Norton, 1994).

4. Monnet, *Memoirs*, p. 222.

5. For a comprehensive history of European integration and the European movement, see Walter Lipgens, *History of European Integration*, 2 vols. (London: Oxford University Press, 1981 and 1986); and Raymond Poidevin, ed., *Origins of European Integration: March 1948–May 1950* (Brussels: Bruylant, 1986).

6. On the pan-European idea and the origins of the European movement, see Richard Coudenhove-Kalergi, *Pan-Europa* (Vienna: Pan-Europa-Verlag, 1923); Arnold Zurcher, *The Struggle to Unite Europe, 1940–1958* (New York: New York University Press, 1958); and Peter Stirk, *European Unity in Context: The Interwar Period* (London: Pinter, 1989).

7. Altiero Spinelli, "European Union and the Resistance," in Ghita Ionescu, ed., *The New Politics of European Integration* (London: Macmillan, 1972), pp. 5–7.

8. Lipgens, *European Integration*, vol. 1, p. 319.

9. Pierre Gerbert, "The Origins: Early Attempts and the Emergence of the Six (1945–52)," in Roy Pryce, ed., *The Dynamics of European Union* (London: Croom Helm, 1987), pp. 40–44.

10. Monnet, *Memoirs*, pp. 286, 304–305.

11. Monnet's *Memoirs* opens with a description of the offer of Anglo-French union, pp. 17–35.

12. Ibid., p. 225; Robert Marjolin, *Architect of European Unity: Memoirs, 1911–1986* (London: Weidenfeld and Nicolson, 1989), pp. 228–229.

13. For an account of the Marshall Plan and its relationship to European integration, see Michael Hogan, *The Marshall Plan: America, Britain and the Reconstruction*

of Western Europe, 1947–1952 (Cambridge: Cambridge University Press, 1987); Alan Milward, *The Reconstruction of Western Europe* (London: Methuen, 1984); Forrest Pogue, *George C. Marshall*, vol. 4: *Statesman, 1945–1959* (New York: Viking Press, 1987); and Imanuel Wexler, *The Marshall Plan Revisited: The European Recovery Program in Economic Perspective* (Westport, CT: Greenwood Press, 1983).

14. Office of the Historian, *Foreign Relations of the United States* (hereafter cited as *FRUS*), vol. 3 (Washington, DC: U.S. Department of State, 1947), pp. 230–232, 237–239.

15. Zurcher, *Struggle to Unite Europe*, pp. 13–16.

16. Walter Isaacson, *The Wise Men: Six Friends and the World They Made* (New York: Simon and Schuster, 1986), p. 122.

17. Hogan, *Marshall Plan*, p. 52.

18. See Alan Milward, *The European Rescue of the Nation State* (London: Routledge, 2000).

19. On the failure of the OEEC, see Milward, *Reconstruction,* pp. 466–469.

20. See John W. Young, *France, the Cold War, and the Western Alliance* (New York: St. Martin's Press, 1990); and F. Roy Willis, *France, Germany and the New Europe, 1945–1967* (Palo Alto, CA: Stanford University Press, 1968), pp. 7–31.

21. Isaacson, *Wise Men,* p. 236.

22. On the change in French thinking that led to the Schuman Plan, see Milward, *Reconstruction,* p. 492; and Raymond Poidevin, *Robert Schuman: Homme d'Etat, 1866–1963* (Paris: Imprimerie Nationale, 1986), pp. 32–58.

23. Monnet, *Memoirs,* pp. 298–306. For an account of the historic declaration, see Roger Bullen and M. E. Pelly, *The Schuman Plan, the Council of Europe and Western European Integration* (London: Her Majesty's Stationery Office, 1986); William Diebold, "Imponderables of the Schuman Plan," *Foreign Affairs* 29, no. 1 (October 1950): 114–129; and Mark Roseman, *Recasting the Ruhr, 1945–1958: Manpower, Economic Recovery, and Labor Relations* (New York: Berg, 1992).

24. On Schuman's life and career, see Poidevin, *Schuman.*

25. Konrad Adenauer, *Memoirs, 1945–1966* (Chicago: Henry Regnery, 1966), pp. 244–248. On Adenauer's commitment to European integration, see also Dennis Bark and David Gress, *A History of West Germany,* vol. 1: *1945–1963* (Oxford: Blackwell, 1989).

26. *FRUS,* 1949, vol. 3, p. 625.

27. Dean Acheson, *Present at the Creation: My Years in the State Department* (New York: W. W. Norton, 1969), pp. 383–384.

28. John Gillingham, *Coal, Steel and the Rebirth of Europe, 1945–1955: The Germans and French from Ruhr Conflict to Economic Community* (Cambridge: Cambridge University Press, 1991), p. 235.

29. Ibid., p. 231.

30. Monnet, *Memoirs,* p. 293.

31. Marjolin, *Memoirs,* p. 126.

32. Milward, *Reconstruction,* p. 255.

33. For a discussion of British policy toward postwar Europe, see Alan Milward, *The United Kingdom and the European Community,* vol. 1: *The Rise and Fall of a National Strategy, 1945–1963* (London: Frank Cass Publishers, 2002); Richard Ovendale, *Foreign Policy of the British Labour Government, 1945–1951* (London: Pinter, 1984); and John Young, *Britain, France and the Unity of Europe, 1945–1951* (Leicester, UK: Leicester University Press, 1984).

34. See Alan Bullock, *The Life and Times of Ernest Bevin,* vol. 3: *Ernest Bevin: Foreign Secretary, 1948–1951* (London: Heinemann, 1983), pp. 731–733; and Dean

Acheson, *Sketches from Life of Men I Have Known* (New York: H. Hamilton, 1961), pp. 38–41.

35. Milward, *Reconstruction,* p. 404.

36. Theodore White, *In Search of History: A Personal Adventure* (New York: Harper and Row, 1978), pp. 438–439.

37. Gillingham, *Coal, Steel,* p. 229.

38. Monnet, *Memoirs,* p. 329.

39. See Edward Fursdon, *The European Defense Community: A History* (New York: St. Martin's Press, 1980).

40. On the political community negotiations, see Rita Cardozo, "The Project for Political Union (1952–54)," in Pryce, ed., *Dynamics,* pp. 49–77.

41. See Raymond Aron, *France Defeats EDC* (New York: Praeger, 1957).

42. Gillingham, *Coal, Steel,* pp. 297–298.

43. Monnet, *Memoirs,* p. 400.

44. Walter Yondorf, "Monnet and the Action Committee: The Formative Years of the European Communities," *International Organization* 19 (1965): 909; see also Pascal Fontaine, *Le Comité d'Action pour les Etats Unis d'Europe de Jean Monnet* (Lausanne: Centre de Recherches Européennes, 1974).

45. *FRUS, 1955–1957,* vol. 4, p. 323.

46. Marjolin, *Memoirs,* p. 284.

47. See Yondorf, "Monnet and the Action Committee," pp. 896–901.

48. Marjolin, *Memoirs,* p. 296.

49. Hanns-Jurgen Küsters, "The Treaties of Rome (1955–57)," in Pryce, ed., *Dynamics,* p. 94.

50. Marjolin, *Memoirs,* p. 306.

2

Uncertain Terrain, 1958–1972

Three individuals, all French, contributed most to shaping the European Union (EU). Yet if the EU ever built a pantheon for its heroes, only two of them would be buried there. The first, Jean Monnet, would have pride of place. The second, Jacques Delors, Commission president between 1985 and 1995, would repose beside Monnet in almost equal esteem. But the third, Charles de Gaulle, would never be considered for interment in the EU's hallowed ground. On the contrary, de Gaulle would be relegated to the rogues' gallery of EU villains. For in the popular opinion of European integrationists, de Gaulle's anachronistic championing of the nation-state destroyed the European Community's development in the 1960s and stunted its institutional growth until the Single European Act of 1986 and the Maastricht Treaty of 1992.

In fact, de Gaulle's contribution to European integration was far from negative. The Common Agricultural Policy (CAP), though subsequently denigrated as a drain on EU resources and an impediment to international trade accord, owes its existence to de Gaulle. In the 1960s, the CAP proved a vital instrument of solidarity and helped restructure declining Western European agriculture. More important, without the CAP there would not have been a community of any kind. Just as the French parliament had successfully insisted on agricultural provisions in the Rome Treaty, so, too, had de Gaulle demanded implementation of those provisions as a condition of implementing the treaty as a whole. The customs union came into being because of, not despite, the CAP.

De Gaulle is best known in the context of the European Community (EC) for keeping Britain out and for curtailing the powers of the European Parliament and the Commission. Once again, both seem negative achievements. But allowing Britain to join in the early 1960s would in all likelihood have thwarted the CAP, undermined the Community, and turned the customs union into a broad free trade area. De Gaulle's stand against the Commission in

1965 epitomized his hostility to supranationalism. Yet intergovernmentalism, which de Gaulle so bluntly asserted, laid the basis for the EC's survival in the 1970s and reinvigoration in the 1980s. Ironically, as Stanley Hoffmann observed, the EU of the 1990s was "an improbable, yet not ineffectual, blend of de Gaulle and Monnet."[1]

After the political frustrations of the 1960s, the EC seemed set to shake off the shackles of Gaullism and begin an invigorating new phase of its development. "Completion, deepening, enlargement," a slogan popularized by French president Georges Pompidou and endorsed by the Six at the Hague summit of 1969, summed up the optimism of the post–de Gaulle era. Imbued with the so-called spirit of The Hague, the EC completed unfinished business, launched new initiatives, and finally concluded accession agreements with Britain, Denmark, and Ireland, which joined the EC in January 1972 (Table 2.1). Nevertheless, solidarity was sorely tested on the eve of enlargement by Franco-German differences over monetary policy, a harbinger of difficulties in the decade ahead as the EC endured the impact of British accession and severe economic recession.

Table 2.1   Chronology, 1958–1972

1958	January	Launch of the EEC and Euratom
	May	Collapse of the French Fourth Republic
	June	Charles de Gaulle forms a provisional government
	July	A conference in Stresa, Italy, lays the foundations for the Common Agricultural Policy (CAP)
	September	A referendum endorses the establishment of the French Fifth Republic
	December	De Gaulle is elected president of France
1959	January	First stage of transition to a common market begins
1961	August	Britain applies to join the EEC (followed by Denmark, Ireland, and Norway)
	November	France drafts a treaty for a political community (Fouchet Plan)
1962	January	Second stage of transition to a common market begins
	April	Fouchet Plan collapses
	July	U.S. president John F. Kennedy outlines a "grand design" for U.S.-European relations
1963	January	De Gaulle vetoes Britain's EEC membership application; de Gaulle and Konrad Adenauer sign the Elysée Treaty; accession negotiations with Britain (and Denmark, Ireland, and Norway) end
	July	Yaoundé Convention between the EC and seventeen African states and Madagascar is signed
1965	April	Merger Treaty, fusing the executives of the EEC, ECSC, and Euratom, is signed
	July	Empty chair crisis begins
1966	January	EC enters the third and final stage of transition to a common market; agreement is reached in the Luxembourg Compromise, ending the empty chair crisis

continues

Table 2.1   *continued*

1967	May	Britain applies a second time for EC membership (followed by Denmark, Ireland, and Norway)
	July	The Merger Treaty enters into force
	November	De Gaulle vetoes Britain's application a second time
	December	Accession negotiations with Britain (and Denmark, Ireland, and Norway) are suspended
1968	May	Student and worker riots in Paris
	July	The customs union is completed eighteen months ahead of schedule
1969	April	De Gaulle resigns
	July	Britain, Denmark, Ireland, and Norway reactivate membership applications
	December	At a summit in The Hague, EU leaders decide to revive the EEC
1970	April	Agreement to finance EC through "own resources"
	June	Accession negotiations with Britain, Denmark, Ireland, and Norway resume
	October	Pierre Werner presents plan for economic and monetary union
		Foreign ministers adopt Davignon Plan for European Political Cooperation (foreign policy cooperation)
	November	Foreign ministers hold first European Political Cooperation meeting (foreign policy cooperation)
1971	January	Second Yaoundé Convention and Arusha agreement enter into force
	August	United States announces the suspension of dollar convertibility, formally ending the Bretton Woods system
1972	January	Accession treaties signed in Brussels
	March	Launch of the monetary "snake"
	September	Norwegians reject EEC membership in a referendum
	October	At Paris summit, EEC leaders agree "to transform the whole complex of . . . relations [between member states] into a European Union" by the end of the decade

▨ France, Germany, and the European Community

De Gaulle's first contribution to the EC was to bring France, then the politically and economically most important member state, back from the brink of catastrophe. Since the end of World War II a series of bitter colonial conflicts, first in Indochina and later in North Africa, had progressively undermined the already precarious Fourth Republic. In May 1958 a revolt by French army officers in Algiers, sparked by rumors of impending negotiations between the French government and the Algerian nationalists, proved the last straw. Threatened by a right-wing coup, the government collapsed. Despite numerous new governments and cabinet reshuffles during the Fourth Republic's brief, unhappy history, the country's hitherto resourceful politicians seemed suddenly paralyzed by fear.

Twice before at times of national crisis de Gaulle had come to the rescue: first when he rejected the armistice of June 1940 and set up the Free French

Movement; second when he bridged deep political divisions and established a provisional government in the newly liberated France in August 1944. Fourteen years later, only de Gaulle wielded the moral authority and commanded the national respect necessary once again to save the nation. Exploiting the legend of 1940 and the lessons of 1944, de Gaulle began negotiations with the political parties (minus the Communists) about forming not only a new government but a new regime. Few argued with his demand that the new republic possess a strong presidency insulated from parliamentary factionalism and having almost exclusive responsibility for foreign policy and defense. In September 1958 a grateful electorate ushered in the Fifth Republic by overwhelmingly endorsing de Gaulle's constitution. In 1962, having survived another army revolt triggered by his acceptance of Algerian independence, de Gaulle held a referendum on direct elections for the presidency, the success of which completed the constitutional construction of the Fifth Republic.

Monnet understood the importance for the EC of a politically stable France. In the run-up to the 1958 referendum, Monnet wrote that "to safeguard our future we must now put an end to the Algerian crisis and ensure governmental stability and authority. These two imperatives are linked." Similarly, Monnet voted yes in the referendum on direct elections for the presidency in order to "give the executive greater legitimacy and also facilitate the decisions required for the unification of Europe. For sovereignty to be relegated, authority must be well-established."[2] Of course de Gaulle was averse to surrendering any sovereignty whatsoever. For that reason Monnet voted against de Gaulle in that year's presidential election. But Monnet's point about a strong executive forming the necessary basis for the sharing of sovereignty was prescient, for it was precisely from such a position that President François Mitterrand advanced European integration so effectively in the mid- and late 1980s.

De Gaulle's concomitant financial and monetary reforms proved equally essential for the success of the EC. Without de Gaulle's drastic devaluation of the franc in 1958 and related government expenditure cuts and taxation hikes, the fragile French economy could not have survived intra-EC tariff reductions. Nor might the first round of tariff cuts, due to be implemented in January 1959, have taken place had the French franc remained so overvalued. There is some truth to de Gaulle's later assertion that when the EC came into being, "it was necessary—in order to achieve something—that we French put in order our economic, financial and monetary affairs. . . . From that moment the Community was in principle viable."[3]

The Economic Advantage of Europe

European Community membership may have provided a pretext for financial and monetary measures that would otherwise have proved politically impossible (as was the case with a number of member states four decades later in the run-up to monetary union). But the EC meant much more than that to de Gaulle. Despite its implications for French sovereignty, membership offered de Gaulle a valuable opportunity to promote two overriding objectives: economic modernization and an institutional framework in which to embed Franco-German rapprochement.

During the debate on economic integration in the mid-1950s, de Gaulle, then in the political wilderness, said little publicly. Privately, he reportedly told an associate that "we shall tear up [the Rome Treaty] when we come to power."[4] When he did come to power, de Gaulle unequivocally supported key EC objectives on pragmatic political and economic grounds. Accordingly, the EC flourished in its early years not because de Gaulle reluctantly acquiesced in it—for legal reasons, or because his government depended on the support of the pro-EC parliamentarians, or because he was preoccupied with Algeria—but because he strongly supported a certain amount of economic integration. As David Calleo noted at the time, "Of all the national governments, it is de Gaulle's France which has supported most vigorously and constantly . . . the creation of a genuinely integrated European economy."[5]

In his memoirs, Harold Wilson, Britain's prime minister in the mid-1960s and again in the mid-1970s, told the story of de Gaulle dismissing the discipline of economics as "quartermaster stuff."[6] Despite his fashionable denunciation of the dismal science, de Gaulle appreciated the importance of good quartermasters for the successful functioning of a modern army. Although he had no formal training in economics, de Gaulle took a keen interest in financial and monetary affairs. In 1946 he appointed Monnet to head the new office of economic planning; in 1958 he resolved to make France a leading industrial power. As de Gaulle remarked in his own memoirs, "International competition . . . offered a lever to stimulate our business sector, to force it to increase productivity . . . hence my decision to promote the Common Market which was still just a collection of paper."[7] De Gaulle's main interest lay in the international arena, but he remained acutely aware that only if France were economically and socially stable could his foreign policy succeed. Paradoxically, it was economic weakness and social discord that blighted de Gaulle's foreign policy and ultimately prompted his resignation in 1969.

Apart from seeking industrial rejuvenation, de Gaulle saw in the EC a great opportunity to modernize the large and cumbersome French agricultural sector. "How could we maintain on our territory more than two million farms," de Gaulle wondered, "three-quarters of which were too small and too poor to be profitable, but on which, nonetheless, nearly one-fifth of the French population live? How, in this day and age, could we leave the agricultural profession to stumble along, without the benefit of technical training, organized markets, and the support of a rational credit system required for it to be competitive?"[8] The solution lay in the proposed Common Agricultural Policy, which would provide an EC-wide outlet for French produce, guarantee high agricultural prices regardless of low prices on the world market, and subsidize the export of surplus produce outside the EC itself. In effect, de Gaulle sought to get the EC to prop up French agriculture. His quid pro quo was Germany's expected profit from the lowering and ultimate abandonment of intra-EC industrial tariffs. The negotiations ahead would be arduous and acrimonious, but the advantage for France was clear. Hence de Gaulle's admission that "if, on resuming control of our affairs, I indeed embraced the Common Market, it was as much because of our position as an agricultural country as for the progress it would impose on our industry. . . . The CAP was a sine qua non of [our] participation."[9]

Britain's proposal to establish a European free trade area to incorporate and possibly supplant the EC threatened to abort the CAP. Having decided not to join the EC, Britain sought instead to enjoy the benefits of free trade in Europe while eschewing a common external tariff, a common agricultural policy, and any form of economic integration. EC member states resented what they saw as Britain's efforts to undermine European integration by diluting the nascent EC in a wider free trade area. Robert Marjolin, a vice president of the new Commission, saw the proposal as "a great danger, that of being more or less sucked into a vast European free trade area in which [the Community] would have lost its individuality, and which might have prevented it from fully establishing itself according to the terms of the Treaty of Rome."[10]

De Gaulle especially feared the proposal's implications for agriculture, a sector specifically excluded from the free trade offer. Although talks about a possible free trade area had continued since the second half of 1956, de Gaulle brought them to an abrupt end soon after coming to power. Britain pressed ahead and in November 1959 formed the European Free Trade Association (EFTA) with Austria, Denmark, Norway, Portugal, Sweden, and Switzerland. EC member states rejected an early EFTA overture for some kind of economic association, resolving instead to continue with closer integration. This proved so successful by the early 1960s that Britain applied for EC membership.

Adenauer and de Gaulle

De Gaulle's position on the EC complemented his policy toward Germany. In September 1958 German chancellor Konrad Adenauer visited de Gaulle for the first time. Whereas de Gaulle had advocated a punitive policy toward a weak, divided Germany when he had left the political stage in 1946, he returned in 1958 to a radically altered European scene. With Germany reindustrialized and rearmed, de Gaulle abandoned his earlier position and espoused instead the then-orthodox French policy of reconciliation and rapprochement.

The remarkably warm relationship that immediately blossomed between the octogenarian chancellor and septuagenarian president confirmed both leaders in the belief that their countries' future, and the future of Europe, depended above all on close Franco-German accord. At their second meeting, in November 1958, de Gaulle assured Adenauer of France's commitment to the Rome Treaty and won German support for the CAP.

During the remaining years of Adenauer's tenure, neither leader allowed a myriad of political and economic issues to come between France and Germany. Key international developments in the late 1950s and early 1960s convinced Adenauer of the wisdom of sticking to the Franco-German course. For instance, when Soviet president Nikita Khrushchev threatened unspecified action unless the Western powers revised the status of Berlin, the divided former capital of Germany, de Gaulle immediately offered Adenauer his full support, a position from which France never wavered during the protracted Berlin crises of the coming years. Hans von der Groeben, a commissioner in the 1960s and later a historian of the EC, identified Khrushchev's ultimatum as being "of crucial importance to further political development and to the establishment of the process of integration."[11] In return for de Gaulle's support in the face of crude Soviet threats, Adenauer supported de Gaulle's controversial positions on the CAP and on Britain's membership application. More important, he also supported de Gaulle's plans for a new European security community.

At issue were de Gaulle's conception of the EC and his espousal of a "European Europe." In de Gaulle's view, European integration should be limited to the technical aspects of the Rome Treaty. But these could succeed only in a broader framework of intergovernmental cooperation on political and security affairs. Such cooperation was an essential prerequisite for the emergence of an economically strong, politically assertive, and militarily independent Europe. Accordingly, de Gaulle sought to establish a "Union of States," both as a central plank of his European policy and as a prerequisite for subsequent efforts to challenge the United States and break down global bipolarity.

Having consulted Adenauer, de Gaulle launched his initiative for a new European security community in Paris in September 1960. Despite the small member states' misgivings, a committee under the chairmanship of Christian Fouchet, French ambassador to Denmark, eventually drafted a design for a confederation of European states. With the goal of a common foreign and defense policy, as well as cooperation on cultural, educational, and scientific matters, the Fouchet Plan outlined an institutional framework that included a ministerial council, a commission of senior foreign ministry officials, and a consultative assembly of delegated national parliamentarians.

The Fouchet Plan was clearly incompatible with European integration as envisioned by the EC's founders. Although Monnet and other leading Eurofederalists had commented favorably on de Gaulle's original idea, their opposition grew as the plan took shape. Fearing French or Franco-German hegemony in a putative European organization that lacked the safeguards of supranationalism, other member states followed the Netherlands' lead and fiercely resisted the idea. A series of acrimonious meetings in early 1962 caused the Fouchet Committee to collapse.

De Gaulle salvaged an institutionalized Franco-German alliance from the wreckage. By contrast with the indifference and hostility of the smaller European partners, Germany had resolutely backed de Gaulle's scheme. To be more precise, Adenauer had resolutely backed the Fouchet Plan. With Adenauer's political and temporal life obviously drawing to an end (the chancellor was then eighty-seven years old), de Gaulle borrowed the Fouchet Plan's infrastructure to cement Franco-German rapprochement. Thus, de Gaulle proposed regular meetings of the French president and the German chancellor, with their relevant ministers, to discuss cultural, economic, educational, and international issues. In the ensuing Franco-German Treaty of Friendship and Reconciliation, signed at the Elysée Palace in January 1963, both sides pledged "to consult each other, prior to any decision, on all questions of foreign policy . . . with a view to reaching an analogous position."[12]

The Elysée Treaty was the pinnacle of Adenauer's diplomacy, symbolizing as it did Franco-German reconciliation and accord. But bitter political controversy in Germany came to a head during the ratification debate in May 1963, robbing the treaty of much of its value for de Gaulle. Alarmed by Adenauer's apparent willingness to go along with de Gaulle's idiosyncratic European initiatives, a majority within the chancellor's own Christian Democratic Party joined with the Social Democratic opposition to attach a codicil to the treaty asserting Germany's overriding commitment to existing NATO obligations. To make matters worse for de Gaulle, Adenauer resigned in April 1963. His successor, Ludwig Erhard, was a steadfast Atlanticist whose tenure as chancellor, from 1963 to 1966, saw a steady deterioration in Franco-German relations. "There is no point deceiving ourselves," de Gaulle remarked after a meeting with Erhard in July 1964, "the [Elysée] Treaty has not yet developed as we had hoped. . . . Europe will only be a reality when France and Germany are truly united."[13]

Ironically, the Elysée Treaty would achieve its potential and prove its worth as a cornerstone not of intergovernmentalism in the EC but of closer political and economic integration. Despite his dislike of Erhard, de Gaulle continued to attend regular bilateral meetings under the terms of the treaty. Subsequent French presidents and German chancellors, as well as a host of government ministers and officials, similarly stuck to a fixed schedule of bilateral meetings. With the rapid improvement of Franco-German relations in the 1970s and a growing consensus in both countries about the utility of European integration, these frequent, institutionalized contacts became a major driving force of European integration.

■ Constructing the Community

Franco-German rapprochement in the late 1950s, de Gaulle's benevolence toward certain provisions of the Rome Treaty, and an extremely buoyant European economy helped get the EC off to a strong start. Robert Marjolin recalled the EC's first four years as "a honeymoon . . . a time of harmony between the governments of the member countries and between [EC] institutions."[14] Walter Hallstein, a former German state secretary for foreign affairs and an early collaborator of Jean Monnet's, presided over the first Commission. With nine members (two each from Germany, France, and Italy and one each from the other member states), the Commission spent the first few months of its existence settling into temporary quarters in Brussels, allocating responsibilities and portfolios among its members, and organizing the necessary staff and services.

The Council, the EC's legislative body, began regular meetings in Brussels and located a small secretariat there. The Council also organized the Committee of Permanent Representatives (Coreper), consisting of ambassadors resident in Brussels and able to promote their countries' interests on a day-to-day basis. In Luxembourg the Court of Justice began to produce an impressive body of EC case law that would profoundly affect the course of European integration. The Assembly of the European Community, later to call itself the European Parliament, met for the first time in Strasbourg in January 1958 and, initially at least, was the Cinderella of the new Community.

The first Commission's nine portfolios, one for each commissioner, are a useful indicator of the early agenda. In addition to one covering administration, there were portfolios for external relations, economic and financial affairs, the internal market, competition, social affairs, agriculture, transport, and overseas countries and territories. In some of these areas the treaty dictated a specific timetable for implementing certain measures; in others, it provided no more than general guidelines and statements of principle. The most immediate task was to establish the customs union. Thanks to French financial and economic reforms, the first intra-EC tariff reductions took place, on schedule, in January 1959. As other rounds of tariff cuts and quota increases followed, member states put in place a common external tariff. The customs union came into being in July 1968, eighteen months earlier than stipulated in the treaty.

The late 1950s and the early 1960s were years of extraordinarily high and sustained rates of economic growth in Western Europe, in large part because of an enormous escalation of international trade. From 1958 to 1960 alone, trade among the Six grew by 50 percent, a dramatic rise that was as much a result of "the increased activity of businessmen as [of] the actual reduction of tariffs. As soon as managers were convinced that the common market was going to be established, they started to behave in many ways as if it was already in existence."[15] High growth rates, a healthy balance of payments, and relatively stable prices provided incentives to coordinate member states' economic policies, a step the treaty merely hinted at but that the Commission eagerly pursued.

The EC's economic success facilitated the assertion and general acceptance of its international identity. With the exception of the Soviet Union and its satellites, other countries quickly acknowledged the Commission's responsibility for commercial policy and opened diplomatic missions in Brussels. The EC's early external initiatives pointed in two directions: multilateral trade negotiations and global development. Under the former, the Commission assumed responsibility for member state participation in the General Agreement on Tariffs and Trade (GATT). Under the latter, in 1964 the EC concluded the Yaoundé Convention with seventeen African states and Madagascar.

Successful first steps in commercial policy and external relations contrasted with the difficulty of fulfilling other treaty objectives. Whereas tariff barriers between member states could easily be identified and eliminated, policies in areas such as competition, social affairs, transport, and energy were harder to formulate. Progress was impeded by a combination of sometimes vague treaty provisions, member state apathy or outright opposition, and philosophical and ideological differences between and within the Commission and Council—factors that are as cogent in the EU today as they were in the early years. The result was a mixed record of policy formulation and implementation.

The EC faced its greatest challenge and enjoyed its first success in agriculture, although arguably at the cost of creating a monster. De Gaulle saw the vagueness of agricultural policy provisions as evidence of French weakness during the treaty negotiations. In his own words, he came to power resolved to "put up a literally desperate fight, sometimes going so far as to threaten to withdraw our membership [in the EC]" until ultimately "France and common sense prevailed."[16] Thanks to de Gaulle's brinkmanship, the foundations of the CAP were laid in a series of marathon negotiations in the early 1960s.

De Gaulle's refusal to acknowledge the Commission's contribution to negotiating the CAP demonstrated his well-known hatred of the Brussels bureaucracy. The extent to which both sides used each other during the CAP negotiations led to a fatal miscalculation by the Commission, which sought to link a further surrender of sovereignty with a successful conclusion of pending negotiations on financing agricultural policy. As it was, the Commission's growing prominence and political influence infuriated de Gaulle. By raising the political stakes, the Commission pushed de Gaulle too far and provoked a crisis that paralyzed the Community.

■ The Empty Chair Crisis

A dispute over the Commission's proposal to fund the CAP for the period between the expiration of the initial financial regulation in July 1965 and the end of the EC's transitional period in 1970 was the proximate cause of what became known as the empty chair crisis. Once fully operational, the CAP was to have been funded by levies on agricultural imports into the EC, supplemented by duties on industrial imports. Together, these would constitute the EC's "own resources." With the common markets due to be completed ahead of schedule in July 1968, the Commission proposed that the EC acquire its own resources at that time. Suggesting that member states give up their import duties early was itself controversial. But, emboldened by the successful implementation to date of the treaty's commercial and agricultural provisions and by de Gaulle's obvious interest in securing a new financial regulation for the CAP, the Commission rashly went too far when it proposed a complex budgetary system in which the Commission itself and the Parliament would greatly enhance their powers.

This plan went far beyond what de Gaulle would ever accept and caused the inherently tense relationship between his government and the Commission to explode into open antagonism in the spring of 1965. As it was, de Gaulle despised the Brussels bureaucracy, dismissing Commission officials as stateless and denationalized. He especially detested Hallstein, who used every opportunity to push European integration along federal lines and enhance the Commission's power.

Marjolin warned his colleagues not to persist with the CAP proposals and violate the Commission's "golden rule" of not taking any action "likely to encounter an outright veto [by a member state] that would have left no room for negotiation."[17] Undeterred, Hallstein pressed ahead and took the additional inflammatory step of first announcing the proposals not to the Council in Brussels but to the Parliament in Strasbourg. Storm clouds immediately appeared, with the French foreign minister warning that "our partners are indulging in wishful thinking by putting forward proposals which they know France will not accept."[18]

France Leaves the Council

Antagonized by de Gaulle's haughtiness and aware of his desire to complete the CAP, other member states prepared to call his bluff. A meeting between de Gaulle and Erhard in early June 1965 failed to avert the crisis. Nor did the other member states act on a French proposal to continue funding the CAP by national contributions, thereby avoiding the contentious question of the Community's own resources. Few seemed alarmed by the looming deadline of June 30. Negotiations on the CAP, after all, had a reputation for running late.

The crucial Council meeting opened on June 28 with France in the chair. Taking a minimalist position, the French foreign minister pressed for a decision only on funding the CAP after July 1. With others insisting that the Commission's proposals would have to be considered as a whole, substantive discussions had not even begun by midnight on June 30. Two hours later, the meeting broke up. The French government promptly recalled its permanent representative and announced that French officials would no longer participate in the Council or its numerous committees.[19]

Faced with an empty French chair, the Community could do little more than conduct routine business. De Gaulle raised the stakes by linking an additional, hitherto unrelated point to the original cause of the conflict. In a typically self-serving press conference in September 1965, full of invective against the Commission and the Parliament, de Gaulle announced that France would not accept a provision of the treaty, due to be implemented in January 1966, introducing qualified majority voting in the Council on a limited range of issues.[20]

De Gaulle's attack on qualified majority voting and insistence on unanimity (in which any nation could unilaterally veto legislation) greatly exacerbated the crisis. Other member states shared France's concern about being outvoted in the Council but argued that important national interests were unlikely ever to be ignored. At a Council meeting held without France in late October, the participants reaffirmed their commitment to the treaty and refusal to renegotiate one of its few supranational provisions. At the same time, they expressed willingness to compromise on the Commission's earlier proposals and offered France every opportunity to return to the negotiating table.

The Luxembourg Compromise

The other member states' solidarity may have been a factor in de Gaulle's decision to resume talks. French public opinion was arguably a more important consideration. Farmers' organizations and business interests feared the consequences of a protracted crisis, and the presidential election of December 1965 gave them an opportunity to express their concern. Although other issues were involved, François Mitterrand, de Gaulle's main rival, called himself "the candidate of Europe."[21] Deprived of an absolute majority in the first round of balloting, de Gaulle and Mitterrand contested the second round alone. As expected, de Gaulle won, but not by a huge margin.

The election result demonstrated the domestic limits on de Gaulle's European policy. Although notoriously insensitive to French public opinion, de Gaulle undoubtedly got the message. A week after the election, France announced its willingness to negotiate an end to the crisis, which was finally resolved at a foreign ministers' meeting at the end of January 1966. There, the Six agreed to adopt an interim financial regulation for the CAP, deferring the question of the EC's own resources and, by extension, the Parliament's budgetary power. Majority voting in the Council remained the outstanding issue. After restating their positions, both sides approved a short declaration, the Luxembourg Compromise, which amounted to an agreement to disagree:

1. When issues very important to one or more member countries are at stake, the members of the Council will try, within a reasonable time, to reach solutions which can be adopted by all members of the Council, while respecting their mutual interests, and those of the Community.
2. The French delegation considers that, when very important issues are at stake, discussions must be continued until unanimous agreement is reached.
3. The six delegations note that there is a divergence of views on what should be done in the event of a failure to reach complete agreement.
4. However, they consider that this divergence does not prevent the Community's work being resumed in accordance with the normal procedure.[22]

The outcome of the crisis was apparently a draw, perhaps even a victory for the EC. After all, the other member states had not reneged on majority voting, and the Council soon resumed full operation. In reality, the crisis ended in victory for de Gaulle. The Council approved temporary funding for the CAP in May 1966, and the Commission's ambitious proposals to revise budgetary procedures sank out of sight. Moreover, the crisis profoundly undermined both Hallstein's credibility and the Commission's confidence. Thereafter, the Commission refrained from asserting itself for over a decade.

Crucially, the Luxembourg Compromise impeded effective decisionmaking in the Council for a long time to come. De Gaulle's insistence on unanimity heightened the member states' awareness of each other's special interests and increased their reluctance to call a vote even when no vital interest was at stake. The Luxembourg Compromise did not disrupt established decisionmaking procedures because majority voting had never been the norm. Instead, as Joseph Weiler observed, "it symbolized a transformation from a 'Community' spirit to a more selfish and pragmatic 'cost-benefit' attitude of the member states. It was a change of ethos, at first rejected by the Five but later, especially after the first enlargement, eagerly seized upon by all. In this sense the danger to the Community, even if not always tangible, was significant."[23]

To some extent the crisis demonstrated that the Community depends on an environment over which it has little control. But the crisis also helped shape the political climate in which the Community operated during the next decade. Six months of near paralysis in Brussels, a heavy blow to the Commission's morale, and a substantial setback to majority voting had an invidious effect. In the final analysis, "the Community and the Western European states moved closer to Gaullist confederal notions, while the European federalists lost ground."[24]

■ Keeping Britain Out

The question of EC enlargement arose for the first time in 1961, when Britain applied to join. By the end of the 1950s it was readily apparent that the Commonwealth was an inadequate vehicle through which to promote British interests. By contrast, the EC was flourishing. Earlier attempts to dissolve the EC into a wider free trade area had emphasized British fears of economic exclusion. The failure of the free trade initiative and the corresponding success of the fledgling customs union convinced Britain's political and business leaders that the country's interests lay in full EC membership.

Yet deep suspicion of European integration tempered British enthusiasm. The opposition Labour Party was deeply divided on the issue. A small group of passionate "promarketeers" balanced a corresponding clique of ardent "antimarketeers," with the bulk of the party either uncertain or moderately hostile to membership. The Conservatives generally favored joining, although Prime Minister Harold Macmillan purged the cabinet of a few antimarketeers and appointed Edward Heath, who ultimately brought Britain into the EC in 1973, to lead the entry negotiations in Brussels.

The Special Relationship

In Macmillan's view, the decision to apply for EC membership complemented his foreign policy priority: restoring and maintaining the Anglo-American "special relationship." No sooner did Macmillan become prime minister in 1957 than he set off to meet President Eisenhower in Bermuda. The two had worked together in Algiers in 1943 trying to coordinate Anglo-American policy toward none other than de Gaulle, then fighting for his political life as leader of the Free French Movement. Coincidentally, while Eisenhower and Macmillan reminisced in Bermuda, leaders of the Six signed the Treaty of Rome, which Macmillan did not even mention in his diaries.[25]

The election of President John F. Kennedy caused Macmillan to fret again about Anglo-American relations. Kennedy's youth, charisma, and Irish ancestry convinced the older, staid Macmillan that the special relationship was imperiled. At their first meeting, in March 1961, Kennedy put Macmillan's fears to rest. For the remainder of Kennedy's brief administration, a remarkably close personal friendship between the president and prime minister cemented Anglo-American ties.

Kennedy's unequivocal endorsement of British membership in the EC strengthened Macmillan's determination to join but aroused de Gaulle's suspicions. Kennedy's "Grand Design" for closer U.S.-EC relations and a stronger Atlantic Alliance, outlined in a famous Independence Day speech in 1962, seemed at variance with de Gaulle's conception of a "European Europe." In de Gaulle's view, an equitable transatlantic relationship was impossible as long as Western Europe was strategically subservient to the United States. By linking British accession and U.S. Atlantic Alliance strategy, Kennedy helped seal the fate of Macmillan's application.[26]

Macmillan tried to overcome these profound differences with de Gaulle by appealing to past friendship and pursuing a close personal relationship. Macmillan visited Paris soon after de Gaulle returned to power. As his biographer noted, "It was a momentous occasion for Macmillan, meeting again the man who had first come into his life in the dark days in Algiers fifteen years previously, and for whose cause he had fought so hard then. But for Macmillan's support for de Gaulle against Roosevelt and Churchill, almost certainly de Gaulle would not have been in Paris, at the helm, in 1958."[27]

Undoubtedly de Gaulle owed Macmillan a huge political debt, but the latter's efforts to overcome de Gaulle's opposition to Britain's EC membership were pitiful. Macmillan's diary entry for November 26, 1961, written after a private visit from de Gaulle, reveals the prime minister's extreme frustration with, and acute misunderstanding of, the French president's position: "De Gaulle was no more conciliatory over the Common Market. . . . The tragedy of it all is that we agree with de Gaulle on almost everything. We like the political Europe that de Gaulle likes. We are anti-federalists; so is he. . . . We agree; but his pride, his inherited hatred of England (since Joan of Arc) . . . above all, his intense 'vanity' for France—she must dominate—make him half welcome, half repel us, with a strange love-hate complex. Sometimes, when I am with him, I feel I have overcome it. But he goes back to his distrust and dislike, like a dog to vomit."[28]

The accession negotiations themselves quickly became mired in a mass of technical detail, mostly over the CAP, the Commonwealth, and the European Free Trade Association. A British government paper outlined the problems in all three areas. In agriculture, Britain's twin policies of buying low-priced food on the world market and paying farmers direct price support were incompatible with the principles of the CAP. As for the Commonwealth, Britain feared the political and economic impact on its former possessions of a sudden disruption of traditional trade patterns. Finally, "given [Britain's] obligations to our EFTA partners, we should not be able to join the Community until [we agreed upon] . . . ways and means of meeting their legitimate interests."[29]

In the event, developments in Anglo-American relations soon overshadowed the enlargement negotiations. Matters came to a head in December 1962 at a meeting in Nassau between Macmillan and Kennedy to negotiate a new Anglo-American missile accord. Under the terms of the Nassau agreement, Britain would use U.S. missiles as the delivery system for British nuclear warheads. Moreover, Britain's nuclear force would be integrated into NATO, except when the government "may decide that supreme national interests are at stake."[30]

For de Gaulle, then struggling to develop the French nuclear force, the Nassau agreement represented a damning surrender of sovereignty. Britain had relinquished to the United States technological and strategic responsibility for a supposedly independent nuclear deterrent. There could have been no more graphic demonstration of Britain's irreconcilability with de Gaulle's "European Europe." After a year of tough bargaining in Brussels, de Gaulle now had a useful pretext to break off the enlargement negotiations.

De Gaulle Says No

He did so dramatically in a press conference in January 1963. In a long, wide-ranging response to a planted question, de Gaulle cataloged the history of Britain's relationship with the EC. Having attempted to submerge the EC in a broad free trade area, Britain now sought to join, "but on her own conditions." Thus far, the entry negotiations had given little assurance that "Britain can place herself . . . inside a tariff which is genuinely common . . . renounce all Commonwealth preferences . . . cease any pretense that her agriculture be privileged, and, more than that . . . treat her engagements with other countries of the Free Trade Area as null and void." More to the point, were Britain to join without fundamentally changing its international orientation, the EC "would not endure for long [but] instead would become a colossal Atlantic community under American domination and direction."[31] De Gaulle's statement amounted to a veto of Britain's EC application.

Paul-Henri Spaak, who had chaired the intergovernmental conference leading to the Rome Treaty, wrote melodramatically that the date of de Gaulle's press conference was "fated to go down in history as the 'black Monday' of both European policy and Atlantic policy."[32] But as another observer remarked, the "crisis atmosphere" provoked by de Gaulle's statement "was not of long duration . . . because the concern of France's partners to push the Community forward was stronger than their irritation with French high-mindedness."[33] Though they regretted how the negotiations had come to an end, many national and EC officials agreed that Britain was not yet ready for accession. As Marjolin remarked in his memoirs, de Gaulle's decision to close the door on Britain "offended France's continental partners possibly more through its form than through its content."[34]

The suspension of Britain's application was a serious setback for Macmillan and contrasted starkly with his apparent success in concluding the Nassau agreement one month before. Nor can Macmillan have failed to notice that de Gaulle was far from isolated in his rejection of Britain's candidacy.

There was nothing for Britain to do but await a favorable time to reapply for membership and review in the meantime why the negotiations had stalled. Dejected, Macmillan resigned in October 1963 because of a purportedly terminal illness—but he went on to enjoy twenty-three years of robust retirement.

Britain Rebuffed Again

When Britain applied again for EC membership, in May 1967, the Labour Party was in power. Prime Minister Harold Wilson was equivocal about joining but, like Macmillan before him, saw no feasible alternative. If anything, Britain's declining political and economic links with the Commonwealth and growing commercial contacts with the continent increased the urgency of accession. Also like Macmillan before him, Wilson hoped to overcome French opposition to British entry by cultivating de Gaulle. Symbolizing a break with the past, Wilson first met de Gaulle at Churchill's funeral in January 1965. In the following months Wilson fostered what he thought was a warm friendship, based in part on his ambivalence about the Anglo-American special relationship. Apart from strategic considerations, Wilson shared French concerns about the long-term implication for European industry of U.S. technological superiority.

While Wilson took various steps to bolster domestic support and allay Commonwealth concerns before formally resubmitting Britain's membership application, de Gaulle reserved judgment. Yet only four days after Britain resubmitted its application, de Gaulle condescendingly claimed that Britain had not yet achieved "the profound economic and political transformation which would allow [it] to join the Six."[35] A period of confusion followed, during which the Commission issued a favorable opinion and preparations went ahead for accession negotiations to resume. In December 1967, during his biannual press conference, de Gaulle announced that Britain's entry "would obviously mean the breaking up of a Community that has been built and that functions according to rules which would not bear such a monumental exception."[36] There was no longer any doubt about the issue. A week later Britain shelved its application.

De Gaulle blocked Britain's second application for essentially the same reasons as before. Despite Wilson's difficulties with Washington, the Anglo-American special relationship remained fundamentally sound and, in de Gaulle's view, a barrier to British membership. In fact, Britain's inclusion in the EC would likely have had little impact on the Cold War and its underlying superpower system. Moreover, Germany, then "an economy in search of a political purpose,"[37] clearly had the potential to displace France as the center of gravity in the EC. British accession might therefore have bolstered

French leadership by providing a bulwark against German economic and political resurgence.

■ De Gaulle's Departure

Domestic and international developments in 1968 abruptly ended the Gaullist illusion. At home in France, social unrest erupted in May 1968 in a series of riots and strikes that threatened to topple not only the government but also the regime. De Gaulle's focus on foreign policy had blinded him to the extent of growing domestic dissatisfaction. Protesting a rigid educational system and declining living standards, millions of students and workers poured onto French city streets. After a month of unrest, the Fifth Republic seemed on the brink of collapse. What saved it, perhaps, was the unwillingness or inability of the Communist Party to exploit the situation fully. The government also survived, but not because of de Gaulle, who fled Paris at the height of the crisis, leaving his prime minister, Georges Pompidou, to find a solution. Pompidou did so brilliantly, largely by gambling on time and capitalizing on the inevitable public reaction against incessant instability. Having dissolved the parliament and called new elections in June 1968, the Gaullists and their allies won an overall majority.

It proved a Pyrrhic victory. The events of May 1968 demolished de Gaulle's personal popularity and fatally compromised his credibility as president. Although his term of office was not due to expire for another four years, after the domestic and international upheavals of 1968 de Gaulle increasingly looked like a lame-duck president. Other member states awaited de Gaulle's departure before taking any new initiatives. That came sooner than expected when, in April 1969, de Gaulle resigned, having staked his presidency on the outcome of two referendums on minor administrative issues. Western European and North American leaders watched de Gaulle go with a mixture of relief and regret—relief because progress within the EC and harmony within the Atlantic Alliance finally seemed ensured; regret because for all de Gaulle's foibles and illusions, few could doubt his eminence or achievements. De Gaulle had done more than restore French pride and self-esteem. He had saved his country's honor during the occupation and collaboration, ensured its stability during the liberation, and rescued its liberal democratic institutions during the Algerian crisis. In addition to leading France to prominence in the postwar world, de Gaulle gave Europe a greater sense of identity and purpose at a time of subordination to the superpowers. Even the Americans, who suffered most from de Gaulle's assertive foreign policy, readily acknowledged his sagacity and statesmanship. As Stanley Hoffmann observed, whatever one's point of view, "it is impossible not to be impressed by de Gaulle's life and works. . . . One does not often come so clearly in contact with greatness."[38]

■ The Spirit of The Hague

Georges Pompidou, de Gaulle's successor as president of France, held the key to the EC's development in the immediate aftermath of the general's resignation. Having served as prime minister for much of the 1960s, Pompidou was steeped in Gaullism but was not a slave to the general's EC policies. He sought to balance Gaullist hostility toward political integration on the one hand with growing resentment throughout the EC against French obduracy on the other. Enlargement posed an obvious dilemma. For Gaullist diehards, the veto of Britain's application had become sacrosanct. Yet for a growing portion of the French public and for France's EC partners, revoking the veto was the only means by which France could possibly retain influence and credibility in the EC.

Regardless of his personal preferences, there was an obvious objective change in France's circumstances in the late 1960s that impelled Pompidou to accept enlargement. The events of 1968 had enfeebled France economically. High inflation and a deteriorating balance of trade had followed de Gaulle's generous wage settlement with the unions and his loose monetary policy to boost recovery and stimulate growth. The result was a run on the franc that culminated in Pompidou's decision to devalue it in August 1969. These difficulties lowered France's international standing and made continued French participation in the EC more important than ever before. Consequently, Pompidou was in a far weaker position than de Gaulle to veto British membership.

Just as France had declined economically in the late 1960s, Germany had surged ahead. Under the new chancellor, Willy Brandt, Germany was also politically assertive. Gone were the days of Adenauer's subservience to de Gaulle. Germany's refusal to arrest the declining value of the franc by revaluing the mark and decision to launch an ambitious initiative toward Eastern Europe and the Soviet Union emphasized the point. The combination of Germany's growing economic power and rising political confidence made British accession a more appealing prospect for Pompidou. Together, Britain and France might counterbalance Germany's increasing weight and establish geopolitical symmetry in the EC.

As foreign minister in the Grand Coalition government of the mid-1960s, Brandt had taken the first tentative steps in the bold new direction of "normalizing" Germany's relations with the East. As chancellor of the Social Democratic–Free Democratic coalition that came to power in September 1969, Brandt elevated what became known as *Ostpolitik* to a central tenet of German foreign policy. The Christian Democrats, in opposition for the first time in the history of the Federal Republic, reacted predictably by denouncing *Ostpolitik* as a sellout of German interests in the East and a threat to Germany's ties in the West.[39]

However unfairly, *Ostpolitik* raised the specter for Germany's allies of a rootless, neutralist Federal Republic loosening its moorings in the West. Allied and internal Christian Democratic concern about *Ostpolitik* obliged Brandt to emphasize his support for European integration, which in any event he genuinely espoused. Moreover, Brandt stressed the importance of British accession as a means of reassuring those member states who feared Germany's resurgence. Prime Minister Harold Wilson used *Ostpolitik* to further his goal of EC entry by arguing that British accession would restrain German nationalist ambition.

The Hague Summit

Apprehensive about the possible impact of *Ostpolitik* and under pressure to launch an initiative of his own in the EC, Pompidou called for a special summit of the EC's leaders in December 1969. The Hague summit—the Netherlands then held the rotating EC presidency—was the first such meeting since the tenth-anniversary celebration of the Rome Treaty in 1967. With de Gaulle gone and enlargement moving toward center stage, most member states anticipated a decisive breakthrough. Indeed, the summit spawned the "spirit of The Hague," a belief that the EC was once more on the move. Especially in view of the Community's difficulties in the mid-1960s and later in the mid-1970s, the summit assumed a retrospective aura of harmony and unprecedented progress. Yet this impression belied the reality of a tense encounter between Pompidou, trying to square the Gaullist circle, and the others, led by an assertive Brandt determined to force the issue of British entry. The EC leaders' endorsement of Pompidou's catchphrase "completion, deepening, enlargement" disguised the continuing tension between France and the others but met the disparate demands of the main protagonists—including Britain, hovering in the wings.

It was no accident that "enlargement" came after "completion" and "deepening." At the summit, Pompidou endorsed enlargement in principle but called first for a strengthening of existing Community competences. "Completion" meant finalizing the financing of the CAP, a cherished French objective put in abeyance since the 1965 crisis. Negotiating a financial regulation for the CAP and funding the EC by its own resources would inevitably involve reopening the debate about the European Parliament's budgetary powers, a price Pompidou seemed willing to pay.

"Deepening" meant extending EC competences beyond existing policies and activities. Specifically, Pompidou advocated a system of foreign policy cooperation through regular meetings of foreign ministers and, possibly, the establishment of a secretariat in Paris. This smacked to the others of a revival of de Gaulle's political plans, although they by no means rejected the idea of attempting to coordinate member states' foreign policies. Especially in the context of *Ostpolitik,* member states quickly grasped the importance of at least exchanging information on foreign policy issues of mutual interest.

The realization that Germany's economy had become the region's driving force prompted Pompidou to propose deepening the EC as well by coordinating the member states' monetary policies. Pompidou realized that further monetary instability would endanger the CAP by exposing farm prices to parity fluctuations. Brandt had little time for the CAP; during the Hague summit he repeatedly attacked the rapid accumulation of agricultural surpluses. Nevertheless, he supported the idea of closer monetary policy coordination if only to demonstrate Germany's commitment to the EC in the face of Allied concern about *Ostpolitik*. But Brandt would not consider monetary cooperation in isolation. An ingrained fear of inflation led him also to urge greater economic convergence in the EC. Pierre Werner, prime minister of Luxembourg, agreed to draft a report on economic and monetary union (EMU) by the middle of the new year.

As for enlargement, Pompidou refused to set a target date for the beginning, let alone the end, of accession negotiations. On the contrary, he insisted that a new system for financing the CAP would have to be agreed to before exploratory talks with the candidate countries could begin. The Dutch countered with the opposite argument—that a financial regulation for the CAP should be concluded only when the EC agreed upon a timetable for enlargement. A bilateral meeting between Pompidou and Brandt on the margins of the summit provided the basis for a breakthrough. It was a classic EC compromise: in return for a commitment from the others to resolve agricultural funding by the end of the year, France promised that enlargement negotiations would begin by June 1970. To save face for the French, the summit communiqué omitted any mention of a timetable for the accession talks, but the Dutch prime minister made no secret in his closing press conference of the French climb-down.

Postsummit Progress

The spirit of The Hague soon bore fruit in an agreement to fund the CAP by granting the EC its own resources, consisting of all levies on agricultural products and duties on industrial goods imported into the EC, plus a small portion (not to exceed 1 percent) of national receipts of value-added tax. By contrast with the original June 1965 proposals that had sparked the empty chair crisis, the agreement granted the European Parliament modest budgetary powers. Europarliamentarians would have an opportunity to modify the budget but could increase its overall amount only within certain narrow limits. Foreign ministers approved the new arrangement in an amendment to the Rome Treaty in April 1970, subject to ratification by the member states.[40] Even in France, ratification proceeded smoothly.

The budgetary agreement marked an important stage of the EC's development. Undoubtedly the acquisition "of clearly defined financial resources accruing directly to the Community and the expansion of the Parliament's budgetary authority were major steps on the path toward political integration."[41] Yet progress on "deepening" the EC proved difficult. Efforts to coordinate foreign, economic, and monetary policies encountered differences of interpretation and enthusiasm among member states as well as an increasingly complex and hostile international environment. The attempt to coordinate foreign policy fared best, with member states agreeing in October 1970 to launch European Political Cooperation, consisting of biannual meetings of foreign ministers and more frequent meetings of their political directors, with the Council presidency managing the procedure and providing the necessary support.[42]

Despite the launch of European Political Cooperation, France remained the most skeptical of Germany's new foreign policy orientation. A desire to reassure France, and thereby indirectly appease the domestic opposition, motivated Brandt's approach to EMU as well as to foreign policy cooperation. In October 1970 Werner presented an ambitious seven-stage plan to achieve EMU within ten years by means of institutional reform and closer political integration.[43] The plan glossed over the contending French and German emphases on monetary measures and economic policy coordination by proposing parallel progress in both spheres. A related difference between the governments in Paris and Bonn soon emerged over the scope and possible implementation of the plan. Although a firm supporter of monetary policy coordination, Pompidou was loath to take any measure likely to advance supranationalism. Brandt and other national leaders, by contrast, saw the plan as an ideal opportunity to achieve closer integration.

■ The First Enlargement

Franco-German friction over EMU and *Ostpolitik* was not unrelated to the enlargement negotiations then under way. Pompidou surely appreciated that once in the EC, Britain would support his gradualist position, whereas Brandt similarly sensed that agreement to quicken the pace of EMU would be harder to get after enlargement took place. As Brandt was willing to sacrifice a bolder position on EMU for the sake of *Ostpolitik* and supported British entry partly for the same reason, the question was moot from Germany's point of view. From the French point of view, Britain's well-known suspicion of supranationalism was a source of comfort. Although, as a good Gaullist, Pompidou had misgivings about the British, he could take some solace from Britain's record of Euroskepticism.

Ironically, Edward Heath, who became prime minister in 1970, was the most Europhilic of British politicians. Heath enthusiastically championed his country's application and deeply regretted the lost opportunity of the early 1960s, when he had negotiated Britain's abortive entry effort. Few of Heath's fellow Conservatives shared the prime minister's ardor for European integration; they saw EC membership largely in negative terms—as Britain's only feasible option. On the other side of the political divide, EC membership continued to split the Labour Party.

Bringing in Britain

The entry negotiations began in June 1970 in Luxembourg and ended almost a year later in Brussels. Familiar issues from Britain's previous applications soon resurfaced. However, the talks were far less contentious and protracted than in the early 1960s. For one thing, Heath was so eager for membership that his approach seemed to be "to gain entry, and then to sort out any differences."[44] For another, Commonwealth and European Free Trade Association concerns about British membership in the EC had abated in the intervening decade. The impact on the Commonwealth of Britain's accession now focused on specific problems, such as imports of Caribbean sugar and New Zealand dairy products. Nevertheless, the negotiations occasionally stalled, particularly on the controversial questions of Britain's budgetary contribution during the transition phase and the related issue of the dubious benefit to Britain of the CAP.

A meeting between Heath and Pompidou in Paris in May 1971 helped resolve the outstanding issues. According to the usually understated *Times* of London, relations between the two leaders reached a "dizzy pinnacle of mutual admiration" at the Paris tête-à-tête.[45] The surprising rapport between Pompidou and Heath led some observers to speculate that France had finally jettisoned its lingering opposition to enlargement. Together with the contemporaneous deterioration in relations between Pompidou and Brandt, it also sparked speculation that the Paris-London axis would replace the Paris-Bonn axis as the main bilateral motor of Community development, or at least that the Paris-Bonn axis might broaden into a trilateral axis that included Britain.[46]

A British government paper published in July 1971 summarized the results of the accession negotiations and extolled the arguments in favor of entry. "Our country will be more secure," the document declared, "our ability to maintain peace and promote development in the world greater, our economy stronger, and our industries and people more prosperous, if we join the European Communities than if we remain outside them." On the sensitive question of sovereignty, the White Paper blithely asserted that "there is no question of any erosion of essential national sovereignty; what is proposed is a sharing and an enlargement of individual national sovereignties in the general interest."[47] Such patent dissimulation infuriated opponents of entry and left a painful legacy for British advocates of greater integration.

The government's proclivity for exaggeration and falsification kindled the highly flammable domestic debate on enlargement. To the government's undisguised joy, the opposition Labour Party suffered most in the ensuing conflagration. Whether motivated by conviction or opportunism, Wilson denounced Heath's entry terms and declared that a Labour government would renegotiate Britain's membership. With ratification of British accession looming in 1972, strife within the Labour Party became more and more pronounced.

Pompidou's surprise announcement in March 1972 of a French referendum on enlargement, to be held the following month, stunned the British government and boosted the antimarketeers. Despite the British government's fears of French backsliding on enlargement, domestic rather than international factors had inspired Pompidou's decision. A snap referendum provided a clever means of splitting the increasingly united opposition by driving a wedge between the Communists, who opposed the mere existence of the EC, and the Socialists, who favored British entry.[48] Referendums were a hallmark of Gaullist government; it seemed especially appropriate for Pompidou to use a widely recognized Gaullist instrument to undermine an equally identifiable Gaullist position on the EC.

The great danger, as de Gaulle's last referendum clearly demonstrated, was that Pompidou could lose. In the event, he won, but not as convincingly as expected. Only 60 percent of the French electorate bothered to turn out, and 32 percent voted against. The result, like the reason for the referendum, should be seen in domestic political terms. The relatively low number of French voters who endorsed enlargement reflected Pompidou's unpopularity more than the merits of Britain's case.[49]

British opponents of enlargement exploited the French referendum to embarrass Heath's government into holding a referendum in Britain on EC membership. With the three other applicant countries—Denmark, Ireland, and Norway—all holding referendums, British antimarketeers cited the French case as an additional reason to adopt such a procedure. Pompidou's decision to consult the electorate directly did nothing to change Heath's opposition to a referendum, but it helped push Wilson into the proreferendum camp.

The Other Applicants

The question of EC membership was even more contentious in Norway, where a narrow majority voted against accession in the referendum in September 1972. Although the result was not binding, the prime minister had already promised to resign in the event of a "no" vote. The government sought to reassure the electorate about the consequences of membership, especially for fishing and agriculture—even more protected in Norway than in the EC— and the fledgling oil industry. After a bitterly contested campaign that polarized Norwegian opinion, 54 percent voted against accession. True to his word, the prime minister resigned two weeks later.

Passions also ran high in Denmark, but the referendum there—held only one week after the Norwegian vote and binding on the government—resulted in an impressive endorsement of membership. Like the British, the Danes were, and remain, skeptical about European integration. Once Britain applied for membership, however, Denmark had little option but to follow suit. With the bulk of the country's exports going to Britain and Germany, it would have been economic suicide for Denmark to stay out of the enlarged EC. Despite familiar fears about the erosion of national sovereignty and the possible severance of traditional ties with the Nordic countries, 63 percent voted in favor of accession.

The Irish referendum, held in May 1972, registered strong support for EC membership. Far more than Denmark's, Ireland's economic fortunes were tied to those of Britain. It would have been absurd economically for Ireland to stay outside the EC once Britain went in. Added to this sense of economic determinism were complementary elements of opportunism and political calculation. The former had to do with the expected windfall for Irish farmers of participation in the CAP as well as a host of other benefits, mostly in the form of grants and loans, that would accrue to Ireland in the EC. The latter consisted of the anticipated impact of EC membership on Anglo-Irish relations. Despite becoming independent in 1922, Ireland remained relatively isolated from Europe, bound up instead in a suffocatingly close relationship with Britain. EC membership gave Ireland the chance to place Anglo-Irish relations in a broader, multilateral context. It was little wonder that a resounding 83 percent endorsed accession in the 1972 referendum.[50]

Therefore, of the four applicants that had signed accession agreements, only three joined the EC in January 1973. The ratification drama continued in Britain until almost the last minute. Having survived a series of procedural hurdles, the act of accession finally won parliamentary approval in October 1972. But that was not the end of either Labour Party posturing or British misgivings about the EC. On the contrary, British—and Danish—aversion to political integration, the inevitable strains of absorbing three new member states, and a hostile international economic environment combined in the mid-1970s to put the newly enlarged EC sorely to the test.

■ Rhetoric Versus Reality

The Paris summit of October 1972, which Pompidou convened to set the agenda of the enlarging EC, marks the high point of Euro-optimism in the post–de Gaulle period. The summit is famous—or infamous—for the last sentence of a "solemn declaration" attached to the concluding communiqué: "The member states of the Community, the driving force of European construction, affirm their intention before the end of the present decade to transform the whole complex of their relations into a European Union."[51] This was an extraordinary statement even by the extravagant standard of Eurorhetoric. Although nobody knew quite what "European Union" meant, the commitment to achieve it within eight years put an unnecessary and ultimately embarrassing onus on the member states. As the 1970s passed and nothing remotely resembling European union appeared on the horizon, the Paris Declaration served only to highlight the extent of the EC's disarray.

Yet at the time, the Paris Declaration played well politically in national capitals. The text was sufficiently warm and woolly to escape excessive criticism even in London and Copenhagen. The communiqué also struck a positive chord by expressing the EC's readiness to launch an impressive array of new initiatives. Apart from referring to monetary union and foreign policy cooperation, the communiqué mentioned regional policy, industrial policy, energy, and the environment. These were striking examples of Community "deepening."

Pompidou's apparent retreat from Gaullism should not be exaggerated, however. A close reading of the communiqué, supplemented by reports of the two-day meeting, suggests that the summit did not represent a radical departure from previous French policy. Pompidou supported the establishment of the European Regional Development Fund mostly in deference to Heath, who badly needed to achieve something at the summit from which Britain might profit directly. Coming in the wake of the bitter accession debate, Heath saw the Paris summit largely in domestic political terms. A promise of financial assistance for depressed industrial and agricultural regions would offset criticism in Britain of the high cost of EC membership.

Pompidou's willingness to help Heath emphasized the rapport between the two leaders and fueled further speculation about a new Anglo-French axis. By contrast, the vaunted Franco-German axis seemed moribund. Personally, Pompidou had little time for Brandt; politically, Brandt's repeated criticism of the CAP greatly angered the French president. In keeping with his complaints about unwarranted EC expenditure, voiced all the more loudly in the prelude to the approaching federal elections, Brandt distrusted the proposed regional fund, which looked too much like "an exercise in old-fashioned, pork-barrel politics rather than a political instrument for the unification of Europe."[52]

The vexing question of economic and monetary policy remained the greatest cause of friction between France and Germany. In the eighteen months before the summit, monetary matters had dominated European and wider international affairs. The collapse of the postwar system of fixed exchange rates had triggered markedly divergent reactions in the two countries. In response to the May 1971 monetary crisis, caused by a reduction of interest rates in the United States and the consequent run on the dollar in favor of the more stable German mark, Brandt had proposed that EC member states together float their currencies. Immediate economic concerns, as well as a desire to appease Washington at a time of growing U.S. annoyance over both *Ostpolitik* and the cost of maintaining troops in Europe, motivated the chancellor. By contrast, Pompidou opposed a joint float because of its likely impact on the competitiveness of European products and because of lack of sympathy with the U.S. plight.

Although Pompidou's position softened in the summer of 1971, President Richard Nixon's announcement in August that year of the suspension of dollar convertibility and the imposition of restrictive trade measures reopened a sensitive subject in Franco-German relations. EC finance ministers failed to agree on a joint response and instead issued a bland communiqué expressing concern about the U.S. action. A more harmonious finance ministers' meeting in September 1971 led to pointed criticism of the United States and presaged a concerted Community approach to the Smithsonian talks of December 1971 that sought to repair the system.

The currency crises of 1971 had long-lasting effects and helped send European economies slipping into recession. Corrective measures in early 1972 had the unfortunate but predictable impact of fueling inflation. Circumstances were hardly propitious for the fledgling EMU, although the collapse of the international monetary system inevitably increased calls among the Six for closer coordination of economic and monetary policy. In April 1972 the Six hatched the "snake," a regimen to keep EC currency fluctuations within a 2.5 percent margin inside the "tunnel" established during the Smithsonian talks. Worried about the consequences of currency fluctuations for the CAP, Pompidou put EMU high on the agenda of the Paris summit. In response to Pompidou's call for exchange rate stability, Brandt stressed the importance of anti-inflationary measures. The result was a reaffirmation at the Paris summit of the need for parallel progress on economic and monetary measures. Echoing the member states' call for European union by the end of the decade, the summit communiqué reiterated their commitment to EMU "with a view to its completion not later than December 31, 1980."[53] As the EC embarked on a turbulent period of enlargement and economic uncertainty, the rhetoric of European integration seemed increasingly at odds with the reality on the ground.

■ Notes

1. Stanley Hoffmann, review of *De Gaulle: The Rebel, 1890–1944,* by Jean Lacouture, *New Republic,* December 17, 1990, p. 34.
2. Quoted in Jean Monnet, *Memoirs* (Garden City, NY: Doubleday, 1978), p. 430.
3. Quoted in *Le Monde,* January 15, 1963.
4. Quoted in Edmond Jouve, *Le Général de Gaulle et la Construction de l'Europe (1940–1966)* (Paris: Librairie Générale de Droit et de Jurisprudence, R. Pichon et R. Durand-Auzias, 1967), p. 253.

5. David Calleo, *Europe's Future: The Grand Alternatives* (New York: Horizon Press, 1965), p. 54.

6. Harold Wilson, *Memoirs: The Making of a Prime Minister, 1916–1986* (London: Weidenfeld and Nicolson, 1986), p. 91.

7. Charles de Gaulle, *Memoirs of Hope: Renewal and Endeavor* (New York: Simon and Schuster, 1971), p. 143.

8. Ibid., pp. 165–166.

9. Ibid., p. 167.

10. Robert Marjolin, *Architect of European Unity: Memoirs, 1911–1986* (London: Weidenfeld and Nicolson, 1989), p. 318.

11. Hans von der Groeben, *The European Community: The Formative Years: The Struggle to Establish the Common Market and the Political Union (1958–66)*, European Perspectives Series (Luxembourg: Office for Official Publications of the European Communities, 1985), p. 32.

12. Edward Kolodziej, *French International Policy Under de Gaulle and Pompidou: The Politics of Grandeur* (Ithaca, NY: Cornell University Press, 1974), p. 316.

13. Quoted in *Le Monde*, July 7, 1964.

14. Marjolin, *Memoirs,* p. 310.

15. John Pinder, "Implications for the Operation of the Firm," *Journal of Common Market Studies* 1, no. 1 (1962): 41.

16. De Gaulle, *Memoirs,* pp. 159, 186–187.

17. Marjolin, *Memoirs,* p. 314.

18. Quoted in Françoise de la Serre, "The EEC and the 1965 Crisis," in F. Roy Willis, ed., *European Integration* (New York: New Viewpoints, 1975), p. 134.

19. See John Lambert, "The Constitutional Crisis, 1965–66," *Journal of Common Market Studies* 4, no. 3 (May 1966): 205–206.

20. *Le Monde*, September 10, 1965.

21. Lambert, "Constitutional Crisis," p. 220.

22. Reproduced in ibid., p. 226.

23. Joseph Weiler, "The Genscher-Colombo Draft European Act: The Politics of Indecision," *Journal of European Integration* 4, nos. 2 and 3 (1989): 134.

24. Kolodziej, *French International Policy*, p. 337.

25. Alastair Horne, *Harold Macmillan*, vol. 2 (New York: Viking, 1989), p. 30.

26. See Alfred Grosser, *The Western Alliance: European-American Relations Since 1945* (New York: Vantage, 1982), pp. 199–208.

27. Horne, *Macmillan*, vol. 2, p. 312.

28. Quoted in ibid., p. 319.

29. The White Paper is reproduced in Frances Nicholson and Roger East, *From the Six to the Twelve: The Enlargement of the European Communities* (Chicago: St. James Press, 1987), pp. 14–21.

30. Ibid., pp. 25–26. On the Skybolt crisis that precipitated the Nassau agreement, see Richard Neustadt, *Alliance Politics* (New York: Columbia University Press, 1970), pp. 52–55.

31. Quoted in Nicholson and East, *From the Six to the Twelve,* pp. 30–32.

32. Paul-Henri Spaak, "Hold Fast," *Foreign Affairs* 41, no. 4 (1963): 611.

33. Lois Pattison de Menil, *Who Speaks for Europe? The Making of a Prime Minister, 1916–1986* (London: Weidenfeld and Nicolson, 1986), p. 136.

34. Marjolin, *Memoirs,* p. 338.

35. Nicholson and East, *From the Six to the Twelve,* p. 49.

36. Ibid., pp. 52–53.

37. Henry Kissinger, *White House Years* (Boston: Little, Brown, 1979), p. 97.

38. Hoffmann, review of *De Gaulle: The Rebel*, p. 29.

39. See Wolfram Hanrieder, *Germany, America, Europe: Forty Years of German Foreign Policy* (New Haven, CT: Yale University Press, 1989), p. 356.

40. European Commission, *1970 General Report* (Luxembourg: Office for Official Publications of the European Communities, 1971), points 515–518, 544–545.

41. Werner Feld, *West Germany and the European Community: Changing Interests and Competing Policy Objectives* (New York: Praeger, 1981), p. 13.

42. "First Report of the Foreign Ministers to the Heads of State and Government of the Member States of the European Community (Luxembourg Report)," in Federal Republic of Germany, *European Political Cooperation (EPC)*, 4th ed. (Wiesbaden: Press and Information Office of the Federal Government, 1982), pp. 28–35.

43. "The Werner Report on Economic and Monetary Union," Bulletin EC S/11-1970.

44. Stephen George, *An Awkward Partner: Britain in the European Community* (Oxford: Oxford University Press, 1990), p. 56.

45. *Times* (London), October 21, 1972, p. 6.

46. Haig Simonian, *The Privileged Partnership: Franco-German Relations in the European Community, 1969–1984* (Oxford: Clarendon Press, 1985), p. 114; Kolodziej, *French International Policy*, pp. 412–413.

47. *The UK and the European Communities*, Cmnd 4715, July 7, 1971.

48. D. Rudnick, "An Assessment of the Reasons for the Removal of the French Veto to UK Membership of the EEC," *International Relations* 14, no. 6: 658–672.

49. Kolodziej, *French International Policy*, pp. 432–438.

50. For an account of the 1972 referenda issues and results in Norway, Denmark, and Ireland, see Nicholson and East, *From the Six to the Twelve*, pp. 97–100, 113–115, 117–133.

51. European Commission, *1972 General Report* (Luxembourg: Office for Official Publications of the European Communities, 1973), point 5.16.

52. Feld, *West Germany*, p. 67.

53. Commission, *1972 General Report*, point 5.1.

3

A Community in Flux, 1973–1984

The terms "Eurosclerosis" and "Europessimism" encapsulate the history of European integration in the mid-1970s. The accomplishments of the early 1970s—the accession of three member states, the adoption of a plan for economic and monetary union (EMU), and the launch of a procedure for foreign policy coordination—soon gave way to severe strains as the European Community confronted a profound transformation in the international economic system. Apart from the impact of enlargement and the shock of the first oil crisis, the EC struggled to cope with fluctuating superpower relations, growing German assertiveness, oscillating exchange rates, and widely uneven economic performance among the member states. The history of the EC in the 1970s and early 1980s is that of a Community in flux, attempting to absorb fundamental changes in the international system and struggling for relevance in a radically altered political and economic environment.

In early 1974 the leadership of the EC's "big three" member states changed hands. First, Harold Wilson returned to office in Britain after Labour's election victory in February. Shortly afterward, Willy Brandt resigned from office following the arrest of his personal assistant on charges of spying for East Germany; Helmut Schmidt, Brandt's finance minister, became the new chancellor. In April Georges Pompidou died; Valéry Giscard d'Estaing won the ensuing election. The new constellation of leaders and the domestic issues they faced had an obvious impact on the EC. Wilson's indifference to the EC and demand for a renegotiation of membership terms inevitably lessened Britain's influence in Brussels. At the same time, Giscard and Schmidt grew increasingly close personally and politically, firmly reestablishing the primacy of the Franco-German axis in EC affairs.

The EC weathered the challenges of the 1970s in part because of the emergence of the European Council—regular summit meetings of national leaders—and the effectiveness of the Paris-Bonn axis under the leadership of Giscard and Schmidt. More important, perhaps, the trials and tribulations of the 1970s convinced leaders in national governments, the Commission, and the Parliament of the urgent need for institutional reform and policy innovation. As a result, the late 1970s formed a critical bridge between the Community's early attainments and later triumphs.

The impending improvement in the EC's fortunes was by no means apparent at the time. The twenty-fifth anniversary of the Rome Treaty, observed in March 1982, was a dismal affair. Remarking on a report that the Council had canceled the official celebration, the president of the European Parliament compared the Community to "a feeble cardiac patient whose condition is so poor that he cannot even be disturbed by a birthday party."[1] Under the circumstances, Greenland's decision in February 1982 to become the first (and so far only) territory to leave the EC seemed entirely appropriate.

The EC's problems were legion: a paralyzed decisionmaking process; a weak Commission; an agricultural policy apparently out of control; a new French president (François Mitterrand) pursuing a "dash for growth" that further strained Community solidarity; and a new British prime minister (Margaret Thatcher) insisting on a budget rebate, an issue that dominated the next five years and fifteen summits. Only when the European Council resolved the British budgetary question in June 1984 did the EC suddenly revel in the impact of other, less perceptible but no less powerful developments that, over the past four years, had gradually generated momentum for greater integration (Table 3.1).

These developments included the trend toward deregulation and liberalization sweeping Europe from the United States; increasing cooperation between the Commission and leading industrialists to boost European competitiveness, especially in the high-technology sector; and growing business interest in the realization of a single market. Such changes, combined with the member states' worries about Europe's apparent impotence during a sudden drop in Cold War temperatures and consensus on the need to improve decisionmaking procedures in view of Mediterranean enlargement, helped set the EC on the road to revival. As Christopher Tugendhat, a commissioner in the early 1980s, remarked at the time, "One has the feeling of ice breaking up and spring approaching."[2]

◼ Britain's Renegotiation and Referendum

Far from celebrating its first enlargement in 1973, the EC instead found itself grappling with serious economic problems. Soaring inflation, rising unemployment, yawning trade deficits, and a worsening oil crisis shook the Community to the core. Continuing exchange rate fluctuations and divergences of member states' monetary and economic policies made nonsense of the 1980 target date for economic and monetary union. A massive hike in oil prices and

Table 3.1   Chronology, 1973–1984

1973	January	Britain, Denmark, and Ireland join EC
	July	Conference on Security and Cooperation in Europe (CSCE) opens in Helsinki
	October	Arab oil producers quadruple the price of oil and embargo port of Rotterdam
	December	EC leaders discuss oil crisis at Copenhagen summit
1974	April	New British government opens renegotiation of membership terms
	September	EC leaders decide to form European Council
	December	EC leaders hold last informal summit in Paris
1975	February	Lomé Convention between EC and forty-six developing countries signed
	March	Inaugural meeting of European Council in Dublin concludes renegotiation of Britain's membership terms
		European Regional Development Fund established
	June	British referendum on continued EC membership
		Greece applies to join EC
	July	Agreement to establish Court of Auditors and strengthen budgetary powers of European Parliament
	August	Thirty-five participating states conclude CSCE
	December	Tindemans Report on European Union
1976	July	Accession negotiations with Greece begin
1977	January	Jenkins Commission takes office
	March	Portugal applies to join EC
	July	Spain applies to join EC
1978	July	European Council agrees to establish European Monetary System (EMS)
	October	Accession negotiations with Portugal begin
1979	February	Accession negotiations with Spain begin
	March	Eight member states launch the exchange rate mechanism of the EMS
	May	Accession treaty with Greece signed in Athens
	June	First direct elections to the European Parliament
	September	Spierenburg Report on Commission reform
	October	Second Lomé Convention signed
	November	"Three Wise Men" report on EC reform
		Beginning of British budgetary question
1981	January	Greece joins EC
	November	Genscher-Colombo proposals
1982	February	Greenlanders decide in a referendum to leave EC
1983	June	Stuttgart Declaration
1984	February	European Parliament adopts Draft Treaty Establishing the European Union
	June	Second direct elections to European Parliament
		At Fontainebleau summit, EC leaders resolve British budgetary question
	December	Third Lomé Convention signed

the imposition of an oil embargo, in the aftermath of the October 1973 Arab-Israeli war, made matters even worse (oil from the Middle East supplied approximately 63 percent of the EC's energy needs). Eager to protect their close relationships with the Arab oil-producing countries, Britain and France strove to stifle discussion of a common energy policy. Meeting in Copenhagen in December 1973, EC leaders failed to restore solidarity or agree on joint action. Germany and the Netherlands, traditionally pro-Israeli, succeeded in toning down some of the more blatant pro-Arab points that Britain and France wanted to include in the summit communiqué.[3]

It was under these inauspicious circumstances that the new British government demanded a renegotiation of the country's accession agreement. Prime Minister Harold Wilson personified Britain's ambivalence toward the EC and led a political party (Labour) bitterly divided on the question of continued membership. Apart from a recalculation of Britain's budgetary contribution, Britain's various demands included reform of the Common Agricultural Policy (CAP) and protection of Commonwealth interests, due apparently to Wilson's personal preference for New Zealand dairy products. The other member states were willing to budge on the budgetary and Commonwealth issues but were unsure of how to respond to Wilson's demand for the retention of British parliamentary sovereignty.

What followed epitomized the EC's languor in the mid-1970s. The renegotiations lasted eleven months, dominated two summits, and drove Britain's partners to distraction. It is difficult to refute an observation by Roy Jenkins, who became Commission president later in the 1970s, that the entire episode "produced the minimum results with the maximum ill-will."[4] At the expense of Britain's prestige in Europe, Wilson seemed to be engaged in a frantic effort to hold the Labour Party together. In the run-up to the October 1974 general election, the second in less than a year, Wilson pledged either another general election or a referendum to validate the renegotiation result. Labour's overall majority in the October 1974 election kept the question of continued EC membership at the top of the political agenda.

Jenkins credits Schmidt not only with successfully concluding the renegotiations but also with convincing a majority of Labour Party members to stay in the EC. Schmidt, a Socialist, visited Britain in November 1974 and made a hugely successful speech at the Labour Party conference. At the same time he coached Wilson privately on the approach to take with Giscard, who strongly disliked Wilson and opposed Britain's renegotiation. Although conceding the validity of Britain's claim that it was contributing too much to the EC budget, Giscard was unconvinced that a successful renegotiation would end British dissatisfaction with the EC. Agreement on the size of the Regional Development Fund, reached at a summit in December 1974, undoubtedly appeased Wilson. In the end, the fund was not as large as Heath had originally hoped, but Britain's share would be a sizable 28 percent, Italy, Ireland, and France being the other main beneficiaries.[5]

The end of the negotiations hove into sight at the end of 1974, when EC leaders charged the Commission with designing a "correcting mechanism" to prevent Britain, or any other member state, from paying too much into the EC. Based on the Commission's formula, EC leaders would decide at their next summit, in Dublin in March 1975, on the size of Britain's refund. As expected, Wilson announced that the government would hold a referendum in June to decide whether Britain would stay in the EC, on the basis of the Dublin agreement.[6]

The Commission published its report, quaintly entitled "The Unacceptable Situation and the Correcting Mechanism," in January 1975. Based on it, a committee of experts worked frantically through the first night of the Dublin summit to come up with an acceptable British rebate. A successful conclusion hinged on satisfying Wilson's demand for assurances about New Zealand dairy imports. Finally, out of tedium or despair, the other eight agreed to accept New Zealand imports and Wilson agreed that the correcting mechanism yielded a reasonable figure on which to base his referendum campaign for Britain to stay in the EC.

Regardless of its impact on public opinion, the result of Britain's lengthy renegotiation had failed to reunite the Labour Party. The Conservative Party, now in opposition, had more than its fair share of Euroskeptics, yet the vast majority of its members favored staying in the EC. Margaret Thatcher's first major speech as the newly elected Conservative Party leader was on the referendum issue. Though deploring the constitutional precedent of a popular referendum, she strongly advocated a "yes" vote. With the leadership of the two main parties and the small Liberal Party urging a positive result, the outcome of the referendum was hardly in doubt. Of the 64 percent of the electorate who turned out, 67 percent voted for and 33 percent against staying "in Europe."

Four days after the referendum, Wilson told the House of Commons that "the debate is now over . . . the historic decision has been made. . . . We look forward to continuing to work with [our partners] in promoting the Community's wider interests and in fostering a greater sense of purpose among the member states."[7] By then it was difficult to repair the damage of the renegotiation either inside or outside Britain. At home, according to Jenkins, "the handling of the European question by the leadership throughout the 1970s did more to cause the [Labour] Party's disasters of the 1980s than did any other issue."[8] Abroad, the renegotiation "added to the spirit of irritation and impatience with Britain that had been growing within the Community" since enlargement.[9] Even before Thatcher came to office in 1979 and promptly reopened the budgetary question, nothing about Britain's behavior after the referendum suggested a willingness to play a positive role in the Community.

▪ Disarray and Damage Control: The European Council

Although relieved to have put Britain's renegotiation and referendum behind it, the EC found itself in a rut in the mid-1970s because of the member states' inability or unwillingness to tackle serious economic and political problems on a Community-wide basis. The Commission was ineffectual, and large member states failed to provide decisive leadership. Germany was strong economically but, for all Brandt's blandishments in the early 1970s, relatively unassertive politically; France was depressed economically and precarious politically, with Giscard under constant threat from left and right; Britain was feeble economically and volatile politically.

Poor leadership and growing divergence among the member states not only undermined political solidarity but also risked jeopardizing current levels of economic integration. Faced with high inflation and unemployment, member states applied an array of nontariff barriers and other protectionist measures that impeded the emergence of a single market. Disputes over budgetary contributions and monetary compensation to farmers for the impact of fluctuating exchange rates on the CAP illustrated the extent of the malaise.

Economic and monetary union (EMU) was an early and inevitable victim of member state unilateralism. The Werner Plan, launched so audaciously in 1972 with a target date for full implementation in 1980, hardly got off the ground. National currencies wiggled in and out of the "snake." The mark, buoyed by Germany's low inflation and large trade surplus, pushed through the top; the pound, franc, and lire, weakened by their countries' high inflation and large trade deficits, fell through the bottom. No wonder that plans for EMU were quietly shelved.[10]

The launch of the European Council in 1975 helped hold the EC together. The move from ad hoc to institutionalized summitry—regular meetings of national leaders (prime ministers and the president of France)—reflected the need for top-level direction in order to maintain the EC's integrity at a time of increasing economic complexity and bureaucratic paralysis. Originally Giscard's idea, regular summits appealed also to Schmidt. With their unrivaled grasp of economic and monetary issues and propensity to deal privately with the other prime ministers, Giscard and Schmidt saw the European Council as an ideal forum in which to dominate the EC. The national leaders' simultaneous decision to hold direct elections to the European Parliament was intended both to satisfy an obligation in the Rome Treaty and to defuse criticism that the European Council would strengthen intergovernmentalism at the expense of supranationalism in the EC's institutional structure.

Meetings of the European Councils provided a stage for the dazzling Schmidt-Giscard show that helped to maintain a modicum of integration during an otherwise inauspicious time. The affinity between the two leaders was not immediate. They had strikingly different characters and personalities—Giscard haughty, Olympian, condescending; Schmidt pretentiously unpretentious, moody, and temperamental, "a figure out of Wilhelm Busch, Elbe bargeman's cap and pipe."[11] But both were shrewd, incisive, and highly intelligent. Before reaching the highest office in their respective countries, they had also been unusually effective finance ministers. Giscard and Schmidt spoke two common languages: economics and English.

The Privileged Partnership, the title of Haig Simonian's book on Franco-German relations in the 1970s, sums up the exclusive relationship between Giscard and Schmidt. Going well beyond the framework of the Elysée Treaty, Giscard and Schmidt got together often for dinner, spoke at least weekly on the telephone, and caucused regularly on the fringes of multilateral meetings. Despite the appearance of an easy Franco-German relationship based on a genuine friendship between the president and the chancellor, both sides worked hard to resolve occasional disputes and ease inevitable friction. As William Wallace observed, "The success of the Franco-German relationship [in the 1970s and 1980s] is a record of determination to accommodate divergent interests through positive political action, to explain and to tolerate differences and to minimize their impact; not a simple record of convergence in economic, industrial, political or security interests and outlooks."[12] It was an approach conspicuously absent from Britain's dealings with other member states at that time.

Yet it would be wrong to suggest that Giscard and Schmidt single-handedly revived the EC. Given the circumstances of the mid-1970s, with the economic recession continuing unabated, it is more apt to speak of damage control. Not surprisingly, few meetings of the European Council held in the mid-1970s are memorable today. Even in the best of times, Giscard and Schmidt's approach to EC affairs would not have facilitated the kind of all-around renaissance that the Community enjoyed in the mid-1980s. Schmidt's reported statement that "Europe can only be brought forward by the will of a few statesmen, and not by thousands of regulations and hundreds of ministerial councils,"[13] was only half right. Schmidt's and Giscard's impatience with the Commission and determination to avoid Brussels in favor of Paris and Bonn contributed to the EC's dysfunctionalism. The two leaders' infatuation with each other also alienated other national leaders.

■ The Community's Malaise

Regardless of the rise of the European Council and the state of relations among national leaders, the inefficiency of the Brussels bureaucracy in the 1970s became a metaphor for the EC's decline. The Commission was dispirited and demoralized. As if to underscore its seeming unimportance, in 1972 the outgoing president, Franco Malfatti, left office early in order to stand for election to the Italian parliament. At the end of the decade Willy Haferkampf, a vice president, brought the Commission into disrepute over allegations about his extravagant traveling expenses.[14] This scandal was relatively trivial, but it reinforced the public image of the Commission as wasteful and mismanaged. Schmidt's intense dislike of the Commission reinforced Germany's reluctance to send top-rate people to Brussels as either commissioners or permanent representatives. For his part, Giscard inherited de Gaulle's antipathy toward the Commission and lost no opportunity to put its president in his place.

More than the Commission's ineffectualness, however, the Council's indecisiveness lay at the root of the Community's institutional immobility. By the early 1970s nearly 1,000 Commission proposals were said to be stuck in the Council's decisionmaking pipeline because of a member state's ability to prevent a vote from being taken, thanks to the Luxembourg Compromise. For all their supposed commitment to the Community, Giscard and Schmidt tinkered with various possible solutions but never injected into the process the political will so desperately lacking.

The fate of the Tindemans Report was typical. Having been charged at the 1974 Paris summit with recommending ways to advance European integration, Belgian prime minister Leo Tindemans focused less on the lofty goal of a federal Europe than on the need for institutional reform and a modest extension of Community competence. The most controversial aspect of the report, published in January 1976, was its exploration of a possible "two-speed Europe," with differing rates of integration depending on the will and ability of each member state.[15]

Britain and France fretted about a further loss of sovereignty; the smaller member states recoiled from the prospect of first- and second-class EC membership. Giscard took the lead and stifled the report with the kind of bureaucratic asphyxiation that Tindemans had so bitterly complained about. National leaders asked their foreign ministers to consider the report; the foreign ministers asked their senior officials to do so. The senior officials reported on the report to their foreign ministers; the foreign ministers reported on the report's report to the national leaders, who thanked Tindemans for his efforts and, as a consolation to him, called for an annual report from the Commission on progress toward European union.[16]

Another high-level report suffered a similar fate: that of the "Three Wise Men." This report had originated in a letter from Giscard to other EC leaders proposing a panel of three eminent Europeans to recommend institutional reforms that would not require changing the treaties. Robert Marjolin, a former Commission vice president, chaired the group. He and his fellow wise men set about the task with enthusiasm, presenting their report on time, a month before the November 1979 Dublin summit.[17]

There, Giscard noted with pleasure the report's criticism of the Commission and its endorsement of the European Council. Beyond that, he did not delve too deep. After all, the report also criticized successive Council presidencies for lack of direction. France's presidency, in the first half of 1979, had been particularly poor, partly because of Giscard's anger with the outgoing European Parliament for having passed its last budget in a form he thought illegal and partly because of his concern that the new, directly elected Parliament would be even more assertive. Nor did Giscard like the report's pointed observation that lack of political will was the main obstacle to the EC's revival. Thus, after a perfunctory discussion at the Dublin summit, the report of the Three Wise Men joined the Tindemans Report in the EC's archive.

Requesting high-level reports and then failing to act on them was a fitting comment on the European Council's activism in the late 1970s. As the decade drew to a close, the EC's fortunes looked unpropitious. Low economic growth, excessive unemployment, and high inflation—collectively called stagflation—plagued the member states. The political will to revive European integration was missing in national capitals. There were few economic, political, or institutional signs that the EC would turn the corner and transform itself dramatically within the next few years.

■ The European Monetary System

The launch in 1979 of the European Monetary System (EMS), an initiative to establish a zone of relative monetary stability in a world of wildly fluctuating exchange rates, was one of the few bright lights on the EC's horizon. After a shaky start, the EMS helped participating member states to fight inflation and recover economic growth. According to the Dooge Report of 1985, the EMS "enabled the unity of the Common Market to be preserved, reasonable exchange rates to be maintained, and the foundations of the Community's monetary identity to be laid."[18] The EMS would also provide a vital underpinning for the single market program.

Peter Ludlow chronicled the origins of the EMS in a masterly monograph that reads like a novel.[19] Jenkins's extensive European Diaries and his later political autobiography verify much of what Ludlow wrote. The story of the EMS has the ingredients of a political thriller: Jenkins's courage and prescience in proposing a monetary initiative after the failure of the Werner Plan and the currency "snake"; Schmidt's sudden espousal of a scheme for exchange rate stability and his determination to see it through despite strong domestic opposition; Giscard's less enthusiastic but nonetheless strong support, and his apparent U-turn at the last moment; the efficacy of the Franco-German alliance in ensuring adoption of the EMS; Britain's refusal yet again to take the plunge; and the value of the European Council for rapid decisionmaking at the highest level. Altogether, the EMS is an excellent case study of EC policy formulation and decisionmaking.

Jenkins's Initiative

Much of the credit for the EMS should go to Jenkins, Commission president from 1977 to 1981. Having spent his entire career in British politics and with little experience in foreign affairs, Jenkins was a Brussels outsider. He would have preferred to stay in London, but his ardent Europeanism at the time of Britain's accession and renegotiation doomed Jenkins's career in the Labour Party. Most member states agreed that Britain, as a large recent arrival, should provide the next Commission president (small member states looked forward to a Commission president from a large member state other than France or Germany). Jenkins's seniority, pro-Community credentials, and underemployment at home made him the Labour government's obvious choice.

Especially because Jenkins succeeded the uninspiring François Ortoli, his arrival in Brussels aroused inflated expectations. In fact, Jenkins got off to a slow and uncertain start, making it look by mid-1977 as if his presidency would be as forgettable as any in the years since Hallstein's resignation. In fact, Jenkins yearned for an initiative that would boost the Commission's morale and reinvigorate the EC. Jenkins's knowledge of economics, experience as chancellor of the exchequer (finance minister) in Britain, and concern about the impact on the EC of oscillating international exchange rates made him want to act in the monetary field. Ortoli, he knew, would be skeptical. Renowned for his hesitancy, enjoying considerable prestige as a former Commission president, and holding the senior portfolio of monetary affairs, Ortoli could have been a formidable potential adversary. Thus, Jenkins proceeded cautiously in the Commission before broaching the subject publicly.

Jenkins used the occasion of a lecture at the Community-sponsored European University Institute in Florence in October 1977 to send up a trial balloon. Apart from making predictable points about advancing European integration and helping to realize the common market's full potential, Jenkins argued that monetary union would help to lower inflation, increase investment, and reduce unemployment. Nor, if properly implemented, would monetary union exacerbate regional economic disparities or intensify institutional centralization in Brussels.[20]

The tension between Jenkins's advocacy of what he called a bold "leap forward" and Ortoli's step-by-step approach resulted in a surprisingly reticent Commission communication on the subject of EMU. Nor was there much discussion of it at the European Council in Brussels in December 1977, where Jenkins noted Schmidt's "benevolent skepticism" and detected "a fair if not tremendously enthusiastic wind behind our monetary union proposals."[21] Despite strong support from the Belgian presidency, who wanted an imaginative initiative in the spirit of the Tindemans Report, by the end of 1977 Jenkins's trial balloon seemed to have fallen flat. To compound Jenkins's disappointment, Germany was one of the least interested member states.

Giscard and Schmidt Take Over

Jenkins's attempt to revive interest in EMU would have withered entirely but for Schmidt's sudden conversion to it, or at least to a modified version of what Jenkins wanted. Schmidt told Jenkins about his newfound enthusiasm for an effort to achieve exchange rate stability during a meeting in Bonn in February 1978. Jenkins was at a loss to explain the reason for Schmidt's sudden change of heart. Was it a function of the chancellor's mercurial personality? Was it an antidote to his domestic security problems? Was it anger with the United States over yet another drop in the dollar's value?[22] One or more of those reasons may explain the timing of Schmidt's espousal of a quasi-fixed exchange rate regime. The fundamental cause of his "conversion," however, went much deeper. Persistent depreciation of the dollar and a corresponding appreciation of the mark cut German industrial competitiveness and fed speculation that a U.S. economic recovery was happening at the expense of German prudence and prosperity.

Overnight, Schmidt replaced Jenkins as the principal proponent of what became the EMS. Yet Schmidt's crucial collaborator was not the president of the Commission but the president of France. Alone or with Jenkins's sole support, Schmidt might not have been able to bring the monetary initiative rapidly to fruition. But with Giscard's backing the proposal quickly gathered speed. Having survived the March 1978 parliamentary elections, Giscard enthusiastically endorsed Schmidt's scheme. The birth of the EMS one year later "came from a clear convergence of French and German interests, confirming the two countries' leading roles in the Community."[23]

Regular meetings of the European Council gave Schmidt and Giscard an opportunity to promote their monetary proposal and a forum in which to approve the EMS at the highest possible decisionmaking level. Giscard and Schmidt possessed enormous powers of political persuasion. When they unveiled their exchange rate idea at a summit in April 1978, only British prime minister James Callaghan expressed serious concern. Resentment of close Franco-German collaboration and doubts about the scheme's validity soon convinced Callaghan not to allow British participation with France and Germany in subsequent planning for the EMS. Thus, the blueprint put before the next summit, in Bremen in July 1978, bore an exclusive Franco-German imprint.

The Bremen summit marked a decisive stage in the gestation of the EMS. Schmidt's forceful chairmanship contributed to a general acceptance of the Franco-German proposal for an exchange rate mechanism as the centerpiece of the EMS, using a parity grid and a divergence indicator based on the European currency unit. By contrast, Callaghan's sullenness presaged Britain's self-exclusion from the system. Britain's decision not to take part was of more than symbolic importance. As Helen Wallace pointed out, "for many of those involved the EMS was viewed, rightly or wrongly, as a critical stage in the development of the EC as a whole."[24]

While Commission and member state officials worked in a number of specialized committees to thrash out details of the scheme, a last-minute political row erupted over compensation for poorer participating countries, with Ireland and Italy demanding an increase in regional development funding and subsidized loans for infrastructural improvements. The problem of resource redistribution came to a boil when France and Britain insisted that their shares of a larger European Regional Development Fund be equal to their shares of the existing fund and Germany balked at paying the bill. Nor would Giscard approve the amount of subsidized loans that Ireland and Italy requested. This did not augur well for the Brussels summit of December 1978, the final European Council before the EMS was to have been implemented in January 1979.

A last-minute compromise by Schmidt at the Brussels summit broke the deadlock. Yet fears of an aborted EMS grew when Giscard unexpectedly demanded abolition of monetary compensatory amounts—funds introduced in the early 1970s to cushion the CAP from exchange rate fluctuations—as part of the EMS package.[25] The compensatory amounts had benefited France little but were popular in Germany, where they helped prop up agricultural prices. Giscard's last-minute intransigence, due more to domestic politics than to international economics, delayed implementation of the EMS. In the event, Giscard's abandonment of the issue was as swift as his embracing of it. Following agreement at a meeting of agriculture ministers in early March 1979 to abolish monetary compensatory amounts without specifying a timetable, Giscard announced his unconditional support for the EMS, which finally came into operation later that month.

The EMS was substantially different from what Jenkins had originally envisioned. What emerged in 1979 was "a hybrid—not entirely Community, nor entirely outside it."[26] Only EC member states could participate in the EMS, although none was obliged to do so. The EMS was not based on the Rome Treaty, although closer monetary coordination, and eventually EMU, were cherished EC objectives. Nor did it emerge from a Commission proposal, although EC institutions, notably the Council of Economic and Finance Ministers (Ecofin), were central to its successful operation. Despite its peculiarities, the EMS represented an important breakthrough for Brussels. Regardless of its subsequent development, the fact of its existence and the relative speed with which it came into being marked an important milestone in the EC's history.

▓ The British Budgetary Question

The launch of the EMS ended an otherwise disappointing decade on a high note. Nevertheless, the long-term beneficial impact of the EMS could not have been predicted in 1979. On the contrary, the emergence that year of the British budgetary question, following Margaret Thatcher's election victory, suggested that the EC was in for another rough time. The EC was no stranger to Thatcher, who had stoutly supported Britain's continued membership in her maiden speech as opposition leader in the House of Commons in 1975. According to one of her senior officials, however, "from the beginning [of her prime ministership] . . . she showed a deep-seated prejudice against the EC."[27] Thatcher also showed ignorance of the EC's institutions and policies and, according to one of her biographers, tended to see the EC as a branch of NATO.[28] But she grasped the potential for British trade of continued EC membership and later became one of the foremost proponents of the single market program. Although the EC seemed moribund in 1979, she also saw the Commission as an agent of supranationalism and enemy of the nation-state. In Thatcher's view, the EC should confine itself to the removal of barriers to trade and investment and the coordination of economic and foreign policies exclusively on an intergovernmental basis.

Thatcher grasped another thing about the EC even before she became prime minister: the obvious unfairness of Britain's budgetary contribution. Simply put, Britain paid too much and received too little in return. That imbalance should have been rectified in the mid-1970s, but Harold Wilson's renegotiation of Britain's membership terms had been largely a cosmetic exercise to appease British public opinion and to try to keep the Labour Party together. Thereafter, special transitional arrangements for Britain cushioned the financial burden of membership. Only at the end of the 1970s did the extent of Britain's overpayment become fully apparent. The figures were striking: Britain's net payments to Brussels averaged £60 million from 1973 to 1976; they amounted to £369 million in 1977, £822 million in 1978, and £947 million in 1979.[29]

Here was a cause dear to Thatcher's heart. Britain's demand for reform was clear-cut, easily comprehensible, and assured of widespread domestic support. How could her EC colleagues possibly not concede the point? Even the Commission's own figures bolstered Britain's case. Thatcher surely had a natural ally in Schmidt, whose country also paid a lot into the EC (although Germany could afford to do so and was unlikely to complain in any event because of lingering war guilt). Righting Britain's wrong would strengthen, not weaken, the EC. Thatcher correctly argued that without budgetary reform the British public, already equivocal about European integration, would turn solidly against the EC and might even insist on withdrawal. For Thatcher, this was not only a question of right and wrong but also a campaign to save the EC from itself.

Under the circumstances it seems surprising that the British budgetary question—what Jenkins called the Bloody British Question, or BBQ[30]—nearly wrecked the EC and filled a reservoir of ill feeling toward Britain in Brussels. Admittedly, Britain's partners were predisposed not to reopen the issue. Wilson's handling of the original renegotiation had left a bitter taste in people's mouths. Yet such was the justice of Britain's case that even the most resentful of Eurocrats and member state officials conceded the fairness of further reform.

Thatcher's Offensive

What turned a relatively straightforward case into one of the most complex and divisive issues in the EC's history was Thatcher's abrasive personality and truculent approach to the negotiations. Being the new kid on the block at European Council meetings, and a woman in a hitherto exclusively male world, may have fired Thatcher's innate aggression. She also suspected the Commission and the other member states of uniformly opposing Britain's position. Thatcher soon discovered that an aggressive approach enhanced her reputation at home as a dogged defender of British interests and increased her political standing at a time of otherwise plummeting ratings.

That set the stage for her first European Council meeting, held in Strasbourg in June 1979. The Strasbourg summit turned into a skirmish during which Thatcher fired a warning shot. According to Jenkins, who attended as Commission president, Thatcher "spoke shrilly and too frequently, and succeeded in embroiling not only Giscard (which maybe was unavoidable), but also in turn van Agt (the Netherlands), Jorgensen (Denmark) and Lynch (Ireland). Then, worst of all, she got into an altercation with Schmidt, whose support was crucial to her getting the outcome she wanted from the meeting."[31]

That summer and fall Thatcher marshaled her forces and prepared for the first pitched battle: the Dublin summit in November 1979. Jenkins tried before that to narrow the ground between Thatcher and everybody else but discovered that the ground had not yet been adequately prepared or defined. Although Thatcher was demanding Britain's money back, neither she nor any of her interlocutors had mentioned a precise sum. Not surprisingly, the Dublin summit degenerated into open combat. Thatcher's tactics were to grind her enemies down by endlessly repeating her main arguments and keeping everyone up late after dinner. Infuriated, the Danish prime minister hurled insults; bored, the German chancellor feigned sleep; disdainful, the French president ignored her; embarrassed, the Irish prime minister wished it weren't happening.[32]

The next summit, in Luxembourg in April 1980, saw a resumption of hand-to-hand fighting. This time precise figures were mentioned for an interim two-year period. Indeed, the difference between what Thatcher demanded and what the others offered (about 400 million European currency units a year) was relatively small. Nevertheless, Thatcher rejected what was on offer and left the battlefield bloodied but unbowed. The other combatants left Luxembourg in despair.

Italy, then in the Council presidency, redoubled its efforts to resolve the problem. The decisive encounter took place at a foreign ministers' meeting in May 1980, where the Eight refined their earlier offer of a truce. The scene of hostilities then switched to the home front, where the British foreign secretary eventually convinced Thatcher to accept the offer. Why Thatcher wanted to reject it is unclear. Her foreign secretary had brought back from Brussels the best deal possible. Rejecting it would have been tantamount to rejecting the EC, which Thatcher claimed not to want to do. Nor could she have gleaned much more political capital from saying no. Public opinion in Britain was already beginning to turn against her European histrionics, which robbed Britain of a potential leadership role in Europe. It is difficult to avoid the conclusion that Thatcher's fierce determination to settle only on her own terms was part of her political pathology.

The 1980 agreement was merely a temporary resolution of the British budgetary question, however. As expected, Thatcher returned to the charge when the interim agreement expired in 1983, the tenth anniversary of Britain's unhappy EC membership. This time she sought a permanent solution, not merely a series of annual remedies. The Stuttgart summit of June 1983 provided the first opportunity for a showdown. Yet the contrast with 1979 was striking. Then Thatcher had been a newcomer in the exclusive European Council club, long dominated by Giscard and Schmidt; now she was a veteran, flanked by François Mitterrand and Helmut Kohl, the relatively new leaders of France and Germany. Both were finding their feet domestically and internationally and had not yet struck up the firm friendship for which they would later become famous. Neither of them could match Thatcher's grasp of detail or passion for the budgetary question; Stuttgart was their baptism by fire.

Two other factors, one domestic and one European, further strengthened Thatcher's position. First, her popularity at home had soared in the aftermath of the Falklands/Malvinas War. Having taken on the Argentineans, Thatcher was set to take on the continentals. This time the British public stood squarely behind her. Even the opposition Labour Party, then committed to pulling out of the EC if it ever got back into office, could hardly criticize her efforts to get a better budget deal for Britain. Second, the EC was financially strapped. In the early 1980s the CAP had run out of control with an obscene accumulation of surplus production for which farmers received guaranteed high prices. The EC would have to reform the CAP and/or increase its overall budget. Thatcher favored

CAP reform, a politically unpalatable option for most other member states. But she was not about to approve a budget increase to cover unrestrained CAP spending unless Britain's contribution was once and for all resolved.

Mitterrand's Statesmanship

There was little progress on the budgetary dispute at the Stuttgart summit or during the remainder of 1983. The situation changed dramatically for the better when France took over the Council presidency in January 1984. Having jettisoned an initial effort to boost employment and economic growth through government intervention and high public spending, Mitterrand was in the process of switching to limited deregulation and market integration. He was eager to end the budgetary impasse and focus member states' attention instead on the need to complete the single market. A special European Council in Brussels in March 1984 afforded an opportunity to thrash out the various budgetary problems three months into the French presidency, but without success.

The French presidency was due to end in June with a European Council just outside Paris in the spectacular setting of the palace at Fontainebleau. Mitterrand launched a concerted diplomatic offensive in the run-up to the summit. Despite these efforts, there was nothing to suggest that a breakthrough on the budget was imminent as the EC leaders converged on Fontainebleau, covered by an army of 1,300 journalists. Talk in previous weeks of a possible "two-speed" Europe, with Britain in the slow lane, had not helped matters; nor had Thatcher's clever definition of what a two-speed Europe meant: "Those who pay most are in the top group and those who pay less are not."[33] Continued squabbling over Britain's budgetary contribution was a pitiful prelude not only to the Fontainebleau summit but especially to the second direct elections to the European Parliament.

Mitterrand's strategy was to avoid the kind of friction that had marred the opening of the previous summit. As the summit progressed, a surprising willingness to compromise gradually became apparent. Thatcher seemed eager to settle the long-standing dispute and move the EC in new directions; the others were equally war-weary and wanted to reach a comprehensive budget agreement. A possible solution emerged based not on previous proposals but on a rebate in the form of a fixed percentage each year of Britain's net contribution. Thatcher held out for 66 percent; Kohl demurred. Finally, after some concessions to Germany on agricultural spending, the chancellor lifted his objections at lunch on the second day of the summit. The British budgetary dispute was over.[34]

Had anything good come of it? Undoubtedly Thatcher's conduct antagonized other EC leaders and protracted the painful negotiations. Yet without her aggressive approach Britain might not have secured such a favorable result (the agreement saved Britain over £10 billion in the remainder of the 1980s).

For all the aggravation and frustration of the previous two years, arguably Thatcher had needed time to build her case, exhaust the opposition, and secure a satisfactory solution. It could also be argued that resolution of Britain's budgetary dispute helped the EC's long-term development, and not only in the obvious sense of removing a persistent irritant in relations among member states, for Thatcher brought home to the Community the folly of overexpenditure and the need to rein in the CAP. Indeed, the European Council resolved the British problem in the context of a wider budget reform, involving a decision to curtail agricultural spending and increase the EC's own resources, effective in 1986, from 1.0 percent to 1.4 percent of the value-added tax collected in each member state.[35]

In a postsummit press conference Thatcher said she now looked forward to "pressing ahead with the development of the Community."[36] The other leaders could not have agreed more. Mitterrand reveled in the success of "his" European Council not only in ending five years of friction over Britain's budgetary contribution but also in clearing the way for new initiatives. At Fontainebleau, Mitterrand had spoken eloquently about the need to revive the EC's policies and institutions and instill a new sense of European identity. Although France would no longer be in the presidency, the Fontainebleau summit created a favorable climate in which to push Mitterrand's objectives of deeper political and economic integration.

■ Toward the Single Market Program

A number of factors in the early 1980s fueled renewed interest in the long-proclaimed goal of a single market, a key element of deeper economic integration. One was the ideological shift then sweeping Western Europe. Its most obvious manifestation was Thatcher's election victory in 1979. After five years of Labour Party rule, a powerful popular reaction against excessive government intervention in economic and social affairs swept Thatcher to power. The new government immediately launched a program of privatization and deregulation to unleash pent-up market forces and stimulate individual enterprise.

Across the Channel, by contrast, Mitterrand pushed a socialist agenda of state intervention and regulation after his election victory in 1981. The consequences were catastrophic: inflation soared; investment slumped; and the value of the franc plummeted, forcing devaluation within the EMS and prompting a tough domestic austerity program. In 1983 pragmatism overcame principle when Mitterrand, at the urging of Jacques Delors, his finance minister, abandoned a doctrinaire approach to economic recovery and began to bend with the prevailing economic wind. Mitterrand's U-turn influenced other socialist leaders, notably Felipe González in Spain and Mário Soares in Portugal, two countries then on their way to joining the EC.

The success of Etienne Davignon, the commissioner responsible for industrial affairs from 1981 to 1985, in rallying European industry to the cause of cross-border collaboration also contributed to the momentum developing for a single, EC-wide market. Davignon's profound knowledge of international politics and economics, high social standing, and previous Brussels experience made him the most formidable member of Gaston Thorn's new Commission. During his second term in the Commission, Davignon made Western Europe's industrial performance and competitiveness a top priority.[37]

Davignon cultivated the CEOs of major European manufacturers in the high-technology sector, advocating the advantages of intra-EC collaboration, something the persistent economic recession in any case predisposed them to do. Commission officials kept discreetly in the background; the last thing Davignon wanted was to scare off big business with a display of bureaucratic heavy-handedness. Davignon's efforts bore fruit in the European Strategic Program for Research and Development in Information Technology (ESPRIT), a basic research program involving major manufacturers, smaller firms, and universities throughout the EC. Technological collaboration, in turn, "created an important and vocal constituency . . . impatient for an end to such things as customs delays at borders, conflicting national standards in data processing or arcane rules on property ownership . . . and pressing for the completion of the internal market, for once these firms had lost their national champions status, it was imperative that they maximized the advantages to be gained from the single market."[38] Guy Gyllenhammer, the head of Volvo, catalyzed such thinking by organizing the European Round Table, a high-level interest group for deeper economic integration, although his own firm was located in Sweden, a nonmember state.

As well as encouraging technological collaboration in the EC, the Commission championed completion of the single market. In its annual report for 1980, the Commission asserted "the need to continue building the common market" and outlined the advantages to be gained from doing so. At the same time, the Commission followed up on a landmark decision of the Court of Justice, in the Cassis de Dijon case, that was to have a profound effect on the integration of the European marketplace. Based on the Court's rejection of a German prohibition on imports from other member states of alcoholic beverages that did not meet minimum alcohol content requirements, the Commission declared that "any product imported from another member state must in principle be admitted . . . if it has been lawfully produced, that is, conforms to rules and processes of manufacture that are customarily and traditionally accepted in the exporting country, and is marketed in the territory of the latter."[39] Thus, the Commission developed the principle of mutual recognition that would avoid the otherwise impossible process of harmonizing the member states' diverse legal norms.

Prodded by the Commission, the European Council declared in June 1981 that "a concerted effort must be made to strengthen and develop the free internal market which lies at the very basis of the European Community."[40] Moving from oratory to action, the Commission urged the Council later that year both to pass a number of proposals to strengthen the internal market and to simplify intra-EC frontier formalities involving customs, taxation, and statistics. Thereafter the Commission sharpened its strategy of putting forward concrete proposals, notably on product standards, and politicizing each problem by prodding the European Council to act. The Commission's approach again bore fruit in 1983 when the Council defined a standardization policy for European industry. The next year the Commission prepared a detailed paper for the Fontainebleau summit on a number of internal market issues ranging from the abolition of customs barriers to the free movement of people, capital, and services.[41]

Thatcher, a leading proponent of market integration, came to the Fontainebleau summit armed with a paper of her own. It contained the classic assertion that "if the problems of growth, outdated industrial structures and unemployment which affect us all are to be tackled effectively, we must create the genuine common market in goods and services which is envisaged in the Treaty of Rome and will be crucial to our ability to meet the U.S. and Japanese technological challenge."[42] By advocating completion of the single market, Thatcher sought to advance deeply held convictions and establish beyond question her pro-EC credentials.

Resolution of the British budgetary question at Fontainebleau removed a major barrier to EC action on a wide range of issues and opened the door to achieving a genuinely single market. During the past few years a consensus had emerged in Brussels and among member states on the need for as much deregulation as possible at the national level coupled with as little reregulation as necessary at the Community level. Ideological, political, and economic transformations had brought about a reemphasis on market integration and paved the way for an imminent breakthrough. Other developments, notably tension in the transatlantic relationship, the assertiveness of the first directly elected European Parliament, and Mediterranean enlargement, drew attention to the necessity of institutional reform in the EC. Those objectives—completion of the single market and a revision of the Rome Treaty—were not unconnected. Each gave added impetus to the other, and both were to combine in the Single European Act of 1986.

■ Transatlantic Tensions

The EC's external relations were every bit as problematical as its internal development in the early 1980s. The sudden heightening of East-West tension in the late 1970s after a decade of relatively benign relations tested the Community's ability to act internationally. European Political Cooperation proved an inadequate instrument for foreign policy coordination, especially in response to crises such as the Soviet invasion of Afghanistan in December 1979 and the imposition of martial law in Poland two years later. At the same time, the unremitting hostility of the United States toward the Soviet Union severely tested EC solidarity and combined with other developments in U.S.-EC relations to put transatlantic ties under great strain. The new Reagan administration saw the Soviet Union as the root of all evil and pressured European allies of the United States to cease most economic and trade activities with the Soviet bloc. U.S. officials cited Western Europe's approach to the question of East-West relations, which was more nuanced than the Reagan administration's, as evidence of weakness and cowardice.

Matters came to a head in June 1982 when the United States announced sanctions against U.S. subsidiaries and license holders in Western Europe involved in the so-called Soviet gas pipeline, a massive infrastructural project to facilitate the export of Soviet gas to Western Europe through a pipeline thousands of miles long. Such arbitrary action galvanized latent anti-Americanism and provided a powerful impetus for high-technology industries to accelerate collaboration in the EC, thereby asserting a European identity and declaring independence from the United States. ESPRIT and other EC-sponsored high-technology research and development programs therefore emerged in a climate of strained U.S.-EC political relations, exacerbated by bitter transatlantic disputes over subsidized steel and agricultural exports from the EC.

At the same time, the United States and its European allies were mired in a political dispute over NATO's deployment in Western Europe of medium-range nuclear missiles in response to a similar Soviet deployment in Eastern Europe. What had begun as a show of Allied solidarity, with NATO adopting the "dual-track" approach of missile deployment and arms control negotiations to counter the new Soviet threat, degenerated into European accusations that the Reagan administration was interested only in deployment and U.S. accusations that the Europeans were giving in to Soviet pressure. The "Euromissile" crisis, played out publicly on the streets of many Western European cities as well as privately in the chancelleries of the Atlantic Alliance, cast a pall over Euro-American relations.

The United States and its allies in the EC also diverged over policy toward the Middle East, an especially sensitive issue for Washington. The United States viewed the member states' declarations on the Arab-Israeli conflict, which tended to criticize Israel and support the Palestinians, as examples of the perniciousness of European Political Cooperation. The so-called Venice Declaration of June 1980, in which the Nine recognized the special position of Palestine in the Arab-Israeli conflict, greatly irritated the United States, as did the resumption of the "Euro-Arab dialogue" shortly afterward. The United

States disliked its European allies' taking an independent and relatively radical position on an issue that was both inherently explosive and part of the wider, all-encompassing Cold War conflict.

Irritation with the United States emboldened the member states to assert themselves internationally. France, well-known for its estrangement from the United States, took the lead. In May 1984, during France's Council presidency, Mitterrand made a famous speech to the European Parliament calling for institutional reform and greater Community competence over internal and external affairs.[43] On external relations, Mitterrand advocated a permanent secretariat for the conduct of foreign policy cooperation and urged member states to make a common defense effort. Hans-Dietrich Genscher, Germany's foreign minister, and Emilio Colombo, his Italian counterpart, launched an initiative to assert the EC's international identity while reassuring the United States about the EC's intentions. Their "Draft European Act," popularly known as the Genscher-Colombo proposals, advocated more effective decisionmaking and greater Community competence in external relations.[44]

Although the Genscher-Colombo proposals soft-pedaled the security implications of a more coherent EC foreign policymaking capacity, the United States expressed concern. Thatcher shared this anxiety. Moreover, for varying reasons a number of smaller member states disliked the proposal's emphasis on closer security cooperation. Despite being a NATO member, Denmark did not want to give the EC competence in the security domain. Under Andreas Papandreou's leadership, Greece (also a NATO member) opposed deeper European integration in general and closer security cooperation in particular. Sensitive to public support for nonmembership in NATO and an ill-defined "neutrality," the otherwise indifferent Irish government objected to any EC initiative on security and defense.

Under the circumstances, the Genscher-Colombo proposals had little direct impact and gave rise only to the "Solemn Declaration on European Union,"[45] a vague statement of the Community's international identity. Efforts to introduce a security dimension nevertheless contributed indirectly to the EC's revival in the 1980s. For example, Mitterrand drew on the Genscher-Colombo proposals in his May 1984 speech to the European Parliament, which in turn contributed to the decision at Fontainebleau to establish a committee to consider the future of European integration. At the very least, the member states' willingness to speculate about a possible security and defense community created a climate conducive to change.

■ The First Directly Elected European Parliament

The activism of the first directly elected European Parliament was yet another factor that prepared the way for the EC's revival in the mid-1980s. The Rome

Treaty provided for a directly elected assembly, but member states had dragged their feet on switching from an appointed to an elected Parliament. As a gesture to counterbalance the creation of the European Council, national leaders decided in December 1974 to hold direct elections "as soon as possible."[46] It took another two years for them to decide on the size of the directly elected Parliament, finally settling on 410 seats, over twice the number in the existing assembly, distributed among member states approximately according to population size. Because of Britain's difficulty meeting the summer 1978 deadline for the elections, the European Council decided to postpone the first direct elections until June 1979.[47]

Britain and France openly disliked direct elections, fearing that a stronger European Parliament would challenge national supremacy in the EC's decisionmaking process. By contrast, Germany, the Netherlands, and Italy traditionally favored a stronger Parliament as a corollary to their support for supranationalism. Similarly, the Commission saw a stronger Parliament as a natural institutional ally. Perhaps because of his years in the British political system, where the government is directly answerable to the parliament, Roy Jenkins especially encouraged direct elections and exaggerated their impact on the Parliament itself.[48]

In the event, the direct elections of June 1979 did not cause a radical redistribution of power in the EC. Only a revision of the Rome Treaty could enhance the Parliament's legislative role. However, direct elections brought a new breed of parliamentarian to Brussels and Strasbourg and noticeably improved the Parliament's morale. For all the excitement surrounding the June 1979 elections, the parliamentarians who convened in Strasbourg later that summer knew only too well that their institution still lacked power or influence. They also appreciated the extent of the EC's difficulties and hoped to revive the process of European integration. Accordingly, between April 1980 and February 1982, the Parliament passed no fewer than eight resolutions advocating institutional and policy reform in the EC.

Spinelli and the Crocodile Club

Altiero Spinelli, the veteran Eurofederalist, was one of the best-known and most influential members of the newly elected Parliament. In 1970 the Italian government had nominated Spinelli to the Commission, but he resigned unexpectedly in 1976 to take a seat in the Parliament. His decision to become a member of the relatively powerless Parliament surprised almost everyone. In fact, Spinelli was positioning himself to become a key figure in the first directly elected Parliament, due to convene at the end of the decade. He interpreted the results of the direct elections as nothing less than a mandate to overhaul the Rome Treaty.

In July 1980 Spinelli gathered together a small number of like-minded parliamentarians, representing a wide spectrum of political opinion, in the Crocodile Restaurant in Strasbourg. By the end of the year the "Crocodile Club," an otherwise heterogeneous collection of parliamentarians dedicated to reforming and reviving the EC, had grown from ten to seventy members. Their ideas ranged from a return to the EC's first principles—the need to complete the internal market—to drafting a constitution for Europe. Gradually a consensus emerged on the urgency of a new treaty to replace the original treaties and for a new European Union to replace the original European Community.

Grown too large to meet in its favorite Strasbourg restaurant, the Crocodile Club moved to a committee room at the Parliament. The group was relatively ineffectual as an unofficial caucus, so in July 1981 Spinelli convinced his colleagues to inaugurate a committee on institutional affairs. The committee met for the first time in January 1983, halfway through the Parliament's five-year term of office. Spinelli served not as chairman but in the crucial capacity of rapporteur (report writer).

Members of the Institutional Affairs Committee appreciated the potential pitfalls surrounding their work. Because the Parliament remained relatively powerless, there was a predisposition in Brussels and in member state capitals to dismiss parliamentarians' agitation for reform as the ravings of reckless, overindulged, and underemployed politicians. Spinelli himself had a reputation for being idealistic and excitable. Because of the Parliament's comparative weakness, national governments expected parliamentarians to demand a larger say for their institution in EC decisionmaking. All in all, the Institutional Affairs Committee risked not being taken seriously.

Yet the crisis in the Community—prolonged economic recession, declining international competitiveness, institutional inertia, and decisionmaking paralysis—lent credibility to the Parliament's efforts to revive European integration, as did the member states' own initiatives along the same lines. Fortunately for the Parliament, the Institutional Affairs Committee's first six months in operation coincided with Belgium's presidency of the Council. Eager to undertake major institutional reform, the Belgians set an important precedent in May 1982 by rejecting the practice of unanimity and calling for a vote in the Council on that year's farm prices.[49] The symbolism of Belgium's action was not lost on the Commission and the member states, and certainly not on the Parliament.

The Draft Treaty Establishing the European Union

Drawing on the support of Belgium and some other member states, the Institutional Affairs Committee proceeded cautiously and responsibly. By the middle of 1982 it had identified the main lines of a reform program and established subgroups to work on them. Issues included the legal personality of a possible new union, its institutional structure, competence, and relationship with the member states. The committee consulted experts throughout the Community in the fall of 1982. With the assistance of some noted jurists, the proposed reforms wound their way procedurally through the committee and the Parliament in 1983, emerging at the end of the year as the "Draft Treaty Establishing the European Union."[50]

The draft treaty sought to substitute a single treaty establishing a European Union for the existing treaties establishing the European communities. The EU would maintain the basic institutional structure and legal competence of the three communities but revise their decisionmaking procedures and add to them new or expanded authority over certain aspects of economic, social, and political affairs. The purpose of decisionmaking reform was both to improve efficiency and to close an emerging "democratic deficit." Allowing for the member states' sensitivity to the centralization of power in Brussels, the draft treaty provided for something that received little attention at the time but became prominent a decade later during the Maastricht ratification debate: the principle of subsidiarity, whereby the EU would be responsible only for tasks that could be undertaken more effectively in common than by the member states acting independently.

In one of the most famous votes ever taken in the Parliament, in February 1984 the draft treaty passed by a resounding 237 to 31 with 43 abstentions.[51] The vast majority of parliamentarians, including the stalwart Crocodile Club members, knew that the draft treaty would never be ratified by the member states. They decided to send it to national parliaments and governments anyway in order to increase the momentum for reform then gathering in the EC. Passage of the draft treaty was especially timely in the run-up to the second direct elections in June 1984: it demonstrated the Parliament's seriousness and commitment to European integration (although most of the electorate took little interest in the Parliament's activities) and constituted a concrete legacy from the first directly elected Parliament to its successors. The vote on the draft treaty also gave Mitterrand, then in the Council presidency and boldly championing deeper integration, additional political ammunition.

Synergy among the European Monetary System, collaborative ventures in high technology, renewed interest in the internal market, concern about international affairs, and eagerness to overcome paralysis in the decisionmaking process paved the way for serious consideration of the EC's potential contribution to Western Europe's political and economic development. Similarly, initiatives such as the Genscher-Colombo proposals, the Stuttgart solemn declaration, and the Parliament's draft treaty were important precursors of the

EC's revival following resolution of the British budgetary question. They provided a climate and a context in which member states could focus on first principles: market integration as originally envisioned in the Rome Treaty. The scene was set for the Single European Act and the single market program, which triggered the EC's resurgence in the late 1980s.

▓ Notes

1. Quoted in Steven Lagerfeld, "Europhoria," *Wilson Quarterly* 14 (Winter 1990): 66.

2. Christopher Tugendhat, "How to Get Europe Moving Again," *International Affairs* 61 (Winter 1990): 421.

3. European Commission, *1973 General Report,* Annex 1 to Chapter II (Luxembourg: Office for Official Publications of the European Communities, 1974), pp. 489–491; "Statement of the Nine Foreign Ministers on the Situation in the Middle East," in Federal Republic of Germany, *European Political Cooperation (EPC),* 4th ed. (Wiesbaden: Press and Information Office of the Federal Government, 1982), pp. 55–56.

4. Roy Jenkins, *Life at the Centre* (London: Macmillan, 1991), p. 375.

5. European Commission, *1974 General Report*, Annex to Chapter I (Luxembourg: Office for Official Publications of the European Communities, 1975), point 24.

6. Frances Nicholson and Roger East, *From the Six to the Twelve: The Enlargement of the European Communities* (Chicago: St. James Press, 1987), pp. 165–180.

7. Quoted in ibid., p. 180.

8. Jenkins, *Life at the Centre*, p. 342.

9. Stephen George, *An Awkward Partner: Britain in the European Community* (Oxford: Oxford University Press, 1990), p. 87.

10. See Loukas Tsoukalis, *The Politics and Economics of European Monetary Integration* (London: Allen and Unwin, 1977.

11. James Goldsborough, "The Franco-German Entente," *Foreign Affairs* 54, no. 3 (April 1976): 499.

12. William Wallace, introduction to Roger Morgan and Caroline Brey, *Partners and Rivals in Western Europe: Britain, France and Germany* (Brookfield, VT: Gower, 1986), p. 4.

13. Jonathan Storey, "The Franco-German Alliance Within the European Community," *World Today* (June 1980): 209.

14. The *Economist* broke the story on January 27, 1979, p. 43.

15. Bulletin EC S/1-1976.

16. See A. N. Duff, "The Report of the Three Wise Men," *Journal of Common Market Studies* 19, no. 3 (1981): 238; and Bulletin EC 11-1976, "Presidency Conclusions," point 2427.

17. European Commission, *1979 General Report* (Luxembourg: Office for Official Publications of the European Communities, 1980), point 8; Bulletin EC 11-1979, "Presidency Conclusions," points 1.5.1–1.5.2.

18. "Ad Hoc Committee for Institutional Affairs Report to the European Council (Dooge Report), March 1985," Bulletin EC 3-1985, point 3.5.1.

19. Peter Ludlow, *The Making of the European Monetary System: A Case Study in the Politics of the European Community* (London: Butterworths Scientific, 1982).

20. Roy Jenkins, "Europe's Present Challenge and Future Opportunity," speech delivered at the European University Institute (Florence), October 27, 1977.

21. Roy Jenkins, *European Diary, 1977–1981* (London: Collins, 1989), p. 183.

22. Jenkins, *Life at the Centre*, pp. 470–471.

23. Haig Simonian, *The Privileged Partnership: Franco-German Relations in the European Community, 1969–1984* (Oxford: Clarendon Press, 1985), p. 277.

24. Helen Wallace, "The Conduct of Bilateral Relations by Governments," in Morgan and Brey, *Partners and Rivals,* p. 154.

25. Bulletin EC 12-1978, "Presidency Conclusions," point 1.14.

26. William Nicoll and Trevor Salmon, *Understanding the European Communities* (Savage, MD: Barnes and Noble, 1990), p. 197.

27. Sir Michael Butler, "Simply Wrong About Europe," *Times* (London), November 26, 1991, p. 3.

28. Hugo Young, *One of Us: A Biography of Margaret Thatcher* (London: Macmillan, 1989), p. 388. For Thatcher's own perspective on the EC and account of the budget dispute, see Margaret Thatcher, *The Downing Street Years* (New York: HarperCollins, 1993), pp. 34–35, 60–64, 78–88, 537–545.

29. *Financial Times,* June 28, 1989, p. 2.

30. Jenkins, *European Diary*, p. 545.

31. Jenkins, *Life at the Centre*, p. 494.

32. Jenkins, *European Diary*, pp. 529–531. Granada Television, a private British television company, produced an entertaining and accurate reenactment of the Dublin summit called "Mrs. Thatcher's Billion."

33. Quoted in the *Daily Express* (London), June 4, 1984, p. 4.

34. For a lively account of the Fontainebleau summit, see John Newhouse, "One Against Nine," the *New Yorker*, October 22, 1984, pp. 64–92. See also Geoffrey Denton, "Restructuring the EEC Budget: Implications of the Fontainebleau Summit," *Journal of Common Market Studies* 23, no. 2 (December 1984): 117–140.

35. Bulletin EC 6-1984, "Presidency Conclusions," point 1.1.1. et seq.

36. Quoted in *Financial Times*, June 28, 1984, p. 14.

37. See Pierre-Henri Laurent, "Forging the European Technology Community," in Michael S. Steinberg, ed., *The Technological Challenges and Opportunities of a United Europe* (Savage, MD: Barnes and Noble, 1990), pp. 59–67; and M. Sharp and C. Shearman, *European Technological Collaboration* (London: Routledge and Kegan Paul, 1987), p. 46.

38. Margaret Sharp, Christopher Freeman, and William Walker, *Technology and the Future of Europe: Global Competition and the Environment in the 1990s* (New York: Pinter, 1991), p. 73.

39. European Commission, *1980 General Report* (Luxembourg: Office for Official Publications of the European Communities, 1981), point 120.

40. Bulletin EC 6-1981, "Presidency Conclusions," point 1.10.

41. European Commission, *1984 General Report* (Luxembourg: Office for Official Publications of the European Communities, 1985), point 133.

42. "Europe: The Future," reproduced in *Journal of Common Market Studies* 23, no. 1 (September 1984): 74–81.

43. François Mitterrand, speech to the European Parliament, May 24, 1984, reprinted in *Vital Speeches of the Day,* August 1, 1984, p. 613.

44. The Genscher-Colombo proposals are reproduced in European Parliament, Committee on Institutional Affairs, *Selection of Texts Concerning Institutional Matters of the Community from 1950–1982* (Luxembourg: Office for Official Publications of the European Parliament, 1982), pp. 490–499.

45. Bulletin EC 6-1983, point 1.6.1.
46. Commission, *1974 General Report*, Annex to Chapter 1, point 18.
47. Bulletin EC 12-1977, point 1.12.
48. Jenkins, *European Diary,* p. 375.
49. Bulletin EC 5-1982, points 2.1.73–2.1.97.
50. "Draft Treaty Establishing the European Union," Bulletin EC 2-1984, point 1.1.2. For a comprehensive assessment of the draft treaty, see Roland Bieber, Jean-Paul Jacqué, and Joseph Weiler, eds., *An Ever Closer Union: A Critical Analysis of the Draft Treaty Establishing European Union,* European Perspectives Series (Luxembourg: Office for Official Publications of the European Community, 1985).
51. Bulletin EC 2-1984, point 1.1.1.

4

From European Community to European Union, 1985–1993

In the mid-1980s the European Community underwent an extraordinary transformation. After years of sluggish growth and institutional immobility, member states concluded the Single European Act (SEA), a major revision of the Rome Treaty that underpinned the single market program. Jacques Delors, who became Commission president in January 1985, is generally credited with the EC's metamorphosis. "Delors is as important to the enterprise today," Stanley Hoffmann wrote at the height of the EC's transformation, "as Jean Monnet was in the 1950s."[1]

Yet Delors's role should not be exaggerated. Undoubtedly he was ambitious, competent, and resourceful. Delors sought to infuse the Commission with a renewed sense of purpose and to deepen political and economic integration. But Delors could not possibly have succeeded had the economic, political, and international circumstances been unfavorable. It was his good fortune to have become Commission president at precisely the time when internal developments (resolution of the British budgetary question, agitation for institutional reform, and pressure to complete the internal market) and external factors (fundamental changes in the global system) made a dramatic improvement in the EC's fortunes almost inevitable. Without Delors, the single market program and the acceleration of European integration might not have happened exactly as they did, but that is not to say that they would not have happened at all.

One of the most remarkable aspects of the EC's transformation is that it coincided with the potentially disruptive Mediterranean enlargement. The accession of relatively impoverished Portugal and Spain (Greece had joined in 1981) threatened to throw European integration further off course. Without compensating mechanisms, completion of the internal market could have aggravated the social and economic divide between the EC's rich and poor member states. The Single European Act was more than a device, therefore, to launch the single market program. It was a complex bargain to improve decisionmaking, strengthen democracy, achieve market liberalization, and at the same time promote economic and social cohesion.

The Single European Act and the single market program sparked a renewed interest in economic and monetary union (EMU). At the same time and in response to similar political and economic pressures, the reform movement in Central and Eastern Europe hastened the collapse of communism. More than any other event, the sudden breach of the Berlin Wall in November 1989 symbolized the end of the Cold War and led to the unification of Germany in 1990. In response to these profound changes, member states negotiated the Maastricht Treaty, which established the European Union (EU).

Yet the new treaty triggered widespread public concern and almost foundered when a narrow majority rejected it in the Danish referendum of June 1992. The ensuing ratification crisis was an inauspicious beginning for the EU. At issue were public alienation from an increasingly complex and intrusive policymaking process, poor democratic accountability in Brussels, and doubts about the EU's ability to cope with unexpected changes in the international political system. Worries about the long-term impact of German unification and eventual EU enlargement to the east contributed to a climate of uncertainty in which the ratification drama unfolded. Implementation of the treaty in November 1993 did not end popular dissatisfaction with the EU but at least allowed European integration to progress beyond the single market program toward monetary union and other important undertakings (Table 4.1).

Table 4.1   Chronology, 1985–1993

1985	January	Delors Commission takes office
	February	Agreement on Integrated Mediterranean Programs
	March	Dooge Committee recommends intergovernmental conference on treaty reform
	June	Portugal and Spain sign accession treaties
		Commission publishes White Paper on single market
		At Milan summit, EC leaders decide to hold intergovernmental conference
	September	Intergovernmental conference begins
	December	Intergovernmental conference ends
1986	January	Portugal and Spain join EC
	February	Foreign ministers sign Single European Act (SEA)
1987	April	Turkey applies to join EC
	July	SEA comes into effect
	September	Finance ministers strengthen European Monetary System (EMS)
1988	January	Balladur memorandum on economic and monetary union (EMU)
	February	Genscher memorandum on EMU
		At Brussels summit, EC leaders agree on Delors I budget package
	June	At Hanover summit, EC leaders decide to establish Delors Committee on EMU

continues

Table 4.1 *continued*

1989	June	Delors report on EMU
		Third direct elections to the European Parliament
	July	Austria applies to join EC
	November	Fall of Berlin Wall
	December	At Strasbourg summit, EC leaders decide to hold intergovernmental conference on EMU and adopt Charter of Fundamental Social Rights for Workers
1990	May	Charter for European Bank for Reconstruction and Development signed
	June	France, Germany, and Benelux countries sign Schengen Agreement
		At Dublin summit, EC leaders decide to hold intergovernmental conference on political union concurrently with intergovernmental conference on EMU, beginning in December 1990
	July	Stage I of EMU begins
		Cyprus applies to join EC
		Malta applies to join EC
	October	German unification
		Britain joins exchange rate mechanism of EMS
	November	U.S.-EC Transatlantic Declaration signed
	December	Intergovernmental conferences begin in Rome
1991	June	Outbreak of war in Yugoslavia
	July	Sweden applies to join EC
	December	Intergovernmental conference ends at Maastricht summit
		Soviet Union collapses
1992	January	EC recognizes independence of Croatia and Slovenia
	February	Foreign ministers sign Treaty on European Union in Maastricht
	March	Finland applies to join EC
	May	EC and EFTA countries agree on European Economic Area (EEA)
		Agreement on CAP reform
		Switzerland applies to join EU
	June	Danes reject Maastricht Treaty in referendum
	September	Britain suspends participation in exchange rate mechanism of EMS as currency crisis deepens
		French narrowly approve Maastricht Treaty in referendum
	November	Norway again applies to join EU
	December	Swiss reject EEA membership in referendum, implicitly rejecting EC membership
		At Edinburgh summit, EC leaders agree on Danish opt-outs from Maastricht Treaty and Delors II budget package
		Completion of single market program
1993	November	Maastricht Treaty enters into force
		EU comes into existence

▓ Mediterranean Enlargement

Having shaken off right-wing dictatorships in the mid-1970s, Greece, Portugal, and Spain sought to join the EC as soon as possible in order to end their relative international isolation, stabilize their newly established democratic regimes, and help develop their comparatively antiquated economies. Thus began a new round of enlargement while the EC was still digesting British,

Danish, and Irish membership. Although Greece managed to join within a relatively short time, the accession negotiations with Portugal and Spain were difficult and drawn out. All were poor countries whose combined population was 20 percent of the existing EC's. The prospect of Greek, Portuguese, and Spanish accession unnerved many member states, not least because of the difficulties caused by the EC's first enlargement. Overall, the EC's southern European expansion confirmed that enlargement was a major test for the EC, both procedurally and substantively.

Greece

Greece succeeded in differentiating itself from the two Iberian candidates, which posed greater economic problems for the EC. Assessing the Greek application on its merits, the Commission advised against early accession. Of the three Mediterranean applicants, Commission president Roy Jenkins considered Greece "the least qualified" to join.[2] By contrast, the Council saw the Greek case primarily from a political perspective and disregarded the Commission's advice. As Germany's foreign minister put it, "Greece, only recently returned to the democratic fold, would march in future with the Community of European nations."[3] Exploiting such sentiments to the full, Greece began accession negotiations in July 1976.

If the EC could have foreseen the problems that Greek membership would subsequently pose, the negotiations might not have concluded so swiftly, if at all. In the event, Greek prime minister Konstantinos Karamanlis skillfully distanced his country from the contemporaneous Iberian negotiations, did not raise any contentious issues, and concluded an accession agreement in April 1979. Signed in Athens in May 1979 and duly ratified in Greece and the member states, the accession treaty came into effect in January 1981, when Greece became the tenth member of the EC.[4]

Portugal and Spain

Realizing that the EC feared the economic consequences primarily of Spanish membership, Portugal also tried to have its application considered separately and concluded swiftly. Portugal applied to join in March 1977, more than a year before Spain lodged its application. Portugal's accession negotiations also began before Spain's, but only four months earlier. Although the EC negotiated separately with each country, the short time between the openings of the two sets of talks indicated the degree to which the EC considered them interrelated.

Portugal ascribed the protracted negotiations to the lumping together of Lisbon's and Madrid's applications and the EC's preoccupation with internal budgetary and institutional problems. Yet a number of factors peculiar to Portugal—notably textiles (which represented over 40 percent of the country's industrial output and 33 percent of its exports), migrant workers, and agriculture—accounted as well for the talks' slow progress. In its opinion of May 1978, the Commission identified a host of economic, structural, and administrative issues that would have to be tackled before Portugal joined the Community. As a result, the Commission refused to recommend a detailed timetable for accession.

British prime minister Margaret Thatcher strongly supported Portuguese accession for traditional British foreign policy reasons: a history of alliance and friendship with Portugal and the desire for a wider and weaker Community. Thatcher delighted the Portuguese prime minister by declaring, during his visit to London in December 1981, that Spain and Portugal need not accede simultaneously and that Portugal could join by January 1984.[5]

As long as France was lukewarm about enlargement (due largely to concerns about the Common Agricultural Policy [CAP]) there was little hope of early Portuguese accession. François Mitterrand, who succeeded Valéry Giscard d'Estaing as president of France in May 1981, refused to endorse enlargement pending an acceptable arrangement for Mediterranean agriculture. Nevertheless, negotiations progressed on a wide range of thorny issues, including capital movements, regional policy, transport, and services. Commission president Gaston Thorn had to remind his hosts during a visit to Lisbon in April 1982 that contentious questions apart from agriculture, such as the issues of textiles, fisheries, and the free movement of labor, remained unresolved.[6]

The formation of a relatively stable administration in Lisbon by the able and energetic Mário Soares in June 1983 increased EC goodwill toward Portugal, not least because the new government soon reached an agreement with the International Monetary Fund that included measures to reduce the country's substantial foreign debt and further restructure the economy. In the following months, Soares embarked on a frantic round of visits to EC capitals and cultivated a close relationship with Mitterrand, a fellow Socialist. Soares impressed his interlocutors with Portugal's determination to become a model member state. Rapid agreement on a number of outstanding issues followed, although (much to Soares's annoyance) the fate of the Spanish and Portuguese negotiations became increasingly linked. Without a breakthrough in the talks with Spain, especially concerning agriculture and fisheries, Portugal's prospects for immediate accession looked poor.

French misgivings about enlargement focused primarily on Spain, whose accession would increase the EC's agricultural area by 30 percent and its farm workforce by 25 percent, thereby further straining the CAP. Nevertheless, France recognized the political imperative of Spanish membership, especially after an attempted military coup in Madrid in February 1981. For its part Spain, despite repeated rhetoric about the country's "European vocation," seemed unwilling to embrace all of the obligations of Community membership, especially the need to introduce a value-added tax, curtail subsidies, and curb protectionism. Spain's reluctance prompted the European Council, meeting in London in November 1981, to urge the Spanish government to "make good use of the period until accession for careful preparations for . . . enlargement by introducing the necessary reforms so that the potential benefits for both sides can be realized."[7]

The situation improved when Felipe González formed a new government in Madrid. González was a passionate Europhile whose overriding goal was to bring Spain into the EC. Young, personable, and able, González emulated Soares by embarking on a series of visits to EC capitals, using personal charm, political savvy, and, where appropriate, ideological affinity to promote Spanish accession. An informal summit of the prime ministers—all Socialists—of the EC's Mediterranean member states and the applicant countries in October 1983 may have paved the way for the first breakthrough on agriculture in the enlargement negotiations.

Whereas an agreement on agriculture seemed within reach, fisheries became increasingly a subject of dispute between the EC on one side and Spain and Portugal on the other. In March 1984, French patrol boats fired on two Spanish trawlers in the Bay of Biscay, about 100 miles off the southwest coast of France but well within the EC's 200-mile fisheries limit. At issue was the EC's effort under the Common Fisheries Policy to limit the access of Spain's fishing fleet, which was larger than the entire EC fleet. Spanish fishermen attacked foreign trucks in protest; French truckers, in turn, blockaded the Spanish border. Such incidents continued throughout the year—thirty-two Spanish trawlers were arrested off the Irish coast alone in 1984.[8]

Iberian Accession

The decisive breakthrough on enlargement came not in the talks themselves but in the EC's internal affairs, notably through resolution of the British budgetary question. As if to signal a new stage in the EC's development, national leaders announced at the Fontainebleau summit in June 1984 that enlargement would take place by January 1986, pending a resolution of the outstanding issues.[9] As Spain had always suspected France of blocking enlargement, Mitterrand's pivotal role in securing the Fontainebleau settlement greatly improved relations between the two countries. In a move calculated to reassure González of French goodwill, Mitterrand flew to Madrid immediately after the summit to report personally on its outcome.[10]

Negotiations between the EC and the applicant countries accelerated thereafter. Yet it was not until March 1985 that foreign ministers resolved the remaining problems in the accession negotiations—fisheries, free movement of Spanish and Portuguese workers in the EC, and the applicant countries' budgetary contributions—at a marathon meeting.[11] At that point enlargement became bound up with Greek demands for an accord by the member states on the so-called Integrated Mediterranean Programs. Originating in a request in 1982 by the new Greek government of Andreas Papandreou for better membership terms, the Integrated Mediterranean Programs called for financial assistance primarily to Greece but also to Italy and southern France to help develop agriculture, tourism, and small business.[12] As the negotiations with Spain and Portugal reached a conclusion, Papandreou linked an agreement on financial transfers to Greece with an agreement on enlargement.

Delors, who became Commission president in January 1985, had to resolve the Integrated Mediterranean Programs before the EC could advance on other fronts. He threw himself enthusiastically into the fray, setting a precedent for his leadership of the single market program. Following intensive negotiations, the European Council agreed in March 1985 to a seven-year program of grants and loans to assist existing Mediterranean regions in the EC "to adjust under the best conditions possible to the new situation created by enlargement."[13] Despite Thatcher's initial opposition, member states finally accepted a figure of €6.6 billion, of which Greece would receive approximately 30 percent. Greece had hoped for a larger share but grudgingly went along with the majority, thus removing the final obstacle to Portuguese and Spanish accession. Regardless of Greek dissatisfaction, the issue showed how a tough-minded member state could leverage a key development in the EC for its own economic advantage.

The outcome of the Brussels summit was a triumph for Delors. Because he had taken personal responsibility for resolving the dispute, failure would have seriously undermined Delors's credibility. After the summit, a relieved Delors declared that "all the family quarrels have been sorted out. The family is now going to grow and we can think of the future."[14] Indeed, for the first time in nearly twenty years the EC's future looked bright. Imminent enlargement provided a psychological boost and an additional rationale for institutional reform. Following the protracted accession negotiations and short but sharp dispute over the Integrated Mediterranean Programs, the decks were cleared for the forthcoming European Council in Milan to consider, as Mitterrand put it, "what Europe will become."[15]

■ Pressure for Treaty Reform

There was a palpable sense in early 1985, after the breakthrough on enlargement, that the EC was about to take off. Concern about the EC's institutional inadequacies and interest in completing the internal market built up pressure for treaty reform. Apart from the internal market, Delors wanted to revitalize the EC by overhauling decisionmaking procedures, launching a new monetary policy initiative, and extending Community competence in the field of foreign and defense policy. As a former finance minister and a committed Eurofederalist,

Delors preferred to concentrate primarily on EMU. Yet Delors sensed that monetary policy lay too close to the core of national sovereignty for an initiative going beyond the European Monetary System to prosper in the mid-1980s. Delors wanted to capitalize on the goodwill generated in the European Council by the successful Fontainebleau summit, not aggravate tension among national leaders by promoting a politically sensitive proposal. Similarly, an outright assault on unanimity in an effort to improve EC decisionmaking would only have raised member states' hackles.

By contrast, the advantages of choosing the internal market option were obvious. By going back to basics and emphasizing one of the original objectives of the Rome Treaty, Delors could hardly be accused of overweening ambition. Regardless of their political preferences and personal opinions of each other, national leaders uniformly sang the praises of a single market. Thatcher was especially eloquent on the virtues of market liberalization. By championing a cause dear to her heart, Delors hoped to reconcile Thatcher to the Community and heal the wounds caused by the protracted British budgetary dispute.

In addition, Delors believed, a single market strategy would indirectly but inescapably result in an improvement in decisionmaking procedures. Political will to complete the internal market could never translate into action unless unanimity gave way to qualified majority voting in the Council. Without reform of the legislative process, single market proposals would ultimately bog down in disputes among member states. A successful single market strategy, in turn, would most likely fuel interest in EMU. How could the market be fully integrated without monetary union and a common economic policy? The logic of a large, vibrant internal market pointed inexorably, Delors thought, toward currency union.[16]

The relationship between market integration, decisionmaking reform, and a further monetary initiative intrigued Delors and underlay the entire single market strategy. Delors was careful not to antagonize Thatcher by emphasizing EMU or majority voting. Nor was Delors sure that Lord Arthur Cockfield, the internal market commissioner, supported more than mere completion of the single market. In the event, Cockfield, a leading British conservative, "went native" in the Commission and became a staunch advocate of greater European integration. Predictably, Thatcher did not reappoint him in 1988 for a second term as commissioner.[17]

Despite their strikingly different political and personal backgrounds, Delors and Cockfield became close colleagues, working tirelessly in early 1985 to draft the famous White Paper on completing the internal market—one of the most important documents ever prepared for the European Council's deliberations.[18] Both understood the importance of maintaining private-sector support. Thus, Delors kept the door to European business leaders ajar and reiterated the Commission's commitment to an active industrial policy. To a great extent the Commission's subsequent proposals for collaborative research and development projects sought to strengthen the Commission-industry alliance in anticipation of the single market program.

European business leaders hardly needed reminding of the virtues of a single market. In 1984 and 1985 alone, three major manufacturers published pamphlets on the need to complete the internal market as soon as possible.[19] The most influential of these was by Wisse Dekker, the head of Philips and a leading member of the European Round Table, a powerful lobby group. Dekker's plan for a single market by 1990 bore a strong resemblance to the Commission's subsequent White Paper, which called for completion of the single market by 1992, the end of two consecutive commissioners' terms of office. It also reminded EC officials that the biggest challenge confronting them from the private sector was not to generate support for the single market but to allay doubts about the Commission's ability to deliver the goods.

The Commission's centrality in planning and implementing a single market strategy was a further reason for Delors's keen interest in the idea. Delors knew the EC's fortunes would never revive without a corresponding increase in the Commission's authority and morale. As incoming president, he wanted to give the Commission direction and leadership. For its part, the Commission looked forward to a new departure after the drift of the previous two decades. A strategy to devise and put in place a fully functioning internal market ideally suited both Delors's and the Commission's aspirations. As a political priority involving most of the Commission's directorates-general, a comprehensive single market strategy would put the Commission at center stage in the EC.

Building on widespread support in political, business, and academic circles, Delors submitted the White Paper to the European Council in June 1985. The White Paper is often caricatured as a typical Commission product: unintelligible, obtuse, and tedious. Indeed, the highly technical nature of the internal market hardly lent itself to lively prose. Yet this White Paper was a surprisingly lucid piece, containing a ringing defense of market liberalization and a clear exposition of how and why the EC should achieve a single market. If anything, the Commission deliberately downplayed the White Paper's style in order to avoid unfavorable political comment. Only in the final paragraph did its authors put the White Paper in historical perspective, proclaim the venture's political significance, and allow free rein to their hortatory impulses.

The White Paper is best known for its appendix listing approximately 300 Commission proposals that the Council of Ministers needed to enact before the internal market could be implemented. Cockfield was able to compile this list in record time because most of the proposals already existed in draft form, a legacy of the Commission's earlier internal market efforts. Nevertheless, Cockfield's job was much more than simply "one of trawling and of sieving."[20] The indispensable novelty of the White Paper's appendix was not the items listed in it but the way Cockfield organized them according to a timetable ending on

December 31, 1992. Thus, the appendix constituted a detailed action plan against which Commission officials, politicians, and businesspeople could measure progress toward a single market (the White Paper is examined in detail in Chapter 13).

Yet the White Paper's appendix represented only part of the large legislative agenda likely to be unleashed by the single market program. As mentioned but not spelled out elsewhere in the White Paper, completing the internal market would impinge directly on a wide range of policies and activities, notably in the fields of competition, research and development, the environment, consumer protection, social affairs, and EMU. Despite the simplicity of the "single market" slogan and the brevity of the Commission's action plan, the White Paper represented a huge leap forward for the EC. It was up to the European Council, meeting in Milan in June 1985, to decide whether the single market program would get off the ground.

As Delors pointed out in a series of speeches before the decisive summit, the European Council's acceptance of the White Paper would not suffice to ensure the success of the single market program. As long as serious procedural problems remained unresolved, the White Paper's detailed proposals likely would languish in the Council. The main challenge for the Milan summit, therefore, was to tackle the politically charged question of legislative reform in the EC, a question already on the Milan agenda not only indirectly in the form of the White Paper but also directly in the form of the so-called Dooge Report, which emerged from the deliberations of the Ad Hoc Committee on Institutional Reform, set up after the Fontainebleau summit and chaired by James Dooge, a former Irish foreign minister.

The Dooge Committee's political significance was evident from the outset. Its composition—senior officials and serving or former ministers—reflected the importance that each member state placed on closer European integration and the approach each would probably take in any negotiation to revise the Rome Treaty. "Spaak II," the committee's informal name, heightened expectations about its deliberations by drawing a parallel between the heady days of European integration in the mid-1950s and the Community's possible resurgence in the mid-1980s. Just as the 1955 Messina Conference had given birth to the Spaak Committee, which in turn had given birth to the Rome Treaty, so EC enthusiasts hoped that the Spaak II Committee would stimulate deeper European integration.

There was consensus in the committee on the importance of completing the internal market. In addition, the committee examined a host of options for improving the legislative process, strengthening the Commission and European Parliament, and ending gridlock in the Council. The committee also considered formally extending EC competence, notably in areas such as competition, research and development, consumer affairs, and monetary policy, and consolidating European Political Cooperation, the procedure for foreign policy cooperation among member states.

The committee's final report, presented to the European Council in March 1985, identified a number of "priority objectives" deemed necessary to deepen integration.[21] Apart from establishing a "homogeneous internal economic area," these included restricting the use of unanimity in the Council, strengthening the legislative role for the Parliament, giving more executive power to the Commission, and launching new initiatives in selected policy areas. Given the nature of the committee's mandate and wide differences among committee members over the future of European integration, the report was replete with reservations and minority opinions. In particular, three committee members—the representatives of Britain, Denmark, and Greece—disagreed with the report's central suggestion that the heads of state and government convene an intergovernmental conference to negotiate a new treaty.

The European Council took up the White Paper and the Dooge Report at the Milan summit, one of the most consequential in the history of the EC. Quick endorsement of the White Paper apparently presaged a smooth summit, but the meeting soon became mired in a difficult procedural discussion. Arguing against a treaty revision, Thatcher advocated informal arrangements to quicken decisionmaking in the Council. Taking a coordinated position, Mitterrand and German chancellor Helmut Kohl urged major institutional reform but disagreed about the Parliament's possible new powers. Prompted by Delors, Italian prime minister Bettino Craxi finally forced the issue by proposing an intergovernmental conference to negotiate a treaty on foreign policy and security cooperation as well as a revision of the Rome Treaty to improve decisionmaking and extend EC competence. Jealous of their national sovereignty, Britain and Denmark objected to holding such a conference, and obstructionist Greece followed suit. Italy again forced the issue by calling for a vote under the treaty article that permitted an intergovernmental conference to be convened if a majority of member states approved. It was unprecedented for the national leaders to vote on anything at a European Council. In the ensuing ballot seven voted in favor of an intergovernmental conference, and three—the British, Danish, and Greek prime ministers—voted against.

It was nothing new for Thatcher, the lone crusader for reform of the EC budget, to be isolated in the European Council, but she found herself in a novel situation at the end of the Milan summit. In the past, Thatcher's intransigence had thwarted the EC's development. Now she was powerless to prevent the EC from holding an intergovernmental conference that could change its character completely. Thatcher felt especially aggrieved because the single market program, at the root of the Community's metamorphosis, owed much to her initiative. She also supported closer foreign policy cooperation—only days before the Milan summit, Britain had circulated a paper proposing new procedures for European Political Cooperation—and appreciated that excessive use of the veto impeded efficient decisionmaking.

The prospect of an intergovernmental conference elicited a mixed response from the "progressive" member states. On the one hand, it was gratifying that the Ten, plus the two candidate countries, were about to negotiate major treaty reform. On the other hand, smarting from their isolation at Milan and renowned for their "minimalist" positions on European integration, Britain, Denmark, and Greece might attempt to sabotage an intergovernmental conference from within. Ultimately, they had too much to lose by pursuing blatantly negative tactics. In the event, the minority member states defended their interests tenaciously in the intergovernmental conference in a creditable and constructive manner.

■ The Single European Act

The Single European Act was the first major treaty change in the EC's history. The intergovernmental conference that brought it about began in September 1985 and ended in January 1986. Foreign ministers conducted the negotiations, assisted by two "working parties" of high-ranking officials. The first, consisting largely of permanent representatives, dealt with treaty revisions. The second, made up of the political directors of the foreign ministries (the "political committee"), tackled European Political Cooperation and also drafted the act's preamble. In addition to member state ministers and officials, commissioners or Commission officials participated at each level of the conference. National leaders resolved the most contentious issues at a summit in Luxembourg in December 1985.[22]

Written submissions from member states and the Commission provided fodder for the conference. One of the Commission's earliest contributions recommended a single concluding document rather than a treaty on foreign and security cooperation and a separate compilation of Rome Treaty revisions. Member states were skeptical, but soon they saw the political advantage of having one document emerge from the conference. Yet it was only at a late stage of the negotiations that foreign ministers endorsed the idea of *unicité* and named the eventual outcome of their deliberations the *Single* European Act.

At a time when intensified Cold War rivalry was gradually giving way to direct U.S.-Soviet bargaining without European involvement, member states generally agreed on the importance of asserting the EC's international identity by shoring up European Political Cooperation. The conference therefore concluded that member states would "coordinate their positions more closely on the political and economic aspects of security" and "endeavor jointly to formulate and implement a European foreign policy." As a sop to the United

States and to those member states—notably Britain and the Netherlands—most sensitive about U.S. opinion, the conference declared that greater foreign policy coordination would not "impede closer cooperation in the field of security" among relevant member states "in the framework of the Western European Union or the Atlantic Alliance."

As for EC policies and procedures, the conference had little difficulty endorsing the goal of an internal market, defined as "an area without internal frontiers in which the free movement of goods, persons, services and capital is ensured." But negotiations on the steps necessary to bring it about were predictably pugnacious. In the end, the conference revised the treaty to allow majority voting on harmonization, but only for approximately two-thirds of the measures outlined in the White Paper. The others—the least tractable ones—still were subject to unanimity. The conference also approved a number of national derogations for aspects of the single market program. As a result, a despondent Delors wondered whether the SEA would suffice to bring about the internal market by 1992.[23]

The conference did not directly confront the Luxembourg Compromise, the informal arrangement whereby a member state could prevent a vote from being taken in the Council. Some member states saw in the agreement to use qualified majority voting for most of the single market program the beginning of a concerted effort to undermine the national veto. Others reached the opposite conclusion by citing the continued applicability of unanimity for the White Paper's most controversial proposals. Undoubtedly member states would remain sensitive to each other's concerns, thus perpetuating "the very strong inclination of the Council to seek consensus irrespective of the voting rules."[24]

The role of the Parliament in the decisionmaking process was an equally sensitive issue. To push the EC more in a federal direction and to increase its democratic legitimacy, Germany and Italy urged greater power for the Parliament; for ideological reasons Britain took the opposite tack, and for a combination of political and practical purposes France opposed strengthening Parliament's legislative role. The issue dominated a number of negotiating sessions, including the December 1985 summit. Eventually the conference agreed to extend "compulsory" consultation between the Council and the Parliament to new policy issues and, more important, to establish a "cooperation procedure" to involve the Parliament fully in the legislative process, notably for most of the single market directives. The conference also gave the Parliament the right to approve future accession and association agreements. As these concessions were limited by comparison with those in the draft treaty, the Parliament, supported by the Italian government, expressed serious dissatisfaction.

During the conference, Delors returned repeatedly to his pet project of including "a certain monetary capacity" in the SEA. This would bring about "an alignment of economic policies" in the EC, "and outside it would enable Europe to make its voice heard more strongly in the world of economic, financial and monetary matters."[25] Finance ministers considered the question at an informal meeting in September 1985, after which Delors submitted a formal proposal, as did the Belgian government. Britain strongly opposed any move toward EMU, France was broadly in favor, and Germany remained equivocal. Without strong support from a large member state, Delors succeeded only in including a new chapter in the treaty that recognized the need to converge economic and monetary policies "for the further development of the Community."

The SEA included significant changes on environmental policy, research and development, and cohesion between rich and poor regions in the EC. National leaders failed to resolve outstanding issues and conclude the SEA at the Luxembourg summit, even after two full days of discussion. A subsequent foreign ministers' session brought agreement closer, but lingering Danish and Italian reservations (the Danes complained that the SEA's institutional provisions went too far, and the Italians complained that they did not go far enough) carried over into the New Year. The wording of an article on working conditions, buried in a subsection on social policy, caused last-minute delays. The final ministerial session of the conference, in January 1986, approved compromises reached in the working party and the political committee.

Ratification of the SEA, which the foreign ministers signed in Luxembourg in February 1986, proceeded relatively smoothly. Despite official British and Danish protestations before and during the conference, there was little popular concern throughout the EC about an excessive loss of national sovereignty or an exorbitant accumulation of power by the Commission. Most national parliaments held lively debates on the SEA, and almost all voted in favor of ratification. Denmark's parliament was the exception, but the positive outcome of the subsequent referendum ensured Danish ratification. (The reverse happened in 1992, when a majority of Danes rejected the Maastricht Treaty following the Danish parliament's acceptance of it.)

Member states and the Commission hoped that the SEA would come into effect by January 1987. In the event, a last-minute upset in Ireland delayed everything when, in December 1986, the Irish Supreme Court ruled that the SEA was unconstitutional, based on a challenge by a citizen concerned about the impact of the act's foreign policy provisions on Irish neutrality. An embarrassed Irish government had no option but to call a referendum to change the constitution. Held in May 1987, the referendum became a vote on whether Ireland should stay in the EC. The predictably positive result removed the final obstacle to ratification of the SEA, which finally came into effect in July 1987.

Revision of the Rome Treaty had proved a messy and protracted affair. For that reason Delors especially disliked the stipulation in the SEA that further steps toward EMU involving institutional change could be taken only in an intergovernmental conference. Yet his confidence in the likely revival of member states' interest in EMU led Delors to talk presciently at the end of 1985 about the possibility of a new conference in a relatively short time.[26] In other respects, too, the SEA disappointed Delors, who felt that member states had been unwilling to take bold initiatives, thus reducing progress to the level of the lowest common denominator. Franco-German leadership had not been decisive; far from pushing a radical reform agenda, Mitterrand and Kohl had seemingly succumbed to Thatcher's minimalist position.

Thatcher's delight and Delors's disappointment indicated the importance attached to the SEA at the time of its negotiation. As the *Common Market Law Review* editorialized in 1986, "Measured against Parliament's Draft Treaty, the results [of the conference] are disappointingly meager. They also fall short of the expectations . . . of the Commission and some of the member states. . . . But they reflect the limits of what was possible at the turn of the year [1985–1986]."[27] Yet the SEA had real potential for the EC's rapid development. First, provision for qualified majority voting could not only expedite the internal market but also encourage the Council to be more flexible in areas where unanimity remained the norm. Second, a successful single market program might advance European integration in related economic and social sectors. Third, the SEA's endorsement of the White Paper and formal extension of EC competence could strengthen the Commission's position. Fourth, the introduction of a legislative cooperation procedure could help close the EC's supposed "democratic deficit" and boost the Parliament's institutional importance. Finally, the SEA's provisions for improved foreign policy coordination procedures might enhance the EC's international standing. Within a short time, proponents and opponents of greater integration would know whether and how the SEA's potential would be realized.

◼ Economic Integration and Geopolitical Change

In the late 1980s, at a time when the historical inevitability of communism was shown to be false, the word "irreversible" crept into the lexicon of European integration. It came to mean the point at which completing the single market program, both legislatively and economically, had become unstoppable. A profile of Cockfield in the *Times* of London in November 1987 claimed that the internal market commissioner aimed to create "a feeling of irreversibility" about the 1992 program in case governments failed to agree on vital parts of it.[28] The following January, in an address to the European Parliament, Delors reported that "progress made to date has lent credibility to the large [single] market. . . . [In the months ahead] the Commission will concentrate on making the process irreversible."[29]

Regardless of when, if ever, completion of the single market program became irreversible, undoubtedly it got off to a flying start in the real world of business and commerce. "Italian businessmen talk about it, the French have visionary dreams about it, the West Germans plan quietly for it." "It," the *Economist* informed the unenlightened in February 1988, "is December 31, 1992, the date by which the European Community is supposed to become a true common market."[30] Entrepreneurs and businesspeople were already enthralled by the single market program. For over two years they had been bombarded by conferences, newsletters, and advertisements organized and disseminated by the Commission, national governments, and the private sector on how to exploit a frontier-free EC. Large enterprises were best able to do so. In 1987 and 1988 "merger mania," part of "a veritable stampede toward big business in Western Europe," swept the EC as companies attempted to realize economies of scale and improve their transnational distribution networks. Sixty-eight major mergers and acquisitions took place in the Community in 1986; by contrast, 300 happened the following year.[31]

A Commission-sponsored research project on the "costs of non-Europe" fueled business interest in the single market program. The purpose of the project, led by Paolo Cecchini, a former Commission official, in 1986 and 1987, was to quantify the cost to the Community of maintaining a fragmented market. Based on data from the four largest member states, Cecchini's team of independent consultants assessed the costs and benefits of maintaining the status quo by analyzing the impact of market barriers and comparing the EC with North America. Cecchini looked at the financial costs to firms of the administrative procedures and delays associated with customs formalities, the opportunity costs of lost trade, and the costs to national governments of customs controls. In early 1988 Cecchini's team produced its optimistic findings in a massive, sixteen-volume publication.[32]

The private sector's love affair with 1992 disguised the program's slow legislative progress. By the end of 1986, the Council had adopted 31 of the White Paper's 300 measures. By March 1987 the Council's record was 56 proposals adopted out of 170 submitted by the Commission. Six months later, the Council had adopted only an additional 8 proposals. The problem lay not only with the complexity and sensitivity of many of the White Paper's proposals—the Council dealt swiftly and easily with the least controversial measures—but also with a looming dispute over a Commission plan for the EC's finances over the next five years. The purpose of the so-called Delors package of budgetary proposals was implicit in its official title: "Making a Success of the Single Act."[33] The SEA had committed the EC to achieving a single market by 1992 and implementing a number of related "flanking" policies without which a single market could not come into existence. Cohesion—closing the economic gap between the EC's rich and poor member states and between rich and poor regions within the member states—was one of those policies.

Economic and Social Cohesion

Cohesion became one of the largest potential obstacles blocking implementation of the single market program in 1987, as the poorer member states (Ireland, Greece, Portugal, and Spain) demanded greater spending on regional and social policy in return for market liberalization. During that time, while the private sector embraced the single market program, the Commission and member states became embroiled in a sharp dispute over how much money to spend on cohesion. Delors himself characterized the budgetary package as a "marriage contract between the Twelve" and struggled throughout 1987 to bring Thatcher to the altar.[34] The British prime minister had an instinctive aversion to increasing the size of the EC's coffers and let it be known that regardless of any budgetary alteration, Britain would retain its current rebate, for which she had fought so hard in the early 1980s. Otherwise, Thatcher applauded Delors's determination to limit spending on agriculture and impose overall budget discipline, two key elements of his financial package.

Thatcher's position brought her into conflict with the Commission and the poorer member states. Matters came to a head at a summit in Brussels in June 1987, where Thatcher complained that the other EC leaders were not sufficiently serious about budgetary discipline and CAP reform.[35] For old-timers at the European Council, this was vintage Thatcher; for newcomers, it was an eye-opener. The poorer member states, apparently acquiescent at the Brussels summit, grew more assertive thereafter in demanding a greater distribution of EC resources. Unofficially led by Felipe González, the Spanish prime minister, they pressed hard for acceptance of the original Delors package. A showdown followed at the Copenhagen summit in December 1987. With Thatcher reverting to her early 1980s negativism, Kohl and Mitterrand reluctant for domestic political reasons to cut the CAP, and González agitating for additional resources, the summit ended in disarray.[36]

Delors was despondent about the progress of the budget negotiations. Member states had tossed his proposals around for nearly a year without reaching agreement. The same concern motivated Kohl to call a special summit in Brussels in February 1988 to try to resolve the impasse. Hoping to turn Germany's Council presidency to domestic political advantage, Kohl wanted credit for breaking the budget deadlock. As a result he was more willing than he might otherwise have been to pay the bill for cohesion. Yet there was no certainty that the Brussels summit would be successful. A month before the event, a concerned Delors warned the Parliament that "the consequences of failure will be extremely serious. It would mean that we could not put our minds to attaining the objectives of the Single Act."[37]

Even more than Kohl's statesmanship, Thatcher's surprising tractability saved the Brussels summit from becoming yet another flop. Although it began badly, with Kohl indecisive, Thatcher strident, and Mitterrand miffed, national leaders eventually got down to the kind of detailed negotiations that should properly have been left to subordinates. After intense bargaining, they agreed to double the structural funds by 1992, to introduce a new method of budgetary assessment, and to reform the CAP. Thatcher's willingness to increase the EC's budget seemed a remarkable climb-down, especially in light of previous budgetary battles. The prime minister may have been grateful for her colleagues' continuing acceptance of Britain's rebate, but most likely a desire to end the dissipating dispute and proceed with the single market program—of particular importance to Britain—convinced her to compromise. Whatever the reason, her decision removed a huge obstacle on the road to 1992.

Toward Monetary Union

Capitalizing on the success of the single market program, interest in which—both inside and outside the EC—increased daily, Delors focused attention on his primary goal of EMU. The idea of monetary union was gaining ground in any case because of the perceived success of the European Monetary System (the road to monetary union is examined in detail in Chapter 15). Primed by Delors, pressed by Mitterrand, and with Kohl's lukewarm support, the European Council decided in June 1988 to instruct a group of experts, chaired by Delors and made up primarily of national central banker presidents, to "study and propose concrete changes" that could result in EMU.[38] Community leaders endorsed the committee's three-stage approach to EMU at their summit in June 1989 and agreed that Stage I, involving greater coordination of member states' macroeconomic policies, the establishment of free capital movement, and membership of all EC currencies in the EMS, should begin by July 1990. They also agreed that an intergovernmental conference to determine the treaty changes needed to launch the subsequent stages of EMU would take place "once the first stage had begun."[39]

France was the most powerful proponent of EMU. Only if monetary policy decisions were taken on an EC-wide basis, the thinking in Paris went, could France hope to regain some of the influence it had lost to Germany in the EMS because of the mark's predominance in the exchange rate mechanism.

For precisely that reason, Kohl was equivocal about EMU. The German central bank, he knew, would not want to lose its predominance in European monetary policymaking. Alone among EC leaders, Thatcher wholeheartedly opposed EMU, seeing it as an unacceptable abrogation of national sovereignty and an effort to aggregate power in Brussels. Opposition to EMU had led in part to Thatcher's infamous speech at the College of Europe in Bruges, a citadel of Eurofederalism, in September 1988. The speech was peppered with barbed attacks against Delors, the Commission, and incipient Eurofederalism as Thatcher presented her view of the EC and of Britain's role in it. "We have not successfully rolled back the frontiers of the state in Britain," she declared, "only to see them reimposed at a European level with a European superstate exercising a new dominance from Brussels."[40]

Yet the prime minister's hostility toward EMU was not widely shared in her own Conservative Party. Nigel Lawson, the chancellor of the exchequer (finance minister), wanted Britain to participate in the exchange rate mechanism and pursued a policy of "shadowing" the mark by maintaining an unofficial parity. Geoffrey Howe, the foreign secretary, feared the impact on Britain of a wholly negative policy toward the EC. Under pressure from Lawson and Howe, Thatcher conceded at the EC summit of June 1989 that Britain would participate eventually in the exchange rate mechanism and reluctantly went along with the decision to launch Stage I of EMU in July 1990. In the words of a senior British official, this was a rare case for the prime minister "of reason triumphing over prejudice."[41]

German Unification and European Union

Reaction to events in Central and Eastern Europe also set Thatcher apart. The most immediate issue was the sudden prospect of German unification following the breach of the Berlin Wall. The challenge for Britain, France, and other member states was to overcome latent fear of a strong, united Germany. The challenge for the EC was both procedural (how to absorb the relatively underdeveloped East Germany) and political (how to retain Germany's commitment to the EC and prevent a united Germany from predominating). The challenge for Germany was to reassure EC partners of its attachment to European integration.

Delors took the initiative in October 1989, a month before the wall came down, in a speech at the College of Europe in Bruges, where Thatcher had issued her infamous antifederalist manifesto the previous year. Citing the rapidly changing situation in Central and Eastern Europe, Delors called for a huge "leap forward" in the EC to meet the challenges ahead.[42] In a key address to the German parliament in November 1989, Kohl sought to assuage restive neighboring states when he proclaimed that "the future architecture of Germany must be fitted into the future architecture of Europe as a whole."[43] Although the relationship between German unification and European integration became a constant theme in official pronouncements, Kohl failed to reassure all of his EC colleagues. Thatcher was the most troubled, but Mitterrand was also anxious.

The Strasbourg summit of December 1989 gave EC leaders an opportunity to thrash things out. Torn between an antipathy toward German unification and an affinity for European integration, Mitterrand forged a link between the two. Obstructing German unification at the Strasbourg summit, the highlight of France's Council presidency, would have tarnished Mitterrand's carefully cultivated image as a European statesman, impaired deeper integration, and possibly undermined the drive for EMU. A key passage in the summit's conclusions outlined Mitterrand's position, to which even Thatcher subscribed: German unity through free self-determination "should take place peacefully and democratically, in full respect of the relevant agreements and treaties . . . in a context of dialogue and East-West cooperation [and] in the perspective of European integration."[44]

It was also at the Strasbourg summit that EC leaders agreed to hold an intergovernmental conference to achieve monetary union. As Mitterrand announced after the summit, the agreement represented "the sole objective link" in the European Council's deliberations between German and European integration.[45] Thatcher did not disguise her opposition but saw no point in being formally outvoted, as she had been at the Milan summit in June 1985.

The outcome of the first free elections in East Germany in March 1990— a resounding victory for Kohl's Christian Democratic Party—signaled the prospect of imminent unification and quickened the momentum for deeper European integration. The time seemed ripe for a major Franco-German initiative on political union. It came in the form of a short letter in April 1990 from Kohl and Mitterrand to the Council president, which linked the need "to accelerate the political construction" of the EC to recent developments in Central and Eastern Europe as well as to moves already under way to achieve EMU.[46] The Kohl-Mitterrand letter was further testimony to the importance of the Franco-German axis in EU history. Yet its significance should not be overestimated. The letter gave considerable impetus to but did not initiate the debate about political union in late 1989 and early 1990.

Meeting in Dublin in April 1990, EC leaders discussed preparations for the intergovernmental conference on EMU (due to open before the end of the year) and the possibility of a parallel conference on political union. Kohl and Mitterrand did not define political union but instead identified four essential elements of it: stronger democratic legitimacy; more efficient institutions; unity and coherence of economic, monetary, and political action; and a common foreign and security policy. Only Thatcher adamantly opposed holding another intergovernmental conference, telling her bemused colleagues that the British monarchy and parliament would survive the EC's efforts to force the pace of European integration. In deference to Thatcher, the European Council postponed until June 1990 the formal decision to hold an intergovernmental conference on political union.[47]

The run-up to the launch of the two conferences in December 1990 saw the member states' understanding of EMU come into sharper focus and their understanding of political union become more blurred. This situation reflected the concrete nature of EMU, especially after publication of the Delors Report, and the imprecise nature of political union. The ultimate goals of EMU—a single monetary policy and possibly a single currency—were obvious, whereas the end point of political union was far from certain. Most member states agreed on what political union could or should include—closing the democratic deficit, strengthening subsidiarity, improving decisionmaking, extending Community competence, and devising a common foreign and security policy—but disagreed on the extent of those changes and how to bring them about.

Moves toward EMU received a further boost at an extraordinary European Council in Rome in October 1990, when eleven member states agreed to launch Stage II in January 1994. The summit's conclusions identified Britain as the odd one out.[48] Thatcher's resistance had an unexpected side effect: it precipitated her ouster as prime minister. With its popularity declining precipitously, the British Conservative Party saw Thatcher's implacable opposition to European integration as a serious liability. By itself, Thatcher's Europhobia would not have caused the Conservatives to lose a general election, but combined with a hugely unpopular tax reform, it threatened to tip the scales in favor of the opposition Labour Party. Thatcher's strident remarks on her return from Rome sparked a leadership struggle the following month, which John Major, her finance minister, surprisingly won. Rarely in EU history had "Community affairs" impinged so dramatically and so directly on domestic politics.

While Britain's political drama unfolded, the crisis in the Persian Gulf, hurtling toward a climax in January 1991 with the Allied liberation of Kuwait, cast a shadow over the impending intergovernmental conferences. Whereas in the summer of 1990 Europhoria apparently knew no bounds, less than six months later attitudes were changing perceptibly. Exhilaration over the revolution in Central and Eastern Europe and its possible spread to the Soviet Union gradually gave way to concern about economic, political, and military instability in the East. Guarded optimism about German unification, which took place in October 1990, rested uneasily with latent fear of the country's resurgence and more realistic anxiety about the high cost of assimilating East Germany into the Federal Republic. At the same time, U.S.-EC economic relations were on a collision course in the Uruguay Round of the General Agreement on Tariffs and Trade (GATT).

Under the circumstances, the European Council inaugurated the intergovernmental conferences in December 1990 with trepidation rather than elation. The presence of a new British prime minister alleviated some of the unease. Although, as the *Economist* facetiously remarked, Thatcher's departure had robbed the Community of "the grit around which the other eleven formed their Euro-pearl,"[49] her erstwhile colleagues were glad to see her go. It was impossible at that stage to judge whether John Major's ascendancy represented more than a welcome stylistic change in Britain's dealings with Brussels. Other EC leaders happily gave him the benefit of the doubt.

■ The Maastricht Treaty

The two intergovernmental conferences began in earnest in Brussels early in the new year and continued until December 1991, culminating in an intensive bargaining session at the regular end-of-presidency summit, held in the southern city of Maastricht in the Netherlands. The Maastricht summit crowned a yearlong series of negotiations among member states with the Commission as a formal participant, the Council secretariat playing a crucial behind-the-scenes role, and the Parliament effectively marginalized. Although the lowest common denominator often prevailed, the conferences and the ensuing treaty nonetheless marked a watershed in the history of European integration.

National and Institutional Interests and Inputs
Each national delegation brought to the table a particular set of expectations and objectives.[50] Germany advocated a close connection between EMU and political union, to the point of threatening to veto EMU without a far-reaching agreement on deeper political integration. The reason, quite simply, was that Germany had the most to lose from EMU and the most to gain from political union. By agreeing to a single currency, Germany would be giving up the mark and surrendering control over European monetary policy, which it currently enjoyed in the EMS. In return, Germany wanted an EU with a familiar federal system of government in which controversial domestic issues (such as asylum policy and defense) might be resolved and in which a more powerful European Parliament (with a large German contingent) would play a greater legislative role.

The central bank rather than the government seemed to determine Germany's position on EMU. Even before the conference on EMU opened, the president of the central bank outlined Germany's objectives in a number of forceful speeches and lectures. His main point was the indivisibility of monetary policy, responsibility for which at the European level would have to reside in a single, independent institution with the unambiguous, statutory mandate of maintaining price stability. In other words, the proposed European Central Bank (ECB) should replicate the German central bank. He also urged a gradual approach to EMU, stressing the need for economic convergence between potential participants. The German central bank's stridency caused a rift in the government, with the finance minister echoing the bank's position and Kohl and the foreign minister taking a more flexible line.

France wanted EMU at almost any cost and did not have an independent central bank counseling caution. Mitterrand was not eager to have an independent ECB but conceded the point early in the negotiations. However, France strongly urged the inauguration of an ECB at the beginning of Stage II rather than Stage III. According to the French, a functioning ECB and a strict timetable for a single currency would spur member states to prepare their economies for EMU. Although overeager for EMU, France had reservations about many aspects of political union. In general, France opposed giving the European Parliament any more power and sought a stronger European Council at the expense of both the Parliament and the Commission.

In a series of speeches in early 1991, Major had promised to put Britain "at the very heart of the Community." The new prime minister's message sounded strikingly similar to Thatcher's statement in November 1990 that "Britain's future lies in the EC: not on the fringes of it, but in the mainstream."[51] Such was the aversion toward Thatcher in the EC, however, that Major's declaration seemed a radical reversal of British policy. In fact, Major adamantly opposed a single currency and an EU organized on federal lines. Britain's performance in both conferences demonstrated the philosophical and ideological distance between it and other EC states. On a range of issues— from EMU to legislative reform to foreign and security policy—Britain took a minimalist position. It was obvious in the run-up to the Maastricht summit that Major was as unyielding in his defense of narrowly defined British interests as Thatcher had ever been.

A prolonged controversy over the "F-word" ("federalism") demonstrated the difference between Britain and its EC partners. A revised draft treaty presented by the Luxembourg presidency in June 1991 described European integration as "a process leading to a Union with a federal goal." The British foreign secretary immediately announced that his country did "not intend to be committed to the implications which, in the English language, the phrase 'federal goal' carries."[52] The issue was not simply linguistic. After all, Americans understood "federalism" to mean something positive and worthwhile. A British Europarliamentarian explained the problem differently: "On the Continent, [federalism] is a harmless label, neither exciting nor controversial. In Britain, it carries connotations of unspeakable disloyalty and unmentionable perversity."[53]

Thatcher, the leading Conservative back-bench Euroskeptic after her ouster as party leader, was like a broken record, warning against an unreasonable concentration of power in Brussels and contrasting the EC's supposed centralization with the Soviet bloc's disintegration. Yet by 1991 the Commission was fully committed to subsidiarity—a federal principle—thanks partly to Thatcher's earlier warnings. Indeed, a desire to enshrine subsidiarity in the new treaty was one of the few issues in the political union negotiations on which every delegation agreed. It was ironic that Thatcher, who had further centralized power in her own already overcentralized state during eleven years as Britain's prime minister, was so wedded to the federal principle of subsidiarity.

With Thatcher hovering in the wings and a general election looming, it was not surprising that the British government protested about the F-word. It was an easy battle to fight because there was nothing of substance at stake. When Major denounced the draft treaty's reference to a "federal goal," the new Dutch presidency merely changed this phrase to "federal vocation." As the conferences gathered speed, Major escalated his campaign to excise the F-word. Eventually his colleagues gave in. "What does the word matter, as long as we have the actual thing?" asked Delors.[54] The word mattered, of course, because Major needed to claim a political victory at home.

Italy and Spain, as well as the smaller member states, had strong national interests but lacked the political clout to influence the negotiations' outcome. Luxembourg—the smallest member state—had unusual leverage by virtue of being in the presidency during the first half of 1991. But as in the pre-SEA negotiations, which coincidentally it had also chaired, Luxembourg scrupulously played the role of honest broker.

No two countries had identical positions on EMU and political union, and no single country—not even Britain—was completely isolated. Regardless of the reason for a country's position—whether principle, pragmatism, tradition, or size—there was considerable scope for ad hoc coalition building, which took place at a series of formal and informal meetings. Such contacts occasionally resulted in formal initiatives at the conferences. For example, a joint declaration reconciling Britain's Atlanticist and Italy's Europeanist positions contributed to the debate on a European defense identity and dispelled the impression that the negotiations pitted Britain against the other eleven on every point.[55] Franco-German initiatives were more common, although the EC's two leading member states disagreed sharply on many institutional and policy issues.

Despite the explicitly intergovernmental nature of the conferences, the Commission participated fully in both sets of negotiations. Given his longstanding interest in the subject and the impact of his committee's report, Delors took a particularly keen interest in EMU. Preoccupied with EMU and with a host of other issues in 1991, however, Delors and the Commission fared poorly in the conference on political union. Early in the negotiations the Commission suggested several treaty reforms with which a majority of member states strongly disagreed. These included a radical increase in the Commission's responsibility for international trade relations and greater powers of policy implementation for Brussels. In addition, Delors made a famous speech in London in March 1991 on security and defense, in which he called for the new EU to subsume the Western European Union and advocated greater independence from the United States.[56] Delors's speech and some of the Commission's proposals caused a backlash in certain member states. Thereafter, the Commission was on the defensive in the conference, fighting a rearguard action to protect its existing prerogatives.

Unlike the Commission, the Parliament was not a participant in the conferences. Instead, the European Council decided in October 1990 to establish regular contacts among the presidents of the Council, the Commission, and the Parliament and allow the president of the Parliament to address ministerial sessions of the conference, measures that the Parliament considered grossly inadequate. The Parliament's institutional and policy objectives included a radical extension of Community competence, more supranational decisionmaking, and, not surprisingly, greater power for the Parliament itself through legislative codecision with the Council and a right to initiate legislation. As the negotiations proceeded and the Parliament's exorbitant demands came nowhere near being met, a torrent of speeches and resolutions condemning the conduct of the conferences flowed out of Strasbourg. Although the Parliament was in a relatively weak position and could not veto the outcome of the conferences, two countries—Belgium and Italy—threatened not to ratify the final treaty unless the Parliament approved it.[57]

Crafting the Treaty

The Luxembourg presidency produced a lengthy draft treaty in April 1990. Its most striking feature was architectural: the putative EU would consist of three pillars capped with the European Council. By keeping the Common Foreign and Security Policy and cooperation on justice and home affairs on an intergovernmental basis outside the Rome Treaty, the presidency hoped to reconcile the two extremes of federalism (supported mainly by Germany, Italy, and the Netherlands) and antifederalism (epitomized by Britain and Denmark).

The presidency also tabled draft treaty provisions for EMU. The length and purpose of Stage II were especially controversial. For practical and symbolic reasons, France and the Commission wanted to establish the ECB at the beginning of a relatively short Stage II. Although a single currency would not be introduced until Stage III, the prior existence of the ECB, together with a deadline for the end of Stage II, would encourage member states to expedite preparations for a single currency. In the meantime, the ECB would reinforce monetary cooperation among national central banks. Germany (specifically, the central bank) saw great danger in establishing the ECB prematurely during Stage II, largely because an underemployed ECB would lack credibility and possibly lose sight of its primary objective: price stability.

The Luxembourg presidency followed Germany's lead and proposed a relatively insubstantial Stage II in which a committee of central bank governors, established toward the end of that stage, would try to coordinate national monetary positions. The Luxembourg proposals sparked the first serious discussion of convergence criteria and of possible opt-outs from a single currency. A consensus gradually emerged that no member state should be allowed for political or economic reasons to prevent others from moving to Stage III. Nor would any member state, notably Britain, be forced to adopt a single currency. That formula proved decisive for the success of the conference.

The European Council was not yet ready to conclude the conferences at the Luxembourg summit of June 1991, although the agreement eventually reached in Maastricht bore a striking resemblance to the draft discussed in Luxembourg. The meeting was overshadowed in any case by the outbreak of war in Yugoslavia, with the troika of foreign ministers flying to Belgrade on the first day of the summit and returning to Luxembourg the following morning. Like the Gulf War six months earlier, the outbreak of war in Yugoslavia emphasized the importance of developing a comprehensive foreign and security policy. Yet, also like the Gulf War, the protracted and—for the EC—much more consequential Yugoslav war would make an effective foreign and security policy far harder to achieve.[58]

The Netherlands' presidency of the Council and chairmanship of the conferences in the second half of 1991 were controversial and, at the outset, ineffectual. Because the prime minister (Ruud Lubbers) and foreign minister were preoccupied with a host of domestic and international issues, Piet Dankert, the junior foreign minister and a former president of the European Parliament, had unusual latitude to chair the conferences. A committed Eurofederalist, Dankert sought to replace Luxembourg's draft treaty with a new draft that included a unitary structure. As word of Dankert's intentions spread, other member states warned the Netherlands to stick to the agreed-upon pillars approach. Predictably, the Dutch draft triggered an angry reaction when presented at a foreign ministers' meeting in late September 1991. Only Belgium supported the text, which Lubbers had earlier proclaimed "acceptable to all our partners."[59] The near-unanimous rejection of the Dutch draft inadvertently put the Luxembourg draft on a pedestal, thereby ensuring that the EU would have a three-pillar structure.

Earlier in September, the Dutch finance minister suffered a similar rebuke in the negotiations on EMU when he proposed that any six member states meeting specific economic criteria by 1996 could establish their own central bank and single currency. Although he did not mention any country by name, there was a general feeling that France, Germany, the Netherlands, Belgium, and Luxembourg were among the top six. Most member states, regardless of economic performance, resented a proposal that could have created a permanent underclass of EU member states. A consensus emerged instead calling for the member states to decide collectively when the EU should move to Stage III and establish a single currency, although not all of them would be economically able or politically willing to participate in the currency union at the outset.[60] The conference finally agreed that the third stage of EMU, involving the introduction of a common currency, would take place by 1999 at the latest.

Despite the Netherlands' poor presidential performance, the success of the Maastricht summit owed much to the prime minister's negotiating skills. Late in the evening of the second day it seemed that the conferences were about to collapse because of Britain's rejection of greater EU involvement in social policy. Lubbers first proposed weakening the provisions on social policy. When Major refused to budge, at Delors's prompting Lubbers proposed removing the new social policy provisions entirely from the treaty and including them in a separate protocol to which the other member states would subscribe, thereby reinforcing the emergence of a "multispeed" Europe already inherent in the provisions for EMU. Such a development may not have been in the EU's interest, but creating the social protocol prevented a British walkout and saved the Maastricht Treaty.

On political union, member states approved new cooperative arrangements for foreign and security policy and for judicial and home affairs. The European Parliament acquired greater political and institutional oversight—including a right of inquiry, a more formal right of petition, and the appointment of an ombudsman—and greater legislative power through the codecision procedure. The treaty redefined or extended Community competence in a number of areas, notably education, training, cohesion, research and development, environment, infrastructure, industry, health, culture, consumer protection, and development cooperation, although with only a limited extension of qualified majority voting.

Some member states had scored more negotiating points than others during the conferences and at the Maastricht summit, but none was an absolute winner or loser. The outcome was more clear-cut for the EU's institutions: the Council and the Parliament gained most; the Commission gained least. As well as being an intensive bargaining session, however, the Maastricht summit was an opportunity to permit each participant, including the Commission, to claim victory on a variety of issues. Clearly, there was something in the final agreement for everyone. Even Major was able to claim "game, set, and match" for Britain.[61]

■ Ratification

Despite their political importance, the intergovernmental conferences had not attracted much public or parliamentary attention in most member states. Britain and Germany were the two main exceptions.

In Britain, an opportunist opposition, a large minority of Euroskeptical members of the governing Conservative Party, and a general election due to take place by mid-1992 ensured that the conferences were newsworthy. Many commentators thought that Major would hold the election before December 1991 in an effort to win an undisputed mandate for the Maastricht summit. By postponing the election until 1992 and emphasizing the unreliability of a new Labour government, Major may have strengthened his position at Maastricht.

In Germany, whereas the lower house of parliament took little interest in the conferences, the upper house pressed the case for subsidiarity from the outset. As the representative of the federal states, the upper house opposed excessive centralization of power in either Brussels or Bonn (later Berlin). The upper house retained a keen interest in subsidiarity after the Maastricht summit, threatening in 1992 to block ratification of the treaty unless the government gave it a greater say in EU affairs.

Only on the eve of the summit did the conferences become a lively issue in Germany, not because of subsidiarity but because of the single currency. Before and during the negotiations themselves, the central bank tried to alert public opinion to the dangers, as it saw them, of EMU: Germany would lose the mark; its central bank would no longer formulate monetary policy but instead would become a regional member of a federal central banking system; the rest of Europe lacked Germany's historical fear of inflation; and the ECB might not be rigorously independent of political control. These harangues stiffened the government's position on EMU but otherwise fell on deaf ears until, in early December, a series of articles in the mass-circulation *Bild* newspaper struck a popular chord. On the second day of the summit, a banner headline proclaimed "The End of the D-Mark." Widespread concern in Germany about the implications of EMU, fueled by the rising costs of unification, came too late to affect the conferences themselves but became a powerful element in the treaty ratification crisis.

There was little public discussion of the conferences in Denmark until the run-up to the fateful referendum of June 1992, which threw the future of the Maastricht Treaty into doubt and shook the EC to its core. Danish opinion seemed evenly divided on the eve of the referendum. Yet the result—50.7 percent against to 49.3 percent in favor—came as a complete shock to the Commission and to national governments. Denmark was known for its ambivalence toward European integration, but the positive results of the 1972 accession referendum and the 1986 referendum on the Single European Act suggested that on polling day, a majority would support the treaty. The Commission and national governments were extraordinarily complacent. Having spent a year negotiating the treaty, they never considered that a majority of Danes, or of any other nationality, would vote against it.

Although they had been oblivious to the possibility of a "no" vote, EC leaders immediately grasped the seriousness of the situation. Unless ratified in each member state, the treaty could not come into effect. There was no question of reopening the Maastricht renegotiations. Clearly groping for a solution, foreign ministers announced soon after the Danish result that other member states would press ahead with ratification in the hope that Denmark would reconsider before the end of 1992.[62]

Fewer than 30,000 votes had determined the outcome of the referendum. Exhaustive analyses indicated a host of reasons for the result. Some were peculiarly Danish, others were common to the EC; some were reasonable, others irrational; some were consistent, others contradictory. Whatever the reasons, the result showed how oblivious national governments had been to growing public resentment toward the EC. The Council seemed secretive and self-serving, the Commission remote and technocratic, and the Parliament expensive and irrelevant. There had been little public interest in the conferences themselves, but Maastricht soon became a topic of popular discourse. Without even having read the treaty, people fretted about its contents. Worries ranged from the desirability of EMU to the rigors of convergence, to voting rights for non-nationals, to the prospect of mass migration, to the likelihood of bureaucratic intrusion from Brussels. In most cases a perusal of the treaty's unintelligible text merely reinforced popular antipathy toward it.

Ireland was the only other member state constitutionally obliged to ratify the treaty by referendum. Coming two weeks after the Danish result, the Irish referendum assumed special significance. Given Ireland's traditional support for European integration, a positive result seemed inevitable and would do little to revive the EC's fortunes. A negative result, however, would have worsened the EC's predicament. The government's referendum campaign concentrated on crude calculations of economic self-interest. Nevertheless, the result was by no means an unequivocal endorsement of the Maastricht Treaty. Of the 57 percent who voted (low by Irish standards), 69 percent were in favor and 31 percent against. Undaunted, the prime minister called the outcome "a tribute to the maturity of the Irish people" and proclaimed that "Eurosceptics do not have much of a following here."[63]

A much more important test for the treaty came in September 1992, when the French electorate went to the polls. Although France could have ratified the treaty by an easily obtainable three-fifths majority of both houses of parliament meeting in joint session, Mitterrand announced immediately after the Danish result that France would also ratify by referendum. Then in the middle of his second seven-year term, Mitterrand was deeply committed to European integration. By winning a resounding referendum victory, he hoped both to breathe new life into the treaty and to give his presidency an indelible "European" imprint. Clearly Mitterrand believed that France's historical contribution to the EC and the electorate's appreciation of the treaty's importance for the future of European integration would produce a comfortable majority and dispel the gloom caused by the Danish result.[64]

Yet developments in France and elsewhere favored the treaty's opponents. The government's popularity slumped as the economic situation worsened and unemployment rose. The deteriorating situation in Bosnia reflected poorly on the EC, whose peace efforts did nothing to stop the fighting. Opinion polls in late August showed that the treaty's opponents were inching ahead and that frustration over the EC's inability to broker a Bosnian cease-fire was a powerful impetus to vote no. The concurrent crisis in the European Monetary System—Britain and Italy dropped out of its exchange rate mechanism in September 1992, and the franc came under heavy pressure—further eroded public confidence. It also fueled a reaction against what looked like a German-designed EMU, although EMU arguably offered the best chance to end currency instability.

The French government went on the offensive late in the campaign, cajoling the electorate to vote in favor of ratification. In keeping with the earlier Danish and Irish campaigns, the government used an unlikely array of arguments to bolster support for the treaty. The normally unexcitable *Le Monde* editorialized on the eve of the referendum that "a 'no' vote would be for France and for Europe the greatest catastrophe since Hitler's coming to power."[65]

Such histrionics may have alienated as many people as they attracted. In the event, Mitterrand's gamble narrowly paid off. In a 70 percent turnout, 51.05 percent voted in favor and 48.95 percent voted against. The result was too close to justify the political and emotional effort invested. Far from boosting Mitterrand or Maastricht, it accelerated the president's political decline—his socialist government lost heavily in the March 1993 general election—and further shook the EC establishment.

The EC's Response: Subsidiarity, Openness, and Opt-Outs

Delors was quick to respond to the Danish referendum result. Alert to the extent of popular alienation from EU policies and institutions, he resolved to break the bureaucratic barrier surrounding Brussels, make the legislative process more transparent, and emphasize subsidiarity, which had already been written into the Maastricht Treaty, as the best way to ensure the EU's compatibility with the political aspirations of its citizens. Thus, subsidiarity would provide guidelines as to where Brussels could or could not act just as similar constitutional provisions determine the proper functioning of U.S. or German federalism.

Even before the ratification crisis erupted, the Commission had started to drop proposed legislation that arguably belonged at the national level. After the Danish result, the Commission redoubled its efforts to concentrate on key policy areas and divest itself of issues best dealt with at lower levels of government. Some member states hoped to use subsidiarity to roll back intrusive but possibly beneficial policies in areas such as the environment and workplace regulation. In Britain, subsidiarity became a political panacea for the EC's manifest ills, a vital safeguard of national sovereignty. For the Commission, by contrast, subsidiarity was a central tenet of Eurofederalism.

At a summit in Lisbon at the end of June 1992, national leaders "stressed the need for [subsidiarity] to be strictly applied, both in existing and in future legislation, and called on the Commission and the Council to look at the procedural and practical steps needed to implement it and to report back to the European Council [in December 1992]."[66] The Commission duly submitted to the Council and the Parliament a lengthy political, technical, and legal analysis of subsidiarity, asserting that the burden of proof as to the need for action and the intensity (proportionally) of action lay with the EU's institutions. Because of its exclusive right of initiative, the Commission accepted special responsibility in that regard. But the Commission also argued that subsidiarity could not become an excuse for member states either to blame Brussels for unpopular actions or to curb the Commission's legitimate legislative and executive authority.[67]

The Commission's report and other contributions set the stage for the December 1992 summit, where national leaders approved a lengthy declaration outlining the basic principles of subsidiarity, guidelines for their application, and institutional procedures and practices as well as concrete examples of pending proposals and existing legislation in light of the "need for action" and "proportionality" criteria. The European Council also called for the EC's institutions to negotiate an agreement on the effective application of subsidiarity.[68]

The development of subsidiarity went hand in hand with efforts to make the EC's legislative process more transparent, with EC leaders adopting specific measures in December 1992. Foremost among them was a decision to televise the opening sessions of some Council meetings and to publish the record of formal votes taken in the Council. Given the Council's history of secretiveness, these seemed remarkable measures. Even more so than the debate about subsidiarity, the European Council's frenzied efforts to make the EU more open and comprehensible to its citizens demonstrated the profound impact on national governments of the Maastricht ratification crisis.

Nevertheless the EC's response to the ratification crisis was intended primarily to make the treaty more palatable to Danish voters. Moreover, the Commission and national governments realized that unless they gave Denmark the right to opt out from specific provisions of the treaty, the electorate was unlikely to ratify it in a second referendum. Opt-outs had the merit of possibly appeasing the Danish electorate without undermining the treaty's validity or salience for the EC as a whole. The Danish government identified a number of sticking points, including the treaty's security policy provisions, the third stage of EMU, EU citizenship, and cooperation on justice and home affairs. The European Council hammered out an agreement at its summit in Edinburgh in December 1992 that included Danish opt-outs from Stage III of EMU (the single currency) and from aspects of the Common Foreign and Security Policy. Based on the Edinburgh opt-outs, a comfortable 56.7 percent voted in favor of ratification in the second Danish referendum in May 1993.

Final Hurdles: Britain and Germany

A combination of weak political leadership, unfortunate timing, and arcane parliamentary procedures almost scuttled ratification of the treaty in Britain. Given Major's supposed triumph in Maastricht and his election victory in

April 1992, Britain should have ratified the treaty without undue delay. Despite the result of the first Danish referendum, which gave a shot in the arm to British Euroskeptics, Major insisted that Britain would ratify the treaty as planned, and nothing seemed seriously amiss when Britain took over the Council presidency in July 1992. Within a short time, however, the currency crisis turned Britain's presidency into one of the worst in the Community's history, a point ruthlessly exploited by the opposition Labour Party. It was difficult for Major to put Britain "at the heart of Europe" after his country left the exchange rate mechanism so suddenly and disastrously in September.

By late 1992 the prime minister was a hostage of the Euroskeptics in his own party, who capitalized on the treaty's growing unpopularity and on the opposition's determination to discomfit the government. When the treaty barely survived a House of Commons vote in November, Major promptly announced that Britain would delay ratification until after the second Danish referendum. The government redeemed its otherwise uninspiring presidential performance by successfully chairing the Edinburgh summit. Moreover, Major grew increasingly assertive in early 1993 when the Labour Party tried to link British acceptance of the social chapter with ratification of the treaty. Considering his rejection of the social chapter at the Maastricht summit, Major was not about to embrace it due to domestic political difficulties. Although peculiar parliamentary procedures gave opponents of the treaty great scope to filibuster, even the staunchest Euroskeptics admitted the unlikelihood of being able to prevent ratification. Yet only after narrowly surviving another vote of confidence did the government finally win ratification of the treaty, in August 1993.

Only in Germany was the treaty still not ratified. There the problem was not parliamentary—in December 1992 large majorities had voted in favor of ratification in both houses of parliament—but legal: opponents of the treaty challenged its constitutionality on a variety of grounds. In a landmark ruling in October 1993, the Federal Constitutional Court upheld the treaty's constitutionality, but not without criticizing the EU's democratic credentials.[69] Despite important implications for Germany's role in the EU, the Constitutional Court's ruling removed the last obstacle to ratification of the Maastricht Treaty, allowing it finally to come into effect in November 1993.

▪ Notes

1. Stanley Hoffmann, "The European Community and 1992," *Foreign Affairs* 68, no. 4 (Fall 1989): 32.

2. Roy Jenkins, *European Diary, 1977–1981* (London: Collins, 1989), p. 199.

3. Quoted in Werner Feld, *West Germany and the European Community: Changing Interests and Competing Policy Objectives* (New York: Praeger, 1981), p. 55.

4. For details of the Greek application and negotiations, see Frances Nicholson and Roger East, *From the Six to the Twelve: The Enlargement of the European Community* (Chicago: St. James Press, 1987), pp. 181–206.

5. Ibid., p. 246.

6. Bulletin EC 4-1982, point 2.1.5.

7. Bulletin EC 11-1981, "Presidency Conclusions," point 1.1.5.

8. Nicholson and East, *From the Six to the Twelve,* pp. 225–226.

9. Bulletin EC 6-1984, "Presidency Conclusions," point 1.1.5.

10. *Le Monde*, June 30, 1984, p. 2.

11. See Bulletin EC 2-1985, point 1.1.2; Bulletin EC 3-1985, points 1.1.1–1.1.4 and 1.2.2.

12. For the original Commission proposal, see Bulletin EC 2-1982, point 1.2.4.

13. Bulletin EC 2-1985, point 1.2.1.

14. *Le Monde,* April 2, 1986.

15. Quoted in Nicholson and East, *From the Six to the Twelve,* p. 229.

16. On Delors's strategy and impact on European integration, see Helen Drake, *Jacques Delors: Perspectives on a European Leader* (London: Routledge, 2000); Ken Endo, *The Presidency of the European Commission Under Jacques Delors: The Politics of Shared Leadership* (New York: St. Martin's Press, 1999); George Ross, *Jacques Delors and European Integration* (Oxford: Oxford University Press, 1995); Jacques Delors, *Mémoirs* (Paris: Plon, 2004), pp. 171–430.

17. See Lord Arthur Cockfield, *The European Union: Creating the Single Market* (Chichester, UK: John Wiley, 1994). For Thatcher's perspective on the single market and the SEA, see Margaret Thatcher, *The Downing Street Years* (New York: Harper-Collins, 1993), pp. 551–554.

18. European Commission, "Completing the Internal Market: White Paper from the Commission to the European Council," June 14, 1985, COM(85)210 final.

19. Wisse Dekker, *Europe 1990: An Agenda for Action* (Eindhoven, the Netherlands: Philips, 1984); Fiat, *La Communauté Européenne et l'Industrie* (Turin: Fiat, 1985); and Ford of Europe, *Building a More Competitive Europe* (London: Ford of Europe, 1985).

20. Nicholas Colchester and David Buchan, *Europower: The Essential Guide to Europe's Economic Transformation in 1992* (New York: Times Books, 1990), pp. 30–31.

21. "Ad Hoc Committee for Institutional Affairs Report to the European Council," Bulletin EC 3-1985, point 3.5.1.

22. For descriptions and analyses of the intergovernmental conference and the SEA, see Jean de Ruyt, *L'Acte Unique Européen: Commentaire* (Brussels: Editions de l'Université de Bruxelles, 1987); Richard Corbett, "The 1985 Intergovernmental Conference and the Single European Act," in Roy Pryce, ed., *The Dynamics of European Union* (London: Croom Helm, 1987), pp. 238–272; Andrew Moravcsik, "Negotiating the SEA: National Interest and Conventional Statecraft in the European Community," *International Organization* 45 (Winter 1991): 19–56; and David Cameron, "The 1992 Initiative: Causes and Consequences," in Alberta Sbragia, ed., *Europolitics: Institutions and Policymaking in the "New" European Community* (Washington, DC: Brookings Institution, 1992), pp. 23–74. For the SEA itself, see Bulletin EC S/2-1986.

23. Delors, *Mémoirs,* pp. 202–228.

24. Roland Bieber, Jean-Paul Jacqué, and Joseph Weiler, eds., *An Ever Closer Union: A Critical Analysis of the Draft Treaty Establishing the European Union* (Luxembourg: Office for the Official Publications of the European Communities, 1985), pp. 372–373.

25. Quoted in Marina Gazzo, ed., *Toward European Union,* vol. 2 (Brussels: Agence Europe, 1985 and 1986), p. 24.

26. See ibid., p. 9.

27. *Common Market Law Review* 23 (1986): 251.

28. *Times* (London), November 16, 1987, p. 15.

29. Bulletin EC S/1-1988, pp. 8, 26.

30. *Economist,* February 13, 1988, p. 11.

31. *Economist,* February 13, 1988, pp. 46–47, and July 9, 1988, p. 30.

32. European Commission, *Research on the "Cost of Non-Europe": Basic Findings,* 16 vols. (Luxembourg: Office for the Official Publications of the European Communities, 1988). For a condensed version of the Cecchini Report, see Paolo Cecchini, *The European Challenge: 1992* (Aldershot, UK: Wildwood House, 1988).

33. Bulletin EC S/1-1987.

34. Bulletin EC S/1-1988, p. 14.

35. Bulletin EC 6-1987, "Presidency Conclusions," point 1.1.5.

36. Ibid., point 1.2.4.

37. Bulletin EC S/1-1988, p. 7.

38. Bulletin EC 6-1988, point 1.1.14. For an examination of the origins and development of EMU in the 1980s, see David Andrews, "The Global Origins of the Maastricht Treaty on EMU: Closing the Window of Opportunity," in Alan Cafruny and Glenda Rosenthal, eds., *The State of the European Community,* vol. 2: *The Maastricht Debates and Beyond* (Boulder, CO: Lynne Rienner Publishers, 1993), pp. 107–123.

39. *Report of the Committee for the Study of Economic and Monetary Union* (Luxembourg: Office of Official Publications of the European Communities, 1989); Bulletin EC 6-1989, "Presidency Conclusions," point 1.1.11.

40. Margaret Thatcher, *Britain in the European Community* (London: Conservative Political Centre, 1988). For her own account of events in the late 1980s, see Thatcher, *The Downing Street Years.*

41. Sir Michael Butler, "Simply Wrong About Europe," *Times* (London), November 26, 1991, p. 10.

42. Jacques Delors, speech at the College of Europe, Bruges, September 20, 1989.

43. Chancellor's press release, 134/1989, pp. 1141ff.

44. Bulletin EC 12-1989, "Presidency Conclusions," point 1.1.20.

45. Quoted in *Le Monde,* December 9, 1989. p. 1.

46. Reproduced in Finn Laursen and Sophie Vanhoonacker, eds., *The Intergovernmental Conference on Political Union* (Maastricht: European Institute of Public Administration, 1992), p. 276.

47. Bulletin EC 4-1990, "Presidency Conclusions," points 1.1–1.12; Bulletin EC 6-1990, "Presidency Conclusions," points 1.1–1.8.

48. Bulletin EC 10-1990, "Presidency Conclusions," points 1.2–1.6.

49. *Economist,* March 23, 1991, p. 15.

50. On the negotiations and their outcome, see Michael Baun, *An Imperfect Union: The Maastricht Treaty and the New Politics of European Integration* (Boulder, CO: Westview Press, 1996); Kenneth Dyson and Kevin Featherstone, *The Road to Maastricht: Negotiating Economic and Monetary Union* (Oxford: Oxford University Press, 1998); Colette Mazzuchelli, *France and Germany at Maastricht: Politics and Negotiations to Create the European Union* (New York: Garland, 1997); and Wayne Sandholtz, "Monetary Bargains: The Treaty on EMU," in Cafruny and Rosenthal, eds., *The Maastricht Debates,* pp. 125–141.

51. Margaret Thatcher, "My Vision," *Financial Times,* November 19, 1990, p. 10.

52. Quoted in *Financial Times,* June 18, 1991, p. 1.

53. Lord O'Hagan, "Federalism," *Manchester Guardian Weekly,* July 7, 1991, p. 12.

54. Quoted in *Agence Europe,* December 6, 1991, p. 4.

55. *Agence Europe,* Documents 1735, October 7–8, 1991.

56. Jacques Delors, speech at the Royal Institute for International Affairs, London, March 20, 1991.

57. See Sophie Vanhoonacker, "The Role of Parliament," in Laursen and Vanhoonacker, eds., *Intergovernmental Conference,* p. 219.

58. See Pia Christina Wood, "EPC: Lessons from the Gulf War and Yugoslavia," in Cafruny and Rosenthal, eds., *The Maastricht Debates,* pp. 227–244.

59. Quoted in *Financial Times,* September 21–22, 1991, p. 3.

60. *Agence Europe,* September 15, 1991.

61. Quoted in *Financial Times,* December 12, 1991, p. 3.

62. Bulletin EC 6-1992, point 1.1.3.

63. Quoted in the *Cork Examiner,* June 20, 1992, p. 1.

64. For a discussion of the French referendum's importance for the EC, see Andrew Moravcsik, "Idealism and Interest in the European Community: The Case of the French Referendum," *French Politics and Society* 11, no. 1 (Winter 1993): 45–56, and Sophie Meunier-Aitsahalia and George Ross, "Democratic Deficit or Democratic Surplus: A Reply to Andrew Moravcsik's Comments on the French Referendum," *French Politics and Society* 11, no. 1 (Winter 1993): 57–69.

65. *Le Monde,* September 20–21, 1992, p. 1.

66. Bulletin EC 6-1992, "Presidency Conclusions," points 1.1.–1.6.

67. European Commission, "The Principle of Subsidiarity," SEC(92)1990 final, October 27, 1992.

68. Bulletin EC 12-1992, "Presidency Conclusions," point 1.4.

69. See Karl M. Meessen, "Hedging European Integration: The Maastricht Judgment of the Federal Constitutional Court of Germany," in *Fordham International Law Journal* 17: 511–530.

5

Enlargement, 1994–2005

Implementation of the Maastricht Treaty seems an obvious turning point in the history of European integration. Yet there was more continuity than change after the launch of the European Union in November 1993. The greatest challenges confronting the EU in the early 2000s—enlargement, economic and monetary union (EMU), and popular dissatisfaction with "Brussels"— had emerged a decade earlier and helped shape the Maastricht Treaty and fuel the ratification crisis.

Plans to implement EMU were already in train when the Maastricht Treaty came into effect, although the criteria and timetable for participation in the final stage (adoption of the euro) preoccupied member states for the remainder of the 1990s. The domestic impact of monetary union demonstrated the inextricable link between Europolitics and national politics, as EMU provided an impetus for governments to rein in public spending, which in turn fueled popular concern about social welfare cuts. Prospects for EMU looked slim in the mid-1990s until an economic recovery made it possible for most member states to meet the key reference point for budget deficits (no more than 3 percent of gross domestic product). The anticipated benefits of launching the final stage of EMU, both positive (improving the EU's global competitiveness) and negative (averting a major political crisis if the venture failed), focused governments' attention and made it necessary for them to stay the course. The successful launch of the euro first as a virtual currency (in January 1999), then as a real currency in people's pockets (in January 2002), was an impressive achievement, politically, economically, and symbolically.

Nevertheless, a public backlash, driven in part by the perception that the quest for EMU exacerbated the problem of unemployment, increased the EU's unpopularity. Member states' determination to proceed with EMU regardless was one of the most striking aspects of European integration in the 1990s. Much of the credit belongs to Chancellor Helmut Kohl, who doggedly advocated EMU despite major misgivings in Germany and weak political leadership elsewhere in the EU. Ironically, having been voted out of office in September 1998 because of widespread dissatisfaction with Germany's economic performance, Kohl did not preside over completion of his cherished goal of monetary union.

Kohl's defeat after sixteen years as chancellor was the most dramatic change in leadership at the end of a decade that saw the departure of nearly every key player in the EU. François Mitterrand left politics in May 1995 at the end of his second presidential term (he died shortly afterward). Jacques Delors had stepped down from the Commission presidency in January 1995 after ten years in office, and in January 1996 Felipe González lost the Spanish general election.

The EU's new leaders included some familiar faces, notably Commission presidents Jacques Santer (1995–1999) and Romani Prodi (1999–2004), and French president Jacques Chirac. But the development of the EU would depend also on the contributions of relatively unknown national leaders. Prime Minister Tony Blair, who came to office in 1997, advocated a more positive British approach toward the EU. Head of government José Maria Aznar (1996–2004) was a dogged defender of Spanish interests. Chancellor Gerhard Schröder, first elected in 1998, personified the ascendancy of domestic German interests within the EU. Personal, political, and ideological differences between Chirac and Schröder put the Franco-German axis to a new test.

EMU was never intended to be an end in itself. Rather, it was supposed to spur widespread economic reform and higher growth in participating member states. By the end of the 1990s, however, the EU's economic performance was once again sluggish, especially in comparison with that of the United States, which experienced a huge increase in productivity and prosperity during that decade. Eager to emulate the record of the United States without abandoning Europe's much-vaunted social welfare system, EU leaders adopted the so-called Lisbon strategy for economic modernization and reform in March 2000. Covering everything from financial services liberalization to extending access to the Internet, the Lisbon strategy set an ambitious ten-year agenda for the EU. In contrast to the single market program of the late 1980s, the Commission was not one of the original driving forces behind the Lisbon strategy, which relied for its success on strong political leadership from the European Council. The Commission's lesser role in this and other policy areas emphasized the institution's relative decline since the early 1990s, a decline dramatically demonstrated by the Commission's enforced resignation under a cloud of alleged corruption in 1999.

Apart from economic reform and monetary union, which are examined in Chapters 13–15, enlargement and treaty change were the biggest items on the EU's agenda for most of the 1990s and the early 2000s. The collapse of communism opened up a hitherto unimaginable enlargement scenario. First the European neutrals, no longer constrained by the Cold War, applied for EU membership. Later the newly independent countries of Central and Eastern Europe, plus Cyprus and Malta, followed suit, while Turkey reactivated its earlier application. Austria, Finland, and Sweden joined relatively quickly, in 1995. Eight Central and Eastern European states, plus Cyprus and Malta, joined in 2004 after a protracted period of preparation and negotiation. The accession of so many mostly small and relatively poor countries was bound to change the EU profoundly. Moreover, Bulgaria, Croatia, and Romania were waiting in the wings while Turkey's eventual membership—increasingly a matter of when, not if—risked causing a major upheaval.

The Amsterdam Treaty of 1997 provided an opportunity to reform the EU's founding treaties in anticipation of enlargement, but member states ducked the most difficult institutional issues. Nor was the outcome of the Nice Treaty of 2001 more satisfactory in that regard. Faced with the inadequacy of Nice, widespread disillusionment with intergovernmental conferences as instruments of treaty change, and the unrelenting pressure of enlargement, EU leaders convened the Convention on the Future of Europe in February 2002 to draft a constitutional treaty intended to equip the Union to meet the challenges of enlargement and international uncertainty. The conduct of the Convention and the outcome of the intergovernmental conference to which it gave rise (intergovernmental conferences were still a legal requirement for treaty change) are examined in Chapter 6.

This chapter examines the enlargement of the EU from twelve member states at the time of the Maastricht Treaty to twenty-five member states at the time of the Constitutional Treaty and looks at the likely accession of more member states. Enlargement has been a central part of the history of European integration almost since the beginning of the European Economic Community. During that time, enlargement helped shape the EU's institutions and policies, which in turn shaped the political, economic, and social character of the existing and acceding member states. More than previous enlargements, however, the 2004 enlargement spurred the EU to accelerate integration in a range of policy areas while, paradoxically, making it appreciably more difficult to manage and implement those policies. As a result, the EU today is more integrated but also more diverse, fractious, and multifaceted than ever before (Table 5.1).

■ The 1995 Enlargement

Compared to enlargements past and still to come, the enlargement of January 1995, when Austria, Finland, and Sweden joined the EU, seemed simple and straightforward. The candidate countries were economically better off than many existing member states; had administrative structures capable of interpreting and implementing EU legislation; and, despite varying degrees of

Table 5.1 Chronology of EU Enlargement

1987	April	Turkey applies
1989	July	Austria applies
1990	July	Cyprus applies Malta applies
1991	July	Sweden applies
1992	March May November December	Finland applies Switzerland applies Norway reapplies Swiss reject European Economic Area membership in referendum, implicitly rejecting EU membership
1993	February April June	Accession negotiations with Austria, Finland, and Sweden begin Accession negotiations with Norway begin At Copenhagen summit, European Council agrees on EU accession criteria
1994	March April June November	Accession negotiations with Austria, Finland, Norway, and Sweden end Hungary applies Poland applies Accession treaties with Austria, Finland, Sweden, and Norway signed Norwegians reject membership in referendum
1995	January June October November December	Austria, Finland, and Sweden join Romania applies Latvia applies Estonia applies Lithuania applies Bulgaria applies
1996	January June	Czech Republic applies Slovenia applies
1997	July December	As part of Agenda 2000, the Commission issues favorable opinions on the applications of the Central and Eastern European countries The European Council endorses the Commission's favorable opinions on the applications of the Central and Eastern European countries
1998	March	Accession negotiations with Poland, Hungary, Czech Republic, Estonia, Slovenia, and Cyprus begin
1999	January December	At Berlin summit, EU leaders agree on Agenda 2000 budget package The European Council agrees to recognize Turkey as candidate for membership
2000	February	Accession negotiations with Latvia, Lithuania, Slovakia, Bulgaria, Romania, and Malta begin
2002	December	Accession negotiations with Cyprus, Czech Republic, Estonia, Hungary, Latvia, Lithuania, Malta, Poland, Slovenia, and Slovakia end
2003	April	Accession treaties with Cyprus, Czech Republic, Estonia, Hungary, Latvia, Lithuania, Malta, Poland, Slovenia, and Slovakia signed in Athens
2004	May December	Cyprus, Czech Republic, Estonia, Hungary, Latvia, Lithuania, Malta, Poland, Slovenia, and Slovakia join The European Council agrees to open accession negotiations with Turkey in October 2005

public opposition, had governments eager to bring them into the EU. Yet, according to the Commission's chief negotiator, the 1995 enlargement involved "the most complex negotiations . . . ever conducted on behalf of the EC."[1] The complexity of the negotiations leading up to the 1995 enlargement provided a foretaste of the far greater complexity of the negotiations that would result in the 2004 enlargement.

The European Economic Area
The accession negotiations for Austria, Finland, and Sweden took a relatively short time (about fifteen months) only because, as members of the European Free Trade Association (EFTA), the three countries had already adopted much of the EU's voluminous *acquis communautaire*. On the internal market alone, this included approximately 1,400 laws covering over 10,000 pages of text. The three countries had begun to adopt the *acquis* in the mid-1980s in an effort to minimize the possible negative consequences for outsiders of the EC's soon-to-be-completed single market program. Dissatisfied with a passive reaction to developments in the EC, EFTA called for a role in formulating single market and related policies that would directly affect its members. When the Commission refused, a number of EFTA countries reached the obvious conclusion and considered joining the EC. Until it had digested the recent Iberian enlargement and fully implemented the single market program, however, the EC was uninterested in acquiring new members. Hoping to fend off applications, in January 1989 Commission president Jacques Delors proposed instead "a new form of [EC-EFTA] association, with common decisionmaking and administrative institutions."[2]

This was the genesis of the European Economic Area (EEA), a huge integrated market intended to encompass the then twelve EC and seven EFTA members (Austria, Finland, Iceland, Liechtenstein, Norway, Sweden, and Switzerland). With 380 million people accounting for 40 percent of global trade, the EEA would be the world's largest and most lucrative commercial bloc. Although meant largely to forestall EU enlargement, the EEA instead became, for most EFTA members, a waiting room for EU accession. Thus, the EEA negotiations constituted a first, unofficial step in the EU's next enlargement. By that reckoning, the 1995 enlargement took almost five years to complete.

The EC's willingness to concede only "decisionshaping" and EFTA's demand for full participation in "decisionmaking" became one of the most contentious issues in the negotiations. Although the EFTA countries scaled back various demands in an effort to expedite an agreement, talks soon stalled over institutional arrangements. They picked up only after the EC agreed in May 1991 to canvass EFTA opinion on draft legislation and to establish a panel of EC and EFTA judges to adjudicate EEA-related disputes.

Fishing rights, alpine trucking, and financial support for the EC's poorer member states nevertheless posed major obstacles to a final agreement. Spain and Portugal demanded generous access to Norwegian and Icelandic fishing grounds, Switzerland and Austria wanted to limit heavy-truck transit from EC member states, and Spain wanted a substantial increase in EFTA's initial offer to the EC's cohesion coffers. Little wonder that the exasperated Council presidency announced in September 1991 that an EEA agreement could prove impossible to reach and was in any case not an EC priority. Clearly, the EFTA countries had more to lose from a complete breakdown of negotiations. Yet Switzerland and Iceland held out until the last moment before accepting final offers on trucking and fishing, paving the way for the agreement to be signed in October 1991. No sooner was the ink dry than the European Court of Justice ruled that a proposed EC-EFTA court would contravene EC law.[3] Renewed negotiations ended in February 1992 with a compromise over the legal mechanism to resolve EEA disputes. Both sides eventually signed the agreement in May 1992, after a last-minute revision of the Austrian truck-transit deal.[4]

From the EEA to EU Accession

Much to the Commission's dismay, the EEA initiative did not deter Austria, Finland, Norway, Switzerland, and Sweden from applying to join the EC. Why were these countries not satisfied with EEA membership? First, although they had generally outperformed their EC counterparts in the past, most of them stagnated economically in the early 1990s and saw better prospects for improvement inside the EC. Second, they were unhappy with the limited decisionshaping offered by Brussels and decided that full EC membership was the only way to acquire decisionmaking power. Third, many EFTA countries feared exclusion from EMU, the EU's new project, and accordingly from EMU-related economic growth (were there to be any).

With the end of the Cold War, neutrality virtually disappeared as an obstacle to EC membership for Austria, Finland, Switzerland, and Sweden. Nevertheless, with the newly negotiated common foreign and security policy very much in mind, the Commission stressed in a report on possible enlargement that "widening must not be at the expense of deepening."[5] Eager to finish current business before beginning the process of enlargement, the European Council decided in June 1992 not to begin accession negotiations until the member states had ratified the Maastricht Treaty and reached agreement on a new budgetary package.[6] Britain appeared eager to open preliminary accession negotiations during its Council presidency in late 1992, prompting suspicion among other member states that, contrary to the Commission's advice, it favored widening over deepening.

Completion of the agreement on the EEA gave the accession negotiations, which eventually began in early 1993, a huge head start. Of the twenty-nine "chapters" or issue areas that made up the negotiations

- eleven (including the single market) had already been covered by the EEA
- five (social policy, energy, the environment, agriculture, and fisheries) were partly covered by the EEA
- six were covered by the EC but not by the EEA (notably external economic relations, regional policy, and taxation)
- four were new "Maastricht issues," such as EMU, foreign and security policy, and justice and home affairs
- the other chapters dealt with general issues such as the budget and institutions[7]

In the event, the most contentious issues were not the EU's intergovernmental policies—the neutral applicants were willing to square their neutrality with the common foreign and security policy and had few serious problems with justice and home affairs—but the chapters only partly covered by the EEA. Some of the fiercest battles involved

- environmental policy (standards were generally higher in the applicant states)
- agricultural policy (price supports and subsidies were higher in three of the applicant states)
- energy policy (Norway was unwilling to relinquish control over its vast oil and natural gas reserves)
- fisheries policy (again, Norway was unwilling to relinquish control over its lucrative territorial waters)

Other difficult dossiers included financial support for remote and sparsely populated areas of the Nordic applicant states, the right of other EU citizens to buy second homes in Austria, alpine transit, the EC's ban on the sale of snuff (to which a large and vocal minority of Sweden's population is addicted), and state monopolies on alcohol sales in the Nordic applicants.

Member states and the Commission adamantly opposed granting the applicants long-term exceptions from the *acquis communautaire*, let alone permanent opt-outs. Under the circumstances, it is ironic that Denmark, which had won opt-outs from the Maastricht Treaty at a summit in December 1992, presided over the opening round of the enlargement negotiations. It is also ironic that the Nordic applicants seemed more enthusiastic than Denmark about European integration, given Denmark's tendency to object to controversial aspects of the Maastricht Treaty on the dubious grounds of "Nordic solidarity."

A call by the European Council to end the accession negotiations by early 1994, in order to give the European Parliament time to approve the results before the direct elections in June that year, put the negotiators under intense pressure to resolve a variety of issues still on the table. Eventual compromises included transitional arrangements for difficult regulatory matters; a decision to create a new category of structural funds for arctic areas; various measures to maintain farmers' incomes following the lowering of agricultural prices in most of the prospective new member states to EU levels; and a promise to review EU environmental directives within four years of enlargement, during which time the new member states could maintain their higher standards. Inevitably the negotiations went beyond the stipulated deadline, but only by four weeks and only on a small number of highly contentious issues, including Norwegian fisheries and truck transit through the Austrian Alps.

One of the bitterest disputes at the end of the negotiations erupted not between the EU and the candidate countries but among the member states themselves over the threshold for a blocking minority in the reweighted system of qualified majority voting. As with previous enlargements, the acceding member states received a number of Council votes roughly proportionate to their populations, and the member states recalculated the number of votes needed for a qualified majority (about 72 percent of the total). This time, however, for reasons of principle and presumed national interest, Britain and Spain insisted on keeping the number of votes needed for a blocking minority at the pre-enlargement level, thereby making it possible for a relatively smaller number of member states to block decisions in the Council. The dispute ended in the so-called Ioannina Compromise whereby the new threshold would remain, proportionately, at its pre-enlargement level, although the Council would "do all within its power to reach, within a reasonable time . . . a satisfactory solution that [could] be adopted by at least 65 votes" (Britain's and Spain's preferred qualified majority).[8]

This seemingly arcane issue showed how institutional disputes could overshadow and possibly derail future enlargement negotiations. Apart from the weighting of Council votes, increasingly troublesome institutional questions included the number of commissioners per member state and the size of national delegations in the European Parliament. Members of the European Parliament had already urged national governments to undertake major institutional reforms before proceeding with enlargement.[9] The unseemly dispute over voting rights strengthened their conviction that large-scale institutional reform was pressing. Although the Parliament delivered a resounding endorsement of the accession treaties in May 1994, parliamentarians made clear their dissatisfaction with the Ioannina Compromise and with the institutional situation in general.[10]

The next step was to win ratification of the accession agreements in the applicant states, where, regardless of the terms of the agreements themselves, the lingering Maastricht crisis had weakened support for EU membership. In addition to general concerns about loss of sovereignty and neutrality (except in the case of Norway, a North Atlantic Treaty Organization [NATO] member), the applicants had various reasons to be wary of joining the EU:

- All complained that the Common Agricultural Policy would hurt their heavily subsidized agricultural sectors.
- Austrians feared an additional influx of foreigners and worried about the anonymity of their bank accounts.
- The Nordics fretted about the integrity of their environmental laws.
- Swedish snuff-takers abhorred the EU's efforts to put a stop to their bad habit.

Hoping to generate momentum for victory in all four countries, the applicants tacitly agreed to schedule their accession referendums in the summer and fall of 1994 so that the more Euroenthusiastic of them would go to the polls first. By the end of 1994, Austria, Finland, and Sweden had voted to join the EU; Norway, where the fault lines of the bitter 1972 campaign had eerily reopened, voted against. Like Norway, Switzerland had applied for EC accession; also like Norway, a narrow majority in Switzerland rejected membership, albeit in a referendum on participation in the EEA. Thus Norway and Switzerland became the only continental countries neither in the EU nor actively seeking to join it.

Norway and Switzerland have other similarities and some striking differences: both are highly nationalistic and wealthy but differ markedly in their security policies, with Norway in NATO and Switzerland doggedly neutral. Both are strongly Euroskeptical, yet a near majority of their populations and the vast majority of their governing and business elites advocate EU membership. Given the strong trend toward regional integration in Europe and elsewhere, nonmembership in the EU may ultimately prove economically unsustainable for Norway and Switzerland. For domestic political reasons, however, their accession seems unlikely in the foreseeable future.

The Impact of Enlargement

The 1995 enlargement changed the EU in a variety of ways. Most obviously, it extended the EU into the far north of Europe and increased its size by 33 percent, although its population by only 6.2 percent. Economically, enlargement brought into the EU three affluent member states, all net contributors to the budget. Politically, as one Commission official predicted that it would during the enlargement negotiations, Finland's and Sweden's accession strength-

ened "traditions of democracy, participation and openness of government"—
a welcome development at a time of widespread public concern about accountability and legitimacy in the EU.[11] In terms of public policy, the new
member states brought into the EU greater concern for environmental issues;
a strong commitment to free trade and global development; progressive social
policies; and a fresh perspective on relations with Russia (Finland's immediate neighbor to the east), the Baltic states (across the sea from Finland), and
Slovenia (across the mountains from Austria).

Enlargement also brought with it another strong streak of Euroskepticism. A majority of Sweden's electorate soon regretted having joined the EU
(the results of the country's first direct elections to the European Parliament
in September 1995 revealed widespread dissatisfaction). Swedish civil servants, used to easy and transparent policymaking in Stockholm, were shocked
by the cumbersome and opaque procedures that awaited them in Brussels.[12]
In deference to public opinion, the Swedish government decided in 1998 not
to participate in the final stage of EMU (a decision validated by the result of
a referendum on EMU participation in September 2003). Deep economic recession and few tangible benefits of membership exacerbated Swedish Euroskepticism. Although it became commonplace by the end of the 1990s to
say that a majority of Swedes would vote to leave the EU, such an outcome
was by no means certain. The EU is still unloved in Sweden (as in other member states), but arguably EU membership is essential for Sweden's long-term
economic welfare (as with other member states).

By contrast, Austria and especially Finland appeared satisfied with EU
membership. Apart from economic considerations, both saw the EU primarily
as a security community. Long dominated by its neighbors and deeply concerned about Russia's future, neutral Finland appreciated the enhanced security that came with EU accession. While geographically less vulnerable than
Finland and also less committed to neutrality, Austria similarly appreciated
the security benefits of belonging to the EU.

The experience of negotiating the 1995 enlargement dampened enthusiasm in the EU (if there had been any to begin with) for Central and Eastern European enlargement. For one thing, the negotiations in 1993 and 1994 showed
how difficult the next round of accession negotiations were likely to be. For another, a last-minute dispute in the negotiations reverberated loudly for the subsequent negotiations with the Central and Eastern European countries. In December 1994, the Spanish government threatened not to ratify the accession
treaties unless the EU agreed to give Spain a fishing deal similar to Norway's.
Foreign ministers resolved the crisis at the end of the month when they agreed
to integrate Spain into the Common Fisheries Policy by January 1996, six
years earlier than the date stipulated in Spain's own accession agreement.
Spain's tactics were an obvious reason for foreboding: during the next round

of enlargement some member states (not least Spain) would surely claim that enlargement threatened their national interests. Would they provoke a dramatic confrontation to win concessions? If so, would other member states be able or willing to buy them off?

The 2004 Enlargement

The unexpected end of the Cold War not only enabled the European neutrals to apply for EU membership but also triggered an avalanche of applications from the newly independent countries of Central and Eastern Europe, plus Cyprus, Malta, and Turkey. The enlargement of the EU to encompass most or all of those countries would be qualitatively and quantitatively unprecedented. Turkey was a case apart, as were Cyprus and Malta because of their exceptionally small size. The Central and Eastern European countries were clearly in a category of their own.

Central and Eastern European Enlargement
All ten Central and Eastern European applicants were economically far worse off than even the poorest EU member state, and all were new democracies. All had been cut off from Western Europe either by incorporation into the Soviet Union (in the case of Estonia, Latvia, and Lithuania) or by Soviet occupation and domination. The end of the Cold War and disintegration of the Soviet Union therefore presented a historic opportunity to restore Europe culturally, politically, and economically. EU enlargement into Central and Eastern Europe was an essential part of that process.

The newly independent Central and Eastern European countries looked to the EU not only for financial support, market access, and technical assistance but also for recognition of their "Europeanness." For its part, the EU had an opportunity and a responsibility to help neighboring countries develop economically and democratically while promoting stability and security throughout the continent and fostering genuinely pan-European integration. In order to succeed, the EU would have to see the potential and not just the pitfalls of eastward enlargement; to look outward at a time of introspection following the Maastricht ratification crisis; to overcome vested interests threatened by Central and Eastern European imports in sensitive sectors like agriculture, steel, and textiles; to restructure its institutions and policies in order to accommodate a diverse group of new member states; and to rethink Europe's future in the post–Cold War world. These were immense challenges. Given its own political and economic constraints, inevitably the EU could not meet all of them in a timely, effective, and generous fashion.

Initial Response. Rapidly unfolding events in the Soviet bloc in the late 1980s forced the EC to confront for the first time its glaring lack of an *Ostpolitik*. For nearly three decades the EC had prospered in a divided Europe, appropriating the name of the entire continent. Despite claims to the contrary, the EC had lost sight of the fact that it represented only a part of Europe. For the EC's founding fathers, European integration was synonymous with *Western* European integration, centered on the Rhine. As a result of the Cold War, to which the EC owed much of its early development, Eastern Europe seemed irrevocably cut off from the West. Thus, the emergence of the Central and Eastern European reform movements in the mid-1980s, leading surprisingly to the end of the Cold War, challenged the EC's assumptions about the meaning and definition of "Europe" and the potential scope of "European" integration.

Given the rapidity of these developments, it is remarkable that the EC initially reacted so well. The European Council first discussed a concerted EC response in December 1988. Seven months later, at the G7 (group of seven most industrialized countries) summit in Paris, the Commission agreed to take responsibility for coordinating Western aid to Poland and Hungary, politically the most advanced countries in the region.[13] In December 1989 the EC launched the so-called PHARE program to support the reform process with financial assistance in a range of sectors and policy areas.[14] Soon afterward, the EC extended the PHARE program to the other Central and Eastern European countries and concluded trade and cooperation agreements with virtually all of them. Other EC assistance included emergency food aid and balance-of-payments loans.

In addition, the EC played a prominent part in the French-sponsored European Bank for Reconstruction and Development, an initiative that aimed to use public money from the West to help develop the private sector in the East. Of the bank's €10 billion capital, the EC, its member states, and the European Investment Bank contributed 51 percent (by contrast, the United States contributed 10 percent). After a political wrangle about the bank's location and president, the European Bank for Reconstruction and Development began operating in London in April 1991.[15]

Coping with the Central and Eastern European challenge and coordinating the concerted Western aid effort had a profound institutional, operational, and procedural impact on the EC. The Commission had to open delegations (embassies) throughout the region and reorganize internally in Brussels. Few of its directorates-general (departments) were unaffected. The European Parliament experienced a similar upheaval as it responded to overtures from Central and Eastern European parliamentarians. A reorganization of the European Parliament's staff and services reflected its enhanced involvement in international affairs as a result of the EC's emerging *Ostpolitik*.

Impressive though it was, the EC's initial response had been improvised and understandably ad hoc. The rapid pace of events made it difficult for the

EC, already coping with the impact of German unification, to devise a coherent strategy. The EC sought to promote stability, democracy, and economic reform in the region but was unable to respond positively to calls for immediate enlargement. The EC was in an invidious position. For thirty years it had decried the division of Europe and called for pan-European integration. It was hardly surprising that with the sudden end of the Cold War, Central and Eastern European countries used the EC's own rhetoric to demand entry. Nor was it surprising that they cited the examples of Greece, Portugal, and Spain, countries that had also sought EC membership to help consolidate economic and political reform and realize a "European" vocation.

The model as well as the rhetoric of postwar integration strengthened the Central and Eastern Europeans' case for membership. Commenting on the fate of the former Soviet bloc, Czechoslovakia's foreign minister remarked in January 1992 (before his country split in two) that "we will be secure only if the relations among all European countries are, let's say, like [those] between Belgium and the Netherlands."[16] The EC had no choice but to endorse the Central and Eastern Europeans' appeals for accession while arguing the impossibility of immediate enlargement.

The obstacles to early accession were formidable. Forty years of communist rule had left an appalling legacy. In order to make a successful transition from command to free market economies, and therefore meet a basic requirement for EC membership, the Central and Eastern Europeans faced a daunting array of legal and business reforms, including the introduction of property rights and a code of business law, the development of banking and financial services, and the privatization of most state-owned companies. In order to lay a foundation for economic growth they needed to overhaul outmoded infrastructures, begin large-scale agricultural and industrial modernization, attract foreign investment, and find new markets. Additional problems requiring expensive solutions included massive environmental degradation and unsafe nuclear reactors. While coping with the social dislocation of wrenching economic reform, many Central and Eastern Europeans had to learn the kinds of basic skills and attitudes taken for granted in the West. Politicians had to learn how to run a government or an opposition along liberal-democratic lines. Government officials at local and national levels had to learn modern administrative methods.

As the high cost and full extent of the reform process became apparent, even enthusiasts of early Central and Eastern European accession realized that further EU enlargement was improbable before the end of the decade. Eleven years had elapsed before Portugal and Spain joined the EC after the restoration of democracy in those countries in 1975. It seemed highly unlikely that any of the Central and Eastern European states would be ready to join the EU—an EU far more economically and politically integrated than the EC of 1986—within eleven years of the fall of the Berlin Wall. The economic disparity between the two halves of Europe was too great for the EU to expand eastward in the immediate future. Going beyond the emergency aid it applied in the aftermath of the Cold War, the EC therefore set about preparing the Central and Eastern European states for the long road to accession by offering additional assistance and crafting comprehensive political and economic packages in the form of special association agreements.

The Europe Agreements. In August 1990 the Commission proposed that the EC conclude "second-generation" agreements with Czechoslovakia, Hungary, and Poland in order to broaden and deepen the scope of the "first-generation" trade and cooperation agreements concluded in the late 1980s. Called Europe agreements to distinguish them from the EC's existing association arrangements, the new accords aimed to strengthen political and economic reform in the three countries, paving the way for their eventual membership. Later made available to all countries in the region, Europe agreements had similar structures but different content according to the needs of each associated state.

Negotiation of the Europe agreements pitted the member states' protectionist proclivities against their political rhetoric. When it came to granting the Central and Eastern European states liberal market access, a number of EU members succumbed to domestic pressure and blocked generous terms. Only when Hungary and Poland embarrassed the EC by threatening to walk out of the talks did the recalcitrant member states—notably France, Spain, and Portugal—come to their senses. The EU eventually signed Europe agreements with most of the Central and Eastern European states by the mid-1990s. These went far beyond existing accords by providing for the eventual establishment of free trade areas, the gradual adoption by the associated states of EU legislation on the single market and related areas, and the launch of a political dialogue. Most important for the Central and Eastern Europeans was an acknowledgment that their "final objective" was to join the EC.

The first Europe agreements were concluded only six days after the Maastricht summit. There was considerable relief among the Central and Eastern Europeans that the Maastricht Treaty would not pose an insurmountable obstacle to joining the EU. If anything, the new treaty's provisions for EMU and for closer political cooperation intensified the Central and Eastern Europeans' eagerness to join lest they be further marginalized outside a more integrated EU. Nor did any of the Central and Eastern European states seem unduly concerned about the diminution of sovereignty inherent in EU membership, welcoming instead the chance voluntarily to join a rule-based organization with obvious economic and political advantages. Only Euroskeptics within some of the existing member states compared the EU to the old Soviet empire.

Just as forming the European Economic Area had failed to deter membership applications from the EFTA countries, the Europe agreements failed to delay applications from the Central and Eastern European states, if that was partly their purpose. Instead, criticism within and outside the EU—notably from the Central and Eastern European states and the United States—of the Europe agreements' limited trade concessions and the EC's self-absorption during the Maastricht crisis prompted the member states to spell out the conditions for eventual eastward enlargement. Thus, the ongoing Maastricht debacle helped the Central and Eastern Europeans because it forced the EC, by appearing to be outward looking and inclusive, to counter criticism that it was too introspective.

Yet the prospect of eastward enlargement was highly controversial among the member states. Whereas Britain hoped that early accession would weaken political integration, most member states feared that an ill-prepared enlargement could turn the EU into a glorified free trade area. There were different points of view about the ideal speed and extent of enlargement even among the more enthusiastic member states. Eager to fill a new strategic void on its eastern border, Germany wanted to bring the Czech Republic and Poland into the EU as soon as possible and supported Hungary's accession largely as a reward for that country's contribution to the fall of the Berlin Wall. Otherwise, Germany seemed lukewarm about enlargement. For its part, France fretted about the economic implications of enlargement and also about the political implications of a German sphere of influence in the eastern part of an enlarged EU. The cohesion countries—Spain, Portugal, Greece, and Ireland—worried about the consequences for them of having to compete for structural funds with new, more deserving member states.

The Copenhagen Criteria. Although member states continued to ponder the practical implications of enlargement, mounting moral and political pressure for a commitment led the EU formally to acknowledge the inevitable and describe the preconditions for its occurrence. In June 1992 the Commission itemized the factors that would influence the EU's consideration of each country's application. These included geographical location (despite the impossibility of defining precisely where Europe ended); a democratic political system; a commitment to human rights; a functioning and competitive free market economy; an adequate legal and institutional framework; acceptance of the *acquis communautaire*; and a willingness to participate in the EU's putative foreign, security, and even defense policy.[17] The European Council welcomed the Commission's report but, preoccupied with the Maastricht crisis, did not get around to discussing it for another year, until the Copenhagen summit in June 1993.

There, the European Council declared unequivocally that "the associated countries in Central and Eastern Europe which so desire shall become members of the European Union" and spelled out the so-called Copenhagen criteria by which candidate countries would be judged for accession:

- stability of institutions guaranteeing democracy, the rule of law, human rights, and respect for and protection of minorities
- existence of a functioning market economy as well as the capacity to cope with competitive pressure and market forces within the EU
- ability to take on the obligations of membership, including adherence to the aims of political, economic, and monetary union

Recognizing the likely impact of enlargement on the EU itself, the European Council also stipulated that "the Union's capacity to absorb new members, while maintaining the momentum of European integration, [would be] an important consideration" in the accession process.[18] Critics saw this statement as a possible pretext for postponing enlargement indefinitely.

The Structured Dialogue and White Paper on Joining the Single Market.
Germany placed special emphasis on eastward enlargement during its otherwise lackluster Council presidency in the second half of 1994. As a result, the European Council decided in December 1994 to accelerate the process by launching a "structured dialogue" between the soon-to-be EU Fifteen and the Central and Eastern European countries, most of which had just applied or were about to apply for membership.[19] Covering a wide range of policy areas, the structured dialogue involved regular ministerial-level meetings as well as annual meetings of the leaders of the EU and of the Central and Eastern European countries on the margins of the European Council. Impatient to begin entry negotiations as soon as possible, most of the aspiring member states dismissed the structured dialogue as a necessary but nonsubstantive public relations exercise.

More important, perhaps, was a request by the European Council for the Commission to draft a White Paper on preparations by the Central and Eastern European countries for participation in the single market, one of the EU's most complex and far-reaching policy areas. Published in May 1995, the White Paper included detailed guidelines for the Central and Eastern Europeans to map their own route to participation in the single market, sector by sector, and therefore to membership in the EU.[20] The conditions set out in the White Paper were daunting for countries with low levels of economic development, little experience of free market economics, and inadequate administrative structures. Precisely because the challenges were so great, the White Paper also became a means of directing financial, legal, and technical assistance to the Central and Eastern European countries. As a result, the Commission reformed the PHARE program in order to devote more resources to such mundane but essential objectives as establishing competent regulatory and bureaucratic structures in the recipient countries.

Guided generally by the Copenhagen criteria and specifically by the Europe agreements, White Paper, and other Commission documents, the Central and Eastern European applicants set about overcoming the high economic and regulatory barriers to EU membership. In 1996 and 1997 most of them adopted detailed preaccession plans as part of an overall accession strategy, including quantifiable measurements of progress toward the approximation of national and EU legislation in the area of market integration, which is mostly what the EU is all about.

Agenda 2000. While the Central and Eastern Europeans adopted detailed accession strategies, the Commission drafted opinions on all the membership applications and a comprehensive report on the likely impact of enlargement on the EU itself. Collectively, the opinions and report made up Agenda 2000, released in July 1997.[21] The Commission reached the following conclusions about the applicants' suitability for EU membership:

- Democracy and the rule of law: All applicants (except Slovakia) had adequate constitutional and institutional arrangements.
- Functioning market economy, competitive pressures, and market forces: All applicants had made good progress, but structural reforms were far from complete, especially in the banking and financial sectors and in social security.
- The *acquis communautaire:* All applicants had begun to embody the voluminous *acquis* into national law, but all still had a long way to go, not least because of the limited administrative and judicial capacities of the Central and Eastern European states.

Accordingly, the Commission recommended that the EU begin accession negotiations in early 1998 with five of the Central and Eastern European applicants—the Czech Republic, Hungary, Poland, Estonia, and Slovenia—plus Cyprus. The Commission's selection of the Czech Republic, Hungary, and Poland was not surprising, but why Estonia and Slovenia? In part because only a week before the Commission released Agenda 2000, NATO had announced that the Czech Republic, Hungary, and Poland would be invited to join the Atlantic Alliance in 1999. While not wanting to be seen as offering EU accession as a consolation prize for countries rejected for early NATO membership, the Commission also did not want to be seen as endorsing the same three countries tapped to join NATO. The Commission's main concern was the possible perception by Russia and other countries in the region that the EU and NATO were drawing new dividing lines in Europe around the Czech Republic, Hungary, and Poland. The Commission therefore recommended that Estonia and Slovenia, countries with strong support from the existing member states and representing a balance between northern and southern Europe, participate as well in the accession negotiations.

The European Council approved the Commission's recommendation without any dissent in December 1997, together with a related recommendation for individual accession partnerships between the EU and the five "fast-track" applicants to plan, assist, and assess their path to accession.[22] These involved

- precise commitments by the applicants to democracy, stable macroeconomic policies, and nuclear safety
- a national program in each applicant country to adopt the *acquis* within a set time according to priorities identified in the Commission's opinion (the EU would base its financial assistance on the applicant countries' progress)
- a reorganization of EU resources needed to support the applicants' membership preparations
- annual EU reports on the applicants' progress toward accession

Bilateral accession partnerships, constituting a detailed map for each of the fast-track applicants to follow on the road to EU accession, replaced the multilateral structured dialogue (and were later extended to all prospective member states).

The Accession Negotiations. Accession negotiations with the "5 + 1" (the Czech Republic, Estonia, Hungary, Poland, and Slovenia, plus Cyprus) began ceremoniously in Brussels in March 1998, when the foreign ministers of the applicant states held separate opening talks with their EU counterparts. It was a momentous occasion: the culmination of nearly ten years of hard work on both sides and the beginning of the end of the long accession process. Despite optimistic statements about the negotiations' eventual outcome, there were no illusions about the difficulties that lay ahead and few realistic hopes that the talks might end before 2002 at the earliest.

The first stage of the negotiations consisted of an analytical review of the *acquis communautaire* in multilateral sessions conducted by officials of the Commission and the candidate countries. The purpose of this so-called screening process was to examine in minute detail the extent to which each of the candidates met the rules and obligations of membership and to identify difficult or contentious issues likely to arise in later stages of the negotiations. The screening process, Europe agreements, and accession partnerships constituted a continuous program of intensive preparation for membership, conducted alongside the substantive bilateral negotiations themselves. These began in November 1998, on seven of the thirty-one chapters or issue areas covered by the negotiations that had already been screened. As the negotiations progressed, officials checked more and more chapters off an accession negotiation scorecard. (See Table 0.3 for a list of the chapters.)

Fears in some member states that differentiation among the applicants would demoralize the slow-track ones and cause their reform movements to lag proved unfounded. Indeed, the five Central and Eastern European countries that had not begun accession negotiations accelerated their economic, and in the case of Slovakia, political, reforms in an effort to catch up with the first five, though Bulgaria and Romania accepted that they still had a long way to go. So successful were the supposed laggards that in October 1999 the Commission recommended opening accession negotiations with them as well. No doubt impelled in part by the strategic imperative of enlargement—instability in the Balkans, culminating in the Kosovo War of 1999, was an unnerving backdrop to the EU's deliberations—the European Council endorsed the Commission's recommendations in December 1999, paving the way for the opening of negotiations with Latvia, Lithuania, Slovakia, Bulgaria, and Romania in February 2000.[23]

Despite their late start, the second group of candidates (with the exception of Bulgaria and Romania) soon caught up with the first group in the negotiations. Each country progressed at its own speed, depending on the degree of difficulty in closing particular chapters. Although the EU negotiated separately with each country, the relative transparency of the process and publication of the negotiation scorecard pressured the candidates to make progress (none of them wanted to top the list of incomplete chapters). By the end of 2002 only the most contentious issues, such as agriculture and the budget, remained unresolved. Institutional issues (notably the prospective member states' representation in EU institutions) were not included in the accession negotiations but were decided by the existing member states in the intergovernmental conference that brought about the Nice Treaty.

The EU was always wary of setting an official date for enlargement. Only in June 2001, at the end of the strongly proenlargement Swedish presidency, did the European Council finally declare that countries whose negotiations ended successfully by December 2002 could join in early 2004.[24] That would give both sides a year to ratify the accession agreements and allow the candidates to become member states in time to participate in the June 2004 elections to the European Parliament (in the vain hope of increasing the overall turnout for the first time in the history of direct elections).

In a key report on enlargement in October 2002, the Commission recommended accession by 2004 for eight of the Central and Eastern European candidates, the exceptions being Bulgaria and Romania. The Commission pointed out that most of the eight candidates had problems meeting all of the EU's detailed membership requirements but was optimistic that the negotiations would end in December 2002. An agreement on funding the common agricultural policy during the next budgetary cycle (2007–2013), reached by the European Council in October 2002, removed the last obstacle on the EU's side to a successful conclusion of the negotiations.

The negotiations—really a series of diktats by the EU to bring the candidate countries into line for membership—left some ill feeling on both sides. Poland, the largest of the applicant states, behaved at times as if the EU wanted to join it rather than the other way around. Hungary, by contrast, tended to go along with whatever the EU offered. The other candidates, lacking experience and influence in Brussels, were hardly in a position to make a strong case for themselves.

The Poles and other applicants were particularly disgruntled with some of the terms being offered by the existing member states, which seemed to imply blatant discrimination against the Central and Eastern European states. Fearful of domestic public opinion on the politically sensitive issue of free movement of people, for example, the existing member states (led by Austria and Germany) insisted on retaining the right to prevent citizens of the candidate countries from moving into other member states for up to seven years after enlargement. A last-minute row over agricultural subsidies nearly delayed enlargement, as the Poles and others unsuccessfully resisted an EU offer of substantially smaller agricultural subsidies than farmers in the existing member states would receive. The rationale for the EU's offer was that a sudden influx of agricultural subsidies on a level comparable to that in Western Europe would cause massive economic dislocation and social resentment in the new member states. That may have been a legitimate concern, but the EU simply did not have enough money to subsidize farmers in the new member states at the level to which Western European farmers had become accustomed.

After the Danish government managed to get a pledge of a little extra EU money for Central and Eastern European farmers, negotiations with the eight candidates came to an end at the Copenhagen summit in December 2002.[25] This closed the circle of Central and European enlargement "from Copenhagen to Copenhagen": from the announcement of the accession criteria in June 1993 to the conclusion of the negotiations ten years later.

Cyprus and Malta
Cyprus. The EC had concluded an association agreement with Cyprus as long ago as 1973, but it was not until July 1990 that Cyprus applied to join. Cyprus had a good political and economic case for membership, and the Commission issued a favorable opinion in June 1993.[26] Understandably, however, the EU was concerned about the division of the island into the Greek Cypriot south and the self-styled Turkish Cypriot north, a separate entity backed by Turkey, which had invaded the island in 1974 to defend Turkish Cypriots from Greek Cypriot attack. The Turkish Cypriot government hotly disputed the right of the (Greek) Cypriot government to seek EU membership on behalf of the en-

tire island. Thus, the contentious cases of Turkish and Cypriot membership in the EU (Turkey had applied to join in 1987) became bound up with each other and with the historical enmity between Greece and Turkey. Nevertheless, having equivocated for some time, the EU invited Cyprus to begin accession negotiations along with five of the Central and Eastern European applicants in March 1998.

The negotiations with Cyprus went well. The island was economically well off (at least, the southern part was) and politically stable. Apart from partition, the EU's main concern was to reform Cyprus's banking laws, which had attracted an influx of money of questionable provenance and with it a lot of wealthy Russian expatriates. The EU's relations with Turkey loomed over the negotiations, especially as Turkey occasionally threatened to block the reunification of the island unless the EU promised to expedite Turkey's own application for membership.

The EU's willingness to admit Cyprus, regardless of the island's division, robbed Turkey of some leverage. It also robbed the EU of its ability to pressure the Greek Cypriots to press ahead with reunification following a rapprochement in relations between Greece and Turkey and between the Greek and Turkish Cypriot communities in the early 2000s. Much to the EU's embarrassment, a large majority of Greek Cypriots rejected an admittedly imperfect United Nations plan for reunification, which a small majority of Turkish Cypriots accepted in an island-wide referendum in April 2004. Having already signed an accession treaty with Cyprus, the EU could do little except denounce the Greek Cypriot government for its intransigence and offer sympathy and economic support to the Turkish Cypriots, hitherto widely perceived as being unalterably opposed to ending the island's partition. A partitioned Cyprus therefore joined the EU in May 2004 and promptly threatened to block further progress on Turkey's application.

Malta. Malta's conservative government applied to join the EC in 1990. Deeply attached to Malta's status as a nonaligned country, the opposition Labour Party opposed Malta's EU membership. After winning the general election in October 1996, Labour promptly canceled Malta's application. The EU was relieved to have one less application to deal with. The EU was equally nonchalant when the conservatives returned to power in September 1998 and reactivated Malta's application. The Commission reported in February 1999 that Malta could join the accession negotiation already taking place with six applicant states.

The only problem for the EU was Malta's size: the EU did not relish having another member state as small as Luxembourg but without Luxembourg's international standing or tradition of European integration. Nevertheless, Malta moved easily toward EU entry, completing its accession negotiations at the end of 2002. Although a majority approved Malta's membership in a referendum there in March 2003, the fiercely anti-EU Labor Party insisted that the issue be decided in the forthcoming general election. It was held only a week before the signing of the accession treaties in April 2003, and the governing Conservatives easily won reelection.[27]

From Fifteen to Twenty-five and More

The EU and the successful candidates signed the accession treaties in a splendid ceremony in Athens in March 2003. All parties—the existing member states, the prospective member states, and the European Parliament—approved the treaties during the next several months. Nine of the acceding member states (Cyprus was the odd one out) ratified the treaties by referendum. Although the turnout and the margin of victory varied significantly, and although there were both generic and country-specific concerns about joining the EU, the results amounted to an impressive endorsement of accession. As a result, the EU finally enlarged from fifteen to twenty-five member states in May 2004.

The long road to accession had produced "enlargement fatigue" well before May 2004. Public opinion in the EU and the candidate countries had long ago lost whatever enthusiasm for enlargement it had originally possessed. Indeed, opposition to enlargement accounted in part for the resurgence of the far right in Western Europe, notably in Austria, where the extremist Freedom Party formed a coalition government with the Christian Democrats in February 2000, and to a lesser extent in France, where the candidate of the extremist National Front beat the mainstream Socialist candidate in April 2002 and made it into the runoff with Chirac, whose easy victory could not disguise the shock to the French political system that the first-round result had imparted. Ireland's rejection of the Nice Treaty in June 2001 looked like another manifestation of antienlargement feeling, although the referendum was not about enlargement and a variety of reasons accounted for a "no" vote. Opinion in the candidate countries, where many people associated enlargement with enduring social dislocation and economic hardship, seemed equally skittish and helped strengthen populist parties throughout the region, notably in Poland.

The likely impact of enlargement on the institutions, policies, and politics of the EU had gradually sunk in with the existing member states. Clearly, enlargement would have a profound effect on agricultural policy and cohesion policy, the two largest items of EU expenditure, and on decisionmaking procedures. Hence the EU's efforts, beginning with the Amsterdam Treaty and continuing with Agenda 2000 and the Nice Treaty, to prepare for enlargement. These efforts were patently inadequate. The Convention on the Future of Europe, in which representatives of the candidate countries participated (but not as full members with the right to block a consensus from being reached), was a belated effort by the EU to accommodate its institutions to the challenge of enlargement. Although far from ideal, the outcome of the Convention and of the ensuing intergovernmental conference, which produced the Draft Constitutional Treaty and in which representatives of the prospective new member states participated fully, signaled the EU's appreciation of the institutional difficulties ahead. Serious policy reform was another matter, the EU preferring to muddle through until the inevitable row over the next budgetary perspective (2007–2013) would force serious reviews of agriculture and cohesion.

The prospect of enlargement had nonetheless prompted the EU to intensify integration or redirect its attention to other areas. Thus, concerns about the porousness of the Central and Eastern European candidates' eastern borders, which would become the eastern borders of the enlarged EU, triggered an acceleration of cooperation in the area of justice and home affairs, specifically with regard to border control (this issue is discussed in Chapter 17). Similarly, concern about the impact of enlargement on relations between the EU and its new neighbors in Eastern Europe, and concern in the Southern Mediterranean about the EU's apparent neglect of the region because of the demands of enlargement, led the EU to launch the European Neighborhood Policy to encourage stability and economic development in the so-called wider Europe (this issue is discussed in Chapter 16).

Managing enlargement within the institutions was bound to be difficult, not least because of the profusion of official languages. By the time enlargement finally took place, many Central and Eastern European officials had become thoroughly familiar with the functioning of EU institutions (thousands of Central and Eastern European students, many of whom had since become government officials, had served internships in Brussels since the early 1990s). As with previous enlargement, only more so, there was a period of cultural and administrative adaptation as officials from the new member states settled into the Brussels institutions.

Politically, the EU's adaptation to enlargement was somewhat strained. It was difficult for some of the existing member states, none more so than France, to adjust to the new reality. This became obvious to everyone in February 2003, after a special summit to discuss the EU's response to the imminent war in Iraq, when Chirac lambasted the Central and Eastern European states for supporting the United States and for not following France's lead. Chirac's outburst (described in Chapter 17) revealed deep frustration with France's diminishing influence in the EU, a development exacerbated but not necessarily caused by enlargement.

Turkey

Not surprisingly under the circumstances, the possibility of Turkish membership deeply unnerved France. Turkey had long aspired to EU membership but only became a serious contender in the late 1990s as the country stabilized politically and economically. Having applied for EU membership far earlier than any of the Central and Eastern European candidates, and having already signed a customs union with the EU, Turkey pressed for participation in the accession negotiations slated to begin in 1998. This put the EU in a quandary. How could it admit a relatively underdeveloped country that, with over 70 million people, would become the EU's second-largest member state; a country with a questionable human rights record; and a country where, as recently as 1997, the army had helped oust a democratically elected government (admittedly in order to restore a government more acceptable to the West)?[28]

Yet Turkey's European orientation and vocation were undeniable. Moreover, Turkey was a big emerging market; needed positive signals and support from the EU to help counter the rise of Muslim fundamentalism; and had assumed great strategic importance with respect to the Balkans, the Middle East, and parts of the former Soviet Union, all extremely volatile areas. Although Western Europeans had legitimate economic and political reasons to doubt Turkey's suitability in the foreseeable future, many were motivated primarily by anti-Muslim prejudice. All could hide behind the excuse of deep-rooted Greek hostility toward Turkey.

Well aware of the EU's dilemma and discomfiture, Turkey knew exactly what buttons to press. "Will the future of the European Union be limited by religious and ethnic considerations, or will it be one that reaches out and boldly contributes to diversity and unity?" asked Turkey's foreign minister only days before the summit in December 1997 at which the European Council decided to open negotiations with certain applicant countries.[29] Apart from seizing the moral high ground, Turkey had a more pragmatic card to play: its ability to influence the negotiations on Cypriot accession through its suasion over the northern part of the island.

Although it decided not yet to invite Turkey to participate in the accession negotiations, the European Council sought to reassure officials in Ankara that the EU's door was still open. In effect, the European Council put Turkey's application on hold, placing it behind all the other applications in the accession queue. Deeply affronted because the EU had deemed it less worthy than countries such as Bulgaria and Romania, Turkey retaliated by freezing its official ties with the EU. More ominously, Turkey threatened to block progress on the reunification of Cyprus unless the EU reconsidered its candidacy. This reaction to the European Council's decision may have convinced many EU leaders that they were right to keep Turkey at arm's length.

A rapprochement between Greece and Turkey in the new decade, together with valiant Turkish efforts to meet the Copenhagen criteria, nevertheless kept Turkey's application at center stage. Turkey protested so vehemently against its exclusion from the enlargement process and strove so hard to improve its membership prospects that the European Council officially recognized it as a candidate country in December 1999. Yet Turkey was again outraged in October 2002 when the Commission recommended that the EU admit ten countries by 2004 while in Turkey's case offering merely to increase preaccession assistance. In December 2002, having endorsed the Commission's recommendations on enlarging the EU, the European Council announced that it would decide by December 2004 whether to open accession negotiations with Turkey, a decision eagerly awaited by Ankara and by the United States, Turkey's strongest supporter in the West.

A change of government in Turkey in November 2002 greatly improved its prospects. Despite being Islamist-leaning, the new government of Prime Minister Recep Tayyip Erdogan, who assumed office in March 2003, pushed through numerous economic and social reforms, cultivated closer relations with Greece, and moderated Turkey's position on Cyprus. The Commission rewarded Erdogan's efforts with a recommendation in October 2004 that the European Council agree to open accession negotiations with Turkey sometime in the new year. The Commission did not suggest that the negotiations would be either short or trouble-free; on the contrary, it held out little hope of Turkish accession before 2014.

In the run-up to the December 2004 meeting of the European Council, the Turkish question assumed enormous importance in the EU. Chirac took a hard line, acknowledging that negotiations would probably have to begin but pointing out that they might not necessarily end in full membership for Turkey. Moreover, Chirac promised a referendum in France on future EU enlargements (clearly he had Turkey in mind). The political climate at the time was soured by growing tension over the assimilation (or nonassimilation) of Muslim minorities in Europe. Lurking behind the rhetoric of Chirac and other conservative politicians throughout the EU was deep-seated concern about the social and cultural impact of Turkish membership, even if Turkey met the political and economic criteria.

The Limits of EU Enlargement?

Where and when will EU enlargement end? Bulgaria and Romania were slated to join in 2007. Croatia's application, submitted in February 2003, was a reminder that most, if not all, of the Balkan countries wanted to join the EU. Countries in far eastern Europe, varying in size from Ukraine to Moldova, are potential members. Even Russia might one day meet the Copenhagen criteria, although it is unlikely ever to want to join, seeing itself instead as equal in power and prestige to the EU. An EU of more than thirty member states is nonetheless quite likely in the not-too-distant future.

Growing opposition within the EU to Turkey's membership, especially in center-right political circles, reflects particular concerns about Turkey itself and general concerns about unfettered enlargement. Nevertheless, the EU seems destined to grow. How could it deny admission to European countries that meet the economic and political conditions for membership? It could question an applicant's claim to being European, but Europe lacks precise geographical and cultural boundaries.

The key question, therefore, is what kind of EU will exist in the future. An increasingly large and diverse EU will become more and more difficult to manage. With proliferating national preferences, it is harder for the EU to reach common positions in many policy areas. Enlargement brings with it an obvious risk of institutional sclerosis and policymaking paralysis. Differentiated integration may be the solution, but it is also problematical. In the meantime, member states have been attempting to cope by negotiating a series of treaty reforms, beginning with the Amsterdam Treaty of 1997 and culminating in the Constitutional Treaty of 2004. The conduct and outcome of the treaty reform process are examined in the next chapter.

■ Notes

1. Quoted in the *International Herald Tribune,* February 15–16, 1992, p. 1.
2. Bulletin EC S/1–1989, p. 17.
3. See Trevor C. Hartley, "The European Court and the EEA," *International and Comparative Law Quarterly* 41 (October 1992): 84–88.
4. Bulletin EC 5–1992, point 2.2.1. See also Finn Laursen, "The Community's Policy Toward EFTA: Regime Formation in the European Economic Space," *Journal of Common Market Studies* 28, no. 4 (June 1990): 320–325; and Clive Church, "The Politics of Change: EFTA and the Nordic Countries' Response to the EC in the Early 1990s," *Journal of Common Market Studies* 28, no. 4 (June 1990): 408–410.
5. European Commission, "Report on Enlargement," Bulletin EC S/3-1992, p. 13.
6. Lisbon European Council, "Presidency Conclusions," Bulletin EC 6-1992, points 1.3–1.4.
7. Francisco Granell, "The European Union's Enlargement Negotiations with Austria, Finland, Norway, and Sweden," *Journal of Common Market Studies* 33, no. 1 (September 1995): 122.
8. Bulletin EC 3-1994, point 1.3.27.
9. Klaus Hansch, "Report of the Committee on Institutional Affairs on the Structure and Strategy for the European Union with Regard to Its Enlargement and the Creation of a Europe-Wide Order." European Parliament Session Documents PE 152.242 final, May 21, 1992.
10. Debates of the European Parliament, 1994/1995 Session, Report of Proceedings from May 2–6, 1994, *Official Journal of the European Communities* 3-448: 123–144, 157–166, 167–177.
11. David Spence, "Towards Enlargement of the European Union," unpublished paper, p. 24. On the negotiations and their aftermath, see John Redmond, ed., *The 1995 Enlargement of the European Union* (Aldershot, UK: Ashgate, 1997); Lee Miles, ed., *The European Union and the Nordic Countries* (New York: Routledge, 1996); Granell, "European Union's Enlargement Negotiations"; and P. Luif, *On the Road to Brussels: The Political Dimension of Austria's, Finland's, and Sweden's Road to Accession to the European Union* (Vienna: Austrian Institute for International Affairs, 1995).

12. For the perspective of Swedish officials, see "Views and Experiences of Swedish Civil Servants Regarding the Structure and Working Methods of the EU," in Statskontoret, 1996/6; see also Sieglinde Gstöhl, *Reluctant Europeans: Norway, Sweden, and Switzerland in the Process of Integration* (Boulder, CO: Lynne Rienner Publishers, 2002).

13. Bulletin EC 7/8-1989, points 1.1.1–1.1.6.

14. Council Regulation (EEC) 3906/89, December 18, 1989.

15. See John Pinder, *The European Community and Eastern Europe* (London: Royal Institute of International Affairs, 1991), pp. 87–88.

16. Quoted in the *New York Times*, January 26, 1992, p. 10.

17. European Commission, "Report on Enlargement," Bulletin EC S/3-1992, pp. 11–12.

18. Copenhagen European Council, "Presidency Conclusions," Bulletin EC 6-1993, point 1.4.

19. Essen European Council, "Presidency Conclusions," Bulletin EC, 12-1994, point 1.1.10.

20. COM(95)163 final.

21. European Commission, *Agenda 2000: For a Stronger and Wider Europe,* Brussels, July 16, 1997, COM(97)2000 final.

22. Luxembourg European Council, "Presidency Conclusions," Bulletin EC 12-1993, points 1.3–1.4.

23. On the road to enlargement and the opening of the accession negotiations, see Michael Baun, *A Wider Europe: The Process and Politics of European Union Enlargement* (Lanham, MD: Rowman and Littlefield, 2000). On the enlargement process as a whole, see Graham Avery and Fraser Cameron, *The Enlargement of the European Union* (Sheffield, UK: Sheffield Academic Press, 1998); Marise Cremona, ed., *The Enlargement of the European Union* (Oxford: Oxford University Press, 2003); Neill Nugent, *European Union Enlargement* (Basingstoke, UK: Palgrave Macmillan, 2004); and Alan Mayhew, *Recreating Europe: The European Union's Policy Towards Central and Eastern Europe,* 2nd ed. (Cambridge: Cambridge University Press, 2002).

24. Bulletin EU 6-2001.

25. Bulletin EU 12-2002.

26. Bulletin EC S/5-1993; on the subsequent negotiations and accession, see A. Theophanous, "The Cyprus Problem: Accession to the EU and Broader Implications," *Mediterranean Quarterly* 14 (February 1, 2003): 42–67.

27. On Malta's application, negotiation, and accession, see Pace Roderick, "A Small State and the European Union: Malta's EU Accession Experience," *South European Society and Politics* 7 (Summer 2002): 24–43.

28. On the Turkish case, see Ali Carkoglu and Barry Rubin, eds., *Turkey and the European Union: Domestic Politics, Economic Integration and International Dynamics* (London: Frank Cass Publishers, 2003); Mujeeb R. Khan and M. Hakan Yavuz, "Bringing Turkey into Europe," *Current History* 102 (March 2003): 119–124; M. Muftuler-Bac and L. McLaren, "Enlargement Preferences and Policy-Making in the European Union: Impacts on Turkey," *Journal of European Integration* 25 (2003): 17–31; M. Muftuler-Bac, "Turkey in the EU's Enlargement Process: Obstacles and Challenges," *Mediterranean Politics* 7, no. 2 (Summer 2002): 79–96; S. Sozen and I. Shaw, "Turkey and the European Union: Modernizing a Traditional State?" *Social Policy and Administration* 37, no. 2 (April 2003): 108–121.

29. "Isn't Europe Ambitious Enough to Admit Turkey?" *International Herald Tribune,* December 10, 1997, p. 10.

6

Constitutional Change, 1994–2005

The European Union is based on international treaties but is much more than a traditional international organization. It is a political entity and system, but is much less than a traditional nation-state. Reflecting the EU's peculiar nature, the European Court of Justice has long interpreted the founding treaties as constitutional texts, although national governments (the masters of treaty reform) have always shied away from drafting a statelike constitution for the EU, which would be a bold and controversial move as well as (most likely) a political impossibility. In a far-reaching step that emphasized the EU's growing political character and stature, EU leaders nonetheless signed a *constitutional treaty* in October 2004. Given the strength of Euroskepticism in some member states and the variable support among them for deeper integration, this was a remarkable achievement.

EU treaty reform requires an intergovernmental conference (a negotiation among representatives of the national governments), unanimous agreement by national leaders, and approval by the member states according to their constitutional requirements for treaty ratification. Clearly, the threshold for EU treaty reform is high.[1] Pressure for deeper economic and political integration in the late 1980s and the early 1990s nonetheless sufficed to bring about major treaty changes, notably with the Single European Act and the Maastricht Treaty. Negotiations leading to both agreements were intense as member states fought their corners and struggled for national advantage. The outcomes were probably the best that could have been expected under the circumstances.

Subsequent intergovernmental conferences were every bit as hard fought but different in their origins and character. In particular, the post-Maastricht conferences took place almost exclusively to improve the EU's efficiency and legitimacy, especially in view of looming enlargement to the east. The intergovernmental conference of 1996–1997 was initially intended to review some of the changes introduced by the Maastricht Treaty. It was dominated instead by the specter of enlargement as EU leaders began to appreciate the likely institutional impact of acquiring ten or more new member states.

The need for institutional reform in light of enlargement opened a can of worms in the EU as member states negotiated highly contentious issues such as the weighting of votes in the Council of Ministers, the size and composition of the Commission, and the size and apportionment of seats in the European Parliament. These issues were all about power: the power of national governments to shape EU legislative decisions. Not surprisingly, therefore, a split emerged between the big and the small member states, with the big member states wanting to increase their share of Council votes and reduce the size of the Commission and the small member states wanting to keep their share of Council votes and maintain national representation in the Commission. Moreover, because the agendas of these intergovernmental conferences were so narrowly focused, there was little opportunity for side bargains or trade-offs on policy issues among member states.

Member states failed to make any headway on institutional reform at the 1996–1997 intergovernmental conference, which resulted in the Amsterdam Treaty. They tried again in 2000, but the outcome of that intergovernmental conference, which resulted in the Nice Treaty, was highly unsatisfactory—so much so that it cast the process of treaty reform into serious disrepute. That result prompted national governments to prepare the next round of treaty reform in a novel way, by holding a convention of representatives of various national and EU institutions. The Convention on the Future of Europe, which met in 2002–2003, produced the draft Constitutional Treaty.

Because the treaties could only be amended by means of an intergovernmental conference, member states held the requisite negotiations in 2003–2004 to consider the draft Constitutional Treaty. The sticking points, once again, had to do with institutional representation. The highly personal nature of intergovernmental conferences, which take place at the level of the European Council as well as at lesser political and official levels, complicated the negotiations, especially after EU leaders had a bitter falling-out over the war in Iraq. Following the spectacular breakdown of the intergovernmental conference at a contentious meeting of the European Council in December 2003, negotiations resumed in the new year and eventually ended in June 2004 with an agreement on the Constitutional Treaty.

The Constitutional Treaty rolled the existing treaties into a single document and introduced important institutional reforms. It also included significant changes in the areas of foreign policy and defense as well as in justice and home affairs. Regardless of the merits of these reforms, in one respect the Constitutional Treaty was a disappointment, as it failed to grab the interest or imagination of most Europeans. Indeed, the convention, launched in large part to popularize the process of treaty change, passed almost unnoticed outside

Brussels. Given widespread indifference about integration and the prevalence of Euroskepticism throughout the EU, the fate of the Constitutional Treaty, which required ratification by each member state, was questionable.

■ The Amsterdam Treaty

The Maastricht Treaty mandated that a follow-on intergovernmental conference would take place in 1996 in order to adjust the treaty's new decision-making procedures, especially in the area of foreign and security policy. By the mid-1990s, however, the institutional implications of enlargement overshadowed preparations for the new intergovernmental conference. Even before Austria, Finland, and Sweden joined in 1995, the European Council had conceded the inevitability of further enlargement, but without specifying a timetable. A future EU of twenty-five or more member states seemed unworkable without major institutional reform.

Preparation

Thanks to the lessons of the Maastricht ratification crisis, if anything the 1996–1997 intergovernmental conference was overprepared.[2] The EU's main institutions, most national governments, and numerous nongovernmental organizations submitted a host of preparatory reports. In addition, EU leaders decided to establish the so-called Reflection Group, a high-level committee to prepare the conference, to which national governments appointed one representative each (the group also included a commissioner and two members of the European Parliament).

The Reflection Group met for the first time at a special gathering of foreign ministers in Messina, Sicily, in June 1995, to celebrate the fortieth anniversary of the Messina conference that had relaunched European integration in the mid-1950s. The fact that the original Messina conference had helped to bring about the Rome Treaty seemed auspicious for the group's deliberations, but the cloud of war in not-too-distant Bosnia and the member states' preoccupation with meeting the monetary union convergence criteria overshadowed the work of the group, and later of the intergovernmental conference.

The group's remit was not to negotiate on the member states' behalf but to draw up a manageable agenda and identify areas of likely agreement. Member states' different approaches and ambitions were evident from the outset, with the more integration-minded countries (notably Belgium, Germany, Italy, Luxembourg, and the Netherlands) ranged against those less inclined toward supranational solutions, especially Britain. Indeed, the extreme Euroskepticism of Britain's Conservative government hobbled the group's work, just as it would hobble all but the final stage of the conference itself.

Without making precise or dramatic recommendations, the group's report identified three main areas for reform: making the EU more relevant to its citizens (for example, by promoting human rights, internal security, employment policy, and environmental protection); improving the EU's efficiency and accountability (in effect, closing the democratic deficit); and improving the EU's ability to act internationally (notably by strengthening foreign and security policy).[3] Overall, the group tried to organize the large number of institutional and policy issues that member states raised in the run-up to the conference.

The possibility of institutionalizing differentiated integration as a basic principle rather than an ad hoc arrangement emerged during the group's deliberations as one of the most important and contentious issues likely to dominate the conference. Three main factors accounted for the timing and intensity of the debate over so-called flexibility: British obstructionism, the likelihood that only a minority of member states would be able to participate in the final stage of economic and monetary union, and the prospect of Central and Eastern European enlargement. The budding debate burst into the open in September 1994 when the parties in Germany's conservative coalition government published a paper claiming that "the existing hard core of countries oriented to greater integration and closer cooperation must be further strengthened" and that "the further development of the EU's institutions must combine coherence and consistency with elasticity and flexibility." Not only did the authors use contested terms such as "hard core" and "flexibility," but they went on to identify the core group as Germany, France, Belgium, Luxembourg, and the Netherlands—in other words, the original EC member states minus Italy. As for Britain, the authors argued that "determined efforts to spur on the further development of Europe are the best means of exerting a positive influence on the clarification of Britain's relationship to Europe and on its willingness to participate in further steps toward integration."[4]

Already sensitive to criticism of its seeming inability to meet the monetary union convergence criteria and embroiled in post–Cold War political upheavals, Italy was deeply offended. The smaller member states, even the three Benelux countries included in the putative hard core, shared Italy's fear that the paper presaged a Franco-Belgian scheme to pursue closer political integration outside the EU system. Nor was the main thrust of the paper lost on the British government. For some time Prime Minister John Major had been talking cavalierly about flexibility, by which he meant an à la carte, pick-and-choose EU. In response to the German paper, Major rejected the idea of an EU "in which some (member states) would be more equal than others." By arguing against a two-tier EU and advocating instead a system in which member states could opt in and out of certain policies, Major drew one of the most important battle lines of the forthcoming intergovernmental conference.[5]

Buried under more preparatory documents than had been generated by all the previous rounds of treaty reform put together, member states launched the intergovernmental conference at a special summit in Turin in March 1996. There was no prearranged date for it to end, although negotiations were expected to continue into the new year. The performance of Britain's representative in the Reflection Group convinced most other participants that the conference would make little progress until after the next British election, due by May 1997 at the latest, which the Conservatives were widely expected to lose. In the event, the conference ran until the Amsterdam summit of June 1997.[6]

Negotiation

France and Germany took a number of joint initiatives in the conference, notably on flexibility and foreign policy. But Franco-German leadership was noticeably weak in the mid-1990s as each country struggled with domestic and European problems. Jacques Chirac, who had replaced François Mitterrand as president of France in May 1995, had been evasive during the election campaign about both monetary union and deeper European integration and seemed lukewarm about relations with Germany. The few Franco-German initiatives taken during the conference barely concealed the personal differences between Chancellor Helmut Kohl and Chirac or disguised the fact that neither leader seemed particularly keen on the proceedings.

As for the other large member states, Britain had marginalized itself and lost all influence in EU affairs until the election of May 1997, when Labour swept the Conservatives from office, as other member states had hoped would happen. The change of government helped the intergovernmental conference, allowing breakthroughs on a number of important issues. Italy's influence in the EU was minimal throughout, as the government focused its attention almost exclusively on the economic reforms necessary to adopt the euro. By contrast, Spain was unusually assertive under the leadership of José Maria Aznar, who had replaced Felipe González, one of the EU's most experienced statesmen, in January 1996.

The small member states invested proportionately more effort in the conference than the big member states, although inevitably their influence was limited. By chance, two small member states (Ireland and the Netherlands) were in the presidency during the conference's substantive stages. The Dutch were haunted in 1997 by their mishandling of the 1991 intergovernmental conferences. Nevertheless, having inherited from the Irish the most difficult agenda items—notably flexibility, institutional reform, and better cooperation on justice and home affairs—the Dutch steadfastly set about narrowing member state differences and drafting the final text. They did so by circulating various "nonpapers" and by convening the European Council for a special summit in May

1997. With the new British government fully on board, the conference gathered speed in the run-up to the Amsterdam summit.

Although they were dealt with separately in the intergovernmental conference, the large number of issues on the table inevitably became linked in the give-and-take of the negotiations, especially toward the end of the conference as member states brokered agreements and constructed package deals. The conference was not a zero-sum game; there were no absolute winners and losers. On the key institutional and policy issues, all parties in the process—whether national governments, the Commission, or the European Parliament—could fairly claim satisfaction with the outcome. Whether the outcome was worth the effort, and whether it greatly benefited the EU, was another matter.

With regard to flexibility, the three factors that drove the initial debate—British obstructionism, the likely size of the euro zone, and concerns about enlargement—changed significantly during the course of the conference. By mid-1997 the British Conservatives were out of power, the euro seemed set to start in January 1999 with a majority of member states, and enlargement looked likely to be staggered over a lengthy period. Whereas in 1994 there had been a sense of urgency about the need for flexibility, three years later the issue aroused more academic interest than political passion. Although some member states remained wary, a consensus emerged during the conference that, in principle, flexibility should be included in the treaty as long as it was limited, in practice, to precisely defined conditions that would not endanger the *acquis communautaire*.

Member states eventually agreed to a compromise that included both general "enabling" clauses for countries wishing to cooperate more closely and particular provisions governing the use of flexibility in certain policy areas. One of these, which would allow any member state to block the others from cooperation more closely by claiming that its "national interest" was at stake, harked back to the days of the Luxembourg Compromise. It also showed that Britain's Conservatives need not have been too concerned about the applicability of flexibility.

As for legislative decisionmaking, most member states favored the possibility of extending qualified majority voting to additional policy areas. This issue became bound up with the seemingly technical but politically sensitive question of the reweighting of Council votes. The big member states favored either an increase in the number of their votes or the introduction of a double majority, combining the traditional requirement of a qualified majority with a new demographic criterion. Without such a change, they argued, a qualified majority could be formed following the next round of enlargement by a group of member states that together did not represent a majority of the EU's population. As French prime minister Edouard Balladur had pointed out well before the conference began, voting in an enlarged EU could mean that "the five big states representing four-fifths of the [EU's] population and wealth could be put in a minority."[7]

Negotiations about the reweighting of votes inevitably became enmeshed in another controversial institutional issue: the size of the Commission. Intellectually, every member state conceded that the Commission was too large; politically, few would countenance a Commission with fewer representatives than the total number of EU member states. Not least because large member states wanted to increase their relative weight in Council voting, small member states adamantly opposed the possible loss of "their" commissioner. With varying degrees of enthusiasm, large member states expressed a willingness to give up at least their second commissioner, but only in return for a reweighting of votes in the Council. France alone favored a radical reduction in the Commission's size, not least because it wanted to reduce the Commission's authority.

The European Council negotiated far into the night in Amsterdam, well beyond the summit's scheduled end, in an unsuccessful effort to reach a lasting agreement on institutional issues. EU leaders settled on a temporary solution: a protocol attached to the treaty stipulated that the Commission would comprise one representative per member state as soon as the next enlargement took place, provided that Council votes were reweighted in order to compensate large member states for the loss of a second commissioner. The protocol also stated that at least one year before the EU enlarged to twenty-one member states, another conference would be convened "to carry out a comprehensive review of the provisions of the treaties on the composition and functioning of the institutions" (in order to decide, specifically, how to apportion twenty commissioners among more than twenty member states).

Issues relating to the European Parliament—its size, location, and legislative powers—proved relatively painless to resolve. The conference accepted the Parliament's own proposal to set a ceiling of 700 members and agreed to enshrine in the treaty an earlier political agreement to hold the bulk of the Parliament's plenary session in Strasbourg (a persistent French demand). Following the change of government in Britain, the conference agreed to the Parliament's request that the number of legislative procedures be reduced to three: consultation, a simplified form of codecision, and assent. The extension and simplification of the codecision procedure would greatly enhance the Parliament's legislative power and political influence.

Other important institutional issues covered in the conference ranged from the role of national parliaments in EU decisionmaking to subsidiarity, transparency, and openness. Important outcomes included

- a protocol on the role of national parliaments, giving the Conference of European Affairs Committees of national parliaments the right to

send comments on EU legislative proposals to the Commission, Council, and European Parliament
- incorporation of a previously agreed-upon subsidiarity protocol into the treaty
- a new transparency clause in the treaty stipulating that any natural or legal person residing in the EU has a right of access to EU documents

The treaty also included a number of important changes in policy areas such as internal and external security, which are examined in Chapter 17.

Significance

Judged by the main reason given by politicians for embarking on another intergovernmental conference—the need to adapt the EU to meet the challenge of enlargement—the Amsterdam Treaty was a disappointment. Giving more power to the European Parliament and extending the range of qualified majority voting were important changes but were unlikely greatly to enhance the EU's efficiency, credibility, or legitimacy. Instead, by deferring the hard institutional questions about the Commission's size and member states' weighted votes until another conference, the EU sent a negative signal to its own citizens and to the applicant states.

The treaty was noteworthy mostly because it included "the first institutionalization of the concept of flexibility as a *basic principle* in the Treaties."[8] Surrounded by qualifications and safeguards, however, flexibility would be difficult to put into practice. What emerged in the treaty was a far cry from what some countries favored and others feared: a two-tier EU. Yet most member states expressed satisfaction with the treaty's flexibility provisions. For the presumed hard core, having the principle of flexibility written into the treaty was a step forward; for the others, what mattered most was having a seat at the decisionmaking table if and when flexibility was ever invoked.

Partly in response to the challenge of enlargement but largely in response to the alienation of ordinary Europeans, national governments sought to give the EU a more political character. Therefore, they inserted into the Amsterdam Treaty a key affirmation: "The Union is founded on the principles of liberty, democracy, respect for human rights and fundamental freedoms, and the rule of law, principles which are common to the member states." Whereas the EU and the communities that preceded it were political constructions, member states had not explicitly imbued them with core political values. In the Amsterdam Treaty, by contrast, member states clearly stated what those values were.

The treaty also included a provision to sanction a member state that deviated from the EU's core values. Should it determine "the existence of a serious and persistent breach . . . of principles mentioned [in the treaty]," the European Council could decide by a qualified majority "to suspend certain of the rights deriving from the application of [the treaty] to the Member State in question, including the voting right of the government of that Member State in the Council." Member states drafted that provision with the Central and Eastern European applicants in mind. Indeed, it was one of the few provisions of the Amsterdam Treaty that owed its existence to impending enlargement.

Ironically, the possible suspension of membership rights became a pressing political issue soon afterward, not in relation to enlargement but because the Christian Democratic Party in Austria formed a coalition government in February 2000 with the far-right Freedom Party. To signal their displeasure, the other member states cited the Amsterdam Treaty and unofficially imposed mild sanction against Austria, but backed down at the end of the year when the Austrian government threatened to call their bluff by holding a referendum on EU participation unless the sanctions were lifted. Sensing that the result of the referendum would have been a huge embarrassment to the EU, Austria's partners soon relented.[9]

Regardless of its political and other significance, the Amsterdam Treaty's length and language were by no means citizen-friendly. With more than fifty pages of text, including numerous references to existing provisions, the treaty was not an easy read. Ironically, a treaty intended to make the EU more intelligible to its citizens was almost unintelligible even to experts. Overall, the Amsterdam Treaty was a fitting testimonial to the impossibility of reconciling the complexity of EU governance with citizens' demands for greater simplicity and comprehensibility.

Ratification

Given what had happened with the Maastricht Treaty, the specter of another ratification crisis loomed over the Amsterdam negotiations. Accordingly, governments handled ratification warily, dragging the process out until well into 1999. Only Denmark and Ireland held referendums this time around. The resolution of the Maastricht Treaty showed that a "no" vote in Denmark would not necessarily have derailed the Amsterdam Treaty. Still, member state and EU officials breathed a sigh of relief in May 1998 when the result of the Danish referendum showed 55.1 percent in favor.

A week before that, Irish voters endorsed the treaty by a vote of 61.7 percent in favor. Although this was a comfortable majority by any standard, a low voter turnout demonstrated both the treaty's unpopularity and growing disillusionment with the EU as a whole. Many of those who voted against the treaty complained that they did not know enough about it. Undoubtedly the treaty was difficult to understand, but a surfeit of comprehensible information on its nature and content was easily available to interested voters. The perception of an information deficit at a time of information overload confirmed the public relations problem facing the EU in the prevailing climate of skepticism and distrust.

▨   The Nice Treaty

The EU embarked on another intergovernmental conference in 2000 to tackle the so-called Amsterdam leftovers (extension of qualified majority voting, reweighting of Council votes, and size and composition of the Commission). As part of a general institutional reshuffle, member states also addressed the number of seats and votes for the prospective new member states, issues that ordinarily would have been included in the accession negotiations. Member states did not include Turkey in their calculations. Had they done so, they might have been forced to revise drastically the EU's institutional structure (on the basis of the existing system Turkey would warrant the second-largest representation in the EU).

The narrowness of the conference agenda was inherently unsatisfactory. A group of "wise men," convened by the Commission to draft a report on the conference, recommended broadening its agenda to include many more issues, but member states preferred to stick to the institutional implications of enlargement. No sooner had the intergovernmental conference begun, however, than prominent national politicians started to outline their visions for the enlarged EU in ways that went well beyond the scope of the negotiations then taking place. What became known as the post-Nice debate on Europe's future began well before the Nice summit of December 2000, where the treaty was concluded, suggesting that for many national leaders Nice was never intended to be more than a stopgap measure.

An Acrimonious Intergovernmental Conference
The division between big and small member states, inherent in negotiations about voting weights and Commission size, deepened as the conference progressed. France was the leading proponent of an institutional rebalance in favor of the big member states, using (or abusing) its position as Council president in the second half of 2000 to advance its interests. That caused a spectacular row among EU leaders at an informal summit in October, their first detailed discussion of institutional issues since the rancorous Amsterdam summit in June 1997. France especially incensed the small member states by proposing a radical reduction in the size of the Commission while promising a system for the selection of a smaller group of commissioners that would ensure equality among all member states. The small countries were reluctant to agree, distrusting France and fearing that the big member states would skew the proposed new system against them. France claimed that the sharp ex-

change over the Commission's size cleared the air in the intergovernmental conference. In fact, it led the small member states to dig in their heels and set the stage for a bruising battle on institutional representation at the Nice summit in December 2000.

The discussion of voting weights also opened deep divisions between the big and small member states. France was determined to keep the same number of Council votes as Germany, a far more populous country. Chirac, a Gaullist, even cited Jean Monnet, the founding father of the EU, to bolster his argument that equality between France and Germany in the distribution of Council votes was an inviolable part of the original Franco-German bargain. German chancellor Gerhard Schröder, participating in his first intergovernmental conference, conceded the point in return for the addition of a demographic criterion for qualified majority voting. As for the small member states, the Netherlands infuriated Belgium, its less populous neighbor, by demanding more Council votes, thereby ending the traditional parity between the two countries.

Member states spent most of the conference reiterating well-known positions. When they convened in Nice, EU leaders were far apart on the main agenda items. It looked to two officials involved in the conference "as if eighteen months of preparation had been thrown out of the window and the negotiations [re]started from scratch."[10] After spending two days on other EU business, the European Council spent the next three days concluding the conference, making the Nice summit the longest in EU history.

The length of the summit and of the conference as a whole hardly justified the effort. EU leaders haggled until the final minutes of the summit over the reallocation of Council votes. Still refusing to accept fewer votes than the Netherlands, Belgium was finally bought off with the promise of hosting all meetings of the European Council in Brussels. France managed to keep an equal number of votes as Germany (both got twenty-nine), but the addition of a demographic criterion gave Germany extra voting weight. The final bargain struck on Council decisionmaking was especially inglorious. Far from making voting simpler and easier for ordinary Europeans to understand, it changed the system in a way that seemed entirely illogical. According to the new rules, a legislative proposal would pass if it received a qualified majority (72 percent) of votes, representing an absolute majority of member states and, subject to a specific request by a member state, a qualified majority (62 percent) of the EU's population. Less controversially, the Nice Treaty also extended the number of policy areas subject to qualified majority voting.

The small member states resented the big member states' acquisition of more voting weight in the Council, making them more determined than ever to maintain national representation in the Commission (although the Commission is not supposed to represent national interests). All agreed in the end to have one commissioner per member state until the EU reached twenty-seven members (a number based on the existing fifteen plus the twelve candidates). At that time the member states would rotate commission appointments according to a system to be worked out later. The provisions on the size and composition of the Commission constituted an implicit Nice leftover, in contrast to the explicit Amsterdam leftovers.

Whereas the Amsterdam Treaty capped the size of the Parliament at 700, member states agreed in the Nice Treaty to exceed the cap when reallocating parliamentary seats in order to accommodate an EU of up to twenty-seven member states. Existing member states grudgingly accepted a reduction in the size of their national delegations in the enlarged EU.

Significance and Ratification

Signed without much fanfare in February 2001, the Nice Treaty succeeded only to a limited extent in preparing the EU institutionally for enlargement. Arguably its most important provision was to relax the criteria under which flexibility (closer cooperation among like-minded member states) could be used. Having agreed to include flexibility in the Amsterdam Treaty, the member states that worried about its possible impact had already conceded an important point of principle, which made it easier for them to discuss ways to allow flexibility to work better in practice. As a result, governments agreed in the Nice Treaty to remove the national veto on the use of flexibility and reduce the number of member states allowed to initiate the procedure.

In general, the paltry outcome of the conference brought the EU and the process of treaty reform into disrepute. When the Irish electorate rejected the treaty in June 2001 by a convincing margin (64 percent against), it was difficult to regret the result. Far from being concerned about the timetable for enlargement, the European Council announced only a week after the referendum that the EU would enlarge regardless, probably in early 2004. Encouraged by other governments and by the Commission, the Irish government pressured its electorate to approve the treaty in a second referendum in October 2002. Meanwhile, the Convention on the Future of Europe, intended to prepare yet another intergovernmental conference, was meeting in Brussels. As the purpose of the next conference was to consider the EU's form and structure after enlargement, it was hard to understand why the EU put such emphasis on the Nice Treaty. To the relief of the EU establishment and the candidate countries, the Irish endorsed the treaty in the second attempt by a majority of 63 percent, thanks to a much higher turnout.

The political legacy of Nice was more enduring than the treaty's institutional provisions. The conduct of the conference soured the public's and the politicians' appetite for negotiations on treaty reform. Distrust between big and small member states and bitterness between particular member states were an equally enduring legacy. Small countries, both current and aspiring member states, realized that the EU was moving in a more intergovernmental direction dominated by the big member states. They especially resented the behavior of France during the intergovernmental conference. Indeed, by engendering the antipathy not only of the small member states but also of Germany, France may have weakened its position in the EU in the long term.[11]

▧ The Constitutional Treaty

Even as the Irish electorate decided the fate of the Nice Treaty in October 2002, representatives of national and EU institutions were meeting in Brussels in the Convention on the Future of Europe to draft a new treaty for the EU. The launch of a "post-Nice debate" in the pre-Nice period by politicians such as German foreign minister Joschka Fischer and French president Chirac indicated widespread disillusionment with the narrow focus of the 2000 conference. In a declaration attached to the Nice Treaty, member states therefore called for a "deeper and wider debate . . . about the future of the [EU]" as a prelude to yet another conference, in 2004, which would deal specifically with the role of national parliaments in the EU system; simplification of the treaties; the delimitation of competences (responsibilities) between the EU and the member states; and the status of the Charter of Fundamental Rights, a nonbinding document that EU leaders had endorsed in December 2000.

The Nice declaration also called for the European Council to issue a follow-up declaration at its meeting in Laeken (Belgium) twelve months later, "containing appropriate initiatives for the continuation of the process [of treaty reform]." In the run-up to the Laeken summit, reform-minded member states pressed successfully to broaden the agenda of the next conference. Widespread disappointment with the Nice Treaty, together with the shock of the Irish referendum result in June 2001, helped their case considerably. Awareness of the likely impact of enlargement and of the extent of public alienation from the EU finally convinced national leaders that the next conference could not be conducted like the previous one.

The Convention and Draft Constitutional Treaty
Accordingly, the European Council agreed in Laeken not only to widen the agenda of the conference but also to prepare for it in a different way. Drawing on the method used to draft the Charter of Fundamental Rights in 2000, the European Council announced that representatives of various national and EU institutions would meet in a convention to prepare the intergovernmental conference "as broadly and openly as possible." The composition of the convention reflected a consensus on the need to diversify participation in the process of EU treaty reform. Thus, the convention would consist of

- fifteen representatives of the national leaders (one from each member state)
- thirty representatives of the national parliaments (two from each member state)
- two representatives of the Commission and sixteen members of the European Parliament

The candidate countries would be represented in the same way as the member states, but representatives of the candidate countries would not have a decisionmaking role.[12]

The convention was to have a high-ranking, influential chairman. Chirac announced that either the chairman would be French or the convention would not take place. He proposed Valéry Giscard d'Estaing, a former president of France, largely because he wanted to remove Giscard from the domestic political scene during the forthcoming national elections. The small member states remembered Giscard's lack of interest in them and dislike of the Commission when he had been president of France but felt powerless to block his appointment by the European Council. And so the septuagenarian Giscard, an archdefender of the interests of big member states, came to personify the future of Europe.

Conducting the Convention. The convention opened in Brussels in February 2002 and ended in June 2003. During the first six months its members conducted wide-ranging discussions about various policy and institutional issues. In addition to the plenary sessions, Giscard organized working groups on topics ranging from economic governance to external relations. The convention got down to serious business later in the year, after the French and German elections and after the second Irish referendum on the Nice Treaty.

The convention soon became known as the Constitutional Convention because of Giscard's intention to draft not simply a new treaty but a constitution for the EU. Yet because of the nature of the EU (a hybrid international organization and statelike entity), the convention could only propose and national governments could only approve a constitutional treaty (an agreement among sovereign states with constitutional characteristics). On the one hand, the decision to draft a constitutional treaty was of greater symbolic than real importance, given that the Court of Justice already interpreted the existing treaties as constitutional texts. On the other hand, drafting a constitutional treaty was far more than a mere tidying up of the existing treaties, as the British government, fearful of Euroskeptical opinion among its citizens, claimed that it was. For instance, incorporating the Charter of Fundamental Rights would give the EU the equivalent of a Bill of Rights, an important constitutional element.

The plenary sessions, which took place more often as the deadline for ending the convention approached, were large and unwieldy affairs. Their most striking feature was a palpable sense of enthusiasm: most of the delegates were optimistic about the eventual outcome. Altogether, delegates drafted hundreds of proposals and amendments. The governments of the existing member states submitted proposals on most agenda items, and national parliamentarians in many cases endorsed their governments' positions. Indeed, although the purpose of the convention was partly to curb the member states' monopoly of treaty reform, discussions in the plenary sessions and in the presidium (the convention's governing body) increasingly reflected national priorities as the deadline for completion approached.

If not masters of the convention, national governments nonetheless made most of the running. Institutionally, they were best equipped to do so, having the resources of government ministries behind them. Also, as Giscard occasionally reminded some of the more disputatious delegates, national governments would ultimately decide the fate of the draft Constitutional Treaty in the intergovernmental conference.

True to his usual autocratic form, Giscard provided forceful leadership, dominating the presidium and submitting draft articles to the convention floor. Giscard's priorities were reform of the Council presidency, a smaller Commission, and a new assembly linking the European Parliament and national parliaments. He also wanted to include a religious reference in the preamble. Giscard was realistic about what he could achieve, although he misjudged the fierce attachment of most of the small member states to maintaining national representation in the Commission and widespread resistance to establishing a new EU-level body.

Big Versus Small Member States. The big-small member state divide, which had opened so alarmingly in the run-up to the Nice summit, was bound to resurface in the constitutional convention, especially when it addressed contentious institutional questions. Other EU developments in 2003 exacerbated tension between the big and small countries. At the beginning of the year, the Iraq crisis caused a rift among the big member states and also between two of them (France and Germany) and most of the small member states. At the end of the year, French and German disregard for the Stability and Growth Pact, which supposedly underpinned economic and monetary union, alienated many of the other member states in the eurozone.

A joint proposal by France and Germany in January 2003—an important element in the celebrations of the fortieth anniversary of the Franco-German Elysée Treaty (a pivotal event in the history of European integration)—brought the big-small country divide starkly to the fore. Its main features were an endorsement of the call, already made by Britain, France, and Spain, for a standing president of the European Council (for a period of up to five years) and for the election of the European Commission president by the European Parliament (a perennial German demand). Many of the small member states (plus the Commission) immediately cried foul, resenting what looked like a Franco-German diktat. They presumed that the standing president of the European Council would come from a big member state and feared that the proposed new position would undermine the Commission presidency and therefore weaken the Commission, traditionally a champion of the small member states.

Britain and Spain supported the call for a standing president of the European Council but rejected the idea of the European Parliament electing the Commission president. They favored the status quo: Europarliamentary approval of the Commission president, who would be selected (if necessary, elected) by the European Council. The avowed support of the biggest member states (Italy and Poland were also on board), together with Giscard's enthusiasm, ensured that the convention would call for an elected European Council president. The opposition of three of the biggest member states, together with Giscard's lack of enthusiasm, ensured that the convention would *not* call for election of the Commission president by the European Parliament.

There was general agreement among all member states that a new position—that of EU foreign minister—should replace those of high representative for the Common Foreign and Security Policy and commissioner for external relations. The same person would therefore chair meetings of a new External Relations Council and coordinate the Commission's external relations responsibilities. The advent of the elected European Council president and the EU foreign minister would mean the end of the rotating Council presidency, as currently constituted. Other Council formations would still need presiding over, but the six months' rotation would be replaced with a new system that would provide greater continuity and predictability, or what Giscard called "stability."

If they had to give up the rotating presidency, the small member states were more determined than ever to maintain another symbol of equality in the EU: representation in the Commission. Most of the small member states mounted a fierce rearguard action to scrap the provision in the Nice Treaty that broke the link between the number of member states and the number of commissioners, asserting their right always to nominate a full commissioner.

With the support of the big member states, Giscard nevertheless pushed through a provision for a college of thirteen commissioners, selected on the basis of equal rotation among member states, plus the Commission president and the EU foreign minister (the Commission vice president). The Commission would also include nonvoting members from the other countries, selected on the basis of equal rotation. Having lost the battle over the Commission's size and composition in the convention, however, the defenders of one commissioner per member state resolved to fight on in the intergovernmental conference.

Other Differences. Despite these differences between the big and small member states, neither group was united on more than a few key issues. As the convention proceeded, the essential distinction seemed to be not between the big and the small countries but between the original six (the founding member states) and the rest, particularly those about to join in 2004. Just as the image of a confrontation in the convention between united groups of big and small member states was misleading, so too was the supposition that, on most other issues, Britain stood alone. Peter Hain, the British government's representative, was pilloried in London for surrendering sovereignty and pitied in Brussels for sticking rigidly to archaic positions. Indeed, British Euroskepticism cast a shadow over the convention, where most of the delegates sympathized with Hain's predicament.

Hain's utter rejection of the "F-word" ("federalism"), reminiscent of Prime Minister John Major's equally allergic reaction during the Maastricht negotiations, drew a predictable response in the convention. While acknowledging that the EU had obvious federal features, most delegates were willing to sacrifice the "F-word" itself in order to help out Hain and mollify the Euroskeptics baying for his blood. Hain's other protestations elicited a mixed response. Oversensitive to Euroskeptical complaints, at one point Hain objected to a reference in the draft document to the supremacy of Community law, a principle first established by the Court of Justice some forty years earlier. The other delegates refused to humor him on that score.

Also in deference to Euroskeptics, the convention dropped the well-known phrase "ever closer union" from the treaty (while keeping it in the Charter of Fundamental Rights), substituting for it a vague reference to the "peoples of Europe . . . united ever more closely." The most striking change intended to mollify Euroskeptics, however, was the inclusion of an exit clause: an elaborate procedure for a country to withdraw from the EU. This was intended to nullify the argument that the EU was a prison from which there was no escape.

Although often on the defensive in the convention, Hain was rarely in a minority of one. The French and German representatives were in a stronger position, not least because they held the rank of foreign minister. Although the French and German foreign ministers may not have attended every plenary session, their participation in the convention lent additional weight to their countries' inherently influential positions. French and German officials worked closely together, giving the appearance at the convention of a concerted Franco-German drive, despite differences between the two countries on a range of issues.

In keeping with Prime Minister Aznar's generally forceful approach to EU issues, the Spanish government pushed certain points, notably preservation of the voting weights agreed to in the Nice Treaty. Thus, Spain resisted a key Franco-German proposal, supported by Giscard, for a new, simpler definition of a qualified majority in Council decisionmaking: a majority of member states and at least three-fifths of the EU's population. Having secured twenty-seven Council votes (compared to twenty-nine for Germany) in the Nice Treaty, Spain's position was understandable.

Institutional issues—whether or not mandated by the Laeken Declaration—predominated toward the end of the convention but were by no means the only sticking points. Other items proved equally contentious. In particular, the question of EU competences and responsibilities—one of the convention's main undertakings, according to the Laeken Declaration—preoccupied the convention in early 2003 and demonstrated the difficulty of demarcating EU-level and national powers in a process as politically and historically muddled as that of European integration. The convention eventually agreed on a short list of exclusive responsibilities (such as monetary policy and trade policy) and a long but not exclusive list of shared responsibilities (ranging from agricultural policy to economic and social cohesion). In addition, the EU could promote and coordinate national economic and social policies and define and implement a common foreign and security policy, including the progressive framing of a common defense policy. Finally, the EU could take supporting, coordinating, or complementary action in areas such as industry, culture, and civil protection. The limits of EU competences were governed by the principle of conferral (at British insistence, conferral by the member states), and the use of competences by the principles of subsidiarity and proportionality.

The values and objectives of the EU were relatively uncontroversial, apart from a heated discussion about whether and how to recognize the EU's religious heritage. The Catholic Church took a keen interest in the convention, especially in this issue. It did not go unnoticed that mention of an explicit Christian heritage would hinder (if not prevent) Turkish accession to the EU. In the end, the preamble merely included a reference to Europe's religious "inheritance." Membership in the EU would be open to all European states that respected the EU's values and were committed to promoting them together—hardly clear-cut criteria, either geographically or normatively.

Most delegates wanted to include the Charter of Fundamental Rights directly in the Constitutional Treaty in order to emphasize the EU's values and possibly increase the EU's appeal to citizens. The British and Irish governments were unenthusiastic about the Charter, doubting that it would have any effect on public opinion (excerpt perhaps to provide more ammunition to Euroskeptics) and fearing that strict adherence to it would raise business costs in the EU. But the Charter's inclusion in the Constitutional Treaty, whether as an integral part or in a protocol, did not become a make-or-break issue. Notwithstanding the Charter's incorporation into the Constitutional Treaty, a majority of delegates agreed that the EU should accede to the European Convention for the Protection of Human Rights and Fundamental Freedoms.

Bringing the various bits and pieces together and concluding the draft document was a Herculean task for a convention of over 100 members from 28 countries. Undoubtedly democratic, the convention method was unavoidably awkward. It needed strong leadership to succeed. Giscard was determined to give EU leaders a single draft text instead of alternative versions of controversial provisions. He could not hope for unanimity, only for majority support from each of the convention's constituent parts. By emphasizing the convention's historic importance as the deadline approached, Giscard won the approval, grudging or otherwise, of most of the delegates for the final text (only a diehard faction of Euroskeptics formally dissented).

By producing a single, reasonably understandable (although long) text, the convention was a qualified success. In one important respect, however, it failed to meet the European Council's and the convention's own expectations. Far from following the work of the convention, ordinary Europeans seemed to know little and care less about it. Media coverage was generally sparse, apart from a flurry of alarming articles in the British tabloid press. Even under the best of circumstances, it would have been difficult to interest the vast majority of citizens in the vagaries of majority voting or other arcane institutional issues. If anything, the convention reinforced a widespread public perception that European integration, and especially political union, were driven entirely by elites.

The Intergovernmental Conference

Meeting in June 2003, the European Council welcomed the draft constitution as "a good basis for starting" the intergovernmental conference, which began four months later.[13] In the meantime, governments sharpened their positions. Most wanted to reopen the Nice package in some way or other. For many of the small member states, especially those about to join the EU, the intergovernmental conference presented an opportunity to reclaim the right to representation in the Commission even after the EU expanded to twenty-seven countries. For Spain and Poland, the Nice agreement on voting weights was a major and, in Spain's case, hard-fought victory. Why should Spain surrender such an advantage, to which the other member states had agreed, especially as the Laeken Declaration had not specifically put the Nice package on the convention's agenda? The Poles were equally justified in claiming that, having recently won a referendum on the terms of EU membership, it would be wrong (and politically risky) to give away the prize of near equality of voting weights with France and Germany. For their part, France and Germany were determined to scrap the Nice arrangement in favor of the proposed new double majority system.

Having played no part in the convention, the Council presidency played a pivotal role in the intergovernmental conference, at the beginning of which Italy was in the chair. Desperate to conclude the conference by December, Italy—or, more specifically, Prime Minister Silvio Berlusconi—tried to ram through the draft Constitutional Treaty instead of mediating among member states and attempting to broker a compromise. To some extent Italy's approach was understandable: revisiting the convention's institutional proposals meant opening a Pandora's box. Yet the strength of national positions meant that a negotiation of institutional arrangements could not be avoided. Italy wasted precious time denying the existence of deep divisions among the member states. When Italy eventually took its responsibilities seriously, it was probably too late to rescue the December summit from failure, although the depth of French and Spanish feelings in any case made a breakdown seem inevitable.

Failure to reach agreement at the December summit did not mean the complete collapse of the intergovernmental conference, which would resume in the new year. Nevertheless, the impasse in the negotiations mirrored the rancorous state of the EU as a whole. Apart from any larger lessons, the course of the intergovernmental conference, in which twenty-five countries participated, illustrated the difficulties awaiting the EU after enlargement.

Threats by France and Germany to link the outcome of the intergovernmental conference to the upcoming budget negotiations (by implication cutting funds to Spain and Poland) and to forge ahead with a "core" or "pioneer" group of like-minded member states (by implication excluding Spain and Poland) were not helpful. Spain drew a more pertinent parallel between the pious incantations of France and Germany in the intergovernmental conference and their disregard for the Stability and Growth Pact outside it. As Aznar observed, perhaps there already was a two-tier EU, with the key distinction being between the economic reformers and the laggards—between member states that were improving employment, growth, and productivity and those that were not.

The incoming Irish presidency lost little time sounding out the other delegations and quietly getting the negotiations going again. Changes of government in Spain and Poland (for reasons unrelated to the intergovernmental conference), the two holdouts over the new voting formula, improved the chances of success. Wanting to signal a more accommodating policy toward the EU, the two countries' new governments were willing to reach a compromise on the proposed new formula for majority voting. Although many other sensitive issues remained on the table, an agreement on the Constitutional Treaty seemed possible by June 2004.

Altogether, the intergovernmental conference approved eighty amendments to the convention's draft. Britain introduced nearly half of these and, according to the foreign secretary, achieved all of its key demands.[14] The small member states eventually agreed to a much smaller Commission, but only in two Commissions' time (2014). The new double majority was set at 55 percent of the member states and 65 percent of the population (as opposed to the convention's proposal of 50 percent of the member states and 60 percent of the population), making it relatively easier for countries to form a blocking minority but without allowing the three biggest member states to do so by themselves. Overall, the Constitutional Treaty bore a close resemblance to the convention's draft, although many of the last-minute deals on institutional provisions were retrograde steps.

The other governments were fulsome in their praise for the Irish presidency, which worked tirelessly to broker the final agreement. The conduct of the intergovernmental conference had demonstrated the strength (in Ireland's case) and the weakness (in Italy's case) of the rotating presidency, an institution destined to change fundamentally under the terms of the Constitutional Treaty.

Outcome

The Constitutional Treaty comprised a preamble and four parts:

- Part I, the quasi-constitutional part, covered such key provisions as the EU's competences, institutions, membership, objectives, and values.
- Part II came ready-made in the form of the Charter of Fundamental Rights.
- Part III consisted mostly of the existing treaties, with some important changes.
- Part IV (general and final provisions) included protocols and other ancillary material.

The Constitutional Treaty proclaimed that the EU was based on democracy, the rule of law, and respect for human rights and fundamental freedoms. It outlined the EU's key organizing principles: conferred powers, subsidiarity, proportionality, and loyal cooperation among member states. It also clarified the division of powers or allocation of competences within the EU. Although it did not include the word "federal," the Constitutional Treaty pointed to a further federalization of the EU while at the same time affirming the EU's special political character.

The new treaty was inelegant and ungainly, rather like the EU itself. Nevertheless, merging the existing treaties into a single text, abolishing the pillar structure, and granting the EU legal personality were important steps forward. In general, the Constitutional Treaty's provisions were a marked improvement on what currently existed. The Constitutional Treaty promised a more intelli-

gible, efficient, and transparent EU. Although its institutional and other reforms were bound to be inadequate, the Constitutional Treaty was nonetheless
a harbinger of better governance.

But would it be ratified? European electorates would have ample opportunity to express their dissatisfaction with the EU and the Constitutional
Treaty in numerous ratification referendums. Given the strength of Euroskepticism, or simply of indifference toward the EU, the fate of the Constitutional
Treaty seemed uncertain. Not that the EU was in danger of falling apart without it. The Constitutional Treaty was desirable but not essential. Without it,
the EU would be relatively weaker but by no means unworkable. Even with
the Constitutional Treaty in place, strong national interests, a willful European
Parliament, and a weak Commission would continue to impair the EU's effectiveness. Arguably, the EU needed better leadership and a more congenial
political and economic environment, not simply a Constitutional Treaty, to restore its luster and sense of purpose.

■ Notes

1. See Brendan P. G. Smith, *Constitution Building in the European Union: The Process of Treaty Reform* (The Hague: Kluwer Law International, 2002).
2. See Finn Laursen, "The Lessons of Maastricht," in Geoffrey Edwards and Al-
fred Pijpers, eds., *The Politics of European Treaty Reform: The 1996 Intergovernmental Conference and Beyond* (London: Pinter, 1997), p. 62; and Finn Laursen and Sophie Vanhoonacker, eds., *The Ratification of the Maastricht Treaty: Issues, Debates
and Future Implications* (Maastricht: European Institute of Public Administration,
1994).
3. The Reflection Group report, and the reports that the institutions presented to
it, are in European Parliament, *White Paper on the 1996 IGC*, vol. 1: *Official Texts of
the EU Institutions* (Luxembourg: European Parliament, 1996).
4. Christian Democratic Union/Christian Social Union Group in the German
Lower House, "Reflections on European Policy," Bonn, September 1, 1994.
5. John Major, "Europe: A Future That Works," William and Mary Lecture, Leiden University, September 7, 1994.
6. On the intergovernmental conference and its outcome, see Finn Laursen, ed.,
*The Amsterdam Treaty: National Preference Formation, Interstate Bargaining and
Outcome* (Odense, Denmark: Odense University Press, 2002); Bobby McDonagh,
*Original Sin in a Brave New World: The Paradox of Europe: An Account of the Ne-
gotiation of the Treaty of Amsterdam* (Dublin: Institute for European Affairs, 1998); J.
Monar and W. Wessels, eds., *The European Union After the Treaty of Amsterdam* (Lon-
don: Continuum, 2001); and Anna-Carin Svensson, *In the Service of the European
Union: The Role of the Presidency in Negotiating the Amsterdam Treaty, 1995–1997*
(Uppsala, Sweden: Acta Universitatis, 2000).
7. Quoted in *Le Monde*, November 30, 1994, p. 1.
8. Alexander C.-G. Stubb, "The Amsterdam Treaty and Flexible Integration,"
ECSA Review 11, no. 2 (Spring 1998): 1–5 (emphasis in original).

9. On the Austrian situation, see Desmond Dinan, "Governance and Institutions: Edging Toward Enlargement," *Journal of Common Market Studies* 39, *Annual Review of the EU 2000/2001* (September 2001): 36–41.

10. Mark Gray and Alexander Stubb, "The Treaty of Nice—Negotiating a Poisoned Chalice?" *Journal of Common Market Studies* 39, *Annual Review of the EU 2000/2001* (September 2001): 13.

11. On the significance of the Nice Treaty, see Martyn Bond and Kim Feus, eds., *The Treaty of Nice Explained* (London: Federal Trust for Education and Research, 2001); Koji Fukuda and Hiroya Akiba, eds., *European Governance After Nice* (London: RoutledgeCurzon, 2003); D. Galloway, *The Treaty of Nice and Beyond: Reality and Illusions of Power in the EU* (Sheffield, UK: Sheffield Academic Press, 2001).

12. On the conduct and outcome of the convention, see Desmond Dinan, "Governance and Institutions: Anticipating the Impact of Enlargement," *Journal of Common Market Studies* 41, *Annual Review of the EU 2002/2003* (September 2003): 29–37; Desmond Dinan, "Governance and Institutions: The Convention and the Intergovernmental Conference," *Journal of Common Market Studies* 42, *Annual Review of the EU 2003/2004* (September 2004): 26–39; Erik Oddvar Eriksen, John Erik Fossum, and Agustín José Meníndez, eds., *Developing a Constitution for Europe* (London: Routledge, 2004); Simon Serfary, ed., *The Finality Debate and Its National Dimensions* (Washington, DC: CSIS Press, 2002); and Jo Shaw, ed., *The Convention on the Future of Europe: Working Towards an EU Constitution* (London: Federal Trust for Education and Research, 2003).

13. On the conduct of the intergovernmental conference, see Dinan, "Governance and Institutions: The Convention and the Intergovernmental Conference," pp. 40–42.

14. "Jack Straw, by Invitation," *Economist*, July 10, 2004, p. 46.

Part 2

Institutions

7

The Commission

The European Union has a singular governmental structure. Superficially, it resembles that of a familiar polity, with a council, a parliament, and a court of justice apparently resembling a national government's executive, legislative, and judiciary branches. Yet the similarity is misleading. The Council, made up of member states' government ministers, shares legislative authority with the directly elected European Parliament, which, unlike most national parliaments in Europe, does not determine the composition of the government (not least because the EU does not have a government analogous to a national government). Only the Court of Justice, consisting of judges appointed by the member states, approximates its national counterparts.

The EU has another institution—the European Commission—with no analog in national governmental systems. With its members nominated by national governments but pledged to act in the EU's interests, its multinational civil service, its exclusive right to initiate legislation in most policy areas, and its quasi-executive authority, the Commission epitomizes supranationalism and lies at the center of the EU system. Not surprisingly, the Commission and the Berlaymont, its headquarters building in Brussels, are synonymous with the EU itself.

The Berlaymont—a large, star-shaped glass and concrete structure in the heart of the "European Quarter" in Brussels—is a potent symbol of the Commission's fluctuating fortunes. Like the name "Commission," the building appears aloof and uninviting. Moreover, the Berlaymont's fate epitomized the Commission's apparent decline in the wake of the Maastricht Treaty. In 1991, as the treaty was being negotiated, the Commission evacuated the Berlaymont "on the grounds that health and safety conditions had become altogether unsatisfactory."[1] During a decade-long renovation, the Berlaymont stood empty, directly across the street from the Council's huge new office complex and not far from the Parliament's new assembly rooms and offices. The emptiness of the Berlaymont starkly symbolized the Commission's institutional retreat in the face of a more assertive Council and ascendant Parliament.

Yet the Berlaymont's emptiness and the Commission's relative weakness were at odds with a widespread perception, throughout the EU and abroad, that the Commission was greedy for power and eager to acquire as many of the prerogatives of a national government as possible. The Commission's efforts over the years to harmonize product standards were undoubtedly heavy-handed and occasionally intrusive, and its poor press increased dramatically during the Maastricht ratification crisis in 1992 and 1993. Ironically, the Commission neither played a prominent role in the Maastricht negotiations nor benefited greatly from their outcome. But that did not prevent national politicians and the press from blaming the Commission for the treaty's defects.

By the mid-1990s the Commission had fallen from the height of its influence ten years previously under Jacques Delors, the most successful president in EU history. For many advocates of deeper integration, Delors was a hero without whom the EC's transformation might never have happened, or would certainly not have happened as it did. According to Stanley Hoffmann, one of Delors's admirers: "While the Community's progress . . . depended on a series of bargains among its main members, Delors . . . skillfully prodded them and enlarged the opportunities for further integration."[2]

Subsequent Commission presidents have lacked Delors's drive and ability to shape major EU developments. Jacques Santer (1995–1999) and Romano Prodi (1999–2004) provided poor leadership. Nothing illustrated the Commission's waning fortunes more than the resignation of the entire college of commissioners in March 1999 in the face of withering charges of corruption and mismanagement. Faced with a vote of censure in the Parliament, a vote that it was bound to lose, the Commission jumped before being pushed. The new Commission made administrative reform a political priority, although the process preoccupied the institution internally and further weakened staff morale.

José Manuel Barroso, who became Commission president in November 2004, set out to restore the institution's prominence and sense of purpose, despite a shaky start when one of his commissioners-designate stood down in the face of withering criticism from the European Parliament. Personal energy and ambition are unlikely to overcome the Commission's relegation since the mid-1990s to a tertiary role in the policymaking process, behind the Council and the Parliament, but in one respect the timing of Barroso's appointment seemed fortuitous. The Berlaymont's prolonged and expensive renovation came to an end in 2004, in time for Barroso and his team of commissioners to move into the building at the beginning of their term in office. Bright and airy on the inside and gleaming on the outside, the Berlaymont no longer represented the Commission's fall from grace but instead symbolized the prospect of an institutional renaissance.

■   **The Once Powerful Presidency**

The Commission—in the sense of the commissioners themselves—is supposed to be collegial (commissioners comprise the "college" of the Commission). As "first among equals," the Commission president sets the tone for the Commission's term in office. Not surprisingly, Commissions are generally known by the president's name. In the mid-2000s, people routinely speak of "the Barroso Commission."

Apart from personifying the Commission and the EU itself, the president has various roles and responsibilities. These include

- mediating disputes and forging agreement within the Commission
- announcing to the European Parliament the Commission's annual legislative and work program
- launching major policy initiatives
- representing the Commission in meetings of the General Affairs and External Relations Council
- representing the Commission in meetings of the European Council
- representing the Commission in key international forums, notably annual group of seven/eight (G7/8) meetings and biannual U.S.-EU summits

A president's performance of these and other duties depends on a variety of personal, political, and economic circumstances such as individual experience, expertise, and acumen; relations with other commissioners and with national government leaders; prevailing political support for further integration; and current economic conditions. Presidential performance has varied widely over the years, and presidents have generally been judged by the perceived strength or weakness of their political leadership (Table 7.1).

Profile and Selection

When he became Commission president, Barroso fit the profile of previous incumbents: all were male, middle-aged, and thoroughly immersed in their own country's political processes. Although unusual because he emerged apparently out of nowhere to take the top job, Barroso's appointment serves as a useful guide to the abstruse politics of choosing a Commission president.

The heads of state and government select the Commission president-designate. With the entry into force of the Nice Treaty in February 2003, they could do so by a qualified majority vote (before that they could do so only "by common accord," or unanimity). Given the political sensitivity of choosing a new president, however, there was little likelihood that national leaders would ever vote, preferring instead to seek consensus. Nevertheless, as in other areas

Table 7.1 Commission Presidents

Name (years served)	Member State	Highest Prior Position in National Government	Type of Leadership
Walter Hallstein (1958–1967)	Germany	State Secretary, German Foreign Ministry	Strong
Jean Rey (1967–1970)	Belgium	Minister of Economic Affairs	Weak
Franco Malfatti (1970–1972)	Italy	Minister for Posts and Telecommunications	Weak
Sicco Mansholt (1972)	The Netherlands	Minister of Agriculture	Weak
François-Xavier Ortoli (1973–1977)	France	Minister of Finance	Weak
Roy Jenkins (1977–1981)	United Kingdom	Chancellor of the Exchequer	Strong
Gaston Thorn (1981–1985)	Luxembourg	Prime Minister	Weak
Jacques Delors (1985–1995)	France	Minister for the Economy, Finance and Budget	Strong
Jacques Santer (1995–1999)	Luxembourg	Prime Minister	Weak
Manuel Marin (1999)	Spain	State Secretary, Spanish Foreign Ministry	Weak
Romano Prodi (1999–2004)	Italy	Prime Minister	Weak
José Manuel Barroso (2004–)	Portugal	Prime Minister	—

of EU decisionmaking, the possibility of taking a vote helps to forge a consensus.

According to the unofficial rota for the selection of the Commission president, it was the turn of a right-of-center candidate from a small member state to succeed Romano Prodi, a left-of-center former prime minister of Italy. Ireland, in the Council presidency in early 2004, was responsible for shepherding the selection process through the European Council. Early favorites included former Belgian prime minister Jean-Luc Dehaene, current Belgian prime minister Guy Verhofstadt, and current Luxembourg prime minister Jean-Claude Juncker. Once Juncker took himself out of the running, Verhofstadt led the pack. But other national leaders resented his close ties to French president Jacques Chirac and German chancellor Gerhard Schröder. In the face of strong British and Italian opposition, Verhofstadt withdrew from the race. Members of the European Council, especially Chirac and Britain's Tony Blair, whose personal relationship had deteriorated badly when they took opposite sides over the war in Iraq, could not agree on any of the other candidates. Having failed to resolve the issue at the EU summit in mid-June 2004, the Irish prime minister searched about for another possible candidate. Barroso's name then began to circulate.

Barroso's relative obscurity was an advantage, although his qualified support for the war in Iraq seemed likely to incur Chirac's wrath. By contrast, Barroso's reputation as an economic reformer appealed to Blair, who campaigned behind the scenes for his appointment. Perhaps because there were so few good candidates left, and because Barroso satisfied the key French criterion that the new president-designate come from a country within the eurozone, Chirac relented (Barroso also speaks excellent French). Moreover, Chirac was probably appeased by the reappointment that week of Pierre de Boissieu as de facto head of the Council secretariat—an indicator of where France thinks institutional power in the EU lies. Whatever the reasons, Chirac's acquiescence allowed the Irish prime minister to announce, after a special summit at the end of June 2004, that the heads of state and government were putting Barroso forward for the job.

Once nominated, Barroso had to be approved by the European Parliament. This was by no means a formality in a Parliament jealous of its prerogatives. Indeed, the Parliament had shown nearly ten years previously that it could not be taken for granted when it endorsed Jacques Santer by only a narrow margin. Although dissatisfied with the method of Barroso's selection, most Europarliamentarians were not about to pick a fight with the national leaders. It helped that Barroso belonged to the political group to which a majority of Europarliamentarians belonged. Accordingly, in one of its first important votes, the newly elected Parliament approved Barroso's nomination by a large margin (413 votes to 251) in July 2004.

Despite this resounding endorsement by the European Parliament, the nature of Barroso's nomination and appointment raised questions about his legitimacy as Commission president as well as the legitimacy of the Commission itself. At least Barroso had held the highest political mandate in his native Portugal. For all his positive attributes, by contrast, Delors had never been elected to high national office in France. This became a liability toward the end of Delors's presidency, when concerns about the Commission's legitimacy came to the fore.

Concerned about ordinary Europeans' alienation from the Commission, the Convention on the Future of Europe considered various ways to boost the institution's legitimacy and popularity. One idea was to hold a presidential election throughout the EU every five years. Aware of the unlikelihood that such elections would generate much interest, however, most members of the Convention thought that the president should be indirectly elected—and not simply approved—by the European Parliament. But who would select the candidates for the Parliament to elect? National leaders were not about to surrender that political plumb. Nor were they willing to countenance a major change in the existing procedure for the appointment of the Commission president. Accordingly, national leaders decided in the 2003–2004 intergovernmental conference to maintain the status quo.

Performance

National leaders were not looking for a Commission president in the mold of Delors but for someone who could restore the Commission's credibility and manage the institution effectively. Without necessarily wanting to enhance the Commission's influence, they certainly wanted to rehabilitate the Commission's reputation after Prodi's lackluster performance. Avuncular, long-winded, and often incomprehensible (in any language), Prodi had failed to make the Commission's presence felt either within the EU or internationally. He had no rapport with Chirac or Schröder, still the EU's most influential national leaders. Despite having voted for him, the European People's Party (the largest group in the European Parliament) resented the fact that the Commission president was not a Christian Democrat, which complicated the relationship between Prodi and the Parliament. Prodi's apparent eagerness to return to Italian political life undermined his position in Brussels. To cap it all, Prodi was prone to gaffes and political blunders. From the point of view of Euroskeptics, he was the ideal Commission president.

Barroso was more surefooted, politically adroit, and articulate (in four of the EU's official languages). Nevertheless, a comparison between Barroso's and Delors's qualities and circumstances illustrates the limits and the potential of the Commission presidency. Delors had a profound impact on the office that he held for ten years—longer than any other Commission president (there are no term limits). He brought unique attributes and skills to the job. Delors was an experienced and able administrator, had shrewd political judgment and a firm grasp of economics, and was an inspiring speaker. Moreover, Delors had a vision to communicate: the vision of a strong EU organized on federal lines, constituting a cohesive "social space" and asserting itself internationally, especially with respect to the United States. When the Cold War came to an abrupt end, Delors's vision soared: the EU would anchor the New Europe and form the inner of a series of concentric circles radiating outward geographically, economically, and strategically. Delors believed strongly in his and the EU's destiny and collective place in history.[3]

Delors had other advantages that he exploited to the full, notably a formidable reputation as a powerful politician with a future in French national politics and close friendships with a number of key EU leaders, especially then German chancellor Helmut Kohl. The prospect of an important career in national politics distinguished Delors from other Commission presidents, with the exception, ironically, of Prodi. Apart from Franco Malfatti, a previous incumbent who had resigned from the Commission in order to contest national elections, other Commission presidents were political has-beens, which weakened their credibility when dealing with forceful leaders in the member states.

Whereas both Malfatti and Prodi returned to political life in Italy, Delors had the prospect of returning to political life in France, one of the two most important EU member states. Moreover, Delors was tipped to return either as prime minister or as a candidate for the French presidency, which he seemed to have had a good chance of winning until the Maastricht ratification crisis damaged his political prospects. The perception of Delors as a potential president of France, not merely president of the Commission, enhanced his stature immeasurably.

Building on this solid foundation, Delors contributed greatly to the Commission's and the Community's transformation in the late 1980s. Delors viewed the Commission as the indispensable "engineer of European integration"; without a revitalized Commission, the EC would remain moribund.[4] Thus, the EC's achievements at that time—the breakthrough on Iberian enlargement, negotiation of the Single European Act, agreement on the budget, success of the single market program, and the launch of economic and monetary union—owed much to Delors's personal and the Commission's political leadership.

Delors's prominence and forcefulness in the late 1980s became particularly apparent at meetings of the European Council. Roy Jenkins had won for the Commission a right to participate fully in these summits. Former Luxembourg prime minister Gaston Thorn, Commission president between Jenkins and Delors, dutifully attended European Council meetings but never made much of an impression. Nor did Thorn's compatriot, Jacques Santer. Despite having been a member of the European Council when he was prime minister of Italy in the mid-1990s, Prodi was uncomfortable in the European Council in the role of Commission president. Delors, by contrast, reveled in the limelight. Some of his and the Commission's greatest triumphs came at European Council meetings.

Similarly, Delors capitalized on his reputation as architect of the single market program and his unrivaled grasp of complex economic affairs to assert the Commission's identity on the broader international stage. Once again, Jenkins had fought hard to win the right to participate in the annual summits of the world's most industrialized countries (then the G7). It was appropriate that the Commission received its greatest international recognition at the G7 summit in July 1989, when the United States asked it to lead the Western aid effort for Hungary and Poland. The Transatlantic Declaration of November 1990, which institutionalized meetings among the U.S. president, the president of the Council, and the Commission president, was a further tribute to Delors's and the Commission's growing international stature.

Delors's achievements prove the point that a Commission president's performance depends not so much on the attributes of the office itself as on prevailing economic and political circumstances; the incumbent's personality, country of origin, and national political experience and prospects; and the caliber of the president's close advisers (Pascal Lamy, later a highly successful commissioner, was Delors's ruthless *chef de cabinet*). The experiences of Walter Hallstein and Roy Jenkins, the Commission's other strong presidents, are similarly revealing. Hallstein, a forceful individual from a large member state (although Germany was then politically meek), had considerable political experience as a senior government official but no prospect of a future career in politics. Like Delors, Hallstein served as Commission president during a period of sustained economic growth when the Commission was responsible for implementing an economic program—the customs union—supported by all the member states.

Also like Delors, Hallstein pushed hard to increase the Commission's power and promote supranationalism. But unlike Delors, Hallstein had to contend with the leader of the EC's most important country (Charles de Gaulle in France), who abhorred political integration. (Because of Britain's relative weakness within the EC, Delors's confrontation with Prime Minister Margaret Thatcher cannot fairly be compared to Hallstein's confrontation with de Gaulle.) Jenkins was the only other incumbent on a par with Hallstein and Delors, although he presided over the Commission at a time of economic recession and political gloom. Moreover, Jenkins tried too hard to appease both his Commission colleagues and the powerful partnership of French president Valéry Giscard d'Estaing and German chancellor Helmut Schmidt.

The lessons of previous Commission presidencies are clear: an assertive, self-assured leader with a sound political past, and ideally with good political prospects in a leading member state, is best suited to advance the Commission's interests and engineer deeper European integration. The existence of a compelling project, in which the Commission is a key player, greatly helps the Commission president's prospects. In the rough-and-tumble world of intra-EU bargaining, a Commission president needs to be forceful, authoritative, and direct. It is difficult for a Commission president to act decisively in the European Council and on the broader international stage without being equally decisive in the Commission itself.

Partly in acknowledgment of that fact, member states agreed in the Amsterdam Treaty of 1997 to strengthen the Commission president's political authority and to allow him or her greater discretion in allocating and reshuffling commissioners' portfolios. The Nice Treaty of 2001, negotiated in the wake of the Commission resignation scandal, went further. Under its terms, the president could demand a commissioner's resignation, subject to the Commission's approval.

Despite these procedural changes, the political reality is that national leaders were not looking for another Commission president like Delors. Though they pay lip service to the importance of a strong Commission and strong Commission leadership, national leaders do not want to be overshadowed by the Commission president. Nor do they want the Commission to be in the driver's seat of European integration. While wishing Barroso well, national leaders know that he cannot overreach himself. As the "accidental president" who emerged after a host of other candidates had been rejected, as a politician from a small country, as a president lacking a compelling project for which the Commission could provide indispensable leadership, and as the head of an unwieldy twenty-five-person executive body, Barroso has limited prospects. Compared to his immediate predecessors, he may shine, but compared to Delors during the golden years of the late 1980s, he is likely to disappoint.

▪ The Uncollegial Commission

Platitudes about the Commission's collegiality notwithstanding, in reality commissioners are far from equal in influence and authority. The way commissioners are popularly known emphasizes the point. Rather than using names, commentators frequently refer to nationality: the "Portuguese commissioner," the "Dutch commissioner," the "German commissioner," and so on. Because Germany is a far more powerful country than either Portugal or the Netherlands, the German commissioner generally has more influence than his Portuguese and Dutch counterparts. Yet hailing from a large country is not a precondition for success in the Commission; commissioners from small member states often fare well.

Commissioners' responsibilities include

- providing political direction to the Commission's directorates-general (departments) and services
- representing the Commission at meetings of the Council of Ministers
- accounting for the Commission's activities before the European Parliament
- publicizing the Commission's work
- exchanging information and ideas between the Commission and the highest levels of national government

The Commission's size, effectiveness, and collegiality are obviously related. The more commissioners there are, the more difficult it is for the Commission to be truly effective or collegial. As Table 7.2 shows, the number of commissioners has grown over the years from a cozy nine to an unwieldy twenty-five (there were thirty commissioners during an interim period in 2004, immediately after enlargement). In order to limit the size of the Commission that took office in November 2004 to twenty-five (one per member state), the big member states had to agree to give up their right to appoint two commissioners each, a right that they had exercised since the launch of the European Community in 1958.

The larger the EU, the less sustainable was the practice of having two commissioners per big member state. The accession of Austria, Finland, and Sweden in 1995 and the anticipated accession of as many as ten Central and

Table 7.2   Commissioners per Member State

Dates	Number of Member States	Number of Commissioners for Each Member State	Total Number of Commissioners
1967[a]–1972	6	France, Germany, Italy (2 each); Belgium, the Netherlands, Luxembourg (1 each)	9
1973–1980	9	France, Germany, Italy, **Britain** (2 each); Belgium, the Netherlands, Luxembourg, **Denmark, Ireland** (1 each)	13
1981–1985	10	France, Germany, Italy, Britain (2 each); Belgium, the Netherlands, Luxembourg, Denmark, Ireland, **Greece** (1 each)	14
1986–1994	12	France, Germany, Italy, Britain, **Spain** (2 each); Belgium, the Netherlands, Luxembourg, Denmark, Ireland, Greece, **Portugal** (1 each)	17
1995–2004	15	France, Germany, Italy, Britain, Spain (2 each); Belgium, the Netherlands, Luxembourg, Denmark, Ireland, Greece, Portugal, **Austria, Finland, Sweden** (1 each)	20
May–Nov. 2004	25	France, Germany, Italy, Britain, Spain (2 each); Belgium, the Netherlands, Luxembourg, Denmark, Ireland, Greece, Portugal, Austria, Finland, Sweden, **Cyprus, Czech Republic, Estonia, Hungary, Latvia, Lithuania, Malta, Poland, Slovakia, Slovenia** (1 each)	30
Nov. 2004–Nov. 2009	25	France, Germany, Italy, Britain, Spain, Belgium, the Netherlands, Luxembourg, Denmark, Ireland, Greece, Portugal, Austria, Finland, Sweden, Cyprus, Czech Republic, Estonia, Hungary, Latvia, Lithuania, Malta, Poland, Slovakia, Slovenia (1 each)	25

Notes: a. Under the terms of the Merger Treaty, which came into effect on July 1, 1967, the ECSC High Authority combined with the Commissions of the EEC and Euratom to form the Commission of the European Communities. Subsequent changes resulted from the accession of new member states (identified in bold) and from implementation of the Nice Treaty (with respect to the Commission formed in November 2004).

Eastern European countries, plus Cyprus and Malta, within the next decade finally brought the Commission's size onto the agenda of treaty reform. Member states addressed the matter for the first time in the intergovernmental conference of 1996–1997. However, the refusal of most member states to reduce the Commission's size below a number that would make it impossible for each of them in future to appoint at least one commissioner emphasized the political sensitivity of the issue. Unwilling to make a painful decision, EU leaders essentially maintained the status quo in the Amsterdam Treaty.

It was only in the Nice Treaty, concluded at a time when Central and Eastern European enlargement appeared imminent, that national leaders agreed to cut the link between the EU's size and the Commission's size once the EU enlarged to twenty-seven member states. The big member states conceded that, in the meantime, each member state would appoint only one commissioner. The Convention on the Future of Europe proposed a college of just fifteen commissioners, based on a system of equal rotation among the member states with due regard to demographic and regional balance, with the remaining member states allowed to have nonvoting commissioners. In the ensuing intergovernmental conference, however, most of the small member states, especially those just coming into the EU, fiercely defended the principle of a unitary Commission with one commissioner per member state. They were motivated by calculations of national interest and prestige and by concerns that the big member states would dominate a restricted college.

National leaders agreed in the Constitutional Treaty to keep the current composition of the Commission—one commissioner per member state—until 2014, at which time the Commission would be limited to a number of commissioners corresponding to two-thirds of the number of member states. Members of the smaller Commission would be chosen according to the principles agreed to in the Nice Treaty.

Although controversy over the Commission's size has consumed a lot of time and energy since the mid-1990s, radical reform was not necessarily in the Commission's interest. Arguably, it was more important for member states, their citizens, and the Commission to have direct, high-level channels of communication via "national" commissioners than to go through the politically painful and potentially unrewarding exercise of drastically reducing the Commission's size. As Niels Ersbøll, a former secretary-general of the Council secretariat, observed, the fact that each member state has at least one of its senior officials or politicians in the Commission "undoubtedly contributes to . . . general confidence in the Commission and the acceptance of its wide powers."[5] In other words, given that the Commission derives some legitimacy from the commissioners' connections to national governments, retaining the principle of one commissioner per member state may not have been such a bad idea, regardless of the challenge it posed for the Commission's collegiality and manageability.

Selection

Each national government nominates its commissioner, supposedly in consultation with the Commission president-elect (or Commission president, if the president's mandate is being renewed). Throughout much of the EU's history, national governments nominated commissioners without consulting anyone, and the Commission president simply accepted the national governments' nominees. Nor were nominees subject to approval by the European Parliament until the mid-1990s. As a result of treaty changes and political precedent since then, governments have lost some of their freedom to maneuver with regard to nominating commissioners.

Member states generally announce their nominee three or four months before the current Commission's term expires. Domestic political considerations, rather than ability or merit, determine a government's choice of nominee for a lucrative and prestigious commissionership. It is hardly surprising that nominees rarely come from outside the governing party or coalition of parties. Most now are career politicians whose standing at home enhances their status and, ideally, their performance in Brussels. Indeed, having held senior elected office has become an informal prerequisite for appointment to the Commission in order to enhance vicariously the Commission's democratic credentials.

The nomination of commissioners from the ten new member states in May 2004 was atypical because those nominees would serve for only six months (from the date of accession until the end of the Commission's term in office in November), although the presumption was that most would be renominated for the next Commission (November 2004–November 2009). Prodi discussed the nominations with the governments of the acceding member states and asked that, at a minimum, three of the nominees be women (only five of the twenty members of the Commission at the time were women).

There was not much consultation between national governments and Barroso on the composition of his Commission, although he too asked that at least eight of the twenty-four nominees (he was the twenty-fifth) be women, a minimum threshold that he attained. Reflecting the rising political prominence of Commission nominees despite the Commission's declining influence, the Barroso Commission-designate included three former prime ministers, five former foreign ministers, and three former finance ministers.

Commissioners may be reappointed any number of times. Hans von der Groeben, a German commissioner, served for fourteen years. It is not unusual for commissioners to serve two full terms (now ten years). Commissioners may resign from office but may not be recalled by their member states. Nor must they step down if their political patrons at home lose an election or otherwise leave office. When a commissioner resigns, the member state in question simply nominates a substitute, who usually receives the same portfolio.

Accountability

The Commission is accountable to the European Parliament. By a two-thirds majority the Parliament may sack the entire Commission, but it may not dismiss individual commissioners. Parliament has never voted the Commission out of office, but it came close to doing so over allegations of corruption and cronyism in the Santer Commission. As noted earlier, knowing that it would not survive a vote of censure following the release of a highly critical investigation by independent experts into its activities, the Commission resigned in March 1999. Nevertheless, Parliament's assertiveness on that occasion, together with withering media criticism and widespread public disapproval of the Commission's performance, taught the Commission a lesson about the importance of political accountability.

Under the terms of the Maastricht Treaty, the commissioners' term of office increased from four to five years beginning in January 1995, bringing them more closely into line with the Europarliamentarians' five-year term. Although the Santer Commission resigned in March 1999, it stayed on in a caretaker capacity until November, when the Prodi Commission took over. As a result, a Commission's term in office now starts in November of the same year in which direct elections to the Parliament take place, thus giving the newly elected Parliament a convenient five-month period (although it includes the summer holidays) to vet the new Commission-designate. Parliament's right to do so is also based on a provision of the Maastricht Treaty, which stipulated that the Commission president-designate be approved by the Parliament and the commissioners-designate "be subject as a body to a vote of approval" by the Parliament. Once approved by the Parliament, the commissioners would be appointed "by common accord of the governments of the member states."

The Parliament carried out its post-Maastricht investiture responsibilities for the first time in 1994, although it had taken nonbinding votes of confidence on all three of Delors's Commissions (1985–1989, 1989–1993, and 1993–1995). Reacting against the manner of his selection, the Parliament endorsed Santer by only a narrow majority in July 1994.[6] Then, to the dismay of the Commission and some member states, Parliament successfully interpreted the investiture procedure to require that it not only vote on the Commission-designate (as a college) but also hold hearings on each of the commissioners-designate. These took place in January 1995 for the Santer Commission, in October 1999 for the Prodi Commission, and in October–November 2004 for the Barroso Commission.

Parliament uses the investiture procedure to question the Commission president's and the commissioners' suitability for the job and to assert its right to hold the Commission accountable. In October 2004, Parliament's Social Affairs Committee narrowly voted not to approve the commissioner-designate for social affairs, a conservative Catholic with traditional views about women and gays, who happened to be Italian, thereby presenting Parliament as a whole and Commission president-designate Barroso with a quandary. Should Barroso appease Parliament by sacrificing the commissioner in question or insist that Parliament vote on his entire college, as stipulated in the treaty? When it became clear that the Parliament would vote against the Commission, Barroso withdrew his support from the embattled commissioner-designate, who withdrew from nomination. The episode delayed the investiture of Barroso's Commission and signaled Parliament's powerful oversight of Commission affairs.

Apart from the investiture proceedings, regular appearances by commissioners before plenary sessions and committees give the Parliament a regular opportunity to hold the Commission to account.

Allocation of Portfolios

The European Parliament has no authority to decide which commissioner gets what job, or portfolio. Those important decisions remain with the Commission president and the national leaders. There have always been more commissioners than substantial portfolios. As early as 1977, only four years after the EC's first enlargement, British prime minister Harold Wilson remarked on "the excessive number of Commissioners" and their "continuing search for work."[7] As former Commission president Roy Jenkins observed many years later, "the position of too many Commissioners chasing too few jobs, with which I was confronted [as Commission president] in 1977, was exacerbated by the Greek entry of 1981 and the Spanish and Portuguese entry of 1986."[8] Later rounds of enlargement expanded the Commission's size but not the number of significant portfolios, apart from some changes due to the extension of the EU's policy scope.

Agriculture and trade policy have always been weighty portfolios. Various economic portfolios became much more consequential as a result of the single market program in the late 1980s and the march toward monetary union in the 1990s. Environmental policy became a desirable portfolio when the EC acquired competence in that area under the Single European Act of 1986. Similarly, regional policy became a politically significant portfolio following the reforms of the structural funds (including a generous appropriation of money) in the late 1980s. Foreign and security policy became an area of EU interest in the early 1990s, although largely beyond the Commission's control. Nevertheless, it soon became one of the most desirable Commission portfolios, for reasons of prestige rather than power.

The growing gap between the number of commissioners and the number of worthwhile portfolios, despite the EU's increasing policy remit, forces national governments to compete fiercely for particular portfolios, regardless of the Commission president's formal responsibility for deciding who does what.

The scramble for portfolios at the beginning of each new Commission suggests that commissioners are not "completely independent in the performance of their duties," as the treaty claims that they should be and as commissioners swear that they will be. Yet there is a big difference between recognizing and upholding a national interest and taking instructions from a national government. The Commission functions best when commissioners thrash out proposals from their own ideological, political, and national perspectives as well as on the abstract basis of what is best for the EU. It is not to the EU's discredit or disadvantage that commissioners "are national champions who defend their national positions in the Commission."[9]

Barroso caused a stir in August 2004 when he allocated portfolios seemingly without regard to national preferences (see Table 7.3). His move was all the more surprising because of the presumption that, having won the grudging approval of the French and German leaders, Barroso would award important portfolios to the French and German nominees. Schröder, in particular, had pressed for the creation of a superportfolio for economic modernization, to be given to Günter Verheugen, his nominee to the Barroso Commission and a holdover from the Prodi Commission. Instead, in a striking declaration of independence, Barroso did not combine the economic portfolios and allocated them to other nominees, mostly from small member states, with track records as reformers. He relegated the French and German nominees to lesser (but not insignificant) portfolios, while taking the political precaution of appointing them Commission vice presidents. Barroso's quick and surprising allocation of portfolios, undertaken when most national leaders were on their summer holidays, helped to establish his authority among the new commissioners and with the member states.

Organization of the College

Commissioners often use their cabinets (groups of private advisers) to absorb excessive national pressure and conduct domestic public relations campaigns. The cabinet system reflects a strong French influence on the EU's administrative apparatus. Over the years, cabinets have grown larger and more powerful. Most commissioners have a seven-member cabinet that includes career Eurocrats and appointees who came to Brussels with the commissioner. A good cabinet can boost the standing of an otherwise poor commissioner, and a poor cabinet can pull down an otherwise good commissioner. It is no coincidence that the most effective commissioners have the best-staffed and best-organized cabinets.

For much of its history the Commission had six vice presidents, positions that the big member states usually managed to grab, though at least one usually went to a small member state. That changed with the Maastricht Treaty, which authorized the Commission to have only one or two vice presidents.

Table 7.3   The Barroso Commission

Commissioner	Country of Origin	Portfolio
José Manuel Barroso	Portugal	President
Margot Wallström	Sweden	Institutional Relations and Communication Strategy (Vice President)
Günter Verheugen	Germany	Enterprise and Industry (Vice President)
Jacques Barrot	France	Transport (Vice President)
Siim Kallsa	Estonia	Administrative Affairs, Audit and Anti-Fraud (Vice President)
Franco Frattini	Italy	Justice, Freedom and Security (Vice President)
Viviane Reding	Luxembourg	Information Society and Media
Stavros Dimas	Greece	Environment
Joaquín Almunia	Spain	Economic and Monetary Affairs
Danuta Hübner	Poland	Regional Policy
Joe Borg	Malta	Fisheries and Maritime Affairs
Dalia Grybauskaité	Lithuania	Financial Programming and Budget
Janez Potočnik	Slovenia	Science and Research
Ján Figel'	Slovakia	Education, Training, Culture and Multilingualism
Markos Kyprianou	Cyprus	Health and Consumers Protection
Olli Rehn	Finland	Enlargement
Louis Michel	Belgium	Development and Humanitarian Aid
László Kovács	Hungary	Taxation and Customs Union
Neelie Kroes	The Netherlands	Competition
Mariann Fischer Boel	Denmark	Agriculture and Rural Development
Benita Ferrero-Waldner	Austria	External Relations and European Neighborhood Policy
Charlie McCreevy	Ireland	Internal Market and Services
Vladimír Špidla	Czech Republic	Employment, Social Affairs and Equal Opportunities
Peter Mandelson	Britain	Trade
Andris Piebalgs	Latvia	Energy

The Nice Treaty, in turn, authorized an increase in the number of vice presidents, in keeping with the anticipated increase in the Commission's size following the 2004 enlargement. There are five vice presidents in the Barroso Commission, the senior of whom accompanies the president to meetings of the European Council and sometimes stands in for him on other occasions.

Commissioners meet every Wednesday in Brussels, or in Strasbourg if the Parliament is in plenary session there, to discuss and resolve various initiatives, including legislative proposals. Usually the president gets his way, although Commission meetings sometimes become bruising battles that the president does not always win. The most notable struggles have been over competition policy, trade, and agriculture. Under the Commission's rules of procedure a simple majority vote may finally decide an issue, although commissioners rarely vote. The increasing uncollegiality of the Commission does not always work to the president's advantage. Just as a strong president has a lot of discretionary power, a strong commissioner may also act independently. Commissioners occasionally make speeches or release statements that are intended to annoy the president or score domestic political points rather than elucidate Commission policy.

▓ The Unloved Civil Service

The Commission's civil service is surprisingly small. Despite the picture that Euroskeptics paint of a vast bureaucracy extending its reach throughout the EU, the Commission has a staff of fewer than 25,000, including more than 3,000 personnel of the Joint Research Center and several thousand interpreters and translators (the EU works in twenty official languages). Altogether, the Commission comprises about thirty-five directorates-general and services, corresponding roughly to its activities, responsibilities, and organizational needs (Box 7.1).[10]

Neither the number nor the responsibilities of the directorates-general and services correspond to the number or the portfolios of the commissioners. Thus, a commissioner may have more than one directorate-general in his/her portfolio, and the responsibilities of a directorate-general may be spread over the portfolios of more than one commissioner. Conversely, a commissioner may not have a directorate-general at all.

The Commission's secretariat-general is first and foremost the commissioners' own secretariat. For that reason, the secretary-general is one of a handful of noncommissioners allowed to participate in the Commission's formal meetings (apart from a *chef de cabinet* standing in for a commissioner). The secretary-general also presides over the regular Monday-morning meeting of *chefs de cabinet* and the regular Thursday-morning meeting of directors-general and attends European Councils with the Commission president.

Box 7.1   Commission Directorates-General and Services

Policies	*External Relations*
Agriculture	Development
Competition	Enlargement
Economic and Financial Affairs	EuropeAid–Co-operation Office
Education and Culture	External Relations
Employment and Social Affairs	Humanitarian Aid Office–ECHO
Energy and Transport	Trade
Enterprise	
Environment	*General Services*
Fisheries	European Anti-Fraud Office
Health and Consumer Protection	Eurostat
Information Society	Press and Communication
Internal Market	Publications Office
Joint Research Centre	Secretariat General
Justice and Home Affairs	
Regional Policy	*Internal Services*
Research	Budget
Taxation and Customs Union	Group of Policy Advisers
	Informatics
	Infrastructure and Logistics
	Internal Audit Service
	Interpretation
	Legal Service
	Personnel and Administration
	Translation

Physically, the Commission is quite spread out. A majority of its officials work in Brussels, but some are based in Luxembourg, and the staff of the Joint Research Center work in a number of institutes throughout the EU. In Brussels itself, the Commission is dispersed in more than sixty buildings rented from or through the Belgian government. During the more than decade-long renovation of the Berlaymont, the Commission president, his cabinet, and the secretariat-general moved to the Breydel building, a short walk from the larger and more imposing Council and Parliament buildings. In order to symbolize decentralization and connect the commissioners directly with their directorates-general, Prodi threw the other commissioners and their cabinets out of the Breydel and lodged them in the buildings of the key directorates-general. The inconvenience of having the commissioners spread all over Brussels may have outweighed its presumed public relations and internal organizational advantages, however. In any case, Barroso moved the commissioners and their cabinets back into the Berlaymont when it reopened at the end of 2004.

Recruitment and Promotion

The Commission recruits civil servants for its administrative grades through a highly competitive, EU-wide selection process (the *concours*) for university graduates. The small number of successful candidates who pass the aptitude tests, written examinations, interviews, and language proficiency tests begin work mostly at the lower end of the administrative cadre of Commission staff. Some may already have gained experience in the Commission as *stagiaires* (paid student interns). Based on previous experience or personal predilection, a new recruit may ask to work in a particular directorate-general or service but is unlikely to get the assignment of his or her choice.

From the beginning of their careers, Commission civil servants enter a world of unstated but finely balanced national quotas, or what the Commission euphemistically calls "respect for geographical balances." Because the Eurocracy needs to reflect the population distribution and size of the EU's member states, the intake of new recruits and their promotion through the ranks are subject to an unofficial allocation of positions among each member state's nationals at each rung of the ladder. Enlargement requires these quotas to be recalculated, as nationals of new member states need to be accommodated at all levels of the correspondingly expanded civil service.

Women are poorly represented in the Commission's administrative grades, especially at the senior levels. As a result, the Commission introduced a policy in the mid-1990s of discriminating in favor of women, although with different targets for two groups of member states. For the fiercely egalitarian Nordic member states (Denmark, Finland, and Sweden), the Commission aimed to achieve parity among men and women at the top levels. For the other member states, the Commission set a less ambitious but more challenging goal of 25 percent women in the top positions. Progress has been slow. As the commissioner responsible for human resources commented in 1998, "The initial [gender] gap was so great that a few good years are not sufficient to redress the imbalance inherited from the past."[11]

It is difficult to say precisely what motivates people to join the Commission. Money is probably the deciding factor. Commission civil servants are extremely well paid and enjoy many fringe benefits unavailable to their national counterparts. That probably explains why over 30,000 people routinely compete for a few hundred positions in the Brussels bureaucracy. Idealism may also play a part, although rampant cynicism in parts of the Commission would soon cause even the most idealistic new arrivals to rethink their commitment to European integration. A desire to live and work abroad may prompt some candidates (excluding Belgians) to take the *concours,* although Brussels is by no means Europe's most appealing city. High regard for public service could also point toward a Commission career. Yet there are greater opportunities for advancement and for assorted assignments in national bureaucracies, and some countries with strong bureaucratic traditions, such as Britain and France, encourage their brightest people to eschew the Commission in favor of the national civil service.

Promotion through the junior and midcareer grades is generally predictable and uncontroversial and is based largely on seniority. However, entry into the senior grades is highly politicized and extremely difficult. Not only is there a smaller number of jobs available than at lower levels, but national civil servants and others who "parachute" into the senior ranks of the Commission—for instance, as part of a commissioner's cabinet—reduce the availability of senior jobs for career Eurocrats. Despite a Court ruling as long ago as March 1993 that the Commission was breaking EU rules by using national quotas rather than merit to recruit high-ranking officials, an unofficial quota system still applies at the higher levels. Thus, promotion to the highest grades tends to be granted as part of a package involving a number of people that is negotiated by the commissioners, their *chefs de cabinet,* and the heads of the directorates-general, with barely concealed interference from the member states.

The difficulty of progressing engenders a lot of frustration and resentment at the midcareer level of the Commission. The politicized nature of promotion and an obsession with national quotas at the senior level mean that competence and merit become less relevant at the top. In an infamous address to the Commission's directors-general in March 1991, Delors reportedly warned that some were doing a bad job, that he knew who they were, and that he would, if he could, fire them.[12] But the president's inability to get rid of poor performers and the stranglehold that national governments have on certain senior positions expose some of the Commission's serious administrative weaknesses. The Spierenburg Report on Commission reform pointed those problems out as early as 1979, but most of its recommendations were never implemented.

Although the Commission is generally portrayed as a unitary actor, inevitably its officials have varying outlooks, ideological orientations, and policy preferences. Based on numerous interviews and questionnaires, one scholar described senior Commission officials as constituting "a special microcosm of the European public space: less nationalist than most citizens, but divided on the mix of intergovernmental and supranational architectural principles; center-left of the average political actor, but disagreeing on the desirable mix of market and state, opportunity and equity."[13] Orientations and preferences vary from directorate-general (DG) to directorate-general. For example, DG Competition inevitably attracts officials with a commitment to, or at least a predisposition toward, neoliberal principles, whereas the ethos and culture of DG Regional Policy are less enamored of the free market and more inclined toward state intervention.

Reform

The preoccupation with national prerogatives that stymies promotion also reduces mobility in the Commission. Over the years, commissioners and directors-general have understandably stuck to existing staff levels even as the Commission's priorities have shifted dramatically. Thus, the Commission itself is far from overstaffed, but certain parts of it have become bloated while others, notably the external relations directorates-general and DG Competition, have remained seriously understaffed. Nor are all member states likely to sanction a sizable increase in the civil service, especially at a time of budgetary cutbacks and public hostility toward European institutions.

Delors's success as president in the late 1980s raised the Commission's morale, yet by the end of the decade Eurocrats identified Delors himself as part of the Commission's problem. Delors's disregard for fellow commissioners, disdain for many directors-general, and aggrandizement of power in his cabinet fueled so much resentment and backbiting that, according to a retired high-level official, "internally the Commission [had] come to resemble Tammany Hall with a French accent."[14] With the unexpected rise in the Commission's responsibilities in the early 1990s and no commensurate increase in its size or efficiency, many officials feared that the institution would soon self-destruct. During the Maastricht ratification crisis, when the Commission unfairly came under widespread attack, the institution's morale reached rock bottom.

The Commission's structural and managerial problems were rooted in the member states' determination to retain as much control as possible over the Commission and were compounded by successive enlargements, the proliferation of portfolios, and the excessive power of the cabinets. Staff policy was underused as an instrument of internal reform, new management techniques were rarely introduced, and a decentralization initiative launched in the early 1990s had only mixed results. Delors made a belated effort to streamline the Commission, but his management style made matters worse. As a result, Jacques Santer, Delors's successor, put internal reform at the top of his presidential agenda.

Working with the commissioners from Finland and Sweden, who because of their countries' reputations for integrity in public life were presumed to be best suited to putting the Commission's house in order, Santer launched a three-pronged reform effort. The first, "Sound and Efficient Management," aimed to improve financial affairs by separating operational and financial management structures within the directorates-general. By the late 1990s the program had increased but not necessarily improved financial control in the Commission, often at a cost of additional bureaucratization and delays in payments to contractors. The second prong was "Modernizing the Administration and Personnel Policy," an attempt to improve administrative practices and personnel policy by means of decentralization, rationalization, and simplification. Easier said than done, its implementation was uneven and aroused the hostility of Commission officials and their unions, resentful of what they saw as yet another top-down management initiative with little serious input from the staff itself. The third prong, an ambitious initiative called "The Commission of Tomorrow," dealt with more politically sensitive issues such as strengthening the Commission presidency, consolidating and reducing the number of portfolios, curbing the power of the cabinets, and basing promotion into the Commission's senior ranks on merit rather than country of origin.

Ironically for a president genuinely interested in internal reform, Santer will forever be remembered for corruption and maladministration. Despite the reform effort that he launched, Santer became mired in allegations of financial irregularities in the Commission that gathered momentum in the late 1990s. Santer himself was never accused of financial impropriety, but he failed to act decisively against the commissioners who were. The most conspicuous case, although it involved a relatively small amount of money, concerned Edith Cresson, a commissioner and former prime minister of France who allegedly awarded a contract to a friend who was unqualified to carry out the work. Smelling blood, the European Parliament made a meal of the issue and demanded Cresson's resignation. Santer lacked the will or ability to dismiss Cresson, especially as the French government backed her to the end.

The Commission escaped censure and removal from office in January 1999 when the European Parliament failed to muster the necessary two-thirds majority to throw the rascals out. Parliament decided instead, with the Commission's agreement, to establish a committee of independent experts to investigate the allegations. The committee's report, published in March 1999, was damning. One widely reported sentence could not have been more injurious: "It is becoming difficult to find anyone [in the Commission] who has even the slightest sense of responsibility."[15] Once the Parliament made it clear that a Commission that still included Cresson would not survive another censure motion, the Commission accepted the consequences of its supposed collegiality and resigned as a body.

Romano Prodi, Santer's successor, redoubled the reform effort and took steps immediately to show the seriousness of the situation. For example, he strengthened the recently approved codes of conduct for commissioners and senior officials, launched a major shake-up of the directorates-general, and radically reorganized the commissioners' portfolios. One seemingly unimportant but highly symbolic change was that instead of being known by number, as had been the case throughout the EU's history, directorates-general henceforth became known by function (thus "DG VI" became "DG Agriculture"). Although difficult for old EU hands to relearn, the new nomenclature helped to demystify the Commission.

The Prodi reformation was fundamental and far-reaching.[16] Prodi chose Neil Kinnock, ironically a holdover from the disgraced Santer Commission, to head a new reform portfolio. Kinnock, a loquacious former leader of the British Labour Party, threw himself enthusiastically into a difficult and thankless task. Following consultations with Europarliamentarians, other commissioners and commission officials, and representatives of national governments, Kinnock released a White Paper on administrative reform in March 2000, on the basis of which the Commission adopted a detailed "road map" six months later.[17] In subsequent years, using the road map, the Commission introduced a number of changes, including new methods of auditing and financial control; a system of activity-based management (intended to match responsibilities and resources); and new recruitment, promotion, and disciplinary procedures. In general, the Prodi reformation drew heavily on British and Scandinavian models of public administration, in contrast to the French model on which the Commission had largely been built.

In a related development, Prodi issued a White Paper on governance in July 2001, following more than a year of consultations with politicians, officials, and representatives of civil society.[18] Whereas the White Paper on administrative reform attempted to shake up the Commission, the White Paper on governance sought to reassert the Commission's centrality in the EU system. It was therefore somewhat defensive in tone, while also advocating new policy instruments and modes of governance that were not necessarily in the Commission's best interest, such as coregulation, the open method of coordination, and the role of executive agencies. By the time the White Paper appeared, the "post-Nice" debate on the future of the EU, which preceded the conclusion of the Nice Treaty, had already begun. The White Paper was therefore swamped by the contributions of German foreign minister Joschka Fischer and other leading national politicians. Ultimately, the White Paper was too wordy and insubstantial to have an impact on the post-Nice debate.

Regardless of the broader governance debate, Prodi's efforts to reform the Commission were urgent and important. But they were not successful. Although they moved the Commission in the right direction, the Prodi reforms faced several entrenched obstacles. One was the inertia and even outright opposition of some parts of the bureaucracy itself. Prodi and Kinnock dared to question EU officials' generous pay and pensions and to link remuneration to performance. That stirred up a hornets' nest and provoked a number of work stoppages and strikes. Another, more serious consideration was the member states' reluctance to give up their stranglehold on key aspects of the Commission's structure and staff policy. Despite rhetorical flourishes to the contrary, member states jealously guarded what they saw as their right to influence the appointment of senior officials, a not-so-subtle way of pushing national interests in the EU.

As a singular institution in a singular polity, the Commission clearly faced major trials and tribulations in the mid-2000s. The challenge for Barroso, as for Prodi and Santer before him, is to enhance the Commission's efficiency to the maximum extent possible within the limits set by the institution's multinational, multicultural, and multilingual character, and by the nature of the EU system in which the Commission is embedded. Because he faces public disgruntlement and an unsympathetic Parliament, this is a pressing but problematic task.

▓ The Commission's Roles and Responsibilities

Informally, the Commission is called the "motor" of European integration, not only because of its almost exclusive right to initiate legislation in most policy areas but also because of its history, composition, culture, and European rather than national outlook.[19] Indeed, according to the Constitutional Treaty, the Commission is obliged to promote "the general European interest" (Article I-25.1). In addition, the Commission upholds EU law and traditionally defends the interests of small member states. As stipulated in the treaties and developed over time, the Commission's primary responsibilities include

- proposing and shaping legislation
- initiating and managing the budget
- executing and implementing policy
- policing EU law
- conducting external relations
- contributing to enlargement and treaty reform
- monitoring and reporting on major EU developments
- pointing the way forward

In an effort to improve the interinstitutional policymaking process, since 2002 the Commission has set out its main priorities in a report called the "Annual Policy Strategy," which it releases early each year (usually in February). Later in the year (usually in October), the Commission adopts a legislative and work program (known as the "Work Program") for the following calendar year, highlighting the practical steps necessary to achieve those priorities. The Annual Policy Strategy and follow-up Work Program are useful guides to the Commission's activities and objectives.

Legislative Role

It is an old axiom that "the Commission proposes [legislation] and the Council disposes," but this view omits the European Parliament's role as codecisionmaker with the Council. The treaty authorizes the Commission to flesh out the treaty's skeletal framework by formulating recommendations, delivering opinions, and proposing legislation. Most of the Commission's legislative proposals have a clear legal base in the founding treaties that established the European Community and the European Union, or in amendments to the treaties. Others flow from legislation already adopted under the treaties or from judgments of the Court. Member states sometimes dispute the legal base of a Commission proposal either because of a genuine difference of interpretation or for political reasons: they may not want the EU to involve itself in certain matters or may not want a legal base that involves qualified majority voting in the Council.

The volume of Commission proposals diminished in the aftermath of the single market program's heavy legislative schedule and in the post-Maastricht climate of suspicion toward the EU's institutions and legislative agenda. Capitalizing on prevailing anti-EU sentiment, some national governments invoke subsidiarity (the principle that decisions should be taken at the lowest level practicable) in order to prevent the enactment of legislation at the European level and the implementation of EU legislation at the national level. By the same token, the Commission often invokes subsidiarity to dispel the popular perception that it has an insatiable appetite for new legislation.

Reacting to the popular and political mood, Santer vowed that during his presidency the EU would legislate less and legislate better. In other words, the Commission would produce fewer legislative proposals, and the proposals that it did produce would be of a higher quality. Put on the defensive by carping member states, the Commission responded at the Cardiff summit in June 1998 with a document titled "Legislate Less to Act Better: The Facts." Prodi went a step further, promising to cut back drastically the 14,000 or so legal acts that make up the *acquis communautaire*. The Commission launched a plan to that effect in February 2003, proposing to reduce the volume of EU law by one-third before the end of 2005. That was easier said than done. As the Commission admitted in a progress report in October 2003, it is difficult to agree on which laws should be repealed, simplified, and consolidated, and almost impossible to find the resources necessary to implement the plan.

As part of a "better regulation" initiative, in June 2002 the Commission established a new, integrated procedure to assess the likely impact of major proposals and improve the quality and coherence of the policymaking process. The Commission now uses the procedure to analyze the possible economic, social, and environmental impact of major proposals in the context of sustainable development (an overarching EU objective), and also with regard to subsidiarity and proportionality.

Apart from the Commission's own efforts to reduce the quantity of EU legislation, the member states' preference for soft law rather than hard regulation in pursuit of the so-called Lisbon strategy for economic modernization and reform has also diminished the Commission's traditional legislative role. By endorsing the open method of coordination in a range of policy areas intended to make the EU the most dynamic and successful regional economy by 2010, the European Council explicitly relegated the Commission to a lesser role. Despite poor progress in implementing the Lisbon strategy, member states have shown little inclination to revert to the traditional Community method of legislative decisionmaking to achieve the Lisbon goals.

Regardless of the legal and political limits that subsidiarity and the open method of coordination impose, the Commission jealously guards its right to propose legislation where legislation is warranted, based on the principle that the Commission alone can best articulate and defend the EU's collective interest. Since the introduction of direct elections in 1979, the increasingly assertive European Parliament has occasionally attempted to win for itself a similar right of initiative. Although the Commission has successfully resisted these efforts, Parliament and the Council may request that the Commission submit a proposal. So too, according to the Constitutional Treaty, may EU citizens invite the Commission to initiate legislation, as long as they muster at least 1 million signatures. The Commission has a shared right of initiative in the Common Foreign and Security Policy, which is more of an intergovernmental than a supranational undertaking and has gradually extended its right of initiative, either exclusive or shared, in the area of justice and home affairs, also traditionally an intergovernmental sphere.

Apart from a request from the Council or Parliament for the Commission to initiate legislation, proposals may originate in a number of ways. A zealous Commission president, commissioner, director-general, or section director might ask his/her subordinates to prepare legislation, or an ambitious and energetic midlevel Commission official could send his/her superiors suggestions for draft proposals. Similarly, a proposal could come as a result of a widely perceived need to develop EU policy in a certain area, or in response to the suggestion of a member state or an interest group.

However they originate, proposals must work their way through the Commission bureaucracy. A network of internal and external committees assists the Commission's work. Internal committees are mostly ad hoc and are convened to ensure coordination among various parts of the Commission if a proposal cuts across departmental boundaries. The secretariat-general plays a key coordinating role, as do the commissioners' cabinets. Of course, there is frequent informal coordination among commissioners, members of their cabinets, and other senior Commission officials, which may take place casually in a corridor, at lunch, or over coffee.

External committees, most of which are chaired and serviced by the Commission, are of two kinds: expert committees and consultative committees. Expert committees consist of specialists from inside and outside the government, who are appointed by the member states. These committees are especially important not only because they provide useful technical advice but also because some of the national civil servants who sit on them may also sit in the working groups that will evaluate the proposal when the Commission formally submits it to the Council. The consultative committees are larger and more diverse and consist entirely of Commission nominees drawn mostly from interest groups and professional associations. Consultative committees are also valued for their technical advice and help the Commission keep in tune with the real world of business and commerce.

In an effort to improve transparency and shore up public trust, the Commission has attempted to disseminate information about impending proposals as widely as possible and to solicit the views of all interested parties. To that end, the Commission publishes a large number of Green Papers, which outline the Commission's ideas about possible legislative proposals. Green Papers trigger responses from interest groups, nongovernmental organizations, and even the general public. They often form the basis for White Papers, which generally contain a legislative agenda.

The consultation and proposal-drafting stage is an opportune time for interested parties to try to modify the shape and content of the contemplated legislation. The Commission is a relatively open organization; its officials are easily contacted and are generally susceptible to outside influence. This is also the stage when small member states, whose power in the Council is relatively limited, make a sustained lobbying effort—outside the formal committee structure—often including contacts between government ministers and "national" commissioners.

Ideally, the college of the Commission would discuss and approve proposals before formally submitting them to the Council and the Parliament. But the pressure of other business makes that impossible. To expedite the process and cut down on the commissioners' workloads, draft proposals that seem uncomplicated and uncontroversial are circulated among the commissioners and, if not objected to within one week, are adopted by default. Alternatively, a subgroup of commissioners may agree to deal with routine proposals on behalf of their colleagues. Either way, the commissioners' cabinets play a decisive role.

The advisory committees' input, as well as the political astuteness of most of the commissioners and their cabinets, usually ensures that the Commission does not submit a proposal that the Council would be likely to reject outright. The Commission is reluctant to alienate the Council and risk paralyzing the legislative process. But the Commission is not servile or afraid to introduce controversial proposals. While not wanting to isolate or embarrass member states, the Commission appreciates that, inevitably, certain member states are likely to oppose certain proposals. Overall, the Commission has to weigh prevailing political realities against essential treaty obligations.

The Commission's role in shaping legislation as a proposal works its way through the decisionmaking process is discussed in Chapter 11.

Budgetary Role

The Commission starts the ball rolling for the annual (general) budget and the multiyear financial perspective—the framework within which the annual budget is decided. Member states concluded the first financial perspective (known as the Delors I package) in 1988 and the second (known as the Delors II package) in 1992. The negotiation of financial perspectives has become a major political event in the life of the EU. Although it is essentially an inter-governmental process, the fact that the first two perspectives unofficially bore the Commission president's name attests to the centrality of the Commission's role in it and to Delors's extraordinary influence. The third perspective, concluded at an acrimonious summit in Berlin in March 1999, was known not as the Santer package but as Agenda 2000 (reflecting Santer's low standing as well as a tendency at the time to name everything after the millennium).

Submitting Proposals. In February 2004, under difficult political circumstances, Prodi unveiled the Commission's proposals for the 2007–2013 financial perspective. The EU's six net contributors (the countries that pay more into the EU's budget than they get out of it) had just served notice that they wanted EU expenditure restricted to 1.0 percent of the member states' combined gross national income instead of the current ceiling of 1.24 percent. Apart from wanting to reduce their financial transfers to Brussels at a time of domestic belt-tightening, two of the net contributors—France and Germany—were signaling their displeasure with Poland and Spain, the countries earmarked for the lion's share of EU expenditure on regional policy, for refusing to accept the provisions of the draft Constitutional Treaty on a new voting system in the Council. Ignoring the net contributors' complaints, Prodi proposed increasing the budget to as much as 1.27 percent of gross national income. Although partly a negotiating ploy, Prodi's proposals—and Barroso's subsequent calls for higher expenditure—reflect the Commission's traditional extravagance and understandable preference for a bigger EU budget.

With much less fanfare, early each year the Commission submits a preliminary draft budget to the two arms of the EU's budgetary authority, the Council and the Parliament, which usually reach agreement by December.

Overseeing Expenditure. The Commission has some obligations on the revenue side—namely, overseeing the collection of the EU's own resources and member states' contributions—but its responsibilities lie primarily on the expenditure side. These include administering appropriations for:

- the Guarantee Section of the European Agricultural Guidance and Guarantee Fund (the main mechanism for financing agricultural policy), which still accounts for approximately 45 percent of total expenditure

- structural funds—made up of the European Social Fund, the Guidance Section of the European Agricultural Guidance and Guarantee Fund, and the European Regional Development Fund—which account for approximately 35 percent of total expenditure
- the EU's external relations, including development and humanitarian assistance

As mentioned earlier, the Commission has a poor record of financial management and a reputation for profligacy. Given that payments for EU policies and programs are made by national authorities on the EU's behalf, most fraud takes place at the national level. Nevertheless, a number of Commission officials have been implicated. Frequent censure of the Commission by the Court of Auditors, the EU's accounting watchdog, fuels unfavorable media coverage and persistent parliamentary questions. It was a Court of Auditors' report, for instance, that triggered the events in late 1998 and early 1999 that led to the Commission's resignation.

In order to fight fraud involving EU funds, the EU's institutions established the European Anti-Fraud Office (known by its French acronym, OLAF) in 1999. Although located in the Commission, OLAF has independent investigative authority.

Executive Responsibilities

The Commission is often described as the EU's executive body, yet it has only limited executive power. The Commission conspicuously lacks the ability to implement EU policy "on the ground." There is no EU customs service, immigration service, veterinary service, or most of the myriad other services that would be necessary to give real effect to EU legislation. Instead, the Commission depends heavily on the member states' civil services. Without assistance from the member states' agriculture departments, for instance, the Commission could not possibly make the Common Agricultural Policy work. At the level where EU legislation should matter most—on farms, in factories, at airports and docks—the Commission depends almost entirely on national officials. Yet national officials can be notoriously recalcitrant when it comes to implementing EU legislation, either because they do not want to lose their jobs (as in the case of customs services), because they resent interference from Brussels, or because they genuinely misunderstand the latest Commission regulation.

The Commission's executive powers therefore refer not to ground-level implementation but to the enactment of innumerable rules and regulations necessary to give EU legislation (as decided by the Council and the Parliament) practical effect. Thus, the Commission issues several thousand directives, regulations, and decisions annually (although these are qualitatively different from Council acts bearing the same name), dealing mostly with highly technical aspects of common policies. The increasing encroachment of Commission regulations, directives, and decisions into everyday life in the EU is a major reason for growing public hostility toward the Brussels bureaucracy. The Commission is too easily caricatured and reviled for its real or supposed rules on such arcane issues as the length of a British sausage, the local environmental impact of a public works project, or the size and shape of potted plants. As the *Economist* uncharitably remarked, for the Commission "to disavow its regulatory lusts would be a prodigious act of self-denial."[20] Despite its apparent addiction to overregulation, the Commission lacks a free hand in implementing EU policy thanks to the arcane "comitology" procedure, which is explained in Chapter 11.

The Commission alone is responsible for implementing EU competition policy, which includes measures to curb excessive state subsidies and abuse by companies of a dominant position in the marketplace. Because a vigorous competition policy is essential for the proper functioning of a single market, the Commission fought tenaciously after the launch of the single market program to win sole authority to approve or block large mergers and acquisitions that could distort the marketplace. The Commission has a large merger task force, whose relatively expeditious handling of many complicated and sensitive cases has generally won the respect of European companies and national competition watchdogs, although some member states have expressed annoyance with the task force's methods and recommendations. Despite political pressure from national governments in particular cases, the Commission (as a college) invariably supports the task force. Some member states have threatened to try to take merger control at the EU level away from the Commission and give it instead to an independent agency but have not yet succeeded in doing so. (Competition policy is discussed in detail in Chapter 13.)

The Commission helps to administer EU policy in a number of other ways. For example, the Commission is an important player in the treaty-mandated "multilateral surveillance" of member states' economic and budgetary policies. In particular, the Commission encourages member states to maintain fiscal discipline and undertake economic reforms to ensure the success of Economic and Monetary Union and implementation of the Lisbon strategy. Each year, the Commission assesses the member states' stability or convergence programs (eurozone members have stability programs; the others have convergence programs), including recommendations for improvement. More generally, the Commission drafts the Broad Economic Policy Guidelines, a key document for economic policy coordination in the EU. First issued in May 1998, shortly after the decision to launch the final stage of economic and monetary union, the Broad Economic Policy Guidelines consist of both general and country-specific recommendations and now cover a three-year period. The Commission follows up with an annual implementation report to see how well member states are following the guidelines.

Policing Community Law

The Commission is sometimes grandiloquently called the "guardian" of the treaties. This means that the Commission may bring a member state before the Court of Justice for alleged nonfulfillment of treaty obligations. Member states generally respect the treaties; otherwise the EU would cease to function. Most member state violations result from genuine misunderstandings or misinterpretations or from delays in transposing Community legislation into national law. Deliberate noncompliance nonetheless exists, notably in the area of competition policy and the internal market. For political and public relations reasons, member states and the Commission are reluctant to pursue cases all the way to the Court, and most disputes are resolved at an early stage.

The Commission may become aware of a possible infringement for any number of reasons. An individual, an enterprise, or another member state may complain, or an investigation by Commission officials could uncover possible violations. If the Commission decides to take action, it first sends a "letter of formal notice" asking the member state concerned to explain the alleged breach. The member state has about two months to reply. If it fails to reply or does not provide a satisfactory explanation, the Commission issues a "reasoned opinion" outlining why it considers the member state to be in violation of the treaty. Again, the Commission usually gives the member state two months to comply. Most cases end with a letter of formal notice or a reasoned opinion. The Commission generates approximately 1,000 letters of formal notice annually.

Compliance with Community law is a sensitive political issue both for member states and for the Commission. Member states resent being taken to court, and the Commission is reluctant to risk antagonizing them. Although the Commission realizes that noncompliance by one member state is unfair to the others and that the EU's credibility may be at stake, examples of political deals between the Commission and the member states abound. As a rule, the Commission acts slowly and deliberately in dealing with infringement.

External Relations Responsibilities

The Commission is an international actor whose stature has increased dramatically since the early 1990s, following the end of the Cold War, when it took responsibility for coordinating the Western assistance effort to the newly independent countries of Central and Eastern Europe. Despite being an area primarily of intergovernmental activity, the Common Foreign and Security Policy, launched by the Maastricht Treaty and revised in the Amsterdam Treaty, added a new dimension to the Commission's international involvement. Also in the 1990s, the Transatlantic Declaration and the New Transatlantic Agenda strengthened the Commission's role in U.S.-EU relations, while the conclusion of the Uruguay Round of the General Agreement on Tariffs and

Trade and the launch of the World Trade Organization highlighted the Commission's importance as an international trade negotiator. Moreover, the Commission conducts the EU's development policy, including the Cotonou (formerly Lomé) agreement for assistance to over seventy African, Caribbean, and Pacific countries. Most other countries and international organizations have diplomatic relations with the EU, and the Commission maintains more than 150 delegations and offices throughout the world.

Despite—or perhaps because of—its burgeoning responsibilities in the area of external affairs, the Commission has had great difficulty adequately organizing its international relations portfolios and directorates-general. In 1993, anticipating the launch of the Common Foreign and Security Policy, Delors established a new directorate-general for external political relations, thereby restricting the long-standing external relations directorate-general to economic affairs, apart from development policy, which remained a separate directorate-general. Two years later Santer reorganized external relations along geographical lines and established yet another directorate-general to help manage the Commission's external relations responsibilities. The regular reorganization of external relations portfolios and directorates-general did not enhance the Commission's international image or effectiveness and fueled internal turf wars among jealous commissioners and directors-general.

Prodi restored some sanity to the situation when he established a single, overarching portfolio for external relations and a separate portfolio for enlargement, while keeping the long-standing portfolio for development. The European Community Humanitarian Office, established in 1992 to provide urgent international humanitarian assistance, is a separate Commission service, as is the EuropeAid Co-operation Office, established in 2001 to coordinate the management of EU external assistance funded by the EU budget and the European Development Fund, to which member states contribute directly.

The rationalization of external relations responsibilities within the Commission reduced the turf wars among commissioners and senior officials, although the establishment in 1999 of the office of high representative for the Common Foreign and Security Policy within the Council of Ministers institutionalized some friction between the Commission's external relations directorate-general and the high representative's office. Fortunately for the EU, Javier Solana, the high representative, and Chris Patten, the commissioner in charge of external relations, had a good working relationship, as do Solana and Benita Ferrero-Waldner, Patten's successor. The office of EU foreign minister, provided for in the Constitutional Treaty, would combine the positions of high representative and commissioner for external relations, thereby streamlining the process of EU foreign policy formulation and implementation. Despite being a combined Council-Commission position, an EU foreign minister would shift the balance of EU external policymaking and representation away from the Commission and toward the Council, which is determined to keep a firm grip on EU foreign relations.

Nevertheless, the Commission remains responsible for conducting EU trade policy, while keeping the Council closely involved in the process. The Council approves the Commission's negotiating mandate and endorses the final agreement, officially by qualified majority vote but in practice by unanimity. As well as setting negotiating directives and endorsing the final agreement, member states exert considerable influence over the Commission's conduct of international trade negotiations themselves. The so-called 133 Committee of member state civil servants meets regularly with Commission officials to approve the Commission's negotiating strategy and proposals. Although members of the committee do not participate directly in most negotiations, their presence behind the scenes ensures that Commission negotiators stick to the agreed-upon Council position. Commission negotiators often turn such oversight to the EU's advantage by pointing out to their interlocutors the impossibility of accepting a proposal without first getting the member states' approval.

The Commission's competence to negotiate and conclude international trade agreements does not extend to trade in services or trade-related aspects of intellectual property rights. The Commission overstepped its competence when it attempted to conclude the agreements in these areas in the Uruguay Round. The Commission sought to extend its competence during the intergovernmental conference on treaty reform in 1996–1997, but member states could not agree among themselves to make the necessary changes. As a result, with the new international trade agenda dominated by disputes over services and intellectual property rights, the Commission's influence in the realm of external economic relations has been considerably curtailed. In addition to negotiating trade accords, managing development policy, and liaising internationally for the EU, the Commission negotiates association agreements with third countries and plays an important part in the process of EU enlargement.

Contributing to Enlargement and Treaty Reform

Enlargement and treaty reform, developments that often go hand in hand, change the EU's contours and character. Both are primarily intergovernmental processes. Indeed, accession negotiations are formally known as intergovernmental conferences. Accordingly, the Council is the lead institution in the enlargement process, with the Council presidency conducting the negotiations on behalf of the existing member states. Yet the Commission plays a key role as well. First, the Commission prepares an "opinion" on the suitability of an applicant country for EU membership. Accession negotiations cannot begin without the Commission's opinion, although the Council is not obliged to take it into account. In 1978, for example, the Council disregarded the Commission's recommendation that the EC delay opening accession negotiations with Greece. The country's economic and political difficulties in the early years of EC membership vindicated the Commission's position.

In that case, the Commission based its recommendation on an honest appraisal of Greece's situation. Indeed, the Commission prides itself on being an honest broker in the enlargement process, telling each side—the existing and the prospective member state(s)—the truth about the other. Whereas national leaders sometimes succumbed to flattery when visiting candidate countries during the Central and Eastern European enlargement and made unrealistic statements about when those countries might eventually accede, commissioners tend to be more reserved and circumspect. The Commission's annual monitoring reports on the candidate countries' preparedness for membership, issued every November, provide refreshingly frank assessments (too frank, some of the candidates complain). Other aspects of the Commission's role in the enlargement process include conducting a screening exercise (assessing the compatibility of the candidates' laws with existing EU laws), publishing a scorecard on the state of play of the negotiations (thereby encouraging the laggards to catch up with the front-runners on the candidates' side), and helping the candidates meet the requirements of EU membership.

Treaty reform is another, more overtly intergovernmental process (the term "intergovernmental conference" is synonymous with it). Here again, the Commission helps to start the formal process by submitting a report on the advisability of holding an intergovernmental conference. Not being a government, however, the Commission cannot be a full participant in the conference itself. Instead, the Commission submits proposals and draft treaty changes, and Commission representatives (usually two commissioners) attend ministerial meetings of the intergovernmental conference. The Commission often helps to broker an agreement in the conference but cannot block an agreement from being reached even if it strongly opposes the proposed changes. The reform process culminating in the Constitutional Treaty was unusual in that a convention drawn from representatives of various national and European institutions, including the Commission, preceded the intergovernmental conference. Thus, the Commission played a primary role in preparing the draft Constitutional Treaty (although its influence was limited) but only a secondary role in the intergovernmental conference that followed.

Depending on the political climate and the caliber of the commissioners involved (including the president), participation in the processes of enlargement and treaty reform affords the Commission an opportunity to assert itself institutionally. Yet enlargement, in particular, imposes a considerable organizational burden on the Commission. Central and Eastern European enlargement was a striking case in point. In January 1999 the Commission established a major new unit, the Task Force for the Accession Negotiations, in anticipation of the formal opening of negotiations in March. Soon afterward the task force became a full-fledged directorate-general, drawing personnel and other scarce resources from elsewhere in the Commission.

Reporting on EU Developments

In order to carry out its various responsibilities, the Commission generates thousands of reports annually. Most of these are narrowly focused and rarely resonate outside the directorate-general or service in which they are written. However, the Commission also produces a number of reports on major EU developments that have a wider interest and readership. In some cases these are part of the Commission's regular responsibilities; in other cases they are the result of specific mandates from the European Council. Examples include

- The "Spring Report" on the Lisbon strategy: a report produced for the annual spring meeting of the European Council, at which EU leaders review progress on the Lisbon strategy and set goals for its realization. The "Spring Report" is a thorough examination of almost all of the EU's economic, social, and environmental activities.
- The "Cohesion Reports": detailed reports on economic and social cohesion, a key policy area. The Commission adopted the "First Cohesion Report" in 1996, the "Second" in 2001, and the "Third" in 2004. Each became the basis for specific policy proposals and large-scale EU expenditure. The Commission presented the "Third Cohesion Report" at a forum in the European Parliament, in May 2004, in which representatives of EU institutions, national governments, regional authorities, and nongovernmental organizations participated.
- The "Regular Reports on Enlargement": annual reports on the progress of the candidate countries toward EU membership, produced every autumn since 1998. Candidate countries eagerly await these so-called Regular Reports, which form the basis for decisions by the member states on the pace and possible conclusion of the accession negotiations.

Pointing the Way Forward

One of the Commission's most important roles is unstated but extremely important. As Jacques Delors put it during a celebration in Rome in March 1987 to mark the EC's thirtieth anniversary, the Commission has a "strategic authority" to "guarantee the continuity of the [integration] project despite the political or geopolitical hazards." Acting as a "custodian of European interests [and] as a repository of past achievements," Delors declared that the Commission has a cherished obligation to point "the way to the goal ahead."[21] Later Delors explained that "the Commission itself cannot achieve much but it can generate ideas. Its main weapon is its conviction."[22]

The history of the EU is replete with examples of the Commission pointing the way forward, notably during the Hallstein, Jenkins, and Delors presidencies. The single market program and monetary union stand out. Capitalizing on the member states' eagerness to complete the internal market, the Commission put the necessary package of proposals together and mapped out a strategy to succeed. The Commission provided the encouragement, explication, and enthusiasm to see the program through. Similarly, the Commission took the initiative in the late 1980s to draft a plan for economic and monetary union and contributed decisively to the outcome of the 1991 intergovernmental conference on monetary union. By contrast, the EU tends to stagnate when the Commission is either unable or unwilling to lead, as has been the case since the late 1990s.

The Maastricht ratification crisis fueled speculation that "the motor [of European integration] has all but stalled."[23] Undoubtedly developments in the early 1990s shattered the Commission's self-confidence. At a time of economic recession and political uncertainty it was difficult for the Commission to regain the initiative and forge ahead. Invidious comparisons were made between the setback to the Commission caused by the empty chair crisis in 1965 and the Maastricht ratification crisis in 1992–1993. The unexpected resignation of the Commission in 1999 dealt a further blow to the institution's image and influence, from which it has yet to recover. In the prevailing climate of Euroskepticism and resurgent intergovernmentalism, it is difficult for the Commission to regain its old authority and promote its overriding goal of deeper political and economic integration.

▨ Notes

1. European Commission, *1991 General Report* (Luxembourg: Office for Official Publications of the European Communities, 1992), point 1196.

2. Stanley Hoffmann, "The Case for Leadership," *Foreign Policy* 81 (Winter 1990–1991): 24.

3. On Delors's strategy and impact on European integration, see Helen Drake, *Jacques Delors: Perspectives on a European Leader* (London: Routledge, 2000); Ken Endo, *The Presidency of the European Commission Under Jacques Delors: The Politics of Shared Leadership* (New York: St. Martin's Press, 1999); George Ross, *Jacques Delors and European Integration* (Oxford: Oxford University Press, 1995); Jacques Delors, *Mémoirs* (Paris: Plon, 2004), pp. 171–430.

4. Jacques Delors, address to the European Parliament, January 20, 1988, Bulletin EC S/1-1988; Delors, *Le Nouveau Concert Européen* (Paris: Editions Odile Jacob, 1992), p. 8.

5. Niels Ersbøll, "The European Union: The Immediate Priorities," *International Affairs* 70, no. 3 (1994): 413.

6. See Simon Hix and Christopher Lord, "The Making of a President: The European Parliament and the Confirmation of Jacques Santer as President of the Commission," *Government and Opposition* 31 (1996): 62–76.

7. Quoted in the *Times* (London), June 28, 1977, p. 16.

8. Roy Jenkins, *A Life at the Centre* (London: Macmillan, 1991), p. 376.

9. Peter Ludlow, "The European Commission," in Robert Keohane and Stanley Hoffmann, eds., *The European Community: Decisionmaking and Institutional Change* (Boulder, CO: Westview Press, 1991), p. 91.

10. On the Commission's internal organization and staffing, see Michelle Cini, *The European Commission: Leadership, Organisation, and Culture in the EU Administration* (Manchester, UK: Manchester University Press, 1996); Liesbet Hooghe, *The European Commission and the Integration of Europe: Images of Governance* (Cambridge: Cambridge University Press, 2001); and A. Stevens with H. Stevens, *Brussels Bureaucrats? The Administration of the European Union* (Basingstoke, UK: Palgrave Macmillan, 2001)

11. European Information Service, *Monthly Report on Europe,* April 1998, p. III.5.

12. See Ross, *Jacques Delors*, p. 154.

13. Liesbet Hooghe, "Serving Europe: Political Orientations of Senior Commission Officials," paper presented at the Fifth Biennial Conference of the European Community Studies Association, Seattle, WA, May 29–June 1, 1997, p. 1.

14. Roy Denman, letter to the editor, *Times* (London), January 27, 1992, p. 10.

15. Committee of Independent Experts, First Report on Allegations Regarding Fraud, Mismanagement and Nepotism in the European Commission, Brussels, March 1999, point 1.6.2.

16. On the Prodi reformation, see Desmond Dinan, "Governance and Institutions: Edging Toward Enlargement," *Journal of Common Market Studies* 39, *Annual Review of the EU 2000/2001* (September 2001): pp. 26–31.

17. European Commission, "Reforming the Commission: A White Paper—Part 1," Brussels, 2000; European Commission, "Reforming the Commission: A White Paper—Part 2 Action Plan," Brussels, 2000.

18. European Commission, "European Governance: A White Paper," COM (2001)428 final, Brussels.

19. On the Commission's roles and responsibilities, see Neill Nugent, ed., *At the Heart of the Union: Studies of the European Commission,* 2nd ed. (Basingstoke, UK: Palgrave Macmillan, 2000); and Neill Nugent, *The European Commission* (Basingstoke, UK: Palgrave Macmillan, 2001).

20. *Economist*, March 17, 2001, p. 50.

21. Jacques Delors, speech on the occasion of the thirtieth anniversary of the signing of the Treaty of Rome, March 25, 1987, Bulletin EC S/2-1987, p. 10.

22. Delors, address to the European Parliament, January 20, 1988, p. 9.

23. *Economist*, October 10, 1992, p. 66.

8

The European
Council and the
Council of Ministers

The European Council and the Council of Ministers (officially called the Council of the European Union and generally known as the Council) are related but separate entities. The Council of Ministers consists of government ministers and a European commissioner who meet frequently to reconcile national interests and enact EU legislation (only the ministers may vote). By contrast, the European Council consists of each country's top political leaders (heads of state and government) and the Commission president. The purpose of the European Council is to resolve otherwise intractable problems and to lead the EU at the highest political level.

Many meetings of the European Council (summits) stand out as key events in the EU's history, such as Maastricht in 1991, Amsterdam in 1997, and Nice in 2000 (agreement on the treaties of the same name); Copenhagen in 2002 (agreement on Central and Eastern European enlargement); and Brussels in 2004 (agreement on the Constitutional Treaty). Some of the most prominent and portentous meetings of the heads of state and government took place even before the European Council formally came into existence in 1975: the 1969 Hague summit that endorsed "completion, deepening, enlargement" and the 1972 Paris summit that called for economic and monetary union by the end of the decade.

That partial list of historical landmarks indicates the political importance of EU summitry. Without regular working sessions of government leaders, the European Community might not have survived Eurosclerosis in the 1970s or successfully launched the single market program in the mid-1980s. Nor could the EU have adjusted, however hesitatingly, to a radically altered international environment in the 1990s. Thus, the European Council is far more than a glorified meeting of the Council, although it sometimes runs the risk of merely doing the Council's work.

The Council of Ministers combines elements of intergovernmentalism and supranationalism (it consists of member states' representatives, who agree in most cases to reach decisions on the basis of qualified majority voting). The European Council is more avowedly intergovernmental, despite the Commission president's participation in it. Ardent Eurofederalists (if they exist anymore) often lament the European Council's ascendancy. Yet the European Council's emergence in the 1970s coincided with a gradual strengthening, rather than weakening, of supranationalism in the then EC. Aware of the threat to supranationalism that regular summitry could pose, the heads of state and government decided, when they agreed to launch the European Council in 1974, to organize direct elections to the European Parliament as a counterweight to more intergovernmentalism in the EC. Member states took other steps to strengthen supranationalism—expansion of the Parliament's powers and greater use of majority voting in the Council—at subsequent EU summits. Thus, the European Council's appearance in the 1970s generated a dynamic interrelationship between intergovernmentalism and supranationalism that contributed to the EC's transformation in the mid-1980s and continues to this day.

■ The Presidency

The rotating presidency of the European Council and the Council of Ministers is one of the EU's most distinctive features. The organization and nature of the presidency may change radically under the terms of the Constitutional Treaty (see below). In the interim, the presidency continues to change every six months when, on the first of January or July each year, a different country assumes the leadership of both the European Council and the Council of Ministers. The six-monthly rotation used to be based on the alphabetical listing of the name of each country in its own official language. It has since been reconfigured a number of times to ensure a sequence of big and small, old and new member states and to ensure that the presidency's workload is distributed evenly among member states. Because EU governance virtually ceases during the sacrosanct summer holidays in August and accelerates rapidly at other times of the year according to a fixed legislative calendar in key areas, it would be unfair for the same countries always to be in the presidency either in the first or the second half of the year.

Accommodating the presidential rota to the vagaries of the EU's legislative calendar suggests that the president's work is preordained, and to a certain extent it is. Particular EU business must be transacted at definite times of the year—for instance, farm price negotiations (each spring) and a budget agreement (each fall). Also, specific EU programs (such as completing the single market in the late 1980s and the three-stage monetary union process in the 1990s) have relatively rigid timetables regardless of the country in the

Council presidency. See Table 8.1 for a list of the Council presidency rota through 2006.

Nevertheless, for three main reasons it can matter a great deal which country holds the presidency at any particular time. First, each country's approach to even the most routine and uncontroversial EU business is bound to be slightly idiosyncratic. Second, countries have preferences for certain EU policies, programs, or activities. Third, changing circumstances inside and outside the EU sometimes confront a presidency with unexpected challenges that call for quick responses. Accordingly, the variables most likely to determine a country's presidential performance are size and resources, diplomatic experience and tradition, familiarity with the EU system, degree of commitment to European integration, and domestic political circumstances.[1]

The presidency's importance has grown steadily throughout the EU's history because of a number of related developments: the progressive deepening of European integration, the profusion of technical or sectoral councils, the corresponding expansion of the influence and authority of the Committee of Permanent Representatives (made up of member states' ambassadors to the EU), the proliferation of Council working groups, the emergence and growing prominence of the European Council, and the impact of intergovernmental cooperation in the fields of foreign and security policy on the one hand and justice and home affairs on the other. As a result, the presidency's roles and responsibilities have expanded over the years and now include

Table 8.1   The Council Presidency Rota, 1998–2006

Member State	Semester
Britain	January–June 1998
Austria	July–December 1998
Germany	January–June 1999
Finland	July–December 1999
Portugal	January–June 2000
France	July–December 2000
Sweden	January–June 2001
Belgium	July–December 2001
Spain	January–June 2002
Denmark	July–December 2002
Greece	January–June 2003
Italy	July–December 2003
Ireland	January–June 2004
The Netherlands	July–December 2004
Luxembourg	January–June 2005
Britain	July–December 2005
Austria	January–June 2006
Finland	July–December 2006

- arranging and chairing meetings of the European Council (summits)
- preparing and chairing meetings of the Council and its subcommittees—the Committee of Permanent Representatives (Coreper), various special committees, and a large number of standing or ad hoc working groups
- brokering deals in the Council in order to reach agreement on a particular legislative proposal or on a package of legislative proposals
- launching strategic policy initiatives
- coordinating member states' positions at international conferences and negotiations in which the EU participates
- representing the EU internationally
- acting as an EU spokesperson
- leading the EU side in enlargement negotiations
- chairing intergovernmental conferences on treaty reform

In the Chair

In Eurospeak, the terms "presidency" and "chair" are often synonymous because the foremost responsibility of a country in the presidency is to chair the European Council, the Council of Ministers, and the Council's numerous subcommittees. The Council's rules of procedure for the presidency include such routine functions as planning the Council's six-month calendar, convening meetings, preparing agendas and minutes, and drafting conclusions. Member states judge presidential performance primarily by how a country manages European Council and Council of Ministers meetings during its six months in the chair.

Running a good meeting is not purely procedural but also involves crafting compromise agreements and steering participants toward a decision. A country may organize meetings well, but unless it knows the issues thoroughly; understands other countries' points of view; appreciates how a discussion is developing; and judges properly when to call for breaks, adjournments, or decisions, the best-prepared meetings can end inconclusively or disastrously. Brokering not just a single agreement but a whole package of agreements is an indispensable task of the presidency.

Countries in the presidency play a dual role in Council meetings and have a split personality. They seek both to advance their own positions and to act as impartial arbiters; they are biased and neutral at the same time. That dichotomy is formally recognized in the seating arrangements for Council meetings, where the country in the presidency not only sits at the head of the table but also maintains a separate national representative who sits next to the president, on the right-hand side of the table.

Yet the difference between a country's national and presidential roles should not be exaggerated. Of the two representatives present, the most senior minister or official always wears the presidency hat, and countries generally see presidential service as being in their national interest. As part of their preparations for holding the presidency, countries coordinate interministerially in order to reconcile national and presidential interests, and if necessary subsume national under presidential interests. Thus, it is rare for countries in the presidency to vote in their own national interest in order to produce the required majority. As a longtime senior adviser to two British prime ministers observed, "The accepted wisdom is that holding the presidency makes it harder, not easier, to pursue specific national aims."[2]

Responsibility for organizing, chairing, and running hundreds of meetings during a Council presidency puts enormous pressure materially and politically on the member state in question. Large countries have an obvious advantage: their big bureaucracies provide solid infrastructural support. By contrast, it is sometimes difficult for small countries to find enough qualified people to chair all the meetings that take place during a six-month period, especially when unforeseen circumstances increase the presidency's workload. Most small countries, such as Greece in early 2003 and Ireland in early 2004, radically reorganize their bureaucracies in order to absorb the shock of the presidency, often at the cost of diminishing domestic government service. Despite the strain that holding the presidency puts on small countries, it is commonly conceded that small countries make more of an effort and generally run better presidencies than do big countries.

Without compromising its neutrality or credibility, the presidency can influence the conduct of EU business in a number of ways. Organizing the Council's agenda and chairing Council meetings afford the presidency considerable control over the pace of EU legislation. The observations of a Brussels insider in 1988 are as valid now as they were then: if the presidency wants progress on a certain issue, "it will secure determined support from the Commission, as well as from some other member states. And it will put into place an active and capable working group chairman."[3]

Agenda, Initiatives, and Representation

Member states outline their presidential priorities in a document circulated at the beginning of the presidency and in an inaugural address by the prime minister or foreign minister to the European Parliament. In an effort to improve coordination among succeeding presidencies, the European Council decided in June 2003 that, beginning in January of the following year, groups of six consecutive presidencies would adopt a multiannual strategic program. The first of these (and possibly the last if the Constitutional Treaty goes into effect) was prepared by Ireland, the Netherlands, Luxembourg, Britain, Austria, and Finland for the period 2004–2006. Moreover, the two countries in the presidency during each of these years develop an annual operating program within the framework of the multiannual strategic program. The evidence so far suggests that cooperation among countries in the conduct of the presidency is more rhetorical than real.

Each country's presidential priorities include predictable promises about strengthening European integration. More specifically, they outline what a country hopes to achieve during its six months in office. Of course, there is no guarantee that the presidency's legislative objectives will ever be realized. Much depends on the prevailing political and economic climate and on the prestige, popularity, and skill of the country in the presidency.

Whether in speeches to the Parliament or elsewhere, the Council president may also launch strategic policy initiatives, a prerogative shared with the Commission president. Just as some Commission presidents are more active than others, some countries are more likely to launch major initiatives than others, and prominent politicians in a particular country inevitably differ in their degrees of interest in and enthusiasm for the EU. The coincidence of a dynamic Commission president, a country in the Council presidency with a reputation for promoting European integration, and imaginative leaders in that country can benefit the EU greatly. The late 1990s and early 2000s have been conspicuously bereft of such occasions.

Along with the Commission president, the Council president speaks on behalf of the EU. Each president supposedly deals only with specific subjects, depending on whether they come under exclusive EU competence or shared (member state and EU) competence. The Commission and Council presidents customarily give a joint press conference at the end of each summit, often presenting noticeably different accounts and interpretations of the same negotiations from their respective institutional perspectives.

External Affairs

Dual representation is particularly prominent and perplexing in the EU's external relations. Nowhere is it more evident than in dealings with the United States. Under the terms of the 1990 Transatlantic Declaration, the president of the United States meets every six months with the presidents of the Commission and the Council. Similarly, the Council and Commission presidents represent the EU at the annual group of seven/eight (G7/8) summits. As long as one of the four EU countries in the G7/8—Britain, France, Germany, and Italy—happens to be in the Council presidency, such dual representation hardly matters. But when one of the smaller EU member states is in the presidency during a G7/8 summit, the EU's dual representation seems anomalous.

On security and defense policy, the Council president is unencumbered by joint Commission representation. As long ago as 1974, the heads of state and government stipulated that "the President-in-office will be the spokesman for the [member states] and will set out their views in international diplomacy.

He will insure that the necessary consultations always take place in good time."[4] The Single European Act established a legal basis for the presidency's role in European Political Cooperation, the forerunner of the Common Foreign and Security Policy, and codified existing practices whereby the Council president managed the process of political cooperation. Furthermore, the Single European Act established a small foreign policy secretariat, housed in the Council building, and put it under the authority of the presidency. The Maastricht Treaty, which inaugurated the Common Foreign and Security Policy, strengthened the presidency's role in EU foreign and security policy representation.

As part of an effort to strengthen the Common Foreign and Security Policy, member states established the position of high representative for the Common Foreign and Security Policy in the Amsterdam Treaty of 1997 and appointed the first high representative in June 1999. Having a standing high representative provides a welcome degree of continuity in foreign and security policy regardless of the rotating presidency, although at the risk of occasional friction between the high representative and the foreign minister of the country in the presidency. Despite being a servant of the Council and therefore of the presidency, the high representative often upstages the president in office, especially when they travel together outside the EU. The advent of a foreign minister for the EU, combining the positions of high representative and commissioner for External Relations, as provided for in the Constitutional Treaty (discussed later in this chapter), would end the rotating presidency with regard to foreign and security policy.

Notwithstanding the existence of the high representative, the presidency's prominence in security and defense policy is burdensome for small countries and highlights some disadvantages of the rotational system. The large number of foreign policy working groups calls for a sizable pool of competent chairpersons, which small member states have difficulty providing. In addition, the presidency's responsibility to represent the EU internationally can be detrimental to the EU's status and influence when a small country is in the chair. For instance, having Greece in the presidency in 2003 during the Iraq War may have reinforced the international image of a weak and indecisive EU response to the conflict. Given the depth of the division among the big member states, however, it may have been better for the EU to have had a small member state in the presidency at that time.

The Council Secretariat

Small countries in the presidency depend heavily for logistical support on the Council secretariat. With a staff of approximately 2,000 people, including about 300 administrative level officials, the Council secretariat assists the Council by helping to draft the six-month legislative program, providing legal advice, briefing government ministers on current EU issues, preparing the agenda for Council meetings, and drafting the meetings' minutes. Nearly two-thirds of the Council staff are translators and interpreters. Like the Commission secretariat, the Council secretariat is divided into directorates-general, although along different lines.

The legal service represents the Council before the Court of Justice, ensures that all texts adopted are in order, and advises the Council at all levels. Indeed, a representative of the legal service sits to the right of the president during Council meetings and often intervenes, especially during discussions on intergovernmental policy areas. Given the presidency's importance in the process of treaty reform, the Council's legal service plays a critical role on such momentous occasions. For instance, the Council's legal service drafted the opt-outs granted to Denmark at the December 1992 summit, which paved the way for ratification of the Maastricht Treaty, and also drafted the key article on flexibility in the Amsterdam Treaty.

The Council secretariat describes itself as "entirely at the service of the Presidency, supporting it in its efforts to find compromise solutions, coordinate work or arrive at an overall view."[5] Indeed, the presidency is the presidency plus the Council secretariat. What is involved is much more than close cooperation; it is a form of common action or symbiosis in regard to preparing and carrying out the presidency program. A member of the secretariat always accompanies the president unless a particular bilateral issue is being discussed.

The Council secretariat has acquired a higher political profile following the acceleration of European integration in the mid-1980s. The Council secretariat successfully took on new tasks during successive rounds of negotiations on treaty reform, acting in support of the Council presidency. Insofar as national leaders treat the secretary-general as a preferred adviser, the Commission president and his colleagues often charge that the secretary-general is exercising undue influence, not least when the European Council and the Council of Ministers decide not to follow the Commission's advice. The Commission also resents the Council secretariat's higher institutional profile since the Maastricht Treaty, which included a reference to the Council secretariat for the first time in one of the founding treaties.

The Amsterdam Treaty changed the role of the Council secretary-general in an important respect. Previously, the secretary-general simply ran the Council secretariat. After Amsterdam, the new position of high representative for the Common Foreign and Security Policy was combined with the old position of Council secretary-general, and the deputy secretary-general assumed responsibility for running the General Secretariat on a day-to-day basis. As high representative, the secretary-general soon assumed a representational and a political role much greater than that of previous secretaries-general.

The Politics of the Presidency

Notwithstanding the onerous responsibilities (even with the Council secretariat's expert assistance) of the Council presidency, most small member states have jealously guarded their right to take a turn at the EU's helm. Despite agreeing in the Constitutional Treaty to establish a standing president of the European Council and an EU foreign minister, small countries generally welcomed the opportunity to play a more prominent part in shaping the EU's agenda and understandably enjoyed being in the international limelight. The presidency could easily be turned to domestic political advantage either by distracting attention from pressing problems or by enhancing the government's prestige and popularity. The presidency hosts numerous events during a six-month term, ranging from informal meetings of government ministers to cultural and academic conferences. Until agreeing in the Nice Treaty to centralize them in Brussels, countries in the presidency also hosted meetings of the European Council, which were a cherished opportunity to showcase national capitals or regional cities. By distributing these spoils throughout the country, the government could score valuable political points. Presidencies also have an important educational function, especially in Euroskeptical countries, where governments use the occasion of the presidency to try to enlighten the public about the presumed benefits of EU membership.

Politically, the presidency can hold a crumbling coalition together. The Dutch coalition government survived a political crisis in August 1991 over social welfare partly because all parties agreed that the cabinet's collapse would have damaged the country's presidency. The Danish government was not so lucky in January 1992, when holding the Council presidency did not prevent it from falling as a result of a domestic political scandal. National elections sometimes coincide with a country's turn in the presidency, generally to the presidency's detriment. Such was the case during Germany's presidency in late 1994 (federal elections took place in October) and during France's presidency in early 1995 (presidential elections took place in May). On each occasion, the German or French leaders were preoccupied with electoral politics at the expense of Europolitics.

In their eagerness to trumpet presidential achievements, member states take credit for agreements reached during their term in office even if the necessary preparatory work took place during a previous presidency. Countries about to assume the presidency may be tempted to obstruct decisionmaking during the dying days of their predecessors' presidencies in order to delay agreement until they themselves are sitting in the Council chair. However, the risks are great that such behavior would rebound on the incoming presidency. As a result, member states almost always play by the rules.

Also for domestic political reasons, the country in office is more likely than other member states to make concessions, especially during a meeting of the European Council, in order to increase its presidency's productivity and prestige. Such was the case in Berlin in March 1999, when Gerhard Schröder, the newly elected chancellor of Germany, dropped his earlier opposition to increasing Germany's contribution to the EU budget, thereby facilitating an agreement on the Agenda 2000 package and resolving an issue that threatened to spoil the summit and the German presidency.

Roy Jenkins, Commission president in the late 1970s, observed in his *European Diary* that "the authority of Council presidencies varies substantially. A new member country can be overawed, a small country over-strained and even a big old member country like Germany can suffer from a lack of coordination within its government. France was neither new nor small and its government, whatever else could be said about it, did not suffer from a lack of coordination. The tradition and the expectations therefore were that France provided the most authoritative Presidency."[6] Jenkins experienced a particularly bumpy French presidency in early 1979, when Valéry Giscard d'Estaing was at his most ambivalent about European integration. Two subsequent French presidencies proved extremely productive: under François Mitterrand, France provided excellent leadership in early 1984 during the final stages of the British budgetary question and in late 1989 during the revolution in Central and Eastern Europe. In late 2000, however, France under President Jacques Chirac ran a notoriously poor presidency, which contributed in part to the unsatisfactory nature of the Nice Treaty. Similarly, Prime Minister Silvio Berlusconi ran an equally bad Italian presidency in late 2003, with predictable consequences for the conduct of the intergovernmental conference on the draft Constitutional Treaty (talks broke down at the end-of-presidency summit in December).

Britain has a mixed record as Council president but has a well-deserved reputation at least for running good meetings. Britain's presidency in early 1998 was especially noteworthy because of the new Labour government's self-proclaimed support for European integration despite a continuing reservation on the question of a single currency. The Labour Party's long period in opposition (between 1979 and 1997) put the new government at a disadvantage in the Council: few ministers had any experience of Council meetings or much acquaintance with ministers from other member states. Nevertheless, Britain's renowned organizational and negotiating skills helped the government make progress in one of its priority areas: completion of the single market (despite the 1992 deadline, a number of proposed directives had not been enacted and many directives had not been implemented). Britain was able to bask in the glory of two ceremonial events: the launch of enlargement negotiations and the selection of eleven member states (excluding Britain itself) for participation in the final stage of monetary union.

In other respects Britain's presidential record has been varied, mostly because of circumstances beyond the country's control. For instance, Britain was unfairly criticized for not having brokered an agreement between France and Germany over the selection of the first president of the European Central Bank at the Brussels summit in May 1998. Usually in such circumstances, it is incumbent upon the presidency to come up with a compromise and head off a crisis. Britain failed to do so not because of indifference or neglect but because of the entrenched and highly publicized positions of France and Germany.

Despite or perhaps because of the obvious disadvantages owing to their size, small member states usually make a prodigious effort to run a successful presidency. In contrast to the mixed record of the big member states, small member state presidencies generally receive favorable reviews. Following Italy's pitiable presidency in late 2003, the other member states were relieved to see Ireland take over in January 2004. Despite having unexpectedly inherited an incomplete intergovernmental conference on the draft Constitutional Treaty, Ireland ran an excellent presidency, even managing to bring the intergovernmental conference to a successful conclusion in June 2004.

Reforming the Rotating Presidency

The rotating presidency is a powerful symbol of equality among member states. It also brings home to each government "the full responsibilities of Community membership."[7] Yet the system is inherently inefficient: some small countries have great difficulty managing a successful presidency, six months is arguably too short a term to pursue a particular legislative program, and frequent rotation impedes the continuity of some EU activities. Member states tackled the problem of continuity by establishing the "troika," a system whereby ministers or officials from the foreign ministries of the current, immediately preceding, and immediately succeeding presidencies cooperated closely and continuously, with the assistance of the Commission (thereby turning the troika into a foursome). Later the troika was reorganized to comprise the president in office, the succeeding president in office, the high representative, and the commissioner for External Relations (or officials representing them).

The EU has frequently addressed the problems of the rotating presidency in more fundamental ways. The 1975 Tindemans Report advocated extending the presidency to twelve months, but to no avail.[8] A twelve-month presidency would mean that countries would have to wait twice as long for their turn in the limelight (a wait of twenty-five years in a twenty-five-member-state EU), a prospect uncongenial to politicians and national civil servants alike. It was the imminence of a twenty-five-member-state EU—an EU that would include a country as small and administratively underresourced as Malta—that finally focused attention on the need to reform the rotating presidency. British prime minister Tony Blair and his Spanish counterpart, José Maria Aznar, castigated the inefficiency of the rotating presidency and led the charge for a radical change.

Pushed by Britain and Spain with the support of France and Germany, the small member states grudgingly agreed in the Constitutional Treaty to do away with the rotating presidency of the European Council by establishing instead the office of EU president, which the heads of state and government would fill by electing an individual for a two-and-a-half-year term (renewable once). The EU president would not hold a national mandate but presumably would be a former national prime minister or president. The Constitutional Treaty also provides for an EU foreign minister, to be appointed by heads of state and government, who would chair the External Relations Council. The presidency of the other Council formations would continue to rotate among member states for a six-month period, according to a new rota based on groups of three member states, with each group containing a big and a small member state and at least one new member state (see Table 8.2).

Table 8.2   The Council Presidency Rota, 2007–2020

Member State	Semester
Germany	January–June 2007
Portugal	July–December 2007
Slovenia	January–June 2008
France	July–December 2008
Czech Republic	January–June 2009
Sweden	July–December 2009
Spain	January–June 2010
Belgium	July–December 2010
Hungary	January–June 2011
Poland	July–December 2011
Denmark	January–June 2012
Cyprus	July–December 2012
Ireland	January–June 2013
Lithuania	July–December 2013
Greece	January–June 2014
Italy	July–December 2014
Latvia	January–June 2015
Luxembourg	July–December 2015
The Netherlands	January–June 2016
Slovakia	July–December 2016
Malta	January–June 2017
United Kingdom	July–December 2017
Estonia	January–June 2018
Bulgaria	July–December 2018
Austria	January–June 2019
Romania	July–December 2019
Finland	January–June 2020

■ Europe's Most Exclusive Club

In a press conference at the end of the December 1974 Paris summit, French president Giscard d'Estaing declared with a rhetorical flourish that "the European Summit is dead, long live the European Council."[9] The EC's leaders had just decided to replace their ad hoc meetings with regular triannual get-togethers. Nevertheless, the newly formed European Council did not become a formal institution on a par with the Council of Ministers, the Commission, or the Parliament. The Single European Act merely recognized the European Council's existence and importance, whereas the Maastricht Treaty codified its composition and number of annual meetings. The Maastricht Treaty also specified that "the European Council shall provide the Union with the necessary impetus for its development and shall define the general guidelines thereof." The Constitutional Treaty was more specific, declaring that the European Council "shall define [the EU's] general political directions and priorities" (Article I-20).

It seems paradoxical that the Maastricht Treaty recognized the European Council's political importance but failed to formalize its institutional status. From the outset, however, informality and spontaneity have characterized the European Council and contributed to its effectiveness. Although meetings of the European Council inevitably became more methodical, structured, and stylized over the years, their relative freedom from legal rules and regulations remained a key ingredient of their success. Nevertheless, the EU's increasing size has robbed the European Council of its intimacy, with many more national leaders and foreign ministers sitting around the table.

Member states were long reluctant to tip the EU's constitutional balance by formally institutionalizing the European Council and implicitly reinforcing intergovernmentalism in the EU system. Only in 2004, by which time it was obvious that the European Council was politically the most important body in the EU and that its prominence had not weakened supranationalism, was the European Council given formal institutional status in the Constitutional Treaty. The Constitutional Treaty also specified that the European Council should meet quarterly, which was already the case—a meeting at the end of each Council presidency (in June and December) and midsemester meetings in March and October or November. EU leaders decided at the Lisbon summit in March 2000, when they launched the "Lisbon strategy" for economic modernization and reform, that they would devote their annual March meeting to economic and financial affairs. Often more immediate issues intrude on the planned agenda of a meeting of a European Council, however. Instead of discussing the Lisbon strategy at its meeting in March 2003, for example, the European Council found itself embroiled in a discussion of the situation in Iraq.

Political Development

In its early years, the European Council dealt less with emergency matters than with prevailing economic and political problems. With decisionmaking in the Council thrown into low gear by the Luxembourg Compromise and member states suffering from stagflation, the European Council helped keep the EC together. These were the years of undisguised Franco-German predominance, personified by the Giscard's and Chancellor Helmut Schmidt's duopoly of EC affairs. The French and German leaders dominated European Council proceedings with masterful, impromptu presentations on international issues. They barely tolerated the Commission president's attendance.

In his diary, Commission president Jenkins recalls a summit at which Schmidt took Jenkins aside while Giscard was speaking: "Giscard allowed this to go by without comment or sign of umbrage. If one is so foolish as to believe in the equality of the [European] Council," Jenkins remarked, "one has only to think how differently he would have reacted if it had been, say, [Irish prime minister] Lynch or [Luxembourg prime minister] Thorn who had come round the table and taken me away."[10] More than twenty years later, the inequality inherent in such an ostensibly egalitarian body was obvious when Chirac and German chancellor Helmut Kohl ignored their colleagues for several hours at a summit in May 1998, preferring to argue privately over the selection of the president of the European Central Bank. The French and German leaders' behavior led Jean-Luc Dehaene, prime minister of Belgium and host of the summit, to quip that the other participants should leave Chirac and Kohl to their own devices and go downtown for lunch.[11]

In the early 1980s, the European Council's composition, rationale, and internal dynamics changed dramatically. Over a three-year period Mitterrand and Kohl replaced Giscard and Schmidt. The Franco-German alliance continued to predominate, but Mitterrand and Kohl lacked their predecessors' intellectual sharpness and, initially at least, their personal closeness. For five years, while the European Council was bogged down in the British budgetary question, EC leaders found themselves debating the minutiae of agricultural prices and member states' financial contributions. Resolution of the budgetary dispute in June 1984 finally allowed the European Council to revert to its original role as a forum for discussion of the EC's long-term political and economic direction. Nevertheless, the European Council remained directly involved in the EC's immediate development and became "the decisive actor, the final arbiter, in the development of the internal market."[12] Reflecting the changing nature and rising political stakes of European integration, national leaders immersed themselves, in the European Council, in detailed negotiations during the concluding summits of successive rounds of treaty reform, namely the Single European Act (December 1985), Maastricht Treaty (December 1991), Amsterdam Treaty (June 1997), Nice Treaty (December 2000), and Constitutional Treaty (June 2004).

The European Council operates almost exclusively on the basis of consensus. Although participants may disagree strongly on many issues, regular voting would sour the atmosphere and alter the dynamics of the cozy Euroclub. Only rarely has the presidency called for a vote in the European Council. The most notable occasion was in June 1985, when EC leaders voted by 7 to 3 (there were then ten member states) to hold the intergovernmental conference that resulted in the Single European Act. Subsequent treaty changes provided for qualified majority voting in the European Council for key EU appointments, such as Commission president (Nice Treaty) and the proposed EU president (Constitutional Treaty). The Amsterdam Treaty included a provision allowing the European Council to decide, by a qualified majority, to sanction a member state that deviated from the EU's core values. Nevertheless, it is hard to imagine the European Council ever holding a vote on these potentially divisive issues.

Roles and Responsibilities

Apart from a few specific decisionmaking functions, such as selecting the Commission president-designate and the head of the European Central Bank or deciding if a member state qualifies for adoption of the euro, the European Council's primary purpose is to provide strategic direction by considering the EU's and the member states' policies and priorities as an organic whole rather than as separate and competing ingredients. Other functions that have either existed from the outset or developed over time include

- acquainting the heads of state and government with each other and with each other's views on economic, social, and political issues
- discussing current international developments and issuing important foreign policy statements and declarations
- reconciling differences between the EU's external economic relations and the member states' foreign policies
- resolving extraordinary budgetary disputes and reaching agreement on the multiannual budgetary framework
- setting the agenda for further integration
- negotiating key treaty revisions during intergovernmental conferences

Because of their political sensitivity, these roles and responsibilities are peculiar to the European Council and could not be performed by any other EU body. But the European Council serves another purpose that possibly reduces its effectiveness and weakens the EU system. By acting as a "court of appeal" for the Council of Ministers, the European Council undermines its own and the Council's efficiency. Although the European Council must take ultimate responsibility, too often it becomes involved in deciding issues that should have been settled at a lower level.

The "Three Wise Men" advised in 1979 that the European Council should not allow regular decisionmaking to dominate its agenda lest it become merely "an extension of the Council of Ministers."[13] Six years later, the Dooge Report warned emphatically that "the trend toward the European Council becoming simply another body dealing with the day-to-day business of the Community must be reversed."[14] The increasing use of qualified majority voting since the early 1980s has reduced some of the pressure on the European Council to replicate the Council of Ministers' work, but a continuing need for unanimity on certain issues ensures that to some extent the European Council will always be the final decisionmaking authority.

Procedures

The European Council's agenda is prepared by member state civil servants, Commission officials, and officials of the Council secretariat under the direction of the Council presidency. An informal agenda and a draft set of summit conclusions begin to take shape at meetings of Coreper and of other special committees and are discussed at length by the General Affairs Council (of foreign ministers) about two weeks before each summit. Traditionally, a few days before the European Council the prime minister or president of the country in the presidency sends a letter to the other summit participants outlining the principal themes and agenda items for the meeting. In keeping with the European Council's supposed informality, however, participants decide the final agenda themselves at the opening session.

Regardless of its functions, the European Council's format has not changed much over time. Most summits are two-day affairs, usually beginning with lunch on day one and ending on the afternoon of day two. Extraordinary summits, convened by the presidency to discuss specific issues or developments (such as the summit called by the Irish presidency to nominate José Manuel Barroso as Commission president-designate in June 2004), tend to be shorter, lasting no more than a day or even a single evening. The heads of state and government, their foreign ministers, the Commission president, and a Commission vice president participate in almost all of the sessions, and the Council and Commission secretaries-general are present throughout. The president of the Parliament makes a statement before the opening session of each European Council (but does not attend the summit proper), setting forth Parliament's views on the various agenda items. Because unemployment is one of the most important items on the EU agenda, the troika of heads of state and government meets representatives of the social partners (industry and labor leaders) on the evening before the March summit begins.

Although the principals meet in a relatively small group, an army of advisers and handlers is never far away. Permanent representatives, members of other special committees, and numerous high-level officials cluster in groups in adjoining rooms, furiously drafting bits of the conclusions that, piece by piece, come before the European Council for adoption. The Danish presidency set a precedent in 1978 by asking the Council secretariat to provide note-takers at the main sessions. However, the note-takers' most important function is unofficial: after their twenty-minute spells with the EU leaders, they immediately tell accompanying officials what transpired in the meeting. Including interpreters, a relatively small number of people—usually about seventy-five—are privy to the European Council's deliberations.

Dinner at the end of day one is restricted to the heads of state and government and the Commission president. Depending on the length of the preceding session, dinner can begin late and end in the early hours of the morning. Time permitting, it is usually followed by the traditional "fireside chat," when EU leaders are supposedly at their most relaxed and informal. The halcyon days of the fireside chat were in the late 1970s, when the EC had only nine member states. Since then, EU leaders have often canceled these intimate sessions in order to continue ordinary business.

Most summits officially end with the Council and Commission presidents' press conference after the morning session on day two. Since December 1994, EU leaders have invited their counterparts from the candidate countries to join them for the concluding lunch at one European Council annually. Occasionally summits run late into the afternoon or evening of day two. Such was the case at Maastricht in December 1991, where agreement on the social chapter proved elusive. In addition to making various political and intellectual arguments, Ruud Lubbers, the Dutch prime minister, used hunger, fatigue, and exasperation to coax a settlement and save the Maastricht Treaty. The relatively youthful Lubbers and Major had considerably more stamina than their older colleagues, notably the septuagenarian Mitterrand. Something similar happened at Amsterdam in June 1997, although there the EU leaders failed to reach agreement on far-reaching institutional reform and decided to conclude the Amsterdam Treaty without it.

Personalities, Politics, and Publicity

EU leaders meet often in the European Council and get to know each other well. They rarely miss a summit. EU leaders also participate in a dense network of bilateral and multilateral meetings. Some are institutionalized; others are not. Examples include separate meetings between the Council president and the other EU leaders before each European Council; summits of European political party leaders, also held regularly before each European Council; and frequent Franco-German summits held under the auspices of the 1963 Elysée Treaty. In addition, many EU leaders meet at other international events, such as NATO summits, G7/8 summits, Organization for Security and Cooperation in Europe summits, and Asia-Europe meetings.

Despite personal and political differences, national leaders have a powerful common denominator: all have been elected to their country's highest office. Well aware of the perils and pitfalls of political life, knowing each other extremely well, and enjoying membership in Europe's most exclusive club, they are careful never to do or say anything that could weaken their colleagues' domestic positions. Even Margaret Thatcher and John Major, who routinely infuriated other members of the European Council, enjoyed the respect of their political peers. Only Greek prime minister Andrea Papandreou, a vituperative critic of the EU, was disliked in the European Council to the point that other leaders longed for his political downfall. Silvio Berlusconi, Italy's mercurial prime minister in the early 2000s, was also extremely unpopular with many of his fellow national leaders and conducted an open feud with Commission president Romano Prodi, a once and future rival for leadership of the Italian government.

Clearly, personalities are important in politics, especially at the rarified level of the European Council. Indeed, the strength of the European Council—regular, close encounters of the EU's leading politicians—is sometimes also its weakness. Highly successful, headstrong national politicians, used to getting their own way at home, often grate on each other in the European Council, with unfortunate results. Thus, the national leaders most centrally involved in the negotiations on provisions for qualified majority voting in the draft Constitutional Treaty—Aznar of Spain, Chirac of France, and Berlusconi of Italy—could not get along together and caused the intergovernmental conference to break down at the summit in December 2003. Rarely have personal factors contributed so negatively to a decisive political development.

Being astute politicians, EU leaders appreciate the European Council's publicity value. As one observer noted early in the history of the European Council, "all summit meetings are to a greater or lesser degree public relations exercises."[15] Indeed, European Councils have turned into huge media events, with over 1,500 journalists covering important summits. Although intimate and supposedly private, summit deliberations are far from confidential. Even as discussions continue, the note-takers' reports to officials quickly make their way to waiting journalists and into news bulletins. During session breaks and immediately after the summit, ministers and officials brief journalists—especially journalists from their own countries—on what transpired. An observation made by Roy Jenkins in 1979 is as valid today as it was then: The European Council is "a restricted meeting with full subsequent publicity, which is perhaps not a bad formula."[16]

◼ The Council of Ministers

By contrast with the European Council, the Council of Ministers' deliberations were rarely disclosed to the public before the upheaval caused by the Maastricht ratification crisis. The Council's opaqueness was a major cause of the democratic deficit and undermined public confidence in the EU. Government ministers were never shy about publicizing their achievements in the Council, but they usually did so in a way that increased the perception of its remoteness and unaccountability. As the Council secretary-general later commented, only one country, the Netherlands, was aware during the 1991 negotiations on treaty reform that there could be a transparency problem. In fact, "all the other countries tried to strangle the Dutch attempt" at openness.[17] In a bid to regain public confidence after the Danish rejection of the Maastricht Treaty, EU leaders promised to open up the work of Council and other institutions.

Pressure from the Dutch, from the public, and from other institutions (notably the Parliament) for transparency in EU decisionmaking unnerved Coreper, the Council secretariat, and many of the ministers themselves. As far as most national and Council civil servants were (and still are) concerned, public involvement would distract decisionmakers and impair the Council's efficiency. As for the ministers, the confidentiality of Council deliberations was a welcome alternative to the intrusive media and public attention that generally pervades domestic political decisionmaking. Given that neither body wanted to open its doors, it is ironic that the Council charged Coreper with finding ways to implement the EU leaders' promise of greater transparency. Nor is it surprising that Coreper's recommendations and the Council's actions were so timid.

In its defense, the Council could legitimately claim that it is not only the EU's colegislator but also an intergovernmental negotiating forum. Critics point out that the Council is the only legislature in the Western world that severely curtails public access to its deliberations; the Council contends that its diplomatic nature precludes full disclosure of its activities. The Council and its critics have attempted to tackle the transparency problem by providing access to Council documents and meetings, although the Council is unenthusiastic about doing either. Access to meetings is severely restricted. Media representatives and members of the public may not attend the meetings themselves but may view a small number of "public ministerial debates," televised live in an auditorium in Brussels (or in Luxembourg if the Council meets there), only if they have received permission in advance to enter the auditorium. (Some of the debates are also broadcast live or later by the Commission's audiovisual Europe by Satellite information service.)

Inevitably these broadcasts have a small audience (few people would want to go to Brussels or Luxembourg to watch them, and Europe by Satellite is not widely available). Few people might watch them even if they were widely broadcast, although the popularity of C-Span in the United States shows that even the most arcane political discussions have a peculiar fascination. Yet the limited openness of Council meetings reveals little of how the Council really works because ministers restrict themselves while on television to bland, predictable statements. John Palmer, doyen of the Brussels press corps and a persistent critic of the Council, complained in 1995 that "the decision to open certain sessions of the Council of Ministers is in danger of becoming an irrelevant circus where ministers read from texts and do not engage in any debate or exchange whatsoever. This is actually making a mockery of the openness principle."[18] The situation is not much better today.

What some ministers see as an assault on their privacy has led them to seek refuge in a sacred Brussels institution: the working lunch. Not only are ministers free of cameras at lunchtime, they are also free of the hordes of officials who attend them in meetings. This dual freedom allows ministers to be unusually frank with each other and to make concessions that they might not otherwise make. Sometimes even the most senior officials are absent from the detailed discussions that take place in that setting. Apart from complicating the officials' work (minutes of the lunchtime discussions need to be constructed from the ministers' often unreliable memories), the ministers' lunchtime seclusion means that officials cannot brief reporters on the course of the discussions (an indirect way of broadcasting Council meetings).

Whereas public access to Council meetings remains extremely limited, Council documents are far more widely available since the early 1990s. By a declaration annexed to the Maastricht Treaty and by a decision of December 1993 on public access to its documents, the Council established a right of access to information and a procedure for those wanting to exercise that right. Angered by the Council's refusal to grant access to documents requested by it, Britain's *Guardian* newspaper took the Council to the Court of Justice in 1994 with the support of the Parliament, the Netherlands, and Denmark. The *Guardian*'s victory (the Court ruled in October 1995 that the Council had failed to strike a balance between the public's need for access and the Council's need for confidentiality) led the Council to revise and relax its policy toward transparency.

Under further public pressure and also under internal pressure not only from the Netherlands but also (since 1995) from Finland and especially Sweden, member states included a "transparency clause" in the Amsterdam Treaty. This stipulated that "any citizen of the Union . . . shall have a right of access to European Parliament, Council or Commission documents" subject to certain principles and conditions (Article 255 TEC). A separate treaty article clarified this clause with reference to the Council's dual nature as a legislative and a diplomatic body: "The Council shall define the cases in which it is to be regarded as acting in its legislative capacity, with a view to allowing greater access to documents in those cases, while at the same time preserving the effectiveness of its decision-making process. . . . When the Council acts in its legislative capacity, the results of votes and explanations of votes as well as statements in the minutes shall be made public" (Article 207.3 TEC).

Nevertheless, the quality of Council documents released to the public remains poor, as they do not include substantive accounts of bargaining and negotiating. A scholar of EU decisionmaking noted in 1996, during negotiation of the Amsterdam Treaty, that "with its notorious and contested secrecy, there is very little knowledge about what really happens in Council meetings."[19] Not a lot has changed since then, as the Council seems to be incapable of opening up entirely.

The Constitutional Treaty calls for the Council and other institutions to "conduct their work as openly as possible" and for the Council to meet in public "when it is examining and adopting a legislative proposal." Of course, this provision does not cover the myriad of groups working under the direction of the Council, where much of the preparatory work is done. Nor is it likely to bring about a sea change in the Council's methods of operation.[20]

Composition and Subcommittees

The original EC treaty stipulated that "each government shall delegate to [the Council] one of its members." The Maastricht Treaty used a new form of words, describing the Council as consisting of "representatives of each member state at ministerial level authorized to commit the government of that member state" (Article 203 TEC). The reason for the change was to accommodate federations, such as Germany and Belgium, where members of regional governments had insisted on representation in the Council when the Council discussed issues that, in their own countries, were the responsibility of regional rather than federal government. Thus, members of subnational as well as national governments occasionally sit around the Council table.

Although legally there is only one Council, in practice there are various Council formations organized along horizontal (for example, foreign affairs, finance) and sectoral (for example, agriculture, competitiveness) lines. All are technically equal, but some are more equal than others. Because of the EU's expanding competence, the number of these councils grew steadily over the years to more than twenty in the late 1990s. The multiplication of councils supposedly increased efficiency by allowing government ministers to decide issues in their particular areas of expertise and also to distribute responsibility for EU decisionmaking among a wider circle of cabinet colleagues. In fact, too many council formations impeded the EU's effectiveness, forcing member states to overhaul the system as part of a reform of the Council that began in 1999. Based on the so-called Trumpf-Piris Report (named after two senior officials in the Council secretariat), the European Council decided to strengthen the coordinating role of the General Affairs Council, reduce the number of Council configurations, and improve preparatory work at all levels. As a result, the number of Council formations was cut back to nine, including a revamped General Affairs and External Relations Council (see Table 8.3). Large numbers of government ministers still come to Brussels for Council meetings, but they participate in fewer Council formations.

The number of council meetings held annually depends on the scope and intensity of EU business and on the political momentum behind a particular issue. Most councils meet monthly. Regardless of which sector or issue it cov-

Table 8.3   Council Formations

Formation	Responsibilities	Preparatory Committees
General Affairs and External Relations		
General Affairs function	General EU affairs; cohesion, enlargement, financial perspectives	Coreper
External Relations function	Foreign and security policy, trade, development	Coreper; Political and Security Committee
Economic and Financial Affairs	Economic and fiscal policy coordination; budget	Coreper; Economic and Financial Committee
Eurogroup[a]	Economic coordination among countries using the euro	Economic and Financial Committee
Justice and Home Affairs	External border control, visas, asylum, police cooperation, judicial cooperation	Coreper; Coordinating Committee
Employment, Social Policy, Health and Consumer Affairs	Employment, working conditions, public health, consumer protection	Coreper
Competitiveness	Internal market, industry, research	Coreper
Transport, Telecommunications, and Energy	Transport, telecommunications, energy	Coreper
Agriculture and Fisheries	Common Agricultural Policy, Common Fisheries Policy, food safety	Special Committee on Agriculture
Environment	Environment, sustainable development	Coreper
Education, Youth and Culture	Education, vocational training, cultural protection	Coreper

Note: a. This is an unofficial Council formation restricted to member states that have adopted the euro.

ers, a council has supreme decisionmaking authority. It is also empowered to make decisions relating to issues beyond its particular area of expertise. A council automatically approves any "A" points on its agenda whether or not those points pertain to that council's area of responsibility ("A" points are items already agreed to at a lower level that Coreper places on the Council's agenda for formal approval). The Council may also approve without a vote (although usually after considerable discussion) some of the "B" points— items thoroughly discussed at a lower level but on which Coreper was unable to reach agreement—or may send some of them back to Coreper for further deliberation. Occasionally the president will call for an "indicative vote" on contentious B points to see where each country stands. Depending on the outcome, the president may resume discussion and try to reach consensus, call for a definitive vote, or postpone the issue until another meeting.

Despite the official pretense of equality, there is an unwritten hierarchy of councils based on political and economic importance. The General Affairs and External Relations Council, consisting of foreign ministers, is at the top. This placement harks back to the early days of European integration, when countries saw EC membership fundamentally as a foreign policy concern. As European integration covered more and more policy areas, however, it became impossible to distinguish between the foreign and domestic implications of EU membership. Accordingly, finance and economics ministers, who make up the Economic and Financial Affairs Council (known as Ecofin), demanded a greater say in EU affairs and, in many member states, challenged their foreign affairs colleagues for preeminence in domestic interministerial coordination. National bureaucratic rivalry over policymaking toward Brussels, and over decisionmaking in Brussels itself, remains endemic. Monetary union has greatly enhanced Ecofin's prominence in Brussels and finance ministers' influence in the coordination of national policy toward the EU. As a result, foreign ministers are struggling to retain their predominant bureaucratic positions.

The General Affairs and External Relations Council is really two councils in one. Meeting under the rubric of general affairs, its members prepare EU summits, coordinate the work of other councils, and take legislative decisions in a range of policy areas (on the ground that foreign ministers possess a broad political and economic perspective on European integration that other ministers lack). The agenda of meetings on general affairs includes "high political issues" that cut across sectoral lines as well as issues that the sectoral councils could not decide. Here the General Affairs Council runs the same risk as the European Council: issues that should be settled at a lower level are pushed up to a higher level. The tendency of the General Affairs Council to become a glorified sectoral council or even a glorified Coreper diminishes its effectiveness and tends to increase absenteeism. Meeting under the rubric of external relations, the foreign ministers discuss foreign and security policy issues and take decisions on trade and development policy.

Foreign ministers' heavy travel schedules also explain why they sometimes miss regular meetings of the General Affairs and External Relations Council, or at least that part of it dealing with general affairs, which usually takes place during the first morning of the two-day council session. In addition to attending numerous bilateral and multilateral meetings under the EU's auspices, foreign ministers participate in a host of other meetings—for instance, meetings of the United Nations, the Organization for Security and Cooperation in Europe, and NATO. At these gatherings, they have additional opportunities to conduct EU business and to get to know each other better (personal considerations and political empathy are as important in the General Affairs and External Relations Council as in the European Council). Although they see each other often, foreign ministers have far less intimate meetings in the General Affairs and External Relations Council than their bosses have in the European Council.

Whereas attendance at the European Council is strictly limited, General Affairs and External Relations Councils include large numbers of officials. Each delegation has three seats at the council table and six seats behind, although sometimes as many as ten additional advisers accompany each delegation's top three (the foreign ministers, the most senior foreign ministry adviser, and the Brussels-based permanent representative). The Council president can cut down on the number present by calling for a restricted session—usually "inner table only," occasionally ministers and commissioner only. As already noted, lunch affords an opportunity for a restricted gathering of the meeting's principals.

Offended by the "football-pitch atmosphere" prevalent in the General Affairs Council, British foreign secretary David Owen tried to reduce the attendance at General Affairs Councils during Britain's presidency in 1977.[21] Using the same metaphor, Roy Jenkins described the General Affairs Council as having "up to 300 people present in a huge room, talking from one end of the table to the other as though across an empty football pitch."[22] The situation only got worse with successive rounds of enlargement. Anticipating the organizational impact of the accession of ten new member states, the Irish presidency called in early 2004 for better preparation of Council meetings, improved coordination by the secretariat-general, and shorter speeches by the ministers themselves (politicians, like professors, are rarely succinct).

Once during each presidency, the foreign ministers and the Commission president or vice president escape with a few aides for an informal discussion of foreign and security policy. The first such event was at Schloss Gymnich during Germany's presidency in early 1974. These biannual retreats are now known as "Gymnich-type" meetings and always take place in lavish settings and surroundings. Most are memorable for their cuisine and conviviality rather than for serious work.

Ecofin is almost on a par with, but is still perhaps one rung immediately below, the General Affairs and External Relations Council, followed by the Agriculture Council and the Competitiveness Council. Despite the steady decline in EU spending on agriculture (relative to the size of the EU budget), it would be wrong to think that the Agriculture Council's importance has greatly diminished. Protracted debate in the early 1990s about agricultural policy reform, especially in the context of the Uruguay Round negotiations of the General Agreement on Tariffs and Trade, maintained the Agriculture Council's political prominence, as did debate in the late 1990s and early 2000s about further reform in the context of enlargement. Of the rest, the Competitiveness Council is especially important. It began life as the Internal Market Council in 1983 to help remove nontariff barriers to intra-EC trade and was instrumental in launching and sustaining the single market program. It became the Competitiveness Council following the launch of the Lisbon strategy for economic modernization and reform.

The Constitutional Treaty includes a further radical revision of the Council system. As well as effectively scrapping the rotating presidency, the treaty proposes only two councils, although it provides for the European Council to establish additional formations along sectoral lines (see Table 8.4).

The Committee of Permanent Representatives

Coreper plays a vital part in preparing council meetings and in behind-the-scenes EU decisionmaking. It has become more prominent and powerful throughout EU history. Even before the Rome Treaty was implemented and the EC came into existence, member states appreciated the need for resident national representatives, at ambassadorial level, to manage Council business in Brussels. Among other things, the Merger Treaty of 1965 recognized

Table 8.4   Council Formations Under the Constitutional Treaty

Formation	Responsibilities	Presidency
Legislative and General Affairs		Government minister[a]
Legislative function	Enact EU Laws	
General Affairs function	Prepare meetings of the European Council	
Foreign Affairs	Conduct/coordinate external relations	EU foreign minister
Others as approved by the European Council		Government minister[a]

Note: a. On basis of the rota shown in Table 8.2.

Coreper's existence and responsibilities. The Luxembourg Compromise of January 1966 boosted the institutional position of the Council vis-à-vis the Commission and in the process strengthened Coreper's role. At the Paris summit in December 1974, the heads of government decided to give Coreper additional power "so that only the most important problems need to be discussed in the Council."[23]

The Commission has always looked askance at Coreper, a highly influential committee of the member states' most senior civil servants. Ironically, however, as the Commission's own position revived in the mid-1980s, relations with Coreper improved. Indeed, the harmonious Coreper-Commission relationship—specifically, the relationship between Coreper and the Commission's secretariat-general—was a key ingredient of the Community's transformation in the late 1980s and early 1990s.

The member states' permanent representations (embassies) to the EU include national bureaucrats from a range of government departments on assignment in Brussels. Member states rank the permanent representation among their most important diplomatic missions. The caliber and effectiveness of permanent representation officials determine to a great extent how countries fare in the EU. As for the officials themselves, it may be more prestigious to serve in Washington, D.C., or in the capital of another member state (notably London, Paris, or Berlin), but a posting to the permanent representation in Brussels is a sound career move.

Coreper's huge workload has resulted in two configurations of the committee: Coreper I, consisting of the deputy permanent representatives, and Coreper II, consisting of the permanent representatives themselves. There is a strict separation of responsibilities between the two; once a subject is given to Coreper I, Coreper II has nothing more to do with it. The division between one list of subjects and another is rigid (see Table 8.5).

Coreper's job is to prepare the councils' agendas, to decide what issues go to which council, and to set up and monitor legislative working groups of national officials who are either based at the permanent representation in Brussels or at home in their government ministries (about ten such groups meet on a given workday in Brussels). Each configuration of Coreper meets at least once a week. The permanent representatives also brief visiting ministers and other dignitaries and report regularly to their national capitals on developments in the EU. Like their ministerial bosses, permanent representatives become well acquainted with each other. Also like their senior ministers, they enjoy biannual retreats at the expense of the Council presidency.

The Special Committee on Agriculture substitutes for Coreper by preparing meetings of the Agriculture Council, although Coreper continues to deal with the political implications of agricultural issues (such as Common Agricultural Policy reform or international trade agreements) on behalf of the General Affairs and External Relations Council. The so-called Coordinating

Table 8.5   Coreper

Configuration	Membership	Responsibilities	Assisted by
Coreper I	Deputy Permanent Representatives	Agriculture, fisheries, internal market, industry, budget, research, transport, environment, social affairs, energy, education, cultural affairs, health, consumer protection	Mertens Group
Coreper II	Permanent Representatives	External economic relations, justice and home affairs, treaty reform, enlargement, some aspects of monetary policy, foreign and security policy	Antichi Group

Committee prepares meetings of the Justice and Home Affairs Council, and the Political and Security Committee assists Coreper with foreign and security policy–related issues that come before the General Affairs and External Relations Council. Whereas Coreper prepares a number of Ecofin agenda items, a separate Economic and Finance Committee, made up of officials from national finance ministries and representatives of national central banks, advises Ecofin on monetary policy issues without reference to Coreper. Unlike other Council subcommittees, which adhere to the Council presidency rota, the Economic and Finance Committee elects its president for a twelve-month period.

Coreper escaped criticism during and after the Maastricht Treaty ratification crisis because its existence and functions were little known outside Brussels. Yet Coreper is extremely powerful and even more secretive than the Council. Coreper's ability to shape the Council's agenda and to influence decisionmaking by categorizing items as either ready for automatic approval (A items) or for discussion and decision (B items) illustrates the committee's importance and suggests that, in certain cases, Coreper is the EU's real legislature. Coreper's lack of accountability to the electorate and inaccessibility to the public are key elements in the EU's democratic deficit. Yet Coreper's obscurity continues to shield it from public criticism, while its professionalism ensures generally favorable media coverage.[24]

Decisionmaking

Speaking at the opening session of the intergovernmental conference that preceded the Single European Act, Commission president Jacques Delors denounced "the ball and chain of unanimity that bedevils the whole Community system."[25] By giving member states the right to block voting in the Council by invoking a real or supposed vital national interest, the Luxembourg Compromise of 1966 tied that ball and chain firmly around the EC's ankles. In consequence, decisionmaking slowed to a snail's pace as succeeding presidencies generally refrained from calling for a vote in Council meetings. Legislative paralysis became chronic in the mid-1970s following the first enlargement (Britain and Denmark strongly opposed majority voting) and during a period of prolonged recession when most countries sought national rather than EC solutions to Europe's economic problems.

The legislative situation improved gradually in the early 1980s as political pressure mounted to complete the single market and revive European integration. A plethora of reports and proposals called on member states to expedite decisionmaking by voting rather than vetoing in the Council. In a famous speech to the European Parliament in May 1984, Mitterrand renounced the Luxembourg Compromise, which de Gaulle had been instrumental in bringing about, and advocated a "return to the Treaty" through "the more frequent practice of voting on important issues."[26]

The EC's imminent Mediterranean enlargement and the member states' increasing interest in completing the single market focused attention in the mid-1980s squarely on reform of the Council's decisionmaking procedure. In the Single European Act, national governments not only committed themselves to achieving a single market by the end of 1992 but also agreed to do so largely through qualified majority voting in the Council. By implication, this was the end of the Luxembourg Compromise. Subsequent practice confirmed that countries were indeed willing to play by new rules and risk being outvoted on a wide range of issues. Also, subsequent treaty changes (especially in the Maastricht and Amsterdam Treaties) extended the applicability of qualified majority voting in EU decisionmaking, leaving fewer and fewer policy areas subject to unanimity.

Despite the apparent demise of the Luxembourg Compromise, a similar mechanism found its way into the Amsterdam Treaty with respect to the possible use of flexibility (closer cooperation among member states). According to the new provision, a member state could—"for important and stated reasons of national policy"—prevent a vote being taken in the Council on whether to allow flexibility (Article 11.2 TEC). In such circumstances, the Council could decide by qualified majority vote to send the matter to the heads of state and government for a decision by unanimity. The inclusion of a quasi-national veto in the Amsterdam Treaty with respect to flexibility and, elsewhere in the treaty, with respect to "constructive abstention" in foreign and security policy decisionmaking reflected the extreme political sensitivity of these issues rather than a full-fledged reversion to the Luxembourg Compromise. Although both the Nice Treaty and the Constitutional Treaty eased the restrictions on the possible use of flexibility, the Constitutional Treaty included "emergency brakes," which could be pulled on grounds of alleged endangerment of the national interest in the areas of social security and the harmonization of certain aspects of criminal law.

Whether or not voting takes place in policy areas not subject to an "emergency brake" or the vestigial Luxembourg Compromise, contentious items often become part of a package deal that accumulates during a number of Council meetings. Shortly after becoming Commission president in 1985, Delors deplored what he called "linkage diplomacy": the member states' tendency to link issues in an effort to negotiate the best deal possible.[27] Despite Delors's denunciation of it, linkage diplomacy flourished during the single market program. Indeed, the inherent give-and-take of legislative package dealing facilitated rapid progress toward the 1992 target date and has since become a standard feature of EU policymaking.

After each meeting the Council issues a press release that lists the legislation just enacted (if any). Since the Maastricht ratification crisis, the Council has also revealed how member states voted (if a formal vote took place). Journalists reconstruct what happened in the Council by piecing together information from the national delegations, the Commission's spokesperson, and the Council press office (the Council president and the relevant commissioner usually give a press conference after each Council meeting). Based on the available evidence, it seems that voting is relatively infrequent and that consensus remains the preferred path for decisionmaking in the Council.

The Vagaries of Council Voting

The general demise of the Luxembourg Compromise since the launch of the single market program has not necessarily resulted in many more items actually being put to a vote. In other words, since the late 1980s there has been greater use of qualified majority voting in principle rather than in practice. Member states agree to abide by majority decisions but, ever sympathetic to national sensitivities and imbued with a deep-rooted culture of consensus, rarely want issues to come to a vote in the Council. The presidency may call for a vote, but voting does not always follow. Instead, the country or countries in the minority may simply accept the inevitable and acquiesce in the passage of legislation.

Another paradox of majority voting, whether in principle or in practice, is that it can deepen the democratic deficit. Although majority voting in the Council is inherently democratic, it weakens the already tenuous ties between governments and national parliaments on EU issues. By renouncing the national veto, governments reduce their parliaments' already weak leverage over EU legislation. After all, a national parliament could try to punish its government for not vetoing controversial legislation if the government were able to impose a veto. But a national parliament can hardly hold its government accountable for being outvoted.

Depending on its legal base in the treaty and its stage in the legislative process, a proposal before the Council may be subject to a simple majority vote, a qualified majority vote, or unanimity. As a result of successive treaty changes, qualified majority voting has become the norm. The number of votes per country (also known as the weighting of votes) has traditionally depended on each country's size. The allocation of votes and the threshold for a qualified majority (around 72 percent of the total number of Council votes) have always been contentious issues among member states and have increasingly divided the big from the small countries. Concerned about the greater difficulty that it would have mustering a blocking minority in an enlarged EU (and under intense pressure from Euroskeptical Conservative back-benchers), in 1994 the British government attempted to keep the blocking minority at its existing threshold (twenty-three votes) even after the accession of Austria, Finland, and Sweden, when, based on the experience of previous enlargements, it should have been increased to twenty-six votes. After a bitter dispute, the other member states agreed to the so-called Ioannina Compromise, whereby "if members of the Council representing a total of 23 to 25 votes indicate their intention to oppose the adoption by the Council of a decision by a qualified majority, the Council will do all within its power to reach, within a reasonable time . . . a satisfactory solution that can be adopted by at least 65 votes" (Britain's preferred qualified majority).

The Ioannina Compromise was largely a face-saving device for Britain and had little practical effect on EU decisionmaking. Its real significance lay in what it portended for the next round of enlargement. Britain's government at that time was obstructionist and Euroskeptical. Moreover, together with other large member states, Britain was concerned about the impact on its relative voting weight of the likely accession, sometime after 2000, of many more small member states (ranging in size from Cyprus to Hungary) and only one big member state (Poland). Such concern led the big member states, beginning in the mid-1990s, to advocate an overhaul of qualified majority voting. They wanted either a substantial increase in the number of votes for each of them or the introduction of a double majority system that would combine the traditional requirements of a qualified majority with a new demographic criterion. Without a demographic criterion, the big member states argued, a qualified majority could be formed in the future by a group of member states that together did not represent a majority of the EU's population. In the event, the Amsterdam Treaty of 1997 did not include major decisionmaking reform but stipulated that Council votes would have to be reweighted during the next round of treaty change in order to compensate big member states for the anticipated loss of their second commissioner.

As expected, the Nice Treaty of 2001 radically reallocated the number of votes for each member state (and allocated votes to the acceding member states) in a manner that redressed what the big member states saw as an imbalance in favor of the small member states (Table 8.6 shows the weighting of votes before and after Nice). The Nice Treaty also introduced two additional criteria for a qualified majority:

- at least half (and in some cases two-thirds) of the member states
- at least 62 percent of the total population of the EU (if a member state seeks such confirmation)

The Nice arrangements came into effect in November 2004.

Table 8.6   Weighted Votes in the Council

Country	Population (in millions)	Before May 2004[a]	May–Oct. 2004	After Nov. 2004[b]
Germany	82	10	10	29
Britain	60	10	10	29
France	59	10	10	29
Italy	58	10	10	29
Spain	39	8	8	27
Poland	39	—	8	27
The Netherlands	16	5	5	13
Belgium	10	5	5	12
Greece	11	5	5	12
Portugal	10	5	5	12
Czech Republic	10	—	5	12
Hungary	10	—	5	12
Sweden	9	4	4	10
Austria	8	4	4	10
Denmark	5	3	3	7
Finland	5	3	3	7
Ireland	4	3	3	7
Lithuania	4	—	3	7
Slovakia	5	—	3	7
Luxembourg	.4	2	2	4
Cyprus	.7	—	2	4
Estonia	1	—	2	4
Latvia	2	—	2	4
Slovenia	2	—	2	4
Malta	.4	—	1	3
Total	451.5	87	120	321
Qualified majority		62	87	232
Blocking minority		26	34	90

Notes: a. Date of EU enlargement
b. Date of entry into force of Nice provisions for qualified majority voting

The arithmetic of qualified majority voting means that no single country can block legislation, and even two of the largest countries acting together lack enough votes to constitute a blocking minority. Thus, on any particular proposal, both sides (for and against) need to muster coalitions in order to prevail. The composition of such coalitions varies considerably according to the item under discussion. A country's block of votes is indivisible, although Flemish politicians proposed in 1996 that Belgium's five votes be split between Flanders (three) and Wallonia (two)—they apparently forgot that Belgium has a third regional government: the Brussels capital region. Needless to say, neither the Belgian government nor the other member states supported the proposal.[28]

Reflecting a further shift of power to the big member states and an effort to simplify Council decisionmaking, the Convention on the Future of Europe proposed that a qualified majority consist of:

- at least 50 percent of the member states (casting one vote each)
- at least 60 percent of the total population of the EU

This proposal was picked apart by the small member states in the intergovernmental conference, as a result of which the system agreed to in the Constitutional Treaty was less congenial to the big member states and more complicated than the original proposal. The Constitutional Treaty therefore stipulates that a qualified majority vote will consist of:

- at least fifteen member states
- at least 55 percent of the member states (casting one vote each)
- at least 65 percent of the total population of the EU

However, a blocking minority must be formed by at least four member states, thereby preventing the three big member states alone from doing so. Moreover, harking back to the Ioannina Compromise, the treaty adds that in the event that a group of member states somewhat less than a blocking minority opposes the adoption of a particular measure, the Council will do everything possible to reach a satisfactory compromise and allay the concerns of the group in the minority.

Notes

1. On the significance of the presidency, see K. Kollman, "The Rotating Presidency of the European Council as a Search for Good Policies," *European Union Politics* 4 (March 1, 2003): 51–75; and Jonas Tallberg, "The Power of the Presidency: Brokerage, Efficiency and Distribution in EU Negotiations," *Journal of Common Market Studies* 42, no. 5 (December 2004): 869–1110.

2. Sir Charles Powell, "Few Chances for Heroics," *Financial Times,* January 5, 1998, p. 15.

3. Guy de Bassompierre, *Changing the Guard in Brussels: An Insider's View of the EC Presidency* (New York: Praeger, 1988), p. 12.

4. European Commission, *1974 General Report* (Luxembourg: Office for Official Publications of the European Communities, 1975), p. 297.

5. Council of the European Communities General Secretariat, *The Council of the European Community: An Introduction to Its Services and Activities* (Luxembourg: Office for Official Publications of the European Communities, 1991), p. 29.

6. Roy Jenkins, *European Diary, 1977–1981* (London: Collins, 1989), p. 371.

7. Helen Wallace and Geoffrey Edwards, *The Council of Ministers of the European Community and the President-in-Office* (London: Federal Trust, 1977), p. 550.

8. "Tindemans Report," Bulletin EC S/1-1976, p. 31.

9. Quoted in *Agence Europe,* December 17, 1974, p. 4.

10. Jenkins, *European Diary*, pp. 248–249.

11. Quoted in *Agence Europe*, May 4, 1998, p. 4.

12. David Cameron, "The 1992 Initiative: Causes and Consequences," in Alberta Sbragia, ed., *Euro-Politics: Institutions and Policymaking in the "New" European Community* (Washington, DC: Brookings Institution, 1992), p. 63.

13. Council of the European Communities, *Report on European Institutions Presented by the Committee of Three to the European Council (Report of the Three Wise Men)* (Luxembourg: Office of Official Publications of the European Communities, 1981), pp. 16–17.

14. "Ad Hoc Committee for Institutional Affairs Report to the European Council (Dooge Report)," March 1985, Bulletin EC 3-1985, point 3.5.1.

15. Annette Morgan, *From Summit to Council: Evolution in the EEC* (London: Chatham House, 1976), p. 56.

16. Jenkins, *European Diary,* p. 75.

17. European Commission, *Openness and Transparency in the EU Institutions,* proceedings of a seminar in Brussels, November 22, 1995, p. 22.

18. Ibid., p. 14.

19. M. P. C. M. Van Schendelen, "'The Council Decides': Does the Council Decide?" *Journal of Common Market Studies* 34, no. 4 (December 1996): 531.

20. On the Council in general, see Fiona Hayes-Renshaw and Helen Wallace, *The Council of Ministers* (New York: St. Martin's Press, 1996); Helen Wallace, "The Council: An Institutional Chameleon?" *Governance* 15, no. 3 (July 2002): 325–375; and Martin Westlake, *The Council of the European Union* (London: Catermill, 1995).

21. Quoted in the *Times* (London), June 28, 1977, p. 16.

22. Jenkins, *European Diary,* p. 74.

23. Commission, *1974 General Report,* Annex to Chapter 1, point 8.

24. For an assessment of Coreper's importance, see David Bostock, "Coreper Revisited," *Journal of Common Market Studies* 40, no. 2 (June 2002): 215–235.

25. Quoted in Marina Gazzo, ed., *Towards European Union,* vol. 1 (Brussels: Agence Europe, 1985), p. 26.

26. François Mitterrand, speech to the European Parliament, May 24, 1984, reprinted in *Vital Speeches of the Day,* August 1, 1984, p. 613.

27. Jacques Delors, speech to the European Parliament, March 12, 1985, Bulletin EC S/4-1985, p. 6.

28. See *De Standaard*, March 19, 1996, p. 1.

9

The European Parliament

Just as the Commission has no analog in national political systems, so could the European Parliament easily be misconstrued as the EU equivalent of a national parliament. Most members of the European Parliament think that it *should* have all the powers and prerogatives of a national parliament instead of having to share legislative power with the Council. They argue that the Parliament's limited legislative authority undermines the European Union's democratic legitimacy and have long found it "unacceptable that a union of democratic states should not itself be democratic."[1] Directly elected every five years in EU-wide elections, Europarliamentarians are understandably aggrieved that their institution lacks the political clout of the Council, although it has surpassed that of the Commission.

The history of the Parliament is a history of relentless efforts by its members to increase their institution's power. Using the argument of a lack of democratic accountability in the EU—the so-called democratic deficit—as a potent weapon, Europarliamentarians have sought, especially since the advent of direct elections in 1979, to redress what they saw as the institutional imbalance among the Commission, Council, and Parliament. With the indispensable assistance of genuinely sympathetic or guilt-ridden governments, the Parliament has succeeded since the mid-1980s in obtaining substantially greater legislative and supervisory authority during successive rounds of treaty reform. Paradoxically, however, greater power for the Parliament has not resulted in a higher turnout in direct elections.

By introducing a "cooperation" procedure (the right to a second reading for certain legislation, notably concerning the single market), the Single European Act of 1986 proved a turning point in the Parliament's fortunes. The Maastricht Treaty of 1992 extended the cooperation procedure to other important areas and gave the Parliament a limited form of legislative codecision with the Council. The Amsterdam Treaty of 1997 virtually abolished the cooperation procedure in favor of a simplified codecision procedure, applicable to many more policy areas. Earlier, in the 1970s, national governments gave the Parliament significant budgetary authority. The combination of budgetary and legislative power, an assent procedure for ratification of association and accession agreements, and the right to scrutinize the Commission's activities make the Parliament a formidable player in the EU political system.

Europarliamentarians claim the high moral ground in the ubiquitous interinstitutional struggle over the Parliament's powers. Yet their management of parliamentary affairs weakens their moral authority. The monthly trek between Brussels and Strasbourg, four hours apart by road or rail, is an obvious but important example. Parliamentarians spend three weeks each month in Brussels attending committee and political group meetings and the other week in Strasbourg attending plenary sessions. A large part of the Parliament's secretariat is located in Luxembourg, approximately halfway between Brussels and Strasbourg. The cost and inconvenience of constantly transporting parliamentarians, officials, and innumerable boxes of papers in a 600-mile circuit every month, and of maintaining two massive buildings (in Brussels and Strasbourg) and a smaller office complex in Luxembourg, have seriously and possibly irreparably eroded public confidence in the Parliament.

In their defense, Europarliamentarians say that they would like to move entirely to Brussels and that they have already taken the initiative to hold committee meetings, political group meetings, and occasional plenary sessions there, but that national governments are responsible for the practice of holding regular plenary sessions in Strasbourg and for keeping the secretariat in Luxembourg. Over the years the governments of France and Luxembourg have gone to great lengths, including taking legal action and blocking decisions about where to locate new EU institutions and agencies, to prevent the Parliament's plenary sessions and secretariat from moving permanently to Brussels. For its part, the Belgian government built a lavish facility in Brussels in an effort to lure all of the Parliament's activities there. Not to be outdone, the French government built an equally lavish facility in Strasbourg, where the Parliament had previously shared a more-than-adequate building with the Council of Europe. Both buildings were inaugurated in 1998.

After intense intergovernmental haggling, member states added a protocol to the Amsterdam Treaty (later incorporated into the Nice Treaty) that settled the matter definitively: "The European Parliament shall have its seat in Strasbourg where the twelve periods of monthly plenary sessions, including the budget session, shall be held. The periods of additional plenary sessions shall be held in Brussels. The committees of the European Parliament shall meet in Brussels. The General Secretariat of the European Parliament and its departments shall remain in Luxembourg."

Although parliamentarians can legitimately claim that the decision to stay in Strasbourg was beyond their control, they continue to bear the political brunt of Parliament's monthly migration. Parliamentarians' generous allowances and seemingly lavish lifestyles, as well as the institution's peculiar procedures, linguistic muddle (the EU's twenty official languages are constantly used), and poorly attended plenary sessions, contribute to the low public esteem for the institution. They also generate an endless supply of silly stories, even in the sympathetic press, causing the institution grave political damage.

Undoubtedly a majority of parliamentarians are hardworking, dedicated, and sensitive to popular cynicism about parliamentarians in general and Europarliamentarians in particular. But until the Parliament ends its monthly road show, simplifies its procedures, and reins in its members' spendthrift ways, redressing the institutional imbalance by giving the Parliament more legislative power will not resolve the EU's supposed democratic deficit. After all, the democratic deficit is based on popular perception as well as political reality, and most Europeans tend to see the Parliament as part of the problem, not part of the solution.

Size and Composition

The size of the Parliament grew with successive enlargements as seats were allocated to each new member state. Apart from the proliferation of languages, the proliferation of Europarliamentarians with each wave of enlargement made the Parliament inherently more difficult to manage. Simply put: the larger the Parliament, the less efficient it is likely to be. But how large is too large? With a parliament of 626 seats for fifteen member states following the 1995 enlargement, and in anticipation of the accession of numerous Central and Eastern European countries, member states agreed in the Amsterdam Treaty to limit the number of parliamentarians to a maximum of 700. No sooner was the Amsterdam Treaty implemented than member states again reopened the question of the Parliament's size and composition, agreeing in view of the possible accession of twelve new member states in the near future (ten of them in 2004, with Bulgaria and Romania expected to join a little later) to increase the total number to 732. That meant not only agreeing on the number of seats for each prospective new member state but also reallocating seats among the existing member states.

Apportionment of seats to the acceding member states and reapportionment among the existing member states was a highly contentious issue in the intergovernmental conference that resulted in the Nice Treaty. Ineligible to participate in the conference, the applicant countries furiously lobbied the existing member states—especially in the margins of the Nice summit of December 2000, where the intergovernmental conference came to an end—for as large a parliamentary representation as possible. At the same time, the existing member states fought either to maintain their current level of representation or to minimize the extent of its reduction. Even governments that liked the Parliament least and resisted supranationalism most argued tenaciously for the largest possible national representation, suggesting that the size of a parliamentary delegation is a matter of both national pride and political advantage.

Given its large population and political influence, Germany retained its representation of 99 parliamentarians, by far the largest national representation in the Parliament. Most other member states, by contrast, saw their delegations shrink appreciably. For example, the allocation of seats for Britain, France, and Italy, the three next-largest member states, dropped from 87 to 72 each; the allocation for Ireland, a small member state, dropped from 15 to 12. At the conclusion of the accession negotiations, by which time it was clear that Bulgaria and Romania would not join until 2007, the existing member states and those just about to join decided to apportion among themselves, for the upcoming direct elections, the seats already allocated to Bulgaria and Romania. That led to another round of intergovernmental bargaining, as a result of which many existing and soon-to-be member states received additional seats, albeit temporarily. Thus, the allocation of seats for Britain, France, and Italy went up to 78 each; Ireland's went up to 13 (see Table 9.1).

If Bulgaria and Romania join in the meantime, the apportionment of seats agreed to at the Nice summit will apply to the 2009 direct elections, thereby adhering to the limit of 732 seats. During the period between their membership and the next direct elections, however, Bulgaria's and Romania's delegations would push the total number of seats in the Parliament temporarily to 786, just as the arrival of representatives from the countries that joined the EU in May 2004 pushed the total number of seats temporarily to 788 until the direct elections in June. The accession of other countries would cause similar temporary increases in the Parliament's size and, in the case of a country as large as Turkey, yet another acrimonious negotiation among existing member states on the reduction of their parliamentary delegations.

The Constitutional Treaty introduces another wrinkle by raising the number of seats in the Parliament to 750. It does not provide for their allocation but authorizes the European Council, on a proposal from the Parliament (not the Commission) and with the assent of Parliament, to allocate the seats before the 2009 direct elections. However, the Constitutional Treaty sets a minimum threshold of 6 seats and an upper limit of 96 for member states, thereby requiring Germany to trim the size of its delegation.

As well as the problem of efficiency, the size of the Parliament and apportionment of seats within it raise politically sensitive questions about fairness and proportionality of representation. The distribution of seats among member states, resulting in great differences in the ratio of parliamentarians to population from one member state to another, is one of the most striking

Table 9.1   Allocation of Seats in the European Parliament

Member State	2005 Population (in millions)	1999 Election	2004 Election
Germany	82	99	99
France	59	87	78
Britain	59	87	78
Italy	58	87	78
Spain	39	64	54
The Netherlands	16	31	27
Belgium	10	25	24
Greece	11	25	24
Portugal	10	25	24
Sweden	9	22	19
Austria	8	21	18
Denmark	5	16	14
Finland	5	16	14
Ireland	4	15	13
Luxembourg	.4	6	6
Poland	39	—	54
Czech Republic	10	—	24
Hungary	10	—	24
Slovakia	5	—	14
Lithuania	4	—	13
Latvia	2	—	9
Slovenia	2	—	7
Estonia	1	—	6
Cyprus	.7	—	6
Malta	.4	—	5
Total seats		626	732

Note: Member states Romania and Bulgaria will be allocated 33 and 17 seats, respectively, beginning with the 2009 election.

anomalies in the Europarliamentary system. For example, before unification Germany had a parliamentarian-to-population ratio of 1:984,000. After unification, when Germany's population increased by 17 million, Germany won extra representation in the Parliament, but not without opposition from the other member states, especially Britain, France, and Italy, which had previously enjoyed equal representation with Germany. When the European Council agreed in December 1992 to redistribute and increase the total number of seats in the Parliament, Germany's parliamentarian-to-population ratio declined to 1:805,000. This may seem like a marked improvement, but it still compares ludicrously to Luxembourg's ratio of 1:66,000 (and will move to a greater disparity under the terms of the Constitutional Treaty).

Direct Elections

The adjective "direct" distinguishes the current system for electing members of the European Parliament from the "indirect" system in operation before 1979.[2] Originally, national parliaments nominated a number of their members to sit also as parliamentarians in Strasbourg. The size of each national delegation was vaguely proportional to a country's population, and the composition of each delegation depended on the distribution of seats among political parties in the national parliaments.

The Rome Treaty called for the Parliament to draw up a proposal "for elections by direct universal suffrage in accordance with a uniform procedure in all Member States." The Parliament did so in 1961 and again in 1963 and 1969, but the Council never acted "to lay down [unanimously] the appropriate provisions, which it shall recommend to Member States for adoption in accordance with their respective constitutional requirements." Efforts to move from "indirect" to "direct" elections fell victim to the pervasive struggle between supranationalism and intergovernmentalism in the EU system. Supranationalists hoped, and intergovernmentalists feared, that direct elections would strengthen the Parliament's legitimacy and power and thereby weaken the Council's authority. French president Charles de Gaulle's guardianship of intergovernmentalism and disdain for the Strasbourg Assembly ensured that direct elections did not come about in the 1960s.

The relaunch of European integration after de Gaulle's departure revived the question of direct elections. A decision at the 1974 Paris summit to offset the nascent European Council (an institutionalization of intergovernmentalism) with direct elections to the Parliament (a sop to supranationalism) prompted the Parliament once again to revise its electoral proposals. Parliament adopted new ones in January 1975, and the European Council approved a modified version of them in July 1976. Apart from the lingering reluctance of some old (notably France) and new (notably Britain) member states to risk having the Parliament gain additional authority by moving from indirect to direct elections, governments differed widely on a myriad of organizational and procedural points. As a result, in September 1976 the Council finally authorized direct elections to be held every five years, but not with a uniform electoral system.

Procedural differences among member states regarding the conduct of direct elections include the way that candidates are nominated, the order of names on voting papers, campaign rules, the validation of election results, the filling of vacant seats, and the choice of election day (within a three- or four-day period in mid-June). The most important differences concern the electoral system, eligibility to vote and stand for elections, and the demarcation of constituency boundaries.

- *The electoral system:* For a long time Britain, with its "first-past-the-post system" (except in Northern Ireland), was the odd country out in elections to the Parliament; all the other member states used various forms of proportional representation. The British system was notorious for causing overrepresentation or underrepresentation of political parties in the national parliament and to a lesser extent in the European Parliament. In theory, a small swing in electoral support for a British political party could have resulted in a large gain or loss of seats for that party in Strasbourg and could have determined which political group (coalition of national political parties) formed a majority in the Parliament. Thanks to the cooperation of the Labour government that came to power in May 1997, member states agreed in the Amsterdam Treaty to allow the Parliament to draw up a proposal for elections by direct universal suffrage in accordance with "principles common to all Member States," thereby paving the way for a common, EU-wide electoral system involving some form of proportional representation (the new government also agreed in the meantime to introduce a form of proportional representation in Britain in the 1999 direct elections). The Parliament lost little time drafting an electoral act, for approval by the Council, to govern the direct elections in 2004. Reflecting the difficulty of harmonization among member states, however, the Parliament's proposal left plenty of room for national variations in a supposedly common electoral system. In the 2004 elections, therefore, all twenty-five member states used proportional representation, but not the same form of it.

- *Eligibility to vote and stand for elections:* Apart from the same minimum voting age (eighteen) in all member states, voting rights still differ markedly throughout the EU. Some member states allow absentee voting without restrictions; others extend it only to their citizens resident elsewhere in the EU. The minimum age to stand as a candidate varies throughout the EU. More significantly, for a long time nationality and residency requirements differed from member state to member state, with some restricting the right to vote to their own nationals and others extending it to residents from elsewhere in the EU. Accordingly, the Maastricht Treaty stipulated that the Council had to arrange, by the end of December 1993, to allow "Union citizens" to vote and stand as candidates in elections to the European Parliament regardless of where they resided in the EU. Aware of the sensitivity of voting rights in some member states and acknowledging the unlikelihood of uniform voting rights by the end of 1993, the treaty permitted derogations "where warranted by problems specific to a Member State." Inevitably, such derogations meant that many EU citizens resident in a member state other than their own could not vote in the 1994 direct elections (the first ones after implementation of the Maastricht Treaty). Since then, most member states have abided by the requirement that non-national residents from other member states be allowed to vote in direct elections in their country of residence, although some member states simply disregard it.

- *Demarcation of constituency boundaries:* In some member states the whole country forms a single constituency; in others the country is divided into a number of regional constituencies that do not correspond to the constituencies used in national elections. A drawback of large, national constituencies is the difficulty of developing close relations between constituents and Europarliamentarians in a majority of member states. Parliament wants to make regional constituencies obligatory in large and medium-sized member states (the Labour government obliged by organizing ten regional constituencies in mainland Britain in time for the 1999 direct elections).

Although the Parliament's profile and political power have increased greatly since the first direct election in 1979, the experience of direct elections themselves—in terms of political party behavior and voter turnout—has been hugely disappointing. The EU-wide turnout in direct elections has declined from 62.5 percent in 1979 to 45.3 percent in 2004. European voters seem unaware of or unimpressed by the Parliament's growing significance in the EU system. Much to the dismay of EU leaders, most voters seem to view direct elections as second-order or even third-order elections, of lesser importance than national or regional elections.

Whereas most candidates campaign to some extent on EU issues and proclaim their party group affiliation, inevitably national political parties and issues predominate during direct elections. In some countries, general elections coincide with and completely overshadow the European elections; in others, the European elections invariably become referendums on the performance of the national government (this was especially the case in Germany in 2004, as the Euroelections were the first major nationwide elections since the federal elections of 2002). Just as they dominate the election campaigns, national political parties also dominate the selection of candidates, over 14,000 of whom stood for 732 seats in the 2004 elections.

Candidates (and consequently Europarliamentarians) tend to fall into one of the following categories:

- aspiring politicians who failed to win selection as candidates for national elections
- aspiring politicians who won selection as candidates for national elections but subsequently lost the election

- established politicians who either are temporarily out of national office because of resignation or a government reshuffle or have retired from national politics (this category includes a number of former government ministers and even a former president of France)
- successful regional or local politicians who want to become Europarliamentarians either as an end in itself or as a stepping-stone to national political office
- prominent trade unionists and farmers' leaders
- former officials of EU institutions and, in a few cases, former commissioners
- politicians with or without a background in local, regional, or national politics who choose to make careers as Europarliamentarians
- celebrities eager to exploit their fame by winning a seat in Strasbourg

Regardless of why they stand for election to the Parliament, an increasing number of parliamentarians (although arguably still a minority) take their work seriously. Fortunately for the Parliament, only committed and competent parliamentarians make their way into leadership positions. The high caliber of leadership has contributed to the Parliament's success in acquiring and executing new political powers since the advent of direct elections.

A few Europarliamentarians still hold the "dual mandate," that is, they are members of both their national parliament and the European Parliament. The dual mandate has the advantage of personifying a close relationship between national parliaments and the European Parliament, but the demands of being a member of both bodies make it difficult for someone to hold the two positions simultaneously. Because holders of the dual mandate tend to devote more time to national politics, they unwittingly reinforce a negative stereotype of the Parliament as a publicly supported leisure center. Accordingly, the Parliament disapproves of the dual mandate, and a number of countries and political parties have banned it.

■ Political Groups

The Parliament's rules of procedure and allocation of resources strongly encourage members to join transnational political groups. Parliamentarians from the same member state are no longer allowed to form a political group. The rules have been simplified over the years and now state that "a political group shall comprise Members elected in at least one-fifth of the Member States. The minimum number of Members required to form a political group shall be nineteen." Members join a particular group for reasons of political affinity, shared interest, or convenience (Parliament only questions whether a political affinity really exists if a group member raises the issue).

Many groups in the European Parliament are branches of transnational political parties (Table 9.2). Recognizing the significance of such parties, member states included in the Maastricht Treaty a statement that "political parties at the European level are important as a factor for integration within the Union. They contribute to forming a European awareness and to expressing the political will of the citizens of the Union." This acknowledgment reflected the thinking among the more integration-minded member states that Europe-wide party organizations would bolster federalism in the emerging EU. The implicit encouragement of transnational political party formation was linked to other aspects of the Maastricht Treaty, such as the concept of Union citizenship and the extension of voting rights in local and European elections to Union citizens resident in a member state other than their own (presumably, party activity at the European level would make it easier for cit-

**Table 9.2 Political Groups in the European Parliament
(after the 2004 elections)**

Group	Characteristics	Member States Represented	Number of Parliamentarians
Group of the European People's Party and European Democrats (EPP-ED)	Christian Democrats and conservatives	25	268
Group of the Party of European Socialists (PES)	Social Democrats	23	200
Alliance of Liberals and Democrats for Europe	Liberals and free marketers	19	88
Greens/European Free Alliance	Environmentalists and "representatives of stateless nations" (e.g., Catalan, Scottish, Welsh nationalists)	13	42
Confederal Group of the European United Left/Nordic Green Left	Far left-wing environmentalists, ex-Communists, and Communists	14	41
Independence/ Democracy Group	Disaffected Euroskeptics	11	37
Union for Europe of the Nations Group	Heterogeneous group, mostly members of Italy's National Alliance and Ireland's Fianna Fáil	6	27
Unattached (independents)	Unaffiliated members	8	28

izens throughout the EU, regardless of their national origin, to participate in direct elections).[3]

The number and composition of political groups have varied greatly over time. Following the 2004 elections, which took place in the recently enlarged EU, there were seven groups in the Parliament embracing members of over 100 national political parties, plus almost thirty unattached parliamentarians. From the beginning of the political group system in the mid-1950s, three generic groupings (or families, as they like to call themselves) have eclipsed all others in the Parliament. These are the Socialists, Christian Democrats, and Liberals. Since the third direct election in 1989, the Socialists and Christian Democrats have predominated: both were the only groups to include political parties or individual politicians from each member state (since the 2004 elections, the Christian Democrats/Conservatives alone hold that distinction).

The Socialist and Christian Democratic/Conservatives Groups

The Socialists and the Christian Democrats benefited greatly from successive enlargements, but the sizable British Labour contingent took its seats in the European Parliament only after the successful outcome of the 1975 referendum on whether Britain should stay in the European Community. From then until the 1999 elections the Socialists were the largest group in the Parliament, dominated by large contingents of the British Labour Party and German Social Democratic Party. The Socialists benefited more than other groups from Spanish and Portuguese accession in 1986 and from the accession of Finland and Sweden—two countries with strong social-democratic traditions—in 1995. In a postscript to the end of the Cold War, in January 1993 twenty Communists (mostly Italians) abandoned their sinking ship and joined the Socialist group.

Following the EC's first enlargement in 1973, the Christian Democrats did not enjoy an influx of British and Danish Conservatives, who instead set up their own group, the European Conservatives, which later changed its name to the European Democratic Group. With the Parliament growing in importance as a result of the Single European Act of 1986, the European Democratic Group requested affiliation with the Christian Democratic group immediately after the 1989 elections. However, concern among Christian Democrats about the strength of Euroskepticism in the British and Danish Conservative Parties delayed an alliance between the Christian Democrats and the European Democratic Group until 1992.

Long before that, the Socialist and Christian Democratic groups in the Parliament had become branches of transnational Socialist and Christian Democratic Parties. The Christian Democrats were first to form a transnational party, the European People's Party, in 1976. As a result, Christian Democrats in the European Parliament became the Group of the European People's Party. It was not until the early 1990s, with implementation of the single market program and the conclusion of the Maastricht Treaty, that national parties constituting the European People's Party (including their members in the European Parliament) made a serious effort to turn the European People's Party into more than a mere umbrella organization.

European socialist parties also organized transnationally in the Party of European Socialists. Accordingly, the Socialists in the European Parliament became the Group of the Party of European Socialists. Like the European People's Party, the Group of the Party of European Socialists developed into a well-organized transnational party, using similar methods to influence European integration in a social-democratic direction.

Once they affiliated within the European Parliament, the Christian Democrats and the European Democratic Group became the Group of the European People's Party and European Democrats (EPP-ED). The newly formed EPP-ED group had little success mobilizing participation in European elections but quickly became more cohesive and effective in the Parliament than the preceding loose association of Christian Democrats and Conservatives. At the same time, constituent national parties and the EPP-ED group began working closely together in the transnational party to try to influence EU policymaking in a variety of ways, notably by organizing summits of Christian Democratic and Conservative Party leaders in the run-up to meetings of the European Council. Both the EPP-ED and Group of the Party of European Socialists (PES) sought to influence the outcome of successive intergovernmental conferences by submitting position papers and lobbying national leaders, most of whom were members of one or another of the groups' transnational parties.

Despite the apparent attenuation of ideological differences in European politics since the late 1980s, the EPP-ED and PES groups differ in their approach to key European issues such as the single market, social policy, and aspects of Economic and Monetary Union. Both support deeper economic integration but part company over specific policy prescriptions. In general, the EPP-ED group is more free market oriented, the PES group more interventionist. The PES group is therefore less enamored than the EPP-ED group with the Lisbon strategy, and more concerned about protecting workers' rights and strengthening social welfare.

Other Groups

For a long time the Liberals have been the third-largest group in the Parliament, having about half as many members as the Socialists and the Christian Democrats/Conservatives and twice as many as the smaller groups. For a long time the Liberals were officially called the Group of the European Liberal,

Democratic, and Reformist Party before reinventing themselves after the 2004 elections as the Alliance of Liberals and Democrats for Europe. As a relatively small group, the Liberals were unable to win elections to top leadership positions in the Parliament until they allied themselves with the Socialists during the 1999–2004 parliamentary term, in the second half of which a Liberal (Pat Cox of Ireland) became president of the Parliament. The Liberals are liberal in the economic sense—they support deregulation and private enterprise—although their social policies are certainly also liberal by American standards.

In 1984, newly elected Greens (environmentalists) and advocates of alternative lifestyles joined with a few independents to form the Rainbow Group. Five years later, after the 1989 election, the growing Green contingent formed its own group (the Green Group). In 1999, in an effort to boost their influence in the Parliament, the Greens formed an alliance with "representatives from stateless nations," such as Catalan, Scottish, and Welsh nationalists, and launched the Greens/European Free Alliance. With forty-two members, this became the fourth-largest group in Parliament after the 2004 elections.

A heterogeneous group of the "nonsocialist left," the Confederal Group of the European United Left/Nordic Green Left, almost surpassed the Greens/European Free Alliance in the 2004 elections but came in with one member less. The origins of the Confederal Group of the European United Left/Nordic Green Left go back to the early 1970s, when Communists in Western Europe became reconciled to the existence of the EC, participated in elections to the European Parliament, and formed the Communist Group. Fissiparous tendencies on the far left, especially after the collapse of communism in Central and Eastern Europe, caused the Communists to split after the 1989 election into two separate groups, the United European Left and Left Unity. The United European Left consisted mostly of Italian and Spanish Communists, whereas the small, more doctrinaire Left Unity consisted mostly of French, Greek, and Portuguese Communists.

The decision by twenty Communists to shed their old beliefs and join the Socialist group in 1993 brought the United European Left's existence to an end, and the small Left Unity group disappeared after the 1994 election. In its place, surviving Communists in the Parliament joined some far-left Scandinavian environmentalists to form the Confederal Group of the European United Left/Nordic Green Left. Ironically, the group includes a number of Communists or nominal ex-Communists from Central and Eastern Europe, nostalgic for the good old days of central economic planning, full (under)employment, and universal (albeit minimal) social welfare.

Perhaps the oddest group in the Parliament is the Independence/Democracy Group. Its members are mostly virulent Euroskeptics who want their countries to leave the EU or who want the EU to cease to exist. They are in the unusual position of serving in a parliament whose legitimacy and utility they reject. The largest and most striking contingent in the group is the UK Independence Party, which won twelve seats in the 2004 elections and wants to take Britain out of the EU. Although enjoying a new lease on life, the Independence/Democracy Group emerged out of the anti-Maastricht movement in the early 1990s and is the successor to the Independent Europe of the Nations Group, which consisted mostly of French and Danish Euroskeptics.

With twenty-seven members after the 2004 elections, the Union for Europe of the Nations Group brought up the rear in terms of political group size in the Parliament. It is a motley group whose members have little in common apart from a desire to enjoy the logistical and financial benefits of being in a parliamentary group and an unwillingness to be in any of the other groups. Its main contingents are members of Italy's National Alliance, heir to the far-right Italian Social Movement, and Ireland's Fianna Fáil Party, the largest party in Ireland and the senior member of its coalition government. Fianna Fáil would be more at home in the Christian Democratic/Conservative group, but a rival Irish party is already in that group, making it politically awkward for Fianna Fáil to join. Such are the vagaries of political group membership in the European Parliament.

Fianna Fáil used to be in a group composed mostly of its members and French Gaullists: originally the European Democratic Union, then the European Progressive Democrats, and later the European Democratic Alliance. In 1995 the European Democratic Alliance merged with Forza Europa, a group made up exclusively of members of Forza Italia, the new Italian party of media tycoon Silvio Berlusconi, and renamed itself the Union for Europe Group. In the process, it briefly surpassed the Liberals in size until a number of the Forza Italia members broke away in 1998 and joined the European People's Party group as individual members. A realignment of French politics in 2002, when most center-right parties merged into the Union for a Popular Movement, took the Gaullists into the EPP-ED group.

Political developments over the years spawned new political groups in the Parliament and caused others to disappear. For example, the reemergence of the extreme right in Europe in the mid-1980s manifested itself in the appearance in the Parliament of the Technical Group of the European Right. The prefix "Technical Group" indicated a marriage of convenience: the French National Front had too few seats to form its own group and coalesced uneasily with the German Republican Party, with which it at least agreed on the supposed evils of immigration. The handful of Italian Social Movement members in the Parliament in the late 1980s would ordinarily have joined the European Right group, but the Italian and German rightists fell out over a historical dispute concerning the South Tyrol; accordingly, members of the Italian Social Movement sat as independents. The German Republicans disappeared after the 1994 elections, thus ending the representation of the far right as a separate group in the Parliament.

The Rainbow Group also flourished briefly in the 1980s. When the environmentalists left to form their own group after the 1999 elections, the Rainbow Group became a heterogeneous collection of regional parties, disaffected members of other parties, and a few Danes dedicated to taking their country out of the EC. The Rainbow Group disappeared after the 1994 election; some of its members joined a new group of advocates of regional autonomy in the context of European integration, the Group of the European Radical Alliance, which in turn disappeared (most of its members ending up in the Greens/European Free Alliance).

The Breadth and Diversity of Political Groups

Although organized into political groups, parliamentarians remain acutely conscious of their national identity and allegiance to national political parties.[4] Indeed, members of the Parliament caucus in national delegations. Obviously, some national delegations are larger and more influential than others. For example, forty-nine of Germany's ninety-nine members are in the EPP-ED group, giving them inordinate influence in the Parliament's largest political group. Similarly, thirty-one of France's seventy-seven members are in the Party of European Socialists group, making them the largest national delegation (Germany has only twenty-three members) in a group with a total of 200 members (compared to the EPP-ED group total of 268 members). Most national delegations are concentrated in the EPP-ED or PES group, but some are more diffused than others. Spain's is an example of a highly concentrated delegation: of its fifty-four members, twenty-four are in the EPP-ED group and twenty-four in the PES group. By contrast, Poland's delegation (the same size as Spain's) is spread out in a number of groups.

Clearly, members of the Parliament cover the spectrum of European politics—a much broader spectrum than exists in the United States—from the far left to the far right. It is easy to place the Confederal Group of the European United Left/Nordic Green Left and the unattached neo-Fascists at opposite extremes. The Socialist group is left of center; the Liberals, Christian Democrats/Conservatives, and the Union for Europe of the Nations Group are right of center. The Greens/European Free Alliance are not easy to place: whereas some of the Greens' constituent parties are definitely on the left, others are not, and the "representatives of stateless nations" who make up the European Free Alliance part of the group include many right-wing politicians. Similarly, the Independence/Democracy Group includes both left-wing and far-right-wing Euroskeptics.

With five political groups spanning the political spectrum, one organized along anti-EU lines, and one a marriage of convenience between environmentalists and subnational nationalists, the political group system in the European

Parliament resembles the political party system in national parliaments. Two of the European Parliament's political groups (the Socialists and Christian Democrats/Conservatives) are substantially larger than the others and are on opposite sides of the left-right divide. Nevertheless, ideological rivalry is far from intense and the political group system is by no means rigidly bipolar. Compared to national parties, the European political groups are undisciplined, as the diversity of their composition suggests. Moreover, unlike their national counterparts, political groups in the European Parliament do not form or support a government. This intensifies the mutual interest of the mainstream groups in working closely together to promote the Parliament's institutional agenda and secure the necessary majorities in order to have an impact on the legislative process.

The role of "intergroups" illustrates the difference between the political group system in the European Parliament and the political party system in national parliaments. As the name implies, intergroups consist of parliamentarians from a variety of political groups who share a common interest. Intergroups range in subject matter from specific issues (such as animal welfare) to broad themes (such as controlling weapons of mass destruction). Intergroups—there are about fifty altogether—serve a useful purpose. By linking members of different political groups, they help to build broad support for important initiatives and proposals. Yet their existence, or at least the existence of the overtly political intergroups, highlights the relative lack of political group discipline and emphasizes the difference between the national parliamentary and Europarliamentary systems.

■ Parliament's Roles and Responsibilities

Whatever else may be said of it, the European Parliament cannot be dismissed as a "windy debating chamber." Parliamentarians spend only one week—in effect, three days—each month in full plenary session. Plenary sessions include agenda setting, voting, question time with or without debate, speeches by commissioners or the Council presidency, discussions of emergency issues, and debates on general topics. Speaking time is carefully parceled out to political groups and independent members and strictly controlled—usually by the simple stratagem of turning off the microphone. Parliamentarians rarely have an opportunity to prattle on. Moreover, some Continental political cultures discourage intense parliamentary exchanges. British members, whose domestic political system thrives on fierce debate, find discussions in the Parliament disappointingly tame.

Apart from procedural problems and cultural differences, language is another obstacle to purposeful debate. Not all parliamentarians are fluent in a second EU language. Thus, the EU's twenty official languages are always in use. An anthropologist who observed the Parliament in action was struck most by "the amputation that political speech undergoes during interpretation. . . . To make oneself understood through the interpreter, one must be brief and simplify one's language to the maximum—there is room neither for rhetoric, nor for wit. And despite all this, the message sometimes doesn't get through." The costs of interpreting and translating are exorbitant, accounting for nearly one-third of the Parliament's total staff and about 30 percent of its annual budget. In the anthropologist's opinion, "the inability to choose a single head-quarters for the European Parliament is echoed by the impossibility of finding a common language."[5]

Despite those constraints, debates are an important part of the legislative process in the Parliament and an opportunity for it to try to raise awareness and consciousness throughout the EU of certain important issues. For example, the Parliament prides itself on its advocacy of human rights, always an area selected each month for urgent debate in plenary session. The Human Rights Subcommittee of Parliament's influential Committee on Foreign Affairs monitors human rights in nonmember countries with the assistance of a special human rights unit. The committee's annual report on human rights forms the basis of a major parliamentary debate.

Apart from raising awareness of important political, economic, and humanitarian issues, the European Parliament has a number of well-defined roles and responsibilities in the EU system covering the budget, the legislative process, scrutiny and oversight, and external relations.

Budgetary Powers

Parliaments have the "power of the purse" in liberal democracies. Inspired by that analogy but reluctant to cede too much authority, in the early 1970s member states gave the Parliament some budgetary power when the EC acquired its own resources (funds that originate in the member states but belong to the Community) and became independent of national financial contributions. As a result of amendments to the Rome Treaty in April 1970 (implemented in 1975), Parliament and the Council became the EC's joint "budgetary authority," sharing responsibility for EC spending but not for raising revenue, which is fixed annually by the Council acting alone within a general framework agreed to by the European Council for a multiyear period.

Expenditure consists of two categories: compulsory and noncompulsory. Compulsory expenditure is that necessarily resulting from the treaties or from acts adopted in accordance with them. It consists mainly of:

- agricultural price supports
- various items connected with agricultural and fisheries structural (development) policy

- flat-rate refunds to the member states, such as costs incurred in collecting their own resources
- part of development aid (although most EU development assistance comes from a separate budget financed directly by the member states)

Noncompulsory expenditure covers all other expenditure, the largest part of which goes to the structural funds, to promote social and economic cohesion. Noncompulsory expenditure has increased from about 8 percent of the budget in the 1970s to about 55 percent in 2004.

The European Parliament may propose modifications only to compulsory expenditure but may amend noncompulsory expenditure. Not surprisingly, the Parliament has sought to increase the size of noncompulsory expenditure and, in recent rounds of treaty reform, to abolish the distinction between the two types of expenditure, giving it the right to make amendments in all areas of EU spending. Indeed, the Constitutional Treaty does away with the distinction between compulsory and noncompulsory expenditure and gives the Parliament the final word on the budget as a whole.

Based on a 1975 agreement that became operational in 1977, Parliament has exclusive authority to grant a "discharge" of the general budget. This is the only budgetary power vested solely in the Parliament. The purpose of granting a discharge is to verify the accuracy of the Commission's budgetary management and to determine precise revenue and expenditure for a given year. The discharge procedure is arduous and time consuming and involves close cooperation with the Court of Auditors. The Parliament usually votes on whether to grant a discharge two years after the budget in question. The Parliament's exclusive power to grant a discharge has considerable political implications, especially in relations between the Parliament and the Commission.

Since the early 1970s and especially since the first direct elections in 1979, the Parliament has attempted to use its budgetary authority to raise its political profile and enhance its institutional standing. Yet the Parliament's ability to do so is constrained by the relatively small size of the EU budget. Devoid of responsibility for such big-ticket items as health, social security, defense, and education, the EU's public finances are small compared with those of the member states. This could be an important factor preventing the emergence of an even stronger Parliament. The Parliament may have acquired considerable budgetary authority, but as long as the budget remains relatively insignificant and the Parliament cannot raise any revenue, its power will remain correspondingly weak. As David Coombes observed many years ago, "the history of representative government in Europe and elsewhere suggests that the Community's weakness in public finance" is an important reason for "its failure to develop [strong] parliamentary institutions."[6]

Legislative Powers

In the legislative field even more than in the budgetary field, the Parliament has acquired greater powers over the years. Initially, its legislative powers were limited to the consultation procedure (so called because of the original treaty's stipulation in a number of articles that the Council could enact legislation in such cases only "after consulting the Assembly"). Under the procedure, Parliament had the right to submit a nonbinding opinion before the Council adopted a Commission proposal. With the introduction of new, more far-reaching procedures, the scope of the consultation procedure was correspondingly reduced. Following the Nice Treaty—the latest round of treaty change that resulted in an extension of the Parliament's legislative powers, pending implementation of the Constitutional Treaty—the consultation procedure remains in use but is applicable to only a small number of policy areas over which national governments are reluctant to cede control.

The Single European Act enhanced the Parliament's legislative powers by introducing the cooperation procedure and requiring parliamentary assent in a small number of cases. The cooperation procedure gave Parliament the right to a second reading of certain draft legislation. Originally it applied to ten treaty articles, most dealing with the single market program. The new procedure revolutionized the Parliament's legislative role and introduced a new dimension into EU decisionmaking. It also had a profound impact on the behavior of the political groups, as only they could muster the required number of votes—an absolute majority of parliamentarians—to amend or reject a common position of the Council (the Council's decision at the end of the first reading and the basis for deliberations in the second stage of the procedure).

The cooperation procedure resulted as well in a profusion of lobbying directed at parliamentary committee meetings in Brussels and plenary sessions in Strasbourg. Before the Single European Act, lobbyists had little reason to cultivate parliamentarians. Afterward, when Parliament acquired more power and parliamentarians became proficient at using the cooperation procedure, lobbyists seized the opportunity to try to shape legislation through amendments. In many cases lobbyists alerted parliamentarians to the cooperation procedure's potential and provided them with information about impending legislation that their small staffs were often otherwise unable to obtain. Given the strength of the parliamentarians' attachment to their own countries, industries and interest groups frequently organize lobbies along national lines, at least for the larger delegations.

The Maastricht Treaty extended the cooperation procedure to fourteen policy areas and also introduced the codecision procedure, whereby the Parliament and the Council could adopt legislation jointly in a large number of policy areas. The form of codecision introduced by the Maastricht Treaty disappointed the Parliament, which received only a limited right of rejection rather than a positive right of approval. The new procedure was also extremely complicated. Nevertheless, Parliament's management of the codecision procedure belied those critics (especially in the Council secretariat) who claimed that the procedure was too awkward to work efficiently and expeditiously. Parliament's experience with the cooperation procedure should have shown that the Parliament would also master codecision, which it did.

The Amsterdam Treaty virtually abolished the cooperation procedure in favor of a revised codecision procedure that gave the Parliament far greater legislative power, putting it almost on a par with the Council in legislative decisionmaking. The treaty also more than doubled (from fifteen to thirty-eight) the number of issue areas subject to codecision, which the Nice Treaty further extended to forty-three. The Constitutional Treaty continued in that direction, even changing the name of codecision to the "ordinary legislative procedure."

Despite a "revisionist" academic critique of the Parliament's role in the codecision procedure, most participants and observers agree that codecision greatly enhanced the Parliament's legislative powers.[7] Parliament has generally succeeded in having its legislative amendments accepted by the Commission and the Council. Moreover, successful efforts by the Parliament in successive intergovernmental conferences to extend the scope of codecision, and unsuccessful efforts by the Conservative government in Britain (before Labour came to power in May 1997) to thwart the extension of codecision in the Amsterdam Treaty, suggest that codecision was indeed politically advantageous to the Parliament. Without doubt, changes since the late 1990s in the nature and scope of the codecision procedure have made Parliament a powerful player in the legislative process, the interinstitutional dynamics of which are examined in Chapter 11.

In addition to its other institutional innovations, the Single European Act introduced an "assent" procedure covering a small number of legislative items. Under this procedure the Parliament may not delay or amend proposals, only accept or reject them. The Maastricht Treaty extended the assent procedure to certain policy areas, notably citizenship, specific tasks of the European Central Bank and amendments to its stature, and the structural funds and the Cohesion Fund. Nevertheless, the Parliament is unhappy with the assent procedure in the legislative field because of the procedure's blunt nature.

Parliament does not have the right to initiate legislation, although the Maastricht Treaty formally gave it the same authority as the Council to request that the Commission submit legislative proposals. Such requests (the Parliament has made only a few of them) do not oblige the Commission to act; however, under a code of conduct concluded with the Parliament in 1995, the Commission agreed to take the greatest possible account of them. In collusion with the Council, Parliament may also pressure the Commission to initiate legislation by linking agreement in a codecision case to calls for the Commission to introduce specific proposals, a practice that the Commission strongly resents.

Scrutiny and Supervision

Parliament has a variety of powers and responsibilities to scrutinize the work of the Commission and the Council and to approve the appointment of the Commission president and the college of commissioners. Parliamentarians may submit written and oral questions as a limited means of holding the Council and Commission to account. Additional supervisory powers range from the innocuous (discussion of the Commission's annual *General Report*) to the vigorous (ability to force the Commission to resign as a body by a two-thirds majority). Parliament uses these powers of scrutiny and supervision not only to improve the quality of EU administration and governance but also to maneuver itself into the classic role of a legislature holding the executive to account. The Maastricht Treaty confirmed another supervisory practice that the Parliament had already developed: convening temporary committees of inquiry. At the request of one-quarter of its members, the Parliament may appoint such a committee to investigate "alleged contraventions or maladministration in the implementation of Community law." Because of the impact of these methods of scrutiny and supervision on interinstitutional relations, Parliament's exercise of them is examined in Chapter 11.

Other tools in the Parliament's supervisory arsenal are supposed to assist EU citizens suffering directly from alleged maladministration of Community law. One is an EU citizen's right to petition the Parliament "on a matter which comes within the Community's fields of activity and which affects him directly." Another is the office of the ombudsman, appointed by the Parliament and "empowered to receive complaints from any citizen . . . concerning instances of maladministration in the activities of the Community's institutions or bodies."

Upon receiving a complaint, the ombudsman investigates and makes a report to the Parliament and the institution concerned. The ombudsman receives an increasing number of complaints annually (usually well over 1,000), although not all of them are admissible. The ombudsman's two biggest problems have been a lack of resources and the difficulty of defining "maladministration." Nevertheless, the work of the ombudsman has helped to improve the quality of EU administration from the citizen's point of view.

External Relations

The prominence of its Committee on Foreign Affairs, including the Subcommittee on Security and Defense, suggests that the Parliament is centrally involved in an important area of EU activity. In fact, governments are generally averse to parliamentary involvement in foreign affairs, and EU governments are particularly averse to involving the European Parliament in the Common Foreign and Security Policy, let alone in an emerging defense policy, in any meaningful way. Parliament's restricted role in the Common Foreign and Security Policy is based on its limited involvement in European Political Cooperation, the EC's original procedure for foreign policy cooperation. The old Political Affairs Committee (forerunner of the Foreign Affairs Committee) regularly discussed foreign policy issues, held a special colloquy four times a year with the Council presidency, and organized meetings between its leadership and the political directors of national foreign ministries. In addition, plenary sessions included a short period for foreign policy–related questions to the Council presidency and member state foreign ministers. Yet these forays into the foreign policy sphere were peripheral to the Parliament's main activities, and foreign policy cooperation itself was extremely circumscribed in its scope and effectiveness.

Parliament hoped that the Maastricht Treaty would give the EU a greater capacity in foreign and security policy and with it give the Parliament a policymaking role. It was disappointed on both counts. As a strictly intergovernmental affair, the Parliament's involvement in the Common Foreign and Security Policy was limited to being consulted and kept regularly informed by the presidency and the Commission, being allowed to ask questions of the Council and make recommendations to it, and being obliged to hold an annual debate on foreign and security policy. Parliament's role in this regard was largely unchanged in subsequent treaty reforms.[8]

Surprisingly, given that it lies squarely within the EU's economic realm, Parliament's role in the common commercial policy has been virtually nonexistent. Parliament's Committee on International Trade monitors the conduct of EU trade policy, but Parliament as a whole is not required to approve and may not reject agreements negotiated by the Commission. Knowing the difficulty of reaching agreement among themselves on international trade negotiations, national governments, which decide the Commission's mandate and approve the final agreement, have been averse to sharing their responsibilities with the Parliament. Nevertheless, governments agreed in the Constitutional Treaty to give the Parliament a more prominent role in trade policy, including the right to approve international agreements.

By contrast, the Parliament plays a decisive role in another important foreign policy sphere: EU enlargement and association with third countries. Under the assent procedure introduced by the Single European Act, an absolute majority of parliamentarians must approve accession and association agreements. Initially this provision seemed like a small concession: in 1986, after the third enlargement, the EU's boundaries looked set for several years to come. Nor did a new series of association agreements appear imminent. Yet the success of the single market program and the sudden end of the Cold War soon gave rise to a new round of accession negotiations and association agreements. Moreover, the assent procedure covers revisions or additions to existing association agreements, such as financial protocols. Parliament has repeatedly used the assent procedure to leverage respect for human rights in countries having or wanting association agreements with the EU, such as Israel, Morocco, and Syria. The Maastricht Treaty extended the assent procedure to all international agreements that set up institutions, have major financial implications, or require legislation under codecision.

Internal Organization

Parliament carries out its budgetary, legislative, supervisory, and other responsibilities through an elaborate leadership structure, a strong committee system, and frenzied plenary sessions.

Leadership Structure

The Parliament's leadership structure and responsibilities are as follows:

- The *president* of the Parliament presides over plenary sessions, chairs meetings of the Bureau and the Conference of Presidents, represents the Parliament at interinstitutional meetings, and signs the budget into law.
- *Vice presidents* (fourteen of them) preside over plenary sessions when the president is absent and represent the Parliament in the conciliation committee.
- The *Bureau* (the president and vice presidents) makes key budgetary, procedural, and personnel decisions.
- The *Conference of Presidents* (the president of the Parliament and the heads of the political groups) decides the agenda for plenary sessions; discusses the annual legislative program, interinstitutional relations, and relations with non-EU institutions; and manages the committee system.
- The five *quaestors* (ordinary members of the Parliament) make important day-to-day administrative decisions.

The Bureau, Conference of Presidents, and quaestors meet approximately twice a month—in Strasbourg during plenary sessions and in Brussels during committee or political group meetings.

All are elected positions; elections take place every two and a half years, at the beginning and in the middle of the Parliament's five-year term. Since 1989, the Socialists and Christian Democrats/Conservatives, who together have commanded an absolute majority of seats in the Parliament, shared the presidency between them. Members of other groups rightly denounced this "more or less automatic [presidential] election system," although their claim that it "harms the credibility of the European Parliament in the eyes of the elector" exaggerated the extent of public awareness of the Parliament's internal operations.[9] The pact broke down briefly during the 1999–2004 term, when the Christian Democrats/Conservatives collaborated with the Liberals against the Socialists, resulting in the election of a Liberal as president for the period January 2002–July 2004. The Socialists and the Christian Democrats/Conservatives reverted to their old ways after the 2004 elections, however. Based on their voting weight, Josep Borrell, a Socialist, was elected president with a large majority on the first ballot. The Socialists are expected to return the favor and support a Christian Democratic/Conservative candidate for the second half of the parliamentary term (January 2007–July 2009).

However tactically elected, recent presidents have at least taken the institution seriously and worked hard to raise its political profile both inside and outside the EU. The president's presentation of the Parliament's views at the beginning of each meeting of the European Council testifies to the institution's growing influence and to the importance for the Parliament of having a politically weighty president.

The outcome of the presidential election determines the outcome of the elections for other leadership positions (except for political group leaders, who are elected by political group members). Although other leadership elections are supposedly open, the party groups decide among themselves who gets what. The leadership's composition generally reflects the distribution of seats by political group and nationality.

Committee System

Parliament could not manage its burgeoning budgetary, legislative, and non-legislative agenda without an adequate committee system. The committee system evolved along with the EU, changing over the years to reflect the EU's increasing competence and the Parliament's growing assertiveness and responsibility. For instance, in response to the Maastricht Treaty, the Parliament revamped and renamed its Political Affairs Committee (it became the Committee on Foreign Affairs, Security, and Defense Policy, before becoming the Committee on Foreign Affairs, with subcommittees on human rights and security and defense). It also established a new Committee on Civil Liberties and Internal Affairs (now the Committee on Civil Liberties, Justice and Home Affairs). The Parliament has twenty permanent committees covering every facet of EU activity (see Box 9.1).

Clearly, some committees are more influential than others. For instance, the environment committee and the Committee on Budgetary Control are influential because the Parliament exercises considerable power in those areas. The importance of the budgets committee (as distinct from the Committee on Budgetary Control) is undiminished despite the existence of an interinstitutional arrangement for medium-term financial planning. Other committees,

---

Box 9.1   European Parliament Committees and Subcommittees

Internal Policies
Committee on Budgets
Committee on Budgetary Control
Committee on Economic and Monetary Affairs
Committee on Employment and Social Affairs
Committee on the Environment, Public Health and Food Safety
Committee on Industry, Research, and Energy
Committee on the Internal Market and Consumer Protection
Committee on Transport and Tourism
Committee on Regional Development
Committee on Agriculture
Committee on Fisheries
Committee on Culture and Education
Committee on Legal Affairs
Committee on Civil Liberties, Justice and Home Affairs
Committee on Constitutional Affairs
Committee on Women's Rights and Gender Equality
Committee on Petitions

External Policies
Committee on Foreign Affairs
Subcommittee on Human Rights
Subcommittee on Security and Defense
Committee on Development
Committee on International Trade

Temporary Committees
Temporary Committee on Policy Challenges and Budgetary Means of the
Enlarged Union, 2007–2013

---

such as the Committee on Transport and Tourism, have always been less important, although much sought after by parliamentarians who like to travel (which means, in effect, all parliamentarians).

Thus, a committee's popularity among parliamentarians is not necessarily related to its inherent importance, although popularity can enhance a committee's influence. The environment committee, one of the largest in the Parliament, is popular with parliamentarians not only because of the Parliament's legislative authority in that area but also because environmental issues have growing political and economic salience throughout the EU (and beyond). By contrast, the Committee on Budgetary Control, one of the most powerful in the Parliament, deals with a complicated and colorless issue (discharge of the budget) and has a correspondingly small membership. Foreign policy is as fashionable as environmental policy. Accordingly, the Committee on Foreign Affairs is as large as the environment committee and has an equally powerful chairman but only limited power. The Committee on Constitutional Affairs has no real power either, yet it attracts prominent parliamentarians because of its reputation as a driving force in the process of European integration (a legacy of Altiero Spinelli, the committee's founder).

The Parliament's leadership divides committee seats among political groups according to their strength in Parliament, using a system of proportional representation called the d'Hondt rule. The groups in turn allocate seats to their members based on seniority, personal preference, and nationality. Certain political groups and nationalities have strong preferences for particular committee assignments. Obvious examples are the Greens (environment, energy) and the Poles (agriculture, regional development). Committee assignments are reallocated every two and a half years; there is no time limit on a parliamentarian's committee service.

Parliament designates two weeks of each month for committee meetings. The frequency of each committee's meetings depends on the business before it; most meet at least monthly. Committee meetings take place in the Parliament's labyrinthine Brussels building, a complex of offices and conference rooms near Schuman Circle. Most meetings last the equivalent of one full day. Parliamentarians' attendance is often sporadic. Meetings may also be attended by officials from the Council and Commission and occasionally by commissioners and government ministers (especially from the country in the presidency).

Given their smaller size and less formal nature, committee meetings are less beset by language problems than are plenary sessions. Nevertheless, interpreters not only provide the essential service of making people mutually intelligible but also, because of the costs involved, ensure that meetings do not run over the allotted time. Apart from paying for simultaneous interpretation, committees run up extra costs by producing documents in twenty languages (each step of the legislative process necessitates translation into each official language). The most striking sight on entering a committee meeting, regardless of the committee's size, is a mountain of documents immediately inside the door. The committee leadership structure replicates Parliament's leadership structure: each committee has a chair and three vice chairs, who form the committee's bureau. Each committee also has a coordinator, who marshals its members for key votes, and a rapporteur, who drafts its reports (parliamentary reports are commonly known by the names of their rapporteurs).

In the case of legislative proposals, committees do the preliminary work on which the Parliament as a whole bases its decisions during plenary sessions. Before examining proposals in detail, committees verify the legal base in consultation with the legal affairs committee. For proposals subject to the codecision procedure, rapporteurs follow the draft legislation's progress through the Council's working groups, through Coreper, and through the Council itself. Committee preparation of draft amendments gives interested parties an opportunity to influence legislation. Predictably, certain committees are a target of intense lobbying. As well as its twenty standing committees and occasional committees of inquiry, the Parliament regularly establishes temporary committees to work on important but transient issues.

Plenary Sessions

Plenaries are the most visible and least flattering part of the Parliament's existence. For a week each month (in reality, from Monday afternoon until the following Friday morning, although most members leave on Thursday evening), parliamentarians participate in a full session of the entire body. Plenaries include debates, speeches by commissioners and the Council presidency, question time, and, most important, votes on legislative amendments and other resolutions. A legislative resolution constitutes the Parliament's opinion on draft legislation, indicating whether the Parliament approves, rejects, or amends the relevant proposal. Outside the chamber itself (in Eurospeak, the "hemicycle") but within the cavernous building where plenaries take place (in Brussels or Strasbourg), parliamentarians hold political group, intergroup, and occasional committee meetings; entertain constituents; and parry lobbyists (a corner of the concourse near the entrance to the Strasbourg hemicycle is appropriately called the "lobbyists' bench").

Too much happens during plenaries in too short a time. Voting alone can occupy several hours despite a change of rules reducing the number of amendments (previously about 1,000 per session) that reach the hemicycle. Such is the pressure of voting and the difficulty of knowing what each vote means that many parliamentarians simply stay away. Because amendments require at least a majority of the whole house to pass, rampant absenteeism sometimes causes important amendments to fail. Presidents constantly urge parliamentarians to deal with technicalities in committee and use the plenaries to debate big issues.

Staff

Parliamentarians have an allowance to hire staff (they often hire their own family members). Parliamentarians rely for policy and legislative assistance on the political groups' staff. Each group may hire a staff commensurate with the size of its membership (the Christian Democrats/Conservatives have a staff of more than 50 administrative grade officials and 100 assistants). Committees have small staffs of their own (drawn from Parliament's secretariat) to help rapporteurs draft and write reports; large national delegations also have separate staffs funded by national parties or the transnational political parties of which their groups are members. Parliament's secretariat (civil service), similar to the Council secretariat and Commission civil service, provides the institution with support ranging from research to public relations to translation and interpretation. As in other branches of the EU's civil service, promotion in the upper echelons of the Parliament's secretariat is highly political and depends on ideological affinity as well as nationality.

More Power to the Parliament?

The influence of the European Parliament has increased dramatically since the first direct elections in 1979. Parliament has considerable budgetary and legislative authority but craves more power, ostensibly in order to close the EU's democratic deficit, which it sees as the gap between the powers of the Commission and Council, on the one hand, and those of national parliaments and the European Parliament, on the other. The Single European Act and subsequent treaty changes that transferred responsibility for a wide range of policy areas from the national to the European level of decisionmaking exacerbated the democratic deficit by reducing the role of national parliaments without correspondingly enhancing the power of the European Parliament. The member states' introduction of the cooperation procedure in the Single European Act and extension of it in the Maastricht Treaty, and especially their introduction of the codecision procedure in the Maastricht Treaty and extension of it in the Amsterdam Treaty, went some way to meet the European Parliament's demands, but not far enough. Fundamentally, Parliament resents having to share legislative authority with the Commission (which initiates proposals) and the Council (which codecides).[10]

The Commission and the Council—including those members of it favorably disposed toward the Parliament—agree that the democratic deficit poses a serious problem for the EU but do not agree that the solution necessarily lies in giving more power to the Parliament. After all, the EU is not a state, and its institutional framework and political system will never correspond to those of a classic liberal democracy, centered on the legislature. Similarly, the Commission will never acquire the characteristics of a national executive. Instead, the EU is a singular system with singular institutions; conventional views of the democratic deficit and conventional proposals for its solution overlook that fact. Undoubtedly the Parliament is an essential ingredient of political accountability and representation in the EU, but it is not the sole source of legitimacy. Tackling the democratic deficit therefore requires an imaginative blend of public representation and participation at the regional, national, and European levels, involving parliamentary and other bodies from all three spheres.

In a celebrated speech in September 1994, British prime minister John Major, a Euroskeptic, complained that "the European Parliament sees itself as the future democratic focus for the Union. But that is a flawed ambition, because the EU is an association of States, deriving its basic democratic legitimacy through national parliaments. . . . It is national parliamentary democracy that confers legitimacy on the EU."[11] The EU is much more than simply an association of states, and Major unfairly denigrated the European Parliament's contribution to its democratic legitimization. But he had a point about Parliament's flawed ambition. Most Europeans, if they thought about the EU at all, would doubt that giving more power to the Parliament might help to close the democratic deficit. Indeed, few people outside the Parliament consider it capable of providing a solution to the EU's presumed crisis of democratic accountability. Europarliamentarians are marginal figures at the national level, regardless of their political influence at the European level. Far from clamoring for a transfer of more sovereignty to Strasbourg, most of the Europeans entitled to vote in direct elections choose not to. Indeed, the consistently low turnout (by European standards) in direct elections seriously weakens the European Parliament's image and undermines parliamentarians' arguments in favor of greater institutional authority.

■ Notes

1. "Prag Report on the Cooperation Procedure," as reproduced in *Agence Europe Documents,* 1820/21, January 30, 1993, pp. 10–12.

2. On direct elections and the role of the European Parliament in general, see Richard Corbett, Francis Jacobs, and Michael Shackleton, *The European Parliament,* 4th ed. (London: John Harper, 2000); David Judge and David Earnshaw, *The European Parliament* (Basingstoke, UK: Palgrave Macmillan, 2003); and *The European Parliament at Fifty,* a special issue of the *Journal of Common Market Studies* 41, no. 2 (April 2003).

3. On the composition and development of the political groups and the transnational party system, see Amie Kreppel, *The European Parliament and Supranational Party System: A Study in Institutional Development* (Cambridge: Cambridge University Press, 2002).

4. See Roger Scully, *Becoming Europeans? Attitudes, Behaviour, and Socialization in the European Parliament* (Oxford: Oxford University Press, 2005).

5. Marc Abelès, "Political Anthropology of a Transnational Institution: The European Parliament," *French Politics and Society* 11, no. 1 (Winter 1993): 16–17.

6. David Coombes, "Public Provision in an Economic and Monetary Union: New Functions for the Budget of the European Community," paper presented at the Second Biennial Conference of the European Community Studies Association, George Mason University, Fairfax, VA, May 1991, p. 1.

7. For the revisionist perspective, see George Tsebelis, "The Power of the European Parliament as a Conditional Agenda Setter," *American Political Science Review* 88 (1994): 128–142; George Tsebelis, "Decisionmaking Inside the European Parliament," in B. Eichengreen, J. Frieden, and J. von Hagen, eds., *Politics and Institutions in an Integrated Europe* (Heidelberg: Springer, 1995), pp. 42–64; and George Tsebelis and Geoffrey Garrett, "Agenda Setting, Vetoes, and the European Union's Co-Decision Procedure," *Journal of Legislative Studies* 3, no. 3 (1997). For a convincing rebuttal, see Roger Scully, "The European Parliament and the Co-Decision Procedure," *Journal of Legislative Studies* 3, no. 3 (1997).

8. See Robert Cutler and Alexander von Lingen, "The European Parliament and European Union Security and Defence Policy," *European Security* 12, no. 2 (June 2003): 1–20.

9. Statement by Gijs de Vries and Yves Galland, Members of the European Parliament, quoted in *Agence Europe,* July 18–19, 1994, p. 4.

10. See Dimitris N. Chryssochoou, Stelios Stavridis, and Michael J. Tsinisizelis, "European Democracy, Parliamentary Decline and the 'Democratic Deficit' of the European Union," *Journal of Legislative Studies* 4, no. 3 (1998): 108–129.

11. John Major, "Europe: A Future That Works," William and Mary Lecture, Leiden University, Leiden, the Netherlands, September 7, 1994.

10

Other Institutions and Bodies

The European Commission, Council of Ministers, and European Parliament are the European Union's core decisionmaking institutions, and the European Council is similar to a board of directors. In addition, the EU has a judicial branch, consisting of the European Court of Justice and Court of First Instance (a lower court). It has a Court of Auditors, which is not a judicial court but examines the EU's financial affairs, and two advisory bodies, the European Economic and Social Committee and the Committee of the Regions. This chapter examines these institutions and bodies as well as the European Investment Bank (an autonomous lending institution) and a growing and diverse group of "Community agencies." It also looks at the role of national parliaments in the EU system. The European System of Central Banks (ESCB) and the European Central Bank (ECB) are examined in Chapter 15.

■ The Court of Justice and Court of First Instance

For much of its existence the European Court of Justice (ECJ) was the EU's least-known institution. Located in Luxembourg, far from the political fray in Brussels and Strasbourg, the Court initially received little outside attention as it waded through a growing number of seemingly arcane and unimportant cases. Only gradually did the significance of the Court's rulings become apparent to the nonlegal world. In the 1970s, while the EC seemed to languish politically, economically, and institutionally, the ECJ persevered and produced an impressive amount of case law that maintained the momentum for deeper integration. In doing so, the Court not only defined and shaped a new legal order but also contributed to the EC's revival and transformation in the 1980s. Inevitably, critics accused the Court of judicial activism, testimony to its enormous impact on the EU's political development.[1] Sensitive to such criticism, especially on the part of governments in countries usually thought to favor deeper integration, the Court has grown noticeably less adventurous in recent years.

The Court's principal purpose, according to the EC's founders, is "to ensure that in the interpretation and application of [the treaties] the law is observed" (Article 220 TEC). The original treaties, the treaties of accession, and the various treaty amendments constitute the EU's "primary legislation," whereas laws made in accordance with the treaties constitute the EU's "secondary legislation." Primary and secondary legislation are the main sources of Community law, a "self-sufficient body of law that is binding on [the member states] and on their subjects."[2]

From the outset the ECJ has seen the original treaties not simply as narrow international agreements but, because of the member states' far-reaching decision to share sovereignty, as the basis of a constitutional framework for the EU. "If one were asked to synthesize the direction in which the case law produced in Luxembourg has moved since 1957," Federico Mancini, a member of the Court, wrote in 1991, "one would have to say that it coincides with the making of a constitution for Europe."[3] In a succession of cases the ECJ held that the EU's "constitution" is based on custom and on shared values as well as on EU primary and secondary legislation. The Court first referred explicitly to the EC treaty as "the basic constitutional charter" of the Community in 1986.[4] One of the most compelling stories in the history of European integration is how the ECJ "fundamentally transformed the nature of the bargain struck between the Member States: [changing the EU] from an interstate organization founded on the basis of an international treaty, to a supranational legal order constructed upon a *constitutional* framework."[5]

Fundamental human rights—an essential ingredient of any liberal, constitutional democracy—underpin EU law. Although the original treaties made no mention of human rights, the preamble of the Single European Act acknowledged the Court's repeated emphasis on the issue by declaring the member states' determination "to work together to promote democracy on the basis of the fundamental rights recognized in the constitutions and laws of the Member States, in the Convention for the Protection of Human Rights and Fundamental Freedoms and the European Social Charter, notably freedom, equality and social justice." The Maastricht Treaty did not institute a charter of fundamental rights and freedoms, as the European Parliament had wanted it to, but it did include a new article explicitly stating that "the Union shall respect fundamental rights, as guaranteed by the European Convention for the Protection of Human Rights and Fundamental Freedoms signed in Rome on November 4, 1950, and as they result from the constitutional traditions common to the Member States, as general principles of Community law" (Article 6.2 TEU).

Despite its use of the European Convention for the Protection of Human Rights and Fundamental Freedoms (ECHR) as a source for upholding the fundamental rights of individuals under EU law, the Court ruled in March 1996 that the EC could not, without a treaty amendment, accede to the ECHR.[6] Moreover, the Court expressed concerns about incorporating a separate international legal order into the EU legal system. Based partly on the Court's misgivings, member states decided during the 1996–1997 negotiations on treaty reform that the EU should not accede to the ECHR, although the member states themselves are all signatories to the convention. The solution adopted was to confirm that Community law was subject to the European Convention, but as applied by the Court in Luxembourg.

The EU finally developed its own Charter of Fundamental Rights—a catalog of civil and economic rights—in the run-up to Central and Eastern European enlargement. Proposed by the German government in 1999 during the celebrations of the fiftieth anniversary of the German constitution, negotiations on the charter, involving representatives of various national and EU bodies, proceeded swiftly and relatively smoothly in 2000. In what could "rightly [be] counted as among the Union's legal response to enlargement," EU leaders "solemnly proclaimed" the Charter at their summit in Nice in December 2000 but did not include it in the treaties, deferring further discussion of it until the next intergovernmental conference.[7]

The charter was generally uncontroversial, although the British government and some business leaders objected to the inclusion in it of social rights that could increase labor costs and reduce Europe's global competitiveness. A more subtle critique came from those, such as prominent EU law scholar Joseph Weiler, who questioned the wisdom of enumerating rights in a charter, for possible inclusion in the treaty. Far from protecting European citizens, Weiler argued, the impact of the charter could be counterproductive if, for instance, "each time an innovative concept were argued before the European Court, it would be pointed out that a proposal to that effect was considered in the drafting of the Charter and failed."[8]

Pending the Charter's incorporation into the treaties or into a new, combined EU treaty, how would the Court respond to it? No sooner was it proclaimed than applicants before the Court and advocates-general (senior officers of the Court) began citing the terms of the Charter in a number of cases. The Court itself began referring in 2002 to the Charter in its decisions. Yet the Court seemed reluctant to cite it copiously until the Charter was given legally binding status as a result of a new treaty reform. The first step in that direction was incorporation of the Charter into the draft Constitutional Treaty of 2003. National governments agreed in the ensuing intergovernmental conference to keep the Charter in the Constitutional Treaty, as well as a provision giving the EU the right to accede to the ECHR.

Thus, the human rights component of the original treaties has been immeasurably strengthened, and the constitutional character of the EU is now explicit. The impact on EU law of the Charter's incorporation into the Constitutional Treaty remains to be seen but is likely to be formidable. As a long-standing champion of fundamental rights in the EU, the Court most likely sees the incorporation of the Charter into the Constitutional Treaty as an important step forward. Moreover, the Court is surely pleased that the Constitutional Treaty gives further substance to EU citizenship, especially as the Court developed that concept before member states included it in the Maastricht Treaty.[9]

Basic Rules of EU Law

Apart from identifying the sources of Community law and endowing the treaties with the attributes of a constitution, the Court also developed two essential rules on which the new legal order rests: direct effect and supremacy. These twin pillars emerged in a series of cases early in the EU's history and clarified the working relationship between the national and Community legal orders.

Direct Effect. The Court first ruled on the direct effect of primary legislation in a case that, though technical and tedious, raised a fundamental principle of Community law. In *Van Gend en Loos* (1963), a Dutch transport firm brought a complaint against Dutch customs for increasing the duty on a product imported from Germany. The firm argued that the Dutch authorities had breached the article of the Rome Treaty that prohibited member states from introducing new duties or increasing existing duties in the common market. Thus, the Dutch firm claimed protection, citing the "direct effect" of Community law.

The Court agreed. In a landmark judgment it ruled that the article in question had direct effect because it contained a "clear and unconditional prohibition." Determined to make its mark, the Court declared that any unconditionally worded treaty provision, being "self-sufficient and legally complete," did not require further intervention at the national or Community levels and therefore applied directly to individuals. Not mincing its words, the Court stated that "the Community constitutes a new legal order . . . the subjects of which comprise not only the member states but also their nationals. Independently of the legislation of member states, Community law not only imposes obligations on individuals but . . . also confers rights upon them. These rights arise not only where they are expressly granted by the Treaty, but also by reason of obligations which the Treaty of Rome imposes in a clearly defined way upon individuals as well as upon member states and upon the institutions of the Community."[10]

The Court continued to push the principle of direct effect in cases involving directives (addressed to member states) as well as regulations (addressed to individuals) and treaty provisions. The Court delivered a landmark judgment in *Grad v. Finanzamt Traunstein* (1970) when it ruled that a directive had direct effect if it contained a clear and unconditional obligation on a member state and had not been implemented by that state within the period prescribed in the directive. The reasoning was that "a Member State should not be able to take advantage of the fact that it had infringed the Treaties by failing to implement the directive or by failing to implement it properly. The individual citizen must be able to rely on his legal position under Community law before the national courts."[11]

Supremacy of Community Law. The principle of direct effect would have had little impact if Community law did not supersede national law. Otherwise member states would simply ignore EU rules that conflicted with national rules. Although the Rome Treaty was unclear on the issue, the Court had no hesitation in asserting the supremacy of Community law over national law. The Court's first chance to do so came in *Costa v. ENEL* (1964), only a year after *Van Gend en Loos,* when the Court pointed out that member states had definitively transferred sovereign rights to the Community and that Community law could not be overridden by domestic legal provisions without the legal basis of the Community itself being called into question.[12] The Court expanded on the primacy of Community law in *Simmenthal v. Commission* (1979) when it ruled that "every national court must . . . apply Community law in its entirety . . . and must accordingly set aside any provisions of national law which may conflict with it."[13]

The *Costa, Van Gend en Loos,* and *Simmenthal* cases established the twin principles of direct effect and primacy of Community law, taking the national courts by surprise. Some national courts reacted strongly against what they saw as the encroachment of a new legal order. A major challenge came in the late 1960s when the constitutional courts of Italy and Germany hinted that because Community law arguably guaranteed a lower standard of fundamental rights than national law, the validity of Community law could be called into question at the national level. In a move that not only developed the Community's human rights case law but also warded off a potentially serious threat from national courts, the ECJ held in *Nold v. Commission* (1974) that "fundamental rights form an integral part of the general principles of [Community] law."[14]

Types of Cases
Cases before the Court originate in one of three ways:

1. requests from national courts for "preliminary ruling" on points of EC law
2. actions brought directly to the Court by other institutions, member states, or natural and legal persons (although individuals have only a limited ability to come before the Court to challenge EU legislation)

3. appeals against judgments of the Court of First Instance, the ECJ's "lower court"

The bulk of ECJ cases, and the most important ones in terms of developing a body of EU law, arise out of requests for preliminary rulings and direct actions.

Requests for Preliminary Rulings. Under Article 234 TEC, if an individual argues before a national court that a national law or policy conflicts with EC law, and if the court is unable or unwilling to resolve the dispute itself based on previous EC case law, the court may seek "authoritative guidance" from the Court by making a preliminary ruling reference (request). The parties involved, as well as EU institutions and national governments, may submit legal arguments to the Court. Based on its assessment of the arguments, relevant case law, and relevant treaty provisions, the ECJ issues a ruling, which the national court then applies to the case in question. Requests for preliminary rulings came slowly at first but accelerated in the 1970s and 1980s. In recent years, there have been approximately 250 requests for preliminary rulings annually.

Clearly, the success of Community law depends to a great extent on the willingness of national courts to seek preliminary rulings and abide by them. Under Article 234, lower national courts may seek guidance from the Court in cases involving Community law, but the highest national courts *must* do so. The general complicity of national courts in consolidating EC law is all the more striking because, in most cases, landmark Court judgments have come in response to requests from national courts for preliminary rulings. The original intent of Article 234 was to ensure uniform interpretation and application of Community law in each member state. Almost immediately, however, Article 234 became a powerful tool with which the Court could strengthen Community law and the Court's own role within the EU system. It also became a device that citizens could use to ascertain the compatibility of national and Community law. As a result, "the preliminary rulings procedure is of fundamental importance to the proper functioning of the legal and economic system established by the EEC Treaty. It is in the framework of that procedure that basic principles of the Community legal order, such as direct effect and primacy, have been developed."[15]

The increasing rate of preliminary ruling requests from lower courts has enhanced the stature of the Court, effectively giving it the power to review national law and thereby turning it into a supreme court. Increasingly, the Court has reformulated national courts' questions in order to elucidate what it considers to be the most important points at issue. This allows the Court to address important points of law that otherwise might not come before it. In so doing, Article 234 has gradually undermined the authority of the highest national courts. Why do so many lower national court judges apply for preliminary rulings "given that such judges must attend to their career prospects within hier-archically organized national judicial systems?"[16] According to a former member of the Court of First Instance, the answer may be simply that "the concept of a Community governed by law is naturally attractive to all Judges." Whatever the reason, Article 234 has brought about a special relationship, indeed a close partnership, between national courts and the ECJ. As a result, "the National Judge . . . in his capacity as Community Judge, becomes the upholder of Community Law in his own member state."[17]

Direct Actions. References for preliminary rulings constitute one branch of ECJ case law; direct actions make up the other. Direct actions usually take one of the following forms:

- Cases brought mostly by the Commission against a member state or, rarely, by a member state against another member state for failing to fulfill a legal obligation (Articles 226 and 227): If the Court agrees that the case is well founded, it declares that an obligation has not been fulfilled. The number of such so-called infringement cases has increased steadily over the years and now averages about 100 annually.
- Cases against the Commission, Council, Parliament, or the European Central Bank concerning the legality of a particular regulation (Article 241): These are called "proceedings for annulment" because the Court may annul a particular act. Grounds for annulment include lack of competence, infringement of an essential procedural requirement, infringement of the treaties or of any rules relating to their application, and misuse of powers. The famous *Isoglucose* (1980) ruling—in which the Court annulled a regulation because the Council had acted before the Parliament had delivered an opinion under the terms of the consultation procedure for legislative decisionmaking, thereby infringing one of the essential treaty provisions concerning the allocation of powers—falls into this category.[18]
- Cases brought by member states or other institutions against the Commission, Council, or Parliament for failure to act (Article 232): The most famous case of that kind was *Parliament v. Council* (1985), in which the Parliament brought the Council to court for failing to lay the foundation of a common transport policy (Parliament was only partially successful).
- Cases for damages against the EU for the wrongful act of an EU institution or an EU servant (Articles 235 and 288): These are known as actions to establish liability.
- Staff cases (Article 236): These are brought by EU civil servants for unfair dismissal, unlawful failure to promote, and the like.

Composition and Procedures of the ECJ

Articles 220–245 TEC stipulate the role, composition, location, procedure, jurisdiction, and powers of the Court. The Court's size has increased over time to reflect the EU's enlargement. It now has twenty-five judges and nine advocates-general. The principle of one judge per member state is an important factor in the evolution of Community law and in the acceptance of the Court's rulings by the member states.

The treaty stipulates that judges must act independently, and generally they do. The president—elected by the members of the Court for a period of three years (renewable)—never asks a judge to be rapporteur for a case involving that judge's member state (the rapporteur is responsible for writing the "report for the hearing"—a summary setting out the facts, procedural history, and arguments of the case—for use by the Court as a whole). As the Court's impact on the EU's development became more conspicuous, there were suggestions that the judges' independence would need to be safeguarded. A government's most obvious means to pressure or influence "its" judge is to threaten not to renew the judge's six-year term. With that in mind, the president of the Court suggested as long ago as 1977 that the judges' terms should be lengthened to twelve years, on the grounds that judges need a long time to familiarize themselves with Community law and build essential camaraderie and rapport.[19] The Parliament has also proposed having a say in judicial appointments, supposedly as a way of strengthening the judiciary's independence. However, the manner of appointing judges and their terms in office have not changed over the years.

Judges come from the upper levels of national judiciaries, from the legal profession, and from academia. Nine advocates-general, who have backgrounds similar to those of the judges and are appointed according to an unofficial national rota, complete the Court's membership. Advocates-general consider cases and give opinions for the Court's guidance at the end of the oral procedure. Judges are free to reject an advocate-general's opinion, but in most cases they accept it.

By majority vote, after consulting the advocates-general the judges select a registrar *(greffier)* for a renewable six-year term. As the Court's secretary-general, the registrar is responsible for conducting proceedings before the Court, maintaining records, publishing the Court's judgments, and administering the Court. The registrar meets regularly with members of the Court to schedule cases and decide procedural aspects. The Court has a relatively small staff of about 1,000 officials to provide research, language, and administrative support.

The Court meets either in plenary session (with a quorum of fifteen members) or, more commonly, in chambers. The number and composition of chambers have changed over the years, reflecting the Court's increasing caseload. Chambers now consist of three or five judges each; there is also a grand chamber of thirteen judges, which hears unusually complex and important cases. The Court hears cases two days a week and has an administrative session every two weeks.

The Court gives requests for preliminary rulings a higher priority than direct action cases because national courts must await a result before proceeding with the case in question. Direct action cases involve written proceedings, an investigation or preparatory inquiry, oral proceedings, and the judgment. Requests for preliminary rulings are not contentious and have a less cumbersome procedure than direct actions, although the original parties may submit written observations to the Court and may attend the oral hearing. Cases are heard in the EU's official languages, but French is the Court's working language.

Each judge has a small cabinet of legal secretaries, although most judges draft opinions without assistance after internal deliberations limited exclusively to the judiciary. Judges neither prepare nor issue minority opinions; nor do they indicate how many of them supported a decision, which the Court always announces as unanimous. Understandably, legal scholars complain that this makes it difficult to track the influence of individual judges' preferences and philosophies on the Court's judgments, but much can be divined from occasional speeches and articles by judges, and interviews with them.

Impact of Case Law

Apart from establishing the principles of direct effect and supremacy, EU case law has greatly advanced the objectives of the treaties. Indeed, some of the Court's landmark rulings have been decisive in helping to achieve the EU's economic and social goals. To a great extent, case law is the glue that holds the EU together. It has had a profound impact in the following areas:

- protection of individual rights
- delineation of competences (external and internal); development of the powers of the EU and its institutions; interinstitutional relations
- development of the principles of substantive EU law (such as the free movement of capital, people, goods, and services; sex equality; competition policy; environmental policy; and consumer protection)
- enforcement and protection of EU law

Key cases include:

- *Free movement of people:* In the *Reyners* (1974) case, the Court upheld an individual's right to take up employment in another member state under the same conditions as a national of that state.
- *Free movement of goods:* In the famous *Cassis de Dijon* (1979) case, the Court gave the Commission an opportunity to develop the principle

of mutual recognition, which underpinned the single market program (see Chapter 13).

- *Free movement of services:* The Court's ruling in *Vereniging Bond van Adverteerders v. The Netherlands State* (1988), a case involving cross-border telecommunications services, opened the way to the removal of barriers against the provision of services throughout the EU.
- *Competition policy:* A number of Court rulings have furthered the EU's competition policy, notably by confirming the Commission's powers to order repayment of illegal state aid to industry and by interpreting the treaty's provisions on public enterprises and enterprises granted special or exclusive rights.
- *Sex equality:* The Court's activism in this area is especially marked in the realm of equal pay for men and women. In the *Defrenne* (1971) case, the Court ruled that the treaty's provision for equal pay was directly applicable and that it was the duty of national courts to ensure that all citizens enjoyed the benefit of that principle. This ruling emboldened the Commission to implement a series of directives on women's issues that forced member states to end systematic and blatant discrimination. A subsequent stream of cases dealt with pensions, training, promotions, part-time work, and so forth.
- *External economic relations:* In its judgment in the *ERTA* (1971) case, the Court held that member states were no longer entitled to enter into obligations with third countries affecting common rules, thus establishing the important principle that in the field of external relations the EU's powers are evolving.

Despite the profound impact of EU case law, few Court rulings attract much public attention, especially throughout the EU as a whole. *Union Royale belge des sociétés de football association ASBL v. Bosman* (1995), a case that radically affected nationality and transfer rules in European soccer clubs, was an obvious exception. In a dispute involving a Belgian soccer player unable to transfer to a French club because his former club set an exorbitant transfer fee, the Court threw out the soccer association's transfer rules because they constituted an obstacle to the free movement of workers (Article 39 TEC). Also based on Article 39, the Court rejected rules requiring soccer clubs to field teams with only a limited number of professional players who were nationals of other member states (except for international matches).

Enforcement

Although national courts and member state governments accept the principles of direct effect and supremacy of Community law, the problem of enforcement remains acute. The worst areas of noncompliance are environmental policy, the single market, and agriculture; the worst offenders are France, Italy, and Spain. Many of the new member states are expected to top the non-compliance table in the years ahead, either because of obduracy or, more likely, administrative incapacity and unfamiliarity with EU membership requirements.

The Court is well aware that inability or refusal to implement EU rules and regulations uniformly in each member state will erode public confidence in Community law. In *Johnson v. RUC* (1984), the Court declared that the right to a judicial remedy is a general principle of EC law and continued its assault on the enforcement problem in a series of cases in the early 1990s. The most important of these was *Francovich and Bonifaci v. Italy* (1991), in which the Court held that in certain circumstances, individuals are entitled to sue governments for damages sustained as a result of the government's failure to implement a directive within the prescribed period. In a series of subsequent cases, the Court spelled out what these circumstances were: where the rule of law infringed is intended to confer rights on individuals, where there has been a sufficiently serious breach of that rule of law, and where there is a direct causal link between the breach of the obligation resting on the member state and the damage sustained by the injured party. In *Haim* (2000), the Court extended the scope of *Francovich*-type liability to public law bodies, legally independent of the state, and in *Kobler* (2003) the Court ruled that individuals were entitled to compensation in cases where the highest national courts had not sought a preliminary ruling or had disregarded the Court's interpretation in a preliminary ruling.

Aware of the growing problem of enforcement, member states agreed during the 1991 intergovernmental conference on political union to give the Court some direct enforcement power. As a result, the Maastricht Treaty included a little-known provision allowing the Court to impose fines on member states for refusing to act on a Court ruling that "it failed to fulfill its obligations under the Treaty" (Article 228 TEC). Given the political sensitivity of this provision, the ECJ has been reluctant to make use of it (the Court first fined a member state—Greece—in 2000).

Relations with Other Institutions and with Member States

Because of the far-reaching nature of its rulings, the Court has a unique relationship with the Council, Commission, Parliament, and member states, all of whom are frequent litigants in Court cases. Although the Court has often ruled against the Commission (especially in cases where the Commission has attempted to extend its competence in the field of external economic relations), the Commission is nonetheless an obvious ally; after all, as "guardian of the treaties" the Commission prosecutes many Court cases. The Commission and the Court work closely together to promote economic integration, particularly through the use of infringement proceedings and competition policy instruments.

Similarly, the Court and the Parliament share a common integrationist and supranationalist outlook. Indeed, the Court has generally promoted the Parliament's institutional interests, most notably in the *Isoglucose* case. The Court also corrected the anomaly whereby, under the original Article 173 TEC, the Parliament could not bring proceedings for judicial review of Community acts, a provision that seemed especially incongruous after the Parliament won greater legislative power under the Single European Act. In the *Chernobyl* case (1990), the Court ruled that in order to ensure institutional equilibrium as a result of the Single European Act, the Parliament should have the right to take action against the Council and the Commission in cases involving parliamentary prerogatives. Despite some member states' criticism of the Court's assertiveness, negotiators in the 1991 intergovernmental conference incorporated the operative part of the *Chernobyl* judgment almost verbatim into a revised version of Article 173 (later Article 230). The Nice Treaty further extended Parliament's right of recourse before the Court.

Also as a result of the Single European Act and, later, the Amsterdam Treaty, the Court was inundated with cases concerning the Council and Parliament squabbling over the correct legal base for legislation (the issue being the extent of parliamentary involvement in the legislative process). As one observer put it, "Council and [Parliament] have contrived to waste a considerable amount of time, and European taxpayers' money has been spent on unnecessary legal costs. There should be a procedure by which the legal base can be agreed as part of the legislative procedure before enactment, to save this unnecessary waste."[20] The issue may be redundant, given that the Constitutional Treaty tidied up the legislative process. Nevertheless, in the interinstitutional battles over the correct legal base, the Court did not always side with Parliament.

Nevertheless, the Council and its members (the national governments) generally regard the Court as favoring the Commission and the Parliament, in keeping with the Court's integrationist outlook. Indeed, the Court's relationship with the Council, and especially with certain member states, can be strained. Institutionally, the Council upholds national interests in the EU system, whereas the Court upholds supranationality. The Court's sometimes liberal interpretation of the treaties in order to deepen economic and political integration has occasionally angered the Council. More to the point, specific Court rulings in politically charged cases under media scrutiny have angered particular member states, including those member states generally in favor of further integration.

For example, in the early 1990s the Court came under sharp criticism from the German government for some preliminary rulings protecting the rights of Italian and non-EU migrants. The German government's criticism focused on the right of lower national courts to ask the Court for a preliminary ruling (a fundamental principle of EC law) and on the Court itself for giving preliminary rulings supposedly hostile to national governments' interests. Not surprisingly, Britain's Conservative government was especially sensitive to the Court's behavior. Indeed, there was a national furor in Britain in 1991 when the Court for the first time overruled a British act of parliament. In *The Queen v. Secretary of State for Transport, ex parte Factortame* (1991), the Court ruled that the 1988 Merchant Shipping Act, which stated that 75 percent of directors and shareholders in companies operating fishing vessels in UK waters must be British, contravened EC law. Basing its ruling on the freedom of establishment and freedom to provide services, the Court declared that Britain could not demand strict residence and nationality requirements from owners and crews before granting their vessels British registration.

The ECJ and Post-Maastricht Treaty Reform

The *Factortame* and a number of later judgments led the British government to propose, during the 1996–1997 intergovernmental conference, a number of measures to curb the Court's effectiveness and to establish a right of appeal against the Court's decisions. Combined with other countries' criticism of the Court, this proposal fueled speculation that the Court's prerogatives would be seriously curtailed in the ensuing Amsterdam Treaty, and even that Article 234 (preliminary ruling) might be annulled. For its part, the Court recommended in its submission to the preconference Reflection Group a number of changes in the Court's composition and operations and an extension of judicial review to the EU's two intergovernmental pillars (covering internal and external security).

In the event, most member states were too appreciative of the Court's overall importance to reduce its role in the EU system, and there were no fundamental challenges to the basic tenets of EC law. Moreover, the Labour government that came to power in Britain toward the end of the conference lacked its predecessor's reforming zeal. If anything, the Court emerged from the Amsterdam Treaty slightly better off than before: the treaty brought much of the old third pillar (covering justice and home affairs) into the first pillar, where the Court is fully involved, and extended judicial review to what remained of the third pillar (subject to certain conditions). However, the treaty did not extend judicial review to the second pillar (the Common Foreign and Security Policy). Also, because of several delegations' distrust of the Court, the treaty's new nondiscrimination clause (Article 13 TEC) did not have direct effect and allowed only for secondary legislation.

In response to persistent pressure from the Court to relieve its workload (the Court faced a huge backlog of cases), member states agreed in the 2000 intergovernmental conference to amend the treaty in order to allow the Court of First Instance to take on more cases (see next section). Nevertheless, the Court's workload remains unrelenting, and the duration of proceedings continues to increase. A long-overdue change to the Court's rules of procedure in 2000, introducing the possibility of an expedited procedure for urgent cases, was used for the first time in 2001 (in a case involving the outbreak of foot and mouth disease in the EU). The Court is very sparing in its use, not wanting to disrupt other, ongoing work, which would then take even longer to complete.[21] The Nice Treaty also allowed national governments to make changes to the Court's rules of procedure by qualified majority voting instead of unanimity in the Council, thereby facilitating greater adaptability by the Court to changing circumstances (not least the challenge of enlargement and the unceasing pressure of new cases).

The Court of First Instance

For more than thirty-five years the EU had only one court, responsible for hearing cases involving everything from important issues of Community law to seemingly trivial matters of staff promotion and dismissal. Apart from its wide jurisdiction, the Court's rapidly increasing caseload threatened to become unmanageable. The Court and the Commission appreciated the problem by the early 1970s and asked the Council to help, suggesting it establish a tribunal to hear staff cases. In 1978 the Court formally complained to the Council about its excessive workload, but to no avail. Only in 1985, when member states convened an intergovernmental conference primarily to make the treaty changes necessary to complete the single market, did the Court successfully rekindle the issue of judicial reform. By that time the Court's problems were pressing: as the caseload increased, the time taken to hear cases also increased. The Court's annual caseload had jumped from 79 in 1970 to 433 in 1985, the average length of proceedings for a preliminary ruling rose from six months in 1975 to fourteen months in 1985, and the average length of a direct action increased from nine months in 1975 to twenty months in 1985. As a result, the Court's accumulated backlog went from 100 cases in 1970 to 527 cases in 1985.[22]

In October 1985, shortly after the conference began, the Court's president raised the prospect of a subsidiary court in a letter to the Council presidency. Member states responded by delegating the issue to a group of experts, who proposed amending Article 168 of the treaty "to attach to the Court of Justice a court with jurisdiction to hear [certain cases] and determine [them] at first instance." The Single European Act duly empowered the Council, acting unanimously on a proposal from the Court and after consulting the Commission and the Parliament, to set up a Court of First Instance. In so doing, the Single European Act gave rise to "a hierarchy of judicial institutions at the Community level."[23]

After implementation of the Single European Act, the Court duly presented a proposal to establish the Court of First Instance (CFI). Following lengthy deliberations by an ad hoc committee drawn from the permanent representations, the Council decided in October 1988 on the CFI's composition and jurisdiction. The new court began operating in October 1989, delivered its first judgment in January 1990, and adopted its own rules of procedure in May 1991.

Jurisdiction. The CFI's initially narrow jurisdiction reflected the member states' difficulty in deciding what to divide from the main Court's caseload. Member states were unsure what to entrust to the CFI, apart from staff cases. Their uncertainty was already evident in changes introduced by the Single European Act, which denied the CFI any jurisdiction over cases brought by member states or Community institutions or over questions referred for preliminary ruling under Article 234. Thus, the CFI could hear only "certain classes of action or proceedings brought by natural or legal persons." The Council's October 1988 decision gave the CFI even narrower jurisdiction than that contemplated in the Single European Act. It encompassed

- *Competition cases:* generally actions by firms contesting fines imposed by the Commission under the EU's competition policy
- *European Coal and Steel Community cases:* mostly stemming from the system of production quotas imposed on the steel industry in an effort to deal with recession and overcapacity
- *Staff cases:* ranging from unfair dismissal to failure to win a promotion
- *Claims for damages:* brought by natural or legal persons where the damage allegedly arises from an action or failure to act that falls into one of the three categories just outlined

Shortly after its establishment, the CFI published a paper urging an increase in its jurisdiction.[24] Under renewed pressure from the Court of Justice, member states revised the treaty at the 1991 intergovernmental conference on political union to permit an extension of the Court's jurisdiction. Nevertheless, the Maastricht Treaty reiterated the prohibition against the CFI's hearing requests for preliminary rulings. Accordingly, in June 1993 the Council agreed to expand the CFI's competence by transferring to it all proceedings brought by individuals and companies with the exception of proceedings against EU trade defense measures (such as antidumping). Changes in the Nice Treaty to the composition and jurisdiction of the CFI, intended to relieve some of the pressure on the Court of Justice, helped to raise the status and profile of the lower court. At the same time, the demise of the European Coal and

Steel Community (its treaty expired in 2002) removed a particular category of cases before the CFI.

According to the original Council decision setting up the CFI, the court's purpose was to hear cases that require "an examination of complex facts." For instance, competition cases usually involve intricate technical legislation and detailed questions of fact. Thus, a useful way to understand the difference between the Court of Justice and the CFI was that "the Court of First Instance is the judge of factual matters, while the Court of Justice is in principle the judge of points of law."[25] Although this is still helpful, changes in the jurisdiction of the CFI, giving it competence for all direct actions (especially requests for annulments and damages and claims of failure to act), have blurred the jurisdictional demarcation between the two courts.

Composition and Procedures. Like the main court, the Court of First Instance consists of one judge per member state appointed for renewable six-year terms. It has no advocates-general, but any judge may be asked to perform the task of advocate-general for a particular case. As with their counterparts on the Court of Justice, judges on the CFI must be independent of national governments. In view of the highly technical work they sometimes perform, CFI judges need not come from the legal profession, although in practice almost all of them do. To maintain continuity, a number of the CFI's first judges were closely connected with the Court of Justice. For instance, the CFI's first president was a former Court of Justice advocate-general. The CFI meets in chambers of three or five judges. Judges may also hear cases singly, and in exceptional cases the CFI meets in plenary session. The judges elect one of their members to serve as president for a renewable three-year term; they also appoint a registrar who serves in a capacity similar to that of the main court's registrar.

In providing for the CFI, the Single European Act included a right of appeal to the Court of Justice. However, litigants may appeal to the Court of Justice on a point of law only, such as the CFI's lack of competence to hear the original case, breach of procedure, or infringement of Community law. An appeal must be lodged within two months of notification of the decision.

Assessment. Despite the CFI's existence, the Court of Justice continues to bear a heavy workload. Of course, if the CFI did not exist, the Court of Justice would have the additional burden of hearing all the cases that currently come before the CFI (as it is, the Court of Justice hears about 20 percent of them on appeal). However, the CFI itself was soon even more overburdened, or at least its productivity seemed much lower than that of the Court of Justice. In 1997 the CFI disposed of only 173 cases (compared to 456 cases disposed of by the ECJ), many of which were staff cases. Apart from staff cases, on average the CFI took nearly thirty months to deal with cases, leaving the court with 624 cases in hand at the end of 1997 (up from 220 at the end of 1996). By contrast, the ECJ took an average of twenty-one months to deal with preliminary rulings—the most complicated category of its cases—and had 683 cases in hand at the end of 1997 (not an unusually high amount for the ECJ).[26]

Concerned that its workload was becoming unmanageable, the Court of First Instance requested, in a submission to the Reflection Group before the 1996–1997 intergovernmental conference, that the Council appoint more judges to it and that certain cases be heard by one judge sitting alone.[27] But many national governments (and many lawyers who appear before the court) disliked the idea of single-judge rulings, and no national government relished the prospect of fighting with other governments over the nationalities of a handful of new CFI judges. As a result, the Amsterdam Treaty did not incorporate the CFI's recommendations. Under the unrelenting pressure of more new cases, however, national governments changed the CFI's rules of procedure in May 1999 to allow for single-judge rulings in certain types of cases that hitherto had been assigned to three-judge chambers. And in 2004, with the accession of ten more member states, the CFI increased in size to twenty-five judges.

The CFI's first president remarked at the court's official launch in September 1989 that "this moment does not mark the end of an era in European judicial history, but rather a stage along the road towards the ultimate maturity of the judicial system of the Communities."[28] Since then there have been four rounds of treaty reform, none of which radically revised the EU judicial system. Instead, member states have tinkered with the two courts' composition and jurisdiction in an effort to alleviate the main court's workload. The effect of the changes has been more significant, however. Far from being a shrinking violet, the CFI is "growing in stature, gaining in confidence and developing its own distinctive voice—yet at the same time being reminded of, and responding to, the ECJ's 'senior role.'"[29]

■ The Court of Auditors

The Court of Auditors is not a judicial court; its responsibility lies solely in examining the EU's financial affairs. The problem of inadequate control over Community resources is as old as the Community itself. In an effort to rectify the situation, and as a corollary to the granting of budgetary authority to the European Parliament, the 1975 budget treaty replaced the old Auditor Board with the new Court of Auditors, which began functioning in October 1977. The 1975 treaty extended the court's authority to cover all bodies created by the Community and all payments made before the year's accounts are closed. In a financial regulation of December 1977, revised in March 1990, member states (through the Council) gave the court complete administrative and budgetary autonomy.

Member states agreed in the Maastricht Treaty to elevate the Court of Auditors to the institutional status of the Council, Commission, Parliament, and Court of Justice. Moreover, a declaration attached to the treaty emphasized the Court of Auditors' "special importance" and called on "other Community institutions to consider . . . ways of enhancing the effectiveness of its work." The Court of Auditors' greater stature and significance reflected not only a substantial increase in the EU's revenue and expenditure since the late 1980s but also growing public and political concern about fraud, waste, and mismanagement of EU resources.

The Amsterdam Treaty further emphasized the role of the Court of Auditors in the fight against fraud, empowered it to carry out sound financial management, and strengthened its prerogatives vis-à-vis the other EU institutions. The Nice Treaty confirmed the principle of one member of the Court per member state in the EU and gave the Court the option of organizing in chambers in order to meet its growing workload (especially in view of enlargement). The Constitutional Treaty no longer lists the Court of Auditors as an EU institution. Rather than a downgrading of the Court's stature, however, this change represents an effort by the member states to clarify the EU's institutional structure by highlighting only the core decisionmaking and judicial institutions: the Commission, European Council, Council of Ministers, Parliament, and Court of Justice. Participants in the Convention on the Future of Europe and the intergovernmental conference that followed were at pains to stress the increasing importance of the Court of Auditors.

The court's scrutiny of EU spending has provided telling evidence to substantiate anecdotal accounts of squandering and financial incompetence. By exposing financial irregularities in the EU, the court can exert considerable pressure for reform, especially of the Commission, which is legally responsible for EU spending. Paradoxically, because management of EU spending is highly decentralized, member states themselves are responsible on a day-to-day basis for most EU expenditure, and most fraud takes place at the national or subnational—not the European—level.

The court consists of twenty-five members, appointed for six-year renewable terms, who have experience with the control of public funds in their own countries. In practice, each member state nominates a member of the court. The Council then appoints the members unanimously, after consulting the European Parliament. Here, as elsewhere, the Parliament has attempted to extend its authority by insisting on a right of approval. Parliament's objection to two court appointees in 1989 caused a political furor, as a result of which one member state changed its nominee. However, the Council ignored the Parliament's recommendation against two appointees to the court in 1994.

The court elects one of its members as president to serve a renewable three-year term. A change of president is followed by a general change of portfolios; each member of the court is responsible for a sector of audit work corresponding to a specific area of the EU budget. The court is located in Luxembourg and has a staff of about 750. It is supposed to be completely independent of national governments.

The court publishes an annual report on each year's budget in November of the following year and also publishes special reports and opinions. All are adopted by a majority vote of the court's members. The annual report consists mostly of a financial management assessment, which involves comparing the general goals and specific targets of EU policies and programs with the results obtained. Special reports allow the court more flexibility than do annual reports, and their highly critical assessments of EU policies and programs often attract media attention. The court's opinions are fewer than its special reports but are not necessarily less spirited.

Before adopting its annual and other reports, the court and the Commission engage in what is called the *procedure contradictoire,* whereby the Commission tries to tone down the court's criticisms. Every court publication includes the Commission's reply to the court's findings, which are often politically sensitive. Indeed, the Commission generally objects to what it sees as the court's tendency to make critical political judgments. On a day-to-day basis, the court deals mostly with the Commission's financial controller and with the directorate-general for budgets; on special occasions the president of the court and the budget commissioner engage in the *procedure contradictoire.*

Another innovation in the Maastricht Treaty was its requirement for the court to provide the Council and the Parliament "with a statement of assurance as to the reliability of the accounts and the legality and regularity of the underlying transactions" (Article 248.1 TEC). Beginning in November 1995, the court included such a statement in its annual report. To date, the court's statements of assurance have been far from reassuring, with the court noting too many errors with respect to EU payments to give a positive assurance of their legality or regularity. Although, as the budget commissioner pointed out in the Commission's defense, the court blamed the member states for 90 percent of the substantial errors in payments transactions, Parliament nonetheless took the Commission to task for the court's findings, threatening in 1998 to censure the Commission by not granting discharge of the 1996 budget. Thus, notwithstanding occasional problems involving appointees to the court, and notwithstanding the Parliament's own financial management problems, it would seem that the court and the Parliament are allies in the battle to improve financial management in the EU. The court has helped indirectly to increase the Parliament's budgetary authority, especially in the area of discharge, and the Parliament has helped to boost the court's institutional status.[30]

Other EU institutions, any bodies managing revenue or expenditure on behalf of the EU, and national audit bodies or government departments must provide the court with documents on request. If necessary, the court may examine these "on the spot in the other institutions . . . and in the Member States" or "on the premises of any body which manages revenue or expenditure on behalf of the Community [and] any natural or legal person in receipt of payments from the budget" (Article 248.3 TEC). The court works directly with its national counterparts when carrying out investigations in member states. Special liaison officers ensure that the court and the national audit bodies collaborate as closely as possible. The liaison officers meet in Luxembourg at least once a year, and the presidents of the court and the respective national bodies meet annually either in Luxembourg or in a national capital. In response to sensitivity in some member states about the court's perceived intrusiveness, the Amsterdam Treaty included an amendment to Article 248.3 stating that "the Court of Auditors and the national audit bodies of the Member States shall cooperate in a spirit of trust while maintaining their independence." The Nice Treaty reiterated the importance of cooperation between the Court and national audit bodies.

■ Advisory Bodies

The EU has two bodies that advise it in the legislative process: the European Economic and Social Committee, established when the European Economic Community was founded, and the Committee of the Regions, of more recent vintage. They have an uneasy relationship with each other. The European Economic and Social Committee views the Committee of the Regions as an upstart; the Committee of the Regions views the Economic and Social Committee as an anachronism and resents being condescended to by it. Most members of the Committee of the Regions took exception to a protocol attached to the Maastricht Treaty stating that the two committees "shall have a common organizational structure." Both have the same number of members, drawn in the same numbers from all member states (see Table 10.1). They also share facilities and administrative support.

Within two years of the establishment of the Committee of the Regions, relations between the two bodies were so strained that the Economic and Social Committee's staff staged a strike against the Committee of the Regions, which promptly moved out of the European Economic and Social Committee's premises into another building. The two bodies patched up their differences and once again share facilities in a recently refurbished building that once belonged to the European Parliament. The two committees share a common core of departments and about 520 staffers, although each also has a small staff (of about 100) of its own.

Table 10.1   Membership in the Economic and Social Committee and the Committee of the Regions

Country	Number of Members
Germany, Britain, France, Italy	24 each
Spain, Poland	21 each
Austria, Belgium, Czech Republic, Greece, Hungary, the Netherlands, Portugal, Sweden	12 each
Denmark, Finland, Ireland, Lithuania, Slovakia	9 each
Estonia, Latvia, Slovenia	7 each
Cyprus, Luxembourg	6 each
Malta	5
Total	317

The European Economic and Social Committee

The European Economic and Social Committee (EESC) consists of 317 representatives of workers, employers, and professional and consumer organizations, appointed for four years by the Council on the recommendation of national governments, who meet in plenary session about ten times a year, more frequently in smaller sections. The EESC's purpose is to advise the Commission, Council, and Parliament on social and economic issues, but none of those institutions is obligated to heed the committee's advice. More often than not the committee's opinions sit, unread, in Council meetings; in that way the Council fulfills its legal responsibility to solicit the committee's views on certain kinds of legislative proposals.

The EESC is modeled on national systems for institutionalizing interest group participation in policy formulation and implementation. The committee's raison d'être is to increase democratic accountability, make EU decisionmaking more transparent, and familiarize the economic and social sectors with the Council's legislative output. Originally the EESC had almost the same political stature as the European Parliament, but as soon as the Parliament acquired budgetary authority in the early 1970s, and especially after the introduction of direct elections, the Parliament became far more powerful and prominent.

Members represent a wide variety of social and economic interests in the EU and form three distinct groups of approximately equal size:

- Group I: employers (from industry and the service sector)
- Group II: employees (mostly from national trade unions)
- Group III: representatives of various interests (farmers, environmentalists, consumers, professionals, etc.)

Committee members are unpaid but are reimbursed for expenses. Although the committee has little clout, its members enjoy occasional trips to Brussels and the prestige of being involved in EU affairs. National governments look upon the committee as a means of dispensing patronage.

Despite its relative insignificance, the EESC generally produces readable and relevant reports, either in response to a Commission request or on its own initiative. The Rome Treaty specified that the Council and Commission must consult the EESC on issues specified elsewhere in the treaty (notably agriculture, transport, and social policy). The Single European Act extended mandatory consultations to areas such as the environment, the single market, cohesion, and research and technology. The Maastricht Treaty made the committee more independent of the Council, in particular with regard to adopting its rules of procedure, and gave the EESC authority to meet on its own initiative. The Amsterdam Treaty extended the EESC's scope to include employment policy and gave the committee the right to be consulted by the Parliament. However, the Amsterdam Treaty disappointed the EESC by not granting it the status of an EU institution.

The EESC elects a president every two years to represent it in relations with EU institutions, member states, nonmember states, and interest groups and with national economic and social councils and similar national bodies. In 1998—its fortieth anniversary—the EESC elected its first female president. The bureau, a leadership committee consisting of the president, two vice presidents, and thirty-one other members, assigns committee members to one of six sections, each comprising a mix of nationalities and groups. The sections are:

- agriculture, rural development, and the environment
- economic and monetary union and economic and social cohesion
- employment, social affairs, and citizenship
- external relations
- the single market, production, and consumption
- transport, energy, infrastructure, and the information society

Study groups of about twelve members each draft opinions on behalf of the sections, usually soliciting expert advice on technical matters. Opinions and reports are adopted by a simple majority in the plenary sessions. Needless to say, consensus is almost impossible to achieve in such a diverse body, and committee opinions and reports often include dissenting points of view. The committee adopts about 170 opinions and reports a year, about twenty-five of which are own-initiative reports.

The EESC looks to the Commission for political support. Relations between the committee and the Commission grew especially close in the late 1980s and early 1990s because of Commission president Jacques Delors's trade union background and strong interest in social policy. Delors briefly brought the committee to prominence in 1988 when he asked for its advice on the proposed Social Charter, a list of fundamental workers' rights. Delors presented the Commission's annual program at an EESC plenary session early each year and insisted that commissioners with relevant portfolios attend at least one EESC plenary session annually, which they still do. The Council politely ignores the EESC, although a representative of the Council presidency—usually a junior minister—outlines the presidency's six-month program at an EESC plenary session. For its part, the Parliament no longer sees the EESC as any kind of threat.

Despite its marginal role, the committee serves some useful functions. It brings to Brussels representatives of influential social and economic interests and provides a forum for them to hold regular and systematic exchanges of views on important issues. The EESC also acts as a conduit for information from Brussels to the member states and alerts special interest groups to the implications of social and economic policy. Although it aspires to a greater role in EU policymaking, the combination of a powerful European Parliament and a highly organized lobby of interest groups in Brussels leaves little room for the committee to assert itself.

Even after the establishment of the EEC in 1958, the Consultative Committee of the European Coal and Steel Community—a body analogous to the EC's European Economic and Social Committee—continued to function. When the Coal and Steel Community came to an end in 2002, following the expiration of its treaty, national governments decided to incorporate a new Consultative Committee on Industrial Change, representing steel producers, workers, consumers, and retailers, into the EESC structure.

The Committee of the Regions

"Europe of the Regions" is a popular catchphrase. It describes an EU more inclusive and democratically accountable because of the involvement in its policymaking process of local and regional representatives. In 1985, on the eve of the EC's transformation, individual regions came together on their own initiative and formed the Assembly of European Regions, a pan-European body that sought a formal role in EC affairs. Partly for reasons of democratic legitimacy and partly because it sees regionalism as integral to federalism, the Commission supported the assembly's efforts to give regions and localities a greater voice in the Community system. But the assembly itself was too large and unwieldy to play such a role, and some of its constituent regions were not even within the EC. Accordingly, in October 1991 the Commission submitted a paper to the intergovernmental conference on political union proposing the establishment of a Committee of the Regions (COR) to advise the Council and Commission on relevant policy issues, notably cohesion policy. National governments concurred and included in the Maastricht Treaty a provision to that effect (Articles 263–265 TEC). The committee held its inaugural session in 1994.

The Commission clearly stated in its submission to the intergovernmental conference that the proposed committee's members should hold elective office, but the Maastricht Treaty merely stipulated that the COR should consist of "representatives of regional and local bodies." The Council decided in June 1992 that it was up to each government, using its own criteria, to nominate people to represent regional and local communities (formally, the Council appoints COR members "acting unanimously on proposals from the prospective member states"). Most governments duly nominated elected representatives, but the question of the COR's composition became a vexing issue in Britain, then under Conservative rule. The British government had instinctively opposed the Commission's proposal to establish the committee but reluctantly went along with the idea in the Maastricht Treaty. Moreover, because Britain was then a highly centralized state, there were no elected representatives to designate from mainland Britain's three constituent nations (England, Scotland, and Wales). Understandably perhaps, the government tried to buy off Scottish and Welsh nationalists by overrepresenting Scotland and Wales in Britain's COR delegation.

The Labour government, elected in May 1997, launched a constitutional revolution that included holding successful referendums to establish separate parliaments in Scotland and Wales, thereby bringing Britain more into line with the internal organization of large EU member states. Nevertheless, a fundamental problem with the COR continues to be the great disparity between the size and political power of regions in the EU and the fact that smaller member states themselves constitute single regions. Thus, a relatively small, unitary state such as the Netherlands has little or no interest in the COR. By contrast, regions in the EU's three federal member states (Austria, Belgium, and Germany), and especially in member states where there is a strong movement in favor of federalism (such as Italy and Spain), see the COR as a vehicle to assert their independence vis-à-vis the central government—much to the discomfiture of the member states concerned.

Many members of the committee therefore have a double agenda: to carry out their functions as stipulated in the treaties and to advance regionalism in their own countries and throughout the EU. Potentially, the committee provides a platform for propagating regional autonomy or even independence in the context of market integration and security cooperation at the European level of government. Thus, regionalism and supranationalism complement rather than conflict with each other. Indeed, supranational institutions and regional authorities share a mutual suspicion of national governments, their natural political adversaries.

Role and Structure. Like the Economic and Social Committee, the COR elects a president for a two-year term, but unlike its sister committee it has a "first" vice president and twenty-five other vice presidents (one from each of the other member states). The COR also has a much larger bureau (the president and vice presidents, twenty-five other members, and the chairs of the political groups) than has the Economic and Social Committee. The COR holds five plenary sessions a year.

The Maastricht Treaty tasked the COR with providing advice to the Commission and the Council in five policy areas that have a direct bearing on local and regional government: cohesion, transport, public health, education and youth, and culture. The Amsterdam Treaty extended the committee's consultative role to five other areas: employment, social policy, the environment, vocational training, and transport. The committee's members are distributed among specialized commissions that correspond to its areas of interest:

- territorial cohesion policy
- economic and social policy
- sustainable development
- culture and education
- constitutional affairs and European governance
- external relations

The Maastricht Treaty gave the COR authority to issue opinions on its own initiative, which it frequently does. Like the Economic and Social Committee's opinions, the COR's opinions are useful and informative. As expected, they always reflect regional and local perspectives and emphasize especially the importance of the subsidiarity principle. Also like the Economic and Social Committee's opinions, they go mostly unread in the Council. All opinions, whether own-initiative or mandated by the treaty, are approved by a majority in plenary session.

Political Posturing. The COR pushed hard before and during the 1996–1997 intergovernmental conference to enhance its political profile and agenda. Among other things, the committee requested in its submission to the preparatory Reflection Group that the principle of subsidiarity be redefined in order to refer explicitly to subnational levels of government, that the committee be allowed to bring subsidiarity cases before the Court of Justice, and that the committee be designated an EU institution.[31] In its report to the Reflection Group, the usually sympathetic Commission criticized the COR for "running the risk of casting its net too wide" by making excessive demands and for straying outside the bounds of its mandate in issuing own-initiative opinions.[32] In the event, the Amsterdam Treaty enhanced the COR's position, but not nearly as much as the COR had hoped. Apart from extending the committee's consultative role to new areas, the treaty strengthened the independence of the committee by allowing it to adopt its own rules without reference to the Council and by repealing the protocol in the Maastricht Treaty that called for a common organizational structure for the EU's two advisory bodies.

In a series of written questions in 1992 and early 1993 on the eve of the COR's establishment, members of the European Parliament expressed concern about the committee's relationship with their own institution. In reply, the Council reassured them that the COR "will have no direct dealings with the Parliament" and will not duplicate Parliament's role in any way.[33] Fears that the COR might undermine the Parliament indeed proved unfounded, although members of the Parliament have a reasonable point when they complain that the COR is redundant because parliamentarians are elected to represent local, regional, and national interests (the same is true for the Economic and Social Committee because parliamentarians also represent employers, workers, and other interests). Nevertheless, the Parliament and the COR have had a relatively harmonious relationship, and the Amsterdam Treaty also gave the committee the right to be consulted by the Parliament. Nevertheless, the treaty included a stipulation that "no member of the committee may also be a Member of the European Parliament" (Article 263 TEC).

In September 2004 the committee voted by a large margin for its members to sit in political groups rather than in alphabetical order, as they had since the first plenary session in 1994. The decision reflects the determination of a majority of the committee's members to raise the political profile of their institution. Committee members now sit in political groups similar to those in the European Parliament. Indeed, the committee's inferiority complex vis-à-vis the Parliament arose during the debate on the new seating arrangement, with some of those who advocated a change arguing that by sitting in political groups, committee members would be more effective and be taken more seriously by the Parliament. Some of those against the proposal argued that the committee should not try to replicate, in form or substance, the European Parliament.

■ The European Investment Bank

The European Investment Bank (EIB) is an autonomous public financial body within the EU. Established in 1958 under the terms of the Rome Treaty, the EIB seeks to promote economic development in the EU by offering loans to the public and private sectors, guaranteeing loans from other financial institutions, and putting financial packages together. The Commission and the recipient country's government must confirm that an EIB loan will help to meet national and EU objectives. A sizable number of EIB loans (about 10 percent of the total) are also directed outside the EU in pursuit of the EU's external relations objectives.

EU member states are the EIB's shareholders, with the size of their subscriptions depending on their economic weight. Thus, Britain, France, Germany, and Italy each subscribe about 17 percent of the EIB's capital, whereas Malta subscribes only 0.05 percent. Before the 2004 enlargement, the Bank's capital base was €150 billion; after enlargement it rose to €163.7 billion. The ten new member states account for about 4.6 percent of the subscribed capital, which is guarantee capital; only 7.5 percent is actually paid in. The bank's statute stipulates that aggregate loans and guarantees may not exceed 250 percent of subscribed capital. Accordingly, the EIB may lend and borrow up to about €410 billion.

The EIB raises almost all funds necessary to finance its lending operations by borrowing on capital markets, mainly through public bond issues quoted on the world's major stock exchanges. The bank's enviable record and reputable shareholders give it a top (AAA) credit rating. This allows it to mobilize extensive resources without burdening the budgets of the member states and to channel resources in an economically efficient way to regions and sectors in need of support. The EIB borrows more than any other international financing institution, including the World Bank. It borrows and lends in several currencies, the most important of which is the euro.

The EIB makes long- and medium-term loans (worth about €40 billion a year) in keeping with strict banking management. But the EIB is not a normal bank: it waits for projects to be brought to it and expects them to be largely financed commercially first. The bank can contribute up to 50 percent of a project's cost but typically lends only about 25 percent. Also, the bank's lending rates are highly competitive because of its excellent credit rating and nonprofit status. As well as offering loans, the bank finds cofinanciers and increasingly issues guarantees to commercial banks to encourage them to lend rather than lending directly itself.

The bank is located in Luxembourg and has a staff of about 1,000. It has its own legal personality and a unique administrative structure:

- *Board of governors:* twenty-five government ministers (usually finance ministers); chairmanship rotates in the same order as in the Council but for a full year. Lays down general directives on credit policy; approves the balance sheet and annual report; decides on capital increases; appoints members of the board of directors, management committee, and audit committee.
- *Board of directors:* twenty-six members (twenty-five nominated by the board of governors and one by the Commission); five-year terms. Decides on loans and guarantees, fund-raising, and lending rates; decisions may be taken by majority, but the majority must represent at least one-third of the board and at least 50 percent of subscribed cap-

ital; meets on average ten times a year with the bank's president as chair.

- *Management committee:* nine members (the bank's president and eight vice presidents); six-year terms. Controls all current operations; recommends decisions to the directors and then carries them out.
- *Audit committee:* three members; three-year terms. Verifies that the bank has carried out its operations and kept its books in order.

Like other EU institutions and bodies, the EIB is responding to growing demands, in this case from nongovernmental organizations, to open itself to scrutiny and generally improve transparency. Recent criticism of alleged secrecy and conflicts of interest prompted EU finance ministers to oblige the bank to explain and publish its governing principles, which it did in September 2004.

A number of developments in the late 1980s and early 1990s greatly enhanced the EIB's stature and importance. First, the single market program increased demand for EIB loans to improve the EU's infrastructure and increase industrial competitiveness. Second, the emphasis in the Single European Act on economic and social cohesion, and the subsequent reform of the EU's structural funds, led to massive EIB financing for projects located in regional development areas. Third, German unification further fueled demand for EIB financing, especially for environmental programs. Fourth, the Commission's leadership of the Central and Eastern European assistance effort extended the bank's financing activities in that direction. Between 1990 and 2004, the EIB lent €27 billion to what became the new Central and Eastern European member states, sometimes through cofinancing projects with the European Bank for Reconstruction and Development.

The Maastricht Treaty confirmed the EIB's centrality in the EU system and essential role in financing European integration. Like the articles concerning the Court of Auditors, the articles concerning the EIB were moved to the section on institutions (although the EIB was not designated an EU institution). The treaty reaffirmed that the bank's main task is to provide funding for investment in underdeveloped regions and included a new paragraph instructing the bank to "facilitate the financing of investment programs in conjunction with assistance from the structural funds and other Community financial instruments" (Article 267 TEC). The Maastricht Treaty also called for greater EU involvement in areas in which the bank was already heavily committed: trans-European transport, telecommunications, and energy supply networks; industrial competitiveness; environmental protection; and development cooperation with third countries. Regional development remains the EIB's top priority and accounts for most EIB lending, notably to projects in the EU's less-well-off rural regions (in Portugal, Greece, Spain, Italy, and all of the new Central and Eastern European member states) and in declining industrial areas (in Britain, France, and the Netherlands).

The EIB's activities within the EU can be broken down into the following major categories:

- Improving the transport and telecommunications infrastructure, including highways, airports, railways, and communications networks. The Channel tunnel was the EIB's largest-ever single project. As the EIB's president pointed out during the project itself, "financing the tunnel fits the EIB's task of furthering the development and integration of the EC. It forms a key element in the development of the transport infrastructure necessary to meet the challenges of the single market."[34] Infrastructural projects account for about 45 percent of the bank's lending activity in the EU.
- Protecting the environment. Even before the Maastricht Treaty emphasized the need for environmental protection, the bank had identified this as a priority area. The EIB assesses the environmental impact of all projects under consideration.
- Strengthening the international competitive position of EU industry and promoting cross-border collaboration. The bank assists industry's adjustment to structural change and promotes the growth of enterprise and innovation.
- Supporting the activities of small and medium-sized enterprises through the European Investment Fund (see below).

The vast majority of the EIB's lending activity takes place inside the EU (including the EU's overseas countries and territories). Outside the EU, the bank provides assistance under various financial agreements, mainly with four groups of countries:

1. *Southeastern Europe:* The EIB has been active in the countries of Southeastern Europe, including Bulgaria, Romania, and Croatia, for several years and is progressively increasing its long-term lending in the region.
2. *Mediterranean countries:* The EIB provides loans to the EU's Mediterranean Partner Countries largely through the Facility for Euro-Mediterranean Investment and Partnership, a body that includes a ministerial committee made up of the economics and finance ministers of the EU and the participating Mediterranean states. It forms an essential ingredient of the so-called Euromed partnership and focuses on private-sector development and support for small and medium-sized enterprises.

3. *African, Caribbean, and Pacific countries:* Under the Cotonou Convention, the EIB offers subsidized loans and risk capital assistance to African, Caribbean, and Pacific countries for industrial, agricultural, tourism, telecommunications, and transportation programs.

4. *Asia and Latin America:* The EU first mandated the EIB in 1993 to lend to countries in Asia and Latin America (ALA) with which it has cooperation agreements; the current mandate (ALA III) covers the period 2000–2007.

While upholding its existing obligations inside and outside the EU, the EIB took on even more responsibilities in the early 1990s. As part of an emergency growth package to try to stimulate economic recovery, the European Council asked the EIB in December 1992 to manage a new, supposedly temporary lending facility to help fill the huge, recession-induced gap in EU investment and accelerate the financing of capital infrastructure projects.[35] Accordingly, the EIB and the Commission worked with other financial institutions to establish the European Investment Fund (EIF). The EIB is the major shareholder, subscribing 60.5 percent of the fund's capital; the Commission subscribes 30 percent; European banks and financial institutions subscribe 9.5 percent. The fund was launched in 1995 with the president of the EIB acting as chair of its supervisory board.

In November 2000, as part of the Lisbon agenda to boost competitiveness and employment, EU finance ministers designated the EIF the specialist financial institution for small and medium-sized enterprises, with responsibility for providing venture capital and guarantee investment. The fund does not invest directly in such enterprises but channels money to them mostly through "global loans" concluded with intermediary institutions.

As part also of the Lisbon agenda, the EIB received another new mandate in December 2003 when the European Council endorsed the so-called Growth Initiative (officially the European Action for Growth). This originated in a proposal from the Commission, in cooperation with the EIB, for an initiative to spur growth by increasing overall investment and private-sector involvement in trans-European networks (transport, energy, and telecommunications) and research and development, which became a priority of the Italian presidency in late 2003. The EIB, which already assists infrastructural development in the EU, was particularly pleased to participate in the research and development pillar of the initiative.

▓ Agencies

One of the most striking features of the EU in recent years is the large number of agencies set up by acts of secondary legislation in order to accomplish specific technical, scientific, or managerial tasks. EU agencies range in their roles and responsibilities from think tanks (such as the European Center for the Development of Vocational Training) to a public health information provider (the European Monitoring Center for Drugs and Drug Addiction) to a functional service provider (the Translation Center for the Bodies of the European Union). Reflecting trends at the national level, where there has been a proliferation of independent agencies to help regulate economic and social policy, a few of the EU agencies have regulatory responsibilities.[36] These include the European Environment Agency (EEA) and the European Medicines Agency (EMEA), which are discussed in the relevant policy chapters of this book. The relative paucity of powerful EU agencies reflects the reluctance of member states to confer extensive rulemaking and enforcement authority on independent EU bodies and the lack of an "agency culture" in Europe (in contrast to the United States, for instance).

EU agencies (variously called agencies, authorities, centers, foundations, and offices) have their own legal personalities, organizational arrangements, and governance structures. Those falling under the purview of justice and home affairs (such as Europol, Eurojust, and the European Police College) are discussed in Chapter 17; those relating to foreign policy, security, and defense (such as the European Defense Agency, the European Institute for Security Studies, and the EU Satellite Center) are also mentioned there. Table 10.2 provides basic information on most other agencies.

Inevitably in an entity like the EU, the location of agencies and other bodies is a controversial and politically charged issue. Largely for reasons of prestige, each member state wants a piece of the agency action. This competition resulted in a major row in the early 1990s that held up a decision about the location of the European Central Bank (ECB) and was resolved only at the highest political level: a meeting of the European Council in Brussels in October 1993. As part of a package that centered on an agreement to locate the ECB in Frankfurt (an almost non-negotiable German demand), the European Council decided to move the European Center for the Development of Vocational Training from Berlin (where it had resided since 1975) to Thessaloniki, Greece. The package also allowed the European Environment Agency to open its doors in Copenhagen (the aggressively Green Danish government coveted this agency) and removed a final obstacle to the functioning of the Trademark and Design Office in Alicante, Spain.

Passions and tempers flared again ten years later over the location of a plethora of newly established agencies and bodies, temporarily located in Brussels. Finland and Italy locked horns over the permanent location of the European Food Safety Authority, a plum agency with a three-year budget of €40 million and a staff of 250. Silvio Berlusconi, Italy's mercurial prime minister, insisted on locating the authority in Parma, renowned for its ham and cheese. Matti Vanhanen, Finland's phlegmatic prime minister, made the case for

Table 10.2   EU Agencies

Title	Task	When Established	Where Located
European Center for the Development of Vocational Training (CEDEFOP)	Promotes and develops vocational education and training	1975	Thessaloniki, Greece (since 1995)
European Foundation for the Improvement of Living and Working Conditions (EUROFOUND)	Helps plan and design better living and working conditions	1975	Dublin, Ireland
European Environment Agency (EEA)	Provides information for sound and efficient decisionmaking on the environment	1994	Copenhagen, Denmark
European Monitoring Center for Drugs and Drug Addiction (EMCDDA)	Provides information on drugs and drug addiction	1994	Lisbon, Portugal
Office for Harmonization in the Internal Market (OHIM)	Registers Community trademarks and designs	1994	Alicante, Spain
Translation Center for the Bodies of the European Union (CdT)	Provides translation services for most other agencies and bodies	1994	Luxembourg
European Medicines Agency (EMEA)	Evaluates and supervises medicines for humans and animals	1995	London, UK
European Training Foundation (ETF)	Promotes expertise in vocational education and training in EU partner countries	1995	Turin, Italy
Community Plant Variety Office (CPVO)	Manages a system of plant variety rights	1995	Brussels
European Agency for Safety and Health at Work	Promotes occupational health and safety	1995	Bilbao, Spain
European Monitoring Center on Racism and Xenophobia (slated to become the Human Rights Agency)	Monitors fundamental rights	1997	Vienna, Austria

continues

Table 10.2   *continued*

Title	Task	When Established	Where Located
European Agency for Reconstruction	Manages EU's main assistance programs in Serbia and Montenegro and in the former Yugoslav Republic of Macedonia	2000	Thessaloniki, Greece
European Food Safety Authority	Provides scientific advice on food and food safety	2002	Parma, Italy (since 2005)
European Aviation Safety Agency	Provides technical advice on air safety and certification of certain aeronautical organizations and products	2002	Cologne, Germany
European Maritime Safety Agency	Provides technical advice on the implementation of EU legislation on maritime safety and pollution by ships	2002	Lisbon, Portugal
European Railway Agency	Provides technical advice on rail transport and safety; pending	2004	Lille-Valenciennes, France
European Network and Information Security Agency (ENISA)	Provides advice on matters relating to network and information security; pending	2004	Heraklion, Greece
European Center for Disease Prevention and Control	Educates the public about infectious diseases	2004	Stockholm, Sweden
European Chemicals Agency	To manage the Registration, Evaluation, Authorization and Restriction of Chemicals (REACH) system	Pending	Helsinki, Finland
Community Fisheries Control Agency	To make enforcement of the fisheries rules more effective and uniform	Pending	Spain (in a location to be chosen by the Spanish government)

Helsinki. In a typical outburst, Berlusconi reportedly proclaimed at a European Council meeting in October 2003 that "the Finns don't even know what prosciutto is."[37] EU leaders finally resolved the row at their December 2003 summit, as part of a package deal on the location of several existing and planned agencies. Helsinki got the less charming European Chemicals Agency; the food agency went to Parma, a city soon synonymous not with good food but with corporate scandal, following the collapse into bankruptcy of Parmalat, the Italian dairy-products group based nearby.

EU leaders also agreed to give priority to the new member states in the distribution of the seats of other agencies that might be set up in the future.

National Parliaments

National parliaments are not EU institutions or bodies, but they are an increasingly important part of the EU system. Before direct elections to the European Parliament (first held in 1979), national parliaments delegated their members to sit in the European Parliament. Such parliamentarians held the so-called dual mandate and personified the organic link between national parliaments and the European Parliament. Once that link was broken, national parliaments and the European Parliament went their separate ways: the vast majority of Europarliamentarians had little formal involvement with their national parliaments, and the vast majority of national parliamentarians had little formal involvement with the European Parliament. National parliamentarians generally disapproved of their European counterparts' lifestyles and posturing, and Europarliamentarians disliked not being taken seriously by their national counterparts.

Clearly, closer contact between the two groups was needed not only to improve each institution's perception of the other but also to help close the democratic deficit, which widened in the late 1980s as a result of the procedural reforms introduced in the Single European Act. Specifically, not only did the new cooperation procedure increase the European Parliament's legislative authority, but greater use of qualified majority voting in the Council undermined national parliaments' control over national governments. As long as a country's government could veto proposed legislation at the European level, that country's parliament could hold the government accountable for exercising (or not exercising) the veto. Once governments subscribed to qualified majority voting, however, national parliaments could not reasonably hold them accountable for being outvoted in Brussels and abiding by a majority decision.

Before the increasing use of qualified majority voting, few national parliaments paid much attention to EU decisionmaking. Denmark's was an exception: the Folketing's powerful Committee for Relations with the Common Market held government ministers strictly accountable for their behavior in the Council of Ministers and the European Council. Paradoxically, Denmark's parliament disliked the antidemocratic implications of qualified majority voting and therefore voted down the Single European Act in 1986 (the notoriously Euroskeptical Danish electorate rescued the act in an ensuing referendum).

For its part, the European Parliament was unhappy with the cooperation procedure's relatively narrow scope, especially with the existence after the Single European Act of a number of policy areas subject to qualified majority voting but not subject to the cooperation procedure. As the Council successfully implemented the single market program in the late 1980s, using (or at least threatening to use) qualified majority voting to great effect, national parliaments and the European Parliament became increasingly alarmed by the widening democratic deficit but differed in their suggested solutions to it.

Nevertheless, a number of forums for formal contact between the European Parliament and national parliaments emerged in the late 1980s:

- Conference of Presidents and Speakers of the Parliaments of the EU (meeting every six months)
- Conference of European Affairs Committees of the National Parliaments and the European Parliament (meeting every six months)
- Conference of the Parliaments—the so-called assizes of several hundred Europarliamentarians and national parliamentarians (no fixed schedule)
- bilateral and multilateral meetings between specialized committees to discuss planned and proposed EU legislation (no fixed schedule)

Concerned about the democratic deficit and about national parliaments' estrangement from the EU decisionmaking process, especially as the Maastricht Treaty extended the legislative power of the European Parliament by introducing the codecision procedure, member states attached two declarations to the treaty on the role of national parliaments. The first promised that national governments would send to their own parliaments "proposals for (EU) legislation in good time for information or possible examination" and generally encouraged contact between Europarliamentarians and national parliamentarians. The second encouraged further assizes and promised to "consult" the Conference of the Parliaments "on the main features of the European Union." These anodyne declarations had little practical effect. Some national governments were more assiduous than others about informing their parliaments of impending EU legislation (and some national parliaments were more assiduous than others about insisting on such information). Moreover, the Conference of the Parliaments was too large and unwieldy to play anything other than a symbolic role.

National parliamentary pressure for greater involvement in EU affairs intensified throughout the 1990s.[38] Germany's parliament had pressed the government successfully during the ratification crisis for the right to evaluate draft EU legislation. In 1995, enlargement brought into the EU two Nordic countries (Finland and Sweden) whose parliaments were unwilling to cede control of EU legislation entirely to the Council and the European Parliament.

At the same time, the somewhat Euroskeptical British and Danish parliaments continued to press for more involvement in the EU legislative process.

Under the circumstances it was not surprising that the issue resurfaced during the 1996–1997 intergovernmental conference. There, governments agreed on the need to keep national parliaments better informed but could not agree on the feasibility or desirability of a new body to represent national parliaments at the European level. Finally, member states attached a protocol to the Amsterdam Treaty outlining practical ways in which national parliaments would receive information on developments in the EU and encouraging the Conference of European Affairs Committees (CEAC) of the national parliaments and the European Parliament to "make any contribution it deems appropriate for the attention of the institutions of the EU."

The role of national parliaments emerged again during the Convention on the Future of Europe. Most of the conventioneers agreed that it was essential to increase the participation of national parliaments in EU affairs in order to increase citizens' links to the European level of governance. Indeed, given the continuous decline in the turnout for direct elections, engaging national parliaments more closely in EU decisionmaking seemed vital if the EU was ever to close the gap between the governed and the governing. Valéry Giscard d'Estaing, chairman of the Convention, pressed for a new, joint national-European parliamentary assembly to act as subsidiarity watchdog but inevitably encountered opposition on the grounds that the very citizens to whom it should appeal would balk at the establishment of yet another EU body. The draft Constitutional Treaty nonetheless proposed giving national parliaments the right to vet Commission proposals for conformity with the principle of subsidiarity.

The intergovernmental conference accepted that idea and added a protocol to the Constitutional Treaty on the role of national parliaments in the EU. This stipulates that the Commission must submit all legislative and other proposals simultaneously to national parliaments as well as to the Council and the European Parliament. A national parliament may inform the EU institutions if it considers that a particular proposal violates the principle of subsidiarity. If at least one-third of the national parliaments object, the Commission must review its proposal, presumably with a view to amending or withdrawing it. Although the protocol risks adding another hurdle to the already cumbersome process of legislative decisionmaking, it raises the possibility of turning national parliaments into a locus of debate and lobbying on the EU, thereby stimulating greater citizen interest in what goes on in Brussels.

Despite the difficulty of institutionalizing a role for national parliaments at the European level, national parliamentarians and Europarliamentarians have largely overcome their mutual suspicion and resentment. The most obvious sign of this rapprochement is close collaboration between both groups in transnational political parties such as the Party of European Socialists and

European People's Party. It is also through the work of these parties that national parliamentarians and Europarliamentarians, outside their respective institutions, are most successful in shaping EU policy.

■ Notes

1. See, for instance, Patrick Neill, *The European Court of Justice: A Case Study in Judicial Activism* (London: European Policy Forum, 1995).
2. Klaus-Dieter Borchardt, *ABC of Community Law,* 3rd ed. (Luxembourg: Office for the Official Publications of the European Communities, 1991), p. 38.
3. G. Federico Mancini, "The Making of a Constitution for Europe," in Robert O. Keohane and Stanley Hoffmann, eds., *The New European Community: Decision-Making and Institutional Change* (Boulder, CO: Westview Press, 1991), p. 177.
4. Case 294/83, *Les Verts v. Parliament* (1986), ECR 1339, at 1365.
5. Jo Hunt, "Legal Developments," in *The European Union: Annual Review 2002/2003,* Vol. 41, p. 79 (emphasis in the original).
6. Opinion 2/94, Accession by the EC to the ECHR, ECR I-1759.
7. George Bermann, "Law in an Enlarged European Union," *EUSA Review* 14, no. 3 (Summer 2001): 6.
8. Joseph Weiler, J.H.H., "Editorial: Does the EU Truly Need a Charter of Rights?" *European Law Review* 6, no. 2 (2000): 96.
9. See especially Case 186/87, *Cowan v. Tresor Public* (1989), ECR 195 C-76/90.
10. *Van Gend en Loos* (1963), ECR 29-62.
11. *Grad v. Finanzamt Traunstein* (1970), ECR 825.
12. *Costa v. ENEL* (1964), ECR 6-64.
13. *Simmenthal v. Commission* (1978), ECR 777.
14. *Nold v. Commission* (1974), ECR 372.
15. Anthony Arnull, "Reference to the European Court," *European Law Review* 15 (October 1990): 391.
16. Martin Shapiro, "The European Court of Justice," in Alberta Sbragia, ed., *Euro-Politics: Institutions and Policymaking in the "New" European Community* (Washington, DC: Brookings Institution, 1992), p. 127.
17. Donal Barrington, "Progress Toward European Union: EC Institutional Perspectives on the Inter-Governmental Conferences," paper presented at the Second International Conference of the European Community Studies Association, George Mason University, Fairfax, VA, May 23, 1991, pp. 7–8.
18. *Isoglucose* Case (1980), ECR 125/77.
19. Lord Mackenzie Stuart, "The European Communities and the Court of Law," *Hamlyn Lectures,* 29th Series (London: Stevens, 1977).
20. Nigel Foster, "Legal Developments," *Journal of Common Market Studies* 38, *Annual Review* (September 2000): 84.
21. See Hunt, "Legal Developments," p. 80.
22. See Tom Kennedy, "The Essential Minimum: The Establishment of the Court of First Instance," *European Law Review* 14 (1989): 7–12; and Spiros A. Pappas, *The Court of First Instance of the European Communities,* European Institute for Public Administration (EIPA) professional papers (Maastricht: EIPA, 1990).
23. Phil Fennell, "The Court of First Instance," *European Access* 1 (February 1990): 11.

24. CFI, "Reflections on the Future Development of the Community Judicial System," December 3, 1990, reproduced in *European Law Review* 16, no. 3 (June 1991): 175–189.

25. Pappas, *Court of First Instance,* p. xii.

26. European Court of Justice, 1997 *Annual Report* (Luxembourg: Office for the Official Publications of the European Communities, 1998), pp. 130–131.

27. The CFI's submission to the Reflection Group is published in European Parliament, *White Paper on the 1996 IGC,* vol. 1: *Official Texts of the EU Institutions* (Luxembourg: European Parliament, 1996), pp. 373–382.

28. José Luis da Cruz Vilaca, speech at the official launch of the CFI, September 25, 1989, reproduced in Pappas, *Court of First Instance,* p. 10.

29. Hunt, "Legal Developments," p. 95.

30. See Brigid Laffan, "Auditing and Accountability in the European Union," *Journal of European Public Policy* 10, no. 5 (October 2003): 762–778.

31. The COR's submission to the Reflection Group is published in European Parliament, *White Paper on the 1996 IGC,* vol. 1: *Official Texts,* pp. 415–428.

32. Commission, "Report on the Operation of the Treaty on European Union," SEC(95)731 final, Brussels, p. 15.

33. Written question no. 1250/92, OJ C 247, Vol. 35, September 24, 1992, p. 53, and written question no. 1206/92, OJ C 6, Vol. 36, January 11, 1993, pp. 10–11.

34. Hans-Gunther Bröder (EIB president), interview in *Europe Magazine* (November 1991): 20.

35. Edinburgh European Council, Presidency Conclusions, Bulletin EC 12-1992, point 1.30.

36. See Giandomenico Majone, *Regulating Europe* (London: Routledge, 1996); and R. Daniel Kelemen, "The Politics of 'Eurocratic' Structure and the New European Agencies," *West European Politics* 25, no. 4 (October 2002): 93–121.

37. *Financial Times,* October 31, 2003, p. 1.

38. On the role of national parliaments in the EU, see Richard S. Katz and Bernhard Wessels, eds., *The European Parliament, the National Parliaments and European Integration* (Oxford: Oxford University Press, 1999); Andreas Maurer and Wolfgang Wessels, eds., *National Parliaments on Their Ways to Europe: Losers or Latecomers?* (Baden-Baden, Germany: Nomos Verlag, 2001); and P. Norton, "National Parliaments and the European Union," *Managerial Law* 45, no. 5 (May 1, 2003): 5–26.

11

Decisionmaking and Interinstitutional Dynamics

Brussels is a hive of political and policymaking activity. Most of the action takes place in the sprawling European Quarter of the city, in the meeting rooms and corridors of the Commission, Council, and Parliament, each of which resembles a contemporary urban campus. Restaurants and coffee shops in the warren of nearby streets cater to a multitude of officials, politicians, lobbyists, journalists, interns, and even the occasional academic, all of whom participate to some extent in the EU system. But Brussels, Luxembourg, and Strasbourg (the other seats of EU institutions) are not the only places where EU business takes place. The country in the Council presidency hosts informal meetings of the Council of Ministers as well as hundreds of other meetings, conferences, and seminars. Officials and politicians of national governments and of EU institutions, as well as lobbyists and others involved in EU affairs, are constantly traveling on business throughout the EU. Member states' embassies in other member states devote most of their time to EU business, and the Commission and Parliament have offices in each national capital. Think tanks in Brussels and elsewhere in the EU influence policy, however indirectly, by analyzing issues, hatching ideas, and disseminating information.

Players in the EU game have particular perspectives, shaped by personal, national, cultural, institutional, ideological, political, and professional considerations. Citizens of a particular country will not always agree on what constitutes the national interest. Indeed, political parties contest elections on the basis of contending interpretations of the national interest. Nevertheless, most citizens, regardless of ideological orientation or political affiliation, have a common national perspective and set of values. These often transcend political differences and institutional loyalties in the EU, making it possible for individual actors to share a particular national outlook regardless of political, professional, and institutional differences.

National interests are really the interests of the governments that happen to be in power at any given time. It is those interests that national politicians and officials defend and promote in the EU system, notably in the European Council and the Council of Ministers (including various subcommittees and preparatory bodies) and in dealings with the Commission, Parliament, and other bodies. National politicians and officials tend to think of themselves as having a realistic perspective on EU affairs, in contrast to what some of them see as the Commission's unrealistic Europeanism and the Parliament's unbridled and unreasonable ambition.

As the institutional epitome of European integration and the successor to Jean Monnet's High Authority, the Commission undoubtedly has a more idealistic understanding of the European interest. Many commissioners and Commission officials are hardheaded and politically astute, but the institution as a whole has a vaguely federal view of the EU that exceeds most member states' understanding of what the EU is or should become. Constitutionally, the Commission is the guardian of the treaties. Politically, it is the guardian of the "Community method": the operational assumption that the Commission is at the heart of a historically unprecedented, supranational polity that is moving inexorably toward ever closer union. Depending on their national or political perspectives, individual commissioners may eschew the concept of deeper integration upon their arrival in Brussels. By the end of their tenure, however, it is remarkable how many of them subscribe to the prevailing Commission outlook, which is also ingrained in many Commission officials.

Parliament shares the Commission's general perspective on the historical importance and novelty of the EU system and on its essentially supranational character. But having been an afterthought of Monnet's, and having struggled to get where it is today, the Parliament is a radical institution that is more than willing to agitate for change. Using (or abusing) the fact that, alone of the EU's institutions, its members are elected specifically to play a part in the EU system, Parliament unapologetically exploits every opportunity to increase its power. Parliament's institutional perspective is simple: as a directly elected assembly in a protofederal system, it wants to acquire the authority that it believes it deserves. Individual Europarliamentarians do not necessarily think that way (the Parliament's Euroskeptics certainly do not), but the institution generally has a power-hungry culture and ethos. On a day-to-day basis, ideological affinity and political persuasion inform the behavior of Europarliamentarians, who nevertheless never lose sight of their national origins.

Politicians and officials of the Commission, European Council, Council of Ministers, and Parliament interact with each other all the time, in a variety of forums and for a variety of purposes. Members and officials of the EU's advisory bodies, national parliamentarians, lobbyists, and diplomats from nonmember states contribute to the mix as well. The weekly meetings of the Commission, quarterly meetings of the European Council, monthly meetings of the Council of Ministers, and monthly plenary sessions of the Parliament are the tip of the iceberg—the most publicized part of the EU system. With the exception of the Commission's weekly meetings, all involve a degree of institutional interaction (for instance, the Commission president sits in the European Council, commissioners attend meetings of the Council of Ministers, and commissioners and national ministers attend plenary sessions of the Parliament).

Beneath the surface, the bulk of institutional interaction takes place in hundreds of formal and informal meetings of the principals and officials of the Commission, Council of Ministers, and Parliament mostly in the course of legislative decisionmaking. These meetings range from Council working groups (which Commission officials also attend) to parliamentary committees (which Commission and national officials also attend) to Council-Parliament conciliatory committees (which commissioners and their officials also attend) held to thrash out final legislative texts.

National, ideological, political, and institutional perspectives are constantly in play during the give-and-take of EU policy formulation and decisionmaking. Given the nature of the policy- and decisionmaking process, interinstitutional dynamics are particularly important. It is by virtue of their institutional roles, after all, that individuals make decisions and shape policy in the EU system. Such decisions and policies range from the annual budget and multiannual financial perspective to treaty change to enlargement. Most decisions, however, are of a legislative nature. It is in the legislative arena, in particular, that the Commission, Council of Ministers, and European Parliament are permanently and intensively engaged and in which most other institutions and bodies in the EU system seek to have a say.

▓ Legislative Decisionmaking

In the everyday world of legislative decisionmaking, the Commission, Council, and Parliament are closely engaged with each other throughout the entire process. The Commission and the Council have a special relationship, which is symbolized by the Commission's presence at the other end of the rectangular table from the Council presidency during the various decisionmaking stages, beginning with the Council working groups, continuing through the Committee of Permanent Representatives, and ending with the decisive meeting of the Council of Ministers itself. As a result of its intensive participation in all stages of the legislative process, the Commission learns the member states' positions and the possibilities for maneuvering and compromise (the Commission is supposed to act as a mediator and honest broker).

Despite an inherent tension in the Commission-Council relationship, as well as the Commission's declining influence since the early 1990s, close cooperation between the two institutions is vital for efficient and timely EU decisionmaking. At the beginning of each Council presidency, virtually the entire college of the Commission and the entire government of the country in the presidency meet for a full day to discuss each other's legislative agenda so that the forthcoming presidency can be as productive as possible. During the six months of the presidency itself, officials from the Commission and the country in the presidency meet regularly to iron out policymaking problems, and the presidency's foreign minister usually meets the Commission president and/or relevant commissioners before each meeting of the General Affairs Council. Indeed, a successful presidency involves continuous contact with officials at all levels of the Commission and requires especially close cooperation between the Council secretariat and the Commission's secretariat-general. Given the Commission's importance in the decisionmaking process, "efficient presidencies, as a general rule, are those that have maintained a close and confident working relationship with the Commission."[1]

Even under the best of circumstances, however, Council-Commission relations are prone to occasional outbursts on either side. The Council is less a coherent institution than a collection of national governments eager to prevail against each other, and against the Commission when they disagree with a Commission proposal. These political battles take place not only in committee meeting rooms but also in the public domain, at press conferences, and at other media events. As an unidentified Commission spokesman once complained, "Ministers who hold their own press conferences for journalists from their countries in rooms reserved for national representatives at the top of the Council building have a disgraceful habit of presenting the outcome as a victory of their national delegation against the Commission. That's not the best attitude to adopt if you want to create a European spirit."[2]

Sensitive to media and public criticism of excessive EU intrusion into everyday life, national governments instinctively blame the Commission for unpopular legislation, even though they often press for particular EU-level legislation and are responsible for enacting laws in Brussels. Similarly, some member states use subsidiarity, the principle that decisions should be taken at the European level only if the objectives of the proposed action cannot be sufficiently achieved at the national level, to bash the Commission. A famous letter from French president Jacques Chirac and German chancellor Helmut Kohl to the Council presidency in June 1998 illustrates the point: "Given the tendency of certain European institutions to remain distant from citizens and their daily problems," Chirac and Kohl wrote in a thinly veiled attack on the Commission, "it is important to invite the . . . European Council to hold a discussion on practical implementation of the subsidiarity principle in order to clarify the limits of the competences of the European Union and of the Member States and to examine the extent to which the current level of intervention is suitable."[3]

Personal chemistry and political similarities or differences among government ministers and commissioners can ameliorate or exacerbate Commission-Council relations. The perceived political weakness of successive Commission presidents since the mid-1990s has not helped the Commission in its dealings with the Council of Ministers, let alone the European Council. Despite presidential weakness in recent years, many individual commissioners have been extremely competent and forceful in their dealings with the Council. Particular Council formations often have an affinity with the relevant commissioner because of a common sectoral interest. Agriculture ministers and the commissioner for agriculture usually come from farm backgrounds, for example, and environment ministers and the commissioner for the environment generally sympathize with (or belong to) Green parties.

Below the ministerial and commissioner level, national and commission officials interact frequently and closely in legislative decisionmaking. Commission officials, on the one hand, and the staffs of the member states' permanent representations in Brussels, on the other, are the main points of contact between the Commission and the Council. As permanent officials, they share an interest in moving the decisionmaking process along, although they are often fiercely competitive, tending to see the complex legislative procedure as a game of winners and losers. Deeply immersed in the minutiae of specific policy areas, they haggle over the choice of words or placement of punctuation. For some, telling the story of a particular legislative act is akin to reminiscing about a good soccer match or round of golf.

Whereas the Council and the Commission have had a close and occasionally tense relationship since the launch of the European Community, the Parliament is a relative newcomer in the legislative process. For much of the EU's history the Council was, in effect, the sole legislative decisionmaking body, depending on the Commission to begin the legislative process by submitting proposals. The Parliament had a consultative role in some policy areas, as prescribed in the Rome Treaty, but the Council usually paid little heed to Parliament's opinions.

The Consultation Procedure

The consultation procedure appeared to give the Parliament no more of a legislative role than that of an advisory body such as the Economic and Social Committee. As a harbinger of its determination to maximize its power, the Parliament managed to exact some leverage from the consultation procedure by getting the Commission to amend proposals on the basis of the Parliament's opinion. As the Council could only change an amended proposal on the basis of unanimity, which is notoriously difficult to achieve, it sometimes found itself having to accept the Parliament's amendments rather than reject a proposal entirely. Parliament's success depended on close relations with the Commission, which seemed natural given each institution's supranational ethos.

The treaty did not place a time limit on the Parliament's right to submit an opinion. In a landmark decision in 1980 (in the so-called *Isoglucose* case), the Court of Justice annulled a legislative act because the Parliament had not yet given its opinion in an area covered by the consultation procedure. The Council argued in the case that it had waited for an opinion but that the Parliament had procrastinated; the Parliament counterargued that the Council had proceeded peremptorily. Regardless of what had happened, the Court's ruling gave the Parliament de facto delaying power over legislation subject to the consultation procedure.[4] Clearly, the extent of Parliament's leverage over the Council depended on how badly the Council wanted a particular piece of legislation. For its part, the Parliament did not want to delay legislation indefinitely because it wanted the EU to be able to produce legislation and wanted to avoid being blamed for any failure to do so.

The Cooperation Procedure

Anticipating and hoping to ward off public concern about the democratic deficit, member states agreed in the 1985 intergovernmental conference to increase the Parliament's legislative power and to improve the efficiency of Community decisionmaking. The Single European Act therefore gave Parliament the right to have a second reading of certain draft legislation and extended the use of qualified majority voting in the Council. The new cooperation procedure incorporated both measures and formed "the institutional core of the Single European Act."[5]

Following the introduction of the codecision procedure in the Maastricht Treaty and the extension of its applicability under the Amsterdam Treaty, the cooperation procedure is hardly applicable anymore. Nevertheless, its profound impact on the Parliament's development and on interinstitutional relations is worth mentioning, not least because elements of the cooperation procedure were incorporated into the later codecision procedure. Once again, the Parliament's reaction to the change in legislative decisionmaking demonstrated its determination and ability to increase its power.

Although unhappy with the cooperation procedure's limited applicability, Parliament resolved from the outset to realize the Single European Act's political and institutional potential. In December 1986, Parliament radically revised its rules of procedure to make the most of the new opportunity. Working closely together, Parliament and the Commission had more scope to pressure the Council to accept parliamentary amendments. Parliament used the first reading stage to try to shape the final legislative outcome by apprising the Council of its intentions and by building the coalition of political groups required to amend, or possibly reject, a "common position" (the Council's decision at the end of the first reading, which formed the basis for deliberations in the second reading). For its part, the Council sought to avoid major parliamentary amendments and, especially, the Parliament's outright rejection of its common position, which it could counter only by an often unobtainable unanimous vote. Moreover, the cooperation procedure cast the Commission in the role of arbitrator between the Council and Parliament.

The increasing importance of voting on legislative issues in the Parliament instilled in political groups a greater sense of identity and cohesion and enhanced consensus and coalition-building among them. Nevertheless, political group discipline is lax by the standards of national parliaments, where a government's survival could depend on fierce party loyalty. In addition, the heterogeneity and cultural diversity of political groups militated against strict control of members' behavior. On ideological issues, either the Socialists or the Christian Democrats would nevertheless try to form the core of a parliamentary majority, vying for the support of groups in the center. When issues were not contested along ideological lines, the two major political groups often collaborated to amend or reject a common position in order to assert their institutional authority.

Parliament and the Commission were generally pleased with the cooperation procedure's impact on legislative decisionmaking and on the political process. According to an influential parliamentary report, the cooperation procedure "transformed the role of Parliament in . . . limited though vital fields, and introduced a degree of democratic control over the establishment of a single market by the end of 1992." Nevertheless, the report identified a number of defects in the procedure, especially the Council's "right to adopt legislation in face of Parliament's rejection of all or parts of it."[6] In the view of the commissioner responsible for relations with Parliament, the cooperation procedure "had worked during a period of intense legislative activity," proving that "democracy and efficiency are compatible."[7]

By contrast, some member states were less enamored of the cooperation procedure, seeing it as an opportunity for Parliament to promote its institutional agenda at the expense of effective decisionmaking. Although the procedure required close interinstitutional collaboration to work properly, the Council sometimes stood aloof. For instance, Parliament persistently complained that the Council refused to explain fully its reasons for rejecting parliamentary amendments. This prompted Parliament to call on the Council to reveal "the results of the votes [on common positions] in the Council and the views of each Member State, enabling the peoples and parliaments of the Community to form a view of their governments' position."[8]

Disputes between the Council and the Parliament over the cooperation procedure focused mostly on the choice of "legal base": the relevant treaty article on which the EU should base a legislative action. If the legal base was ambiguous, the Parliament would invariably opt for a treaty article that stipulated the cooperation procedure, whereas the Council would choose the consultation procedure in order to avoid a second reading. Until the Maastricht

Treaty, environmental issues lent themselves to such ambiguity because the Single European Act had extended Community competence to environmental policy subject to the consultation procedure (Article 130s TEC) but had also introduced a new article for the harmonization of national standards subject to the cooperation procedure (Article 100a). Thus, for certain environmental legislation, the Council would favor Article 130s as a legal base, whereas Parliament preferred Article 100a. Despite improvements in the Maastricht and Amsterdam Treaties, plenty of scope remained for disagreement between the Council and Parliament over the choice of legal base in other areas, not least because of the introduction in the Maastricht Treaty of the new codecision procedure for legislative decisionmaking.

The Maastricht Treaty switched some policy areas from the cooperation procedure to the codecision procedure and switched a number of others from consultation to cooperation. As a result, the cooperation procedure remained the most widely used in the enactment of EU legislation until implementation of the Amsterdam Treaty in 1999.

The Codecision Procedure

The European Parliament regarded the cooperation procedure, introduced in the Single European Act, as "part of a preparatory stage in the introduction of genuine co-decision," through which Parliament would receive legislative power equal to that of the Council.[9] By introducing a new legislative procedure—codecision—for a number of policy areas, the Maastricht Treaty went a long way toward meeting the Parliament's demands. The most important innovation in the new procedure was the provision for a conciliation committee, consisting of representatives of the Parliament and the Council, to work out a joint text (if necessary) at the end of the second reading. The joint text would then be subject to approval by the Council and the Parliament in a third reading.

Once again, Parliament confounded its critics, notably in the Council secretariat, by quickly mastering the new procedure and participating in the legislative process in a constructive and timely way. Parliament adopted the vast majority of legislation proposed under the original (Maastricht) version of the codecision procedure without having to convene the conciliation committee. Moreover, Parliament rejected only a handful of proposals either at the second reading stage or after agreement in the conciliation committee, usually in order to make a political point. More often than not the point at issue had to do with the appropriate implementing committee for a particular measure and became bound up in the arcane dispute between the Council and Parliament over "comitology," which is discussed later in the chapter.

Under the original version of codecision, the Council could act unilaterally after the conciliation committee had agreed upon a joint text by adopting the common position it had agreed upon before the conciliation procedure, albeit on the basis of unanimity. This one-sided third reading gave the Council greater power than Parliament in the new procedure and did not amount to "genuine co-decision," for which Parliament continued to press. Parliament's opportunity to achieve its goal came in the 1996–1997 intergovernmental conference on treaty reform, which resulted in the Amsterdam Treaty.

The Impact of Amsterdam. As with previous rounds of treaty reform going back to the Single European Act, member states agreed to strengthen parliamentary involvement in legislative decisionmaking by extending the scope of codecision to many more policy areas and, more important, revising the procedure in order to reinforce Parliament's role in it. One of the most consequential changes to the codecision procedure introduced in the Amsterdam Treaty was the possibility of reaching a decision at the end of the first reading. This gave the Parliament and Council an incentive to cooperate closely in order to expedite the decisionmaking process. An equally important procedural change, and one that increased the incentive for the Council to reach agreement in the first reading stage, was a revision of the third reading obliging the Council to approve or reject the joint text agreed upon in the conciliation committee rather than allowing it to enact the common position upon which it had agreed in the second reading. Altering the one-sided third reading put the Parliament on an equal legislative footing with the Council.

These and other procedural changes, together with the extension of codecision to most policy areas and, correspondingly, the limited applicability of the consultation procedure and near abolition of the cooperation procedure, revolutionized relations among the Commission, Council, and Parliament in legislative decisionmaking. In particular, interaction between the Council and the Parliament has become much more frequent and intense.[10] The Nice Treaty did not include any procedural changes in legislative decisionmaking but extended codecision to yet more policy areas. In recognition of the ubiquity of codecision, the Constitutional Treaty gave the procedure a new name: the "ordinary legislative method" (but otherwise did not alter it).

How It Works. The Commission submits a proposal jointly to the Council and the European Parliament. (The Constitutional Treaty calls for the Commission to submit the proposal also to national parliaments, as pointed out in Chapter 10.)[11]

Parliament's first reading. The relevant committee considers the proposal. The committee's rapporteur drafts a report (opinion) on behalf of the committee, either approving the proposal or proposing amendments to it, together with an explanation of the committee's position. Other committees may also draft opinions. Commission officials attend these committee meetings, where they often answer questions from parliamentarians and defend the Commission's proposal. Drawing on the various committee reports, the lead committee submits a draft legislative resolution, possibly containing suggested amendments to the original proposal. Additional amendments may be tabled during the plenary session, although political groups work closely together to prevent this from happening in order not to overburden plenary sessions.

Council's first reading. If the Parliament approves the proposal in its first reading without amendments, then the Council adopts the measure without further ado. Otherwise the relevant Council working group considers the Parliament's proposed amendments. As a result of intensive contacts among the Council presidency, the Committee of Permanent Representatives (Coreper), the Council working group (which answers to Coreper), the Council secretariat, the Parliament's leadership, and the parliamentary committee (or committees), the Council often accepts the Parliament's amendments. The Commission has the right to amend or withdraw its proposal after the Parliament has adopted an opinion but is unlikely to do so if the Council indicates that it accepts the Parliament's amendments (otherwise the Commission would antagonize both the Council and the Parliament). The ability of the Council and the Parliament to reach agreement on a legislative act during the first reading therefore reduces the Commission's ability to shape EU legislation (the Parliament no longer depends on the Commission to increase Parliament's leverage with the Council). Almost 50 percent of proposals are adopted at first reading.

If it disagrees with the Parliament's amendments, the Council concludes its first reading by adopting a common position.

Parliament's second reading. This stage begins when Parliament receives the Council's common position (accompanied by an explanation of the Council's position and of the Commission's standpoint). There is a time limit of three weeks, with the possibility of a one-week extension, for completion of Parliament's second reading. As in the first reading, the relevant committee considers the common position and makes a recommendation to the Parliament as a whole, which votes on it in a plenary session.

Parliament may:

1. approve the common position, in which case the act is deemed adopted (there is no further action by the Council).
2. reject the common position by an absolute majority of the Parliament's entire membership, which would currently require 367 votes (Parliament has 732 seats); if it does so, the act is deemed not to be adopted.
3. approve amendments to the common position by absolute majority of members of the Parliament, in which case Parliament notifies the Council and the Commission, which prepares an opinion on the matter.

Council's second reading. This stage begins when the Council receives the amendments from the Parliament's second reading. There is a time limit of three weeks, with the possibility of a one-week extension, for completion of the Council's second reading. The Council may:

1. accept the Parliament's amendments (by qualified majority vote or unanimity, depending on what the treaty stipulates), in which case the act is deemed adopted.
2. reject some or all of the amendments, in which case both sides convene the conciliation committee.

The conciliation committee. There is a time limit of six weeks, with the possibility of a two-week extension, for the conciliation committee to complete its work. The clock starts as soon as the first meeting of the committee takes place. Intensive contacts (at all levels) among the Commission (acting as an honest broker), the Council, and the Parliament usually precede the convening of the committee. These include a formal "trialogue" of the committee's two chairpersons—a vice president of the Parliament and a minister of the country in the presidency—and the relevant commissioner. If these contacts are successful, an agreement may be reached at the first meeting.

The committee consists of twenty-five members of the Parliament and twenty-five representatives of the Council and is chaired jointly by the Council presidency and a Commission vice president. Apart from the presidency, which sends a junior minister, national governments send their permanent representatives to conciliation committee meetings. The political groups appoint the parliamentarians on the conciliation committee, most of whom belong to the parliamentary committee that has been considering the proposal from the outset. Parliament also appoints twenty-five substitute members of the conciliation committee, who may attend meetings but do not have the right to vote. At this stage of the codecision procedure the Commission may no longer withdraw its proposal, thereby significantly weakening the Commission's leverage in the bargaining process. Nevertheless, the Commission is represented by the commissioner responsible for the legislation in question.

The conciliation committee works on the basis of the Commission's proposal, the Council's common position, and the Parliament's amendments, together with a joint Council-Parliament working document showing the areas of agreement and disagreement between the two sides. Meetings alternate between the Council's and Parliament's headquarters; all official languages are used. If the committee cannot reach agreement by the end of the time limit, the proposed act is deemed not to be adopted. If the committee approves a joint text, the codecision procedure moves to its final stage, which may last no more than six weeks, with the possibility of a two-week extension (the clock starts from the time that the joint text is approved).

Parliament's third reading. Parliament may approve the joint text by an absolute majority of the votes cast. If it fails to do so, the act is deemed not to be adopted.

Council's third reading. The Council may approve the joint text by qualified majority vote or unanimity, depending on what the treaty stipulates. If it fails to do so, the act is deemed not to be adopted.

If approved by both the Council and Parliament, the act is deemed adopted. Once approved (at this or an earlier stage), the legislative text is revised by the legal/linguistic service of the Council before being sent for signature to the presidents and secretaries-general of the Council and the Parliament. It is then published in the *Official Journal*.

The "ordinary legislative procedure," as the Constitutional Treaty renamed it, is complicated but far from incomprehensible. In general it works well. Given the technical nature of most Commission proposals, it usually lacks excitement and entertainment, but that is true of legislative procedures everywhere. Even the most arcane issue is of interest to some people outside the high priesthood of the Council, Commission, and Parliament, however. Lobbyists for business interests or advocacy groups closely track proposals as they wend their way through the legislative process. Some proposals have a potentially greater impact than others and therefore attract greater media attention. Lobbying by interest and advocacy groups of national governments and the European Parliament, and occasionally by national governments trying to sway the opinions of Europarliamentarians, can be intense. Occasionally, in response to such pressure, Parliament rejects a proposal at third reading (that is, rejects the conciliation committee's joint text). For example, in July 2001 Parliament rejected the so-called Takeover Directive at the final stage of the procedure after the German government applied powerful pressure to German members of the Parliament.

Close and constant contact between the Council and the Parliament, based on extensive preparatory work, is essential for the success of the codecision procedure. Clearly, the Council presidency plays a vital role. So does personal chemistry. Officials of the Council, Commission, and Parliament meet often and get to know each other well. Officials engaged in the same policy areas form strong professional and sometimes personal networks that cut across the three institutions. A host of other networks—national, linguistic, educational, and social—helps to oil the wheels of EU decisionmaking.

Closer Interinstitutional Cooperation

Following the launch of the single market program, the Commission suggested developing an annual legislative program with the European Parliament. The

Commission wanted to help ensure the success of the new cooperation procedure introduced in the Single European Act. In 1991 a representative of the Council presidency participated for the first time in these interinstitutional discussions. The three institutions concurred that legislative programming was indispensable for the EU's decisionmaking procedures to operate effectively. Ten years later, well after the introduction of codecision, the institutions attempted to upgrade their joint legislative programming because of pressure from citizens wanting better environmental, health, and social protection and from businesses wanting less costly and intrusive regulation. The prospect of having many more politicians and officials involved in the legislative process as a result of imminent Central and Eastern European enlargement highlighted possible difficulties ahead and added to the momentum for better interinstitutional cooperation.

The Commission took up the cause of better regulation in the early 2000s, urging the Council and the Parliament to work more closely with it in the legislative process through intensive interinstitutional legislative programming. The Commission took the lead by adopting toward the end of each year an Annual Legislative and Work Program outlining its legislative priorities and proposals for the coming year (the Commission adopted the program in October 2002). The Commission now drafts its work program in consultation with the Council and Parliament. The work program, in turn, represents the Commission's contribution to the Council's annual operating program, the first of which was adopted in January 2003 (covering the Greek and Italian presidencies in that year).

While welcoming the Commission's contribution to the Council's annual operating program, in June 2002 the European Council requested that the Council, Commission, and Parliament adopt an interinstitutional agreement before the end of the year to improve the quality of Community legislation and the conditions, including time frames, for its transposition into national law. Reaching an interinstitutional agreement on better lawmaking proved difficult: the Council of Ministers was wary of reopening a debate on implementation procedures (comitology), while Parliament was concerned about the possible use (or abuse) of so-called soft regulation, such as codes of conduct and the sector-specific agreements among economic actors that were becoming increasingly prevalent in the EU. Far from concluding the interinstitutional agreement by the end of 2002, the Commission, Council, and Parliament reached an accord only by the end of the following year.

Among other things, the interinstitutional agreement on better lawmaking calls for closer coordination in the programming of legislation and the mutual sharing of information at all stages of the decisionmaking process. It also invites members of the Council and the Commission to attend all parliamentary plenary sessions and committee meetings. Despite the ongoing efforts of the

High Level Technical Working Group on Interinstitutional Cooperation, which helped draft the interinstitutional agreement, the sheer size, scope, and diversity of the EU raise daunting challenges for the legislative process.

▉ Comitology

"Comitology" is EU jargon for the complex committee procedures by which the rules and regulations necessary to implement EU legislation are agreed upon. In addition to primary legislation (treaty articles) and secondary legislation (enacted by the Council and the Parliament under the terms of the treaties), a third set of EU legislation stipulates the detailed technical measures that have to be taken in order to execute secondary legislation in the member states. Given the scope of EU secondary legislation—from agriculture to fisheries to the environment to the internal market—the EU produces thousands of implementing acts annually. Although the Commission is the EU's executive body, responsible for executing or implementing EU policy, the Council long insisted that the Commission draft these legislative acts in collaboration with national officials in the comitology committees. It did so because member states were jealous of their national prerogatives and suspicious that the Commission would attempt to alter the Council's acts with its implementing legislation. Member states therefore devised the comitology system to oversee—some would say constrain—the Commission's executive powers.

There are three types of committee: advisory, managerial, and regulatory, and about 250 committees in all, covering almost every aspect of EU activity. As the name suggests, advisory committees merely counsel the Commission on rulemaking. Management and regulatory committees, by contrast, may oblige the Commission to send proposed implementing measures to the Council for review. Management committees were first set up in 1962 to help implement the Common Agricultural Policy, whereas regulatory committees came about to help manage the common external tariff. Regulatory committees later became concerned with a wide range of harmonization issues.

The existence of the committees has always been a source of wounded pride for the Commission, which nevertheless benefits from national experts' advice on the suitability of implementing measures in particular member states and regions of the EU. As a concession to the Commission, member states reiterated in the Single European Act that, as a general rule, EU secondary legislation should confer implementing powers on the Commission. Yet the member states could not agree in the preceding intergovernmental conference on a set of principles and rules to define the exercise of those powers. In March 1986 the Commission proposed to the Council that the three "tried and tested procedures" (the advisory committee, the management committee, and the regulatory committee) remain in use but urged the Council to give the advisory committee predominance in matters concerning the single market.[12] The Parliament delivered a nonbinding opinion in October 1986 expressing concern that comitology might tie the Commission's hands and make implementation of certain single market directives impossible.

It took the Council until July 1987 to decide on new procedures.[13] The Council stipulated that the Commission would exercise powers of implementation either alone or through one of the three types of committee. However, the Council added two variants on the regulatory committee and inserted a safeguard clause, to which the Commission strongly objected. In a speech to the Parliament in January 1988, Commission president Jacques Delors complained that "the Council has not hesitated to resort to institutional guerrilla tactics . . . to impose [procedural changes] which are incompatible with efficient administration and fly in the face of the Single European Act."[14] Delors was particularly put out by the Council's reluctance to allow the Commission to use the advisory committees to implement harmonization legislation in the single market program.

Since then the Council and Commission have sparred over the appropriate procedure for each legislative act. Yet the Council-Commission dispute has become more ritualistic than real. In effect, the Commission has enjoyed a considerable degree of autonomy; the culture of the Commission in any case stressed the importance of legislative initiation rather than implementation; and the efficiency of the various procedures was never an issue (although the variety of procedures available often resulted in protracted and theoretical discussions about which one to use, thereby slowing down the legislative process). Thus, the Commission reached the logical but politically surprising conclusion in a preparatory report for the 1996–1997 intergovernmental conference that, in general, "the implementing procedures operate satisfactorily and present no major obstacles to actual implementation." The Commission also provided a compelling statistic: of the thousands of decisions by comitology committees since 1992, only six had been referred back to the Council, which had then made a decision in each case.[15]

If comitology were still restricted to Council-Commission relations, it would appear only in the lifeless pages of the *Official Journal* and the Commission's *General Report*. But by giving the European Parliament real legislative powers through the codecision procedure, the Maastricht Treaty added a new twist to an already complicated story. Because it championed the Commission's implementing powers and wished, in turn, to control the executive, Parliament had always taken a keen interest in comitology. Until the Maastricht Treaty came into effect, however, Parliament lacked a reason to become directly involved in the procedure. Thereafter the Parliament could argue that it should have equal rights with the Council to monitor implementation by the Commission of legislation enacted jointly with the Council (through codecision). Most member states were aghast at the idea of parliamentary involvement in comitology and claimed that the Council's and Parliament's roles were not comparable in that respect.

The president of the European Parliament warned the Council in July 1994 "not to try to use comitology to deprive Parliament of co-decision rights [to which] it is entitled . . . under the Maastricht Treaty."[16] The intensity of parliamentary feeling became clear shortly afterward when Parliament caused the conciliation phase of the new codecision procedure to fail for the first time (in legislation on voice telephony) because of the Council's refusal to make concessions on comitology. Parliament's concerns about comitology therefore threatened to impair legislative decisionmaking and poison relations between the Parliament and the Council.

An interinstitutional agreement in December 1994 brought about a truce and committed the parties to settle the matter definitively at the forthcoming intergovernmental conference. Although favoring an extension and revision of codecision in order to enhance Parliament's legislative role, the Commission did not advocate parliamentary involvement in comitology but sought instead to devise the simplest procedures with the minimum amount of interference either from the Council or Parliament. In the event, member states agreed to strengthen Parliament's legislative powers by radically revising the codecision procedure. They also attached a declaration to the Amsterdam Treaty calling for a new comitology decision to replace that of 1987.

As it unfolded in 1998 and 1999, however, the comitology battle was fought not between the Council and the Commission or the Council and the Parliament but between the Commission and the Parliament. Parliament was disappointed because the Commission's proposal for a new comitology decision was not radical enough. Rather than advocating a complete overhaul of the system, the Commission merely proposed keeping Parliament better informed of developments in comitology. Parliament pressed for a bigger role and for a clearer distinction to be made between substantive legislation and implementing provisions so that important legislative acts could not be introduced under the guise of implementing measures. Parliament backed up its demands in a way that only it could: it put funding for comitology meetings in a reserve, thereby bringing the system to a standstill.

In the face of Council and Commission intransigence, the usually triumphant Parliament eventually backed down and acquiesced in the new decision, which the Council enacted in June 1999. Under its terms, the Council agreed to involve Parliament more fully in the implementation of acts adopted by codecision, to simplify procedures largely by dropping the variations of the management and regulatory committees, and to provide more public information on comitology. In an additional effort to make the system more transparent, the Council mandated that the Commission produce an annual report on transparency. The Commission and Parliament reached a modus vivendi in

February 2000 when they agreed on procedures for applying the new comitology decision.

The Commission's annual reports on comitology suggest that the system is working reasonably well. The Commission takes the national experts' views into account when drafting implementing legislation and has rarely had to refer measures back to the Council. The Commission has some concerns about the way in which the Council and Parliament occasionally tie the Commission's hands by specifying a particular implementing procedure in the course of enacting a "basic instrument" (a piece of secondary legislation enacted by the Council and Parliament).

■ Negotiating and Discharging the Budget

The Council and the Parliament are the two branches of the EU's budgetary authority. The Commission also plays a part: its proposals get the process going. The Commission and the Parliament tend to aim high in their budgetary requests; the Council tries to rein them in. After all, most of the EU's revenue comes in the form of a percentage of the member states' gross national income (GNI). The larger the percentage of GNI that member states hand over to the EU, the less they have for themselves (even though the percentage in question—1.24—is small, the amounts of money involved are large). In general, the Commission and Parliament want the EU to move in a more federal direction, with an appropriately large budget. Few member states want the EU's budget to grow substantially.

The Financial Perspectives and Annual Budget

Since 1988 the EU has operated within a multiannual financial framework or perspective, within which annual negotiations take place (see Box 11.1). Commission president Delors initiated the multiannual perspectives in part to end the rancor surrounding the annual budgetary procedure. The financial perspectives set binding limits for each main category of expenditure that include a small flexibility margin to cover major unforeseen costs. Finance ministers, foreign ministers, and eventually national leaders (meeting in the European Council) negotiate the financial perspectives, based on a Commission proposal.

In July 2004, the Commission submitted a package of proposals for the 2007–2013 financial perspectives. The Commission asked for a large increase over the seven-year period. Predictably, national governments, especially those whose countries pay more into the EU than they get out of it, balked. That set the scene for protracted and difficult negotiations within the Council of Ministers and the European Council during the following two years until the Commission, Council, and Parliament concluded an interinstitutional agreement to

---

Box 11.1   The Budgetary Procedure

---

1. *Commission draft:* The Commission draws up the preliminary draft budget based on guidelines laid down by Parliament and the Council in the course of an interinstitutional trialogue and sends it to the Council by September 1 at the latest.
2. *Council's first reading:* After conciliation with a parliamentary delegation, the Council adopts the draft budget by a qualified majority and forwards it to Parliament by October 5 at the latest.
3. *Parliament's first reading:* Within a forty-five-day period:
   - Parliament may adopt the draft or decline to take a position, in which case the budget is deemed to be adopted.
   - Parliament may propose modifications to compulsory expenditure (by an absolute majority of the votes cast) and/or make amendments to noncompulsory expenditure (by a majority of the total number of parliamentarians). Noncompulsory expenditure is spending on policies and programs that are not specifically mentioned in the treaties.
4. *Council's second reading:* The Council has fifteen days to respond, during which time it may engage in conciliation with a parliamentary delegation.
   - It may accept Parliament's proposed modifications or amendments, in which case the budget is deemed to be adopted.
   - However, if a proposed modification to compulsory expenditure would increase the overall expenditure of any of the institutions, the Council must expressly accept it by a qualified majority, otherwise the proposal is deemed to be rejected.
   - Acting by a qualified majority, the Council may reject or alter a proposed modification that would not increase the overall expenditure of any of the institutions.
5. *Parliament's second reading:* The Parliament has fifteen days to respond.
   - If it does not take a position during that time, the budget is deemed to be adopted (including the changes made by the Council).
   - Acting by a majority of its members and three-fifths of the votes cast, Parliament may amend or reject the Council's changes. If so, the procedure comes to a close and the president of the Parliament signs the budget into law.
   - Acting by a majority of its members and two-thirds of the votes cast, Parliament may reject the budget as a whole. If so, the entire procedure must begin again, with a new Commission draft. In the interim, the EU operates on the basis of monthly appropriations equal to one-twelfth of the budget of the previous year (the so-called provisional twelfths system).

---

respect the budgetary ceilings and implement the financial perspectives (the agreement of May 1999 covers the period 2000–2006).

Before the advent of the financial perspectives, the Council and Parliament repeatedly clashed during the annual budgetary negotiations. Because of the likelihood of budgetary disputes, the Council and Parliament established a conciliation procedure as early as 1971. This involves biannual Council-Parliament meetings, first when the Council prepares to adopt the draft budget and later when the Council is about to decide on the Parliament's proposed amendments. In addition, the Council president, the budget committee chairman, and the budget commissioner hold "budgetary cooperation meetings" in December during the plenary session at which the Parliament adopts the budget.

The budgetary conciliation and cooperation procedure did not prevent the Parliament and Council from clashing repeatedly in the 1970s and 1980s. Indeed, Parliament rejected the budget in 1979 and 1984 and continually tried to increase the size of noncompulsory expenditure, for which it has the power to make budgetary amendments. Parliament's main concerns were to curb agricultural expenditure and increase spending on policy areas in the noncompulsory category, notably regional policy. Only as a result of the agreement of February 1998 on the first financial perspectives (the so-called Delors I package) and ensuing interinstitutional agreement on budgetary discipline did the situation improve. The Council and the Parliament completed the 1989 budget on time without a major dispute.

The positive impact of Delors I generated momentum for a Delors II package to cover the years 1993–1999, although recession in the early 1990s strengthened opposition in the EU's northern member states to a large Cohesion Fund for the southern member states. Agreement on the Delors II package in December 1992 (followed by a new interinstitutional agreement in October 1993) owed much to the success of the 1988 budgetary reform and ensured that the multiannual financial framework became a fixture of the EU.

Nevertheless, the Council and the Parliament continued to squabble over the distinction between compulsory and noncompulsory expenditure—a squabble that led the European Court of Justice to declare the 1995 budget illegal because the Parliament had changed some of the classifications. Parliament pressed for the issue to be included in the 1996–1997 intergovernmental conference, but, apart from financing the Common Foreign and Security Policy, budget issues were almost wholly absent from the intergovernmental conference and the ensuing Amsterdam Treaty. Several years later, member states followed the recommendation of the Convention on the Future of Europe and agreed in the 2003–2004 intergovernmental conference to abolish the distinction between compulsory and noncompulsory expenditure. This and related provisions of the Constitutional Treaty would considerably enhance the budgetary authority of the Parliament but not necessarily do away with Council-Parliament friction on budgetary matters.

Budget Discharge

Parliament has the sole authority to approve (grant discharge to) the Commission's annual financial statement of accounts. Parliament often uses that authority to enhance its institutional power, although arguably to the detriment of the budgetary and accounting aspects of the discharge function. At a plenary session in July 1979, the budget commissioner opined that refusal to grant a discharge would be "a political sanction . . . an event of exceptional seriousness [that] would have to lead to the dismissal of the existing [Commission] team. I venture to think that we shall never reach that point."[17] Yet five years later, in November 1984, the Parliament refused a discharge of the 1982 budget as a means of censuring the Commission. A political crisis was averted only by the expiration of the Commission's term in office (the Parliament finally granted a discharge for the 1982 budget in March 1985).

In 1998 the Parliament delayed discharge of the 1996 budget to protest the Commission's poor management of successive budgets, based on highly critical reports by the Court of Auditors. This action triggered the events that culminated in the Parliament's highly publicized efforts to vote the Commission out of office in early 1999 (the Commission resigned when it became apparent that the Parliament would be able to muster the requisite number of votes to do so).

■ Holding the Commission and Council to Account

As the way in which it exercises its power to discharge the budget shows, Parliament uses every opportunity to hold the Commission, and where possible also the Council and even the European Council, to account. Parliament may vote the Commission out of office by a two-thirds majority of its total number of members (currently 489 out of 732 members). Only since being directly elected has Parliament contemplated using its power of censure. For much of that time, fearful of provoking a major political crisis that could escalate beyond its control, Parliament was generally reticent about tabling, let alone adopting, motions of censure against the Commission.

For example, Parliament's response to the bovine spongiform encephalopathy (BSE, or "mad cow") crisis in 1996 demonstrated the institution's increasing assertiveness vis-à-vis the Commission but continuing unwillingness to censure the EU's executive. Although Parliament may have had enough votes to pass a motion of censure, its leadership decided instead to adopt a nonbinding resolution of "conditional censure" to pressure the Commission to implement Parliament's recommendations for administrative improvements in the wake of the BSE crisis.[18] In March 1998, at a stormy plenary session, parliamentarians again threatened the Commission with censure, this time over the Commission's alleged mishandling of the EU budget. Amid growing allegations of fraud and financial mismanagement in the Commission, and in the run-up to that year's direct elections, Parliament crossed the Rubicon and voted in January 1999 to oust the Commission. It failed in its first attempt but, as noted above, would probably have succeeded in a second attempt had the Commission not resigned in the nick of time.

Far from being the result of a calculated parliamentary maneuver, the Commission's collapse was the culmination of a series of mistakes and misjudgments in both institutions. But the widespread perception was that Parliament had finally come of age and asserted its authority over an arrogant and corrupt Commission. As perception shapes political reality, the events of early 1999 therefore represented a major institutional advance for the Parliament, although its assertion of accountability did not so much tip an institutional imbalance as redress one. In principle, the Commission was always accountable to Parliament; in practice, it now had to behave accordingly. The Council also emerged triumphant from a follow-on interinstitutional dispute. Emboldened by having forced the Commission out of office, Parliament wanted to install the new Prodi Commission only on an interim basis (to see out the Santer Commission's term) before putting yet another new Commission in place. The Council insisted instead on appointing the Prodi Commission not only for the remaining months of the Santer Commission's term but also for the following five-year period.[19]

Temporary committees of inquiry are another instrument that Parliament uses to hold the Commission to account. Indeed, it was a highly critical report of a temporary committee of inquiry that led the Parliament to censure the Commission conditionally in the BSE case. The use of temporary committees of inquiry, as well as aggressive questioning of commissioners during their routine appearances at plenary sessions, clearly signals Parliament's determination to hold the Commission more accountable than ever before.

Although the Rome Treaty did not give Parliament a role in appointing the Commission, since 1981 Parliament has voted on the investiture of each new Commission. The Maastricht Treaty formalized that practice by mandating that the newly nominated president and other members of the Commission "shall be subject as a body to a vote of approval by the European Parliament" (Article 214.2 TEC). In its usual thrusting way, Parliament interpreted this as meaning that it could vote separately on the presidential nomination (which it did for the first time in July 1994) and collectively on the nominations of the other commissioners following individual "investiture" hearings (which it held for the first time in January 1995). The conduct of the 1994 vote on Jacques Santer's nomination (fearing that the vote would go against Santer, some national governments pressured parliamentarians to vote in his favor) and of the 1995 investiture hearings (parliamentarians quizzed some commissioners-designate aggressively) illustrated the institution's determination to make the Commission more accountable to Parliament.[20] The 1995 hearings were especially memorable for the alleged comment by one commissioner-designate that the European Parliament "was not a real parliament."[21] In general, the hearings contributed to the changing dynamics of Commission-Parliament relations, which, as the increasing recourse to censure motions shows, are becoming less complementary and more conflictual.

The investiture hearings of the Barroso Commission in October–November 2004 provided a striking example of how conflictual those relations were becoming. As noted in Chapter 7, Parliament's social affairs committee rejected the commissioner-designate for social affairs on the grounds of his unsuitability for the justice and home affairs portfolio after the nominee made objectionable remarks about women and gays. In the face of strong opposition from the Parliament as a whole and weak support from national governments, Barroso withdrew his support from the embattled nominee, who obligingly withdrew from nomination. The episode, which delayed the investiture of Barroso's Commission, signaled Parliament's increasingly aggressive oversight of the Commission.

Parliament has much less leverage over the Council. Nevertheless, Parliament acts unofficially as a Council watchdog. The Council presidency reports to the Parliament after each summit and at the beginning and end of each presidential rota, thereby giving the Parliament an opportunity to debate the presidency's performance and priorities. The Council presidency must also answer written and oral questions from parliamentarians. Parliament's showdown with Barroso over the investiture of his Commission was a warning from Parliament to the national governments that they would have to be more careful when nominating commissioners.

▧ Notes

1. Guy de Bassompierre, *Changing the Guard in Brussels: An Insider's View of the EC Presidency* (New York: Praeger, 1988), p. 25.

2. Quoted in *Le Monde,* October 13, 1992, p. 2.

3. The letter is reproduced in *Agence Europe,* June 20, 1998, p. 1.

4. Richard Corbett, Francis Jacobs, and Michael Shackleton, *The European Parliament*, 4th ed. (London: John Harper, 2000), pp. 25–30.

5. John Fitzmaurice, "An Analysis of the European Community's Cooperation Procedure," *Journal of Common Market Studies* 26, no. 4 (June 1988): 390.

6. See "Prag Report on the Cooperation Procedure," as reproduced in *Agence Europe* Documents, 1820/21, January 30, 1993, pp. 10–12.

7. Quoted in *Agence Europe,* January 22, 1992, p. 1.

8. "Prag Report," p. 12.

9. Ibid., pp. 10–12.

10. See Michael Shackleton, "The Interinstitutional Balance in the EU: What Has Happened Since 1999?" *EUSA Review* 17, no. 3 (Summer 2004): 3.

11. This description is based largely on "Codecision 'Step by Step,'" http://europa.eu.int/comm/codecision/stepbystep/text/index_en.htm.

12. OJ C 70, March 25, 1986; Bulletin EC 2-1986, point 2.4.14.

13. OJ L 197, July 18, 1987.

14. Jacques Delors, address to the European Parliament, Bulletin EC S/1-88, p. 10.

15. Commission, *Report on the Operation of the Treaty on European Union,* SEC(95)731 final, p. 22. For subsequent developments relating to comitology, see Morten Egeberg, Gunther F. Schaefer, and Jarle Trondal, "The Many Faces of EU Committee Governance," *West European Politics* 26, no. 3 (July 2003): 19–43; Robin H. Pedler and Guenther F. Schaefer, eds., *Shaping European Law and Policy: The Role of Committees and Comitology in the Political Process* (Maastricht, the Netherlands: European Institute of Public Administration, 1996); and M. P. C. M. Van Schendelen, ed., *EU Committees as Influential Policymakers* (Aldershot, UK: Ashgate, 1998).

16. Debates of the European Parliament, OJ 4-449, July 19–22, 1994, p. 13.

17. Quoted in Daniel Strasser, *The Finances of Europe,* 7th ed. (Luxembourg: Office for Official Publications of the European Communities, 1992), p. 290.

18. See Martin Westlake, "'Mad Cows and Englishmen': The Institutional Consequences of the BSE Crisis," *Journal of Common Market Studies* 35, *Annual Review* (1996): 11–36.

19. See Desmond Dinan, "Governance and Institutions 1999: Resignation, Reform and Renewal," *Journal of Common Market Studies* 38, *Annual Review of the EU 2002/2003* (September 2000): 27–30.

20. See Simon Hix and Christopher Lord, "The Making of a President: The European Parliament and the Confirmation of Jacques Santer as President of the Commission," *Government and Opposition* 31 (1995): 62–76.

21. See *Agence Europe,* January 6, 1995, p. 3.

Part 3

Policies

12

Agriculture
and Cohesion

Agriculture and cohesion (efforts to reduce socioeconomic disparities among regions) are highly distinctive areas of European Union policy. The Common Agricultural Policy (CAP) was put in place in the 1960s as a corollary to the customs union. Although it has changed markedly since then, its original rationale remains the same: the CAP is a welfare program intended to give farmers an income comparable to that of workers in other sectors. This project entails massive financial transfers to the agricultural sector from the EU budget. For a long time the CAP was the largest item of EU expenditure. Its declining share of EU spending is due not to cutbacks in payments to farmers but to the larger size of the EU budget and higher spending on cohesion, the other main category of EU expenditure.

EU agricultural subsidies are visible (and welcome) to the farmers who get the checks but are imperceptible to the population of the EU as a whole, except for high food prices, which consumers do not necessarily ascribe to the CAP. By contrast, the impact of the structural funds (the instruments for promoting cohesion) is more widely and readily apparent. Travelers throughout the EU, but especially in the less developed parts (notably in Central and Eastern Europe), frequently encounter road and rail improvements paid for in part—as the blue signs with gold stars proudly proclaim—by EU structural funds. Workers in transition and the unemployed are also aware that their vocational training courses are paid for to some extent by the structural funds. Apart from monetary union, which puts a common currency in the pockets of residents and travelers in twelve member states, no other policy area has such a discernible impact on the EU.

The CAP has long been pilloried for its extravagance. Asked by the Commission to study the EU budget, a group of outside experts called in July 2003 for a major cut in agricultural spending in order to finance more important priorities such as education and research.[1] Some of those who criticize the CAP for excessive subsidization also criticize cohesion either for misallocating assistance to disadvantaged regions or for spending money on regional development in the first place. The CAP and cohesion are so deeply embedded in the culture and psyche of the EU, however, that their future is probably secure (at least as secure as the future of the EU itself). Both have adjusted to the greatest challenge since their inception: Central and Eastern European enlargement. Rather than making the CAP and cohesion adapt to enlargement, the EU adapted enlargement to the CAP and cohesion. The proposed financial perspective for 2007–2013 maintains approximately the same proportion of spending on the EU's two largest redistributive policies. The CAP and cohesion are therefore unlikely to change radically anytime soon.

■ The Common Agricultural Policy

The CAP is one of the oldest and most controversial EU policies. It covers almost every aspect of farming life in an EU that, with successive enlargements, has acquired an ever more diverse agriculture sector, incorporating small family farms and large factory farms, farms in the plains of Poland and the highlands of Scotland, farms in the frozen north of Finland and the sweltering south of Spain. The range of agricultural products is as diverse as EU farm size and type, ranging from cereals, beef, milk, olive oil, fruit, and vegetables to tobacco and reindeer meat. Agriculture in the EU employs eight million people (5.3 percent of the working population), and agricultural exports account for 8 percent of total EU exports.[2]

Critics of the CAP denounce it as expensive, wasteful, environmentally unfriendly, and trade distorting. It accounts for approximately 45 percent of annual EU spending, causes food surpluses that are warehoused throughout the EU, and contributes to land and river pollution through farmers' excessive use of fertilizers and pesticides. Because of its complexity, the CAP is poorly managed; because of its largesse, it is prey to massive fraud. The CAP is a source of friction in the EU's external economic relations by virtue of its import restrictions and export subsidies. The eruption of the bovine spongiform encephalopathy (BSE, or "mad cow") crisis in 1996 added food safety to the litany of complaints. Little wonder that the CAP is increasingly unpopular with most Europeans, although still beloved by farmers.

Despite its obvious failings, the CAP remains a cherished icon of European integration, and especially of Franco-German friendship. It evokes the heady days of the late 1950s, when Germany supposedly agreed to European subsidization of France's large agricultural sector in return for French acceptance of a common market in industrial goods. The truth was less clear-cut, but French leaders habitually evoke the myth of the EC's constitutive bargain to deflect pressure for far-reaching CAP reform. German leaders invariably perpetuate the CAP for its own sake and for the sake of harmonious relations with France.

Nevertheless, the CAP is changing in important ways. Since the early 1990s the EU has been moving away from a system of price supports to one of direct income supports but is not about to abandon large-scale subsidization of agriculture. At French prompting, the EU rationalizes farm subsidies on the grounds that agriculture in the EU is different from agriculture anywhere else in the world, that the "European agriculture model" with its mixture of social, environmental, and economic elements requires a high degree of government intervention and support.[3] Undoubtedly agriculture is a singular sector—food is a basic need, rural life has a special appeal, and farms have a romanticism about them that factories and offices do not. Perhaps for those reasons, the 95 percent of European workers not in agriculture—many of whom have to survive in the real world of global competition, restructuring, and job losses—are still surprisingly indulgent of their fellow workers on the land.

Looked at purely from an economic perspective, the CAP does not make sense. But it cannot be understood from a purely economic point of view. Rather, comprehending the CAP requires some knowledge of the history and politics of European integration, which favor the status quo—gradual reform but maintenance of the policy's underlying characteristics—rather than radical change. Although its modalities may change over time, the CAP will likely endure forever as a symbol and instrument of EU support for a privileged socioeconomic sector.

Origin and Development

Even before the European Community came into existence in 1958, agriculture was a sensitive issue for most European governments. Near-famine conditions in much of postwar Europe made food security a national priority. The centrality of peasant proprietorship in European political culture, the romantic allure of the land, and the emergence of a highly influential farmers' lobby gave agriculture added political salience. A decline in the relative economic weight of the agricultural sector and a corresponding drop in farmers' incomes raised the political stakes. Not surprisingly, by the mid-1950s agriculture had become a heavily protected and subsidized sector.

Notwithstanding their general support for market integration, governments had no intention of giving up the traditional interventionist measures widely used to protect agricultural price levels and buttress farmers' earnings. Some governments, such as the German and the Dutch, would have been happy to exclude agriculture from the new EC, continuing instead to subsidize it at the national level. The French government, by contrast, wanted to include agriculture in the EC in order to shift the cost of subsidizing France's large and unproductive agricultural sector from the national to the European level. As France made this a condition of accepting a common market in manufactured goods, which it wanted to have in any case, France's partners had little choice but to commit themselves in the treaty to establishing an EC-level agricultural policy.

There was no disagreement among member states on the general objectives of that policy, which were written into the Rome Treaty:

- to increase agricultural productivity
- to ensure a fair standard of living for farmers
- to stabilize agricultural markets
- to guarantee regular supplies of food
- to ensure reasonable prices for consumers

Nor did member states think that agricultural production and trade should be subject to the mechanisms for market liberalization laid down for industrial products. They therefore excluded agriculture from the scope of the treaty's general provisions on competition. Instead, member states agreed to replace various "national organizations" of agricultural markets with one "common organization" that would have at its disposal such interventionist measures as "regulation of prices . . . and common machinery for stabilizing imports or exports" (Article 34 TEC). The treaty charged member states with establishing the new European agricultural regime by developing a Common Agricultural Policy before the end of the transition to the customs union and charged the Commission with taking the first step: convening a conference of member states "with a view to making a comparison of their agricultural policies, in particular by producing a statement of their resources and needs" (Article 37 TEC).

Given the sensitivity of agricultural policy and the nature of the treaty's provisions for agriculture, it is hardly surprising that, according to a key participant, "during the [Community's] first five years the question that dominated all others, by far, was the progressive construction of the CAP."[4] The process began in July 1958 when Sicco Mansholt, vice president of the Commission with responsibility for agriculture, having convened the obligatory conference of Commission, government, and farmers' representatives, proposed the following guiding principles:

- *A single market:* Agricultural produce should be able to move freely throughout the EC.
- *Community preference:* Priority should be given to EC produce over that of other countries.

- *Financial solidarity:* The cost of the policy should be borne by the common EC budget rather than by individual member states.

The Commission then formulated proposals to replace individual member states' systems of customs duties, import quotas, and minimum prices with a harmonized Community-wide market, free intra-Community trade in agricultural products, and common protection vis-à-vis nonmember countries. Detailed negotiations culminated in a series of legendary marathon meetings of the Council in December 1961 and January 1962. By the simple stratagem of "stopping the clock" at midnight on December 31, the ministers ostensibly reached agreement on the CAP by the statutory deadline, although talks continued until mid-January.[5] The result was a package deal that included a common system of price supports covering 85 percent of total EC production, a framework to raise levies on imports into the EC, and the establishment of the European Agricultural Guarantee and Guidance Fund (EAGGF) to underwrite the entire operation. The guarantee section (accounting for the bulk of the fund) would cover the costs of market intervention; the guidance section would pay for structural improvements. The Council agreed to finance the EAGGF by member state contributions only for the first three years, after which a new arrangement would have to be made. Commission proposals to finance the EAGGF from July 1965 on by using the EC's sources of revenue (the so-called own resources) sparked the infamous empty chair crisis; it was only in 1970, as part of a wide-ranging budgetary agreement, that member states finally switched to paying for the CAP through the EC's own resources.

The basic elements of the CAP were:

- *Target price:* the EC-wide guaranteed minimum price for a particular agricultural commodity or product
- *Intervention price:* the price at which specially designated intervention agencies in the member states would buy surplus produce in unlimited quantities (guaranteed withdrawal from the market)
- *Entry price:* the minimum price at which produce could be imported into the EC
- *Levy:* a duty imposed on agricultural imports to raise their prices to the level of the entry price (levies are part of the EU's "own resources")
- *Refund:* a rebate paid to EC exporters to bridge the gap between lower world prices and higher EC prices

The target price was supposed to ensure that farmers had adequate incomes; the intervention system guaranteed the sale of their products regardless of market demand; the entry price protected the EC market from being inundated with cheap imports; and the refund was an export subsidy that enabled farmers to sell their products on the world market, given that the EU's guaranteed minimum price was generally higher than prevailing world prices.

Because the target price and intervention price were the same throughout the EC, the CAP was susceptible to exchange rate fluctuation among member state currencies. Distortions in cross-border pricing because of changes in exchange rates led to the introduction of "green money" for the CAP: a complicated system involving payments to farmers of "monetary compensatory amounts" (border taxes and subsidies to compensate for price differences within the EC caused by fluctuating exchange rates). The introduction of the artificial currency gave farmers in border areas ample opportunity to cheat the system and allowed certain member states to manipulate exchange rates in order to keep support prices higher than they would otherwise have been. Following numerous efforts to reform the agrimonetary system, often linked to major currency fluctuations in the real world and linked as well to implementation of the single market program, the EU decided in 1996 to freeze green exchange rates until January 1999, when the introduction of the euro obviated the need for a contrived agrimonetary system in the eleven member states participating in the single currency (a twelfth member state joined in 2001).

Apart from the peculiarities of the agrimonetary system, annual farm price negotiations in the Agriculture Council (the council of agriculture ministers) are one of the most important and distinctive features of the CAP. The negotiations proceed as follows:

1. The Commission sends the Council a detailed package of proposals early in the year, usually in January.
2. The Special Committee for Agriculture, rather than the Committee of Permanent Representatives (Coreper) as in most other EU policy areas, considers the proposals during the next two or three months in close consultation with the Commission.
3. The European Parliament also considers the Commission's proposals and delivers an opinion. Although its input is based on the consultation procedure, not codecision, the Council and the Commission pay close attention to the Parliament's proposed amendments.
4. The Special Committee and the agriculture ministers try to reach agreement on the price package during the Council's monthly meeting in April or May, but negotiations sometimes continue into June or even into the beginning of a new Council presidency in July.

This brief, dry description belies the monumental effort involved in concluding the annual package of farm prices, a staple of the EU until reforms introduced in the early 2000s, in anticipation of Central and Eastern European enlargement, reduced the annual negotiations to only a few sectors and robbed them of much of their drama. Indeed, the effort is so great that the presidential rota was deliberately constructed so that a member state in the presidency for the first half of the year (and therefore responsible for managing the agriculture negotiations) assumed the presidency for the second half when its turn next came around. In the latter stages of the price-fixing process, negotiations could last several days, taxing the patience and stamina of the negotiators. Price packages sometimes contained fifty or sixty regulations that included not only monetary amounts but also complex changes to already complicated market mechanisms.[6]

Ministers and officials are acutely aware that farmers' livelihoods depend on the outcome of the annual negotiations, not least because farmers often gather outside the Council building to press their case for higher prices. The European farmers' lobby—notably the powerful Committee of Professional Agricultural Organizations of the European Community (COPA)—is active in all stages of CAP policymaking, contacting commissioners, Europarliamentarians, agriculture ministers, and officials (especially the senior officials on the Special Committee for Agriculture). National governments are highly susceptible to pressure from farmers. Despite the popular notion that France is the CAP's most tenacious defender, Germany has proved equally obdurate in perpetuating price-driven support and blocking meaningful reform, thanks largely to the Bavarian farm lobby's immense sway over the Christian Social Union, a small but nationally influential political party.

CAP Reform: From Mansholt to MacSharry

The CAP's market-regulating mechanisms—target prices, intervention, levies, and export subsidies—ensured a number of positive outcomes: agricultural production increased greatly, farmers enjoyed a fair standard of living (although some benefited more than others from the CAP's largesse), agricultural markets were stabilized, and food security was ensured. However, consumers clearly lost out as high prices in shops and supermarkets reflected high target prices for farm products and high levies on imported foodstuffs.

Although the CAP could be judged a success on the basis of its stated objectives, the policy's market-regulating mechanisms caused serious economic, environmental, and political problems:

- Guaranteed prices bore no relation to demand and encouraged massive overproduction.
- Surplus produce had to be stored in "intervention" (Eurospeak for warehoused) throughout the EC at considerable cost to taxpayers (these were the infamous butter mountains, wine lakes, and the like).
- "Big" farmers (those with large farms) produced more and thereby earned more money, whereas small farmers, who most needed assistance, earned less.

- In order to increase output from their already overworked fields, farmers used excessive amounts of herbicides, pesticides, and artificial fertilizers, exacerbating the EC's acute environmental problems.
- The maintenance of quotas, levies, and tariffs in agricultural trade angered exporters to the EC and contrasted unfavorably with the EC's efforts to promote global market liberalization in other sectors.
- Export price supports distorted world prices and undercut non-EC exporters, leading to trade disputes.

All of these problems or potential problems became apparent early in the CAP's existence, prompting Mansholt, father of the CAP, to try to rectify some of its most obvious excesses. The so-called Mansholt Plan of 1968 was the first, ill-fated effort to avoid surpluses yet still provide an adequate income to those who stayed on the land.

Enlargement, Overproduction, and Overspending. The 1973 enlargement made matters worse by bringing into the EC two small countries (Denmark and Ireland) with large agricultural sectors and a large country (Britain) with a small agricultural sector but many big farmers. Britain's accession introduced a new political twist because it had traditionally pursued an agricultural policy that was the antithesis of the CAP (it was even called the "cheap food" policy). Not since the beginning of the Industrial Revolution had Britain attempted to be self-sufficient in food production. Britain's population was too large and its amount of arable land too small to feed everyone on the island solely from homegrown stocks. Accordingly, Britain imported food from the empire and, as the empire shrank, from Commonwealth countries and other inexpensive suppliers—hence Commonwealth concerns about Britain's entry into the EC; hence also Britain's instinctive antipathy to the CAP. Britain therefore became a persistent critic of the CAP and, in the person of Margaret Thatcher in the 1980s, a powerful advocate of CAP reform.

By that time, however, vested agribusiness and rural interests had a firm grip on the CAP and could successfully resist major reform. Farmers maximized political support for the CAP by lobbying effectively and by portraying themselves as a disadvantaged and beleaguered group providing a vital service to society. Despite paying high prices over the counter, the nonfarming sector had relatively little information about or interest in the CAP and failed to appreciate the program's pernicious economic impact. Thus, politicians could win farmers' votes without alienating other social groups and political constituencies. As a result, not just agriculture ministers but also foreign ministers and even heads of state and government aggressively advocated farmers' interests, often invoking the national veto to do so.

The idiosyncratic nature of the Agriculture Council compounded the problem. Apart from convening more often than most other councils, being served by the Special Committee on Agriculture rather than by Coreper, and engaging in the annual price-fixing ritual, the Agriculture Council consists mostly of ministers with strong ties to the rural community and a strong personal and political awareness of the CAP's importance. Harold Wilson, Britain's prime minister in the mid-1970s, often "heard the most powerful heads of government aver that the agricultural cabal in the EEC—their own ministers—have so powerful a leverage that they have become a power center transcending the authority of national cabinets and prime ministers."[7]

Obscene levels of overproduction in the late 1970s triggered a renewed discussion of possible CAP reform. In 1979 the Council introduced a modest change in the system of price guarantees and imposed a "coresponsibility" levy on dairy farmers to help meet the cost of intervention storage and subsidized sales of surplus produce. When the coresponsibility levy failed to curb output, the Commission proposed a production quota. After an intensive series of negotiations at the highest level, which at one point saw the Irish prime minister walk out of a summit meeting, EC leaders agreed in March 1984 on a quota system for milk production.[8]

The milk quota was an inadequate response to the problem of overproduction and did little to reduce spending on the CAP (which by 1984 accounted for over 70 percent of EC expenditure). The possibility of bankruptcy, impending Mediterranean enlargement, and Thatcher's insistence on budgetary reform intensified pressure for radical action. Indeed, as part of the budgetary package agreed to at the June 1984 Fontainebleau summit, the European Council resolved to curtail the growth of CAP expenditure. At the same time, however, it agreed to increase the EC's own resources, thereby eliminating the most compelling reason for far-reaching CAP reform: the threat of running out of money.

Budgetary pressure again brought the question of CAP reform to the top of the EC's agenda in 1987 and 1988. As part of the Delors I budgetary package, introduced in 1987 in the wake of the Single European Act, the Commission proposed a mix of measures to prevent overproduction, limit expenditure, diversify support for farmers, and promote rural development. Germany's fragile government was unwilling to countenance reform until after crucial local elections (curtailing agricultural spending was unpopular with farmers and could have cost the government valuable votes). Once the elections were out of the way, negotiations on the Delors I package came to a conclusion at an extraordinary summit in Brussels in February 1988 held under Germany's presidency of the Council.

Like previous reform efforts, the 1988 package proved only moderately successful. Pressure for effective reform continued to build not only because of the CAP's exorbitant cost but also because the CAP encouraged unfavorable international comment on the recently launched single market program. Although the single market program was popular within the EC itself, it raised

fears abroad about the possible emergence of a "fortress Europe." Undoubtedly, the CAP's abominable international image fueled concern in nonmember countries about the single market's consequences. If the protectionist and
trade-distorting CAP was an example of a common policy in action, the single market would hardly help the rest of the world. Thus, the EC's vigorous
efforts to combat pessimistic prognoses about the single market's external impact intensified internal pressure for agricultural reform.

The Uruguay Round. At the same time, poor progress in the Uruguay Round
negotiations of the General Agreement on Tariffs and Trade (GATT), due
largely to disagreements over agricultural export subsidies, heightened international pressure on the EC to reform the CAP. The inclusion of agriculture in
the Uruguay Round had put the EC on the defensive even before the negotiations opened in September 1986, with the Council insisting that "the fundamental objectives and mechanisms both internal and external of the CAP shall
not be placed in question."[9] Nevertheless, the EC soon came under fierce pressure from the United States and the Cairns Group (an informal association of
agricultural free-traders) to cut subsidies for agricultural production and exports. Developing countries insisted on progress on agricultural trade liberalization in return for concessions in other sectors. Ultimately, such pressure
from the EU's trading partners proved decisive in bringing about CAP reform.

In 1987 the United States set the scene for a protracted quarrel with the
EC by demanding the elimination of all trade-distorting measures within ten
years. The irreconcilable positions of the United States and the Cairns Group,
on the one hand, and the EC, on the other, caused the midterm review of the
Uruguay Round in December 1988 to end in acrimony. The row over agriculture affected other areas: India blocked agreement on intellectual property
rights, and a number of South American countries threatened to reopen negotiations on tentatively agreed-upon issues unless the EC conceded more on
farm trade.[10]

The Uruguay Round made little progress after the midterm review; all
parties to the GATT avoided commitments or concessions until the run-up to
the final ministerial meeting in Brussels, in December 1990, where the round
was to have been wrapped up. After several battles in the Commission and in
the Council—each institution was divided internally on the merits of further
CAP reform, especially if made under international duress—the EC eventually tabled an offer to reduce farm support that was a far cry from its trading
partners' demand. Not surprisingly, the Brussels talks broke down largely because of the EC's refusal to make a more substantial offer on agriculture.

As negotiations resumed in early 1991, mounting pressure from international trading partners provided a powerful impetus for member states to undertake serious CAP reform both to save the Uruguay Round and to rein in a
system plagued by overproduction and spiraling costs.[11] In addition, unrelated

international developments in 1990 and 1991—notably in Central and Eastern Europe and in the Persian Gulf—caused a sharp drop in export prices and aggravated the CAP's imbalances. This was the context in which the Commission for the first time recommended a proposal to break the automatic link between price support and volume of food production. To balance the deepest price cuts ever contemplated by the Community, the Commission proposed full compensation for small farmers and scaled compensation for big farmers, subject to big farmers' removal of large tracts of land from production (so-called set-asides).

The MacSharry Plan. Agriculture commissioner Ray MacSharry was the plan's architect and prime political mover. As Ireland's first-ever agriculture commissioner, MacSharry seemed more suited to maintaining the status quo, but the extent of the CAP's inefficiency genuinely appalled him. "Look at the ... situation that exists in European agriculture today," MacSharry told a sympathetic European Parliament in July 1991. "We have 20 million tonnes of cereals in intervention [that are] going to rise to 30 million tonnes. . . . There are almost 1 million tonnes of dairy produce in intervention and that cannot be given away throughout the world. . . . There are 750,000 tonnes of beef in intervention and rising at the rate of 15,000 to 20,000 per week."[12]

MacSharry was just as passionate about the inequitable distribution of price supports between big and small farmers, not least because his political roots lay in the poor western part of Ireland. The most effective method of CAP reform would have been to replace the system of guaranteed payments entirely with a fair program of income support for farmers. But the visible cost of such a program was politically unacceptable. Farmers like to pretend that they operate in a free market system; direct aid would have exposed the truth. Nor would it have been easy to target assistance to those farmers who needed it most. Accordingly, although the MacSharry Plan included some direct income support, it did not propose to abolish guaranteed prices.

Predictably, agriculture ministers and farmers' organizations almost uniformly opposed the MacSharry Plan. The leader of the Irish Farmers Association compared MacSharry to Oliver Cromwell, the seventeenth-century English general who destroyed Irish towns and slaughtered their inhabitants, and accused the agriculture commissioner of attempting "to destroy the CAP."[13] Representatives of other farmers' organizations were less excitable but equally irresponsible, claiming that the plan would bankrupt small farmers and unfairly penalize big, efficient producers.

Given the unfavorable reaction engendered by the reflection paper, it seems remarkable that the Agriculture Council approved the plan, albeit in a modified form, over a year later. At first MacSharry appeared to lack even the Commission's support. Fearful of alienating French political opinion, Commission president Jacques Delors never backed MacSharry completely. Only after intensive discussion did the Commission eventually approve the plan in July 1991 and forward it to the Council, where discussion of it proved far more contentious. British, Dutch, and Danish ministers complained that the plan discriminated against large producers; Spanish, Greek, Portuguese, and Irish ministers complained that it did not compensate small farmers adequately; and the French government opposed reform of any kind. Unusually, the German government stood up to the farmers' union (there were no elections in Germany at the time) and supported the MacSharry Plan. Hoping to conclude the GATT negotiations as soon as possible, and apprehensive about the impact of German unification on farm policy, the German government abandoned its unconditional defense of the CAP.

The agreement finally reached by the Agriculture Council in May 1992, after a classic fifty-hour meeting, was a triumph for the Commission and for the Portuguese presidency, which got the package through by qualified majority vote.[14] Although smaller than the cuts in MacSharry's original proposal, the price reductions approved by the Council were nonetheless substantial. Most important, the package began the process of shifting the basis of agricultural assistance from price supports to direct income supplements (in this case paid to big farmers in return for land set-asides of 15 percent). As a concession to the French and British governments, the compensation offered to big farmers was substantially higher than MacSharry's original offer.

Paradoxically, the generous compensation package agreed to by the Agriculture Council made the reformed CAP more expensive than the unreformed CAP. But by cutting guaranteed prices and taking land out of production, the reform helped reduce the EU's ruinous agricultural surpluses. At the same time, farmers did not experience the drops in income predicted by their leaders; on the contrary, farm incomes across the board rose steadily in the following years.

The GATT Agreement. Because price cuts would translate into lower (if any) export subsidies within four or five years (depending on world price levels), the MacSharry reforms gave an urgently needed boost to the moribund Uruguay Round, which finally came to an end in December 1993.[15] The agreement on agriculture (converted, when the GATT changed itself into the World Trade Organization [WTO], into the WTO agreement on agriculture) set the framework for global trade in agriculture after the Uruguay Round. The agreement rested on three pillars:

- *Domestic support:* a few categories of temporarily permissible price supports in domestic markets
- *Export subsidies:* limits on export subsidies in terms of base quantities and budget expenditures

- *Market access:* minimum levels of imports into domestic markets plus a commitment to convert all nontariff barriers to tariffs on an equivalent basis.

The agreement also set up the WTO Committee on Agriculture to monitor compliance and called for new negotiations, starting no later than 1999, to continue the process of liberalizing the agricultural sector.

Consumer and Environmental Concerns

Far from being the end of a sporadic reform effort that had begun a decade earlier, the MacSharry Plan represented the beginning of a reform process that accelerated in the face of important internal and external developments. Internally, consumers finally woke up to some of the CAP's inequities not because of high prices but because of concerns about food safety. Whereas food security (meaning self-sufficiency in food production) was one of the CAP's main objectives, for most of the CAP's history farmers and agricultural officials had paid little or no attention to food safety (meaning the quality and healthiness of food). By contrast, consumers gradually grew more concerned about food safety in the 1980s and 1990s, largely as a spin-off of the environmental and ecological movements. European farmers and agricultural officials happily jumped on the bandwagon when it involved issues such as hormones in beef and genetically modified organisms (GMOs), despite a lack of scientific evidence that the use of artificial growth hormones in cattle and the genetic modification of cereals compromised food safety. As such practices were prevalent in the United States rather than in Europe, however, opposing them was a useful way primarily to oppose beef and cereals imports into the EU.

Consumer concerns about hormones in beef and GMOs paled in comparison with concerns about BSE, a disease affecting cattle that appeared in Britain in the 1980s. BSE hit the headlines and caused widespread panic in March 1996 when the British government announced a possible link between BSE and Creutzfeld-Jacob disease (CJD), a human brain condition that affects mostly young people and can be fatal. Here was an indigenous food safety crisis; no one could blame the Americans (the United States was BSE-free). Moreover, European officials had been aware for the previous decade of BSE's existence but had done little or nothing to control or eradicate the disease. Suddenly, the Commission leaped into action, banning exports of beef from Britain to other EU member states or anywhere else in the world. A major political crisis followed, with the Commission being blamed by Britain for punishing it unfairly and by the European Parliament for mishandling the whole affair.[16]

Regardless of its political implications, the British announcement caused an immediate public health scare throughout the EU and depressed the European beef market overnight. Consumers questioned not only the safety of beef generally but also the safety of other products of a system (the CAP) that emphasized mass production and paid little attention to product quality. Although farmers in other member states fell over themselves to present their products as unquestionably safe for human consumption, it was too late to put the genie of consumer criticism back into the bottle. The CAP itself became a target for consumer complaints, forcing farmers and officials to recast it in an environmentally friendly and health-conscious light.

The BSE crisis shook farmers' and agricultural officials' complacency about the CAP and introduced a new dynamic for reform with roots in the environmental movement, which has been a feature of European politics for nearly two decades. The first mention of environmental policy in the EU treaties—in the Single European Act of 1986—had no direct impact on the CAP but served notice of the increasing importance of environmental issues in the EU. The Maastricht Treaty went considerably further by including respect for the environment as a basic objective of the EC, and the Amsterdam Treaty went further again by specifying that such respect meant "a high level of protection and improvement of the quality of the environment" and that "environmental protection requirements must be integrated into the definition and implementation of the Community policies and activities . . . with a view to promoting sustainable development" (Article 6 TEC).

In response to pressure later in the 1990s and early 2000s from consumers concerned about food safety and environmentalists concerned about the ecological consequences of the CAP, farmers and politicians understandably tried to recast the CAP as food-safety conscious and environmentally friendly. Accordingly, the farm lobby now portrays itself as a champion of environmental protection and food safety, while the EU lists these as key policy objectives for the CAP.

Enlargement and Agenda 2000

In the late 1990s the CAP faced an even greater challenge than concerns about food safety and environmental degradation: the prospect of large-scale Central and Eastern European enlargement. Whereas previous EU enlargement had necessitated readjustments of the CAP, for the first time in the EU's history the prospect of enlargement prompted proposals for major CAP reform. That was because, in agriculture as in other areas, Central and Eastern European enlargement was qualitatively different from previous enlargements. Specifically, only 5.3 percent of the EU's workforce was engaged in agriculture, compared to over 22 percent of the workforce in the applicant states. The accession of all ten Central and Eastern European applicant states would result in a doubling of the farm labor force and a 50 percent increase in agricultural land in the EU. Moreover, agricultural prices in Central and Eastern

Europe were much lower than in Western Europe. Thus, extending the CAP to the new member states would necessitate either a big increase in the EU's budget, major cuts in price supports throughout the enlarged EU, or lower subsidies for the new member states than those paid to farmers in the existing member states. Raising the EU budget and cutting the level of subsidies in the existing member states were political impossibilities. The only option left was to subsidize Central and Eastern European farmers at a lower level than their Western European counterparts. This difference would be justified on the grounds that a massive infusion of money into economies lacking the capacity to absorb it would be socially and economically catastrophic.

The impetus of enlargement, together with growing environmental and consumer concerns, underlay the proposals for CAP reform in Agenda 2000, the Commission's strategy "for strengthening and widening the Union in the early years of the 21st century."[17] Released in July 1997, Agenda 2000 included revised policy objectives for the CAP that revealed the influence on agricultural policy of new social movements and economic trends and showed how far the EU had changed in the four decades since the launch of the EC in 1958. Thus, the CAP should

- improve the EU's global competitiveness through lower prices
- guarantee the safety and quality of food to consumers
- ensure stable incomes and a fair standard of living for the agricultural community
- make agricultural production methods environmentally friendly and respectful of animal welfare
- integrate environmental goals into its instruments
- seek and create alternative income and employment opportunities for farmers and their families

In essence, Agenda 2000 proposed that the EU continue the MacSharry reforms by shifting agricultural subsidies from price supports to direct payments. The Commission suggested large cuts in guaranteed prices for a range of agricultural products; farmers would be compensated with direct payments of one kind or another. Indeed, the Commission estimated that the cost of the compensatory payments would exceed the savings from reduced price supports by €6 billion annually. However, anticipated increases in EU revenue (linked to projected annual economic growth) would mean that CAP spending remained within existing guidelines and continued to shrink as a percentage of overall EU spending.

In addition, Agenda 2000 paid particular attention to rural development, stressing the "obligations and opportunities for agriculture" presented by growing environmental awareness and the increasing use of the countryside for recreation. Accordingly, Agenda 2000 proposed a more prominent role for agrienvironmentalism and organic farming. Improving CAP management was another major thrust of the proposed CAP reforms, which particularly emphasized the desirability of giving member states and regions more responsibility for implementation of EU agricultural policy. However, the Commission sought to balance the vogue for decentralization and subsidiarity against the risk of renationalizing the CAP.

The European Council endorsed the general thrust of Agenda 2000 in Luxembourg in December 1997 with a statement that "the process of reform begun in 1992 should be continued, deepened, adapted, and completed."[18] As for the Commission's specific proposals for cuts in guaranteed prices, farmers' reactions were predictably negative. Most national governments also reacted negatively, but not necessarily for the same reasons. For countries critical of the CAP, such as Britain, the proposals did not go far enough to reduce price supports; for others, such as France, they went too far. As on so many occasions in the past, Germany's reaction was moderated by the Bavarian government's unequivocal rejection of Agenda 2000. With a weak Chancellor Kohl facing federal elections in September 1998, the German government was not willing to risk alienating the conservative farmers' vote by wholeheartedly endorsing Agenda 2000.

The Commission followed up the broad outlines of Agenda 2000 with precise legislative proposals in March 1998 that mostly adhered to the guidelines in Agenda 2000. Sensitive to the general perception that many farmers were bilking the system, the Commission also proposed a ceiling on the amount of direct aid that a farm could receive under various support schemes. Additionally, the Commission submitted a legislative proposal for a new regulation on rural development.

As was the case with all proposals for agricultural legislation, the Commission's reform proposals were chewed over by the Agriculture Council and its Special Committee. Early in the process, agriculture ministers signaled their concerns about the extent of the proposed cuts and complained that the various compensatory schemes were inadequate. However, given the overall political importance of Agenda 2000, the General Affairs Council (foreign affairs ministers) staked a claim to oversee the legislative program for CAP reform. Despite deep differences among a number of governments on specific parts of the proposals, foreign ministers were more likely than their agricultural counterparts to take a broader view of things. Moreover, the change of government in Germany in October 1998 augured well for the fate of Agenda 2000. With the farmer-friendly Bavarian conservatives out of the coalition government and the environmentally conscious Greens in, Germany was more inclined to overhaul the CAP's budget and priorities. Ultimately, the European Council would have to resolve the most intractable disputes by the EU's self-imposed deadline of March 1999 for completion of the entire package.

Agriculture ministers reached agreement on the CAP component of the package in early March 1999, although the cost of offsetting their proposed cuts in price supports with direct payments would have increased the cost of the CAP, at least in the medium term. Far from chastising the agriculture ministers and reining in agricultural spending, however, the European Council decided in Berlin at the end of March 1999 to postpone key cuts in guaranteed prices. French president Jacques Chirac, a tenacious defender of the unreconstructed CAP, led the charge against large-scale price cuts. Chirac prevailed over Gerhard Schröder, the inexperienced German chancellor, who may have been more accommodating because Germany was in the Council presidency. Unwilling to stand up to the farmers' lobby, the other EU leaders went along with Chirac and Schröder.

Predictably, the European Council declared the summit, which agreed to some cuts in guaranteed prices and in direct payments, a success. A related decision to limit the EU budget to 1.27 percent of EU gross national product satisfied the net contributors. Enlargement, the ostensible reason for Agenda 2000, hardly intruded on the agreement. By that time the expected date of enlargement was slipping later into the decade, and it still looked as if only five of the Central and Eastern European candidates would join in the first round.

Thus, the Agenda 2000 CAP reform was extremely modest, involving as it did neither a radical shift from a price support system nor a major diminution of farmers' incomes. The agreed-upon price cuts did not go far enough to ensure the manageability of agricultural policy in the postenlargement period, let alone appease critics of EU agricultural protectionism in the WTO. Regardless of prices and protectionism, at least environmental standards in European agriculture were going up and the EU was paying greater attention to food safety. But consumers could be certain of one thing: in defiance of basic economic principles, food prices would remain high in the EU even though supply far exceeded demand.

Subsidies for Central and Eastern Europe

As the enlargement negotiations drew to a close, EU leaders still had to agree on the extent of agriculture expenditure in Central and Eastern Europe. The Commission called for the phasing in of direct payments to farmers in Central and Eastern Europe until 2013, when the next financial perspective would come to an end. EU leaders also agreed at their summit in October 2002 to phase in direct payments for the new member states, beginning at 25 percent in 2004 and ending at 40 percent in 2007, when the new financial perspective would begin. Far from accepting a fait accompli, the candidate countries pressed for larger allocations in the run-up to the next meeting of the European Council, in December 2002, where a final decision on enlargement was due to be made. As anticipated, agriculture therefore became the most contentious and longest-lasting issue in the accession negotiations. The summit ended successfully when the Danish presidency managed to eke out some more money for farmers in the new member states, thus paving the way for enlargement to take place in May 2004. But the entire affair embittered the acceding member states, which resented the second-class citizenship inherent in the CAP agreement.

The Midterm Review

Agenda 2000 mandated a budgetary review in 2003, halfway between 2000 and the beginning of a new financial perspective in 2007. The net contributors to the EU budget, led by a now more experienced Schröder, anticipated the midterm review with a call for radical CAP reform, including the phasing out of direct payments throughout the enlarged EU and the renationalization of agricultural subsidies. Defending the status quo, France led a group of countries, including Greece, Ireland, Portugal, and Spain, that benefited greatly from the existing CAP. Britain, traditionally in the forefront of the CAP reform campaign, was in a difficult position as both sides took aim at its budget rebate, negotiated by Prime Minister Thatcher in 1984 and considered sacrosanct by subsequent British governments, regardless of their political stripe.

The Commission's proposals for the midterm review, submitted in July 2002, sought to strike a balance between the contending French and German positions. On the one hand the Commission upheld the French position that direct payments were an integral part of the EU's *acquis communautaire* and could not be phased out entirely; on the other hand it sided with Germany by proposing cuts in direct payments of 20 percent. In keeping with the direction of CAP reform in recent years, the Commission's proposals linked direct payments to environmental, forestation, and animal welfare measures (so-called cross-compliance), thereby advancing the broader objectives of EU agricultural policy.[19]

Negotiations on the Commission's proposals reverted to their usual pattern of Franco-German dealmaking when Chirac and Schröder reached agreement just before the EU summit in October 2002 to freeze annual expenditure on agriculture in the forthcoming financial perspective (2007–2013) at the 2006 level of approximately €45 billion, with a 1 percent increase for inflation. Much to the consternation of the reform-minded member states, Chirac and Schröder pushed this agreement through at the summit itself. Once again Schröder chose Franco-Germany harmony over discord, perhaps fearing that without a guarantee of continued agricultural largesse, France would delay a final agreement on enlargement. The emerging Franco-German consensus on the deepening crisis in Iraq may also have inclined Schröder toward a compromise with Chirac. Whatever the reasons for it, the agreement on overall

CAP funding postponed difficult decisions about the size and allocation of agricultural subsidies until 2006, when the new financial perspective would have to be negotiated and the existing pie divided among many more member states.

The European Council's agreement on the size of CAP spending for the period until 2013 robbed the Commission's proposals for the midterm review of much of their meaning. Franz Fischler, the agriculture commissioner, gamely announced that he would press ahead, despite Chirac's statement that CAP reform was off the agenda until 2006.[20] Chirac relented in some small ways in order to avoid a collapse of the contemporaneous WTO negotiations, and after the usual haggling, the agriculture ministers reached an agreement in June 2003. Although hailed by the protagonists as a major breakthrough in the history of CAP reform, the outcome of the review was a patchwork of compromises and concessions to obstinate member states like France and Spain. The agreement further decoupled subsidies from production, reinforced cross-compliance, tipped the balance toward a more equitable distribution of payment from big to small farmers, and introduced price cuts in some hitherto unreformed agricultural sectors (although the sacrosanct sugar sector once again emerged unscathed). Essentially, the 2003 reform was a continuation of the MacSharry reform of 1992. It changed the modalities, but not the munificence, of EU agricultural subsidies.

The Doha Development Round

Like the MacSharry reform, the midterm review was driven in large part by the EU's need to curb the trade-distorting impact of the CAP in order to facilitate completion of another round of multilateral trade negotiations, this time under the auspices of the WTO. Even more so than in the early 1990s, the EU's trading partners targeted the CAP as an obstacle to the success of a decisive effort to liberalize global trade and investment. Moreover, because the new round was specifically linked to global development, the EU faced added pressure to change the CAP so that farmers in the developing world would not be disadvantaged by it. Launched in Doha, Qatar, in November 2001, the new set of negotiations was officially called the Doha Development Round.

Developing countries long damaged by the pernicious impact of EU agricultural export subsidies, the Cairns Group of agricultural free-traders, and the United States all took aim at the CAP. The United States lost the moral high ground after massively increasing subsidies to its own farmers under the 2002 Farm Bill, although officials in Washington claimed that the CAP was still much more trade-distorting than its American counterpart. Regardless of its impact on world trade, however, the U.S. Farm Bill was a propaganda coup for the EU, whose politicians and officials seized on it to deflect criticism from the CAP. EU farmers were more impressed by the generosity of the American measure.

Far from letting the EU off the hook, enactment of the 2002 Farm Bill merely put the United States in the dock alongside the EU in the Doha Round. Yet the EU was under more pressure than the United States, not only because EU tariffs and export subsidies obviously distorted global agricultural trade but also because the EU was more sensitive than the United States to the needs of the developing world. Having made north-south global development a cornerstone of its foreign policy, the EU had to do something, or at least be seen as doing something, about the CAP's impact on developing countries. External and self-imposed pressure on the EU to reform the CAP intensified after U.S. and EU intransigence caused the WTO to miss the deadline of March 2003 for an agreement on a framework for the negotiations to reduce farm subsidies.

Growing WTO-related pressure gave the EU a strong incentive to reform the CAP under the auspices of the midterm review. The EU claimed, in turn, that the midterm review, finally agreed to in June 2003, would facilitate a breakthrough in the WTO negotiations on agriculture and in the Doha Development Round as a whole. Indeed, more direct payments to farmers reduced the scope for overproduction, import levies, and export subsidies, thereby lessening the trade-distorting impact of the CAP. Nevertheless, the EU's trading partners remained skeptical, preferring to see concrete proposals for agricultural trade liberalization in the WTO negotiations.

In August 2003, the United States and the EU, hitherto highly critical of the impact of each other's agricultural policies on the prospects for a Doha Round agreement, came together and presented a "joint approach" to agricultural issues in the WTO, dealing with the three pillars of domestic support, export subsidies, and market access. The transatlantic initiative in the WTO was analogous to a Franco-German initiative in the EU: when the two leading players take the lead, the others often have little choice but to follow. On this occasion, however, the joint U.S.-EU initiative was insufficient to ensure the success of the Cancun ministerial meeting in September 2003, the Doha Round's own midterm review.

With the WTO having missed the deadline of January 2005 for completion of the Doha Round, thanks in part to dissatisfaction among the Cairns Group and the developing countries with the Europeans' and Americans' offers of agricultural trade liberalization, the EU came under additional pressure to reform the CAP in 2005 and 2006, during the negotiations for a new financial perspective. The European Council had already agreed on the size of the CAP budget for 2007–2013, the period of the new perspective, but not on how to allocate agricultural expenditure among a considerably enlarged EU, including new member states that deserved more support than most of the old ones. Despite the pressures of enlargement and multilateral trade negotiations, however, the history of the CAP suggested that a core group of member states would ensure that farmers (especially in Western Europe) would continue to receive generous subsidies, albeit for multifunctionality rather than overproduction.

■ Cohesion Policy

Cohesion—the reduction of economic and social disparities between richer and poorer regions—is a fundamental objective of the EU. Not only do such disparities threaten the integrity of the single market and monetary union but their existence is incompatible with the ideals of community and solidarity that supposedly suffuse the movement for European integration. Indeed, an unusual blend of idealism and pragmatism has motivated the quest for cohesion, especially since the Mediterranean enlargements of the early and mid-1980s. Yet concerns about the management and effectiveness of the structural and cohesion funds (the financial instruments of cohesion policy) and the cost of cohesion in an ever-enlarging EU raise serious questions about the future of cohesion policy.

Origin and Development

Cohesion policy encompasses regional policy (to reduce spatial disparities and regenerate old industrial areas), aspects of social policy (to combat long-term unemployment and foster vocational education and training), and a small part of the Common Agricultural Policy (to assist rural development). It developed relatively late in the EU's history. The preamble of the Rome Treaty mentioned the need to reduce regional disparities, but the treaty itself included few redistributive mechanisms. The European Social Fund and the European Investment Bank, established by the treaty, were not intended primarily to promote cohesion but were nonetheless expected to help the EC's poorer regions. Similarly, the treaty declared that national subsidies (state aids) were compatible with the common market as long as they promoted "the economic development of areas where the standard of living is abnormally low or where there is serious underemployment" (Article 87.3 TEC).

Apart from those concessions, the prevailing attitude in the late 1950s was that the common market would, of its own accord, "promote throughout the Community a harmonious development of economic activities" and thereby lessen disparities among regions (Article 2 TEC). After all, the treaty was a package deal to distribute losses and gains among member states, not to redistribute resources between rich and poor regions. In any case, with the notable exception of the south of Italy, regional disparities in the EC of six member states were not as striking as in the enlarged EC of nine, ten, and twelve member states, let alone in the EU of twenty-five member states.

The Impact of Enlargements

Successive enlargements increased regional disparities with regard to income, employment, education and training, productivity, and infrastructure. The EC's growing regional differences manifested themselves in a north-south divide, with Ireland included in the southern camp. The spatial characteristics of the EC's regional imbalance conformed to the core-periphery concept used by economists and social scientists to analyze inequalities between or among regions. As a result, the EC built its cohesion policy in the late 1980s and early 1990s largely on the assumption of a poor periphery (Scotland, Ireland, Portugal, central and southern Spain, Corsica, southern Italy, Greece, and—after 1990—eastern Germany) and a rich core (southern England, northeastern France, the Benelux countries, northwestern Germany, and northern Italy).

A protocol attached to Ireland's accession treaty emphasized the need to end regional disparities in the EC, but the European Regional Development Fund (ERDF) was established only in 1975, largely to compensate Britain for its poor return from the CAP. The EC began coordinating member states' regional aid schemes in the late 1970s, although its own regional aid policy remained rudimentary. The extent of the EC's failure to redress regional imbalances became more apparent after Greek accession in 1981 and in the run-up to Spanish and Portuguese accession in 1986.

Concern that the EC's existing disadvantaged regions in southern Italy and Greece would suffer as a result of Iberian enlargement sparked a row in early 1985, which newly appointed Commission president Jacques Delors resolved by renegotiating the Integrated Mediterranean Programs, an assistance package agreed to earlier in the decade to help Greece cope with the challenge of accession. By introducing an integrated approach to development, programming, and partnership among the Commission, national governments, and regional and local authorities, the Integrated Mediterranean Programs became an important testing ground for what was later applied throughout the EU.[21]

Economic, political, and moral arguments underpinned the Commission's efforts to promote cohesion in the aftermath of the EC's Mediterranean enlargements. Delors had long been aware of a growing rich-poor divide in the EC, which the accession of Spain and Portugal would greatly exacerbate. The Commission's program for 1985 cautioned that regional disparities "could become a permanent source of political confrontation" and urged that the south be given "a fairer share of the benefits of economic development."[22] Delors warned the European Parliament in March 1985 that enlargement negotiations with Greece, Spain, and Portugal had "revealed a tension in Europe which is, let's face it, a tension between north and south. It stems not only from financial problems but from a lack of understanding, from a clash of culture, which seems to be promoting certain countries to turn their backs on the solidarity pact that should be one of the cornerstones of the Community, solidarity being conceived not in terms of assistance, but rather as an expression of the com-mon-weal, contributing to the vigor of the European entity."[23]

The Single Market Program

The single market program greatly boosted the Commission's and the poorer countries' leverage for a vigorous cohesion policy. The gradual worsening of regional disparities since the 1960s suggested that market liberalization would broaden rather than narrow the EC's rich-poor divide. Advocates of a stronger regional policy exploited uncertainty about the distributional consequences of the single market program to press their claims for cohesion. Fear that the single market would make rich regions richer and poor regions poorer and that the dynamic of market liberalization would intensify existing disparities led to an explicit link between cohesion policy and the 1992 program. In the Commission's words, "The reduction of disparities and the strengthening of economic and social cohesion should go hand in hand with the implementa-tion of the large internal market."[24]

Apart from vague notions of solidarity, the likely economic and political impact of greater regional disequilibrium strengthened the case for cohesion. The EC would not prosper, let alone survive, if excessive disparities caused poorer member states to block legislation and impede completion of the single market. Accordingly, during the 1985 intergovernmental conference on treaty reform, the Commission advocated a substantial redistribution of resources to the EC's less prosperous regions. Although one of the attractions of the single market program for a financially strapped EC was its relative lack of cost, the Commission's emphasis on cohesion raised the prospect of a sizable budgetary hike. The intergovernmental conference deferred until later a decision about in-creasing the amount of structural funds, European Investment Bank loans, and other forms of assistance for poorer regions but committed member states to promoting cohesion and reducing regional disparities.

As a result, the Single European Act included a section on economic and social cohesion. It committed the EC to reduce "disparities between the vari-ous regions and the backwardness of the least favored nations," called for co-ordination between other EC policies and cohesion policy, and obliged the Council to reform the structural funds within a year of the act's implementa-tion on the basis of a Commission proposal. Delors described the revised treaty's provisions on cohesion as one of the Single European Act's "funda-mental objectives."[25]

Delors I and Reform of the Structural Funds

In February 1987 the Commission introduced a five-year budgetary package to control agricultural spending, increase the EC's own resources, and impose budgetary discipline. The so-called Delors I package also proposed reform of the structural funds, a doubling in real terms of the resources available through them to promote cohesion, and a particular focus on regions with a per capita income below 75 percent of the EC average. Just as Delors had used the voluminous Cecchini Report to bolster his arguments in support of the single market, he now cited the Padoa-Schioppa Report to make a compelling case for reform of the structural funds. Published in April 1987, the report assessed the "implications for the economic system of the Community of . . . [the] adoption of the internal market program and the latest enlargement." One of its major conclusions pointed out "the serious risks of aggravated regional imbalances in the course of market liberalization" and, in a memorable phrase, warned that "any easy extrapolation of 'invisible hand' ideas into the real world of regional economics in the process of market opening would be unwarranted in the light of economic history and theory."[26]

This was grist to Delors's mill and strengthened the southern countries' determination to win a sizable redistribution of resources. As a staunch economic liberal, however, Thatcher rejected the Padoa-Schioppa Report's advocacy of guiding the "invisible hand." In her view, market liberalization throughout the EC would hasten rather than hinder economic development in the southern member states. Kohl sympathized with the southern states but knew that Germany would have to contribute most of the proposed budgetary increase. Thus, the battle lines were drawn for a protracted dispute that, thanks to Kohl's largesse, the European Council eventually resolved at a special summit in February 1988. A delighted Delors called the European Council's decision to double the structural funds by 1993 "a second Marshall Plan."[27] Despite Thatcher's misgivings, the rich member states' endorsement of the Delors I package demonstrated their acceptance of redistributional solidarity as part of the single market program.

Substantially increasing the structural funds was not enough to redress regional imbalances, however. As Delors told the Parliament in January 1988, "Cohesion is not simply a matter of throwing money at problems. . . . It implies rather a willingness to act at Community level to redress the disparities between regions and between different social groups."[28] Accordingly, the Council reformed cohesion policy later in 1988 in order to turn the structural funds into effective instruments of economic development. In effect, the Council sought to weld regional policy and aspects of social policy and agricultural policy into a powerful means of narrowing the north-south divide.

The 1988 reform radically revised structural policy by introducing a number of new principles and procedures and strengthening existing ones.

- *Additionality:* Structural funds must add to, not substitute for, member state public expenditure.

- *Partnership:* The partnership principle was the key to involving regions, not just national governments, in formulating and implementing structural policy. Because EC operations would complement national measures, there would have to be close consultation and cooperation among the Commission, member states, and regional or local bodies at all stages of a structural program. Eligible member state plans for regional assistance were incorporated into Community Support Frameworks, contractual agreements between the Commission and national and regional authorities. The Community Support Frameworks set out the program's priorities, type of aid, methods of financing, and so on. Operational programs usually would last five years.
- *Programming:* The structural funds reform involved a major switch from project-related assistance to program assistance and decentralized management, putting the emphasis on planning and continuity rather than on ad hoc activities. Under the old system the Commission dealt with thousands of separate projects; under the new system the Commission would oversee a much smaller number of Community Support Frameworks.
- *Concentration:* Instead of spreading the EC's financial resources widely and ineffectively, structural funds would be concentrated on a few major objectives. Functional and geographic concentration would restrict assistance to the five priorities or objectives. These were:

  1. *Objective 1:* assist "regions whose development is lagging behind," that is, regions with a per capita gross domestic product (GDP) of less than 75 percent of the EC average (all of Greece, Ireland, and Portugal; large parts of Spain; and southern Italy, Corsica, and the French overseas departments). Almost 80 percent of the ERDF (by far the largest structural fund) was allocated to Objective 1 projects.
  2. *Objective 2:* promote economic conversion and modernization in declining industrial areas, largely by helping small and medium-sized enterprises in new economic sectors.
  3. *Objective 3:* combat long-term unemployment by assisting workers over the age of twenty-five who have been unemployed for more than one year.
  4. *Objective 4:* integrate young people into the workforce.
  5. *Objective 5:* adjust production, processing, and marketing structures in agriculture and forestry. In 1994, Objective 5 was split into two separate objectives:

     - *Objective 5a:* assist "regions dependent on fishing."
     - *Objective 5b:* support certain "rural areas."

The 1988 reforms had political as well as economic implications, as the principles of concentration and partnership allowed the Commission to work closely with regional authorities, often bypassing national governments. The Commission used these contacts "to act as a lever for regions that are not yet traditionally recognized" and to promote the emergence of new "Euroregions" straddling national frontiers.[29] Most regions opened offices in Brussels and became active in the Assembly of European Regions, a Brussels-based interest group. Increasingly, therefore, the formulation and implementation of cohesion policy strengthened regionalism in Europe and contributed to the emergence of multilevel governance in the EC.[30] It also contributed to the inclusion in the Maastricht Treaty of a provision calling for the establishment of the Committee of the Regions, an EU advisory body that came into existence in 1994 (see Chapter 10).

The Maastricht Treaty

Moves toward monetary union in the late 1980s raised concerns among the poorer countries similar to those prevalent at the outset of the single market program. For Delors, the architect of structural funds reform, monetary union was inconceivable without a sizable increase in assistance for disadvantaged regions. The 1989 Delors Report, which set the stage for monetary union, pointed out that because monetary union would deprive member states of their ability to devalue, it could worsen the balance-of-payments difficulties of poorer countries. Indeed, the need for member states to harmonize their budgetary policies, coupled with a loss of exchange rate flexibility, portended serious problems for less developed regions.[31]

During the 1991 intergovernmental conferences on treaty reform, Ireland, Spain, and Portugal attached the highest priority to strengthening cohesion policy. Without mechanisms to redistribute the benefits of monetary union, they claimed, the more central and prosperous regions would gain disproportionately. Using arguments honed during the Delors I debate, the poorer countries claimed that failure to meet their demands would undermine the EU's foundations. Felipe González, the Spanish prime minister and the poor countries' standard-bearer, fought tenaciously in the run-up to the Maastricht summit to win a greater commitment to cohesion in the new treaty.

From the poorer countries' point of view, the outcome of the intergovernmental conference was highly satisfactory. The Maastricht Treaty provided a framework for extending and deepening EU policies and actions to promote cohesion in parallel with the degree of political, economic, and monetary integration in the EU. It also identified cohesion as one of the EU's main goals and listed rural development as an objective of structural policy. Of more immediate importance, the treaty stipulated that the Council, acting unanimously on a proposal from the Commission and after obtaining the Parliament's assent, would set up a cohesion fund by the end of December 1993. The purpose of the fund was to help poorer countries reconcile the apparent contradiction in the treaty between the budgetary rigor necessary to achieve economic convergence (a prerequisite for monetary union) and the budgetary flexibility necessary to promote cohesion (a key EU objective).

At Spain's insistence, the treaty included a protocol that elaborated upon the treaty's cohesion clauses. The protocol promised a review of the size of the structural funds and specified that the Cohesion Fund would be used for the benefit of member states with a per capita GDP of less than 90 percent of the EU average and a program designed to achieve economic convergence. In effect, that meant Spain, Portugal, Ireland, and Greece. Without mentioning a figure, the protocol earmarked 85–90 percent of the fund to support environmental and transport projects.

Delors II

In February 1992 the Commission sent the Council a draft budget for the years 1993–1999 (the Delors II package).[32] In order to meet the additional cost of implementing the Maastricht Treaty, the Commission proposed increasing the EU's budgetary ceiling from 1.2 to 1.37 percent of GDP by 1997 (an annual budgetary growth rate of 5 percent), including a sizable allocation for cohesion policy. The Commission also proposed improving structural fund operations. Together with the Cohesion Fund, a projected 66 percent increase in Objective 1 funding would boost EU financial support for Spain, Portugal, Ireland, and Greece by 100 percent. Some of the new spending on Objective 1 would go to the five new German states (the former East Germany), which had received a special structural funds appropriation for 1991–1993. Other objectives would receive a 50 percent increase in funding.

The negotiations in 1992 over the Delors II package were every bit as contentious as the negotiations in 1988–1989 over the Delors I package. An EU-wide economic recession, together with Germany's effort to meet the costs of unification, made it difficult to reach an agreement. Ironically, the Maastricht ratification crisis—another gloomy development—may have saved Delors II. Battered by a year of economic and political blows, government leaders wanted to demonstrate their ability to act decisively in the EU's interest. As one observer noted, it was imperative for the EU "to avoid the high costs of a failure whose repercussions would have extended well beyond the budgetary arena."[33] The Delors II package was a good way to show that redistributional solidarity had survived the year's setbacks. Once again, González represented the southern countries' interests; once again, Kohl conceded on most issues at the decisive summit in December 1992. The agreement more than doubled EU assistance for the least prosperous countries. With the Central and Eastern European states about to apply for membership, the southern member states suspected that Delors II was their last chance to get a big share of the cohesion budget.

Enlargement and Agenda 2000

The 1995 enlargement had little effect on cohesion policy, apart from leading to the creation of a new priority, Objective 6, for the development of regions with very low population densities. This was a sop to Finland and Sweden, net contributors to the EU budget that would otherwise not get much from the structural funds. Austria, another net contributor, would benefit from some of the existing objectives, at least enough to give the appearance of a fair return for its money.

In its impact on cohesion policy, however, the 1995 enlargement paled in comparison with the next round of enlargement. The countries of Central and Eastern Europe were underdeveloped compared to the EU's Mediterranean member states, let alone the EU's affluent member states. Their accession would dramatically change the face of the EU. All of the Central and Eastern European states would qualify for Objective 1 funding: all had dilapidated road and rail networks, most had declining industrial regions, and all suffered from serious unemployment and underemployment. Meeting the challenge of Central and Eastern European enlargement would test cohesion policy to the limit (see Box 12.1).

The Commission responded in Agenda 2000 with proposals for funding and reforming cohesion policy in the run-up to enlargement (Agenda 2000 also contained the Commission's budget proposal for the 2000–2006 financial perspective). The Commission planned to keep EU funding for economic and social cohesion at 0.46 percent of the EU's GDP, amounting to €275 billion

---

Box 12.1   Cohesion and the Central and Eastern European Member States (2004)

- Had an average per capita GDP less than half the average in the EU15

- Only 56 percent of those of working age were in jobs, compared to 64 percent in the EU15

- 92 percent of their populations lived in regions with a per capita GDP below 75 percent of the EU25 average

- Accounted for just under 5 percent of the EU's GDP but almost 20 percent of the EU's population, thereby reducing the average per capita GDP in the EU25 by about 12 percent from what it had been in the EU15

- Their poor administrative capacity made it difficult to dispense allocated funds in the run-up to accession and in the early years of membership

Source: European Commission, Third Cohesion Report.

over the period 2000–2006. Of that amount, €45 billion would be earmarked for the new member states, which were likely to join toward the end of the financial perspective, plus €7 billion in preaccession aid. The Commission proposed as well reducing the structural fund objectives to three: a strengthened Objective 1, a redefined Objective 2, and a new Objective 3 (developing a strategy for human resources). In addition to some badly needed administrative and managerial reforms, the Commission further recommended reducing the proportion of the EU population covered by the structural funds from 51 percent to between 35 and 40 percent.

Although the Commission's scenario was modest by the standards of many other estimates of the financial impact of enlargement, Agenda 2000 generated controversy in existing and prospective member states. Net contributors to the EU budget wanted to pay less, recipients of large-scale transfers from the structural and cohesion funds wanted to maintain or increase their share, and prospective member states wanted more than the Commission offered. The inevitable row over cohesion funding began in earnest in March 1998 when the Commission followed up on Agenda 2000 with precise legislative proposals. Almost every member state—not only the poorer ones—pleaded for special treatment. With federal elections looming and popular dislike of the EU growing, Kohl objected to raising the EU's budget and at the same time rejected the idea of cutbacks in financial transfers to eastern Germany.

Gerhard Schröder, Kohl's successor after the September 1998 elections, made similar noises about reducing Germany's contribution to the EU budget, and therefore reducing the size of the budget as a whole. His relative inexperience as chancellor, together with Germany's presidency of the Council during the last stages of the Agenda 2000 negotiations, undermined Schröder's resolve (as Council president, Germany had to moderate its own position while striving to end the negotiations by the agreed-upon deadline of March 1999). Accordingly, Schröder made generous concessions to the cohesion countries during the final negotiating session. Despite expectations to the contrary, the Agenda 2000 agreement therefore stuck closely to the Commission's proposal and did not result in cutbacks for cohesion policy. With enlargement still several years away, member states were not under sufficient pressure to bite the political bullet and radically overhaul one of the EU's most costly policies.

Nevertheless, Agenda 2000 included some important procedural reforms. Given the stronger institutional capacity of many disadvantaged regions and the Commission's administrative overreach, the reforms gave more responsibility for the management of cohesion policy to the member states and regional authorities concerned and reduced the Commission's responsibility for implementing, monitoring, and evaluating programs. Instead, the Commission assumed greater financial control of cohesion policy. To encourage better management, the Commission introduced a financial incentive in the form of a performance reserve, amounting to 4 percent of the structural funds for allocation in 2004, on the basis of the achievement of program targets set at the beginning of the financial perspective in 2000.

The Effectiveness of Cohesion Policy

Spending on cohesion policy accounts for about one-third of the EU's annual budget of over €100 billion (see Table 12.1). That is a lot of money, although it amounts to only 0.4 percent of the EU's total GDP. (By comparison, combined public expenditure in the member states amounts to about 47 percent of total EU GDP.)

Is the money well spent? A recent World Bank report castigated the structural funds for being "ineffective, based on incorrect or at least unsubstantiated economic theory, badly designed, poorly carried out, and in most cases a source of wrong incentives."[34] That criticism seems excessive. Apart from problems with the management of structural and other cohesion funds, economists nevertheless disagree on the usefulness of cohesion policy. Empirical evidence is difficult to distill because of the multifaceted nature of economic growth and decline. The Commission claims that the north-south economic divide in Europe is closing, although with enlargement a new east-west gap has opened. In the enlarged (and ever enlarging) EU, economic differences between rich and poor regions are widening, not narrowing. Some of the poorer countries in the EU of fifteen states (EU15) have benefited greatly from cohesion funding; others have performed poorly. Ireland is the classic success story. Thanks to annual growth well in excess of 5 percent, Ireland's

Table 12.1   Spending on Cohesion Policy (in billions of euro)

1989–1993		1994–1999	
Objective 1	8.8	Objective 1	16
Objective 2	1.2	Objective 2	2.6
Objectives 3 and 4	1.3	Objective 3	2.2
		Objective 4	0.4
Objective 5a	0.8	Objective 5a	1.0
Objective 5b	0.4	Objective 5b	1.1
Community Initiatives	1.0	Community Initiatives	1.0
2000–2006[a]		**2007–2013**[b]	
Objective 1	19	Convergence	37.4
Objective 2	3.2	Competitiveness	8.6
Objective 3	1.6	Cooperation	1.5

Notes: a. Member states revised and reduced the number of objectives in Agenda 2000.
b. Financial perspective and new objectives proposed by the Commission in 2004.

per capita GDP rose from 63.6 percent of the EU average in 1983 to 89.9 percent in 1995, making it ineligible for Objective 1 funding under Agenda 2000. Despite being weaned from large-scale financial transfers from Brussels, Ireland continued to grow economically; by 2004, it had the second-highest per capita GDP in the EU. Of course Ireland's economic takeoff was not due solely, or even exclusively, to cohesion funding. Sound economic management, massive inward investment (thanks largely to the single market program), and a national consensus on moving the country forward and using cohesion funding wisely were essential for Ireland's success. Portugal and Spain fared less well, and Greece remained in an economic rut despite receiving hundreds of millions of euros in cohesion funding. As well as attracting relatively little inward investment (less than 1 percent of its GDP, compared to about 21 percent in Ireland) and failing to undertake macroeconomic policy reforms, Greece reputedly squandered a lot of its cohesion funding through fraud and mismanagement.

Based on the experience of Greece, Ireland, Portugal, and Spain, the key to economic development in the poorer member states would appear to be a combination of sensible macroeconomic policies, a favorable international economic climate, sound management of sizable cohesion funding, and closer coordination in the formulation and implementation of regional policy at the European, national, and subnational levels. Have the countries of Central and Eastern Europe learned that lesson? All of them would like to emulate Ireland's example. Despite being at a disadvantage in many respects, most enjoy higher rates of growth than many of the richer member states, not least because of their wrenching economic reforms in the postcommunist period. Even without large-scale financial transfers from Brussels, the new member states may have a brighter economic future than many of the old ones.

The Future of Cohesion Policy

The Commission's proposals for the next financial perspective, adopted in February 2004, called for higher EU spending, including spending on cohesion policy. The allocation for cohesion would remain approximately 34 percent of a larger EU budget, amounting to €336 billion for the period 2007–2013 (at 2004 prices). The net contributors reacted predictably, with Germany and the Netherlands leading the charge. Apart from their opposition to additional EU expenditure, the net contributors resented the idea of generous financial transfers going to countries that were doing well economically or that allegedly had squandered regional development assistance. The Commission's arguments that cohesion policy works, and that the net contributors benefit from extra public works contracts and other business in the recipient member states, may no longer assuage cash-strapped "donor" governments. Nevertheless, spending on cohesion policy is unlikely to fall below its

1999–2006 level. The moral, political, and economic justifications for cohesion policy are still sacrosanct. If anything, they are more compelling because of Central and Eastern European enlargement. Most of the older member states, including those receiving large-scale cohesion funding and fearful of the impact of enlargement on future funding, acknowledge that the new and aspiring Central and Eastern European member states have a lot of catching up to do and need extensive assistance. Few of the older member states disputed the Commission's call for a 50–50 allocation of cohesion spending between the EU15 and the new member states. Yet few of the EU25 would be well disposed toward allocating billions of euros in regional development assistance to Turkey, should it join the EU.

In its third report on cohesion, published in 2004, the Commission reviewed recent developments and set out its vision for the policy's future (Agenda 2000 stipulated that the Commission must report every three years on progress made toward achieving cohesion).[35] In order to improve the effectiveness of cohesion policy and link it to the Lisbon strategy for economic modernization and reform, the Commission proposed reorganizing cohesion policy under three headings (these would replace the existing objectives):

- *Convergence:* supporting growth and job creation in the least developed member states (regions with a per capita GDP less than 75 percent of the EU average). In effect, this is a continuation of the original and later revised Objective 1.
- *Competitiveness:* promoting economic modernization and improving employment prospects in regions identified by the member states that face particular difficulties
- *Cooperation:* encouraging cross-border cooperation, including cooperation across borders between member states and nonmember states. A new financial instrument, the New Partnership and Neighborhood Instrument, planned as part of the EU's "wider Europe" strategy, would contribute to the achievement of this objective (see Chapter 16).

Although the declared priorities or objectives of cohesion policy have changed (and continue to change) over time, the underlying goal remains the same: to help regions with poor infrastructure, labor skills, and social capital to develop more rapidly than they otherwise would, or even to prevent them from regressing further than they otherwise might. Despite neoliberal critiques of the effectiveness of cohesion policy, most EU politicians are wedded to the concept. Like social welfare within member states, cohesion policy rests on cherished principles of fairness and solidarity. Also like social welfare, the costs of cohesion policy may prove exorbitant, pitting pragmatism against principle in the enlarging EU. The debate over the 2007–2013 financial perspective is instructive in that regard.

▧ Notes

1. Andre Sapir, *Agenda for a Growing Europe: Report of an Independent High-Level Group* (Brussels: European Commission, July 2003).

2. On European agriculture and the CAP, see Wyn P. Grant and John T. S. Keeler, eds., *Agricultural Policy*, vol. 1: *Agricultural Policy in Western Europe* (Cheltenham, UK: E. Elgar, 2000); and Wyn P. Grant, *The Common Agricultural Policy* (New York: St. Martin's Press, 1997).

3. See European Council, "Presidency Conclusions," Bulletin EC 12-1997, point 1.5.11.

4. Robert Marjolin, *Architect of European Unity: Memoirs, 1911–1986* (London: Weidenfeld and Nicolson, 1989), p. 312.

5. For an account of the CAP's origin and development, see Hans von der Groeben, *The European Community: The Formative Years: The Struggle to Establish the Common Market and the Political Union (1958–66)* (Luxembourg: Office for Official Publications of the European Communities, 1987), pp. 70–78. See also Leon Lindberg, *The Political Dynamics of Economic Integration* (Palo Alto, CA: Stanford University Press, 1963), pp. 145–151.

6. See Martin Westlake, *The Council of the European Union* (London: Catermill, 1995), pp. 204–207.

7. Quoted in *Times* (London), June 28, 1977, p. 16.

8. See Michel Petit et al., *Agricultural Policy Formation in the European Community: The Birth of Milk Quotas and CAP Reform* (Amsterdam: Elsevier, 1987).

9. Bulletin EC 3-1985, point 2.2.12.

10. See Finn Laursen, "The EC, GATT, and the Uruguay Round," in Leon Hurwitz and Christian Lequesne, eds., *The State of the European Community: Policies, Institutions, and Debates in the Transition Years* (Boulder, CO: Lynne Rienner, 1991), pp. 378–381; Anna Murphy and Peter Ludlow, "The Community's External Relations," in Peter Ludlow, ed., *The Annual Review of European Community Affairs 1990* (Brussels: Center for European Policy Studies, 1992), pp. 176–179.

11. For an account of the GATT negotiations in 1991 and 1992, see Finn Laursen, "The EC, the U.S., and the Uruguay Round," in Alan Cafruny and Glenda Rosenthal, eds., *The State of the European Community: The Maastricht Debates and Beyond* (Boulder, CO: Lynne Rienner, 1993), pp. 245–264.

12. Debates of the European Parliament, *Official Journal of the European Communities* 3-407 (July 11, 1991): 282.

13. Quoted in *Irish Times*, July 10, 1991, p. 1.

14. Council press release 6539/92, May 18–21, 1992, 1579th Council Meeting (Agriculture).

15. See John T. S. Keeler, "Agricultural Power in the European Community: Explaining the Fate of CAP and GATT Negotiations," *Comparative Politics* 28, no. 2 (January 1996): 127–150.

16. See Martin Westlake, "'Mad Cows and Englishmen': The Institutional Consequences of the BSE Crisis," *Journal of Common Market Studies* 35, *Annual Review* (1996): 11–36.

17. European Commission, *Agenda 2000: For a Stronger and Wider Europe*, Brussels, July 16, 1997, COM(97)2000 final.

18. Council, "Presidency Conclusions," point 1.5.11.

19. Christilla Roederer-Rynning, "Impregnable Citadel or Leaning Tower? Europe's Common Agricultural Policy at Forty," *SAIS Review* 23, no. 1 (Winter/Spring 2003): 133–151.

20. *European Report*, October 19, 2002, p. 480.

21. See Desmond Dinan and Marios Camhis, "The Common Agricultural Policy and Cohesion," in Maria Green Cowles and Desmond Dinan, eds., *Developments in the EU 2* (Basingstoke, UK: Palgrave Macmillan, 2004), p. 132.

22. "Commission's Program" for 1985, Bulletin EC S/1-1985, p. 15.

23. Bulletin EC S/4-1985, p. 5.

24. European Commission, "From the Single Act to Maastricht and Beyond: The Means to Match Our Ambitions," Bulletin EC S/1-1992, p. 9.

25. Jacques Delors, speech to the European Parliament, January 20, 1988, Bulletin EC S/1-1988, p. 11.

26. Tommaso Padoa-Schioppa, *Efficiency, Stability and Equity: A Strategy for the Evolution of the Economic System of the European Community* (Oxford: Oxford University Press, 1987), pp. 3, 4, 10.

27. Quoted in *Economist*, February 27, 1988, p. 41.

28. Jacques Delors, address to the European Parliament, January 20, 1988, Bulletin EC S/1-1988, p. 11.

29. European Commission, *Reform of the Structural Funds: A Tool to Promote Economic and Social Cohesion* (Luxembourg: Office for Official Publications of the European Communities, 1992), p. 18.

30. See Liesbet Hooghe, ed., *Cohesion Policy and European Integration: Building Multi-Level Governance* (Oxford: Oxford University Press, 1996).

31. Jacques Delors, *Report of the Committee for the Study of Economic and Monetary Union* (Luxembourg: Office for Official Publications of the European Communities, 1989).

32. Commission, "From the Single Act to Maastricht and Beyond."

33. Michael Shackleton, "The Community Budget After Maastricht," in Alan Cafruny and Glenda G. Rosenthal, eds., *The State of the European Community: The Maastricht Debates and Beyond* (Boulder, CO: Lynne Rienner, 1993), p. 387.

34. Bernard Funck and Lodovico Pizzati, eds., *European Integration, Regional Policy, and Growth* (Washington, DC: World Bank, 2002), p. 80. For a more positive assessment, see Robert Leonardi, *Cohesion Policy in the European Union: The Building of Europe* (Basingstoke, UK: Palgrave Macmillan, 2005).

35. European Commission, *A New Partnership for Cohesion: Convergence, Competitiveness, Cooperation* (Luxembourg: Office for Official Publications of the European Communities, 2004).

13

Economic Integration: Growth and Competitiveness

Economic integration is the keystone of the European Union. The EU's success depends on the extent of economic integration among the member states and especially on the state of the single market. Originally called the common market, the single or internal market was the raison d'être for the European Economic Community. Despite the success of the single market program in the late 1980s and early 1990s, the single market remains a work in progress. Even with the best political will in the world, it can never be entirely complete. New technologies, products, and production processes require constant attention to ensure the integrity of the single market. But political will to consolidate the single market is often lacking in the member states, especially when it comes to the transposition of EU directives into national law and their enforcement at the national level.

Various EU policies and programs buttress and complement the single market. For example, competition policy ensures that governments and large companies do not distort the marketplace and disadvantage other economic actors. EU efforts to promote enterprise, the information society, research and development, and higher educational standards and to strengthen trans-European transportation and telecommunications networks aim to deepen European integration and enhance economic growth.

Concerned about the EU's sluggish economic performance in the 1990s, EU leaders made a bold—some would say rash—commitment at a summit meeting in Lisbon in March 2000: by 2010 they would transform the EU into "the most competitive and dynamic knowledge-based economy in the world, capable of sustainable economic growth and more and better jobs."[1] Language of that sort was more familiar to American than European ears. Indeed, the Lisbon goal was a tacit acknowledgement that the EU had to adopt a more aggressive, American-style approach in order to achiever higher economic growth. The lesson of the 1990s was plain. Whereas the United States had increased productivity enormously, Europe seriously lagged behind. Moreover, it was the leaders of Britain, Portugal, and Spain, countries that were already in the throes of sweeping economic reform, who urged the so-called Lisbon strategy on their fellow EU leaders.

The Lisbon strategy does not seek higher productivity, improved growth, and more jobs at any cost. Instead, it aims to fashion an EU that is prosperous, socially just, and environmentally sound. The Lisbon strategy therefore includes the goal of "greater social cohesion," a concept alien to the United States but beloved in the EU. Moreover, the adjective "sustainable" before the noun "growth" in the Lisbon declaration refers to environmental sustainability. EU leaders developed that point at their summit in Göteborg, Sweden, in June 2001, when they endorsed a strategy on sustainable development and explicitly linked it to the Lisbon strategy.

Social cohesion and environmentally sustainable growth are laudable goals but may not be compatible with the kind of economic performance to which the EU now aspires. At the very least, meeting the challenges of social cohesion and sustainable development will require an extraordinary increase in productivity throughout the EU. It will also require considerable cooperation among member states in a range of economic and social policy areas. The EU has long been involved in social policy, narrowly understood as employees' rights and regulation of the workplace. Employers and economic liberals complain that EU social policy imposes additional costs, undermines competitiveness, and contributes to unemployment. In an effort to dispel the negative connotation of social policy in the minds of employers and economic reformers, the EU has broadened the policy's scope to "social and employment policy."

This chapter outlines the Lisbon strategy before examining the elements of economic integration on which it rests: the single market, competition policy, enterprise and industry, research and development, the trans-European networks, and education and vocational training. Chapter 14 examines social policy, employment, and sustainable development.

The Lisbon Strategy

By the late 1990s the word "competitiveness" was commonplace in the vocabulary of European integration. Jacque Delors had used it in the title of his last important initiative before leaving office: a White Paper titled *Growth, Competitiveness, and Employment: The Challenges and Ways Forward into the 21st Century*.[2] European political and business leaders appreciated the necessity of boosting productivity in order to become more competitive in the global economy. EU politicians and labor leaders wanted higher productivity and growth to translate into more and better jobs for European workers.

At the same time, the EU began to face a related demographic and economic challenge. Europe's population was declining, while people lived longer. Relatively high unemployment and earlier retirement increased the burden of dependency, meaning that those in the workforce had to support (through taxes) larger numbers of unemployed and retirees, who received generous welfare and other benefits.

Europe's welfare programs, including (mostly) free education at all levels, are generous by American standards. They vary from country to country and are national, not EU, areas of responsibility. Nevertheless, they do not exist in a policy vacuum: countries participating in (or hoping to participate in) the single currency are not supposed to exceed a budget deficit of 3 percent of GDP, which limits the ability of governments to pay for welfare programs as the burden of dependency increases, especially if the international economy is soft.

In order to sustain its welfare programs in the long run, Europe would have to boost its productivity considerably and get many more people into the workforce. In short, it would have to do better than the United States. Although some EU member states performed extremely well in the 1990s (Ireland comes immediately to mind), the EU as a whole continued to underperform and fall further behind the United States. Taking matters into their own hands, British prime minister Tony Blair and Spanish prime minister José Maria Aznar, center-right politicians with a market-oriented, probusiness philosophy, urged Portugal, then in the Council presidency, to convene a special summit to inject new political life into economic integration. The so-called dot.com summit took place in Lisbon in March 2000 and produced an overall goal for the EU, a set of targets, and a strategy for achieving them (see Box 13.1).

The goal of becoming the most competitive and dynamic knowledge-based economy in the world, capable of sustainable economic growth with more and better jobs, was ambitious. Achieving greater social cohesion would entail maintaining or even increasing welfare provision, which Europe could ill afford to do. Moreover, environmentally sustainable economic growth was an expensive objective. On the face of it, the Lisbon goal was audacious in the extreme.

Yet the Lisbon targets were not necessarily new. Indeed, the summit conclusions were a patchwork of preexisting commitments in a variety of policy areas. The Lisbon strategy was part political exhortation and part procedural change. In order to keep up the pressure, EU leaders agreed to hold a special summit every spring to review progress on meeting the Lisbon targets. Politically and procedurally, the Lisbon strategy "raised the level of the European Council's ambitions as the core of the EU executive."[3]

Subsequently, as part of a general overhaul of the Council of Ministers, EU leaders agreed to a new configuration, the Competitiveness Council, to deal with the host of issues on the Lisbon agenda. Later still, incoming Commission president José Manuel Barroso formed a working group of commissioners with responsibility for areas covered by the Lisbon strategy (the Lisbon

Box 13.1   The Lisbon Goal and Strategy

Meeting in Lisbon in March 2000, the European Council set a "strategic goal" for the EU "*to become the most competitive and dynamic knowledge-based economy in the world capable of sustainable economic growth with more and better jobs and greater social cohesion.* Achieving this goal requires an overall strategy aimed at

- preparing the transition to a knowledge-based economy and society by better policies for the information society and R&D as well as by stepping up the process of structural reform for competitiveness and innovation and by completing the internal market;
- modernizing the European social model, investing in people and combating social exclusion;
- sustaining the healthy economic outlook and favorable growth prospects by applying an appropriate macro-economic policy mix.

Meeting in Göteborg in June 2001, the European Council expanded the Lisbon goal to include "sustainable development."

Sources: European Council, Presidency Conclusions, March 2000 (emphasis in the original); European Council, Presidency Conclusions, June 2001.

Strategy Commissioners Group) and put himself at its head. These institutional changes signaled the political importance of the Lisbon process.

Most of the Lisbon targets required legislative enactment through the traditional Community method of EU decisionmaking. The Lisbon summit and the follow-on summits were supposed to generate the political will necessary to overcome blocks in legislative decisionmaking. As well as the Community method, however, the Lisbon strategy included a more flexible policymaking process: the so-called open method of coordination. It involved benchmarking, best-practice, and target-setting, particularly in the areas of employment and social policy, in the hope that peer pressure would achieve progress, especially in areas that did not fall within the EU's competence.

Business leaders strongly supported the Lisbon objectives and strategy but were somewhat skeptical of the chances of success. They knew that EU summits generally produced extravagant rhetoric. Moreover, the fact that French prime minister Lionel Jospin, a doctrinaire Socialist, had signed on to the strategy cannot have been reassuring. French president Jacques Chirac, who was also at the summit, was known to be unsympathetic toward economic liberalization, which the Lisbon strategy implicitly endorsed. Nicole Fontaine, president of the European Parliament, made a typically French remark when she warned EU leaders before the summit not to pursue "untrammeled capitalism and remorseless pursuit of profit at the expense of working men and women."[4]

The Commission enthusiastically endorsed the initiative, or at least internal market commissioner Frits Bolkestein did. A maverick Dutch politician and unabashed economic liberal, Bolkestein once quoted Thomas Jefferson at an informal meeting of the Competitiveness Council: "Were government to direct us when to sow and when to reap, we should soon want for bread." In Bolkestein's view, "the best—and probably the only—way to raise our growth levels is to inject more competition into our markets and ensure that the most productive and innovative companies are generously rewarded."[5]

Bolkestein's economic liberalism may seem surprising, given that right-wing critics of the Commission contend that the EU's executive body has a left-wing, big-government agenda. Yet Bolkestein is exceptional only in his outspokenness. Economic liberals have occupied key portfolios in the Commission, notably the internal market and competition policy portfolios, since the revival of European integration in the mid-1980s. Representatives of big business in Europe, strong backers of market liberalization, have long admired and depended on commissioners such as Bolkestein to advocate their cause in the EU policymaking process.

Bolkestein and like-minded commissioners, such as Erkki Liikanen (enterprise and information society) and Mario Monti (competition), saw the Lisbon strategy as an opportunity to push their reform agendas. Thanks to their efforts, the Commission began to produce scorecards and league tables on the Lisbon strategy and did not hesitate to scold member states that were lagging behind. The Commission plays a vital part in the annual spring summits, having responsibility for drafting the sole report on which EU leaders base their discussions.

■ The Single Market

Of the various policy pillars that buttress the Lisbon strategy, the single market is by far the most important. It rests, in turn, on the customs union, put in place in 1968 to facilitate the free movement of goods among member states. National governments failed to complete the single market in the following decade because of political setbacks (adherence to unanimity in Council decisionmaking) and economic recession. If anything, the European market became more fragmented as member states not only failed to remove nontariff barriers to trade but also put new ones in place. Eventually, confronted by intense international competition in the early 1980s, EU leaders committed themselves in the Single European Act to completing the single market by the target date of 1992 (see Chapter 4).

This section looks at implementation of the single market program, beginning with the Commission's famous White Paper of June 1985, which contained the detailed legislative blueprint for meeting the 1992 deadline. Some of the directives tabled in the White Paper were intended to tidy up previously enacted single market legislation; others came in response to changing technology or changing social and environmental priorities. Completion of the single market also required measures to remove quotas and other trade restrictions imposed by member states in order to protect their markets from nonmember imports. Finally, the success of the single market program prompted member states to liberalize energy and telecommunications, two sectors initially excluded from the program. Two decades after the launch of the White Paper, the single market requires constant monitoring, especially to ensure the transposition and enforcement of single market measures.

The 1992 Program

By identifying the steps necessary to complete the single market, the Commission's 1985 White Paper underpinned the 1992 program. It also served to give new momentum to old proposals by repackaging them as part of an exciting new initiative. Despite its comprehensiveness and seemingly microscopic specificity, the White Paper represented an educated estimate of the measures needed to bring about a single market rather than a revealed truth. Moreover, the White Paper was far from sacrosanct: the number of proposals to complete the single market hovered around 282, but they were not always the same 282. Some were discreetly deemed unnecessary when they failed to win support; others spawned additional measures. Given the complexity of the EC market, it is not surprising that the lines between the Commission's three categories of barriers to integration—physical, technical, and fiscal—were neither neat nor self-evident.

Completing the single market involved intensive interaction between the Commission (which submitted the legislative proposals) and the Council (which enacted them). The European Parliament also played a key part through the cooperation procedure for legislative decisionmaking, introduced in the Single European Act. The following description of the single market program may seem tedious and technical, but it is intended to convey the intricacy and enormity of the operation. Integrating separate national markets into a single market is a Herculean task, even with a customs union and an institutional structure already in place.[6]

Physical Barriers. Physical barriers—customs and immigration posts at border crossings between member states—were the most tangible obstacles to a single market. Border posts impeded the movement of people (due to passport controls and residence restrictions) and goods (due to delays for inspection).

Accordingly, the Commission sought unequivocally "to eliminate in their entirety . . . internal frontier barriers and controls . . . by 1992."

Movement of goods. Ending onerous and costly delays at border crossings proved politically uncontroversial. The Commission took a lengthy, phased approach to the abolition of customs formalities and inspections by the end of 1992. Measures included the consolidation and eventual abolition of all the paperwork needed at frontier posts and a new statistical system for tracking trade among member states once border posts disappeared. By the end of 1991 the Council had adopted all the necessary legislation. In October 1992 the Commission published the Common Customs Code, supplementing it with a long-overdue digest of customs practices.

The removal of physical barriers had a direct bearing on agriculture, as border checks ensured compliance with a wide array of plant and animal health and food safety requirements. Under byzantine Common Agricultural Policy rules, farmers were compensated at internal borders, and border inspections enforced quota arrangements granted to Spain and Portugal at the time of their accession. Sixty-three of the White Paper's proposals covered disease control and livestock trade generally, as well as trade in food products. Another eighteen covered phytosanitary (plant health) and similar measures. Of the eighty-one measures in these two categories, only three remained outstanding at the end of 1992.

Movement of people. Barriers to the movement of people proved the most intractable part of the 1992 program. Essential elements, such as passport and visa requirements, remained the exclusive preserve of member states, some of which agreed to eliminate all border formalities under the auspices of the so-called Schengen regime, outside the treaty framework. Although signed in 1985 by France, Germany, and the Benelux countries, the Schengen agreement was still not operational in 1992. Aware that it was running out of time, in May 1992 the Commission issued a communication describing lack of progress on the free movement of people as "worrying at all political levels" and reminded member states of their commitment under the terms of the Single European Act to abolish all controls at frontiers, without exception, by the end of the year.[7] The legally complicated and politically contentious question of free movement of people became bound up with the provisions of the Maastricht Treaty for intergovernmental cooperation on justice and home affairs, which are examined in Chapter 17.

Technical Barriers. The White Paper used the term "technical barriers" almost as a catchall: proposals under this heading covered product standards, testing, and certification; movement of capital; public procurement; free movement of labor and the professions; free movement of financial services;

transport; new technologies; company law; intellectual property; and company taxation. Not surprisingly, it was by far the largest category of White Paper measures.

Standards, testing, and certification. The use of different product standards, testing, and certification in each member state—and the need for multiple approvals in some areas—traditionally posed major barriers to intra-European trade. Despite a general prohibition on technical barriers in the Rome Treaty, member states frequently abused an escape clause to impose their own product standards for reasons of health and safety. A key treaty provision called on the Council to develop harmonized standards in cases where member state standards differed. However, the arduous and politically sensitive process of harmonization led to a huge backlog of cases by the mid-1980s.

To end the backlog and remove a major obstacle to the free movement of goods, the Commission developed the principle of mutual recognition of national regulations and standards. Instead of trying to harmonize a potentially limitless number of product standards throughout the EC, member states would recognize and accept each other's standards as long as those standards satisfied certain health and safety concerns. Mutual recognition rests squarely on the outcome of the famous *Cassis de Dijon* (1979) case, in which the European Court of Justice overruled a ban imposed by German authorities on the importation of cassis, a French liqueur, because it failed to meet Germany's alcohol-content standards.[8]

Building on the *Cassis de Dijon* judgment, the White Paper proclaimed that "subject to certain important constraints . . . if a product is lawfully manufactured and marketed in one member state, there is no reason why it should not be sold freely throughout the Community." By emphasizing mutual recognition on the basis of treaty obligations and EC case law, the Commission expected to trigger "the withdrawal of numerous harmonization proposals pending before the Council and . . . the abandonment of even more drafts envisaged by the Commission's staff."[9] The Commission hoped that a combination of self-interest, common sense, goodwill, and peer pressure would reduce member states' recourse to the escape clause. Yet there could be no question of member states' forsaking legitimate health and safety concerns about specific products manufactured elsewhere in the EC. The White Paper sought to maximize mutual recognition, not to abolish harmonization. Where harmonization remained essential, the White Paper proposed a two-track strategy: (1) a "new approach" approved by the Council in May 1985, while the White Paper was still being drafted; and (2) the old approach of sectoral harmonization.

The new approach consisted of two parts. The first limited legislative harmonization to the establishment of essential health and safety requirements. Member states would transpose those fundamental requirements into national regulations but could not impose further regulatory requirements on the products in question.[10] The White Paper included "new approach" directives on a wide range of products such as toys, machinery, and implantable medical devices. Because manufacturers could have problems proving that their products met fundamental requirements without the aid of further technical specification, the second part of the new approach required the Commission to contract with European standards organizations such as the European Standardization Committee (CEN) and the European Electrotechnical Standardization Committee (CENELEC) to develop voluntary European standards, so-called European Norms. Manufacturers adhering to those standards would be presumed to be in compliance with the essential requirements set in the directive, and their products would therefore be assured free circulation throughout the EC.

In order for the system to work, member states had to reach agreement not only on the essential requirements themselves but also on the level of proof needed to demonstrate compliance. In other words, they had to reach a consensus on testing and certification requirements. They did so in December 1989 by adopting a "global approach" that described a set of standard "modules" for testing and certification of products, in most cases offering manufacturers some degree of choice.[11] The options ranged from the least burdensome—in which a manufacturer could simply declare that a product met essential requirements—to the most burdensome, where, for instance, a third party (such as a nationally approved laboratory) would test and evaluate the product.

Another option involved a "quality systems" approach, in which a manufacturer's consistent application of quality-control measures from design through production would be certified by an outside body. The rigor of the requirements specified in the "new approach" directives—the modules that manufacturers are required to follow—varies according to the perceived risk attached to the product. Thus, a manufacturer of stuffed animals could simply declare the products to be in compliance with the relevant directive, whereas a maker of cardiac pacemakers would need to seek third-party certification. Where required, "notified bodies"—laboratories or other institutions nominated by national governments—would perform third-party tests or certification. In a further application of the principle of mutual recognition, member states are required to allow free circulation of goods certified by the notified bodies of other member states.

The European conformity, or CE, mark, applied either by the manufacturer or by the notified body certifying the product, would play a key part. CE marks were intended primarily to show customs and regulatory authorities that products complied with essential requirements (they are not quality marks such as those awarded by other national bodies).

Although new-approach directives covering a wide range of products were largely completed by the end of 1992, application of the system ran into trouble. European standards bodies, bureaucratic and slow, soon lagged behind in developing the norms necessary to allow manufacturers to comply with the directives. Some requirements for use of the CE mark turned out to be inconsistent and in some cases incompatible. For example, products subject to more than one directive were not able to comply with each set of requirements. In April 1993, the Council eventually approved a directive on the CE mark retroactively harmonizing existing directives and laying down a single set of rules.

The continuing delay in the development of European Norms was a more serious problem. A 1989 Commission recommendation on ways to remove bottlenecks met with a frosty response from the leadership of CEN and CENELEC and raised concerns outside the EC that hasty setting of standards could lead to divergences between European and international standards. In the end there were few fundamental changes, although the standards bodies agreed to streamline procedures as much as possible. The slow pace at which member states notified testing bodies created another bottleneck in the system, especially because the bodies so notified faced an initial surge in demand as manufacturers rushed to certify their existing product lines.

Recognizing that the new approach could not be applied to all sectors, the Commission kept the old approach of working toward total sectoral harmonization—developing a single, detailed set of technical specifications for a given product that all member states would have to accept—in a number of key areas traditionally subject to intensive member state regulation because of safety risks and/or public concern. In the White Paper, the Commission advocated the old approach for motor vehicles, food, pharmaceuticals, chemicals, construction, and a number of other items.

In the case of pharmaceuticals, where the European market was highly fragmented, the White Paper included fifteen directives addressing such questions as common testing rules, price transparency, patient information, advertising, and, above all, centralized approval of new drugs. The Commission envisioned a European-level agency that would eventually take responsibility for all new drug approvals, backed by a host of new harmonizing directives. Member states finally decided in 1992 to establish the European Medicines Agency, with responsibility for approving all medicines based on biotechnology and all veterinary medicines likely to improve the productivity of farm animals. This peculiar list resulted from a previous debate over the safety of biotechnology generally and over the possible approval of bovine somatotropin (BST), a controversial new drug that improved milk yields of dairy cows.

Movement of capital. Since the 1960s, the EC had achieved considerable liberalization of the initially tight postwar restrictions on capital flows. As member states became richer and more confident of their own stability, many lifted restrictions unilaterally. Three White Paper directives aimed to complete the process with a sequence of measures intended to phase out controls. The first two liberalized rules governing cross-border securities transactions, long-term commercial loans, and admission of corporate securities to capital markets in other member states; the third superseded these and obliged member states to lift all restrictions on capital movements except measures intended to ensure the continuing liquidity of local banks or temporary restrictions in response to major disruptions in foreign exchange markets. The Commission saw enactment of these measures as a final step on the road to "an effective and stable Community financial system"—a prerequisite for monetary union.

Public procurement. Member states made initial moves in the 1970s toward opening procurement, which accounted for as much as 15 percent of Community GDP. For a variety of reasons, however, including active obstruction by local authorities, public procurement remained overwhelmingly the preserve of national suppliers. In 1992, the Commission estimated that only 2 percent of the €600 billion public market had been won by firms from outside the home country.

The Commission correctly characterized such a distortion of competition as "anachronistic" and contrary to the spirit of a free market. Moreover, the Commission had a particular concern about the telecommunications sector, fearing that closed public markets and a cozy relationship between public authorities and cosseted but internationally weak "national champions" would hinder the development of a European telecommunications industry capable of competing in the harsher world market. The need to open public procurement and encourage competition generally became a recurring theme of the Commission's developing industrial policy.

The White Paper proposed seven directives to eliminate distortions caused by local procurement bias. Proposals covered essential elements of an open bidding system, such as transparency, review procedures to penalize violations, use of common standards, and procedures for award of public contracts. The directives also extended the scope of those rules to cover nearly all public procurement above certain thresholds (which vary by sector and by type of contract).

The most important of these directives was the so-called utilities, or excluded-sectors, directive, extending EC public procurement rules to enterprises (not necessarily publicly owned) offering public services in the water, energy, transport, and telecommunications sectors. As well as setting out minimum thresholds for application of its rules and procedures to ensure transparency, the directive required public authorities to evaluate bids on objective and nondiscriminatory criteria—for example, lowest price or most economically advantageous package (an exception to this rule allowing member states to discard bids with less than 50 percent EC content and providing a 3 percent price preference for EC bids later caused trouble with the United States). Other procurement directives applied similar principles to the supply of services and public works, such as construction and similar projects, and developed legal remedies for violations. All were adopted by the spring of 1993.

Free movement of labor and the professions. The White Paper included proposals for putting into practice the right, enshrined in the treaty, of EC citizens to live and work in other member states. Directives extending residency rights throughout the EC to students, retired persons, and other members of the nonworking population came into force in June 1992. Those relating to workers and their families built on a 1968 directive guaranteeing nondiscrimination in employment and a right of establishment. White Paper proposals sought to extend nondiscrimination to various employment-related subsidies and social benefits, as well as granting residence and social and educational rights to non-EC nationals in the extended family of EC national workers.

In order to facilitate the movement of workers among countries, the Commission also took on the task of establishing equivalencies among the various types of professional and vocational training available in each member state and of removing traditional restrictions that prevented members of regulated professions, such as doctors and lawyers, from freely offering their services in other member states. The Council eventually adopted two directives on the recognition of diplomas. In addition, the Commission undertook extensive studies and published comparative lists of member state qualifications and credentials covering over 200 vocations, enabling employers to evaluate qualifications in nonregulated areas.

Free movement of financial services. The Commission followed three basic principles to permit free movement for financial services: harmonization of essential standards; mutual recognition among supervisory authorities; and home-country control, that is, making a financial institution's branches the responsibility of the member state in which the institution's head office is located.

The White Paper proposed eight directives intended to allow banks incorporated in one member state to operate across national borders without having to seek authorization from national regulatory authorities in each member state. Clearly, member states would have to agree to common rules and criteria for judging the soundness of banks in order to develop the necessary mutual confidence to allow the home-country control system to work.

The second banking directive, which entered into force in January 1993, established a single banking license, valid throughout the EU, allowing banks to open branches anywhere without additional authorizations. Overall supervision of a bank with multiple branches is a cooperative venture: the home country monitors solvency, and the country in which a branch is located may monitor the liquidity of the branch and impose local conduct rules. The directive also contained provisions on foreign banks designed to give the Commission leverage in negotiating conditions for EU banks in foreign markets.

The Commission based its approach to creating a single market for insurance services on the principles used in the banking sector. Nine White Paper directives built on an existing body of EC legislation in the insurance area.

Another directive set out the system for a single authorizing procedure, reciprocity with third countries, common prudential rules, cooperation among supervisory authorities, and other necessary elements in the area of investment services. Neither the investment services directive nor a supplementary directive harmonizing member state capital adequacy requirements had been formally adopted when the single market supposedly became operational on January 1, 1993.

Transport. Opening up the EC's highly regulated transport markets required twelve directives covering six discrete and dissimilar sectors including air, road haulage (goods), and maritime transport. Most international air transport markets are regulated by government agreements that usually inhibit competition. The situation in Europe was a particularly egregious example, combining a number of relatively small markets with "national champions" (frequently government owned) protected through market-sharing arrangements, fixed fares, and occasional massive subsidies—all governed by 200 bilateral agreements covering twenty-two countries. Not surprisingly, the result was high consumer costs. The Commission tackled the morass in three stages, with the Council adopting aviation packages in 1987, 1990, and 1992 that gradually liberalized the market in areas such as competition in fares, sharing of passenger capacity, access to routes for all operators, application of EC competition rules, and a right to carry passengers between two locations inside another member state (cabotage) for European airlines, starting in January 1997.

Before the 1985 White Paper, road haulage between member states was generally subject to quotas that restricted rights to carry cargo on the return leg of any journey. As a result, large numbers of empty trucks trundled through the EC, adding to congestion and pollution and raising transport costs. Truckers were also prohibited from engaging in cabotage. In addition, trucks were subject to different and often incompatible work rules or technical specifications. The Commission approached the problem with three initiatives: harmonization to the extent possible of technical specifications and work rules, abolition of all quotas on road haulage between member states, and the gradual introduction of cabotage. Full cabotage rights—the final step in establishing a single transport market—were finally granted in June 1993, when member states agreed on a fair way to assess road taxes on foreign operators.

New technologies. The 1985 White Paper included five directives on "new technologies," focusing on opening markets in areas such as cable and satellite broadcasting. The most important were

- A directive on mutual recognition of member state approvals for telecommunications terminal equipment (telephones, faxes, modems, etc.).
- A framework directive on open network provision in the telecommunications area to ensure access for equipment and service providers to the public telecommunications infrastructure. The directive prohibits public telecommunications networks from restricting access except on grounds of security, data protection, or the need to preserve interoperability. It also provides for a gradual development of mutual recognition of authorizations for service providers.
- A follow-up directive on open competition in the market for nonvoice telecommunications services.
- The television-without-frontiers directive, which liberalized member state television markets by prohibiting discrimination against works from other member states (with the exception of some language quotas). The directive also harmonized advertising standards, including prohibiting the advertising of tobacco, and obliged broadcasters to encourage local talent by showing a majority of EC-origin programming where practicable (a requirement that sparked fierce opposition from the United States).

Other related directives covered mobile telephones, a European code of conduct for electronic payment systems, radio frequencies, data protection, and high-definition television standards. Also included was a Council decision calling on the Commission to develop an action plan for a European information services market.

Company law. The Rome Treaty empowered the EC to take action in the field of company law "to coordinate . . . safeguards . . . required by member states of companies or firms . . . with a view to making such safeguards equivalent throughout the Community." In 1968 the Council adopted the first in a long and often arcane series of directives in this area; as with those that initially followed, its purpose was to approximate member state laws to allow maximum freedom of movement for enterprises. The White Paper went beyond that goal by aiming to create an EC framework regulating cross-border corporate activity. As in the case of the procurement directives, one of the Commission's objectives was to increase the competitiveness of European firms by allowing them to become larger and more efficient.

The White Paper proposed a number of directives in this area, including the European Company Statute, intended to allow enterprises to declare themselves "European companies" subject primarily to EC law, which had already languished for some time in the Council. The White Paper also included a regulation defining the European Economic Interest Grouping, a legal entity created to accommodate firms or other entities wanting to pool their resources for a common goal, but not wanting to merge. Perhaps the best-known example was Airbus Industrie before it became a limited company in 1999.

The Commission enjoyed only some success with these measures. After years of blockage, it made some of the proposals—notably those dealing with corporate structure and voting rights, cross-border mergers, and harmonization of rules on takeover bids—"nonpriority" for the creation of the single market. In a triumph of hope over experience, however, the Commission declared that the European Company Statute remained a top priority for the 1992 program.

Intellectual property. Also under the general heading of removing technical barriers, the Commission proposed nine directives dealing with various aspects of intellectual property rights, only four of which were adopted by the end of 1992. The major disappointment in this area was the legislation establishing the Community Trademark Office, which was thoroughly derailed by nonsubstantive but unresolvable disputes over the location of the office itself and the working languages to be used.

Company taxation. To address the question of differing rates of tax on corporations in different member states, the Council finally adopted three proposals in 1990 that had been on the table for nearly twenty years. One covered taxes on capital gains resulting from mergers, share exchanges, and other forms of company restructuring; the other two concerned the problem of double taxation on intracompany dividend transfers and on profits of affiliated companies. A number of other draft directives remained on the table at the end of 1992 (tax proposals were particularly difficult to adopt because they required unanimity in the Council).

Fiscal Barriers. The White Paper included an ambitious set of initiatives for harmonizing taxation—a prerequisite not only for eliminating borders (where many taxes were assessed) but also for reducing distortion and segmentation of the EC market through disparate tax practices. To take one of the more extreme examples, consumer groups calculated that the cost of a car varied as much as 100 percent across Europe because of excise, value-added, and other tax differentials.

Value-added tax. Of the wide variety of indirect taxes assessed on European goods, value-added tax (VAT) is the most visible and probably the most important. Before 1992, standard VAT rates varied up to 11 percent among member states. Some states charged luxury rates on certain categories of goods and no VAT at all on others. The White Paper called on member states to harmonize VAT rates and to develop a system for charging VAT on cross-border sales once border posts had been eliminated.

The road to VAT harmonization proved especially arduous. Because VAT revenues were in many cases the mainstay of member state social welfare systems, high-VAT countries resisted harmonization downward, even into the broad bands proposed by the Commission. Governments feared having to explain to voters why they were cutting back on prized social security programs for the sake of the single market. There was speculation in 1992 that popular anxiety in that regard contributed to Denmark's narrow rejection of the Maastricht Treaty. Elimination of such local exceptions to VAT as food or children's clothing was equally certain to create political fallout. The alternative, proposed by some member states such as Britain, was to leave VAT unharmonized and let the market force member states to align their VAT rates with those of their neighbors, if need be. This was a prospect only an island nation could face with equanimity; others feared that hordes of consumers, streaming across borders to get the best tax deal, would bankrupt local retailers and cut into the revenues of high-tax states.

Member states eventually adopted a general framework for harmonization, stipulating a standard rate of 15 percent or above in each country as of January 1993. Luxury rates were to be abolished, but member states could apply lower rates, or zero rates, to an agreed-upon list of items during a transition period. Itself a result of political horse-trading, the list yielded a few anomalies: in deference to Britain, for example, member states could apply lower rates to food but had to apply the standard rate to "snacks" (needless to say, consumers were not allowed to make the distinction between food and snacks).

As well as harmonizing rates, member states agreed on rules for who should pay VAT and where. In 1987 the Commission proposed a straightforward system: VAT was to be paid in the country of sale. However, member states insisted on adopting an ungainly "transitional" system in which VAT on cross-border trade must be paid in the country of destination. To make the system work, sellers and buyers were required to declare their cross-border transactions regularly to tax authorities, including such information as the VAT registration number of the buyer, and pay the VAT applicable in their own country on imports from other member states (firms whose cross-border transactions fell below a threshold were exempt from regular reporting). Private consumers shopping in other member states, by contrast, paid VAT in the country of sale—except on mail-order purchases and on cars, for which VAT was payable at registration.

Excise tax. The second aspect of the indirect taxation dossier concerned excise taxes—internal taxes levied mainly on fuels, liquor, and tobacco. In March 1991, the Council adopted a harmonized structure and rates for excise duties. At the end of 1992, the Council decided to eliminate restrictions on cross-border purchases by consumers of items subject to excise taxes, having earlier set "indicative levels" to help enforcement officers distinguish between customers and commercial traders. As a result, travelers could carry up to 800 cigarettes, 90 liters of wine, 110 liters of beer, 20 liters of aperitif, and 10 liters of spirits across borders for their own use.

The logical consequence of removing fiscal frontiers should have been an end to duty-free shops in airports and on ferries. However, politics overcame logic in this case, as many airports and ferry operators gathered a large part of their operating revenues from highly profitable duty-free sales, to which travelers seemed addicted. Accordingly, the Council decided to put off the demise of duty-free shopping until 1999.

Related Measures. In order to eliminate internal borders, the Commission also had to address the problem of quotas and other restraints imposed by individual member states under the Rome Treaty. Nearly 1,000 such measures, including over 100 restrictive quotas, were in place by the late 1980s. Using its power to deny quotas, the Commission managed to phase out all but six of them by July 1992, leading it to dismiss "the too widespread notion that a Fortress Europe is being constructed."[12]

For exporters to the EC of certain products—notably textiles, bananas, and Japanese cars—the Commission's exultation was premature. For instance, Japanese car manufacturers were not destined to enjoy the immediate benefits of an open EU market. Responding to French and Italian consternation at the prospect of losing their harsh import restrictions and the potentially disastrous consequences for their sluggish national champions, the Commission negotiated a voluntary-restraint agreement with Japan, which allowed Japanese car imports a steadily increasing market share, reaching a ceiling of 15.2 percent of the European auto market by 1999, when the EU was expected to lift all restrictions. Although production of Japanese-brand cars in Europe, so-called transplants, was not to be counted as part of the overall ceiling, the agreement effectively protected European producers for most of the decade.

One of the bitterest and more risible rows to emerge from the internal market program erupted over banana quotas. Seeking to protect the market position of high-cost bananas from Caribbean countries with which the EC has a development assistance program (as well as some even more inefficient growers in the Canary Islands), France, Britain, Spain, and Portugal imposed on an indignant Germany and the Netherlands a restrictive tariff quota limiting imports of so-called dollar bananas from Latin America. Outvoted in the Council, Germany, whose per capita banana consumption had hitherto been the highest in Europe, threatened to bring a case to the Court of Justice, and the Latin Americans initiated a GATT challenge to the EC's banana regime. The World Trade Organization (WTO) subsequently concluded that the European system violated world trade rules. Efforts by the Commission to devise a system that preserved protection for Caribbean producers while technically falling within the WTO ruling elicited both internal and external criticism.

Other issues also had the potential to block the full abolition of borders. The most difficult to resolve were those in which some member states were suspicious of the ability or will of other member states to enforce existing obligations or where the disappearance of border controls required member states to develop a framework to carry out each other's decisions. These included controls on trade in endangered species, controls on the movement of waste, and controls on the export of cultural treasures. Because of lack of Community competence over export of dual-use goods (those with military as well as civilian applications), the Commission was confined to proposing procedural measures for carrying out controls at external borders.

Beyond 1992

The official unveiling of the single market on January 1, 1993, happened at an inauspicious time. The EC was in the doldrums, with parts of it, including Britain, in a deep recession. The brisk economic growth of the late 1980s, which had lent credence to extravagant claims for the single market, had suddenly dissipated. It seemed unlikely that merely announcing the official existence of the single market would get the EC economy going again.

Sensing public skepticism and even hostility during the Maastricht ratification crisis, the Commission kept the celebrations low-key. Aside from sponsoring a chain of bonfires across Europe and a fireworks display in Brussels, the Commission's main response was to issue reams of information keyed to perceived citizen concerns about such issues as conditions for transporting horses or the fate of unemployed customs agents. Thus, the long-awaited advent of the single market came almost as an anticlimax. As the bonfires smoldered, the griping began. Businessmen complained vociferously about the computerized VAT reporting system, with smaller firms threatening to stop shipping across European borders. Members of the European Parliament were irate when asked for their passports in the Strasbourg airport, and journalists tried to provoke border guards by walking through border posts carrying armloads of bananas. The only conspicuously happy constituency was the horde of Britons reboarding ferries at Calais with vans full of cheap French wine.

Amid all the bluster were some real grounds for criticism: transition periods and derogations stretching toward the end of the century meant that the single market program was far from being entirely in place. The highly visible failure to abolish border checks on people was bound to tarnish the image of the single market, already under fire from environmental and social groups characterizing it as a heartless sellout to business interests. Important ancillary measures, such as rules on export of dual-use goods or trade in endangered species, were unfinished. Manufacturers of products covered by new-approach directives faced uncertainty and disruption over the pace at which European standards could be developed and introduced. Taxation policies and exemptions from competition rules that prevent cross-border price shopping meant that customers would benefit little from lowered manufacturers' costs brought about by harmonization. Consumer banking charges, especially in the foreign exchange area, remained opaque and disparate. The double-barreled VAT system became a fertile source of confusion.

Beyond the expiration of the 1992 deadline, the success of the single market depended on three things:

- the legislative enactment of those proposals still on the table and new proposals necessitated by changing social, economic, and technical circumstances
- the complete liberalization of the energy and telecommunications sectors, hitherto largely excluded from the single market program
- the level and quality of member state transposition of directives into national law and the Commission's ability to resist the proliferation of new trade barriers

Completing the Legislative Framework. In the mid- and late 1990s the EU enacted most of the remaining 1985 White Paper and related proposals, although a few key items continued to elude agreement. There was a considerable reduction in the number of new legislative proposals, either because most areas had already been covered or because of the vogue for subsidiarity. The most important legislative developments after 1992 involving preexisting and new proposals included

- *Product standards:* The "novel food" regulation, governing the marketing and labeling of novel food and food ingredients (including genetically modified organisms) took effect in May 1997. This represented a major step toward completing the single market for foodstuffs.
- *New technologies:* The Commission revived the Open Network Provision directive (a telecommunications measure) in February 1995 after the European Parliament had rejected the original proposal in July 1994 because of a procedural dispute with the Council. The new proposal included some parliamentary amendments in the area of consumer protection. The Council adopted the long-delayed directive in December 1995.
- *Company law:* In February 1996 the Commission proposed a new streamlined directive on public takeover bids in the EU, replacing the moribund proposal for a thirteenth company law directive, one of the original White Paper proposals.
- *Intellectual property rights:* In December 1995 the Commission presented a new proposal for a directive on the legal protection of

biotechnological inventions after the Parliament had rejected the original proposal in March 1995 because of ethical concerns related to animal welfare. The new proposal was adopted in 1998. In March 1996 the Council adopted a directive on the legal protection of databases, providing copyright protection to computerized and manual databases for the first time, thereby affording legal protection for database creators and investors throughout the EU. Legislation establishing the Community Trademark Office (CTMO) was finally unblocked following a political package deal in October 1993 on the location of EU institutions and agencies. The CTMO opened in Alicante, Spain, in January 1996, allowing companies to file for a single Community trademark for products and services marketed in the EU.

- *Company taxation:* In October 1997 the Commission revived a White Paper proposal to eliminate the double taxation of interest and royalty payments made between parent companies and their subsidiaries in different member states (the Commission had dropped the proposal three years before due to insufficient political support). Reflecting a changed political climate owing to the momentum generated by the impending launch of the single currency, the Council approved the proposal only two months later, in December 1997.

Regardless of these successes, a small number of single market proposals remained doggedly beyond reach of agreement. One of the oldest and most intractable was the proposal for the European Company Statute, a long-standing goal that the Commission had inserted into the White Paper in the hope that the single market euphoria would carry it through. In the event, it foundered once again because of fundamental conflicts among member states over the issues of worker rights and provision for a European works council of union representatives in multinational firms operating under the statute. The proposal was put on hold but sprang back to life when the Commission launched a single market action plan in June 1997 to try to breathe new life into the remaining single market measures. It failed to pass because of member state opposition to accompanying measures on worker participation.

Value-added tax was another area impervious to agreement, with some national governments refusing to go beyond the interim regime established in 1993 for payment of the tax. Thus, a definitive VAT system based on payment in the country of origin rather than the country of destination remains elusive because of concerns about the possible loss of revenue.

Efforts to achieve the free movement of financial services also proved unavailing throughout the 1990s. The Commission enjoyed some successes, such as a directive adopted in March 1997 providing minimum protection for small investors across the EU in the event that an investment firm defaults. This measure substantially reinforced the single market for securities transactions. In November 1997 the Commission proposed a directive tightening supervision of EU insurance groups, complementing existing single market legislation in the insurance sector. Nevertheless, key financial services directives remained on the table, delaying completion of an integrated European capital market and restricting economic growth throughout the EU. In order to provide new political momentum for the financial services sector, in May 1999 the Commission launched the Financial Services Action Plan, which became a key part of the Lisbon strategy.

Energy and Telecommunications. While continuing to work on the single market program, the EU also attempted in the mid- and late 1990s to liberalize energy and telecommunications, two important sectors excluded from the 1992 program except with respect to procurement and, in the case of telecommunications, measures relating to new technologies.

Energy. Traditionally, national energy markets were monopolized by state-owned suppliers because of national governments' concerns about security of supply and the related public service obligation of universal, uninterrupted provision. Efforts to establish a single energy market in the EU, limited to electricity and natural gas, therefore required a fundamental change in attitude based on growing trust among member states and growing acceptance of the economic philosophy of liberalization and competition. The Commission sought to establish a competitive regime, accompanied by the necessary regulation imposing certain indispensable constraints, in order to satisfy the requirement for safe, uninterrupted supply to all parts of the EU.

As an opening gambit, the Commission decided in 1991 that an agreement concluded among a number of electricity companies violated EC competition policy rules insofar as it had the effect of impeding imports and exports by private industrial consumers. Beyond that, the Commission initially took a flexible and gradual approach to energy market liberalization, hoping that the 1992 momentum would push the electricity and gas monopolies into a more competitive environment.

Practical steps necessary to achieve a single energy market included the removal of numerous obstacles and trade barriers, the approximation of tax and pricing policies, the establishment of common norms and standards (mostly through CEN and CENELEC), and the setting of environmental and safety regulations. When work on the further opening of electricity and gas networks bogged down politically, the Commission made completion of a single energy market a top priority in the mid-1990s. Based on extensive investigation and consultation, in 1995 the Commission published a long-awaited White Paper on energy policy. Following an examination of the general political context and market trends, the White Paper proposed a work program and timetable for liberalizing energy markets.[13]

More market-oriented countries such as Britain and Germany criticized the Commission for not going far enough with its proposals, whereas more protectionist countries such as France criticized the Commission for going too far. These political differences were compounded by the existence of two separate systems of electricity market organization in the EU, one of which was peculiar to France. Partly by threatening to use its competition policy powers to break up national monopolies but largely because of the pressure from influential industrial consumers of electricity, the Commission managed to erode national resistance to market liberalization. A breakthrough came in June 1996 when the Council agreed on a common position on the gradual creation of a single market for electricity that would allow industrial users to shop around for the lowest-cost EU provider. The Parliament approved the common position without change, permitting the Council to adopt the directive in December 1996.

Efforts to open national gas markets were equally contentious but followed the same political and economic logic as the liberalization of electricity markets. In February 1998 the Council adopted a common position on a directive to open up the natural gas market, dealing with issues such as transmission, supply, storage, and distribution.

Telecommunications. Like the energy sector, the telecommunications sector in Europe was traditionally the preserve of national monopolies and resulted in such anomalies as calls between member states often costing twice as much as calls of equivalent distance within member states. Unlike in the energy sector, however, the impetus to liberalize telecommunications received an additional boost from rapid technological changes with huge commercial implications, such as the development of the Internet. In October 1994 the Commission issued the first part of a discussion document on telecommunications policy, recommending full liberalization for voice-telephone services by January 1998 (countries with less developed networks had until 2003 to adjust). In June 1994 the Council endorsed the Commission's proposed timetable but could not agree on early liberalization of "alternative networks," such as those owned by railways and utilities.

The second part of the discussion document, issued in January 1995, dealt with the regulatory framework for key issues such as interconnection and interoperability; licensing of telecommunications infrastructures, networks, and services; and the provision of universal service (access to a minimum defined service of specified quality to all users at an affordable price); and third-country reciprocity. The Commission suggested that responsibility for regulation should remain primarily at the national level. Accordingly, EU regulation would provide a framework in which national regulators would operate in accordance with national and EC law and the principles of the single market.[14]

Building on widespread support among interest groups, telecommunications providers, and national governments, the Commission adopted much of the necessary legislation under the treaty's competition policy provisions, including directives to liberalize the mobile telephone sector (the fastest growing in the EU) by January 1996, lift restrictions on the use of alternative infrastructures for telecommunications services, and implement full competition in the EU telecommunications market by January 1998.

As late as November 1997 the Commission brought legal proceedings against seven member states for not abiding by one or more of its market-opening directives. Nevertheless, the single telecommunications market began as planned in January 1998 (although Greece, Ireland, and Portugal had temporary exceptions). Thus, in principle, any telephone company could offer callers in most member states a local or long-distance service. Like the success of the single market program, the success of the single telecommunications market depended on Commission vigilance and member state compliance. It also depended on the ability of new national regulatory authorities to enforce directives in a sector still overshadowed by powerful former monopolies.

Problems of Transposition and Enforcement. Enactment of directives at the EU level was only the first step in establishing the single market. The second step involved transposing those directives into law at the national level within the time prescribed in the directive. Without transposition into national law, the single market could not work on a day-to-day basis. Transposition rates varied from member state to member state and from sector to sector. In some cases governments deliberately delayed transposition in order to gain a temporary competitive advantage or for fear of aggravating domestic constituencies; in most cases delays were the result of the technical complexity of legislation and procedural problems due to decisionmaking processes in the member states themselves.

In the immediate aftermath of the 1992 deadline, the Commission publicly adopted a circumspect tone on member state transposition, with the internal market commissioner even suggesting that gentle encouragement was the best means of moving forward. In private the Commission took a tougher line, backed up with the threat of legal action. As "guardian of the treaties," the Commission could begin infringement proceedings against member states for nonimplementation of single market measures (or other EU obligations, for that matter).

The third step necessary to make a success of the single market was for member states to enforce the national law into which they had transposed EU directives. Just as transposition at the national level depended in large part on the quality and clarity of the relevant directive, so enforcement at the national level depended on the quality and clarity of the legislation to be implemented (claims that transposed directives were vague or unreasonable sometimes gave member states a good excuse to avoid enforcement). It also depended on the participation of national courts, which in turn required that lawyers and judges be trained in EC law. Effective enforcement benefited as well from the development of networks among member states to compare notes on the transposition and implementation of directives at the national level.

In December 1992 the Commission issued a communication adjuring member states to improve their administrative infrastructures in order to transpose single market legislation more quickly and effectively.[15] This was the first of a seemingly interminable number of communications, papers, and reports on implementation of the single market issued by the Commission over the years. Ritualistic statements at successive European Councils about the need for greater member state compliance with directives and regulations were another staple feature of EU efforts to complete the single market.

The Commission's annual reports on the single market contained useful information about the enactment of directives and their transposition (or nontransposition) at the national level. The annual reports showed a steady increase throughout the 1990s in both the enactment of single market legislation and the overall transposition rate in the member states. Transposition was consistently poor in the insurance, intellectual property, and procurement sectors, and Germany and France were often among the worst offenders. Indeed, league tables regularly ranked member states on their level of implementation of directives in force, and the press mulled over the occasional dramatic leaps registered by Italy or the irony that politically refractory Denmark consistently topped the charts.

The Commission began to take a tougher line on implementation in the mid-1990s, as reflected in a steady increase in infringement proceedings in order to correct what it had begun to characterize as the "enforcement deficit."[16] Infringement proceedings were begun in response not only to tardy transposition of legislation but also to complaints from businesses and individuals about poor national application of single market measures. Yet implementation and infringement statistics yielded little real information on the state of the single market, as they failed to reflect the quality of implementing legislation or the likelihood that national authorities would take enforcement measures.

Taking yet another initiative, in June 1997 the Commission launched the single market action plan, a concerted effort to accelerate implementation of the single market in parallel with progress on monetary union.[17] The action plan contained four strategic objectives: making the rules more effective, dealing with key market distortions, removing obstacles to market integration, and making the single market relevant to EU citizens. Specific actions (nineteen in all) were of three kinds:

- taking measures that did not require new legislation, such as transposition of directives
- enacting technically complicated but not necessarily politically contentious proposals still in the EU decisionmaking process, perhaps awaiting approval in the Council or a vote in the Parliament
- enacting politically contentious and perhaps also technically complicated proposals that in some cases had been languishing for years, such as the European Company Statute

The European Council took note of the action plan when it met in June 1997, but it was too preoccupied with concluding the Amsterdam Treaty to do much more. At its meeting in December 1997, however, the European Council put its considerable political weight behind the action plan. What gave credence to the European Council's usual exhortatory references to the single market, however, was the special emphasis on the action plan by the incoming British presidency. Eager to make its mark in the EU and push a liberal economic agenda, the new Labour government was not averse to "naming and shaming" in order to improve its partners' compliance with the single market program. The British presidency focused especially on better implementation, for instance, prodding other member states on mutual recognition and public procurement issues as well as enforcement. The British also sought to broaden the single market "scoreboard" to include market integration indices, such as price-level differentials and volumes of intra-EU trade, alongside the more legalistic yardstick published at the time.

A Job Well Done

Despite all the effort put into its initial completion by 1992 and subsequently throughout the 1990s, the single market remained unfinished, although its patchwork of derogations and transitions steadily disappeared.[18] Nevertheless, the EU marketplace became far more integrated than many people had thought possible. Market integration was a continuing process requiring enforcement of existing rules and the occasional enactment of new ones. Threats came from a variety of sources, such as poor implementation of directives, the slow pace of standards development, and lack of mutual recognition. New trade barriers that could render market integration irrelevant or ineffective, such as certain types of environmental measures that hinder the free circulation of goods, were an additional concern.

Nevertheless, the original White Paper stood up well to the test of time. Notwithstanding a lack of perfection and logic—inevitable in any political process—the White Paper functioned largely as intended. By tying so many elements to a coherent and attractive vision, the Commission managed over the years to push the Council into adopting proposals that would not otherwise have engendered much political enthusiasm. There was also a risk that the Commission would become a victim of its own publicity success, that failure to "complete" the single market precisely on time would deal a crushing political blow to the Commission's credibility. In the event, public reaction was measured, and the Council continued to adopt the remaining proposals at a respectable pace.

The main achievement of the 1992 initiative may well have been psychological. It created a climate in which individuals as well as firms could begin to identify themselves as European and look for opportunities beyond their own borders. It also created an atmosphere in which national governments could contemplate surrendering further sovereignty. Despite the political setback of the Maastricht ratification crisis and lingering citizen anxieties about cultural identity and economic competition, those attitudinal and psychological changes have persisted. The single market program, and the drive and energy displayed by the Commission in pushing it through, restored the image of the EU as a vital and modern entity and paved the way for the successful launch of the single European currency.

Competition Policy

Without rigorous antitrust rules, control of state subsidies, and liberalization of restricted industries, the single market could not function fairly or efficiently. The Rome Treaty therefore identified competition policy as a core area of EC activity in order to buttress the projected common market and create a level playing field. For its part, the Constitutional Treaty lists competition policy as one of only six areas of exclusive EU competence.

EU competition policy comprises two main branches, one dealing with the activities of private enterprises, the other with the activities of member states and state-sponsored bodies. The first covers what is generally referred to in the United States as "antitrust," that is, the prevention of practices by private entities that could inhibit competition and distort the marketplace, such as restrictive agreements or abuse of a dominant position. The second pertains to the control of "state aids" (all forms of public subsidies to firms) and the liberalization of "regulated industries" (companies either owned by or having a special relationship with national governments).

The EU's antitrust efforts draw heavily on the U.S. experience. Indeed, U.S. antitrust doctrine exerted considerable influence over officials in the EC Commission's competition policy directorate-general (DG Competition), many of whom had studied U.S. competition law. Unlike competition policy in the United States, however, competition policy in the EU deals not only with private-sector abuses in the marketplace but also with massive government financial assistance to national enterprises and with utility services—such as electricity, water, and telecommunications—which European governments have traditionally controlled. By including efforts to curb state subsidies to industry and to confront government monopolies, EU competition policy involves much more than antitrust.

In addition, competition policy has a political purpose in the EU that goes far beyond its economic objective in the United States. As well as policing the marketplace, EU competition policy seeks to break down barriers between national markets, thereby promoting European integration. Speaking at the University of Chicago—famous for its scholarship on antitrust law and economics—Sir Leon Brittan, a former competition commissioner, jocosely described the "Brussels School" of competition policy: "It includes rules on state aids and on firms granted special or exclusive rights, and has special concerns to promote market [and European] integration."[19]

As the EC's fortunes fluctuated in the 1960s and 1970s, there was little progress in completing the internal market, let alone in developing a robust competition policy. Only when efforts to complete the single market gained momentum in the early 1980s did attention focus as well on the closely related area of competition policy. Without the vigorous application of competition rules, the benefits of market liberalization might easily have been nullified by price fixing and market sharing between firms as well as by rampant government intervention. As a result, the EU implemented important competition policy reforms in the late 1980s and early 1990s.

The Commission launched a thorough review of competition policy a decade later in anticipation of Central and Eastern European enlargement and in the context of the Lisbon strategy for economic modernization. The imminent accession of so many new member states, most of them having only recently put competition authorities in place, prompted the Commission to reassess the conduct of EU competition policy. In order to prepare for enlargement, officials from the candidate countries began working in DG Competition on a temporary basis before May 2004. The new member states had to apply competition policy rules with only some transitional arrangements for state aid, although their economies were still very different from those of the existing member states. In the event, enlargement increased the Commission's overall state aid workload by about 40 percent.

Apart from the possible impact of enlargement, the Commission attempted to hone competition policy as an instrument of economic reform in order to boost competitiveness and growth. Under the energetic leadership of competition commissioner Mario Monti in the early 2000s, the Commission recommended revising the regulations governing the application of antitrust and pressed member states to curtail the provision of state aid, especially to ailing enterprises. Monti sought especially to ensure that competition policy was grounded in sound economics: instead of taking a narrow, legalistic approach to competition policy cases, the Commission would look at the likely impact of the activity in question on markets and consumers. To that end, the Commission established the new position of chief economist, assisted by a team of industrial economists, to provide independent economic analysis in individual antitrust, merger, and state aid cases throughout the investigation process.

Restrictive Practices and Abuse of Dominant Position

Articles 81 and 82 TEC form the legal basis of EU antitrust policy. Article 81 prohibits agreements and concerted practices that prevent, restrict, or distort competition and that affect trade between member states. This article generally refers to collusion between companies to fix prices or control production. Article 82 prohibits any abuse by one or more undertakings in a dominant position that distorts trade between member states. Such abuse could consist of setting unfair prices, limiting production or markets, applying dissimilar conditions, and making the conclusion of contracts subject to acceptance of supplementary obligations. Dominance is presumed to mean more than 50 percent of market share.

Clearly, EU antitrust law would have little effect without practical measures to implement it. Accordingly, in 1962 the Council adopted Regulation 17, obliging firms to notify the Commission of restrictive agreements and giving the Commission extensive powers of investigation, adjudication, and enforcement.[20] The Commission could grant individual or block exemptions under certain circumstances.

The Commission's ability to counter infringements depends to a great extent on the information at DG Competition's disposal. Most companies under investigation cooperate with the Commission, however grudgingly. In the event that some would not, Regulation 17 authorized Commission officials to arrive unannounced at businesses throughout the Community and conduct immediate on-site investigations. Only after the launch of the single market program did DG Competition's "trustbusters" go on the offensive under the energetic leadership of successive competition commissioners.

Nevertheless, it would be misleading to imagine Commission officials conducting dramatic dawn raids. Unannounced on-site inspections take place during normal working hours and are the exception, not the rule. However, the unexpected arrival of Commission officials usually yields otherwise unobtainable evidence of wrongdoing. In 1980, the Court of Justice upheld the Commission's power to order and carry out investigations without warning companies in advance; since then it has upheld the Commission's right, once inside a company, to carry out an active examination of its files and records without hindrance or restriction.

Until a new regulation came into effect in May 2004 and did away with compulsory notification of restrictive agreements, new cases under Articles

81 and 82 averaged about 500 a year. Approximately 70 percent were notifications by undertakings seeking approval of a practice subject to Commission review, about 20 percent were complaints, and the remainder were cases in which the Commission acted on its own initiative. The Commission resolved most of these cases informally, without launching formal procedures or adopting a formal decision.

If the Commission decides to take formal action, it sends the firm in question a detailed statement of objections. Firms are entitled to respond in writing and to present their case (including witnesses) at a hearing. Not least because of the political sensitivity of some cases and the possibility that firms will appeal to the Court, the Commission deliberates carefully before reaching a decision. If it concludes that there is an infringement, the Commission may impose a fine—not exceeding 10 percent of the firm's total turnover. Substantial though that amount seems—the Commission routinely imposes fines of tens of millions of euros—it is often insufficient to deter large firms from conducting other anticompetitive practices. As a former competition commissioner remarked, "Some firms seem to regard [Commission] fines as just another overhead."[21]

The Tetra Pak case is a good example of Commission action against abuse of a dominant position. Tetra Pak, a Swedish company based in Switzerland, is the largest supplier of cartons for milk and fruit juices. In some cases the company enjoyed a virtual monopoly (95 percent of the market) for machinery and for packaging of "long-life" liquids. A lengthy Commission investigation, based on a competitor's complaint, revealed that Tetra Pak's marketing policy, customer contracts policy, and pricing policy had deliberately infringed Article 82. The Commission ordered Tetra Pak to end its anticompetitive behavior and imposed a fine of €75 million.[22]

The Microsoft case is perhaps the most famous antitrust case prosecuted by the Commission. After an exhaustive investigation, the Commission found Microsoft guilty in 2004 of anticompetitive behavior because it refused to supply interoperability information and incorporated a software product, Windows Media Player, into its operating system. In addition to demanding that Microsoft remove Windows Media Player from the version of its operating system sold in Europe, the Commission fined Microsoft €497 million, the largest fine ever imposed against an individual company.

The new antitrust regulation, approved by the Council in November 2002, came into effect in May 2004, at the time of EU enlargement. The new regulation simplified the enforcement of the treaty's antitrust rules. In a major departure from past practice, firms no longer have to notify the Commission of restrictive agreements (the notification requirement no longer ensured effective surveillance and had became an unnecessary burden on firms and on the Commission, which was spending too much time simply processing notifications). Instead, the Commission will prosecute possible infringements on the basis of complaints and own-initiative investigations. The new regulation also provided for joint enforcement of the rules governing restrictive practices by the Commission, national competition authorities, and national courts. The Commission and the national enforcement bodies—the so-called European Competition Network—work closely together in order to ensure consistent application of the rules.

Mergers

An extensive body of EC case law extended the scope of Article 82 to include structural changes brought about by mergers and acquisitions, which were not specifically mentioned in the Rome Treaty. Accordingly, a firm was judged to have contravened Article 82 if it created or strengthened a dominant position by means of a takeover or merger. Yet the EC's limited merger control was reactive (it applied only to cases where a dominant market position had already been established). Although merger-control reform had been on the EC's agenda since 1973, little progress was made until a plethora of mergers and acquisitions took place in the mid-1980s at the outset of the single market program.

The number, size, and speed of 1992-induced mergers gave the Commission an opportunity to press national governments to cede more regulatory authority to Brussels. Member states appreciated the threat that uncontrolled EC-wide mergers posed to the emerging single market and the advantage for businesses of dealing with a single European competition authority rather than several national ones. Nevertheless, member states disagreed on the criteria for Commission vetting and approval, with Germany and Britain—the countries with the strongest national competition authorities—putting up the strongest resistance. As a result, it was not until December 1989 that the Council adopted a regulation providing for the prior authorization of mergers, thus enabling the Commission to control the buildup of dominant firms.[23] The 1989 merger regulation constituted a cornerstone of the EU's competition policy and single market program.

Based on a number of key principles and provisos, the regulation made a clear distinction between mergers with an EU dimension, where the Commission had the power to intervene, and those that mainly affected a particular member state. An EU dimension existed when all of the following were true:

- The firms involved had an aggregate worldwide turnover of more than €5 billion.
- At least two of the firms involved had an aggregate EU-wide turnover of more than €250 million each.
- At least one of the firms involved had less than two-thirds of its aggregate EU-wide turnover within one particular member state (this was the requirement of transnationality).

For mergers coming under the Commission's scrutiny the crucial test was that of dominant position, taking into account such factors as the structure of the markets concerned, actual or potential competition, the market position of the firms involved, the opportunities open to third parties, barriers to entry, the interests of consumers, and technical and economic progress. The regulation also included compulsory prior notification by the firms concerned and a strict timetable for Commission decisionmaking. The Commission established a merger task force to implement the new regulation, which came into force in September 1990.

The number of mergers above the threshold for notification to the Commission dropped in the early 1990s following the initial single market boom but picked up rapidly in the late 1990s due to the approach of monetary union. On a single day in 1997, plans were announced for six mergers or acquisitions among major European companies involving business worth more than €110 billion.[24] Most of the mergers dealt with by the Commission are in particularly dynamic business sectors such as telecommunications, financial services, pharmaceuticals, and the media.

Of the approximately 140 notifications that it receives annually, the Commission usually clears the vast majority within a month. Only a handful go to a full-scale, four-month, second-stage investigation. If the Commission considers that a proposed merger is incompatible with the single market, it may insist on the merging companies offering "remedies," such as the sale of some production facilities or other assets. Otherwise, the Commission can block the merger. Companies that ignore the Commission's ruling can be fined up to 10 percent of their turnover (subject to appeal to the Court).

A proposed joint venture known as MSG Media Service, between Bertelsmann, the Kirch Group, and Deutsche Telekom, was one of the first deals blocked by the Commission (in November 1994) under the merger regulation. According to the Commission, the venture would have led to the creation or strengthening of a dominant position in three markets, including those for pay-TV and cable networks.[25] The Commission blocked another deal involving Bertelsmann and Kirch in 1998—a planned German digital pay-TV venture—when Bertelsmann rejected a last-minute compromise proposed by DG Competition.[26] Bertelsmann's refusal to make more concessions allowed the Commission to claim that its decision to block the deal was unanimous, whereas the Commission was divided on the issue, not least because of intensive lobbying from the media giants involved and from German politicians.

The Swiss food group Nestlé's takeover of Perrier, France's largest mineral water supplier, is an early example of Commission authorization of a major acquisition subject to remedies. The merger task force challenged the deal on the grounds that it would give two companies, Nestlé and BSN, a duopoly of the lucrative French mineral-water market. After four months of hard bargaining the Commission approved the merger in July 1992 when Nestlé agreed to give up control of about 20 percent of the French market.[27] Although the deal left Nestlé and BSN with more than 65 percent of the mineral-water market, it set a precedent by allowing the Commission to challenge duopolies as well as monopolies. More recently, the Commission allowed Vodafone AirTouch, a British telecommunications firm, to take over Mannesmann, a German one, on condition that Vodafone AirTouch agreed to sell a Mannesmann subsidiary.

From the outset, the Commission worked with representatives of industry, the legal profession, and national competition authorities to ensure that the merger regulation worked well. Firms seemed pleased to deal with a single EU-level procedure instead of having to master a number of procedures at the national level. Most companies complied fully with the notification requirement. Indeed, many firms complained about the high level of the thresholds triggering notification, as those whose mergers and acquisitions fell below those thresholds had to deal with a number of national authorities rather than the Commission's "one-stop shop." In an effort to increase transparency and improve efficiency, in December 1994 the Commission introduced a revised implementing regulation and other administrative modifications. It was not until February 1996 that the Commission suggested, in the face of considerable member state opposition, that the thresholds be lowered.

Member states agreed in May 1997 to a change in the merger regulation, but not involving a general reduction of the notification thresholds, as requested by the Commission. Too many national competition authorities, especially those in Britain and Germany, were jealous of the Commission's control over big competition cases. Nevertheless, the Council agreed to increase the Commission's role by giving it jurisdiction over mergers falling short of the turnover thresholds that required multiple notifications to national competition authorities (subject to new thresholds for those cases). The Council's intent was to obviate the need for companies in certain merger cases to notify and await approval from national authorities in several member states.

A more far-reaching change came in January 2004 when the Council decided on a new merger regulation. Like the new regulation on antitrust enforcement, the new merger regulation came into effect in May 2004, at the time of EU enlargement. The reform specified that "a concentration [that] would significantly impede effective competition in the common market or in a substantial part of it, in particular [but not exclusively] as a result of the creation or strengthening of a dominant position, shall be declared incompatible with the common market." The Commission could therefore intervene against all anticompetitive mergers, not just those that met the old "dominance test." The reform promised greater transparency and efficiency in the conduct of merger investigations, including more interaction among regulators and businesses, giving firms an opportunity to respond to the Commission's concerns before a possible adverse ruling. The reform was also a response to the fact that the ECJ overturned three important Commission merger rulings in 2002.

Subsidies and State-Sponsored Bodies

Control of state aid such as subsidies, tax breaks, and public investments on nonmarket conditions is an even more politically sensitive subject than merger policy. Although member states agreed in the Rome Treaty (Article 87 TEC) that state aid should be prohibited in most circumstances, in practice they have allowed themselves broad latitude under the exceptions included in the treaty—notably for aid to poorer regions—especially during economic recession and when facing political and social fallout from the precipitous decline of industries. Nor have they always informed the Commission in advance of plans to grant or alter aid. The mixed character of the European economy, where government ownership of industry is still considered an acceptable instrument of economic development, means that the precise level of state support is often difficult to determine.

State Aid. Like the lack of an EC-level merger policy, state aid was a chronic problem that became a major issue in the mid-1980s with the launch of the single market program. Article 88 TEC authorized the Commission, in cooperation with member states, to monitor state aid closely. Article 89 allowed the Council, acting by a qualified majority on a proposal from the Commission, to adopt appropriate regulations to prohibit market-distorting public assistance. A weak Commission and a deep recession combined in the 1970s virtually to end EC-level efforts to control state aid. With EC solidarity almost nonexistent and governments vying with each other to prop up infirm industries, state aid was rampant. From 1981 to 1986 member states reported between 92 and 200 cases of state aid each year; the EC acted against less than 10 percent.[28]

A potentially ruinous increase in state aid in the early 1980s, along with national rivalry in the provision of public support, strengthened the Commission's hand. In 1983 the Commission sent a communication to member state governments announcing that it would require them to refund any aid granted without prior notification to the Commission or a prior ruling by the Commission on the aid's compatibility with Article 87. The onset of the single market program further boosted the Commission's position.

Strict control of state aid became as vital as the vigorous application of antitrust law for the success of the single market. By subsidizing companies in their own countries, national governments distorted competition throughout the EC and put nonsubsidized companies at an obvious disadvantage. The Commission began a comprehensive review of state-aid policy with a view to ascertaining the real level of aid being granted, taking strong measures against the most anticompetitive and wasteful subsidies and trying to roll back the general level of support. Based on case law, a more favorable political climate, and a number of specific actions, the Commission began to make an impression.

The Commission also launched a procedure to tackle the problem of aid being granted without prior notification to the Commission. It called for member states to supply full details of the alleged aid within thirty days, sooner in urgent cases. If the member state failed to reply or gave an unsatisfactory response, the Commission would make a provisional decision requiring the state to suspend application of the aid within fifteen days and would initiate proceedings under Article 88.2 to make the member state provide the necessary data. If the member state still refused to comply, the Commission could adopt a final decision of incompatibility and require repayment of the amount of state aid allocated. Should the member state ignore the Commission's decision, the Commission would refer the matter to the Court.[29]

Despite the Commission's apparent feistiness, state aid remained ubiquitous in the EU until recently, amounting to many billions of euros annually in the late 1990s. The four biggest member states—Germany, France, Italy, and Britain—accounted for a growing share of state aid, most of which therefore went to the EU's better-off regions. The Commission received approximately 600 notifications annually of new aid schemes or amendments to existing aid schemes and registered approximately 100 cases annually of unnotified schemes. Yet the Commission raised no objection to the vast majority of these, either because difficult economic circumstances appeared to warrant government assistance to firms in need of restructuring, for example in order to cope with globalization, or because the assistance contributed to EU objectives in other areas such as social, regional, or environmental policy. Of the cases it pursued, the Commission rarely made a negative decision, although it occasionally attached conditions to approvals.

A well-publicized and widely criticized state-aid case that the Commission approved conditionally involved the French government's proposed injection of €3.5 billion of new capital into the state-owned airline Air France. The government notified the Commission in March 1994 that it intended to make the investment as part of a restructuring plan to restore the ailing airline to financial health by the end of 1996. Two months later the Commission began an inquiry to assess the plan's feasibility and compatibility with the single market. In September 1995 the Commission approved the plan but attached conditions to ensure that it did not distort competition while aiding the airline's recovery. The Commission also insisted that this was the last state aid payable to Air France. Other airlines understandably attacked the Commission's decision. Six of them, led by the privatized and highly successful British Airways, brought a successful case against the Commission in the Court (although it was then too late to make Air France give the money back).

The Commission's questionable record of curbing state aid masks the undoubted value of having a state-aid watchdog at the European level. Without the Commission's vigilance, however weak, the problem of national subsidies would be far worse than it is. Intellectually, governments accept that subsidies are often expensive, wasteful, and generally unavailing, but politically they find it difficult to kick the habit. Ironically, it is precisely as a political tool that the Commission's state-aid authority can prove most useful to governments. Once again the case of Air France provides a good example. In June 1998 Air France pilots went on strike to protest government efforts to cut their salaries in order to maintain the airline's renewed profitability. Instead of giving in to the strikers' demands—as French governments usually do—the government held firm and conveniently cited the Commission's "one time/last time" approval of the 1994 aid package as evidence that it could not bail out the airline again. Realizing that they were running Air France into the ground and that the government would not pick up the pieces, the pilots abandoned their strike and went back to work.

Aware of the incompatibility of state aid with its commitment to boost economic growth under the Lisbon strategy, the European Council promised at its summits in Stockholm (March 2001) and Barcelona (March 2002) to reduce overall aid levels and to better target the aid that it provides. The Commission noted a downward trend thereafter in state aid, and also scored some significant successes, such as the removal of state guarantee from German regional banks, thereby allowing other institutions to compete fairly with them. As in other areas of competition policy, the Commission has begun to pay more attention to state aid that has a significant economic impact throughout the single market, for instance by focusing on aid to sectors producing tradable goods and services. The Commission especially opposes the granting of restructuring aid to large companies and is redoubling its efforts to recover aid illegally granted.

Regulated Industries. European governments have traditionally sheltered certain industries from competition because of those industries' fundamental economic importance. In particular, telecommunications, energy (electricity and natural gas), banking, insurance, and transport have usually been highly regulated and in many cases were wholly or partly government owned. In close association with the single market program, the Commission began in the early 1990s to apply competition law to liberalize those sectors, often in the teeth of fierce member state opposition.

Article 86 TEC provides for the full application of treaty rules, including those on competition and free movement of goods and services, to companies owned by or in a special relationship with member states—except where the application of such rules would prevent the companies from carrying out their public service obligations. The Commission applies Article 86 by adopting appropriate directives or decisions without Council approval. The Court has upheld the Commission's right to do so, spelling out in a number of important cases the extent to which member states may grant statutory monopolies or special rights. As a result, there is much less uncertainty now than in the pre–single market period about the proper application of Article 86.

The Politics of Competition Policy

As is obvious from many of the cases already mentioned, competition policy is an extremely sensitive subject for the Commission, which must balance concern for preventing market distortion with the need to avoid overreaching its own political (as distinct from legal) authority with member states. Although striving for integrity, the Commission cannot divorce from politics the process of implementing antitrust law, merger policy, control of state aid, and liberalization of regulated industries. Decisions are taken by the full college of commissioners, which must consider such things as political timing and the need to maintain the appearance of national and regional impartiality. Member states are quick to accuse the Commission of favoritism. Inevitably, commissioners come under intense pressure from their governments and from firms in their countries during contentious competition policy cases.

Arguably the competition policy commissioner is the most powerful person in the Commission. In order to be effective, however, he or she must be able to stand up to powerful business interests and national governments, especially the French government, which seems wedded to supporting national champions and other anticompetitive practices. When talking about France, the *Financial Times* noted in July 2004, the competition commissioner "sounds like a disappointed teacher speaking about a bright but unruly pupil."[30]

Since the original merger regulation entered into force in 1990, the Commission has blocked on average only one merger a year. Some critics contend that this low rejection rate is due to the Commission's susceptibility to political pressure. Whether or not the Commission is politically vulnerable, controversial mergers generate an intense amount of lobbying. The Commission's first-ever rejection of a merger under the new regime—the 1991 bid by France's Aerospatiale and Italy's Aliena to take over Canadian aircraft manufacturer De Havilland—split the Commission, with one side (including the president, Jacques Delors) arguing that the merger would boost European competitiveness by giving manufacturers a footing in the North American marketplace and the other side, led by the competition policy commissioner, claiming that the merger would give Aerospatiale and Aliena a near monopoly in the EU marketplace for turboprop commuter aircraft. Arguments inside the Commission mirrored contending national positions, with the French and Italian governments lobbying hard in favor of the merger and other more market-oriented member states, which did not have a stake in the case, urging a strict interpretation of the merger regulation.

Despite the Commission's decision in the De Havilland case and a small number of other high-profile cases, critics of its alleged weakness and susceptibility to business and national pressures cite the high merger approval rate as a reason to give responsibility for competition policy to a separate authority. A number of observers suggested before the 1996–1997 intergovernmental conference on treaty reform that an independent EU competition authority, along the lines of Germany's Bundeskartellamt (federal competition office), should be established. Claus-Dieter Ehlermann, the formidable former head of DG Competition, accepted the idea in principle but argued that it should not be implemented until the EU's political development made it more likely that such an office could be fully independent, or at least manifestly more independent than DG Competition appeared to be. In the event, the possibility of changing the Commission's responsibility for competition policy was not pursued at the 1996–1997 or any subsequent intergovernmental conference.

Those who criticize the Commission for being too vigorous in its application of competition policy rules have been unrelenting in their attacks, especially during Commissioner Monti's tenure (1999–2004). The French and German governments are among the Commission's harshest critics. France and the Commission became locked in a bitter political battle over government efforts to bail out Alstom, a French engineering group. In what looked like a French victory, the French government eventually won the Commission's approval. The German government is highly partial to providing state aid, against which the Commission has redoubled its efforts. Although the rigorous enforcement of competition policy is a logical plank of the Lisbon strategy, the French, German, and other governments rarely emphasize it. Monti's conviction that in order "to be able to keep some parts of its social model, [the EU] simply has to become more and more similar to the US in its own domestic economic structure . . . more liberal, more efficient, more productive, more competitive," finds little sympathy in Paris or Berlin.[31]

The International Dimension

EU competition rules have an important dimension beyond the EU itself, as they affect the activities of all companies operating in or having an impact on the EU market (subject to business turnover thresholds), regardless of where those firms are based. This situation can cause considerable friction in the EU's external relations, especially with the United States. Moreover, the EU includes competition policy provisions in many of its external relations agreements and is actively pushing for the inclusion of a multilateral agreement on competition in the WTO. In the interim, the Commission is a strong supporter of the informal International Competition Network, a body that sets guiding principles and recommended practices for the control of multijurisdictional mergers.

U.S.-EU friction over competition policy is a staple of the transatlantic relationship, with the U.S. government and U.S. companies highly critical of what they see as an EU competition policy that favors European companies, often at the expense of their U.S. rivals. Although EU competition law is based on U.S. practices and principles, American companies have a dim view of its partiality. As long ago as the mid-1980s, a protracted Commission investigation of IBM fueled "the prevalent American conception . . . that the EC's antitrust policy . . . invariably protects Community industries which are important for the achievement of social and economic goals and . . . promotes anti-competitive business agreements."[32]

American concerns about the partiality of EU competition policy came to the fore in mid-1997 when the Commission threatened to block a merger between Boeing and McDonnell Douglas despite the U.S. Federal Trade Commission's unconditional approval of it. The Commission objected to the deal on the grounds that the new firm would dominate the European market for large airliners, that Boeing's civil business might enjoy defense spillovers, and that Boeing had exclusive twenty-year contracts with a number of U.S. airlines. Boeing took steps to allay the Commission's first two concerns but argued that the third concern was beyond the scope of the merger and was not an issue for the U.S. airlines involved in the contracts. Boeing pointed out that a challenge to its exclusive contracts was in the interests only of its archival, Airbus.

"Airbus" is a dirty word in American aviation and government circles, where it is synonymous with EU protectionism and subsidization. The involvement of Airbus in the dispute, however indirectly, raised the political stakes. Despite intense pressure from Washington, including threats of a trade war, the Commission obstinately refused to approve the deal unless Boeing made extra concessions. Boeing did so at the last moment, agreeing not to sign any new exclusive contracts for ten years and not to enforce the deals it had signed. This concession paved the way for Commission approval of the merger, but at a cost of casting the Commission once again as an unswerving supporter of Airbus and endangering cooperation between the United States and the EU in competition policy.

More recently the Commission's veto of General Electric's $45 billion bid for Honeywell also caused consternation in the United States, whose competition authorities had already approved the deal. Clearly, the Commission's concerns about the consequences of the proposed deal for the aerospace industry reflected different assumptions on both sides of the Atlantic about the impact of mergers on markets and consumers.

American antitrust authorities also vet mergers involving EU companies. Because of their mutual interest in megamergers, the Commission and its U.S. counterpart concluded an agreement in 1991 to cooperate on competition cases (the Court of Justice threw out the agreement in 1994 because the Commission had exceeded its external relations competence; the agreement finally came into effect in 1995 when the Commission and the Council enacted the necessary legislation). Despite some spectacular cases, such as those already mentioned, the U.S.-EU competition accord has operated reasonably well.

Indeed, in February 2004 competition commissioner Monti described cooperation on competition policy as "one of the most important (and perhaps least heralded) success stories in EU-U.S. relations in recent years" and praised the Commission's "quiet and business-like cooperation" with its U.S. counterpart agencies (the Department of Justice and the Federal Trade Commission).[33] The proposed merger between Air France and KLM Royal Dutch Airlines, a deal that would create Europe's largest airline, is a good example of such quiet cooperation. Neither the Commission nor the Department of Justice challenged the merger once the airlines offered to provide substantial remedies.

◼ Enterprise and Industry

Traditional industrial policy is the antithesis of competition policy. Both aim to encourage competitiveness, but in very different ways. Whereas competition policy curbs private practices and public subsidies intended to assist a particular enterprise or sector, industrial policy facilitates state intervention to underwrite specific enterprises or sectors whose survival or success the government deems essential for socioeconomic or strategic reasons. The instruments of industrial policy include "soft" loans, grants, tax concessions, guaranteed procurement contracts, export assistance, and trade barriers. Industrial policy is driven by nationalism rather than ideology, although left-wing governments are often zealous proponents of government intervention in industrial affairs. France in the 1960s is generally cited as the epitome of dirigisme, or economic interventionism (at the time France had right-wing governments).[34] Even if they deliberately eschew direct intervention, governments of all political persuasions have a major impact on industrial planning and production. Public contracts and defense-related procurement are obvious ways in which governments intentionally or unintentionally assist national manufacturers.

Industrial Policy

When it came into being in 1958, the EC inherited a strong interventionist ethos. Indeed, the CAP is a classic example of an intrusive industrial policy. But member states agreed to share responsibility for agriculture for peculiar political reasons and because the agricultural sector was in serious social and economic decline. By contrast, member states retained as much power as possible over other sectors, including the right to nurture "national champions"—national industries that could compete internationally. The Rome Treaty therefore included few provisions for an interventionist, EU-level industrial policy.

Nevertheless, the treaty embodied an industrial policy in the broader sense of mapping out a strategy for industrial development. The projected single market and related competition policy were intended to create an economic framework conducive to industrial growth. In the recessionary 1970s, however, governments pulled back from market integration and liberalization and resorted instead to restrictive practices to protect national champions. National governments allowed the EC to intervene directly to help ailing industries in sectors suffering serious economic trouble: steel, shipbuilding, and textiles. Especially in the early 1980s, the EC provided various kinds of assistance to help sunset industries restructure and survive.[35]

Whereas steel, textiles, and shipbuilding were old, declining industries, the high-technology sector (including computers, consumer electronics, and telecommunications) was new—yet it was also in trouble. *Le Défi Américain* (The American Challenge), the title of a popular book by Jean-Jacques Servan-Schreiber, seemed to sum up the problem. Throughout the 1960s, Europeans had fretted about a supposed "technology gap" between themselves and the United States. *Le Défi Américain* confirmed their fears by portraying the United States as a powerful predator encroaching on Europe's weak and fragmented market in the increasingly lucrative and strategically important high-technology sector.[36] Compared to American industry's enterprise, scale, and international ambition, European firms seemed severely handicapped.

For the next decade European governments responded to the U.S. challenge largely by supporting national champions—huge firms that enjoyed a virtual monopoly in their countries' sizable public-sector markets. France, with a well-deserved reputation for intervention, was not the only culprit. Despite its supposed inclination toward market liberalism, Germany also promoted national champions, as did Britain under Labour leadership for much of the 1970s. Yet by the early 1980s the transatlantic technology gap had widened, and a new chasm was opening between Western Europe and Japan. Poor economic performance during the previous decade exacerbated Europe's predicament. With little economic growth, industries had no incentive to invest heavily in research and development. Nor did the limited and relatively small size of their domestic markets encourage new initiatives.

At the same time European companies undertook a number of collaborative ventures, notably in aircraft manufacturing and marketing. Concorde, the joint Anglo-French effort to produce a supersonic passenger plane, is the most obvious and expensive example. In the early 1960s France and Britain also began to collaborate on Airbus, a project to produce short- to medium-range wide-bodied passenger aircraft in direct competition with Boeing. Germany joined the consortium in 1966, and Britain departed in 1968. Despite its success in the 1980s and 1990s, Airbus began badly, with numerous cost and time overruns. Concorde was already in service by the late 1960s, but the first Airbus still remained on the drawing board. Only in the mid-1970s, when Airbus broadened its base to include Dutch and Spanish participation and received its first non-European orders, did the venture really take off.

The EC did not participate in those collaborative projects, although in 1967 the Commission established a directorate-general for industrial affairs to encourage cross-border cooperation. The birth of the new directorate-general reflected a growing awareness of the need to concentrate resources and promote intra-EC industrial alliances. Early EC efforts to increase European competitiveness were not confined to the member states, however. In 1971 the Community joined with neighboring Western European countries to launch European Cooperation in the Field of Scientific and Technical Research (COST), an institutional framework and source of funds for joint research projects in such areas as informatics and telecommunications.

Notwithstanding such efforts, by the end of the 1970s Europe's high-technology sector seemed as badly off as before. National governments disputed the wisdom and practicability of cross-border industrial cooperation. Within the Commission, DG Competition kept a close eye on DG Industry's interventionist proclivities. Yet the EC's acute industrial difficulties, the soaring cost of research and development, the increasing importance of new technologies—especially in microelectronics and semiconductors—and the continuing U.S. and Japanese threats convinced many European manufacturers, politicians, and government officials that closer collaboration under the EC's auspices, and EC rather than national intervention, held the key to European industry's survival and success. The notion of national champions became increasingly outmoded.

Etienne Davignon, Commission vice president with responsibility for industrial affairs from 1981 to 1985, took the lead in promoting EC-wide technological collaboration. By cultivating the CEOs of major European manufacturers in the high-technology sector, Davignon developed powerful industrial support for cross-border collaboration. European industrialists were especially receptive to Davignon's ideas because of renewed economic recession and the evident failure of the national-champion approach. This was the background for the launch of the EC's first research and development (R&D) programs.

Despite the limited impact of these programs on European industrial competitiveness, Commission-industry collaboration fostered awareness on both sides of the EC's potential for reviving Europe economically. The best approach seemed to be to end the fragmentation of Europe's own market by breaking down the plethora of nontariff barriers that impeded intra-EC business and trade. Big business in Europe encouraged the Commission to promote liberalization, harmonization, and standardization. Far from interpreting industrial policy in an interventionist light, big business saw it in broader terms as a way to help level the playing field for manufacturers throughout the EC. Thus, Davignon's endeavors to promote industrial competitiveness contributed to a growing momentum in the early 1980s for completion of the single market.

Indeed, by giving European industry "a political program on which it could finally base concrete action plans for restructuring operations, for increasing economies of scale, and for improving the efficient use of vital resources,"[37] completion of the single market became an integral part of the EC's industrial strategy. Martin Bangemann, the commissioner with responsibility for industrial affairs, argued that the competitive discipline of the single market would be the best possible medicine for European manufacturers.[38] In the sense that it opened up enormous opportunities for European industry, not least by forcing many national champions to restructure radically, the single market program became the most important instrument of EC industrial policy in the late 1980s.

The single market program represented a triumph for economic liberalism and a setback for state interventionism. The aggressive application of competition policy reinforced the latter point. As the Commission observed after the De Havilland case, "a rigorous competition policy is an essential element in the Community's industrial policy. Maintaining effective competition is one of the key factors in ensuring that Community industry is successful."[39]

While squashing support for national champions, the Commission's aggressive pursuit of competition policy as a means of opening up the marketplace did not result in the emergence of Eurochampions (European firms that could compete and win globally). The problem seemed especially acute in the electronics sector, which encountered serious difficulties in the early 1990s despite market liberalization and the allocation of considerable amounts of R&D funding by the EC. Lobbying by European electronics companies for the Commission to dispense old-fashioned industrial assistance began to grow, not least because the French government owned two such firms (Bull and Thomson).

In response to pressure from the French and other protectionists, and in an effort to lay the ground rules for a post–single market industrial strategy, the Commission produced a key discussion document on competitiveness in November 1990. Following a contentious internal debate that split the college along national and ideological lines, the Commission declined to offer any industrial policy measures in the traditional, interventionist, sense of the term. Instead, in a decisive reiteration of prevailing economic orthodoxy, it issued guidelines rejecting sectoral policies as ineffective and stressing that the EC's role should be to maintain a competitive environment. In elaborating this position, the guidelines accomplished two important Commission objectives: establishing a coherent philosophical framework to justify the policies the Commission was already pursuing in the realm of market integration and dashing expectations that the EC would act to support and protect a given sector, no matter how strategic.[40]

In the Commission's analysis, the role of government (hence that of the EC, with due regard for subsidiarity) should be limited to providing, first, a competitive business climate and, second, "catalysts to encourage firms to adjust rapidly to changing circumstances." The need for a competitive environment as an industrial policy objective implied vigorous competition policy—including strict control of state aid—in addition to macroeconomic stability. Moreover, it required a relatively open trade policy to allow European firms to become seasoned international competitors.

The Commission reiterated the centrality of the single market as the chief catalyst for higher growth and greater industrial competitiveness. It noted the importance of common standards, mutual recognition, and open procurement, for rapid structural adjustment and better economies of scale. On the R&D side, the paper suggested that the EC should aim not only to develop but also to diffuse generic technologies—encouraging greater use of information technology, an area in which Europeans lagged behind both as producers and as consumers.

Emphasizing the importance of a competitive business climate in which firms make key decisions, the Commission stressed that EC assistance would be "horizontal" rather than industry-specific and would consist largely of policing the marketplace to guard against protectionism and private market power. The Commission also reiterated the current conception of industrial policy as a combination of environmental, social, regional, and competition policies contributing to a level playing field for European manufacturers as well as an aggressive trade policy to ensure that the international economic environment was as fair as possible.

The European electronics industry, battered by foreign competition and holding on to less than half of its own domestic market, provided the first testing ground for the Commission's noninterventionist stance. After a spirited tussle between the market-oriented DG Competition and the largely French-influenced (and therefore protectionist) DG Technology, the Commission produced a paper that blamed the feeble state of Europe's electronics industry on market fragmentation and high capital costs.[41] It also advocated the development of the trans-European networks, better training, more market-oriented research and development at the European level, and the pursuit of global trade liberalization as suitable approaches to resolving the industry's problems. Predictably, this report infuriated the French and many in the private sector who wanted outright financial assistance and protection.

The Commission's position against demands for a more interventionist approach was strengthened by a coalition of member states with no national champions to protect. Transcending north-south differences, Britain, Ireland, Spain, and Portugal feared that protection of European industry would hamper foreign investment in their countries, harm consumers, and divert scarce EU resources to giant firms in France, Germany, and the Benelux countries. In the event, it was far from clear where new sectoral subsidies could come from, in either EU or member state budgets. France suggested redeploying existing EU funds, to which an unsympathetic commissioner countered that the EC should start with the CAP. In a clear victory for the free marketeers, in November 1991 the Council adopted a resolution along the lines of the Commission's paper.[42]

Subsequent Commission papers met a much less stormy reception. Perhaps all sides had learned the pitfalls of trying to push an overtly interventionist policy in the EU context. The debate over electronics clearly demonstrated that conflicting member state interests made it impossible to support sectoral initiatives at the EU level, to say nothing of the substantial new funding that such policies would require. Despite their panic at the thought of fully opening markets to the Japanese in 1999 (the long grace period was itself a concession to the need for structural adjustment among overprotected national champions), European auto producers were unable to wring much more from the Commission than some modest worker-training proposals for firms in poorer regions. The Commission applied the same principles to other sectors with increasing confidence and decreasing backlash from firms and member states.

Reflecting the ongoing debate on industrial policy, the Maastricht Treaty contained a new section on the subject. Its language was vague, calling on the EU and its member states "to ensure that the conditions needed to make Community industry competitive are met in a system of open and competitive markets." In order to achieve the objectives of structural change, a favorable business environment, and better exploitation of innovation and research, the treaty stipulated that the Council "may adopt specific measures in support of action taken by member states." However, the Council could act only unanimously, effectively denying the EU more authority in the area of industrial policy.

Later Commission initiatives, ranging from its White Paper on competitiveness, growth, and employment (1993) to a communication titled "Industrial Competitiveness Policy for the European Union" (1994), suggested that the debate about industrial policy in the EU had gone well beyond the old interventionist arguments. Despite renewed recession in the late 1990s, a widening trade deficit with Japan, and growing economic nationalism on both sides of the Atlantic, ardent interventionists mostly failed to make their voices heard. The difficulty of designing a sectoral policy that could give real benefits to the affected sector without distorting competition, undermining cohesion, and drawing fire from member states whose industries would be disadvantaged was the most compelling reason for maintaining the horizontal approach. By the end of the 1990s there seemed to be a general consensus in the Commission and among member states—including France—that a range of liberalizing measures aimed at boosting growth, prosperity, and jobs was the best industrial policy. Symbolizing that consensus, DG Industry changed its name to DG Enterprise.

Enterprise Policy

Rather than intervening to support certain industries or sectors, EU enterprise policy seeks to foster innovation, entrepreneurship, and competitiveness in manufacturing and services by providing a business-friendly climate and supportive regulatory environment. The health of European industry depends on a large number of factors, including its ability to innovate and adapt to the challenges of global competition. Enterprise policy analyzes and monitors developments in a wide range of sectors, from the old economy (such as shipbuilding and textiles) to the new (such as aerospace and biotechnology). Under the auspices of enterprise policy, the Commission produces a steady stream of industry- and sector-specific studies, reports, and recommendations.

Enterprise policy is not a stand-alone area of EU activity but overlaps closely with other policy areas, such as the single market and competition policy. In certain sectors, such as chemicals and pharmaceuticals, it intersects with environmental and health policy. Enterprise and innovation are also closely related to research and development policy, especially with regard to the development and application of new technologies. The appropriate policy response varies from sector to sector. Thus, for knowledge-intensive industries, such as biotechnology and life sciences, the emphasis needs to be on research and product regulation, whereas for old-economy industries, global market access is a primary consideration. Europeans are hardly less imaginative or innovative than others, but they appear to be more risk averse when it comes to launching new businesses. Entrepreneurship is certainly lagging in Europe, especially in comparison with the United States. A willingness to take business risks depends on cultural factors, which vary from state to state, as well as on more obvious issues such as prevailing economic circumstances, the availability of capital, and the regulatory framework. The EU is trying to provide a more conducive economic and regulatory environment for entrepreneurship, focusing especially on opportunities for people to launch and sustain new businesses.

The Commission sees small and medium-sized enterprises (SMEs), which provide most of Europe's jobs, as "the backbone of EU enterprise." In a typically extravagant gesture, the European Council approved the "European Charter for Small Enterprises" in June 2000. This calls upon member states and the Commission to take concerted action to support SMEs in a number of key areas, including

- education and training for entrepreneurship
- cheaper and faster start-up
- better legislation and regulation
- improving Internet access
- taxation and financial matters
- making the most of the single market
- improving the technological capacity of small enterprises

The Innovation Relay Center network, which the Commission partially funds and extends beyond the EU, helps SMEs find partners for research and innovation projects. Euro Info Centers, established in the late 1980s to help SMEs enjoy the benefits of the single market program, are dotted throughout the EU (and beyond). They provide technical information and assistance to SMEs that are trying to comprehend and conform with EU rules and regulations covering particular sectors. Such initiatives are popular with SMEs, which make up a diffuse but nonetheless important business and political lobby. The charter helped focus political attention on the plight and potential of SMEs and has produced some tangible, beneficial results. Arguably the EU needs to focus not only on sustaining SMEs but also on growing them into large, globally competitive enterprises.

Nokia, the Finnish mobile telephone company, is one of Europe's largest and most competitive businesses. Europe has an extremely high density of mobile telephone ownership (Europeans seem constantly to be either talking on cell phones or text messaging—sometimes doing both at the same time). The EU has facilitated the explosion of cell phone use, as well as other developments in information technology, through the single market program and the aggressive implementation of competition policy rules. The old, publicly owned telephone monopolies are gone (although in many cases the former monopolies have retained a dominant position), customers have a wide choice of suppliers and services, and prices have tumbled. The convergence of communications and broadcasting technology as a result of digitization prompted the EU to redraw the regulatory boundaries to cover all electronic communications networks and services in a new directive that came into effect in July 2003.

The Commission is keen to spread the benefits of what it calls the information society throughout the EU and avoid the emergence of a "digital divide" either spatially, socially, or generationally. Internet use in Eastern Europe lags behind that of Western Europe, and Internet use in the EU lags behind that in the United States. But the situation is improving rapidly in both regards. The European Council launched the catchy eEurope initiative in Lisbon in March 2000 as part of the strategy to transform the EU into the most competitive, knowledge-driven economy in the world by 2010. This calls for all businesses and schools in the EU to have broadband Internet access by

2005 and for the provision of broadband access in a number of ways (for example, through third-generation mobile telephony) in order to reduce the dominant position of fixed-line telephone operators.

Resisting a Return to the Past

The Lisbon strategy, with its emphasis on economic liberalization, seemed to sound the death knell of traditional industrial policy and ensure the preeminence of enterprise policy as the best approach to the challenge of Europe's industrial competitiveness. Despite their rhetorical commitment to the Lisbon strategy, however, French and German leaders raised the specter of old-fashioned industrial policy in 2003 and 2004, this time on the basis of joint Franco-German rather than separate national subsidization and support. The French were driven in part by an atavistic attraction to state intervention, the Germans by an inclination to follow the French lead. More particularly, the two countries, among the worst economic performers in the EU, feared the intensification of global competition not only from the United States but also from China and India. They also feared competition closer to home, from the low-wage Central and Eastern European countries poised to join the EU. Echoing similar concerns in the United States, the French and Germans warned of rapid deindustrialization in Western Europe.

Due largely to French and German pressure, the Commission revisited the question of industrial policy, producing a communication on the subject in December 2002. The report made the obvious point that without an internationally competitive industry the EU could not achieve its economic and social goals. The Commission refused to abandon its horizontal approach, while nonetheless taking into account the specific needs of industrial sectors. The Commission followed up with a new communication in April 2004 on industrial policy in an enlarged EU. In this and other communications, the Commission pointed out that there was no evidence of a generalized process of deindustrialization and urged European industry to restructure in the face of global competition in order to survive and ultimately flourish.

Far from being mollified, France and Germany launched a plan in May 2004 "to formulate a joint industrial policy aimed at creating a framework for mergers and joint-ventures between major German and French corporations."[43] The Commission may have nixed the first such effort when it approved the French government's bailout of Alstom, the giant French engineering company. Had it not done so, Siemens of Germany would likely have bought a large part of Alstom's operations, thereby creating a Franco-German champion. The French government's decision to press ahead with the Alstom bailout discomfited Germany, as it signaled France's preference for a national champion (Alstom) rather than a Franco-German champion (an arrangement between Alstom and Siemens).

Characteristically, internal market commissioner Frits Bolkestein castigated the French and German efforts to go back to the future. Writing in the *Financial Times* in June 2004, Bolkestein remarked that, with all the talk in
France and Germany about industrial policy, "I cannot help feeling that I am in
a time warp. I have to pinch myself to make sure that I am not back in the
1960s, 1970s, or 1980s. Or even under the mercantilist regime of Jean Baptiste
Colbert in King Louis XIV's France." In Bolkestein's opinion, "The defenders
of vested interests and cozy corporatist arrangements rarely miss a trick when
it comes to resisting the opening of markets. Warnings of deindustrialization
are just the latest wheeze to try to stave off competition, notably from new
member states, instead of making the most of enlargement's opportunities."[44]

France and Germany also made noises in mid-2004 about the need for a
new, supereconomic portfolio in the Barroso Commission, presumably under
a French or German commissioner, to direct industrial recovery in Europe.
The implication was clear: both countries wanted to revive the old approach
to industrial policy. Barroso, the incoming Commission president, failed to
oblige, although he gave Günter Verheugen, Germany's commissioner, the enterprise and industry portfolio. Barroso added "industry" to the name of the
portfolio "to reflect the renewed importance attached to our industrial heartland."[45] This was a sop to France and Germany.

The Franco-German effort to go back to the future, and the furious reaction
of other member states and of individual commissioners, demonstrate the sensitivity surrounding industrial policy in the EU. The parlous state of the French
and German economies relative to most others in the EU was a poor advertise-
ment for their preferred approach to industrial rejuvenation. Reflecting the prevailing view among most member states, Erkki Liikanen, commissioner for enterprise and the information society, affirmed that "EU industrial policy will
remain market-driven: there is no question of designing specific policies to give
priority to specific sectors—or worse, companies—at the expense of others."[46]
It was precisely the market-driven approach that the EU's leaders had accepted
when they agreed to the Lisbon strategy in March 2000. "But to listen to recent
statements by French and German politicians," Bolkestein fumed in June 2004,
"you would think the strategy had never existed."[47]

■ Research and Development

Research and development (R&D) programs are almost the only holdovers
from the early days of industrial policy. Yet, because R&D is essential for innovation and economic growth, they fit well into the current conception of enterprise and industry policy. Although most R&D spending should and does
come from the private sector, even ardent free marketeers concede that R&D
is one of the few areas (along with education and infrastructure) in which gov-

ernment intervention is essential. Just as private R&D spending in most industrial sectors is an indicator of corporate confidence, public spending on R&D is an indicator of the government's faith in a country's future economic performance.

EC involvement in R&D originated in the Joint Research Center (JRC), established in Ispra, Italy, in 1958 under the auspices of the Atomic Energy Community. There are now seven institutes within the JRC system, located in five member states (Belgium, the Netherlands, Germany, and Spain as well as Italy), conducting research on subjects such as the environment, nuclear measurement, advanced materials, informatics, and safety technology. Though funded by the EU and accountable to the Commission, the JRC is administered by an independent board.

The Commission established a directorate-general for science, research, and development in 1967 and issued a number of calls for EC-level R&D programs in various industrial sectors during the 1970s. It was only thanks to Davignon in the early 1980s, however, that the Commission took a major step forward. In May 1982 the Commission unveiled a proposal for the European Strategic Program for Research and Development in Information Technology (ESPRIT), which the Council, already being lobbied by Davignon's collaborators in European industry, approved the following June.[48] ESPRIT called for major European manufacturers, smaller firms, universities, and institutes throughout the EC to collaborate on "precompetitive" (basic) research. That distinction helped to reduce friction among the industrial participants and satisfy the concerns of the Commission's competition watchdog. A pilot scheme of thirty-eight projects, funded jointly by the EC and the private sector, got under way in 1983 and constituted "the first step toward the development of a genuine, long-term European industrial policy."[49]

Later in the 1980s the EC launched not only a full-fledged ESPRIT but also related research initiatives with catchy names such as RACE (advanced communications technologies), BRIDGE (biotechnology), FLAIR (agroindustry), and COMETT (education and training for technology). In 1985 the EC became a founding member of EUREKA, a French-led effort to develop European technology as a response to the U.S. Strategic Defense Initiative.[50]

These early R&D initiatives helped develop momentum for completion of the single market program. As well as facilitating the enactment of single market legislation, the Single European Act gave the EC a new and explicit basis for R&D policy. With the aim of "strengthening the scientific and technological base of European industry and [encouraging] it to become more competitive at an international level," the Single European Act stipulated that the Council should unanimously adopt "multiannual framework programs" as the main instrument of R&D policy. These programs would delineate the main scientific and technological objectives of R&D policy and define priorities and would be implemented by a series of specific subprograms, most involving cost sharing between the EC and private industry. The only important change to R&D policy in the Maastricht Treaty concerned decisionmaking: henceforth framework programs would be adopted jointly by the Council and the Parliament using the codecision procedure. A further decisionmaking change in the Amsterdam Treaty dropped the unanimity requirement for the adoption of framework programs by the Council.

Activities under the umbrella of the framework programs range from the work of the Joint Research Center to research undertaken by research centers and universities where the EU covers between 25 percent and 100 percent of the cost. The essential prerequisites for EU funding are that the research be of a precompetitive nature and involve at least two organizations in two different member states. In practice, most projects involve about eight partners, with EU financing amounting to several million euros. In addition to the member states, a number of other countries, including Israel, Norway, and Switzerland, participate fully in the framework programs, to which they contribute financially. Candidate countries for EU accession have limited access to the framework programs, as have southern Mediterranean and some other developing countries.

The EU publishes requests for proposals for research projects four times a year in the *Official Journal.* Independent scientific and technical experts evaluate the proposals and try to ensure (unofficially) that organizations in all member states are involved to some extent in these assessments. The Commission runs a network of "innovative relay centers" (Eurospeak for information offices) throughout the EU to promote academic and business awareness of and involvement in the programs. The relay centers devote a lot of attention to SMEs, which might otherwise feel shut out of the process.

The sixth framework program (FP6), covering the period 2003–2006, sets out seven priorities:

- geonomics and biotechnology for health
- information society technologies
- nanotechnologies, new materials, and production processes
- aeronautics and space
- food quality and safety
- sustainable development, global change, and ecosystems
- citizens and governance

Almost 10 percent of the EU's R&D budget is spent on research on nuclear energy, especially on nuclear fusion (an environmentally friendly but technologically challenging alternative to nuclear fission). The EU is engaged in a bitter political struggle with partner countries in the ITER project over the location of the first nuclear fusion device to generate as much electricity as a normal power plant.

Space technology may be the final frontier of EU R&D. The European Space Agency is not an EU body but includes most EU member states (and a number of nonmember states as well). The EU collaborates with the space agency on projects including communication by satellite, human space flight, and microgravity. The EU has also developed Galileo, its own global positioning system, a project driven as much by envy of the preexisting U.S. system as by legitimate economic and security considerations.

Money—not objectives or priorities—has been the biggest obstacle confronting the EU's R&D ambitions. Member states support R&D policy but want to limit spending on it (as on other EU policy areas). The Commission and Parliament, the other key players in the decisionmaking process, inevitably push for a higher budget than the Council is willing to countenance. Despite previous disagreements over the budget for the framework programs, the Council adopted the sixth framework program in June 2002 with significant changes to the Commission's proposal, to which the Parliament also agreed. The budget for FP6, €17.5 billion, represented 3.9 percent of the EU's overall budget and 5.4 percent of all public (nonmilitary) research spending in Europe.

Research and development spending in the EU is still far lower than in the United States. Moreover, EU spending is only a small part of total EU-wide spending on civilian R&D; hence the need for greater coordination between national- and EU-sponsored R&D programs to ensure consistency and value for money. Despite a call in the Maastricht Treaty and frequent appeals by the Commission for more concerted national-EU action, there is still plenty of room for improvement.

Rapid globalization, the EU's increasing economic openness, and faster technological obsolescence are the greatest challenges facing EU R&D policy. Despite over twenty-five years of EU support for high-technology R&D and despite also having some global leaders in the high-technology sector, the EU continues to lag far behind the United States in biotechnology and information technology. Although R&D policy was never intended as a panacea for Europe's high-technology sector or as a substitute for industrywide restructuring, it seems reasonable to observe that EU-sponsored projects have so far produced little commercially useful technology (perhaps because of the emphasis on precompetitive research).

A key goal of EU policy is to close the gap between research work and its downstream commercial application. The EU has also set a target of 3 percent of GDP for overall R&D expenditure by 2010, which would represent a 50 percent increase over current expenditure. Moreover, the EU wants the private sector, not just governments, to pick up much of the additional expenditure, increasing its share from 56 percent in 2000 to 67 percent in 2010.

In any event, R&D is only one element of an overall strategy to boost EU competitiveness, the most important being consolidation of the single market.

By creating conditions conducive to economic growth, the single market will induce firms to invest more in R&D. As Bolkestein reminded national government ministers, "not a single company will [invest more in R&D] because of some exhortation by ministers and bureaucrats. Or because we've set a 3 percent target in [a] Commission document. Companies will only invest more if they expect the market to reward them. So instead of making calls for more R&D investment, we must create the conditions that will make companies want to invest more in Europe."[51]

◼ Trans-European Networks

It goes without saying that the EU needs to be connected by first-rate transport, energy, and telecommunications networks in order to maximize the potential of the single market and thereby boost economic growth and competitiveness. The quality of the EU's rail and road networks is variable. Some countries spend more money on construction and maintenance than others; some (especially those in Central and Eastern Europe) have a lot of catching up to do. Whereas cohesion policy includes financial assistance for infrastructural projects to the poorer member states, the Trans-European Networks (TENs) is a program to help develop a system of top-quality road, rail, telecommunications, and energy networks throughout the EU.

Member states agreed without much discussion to include a section in the Maastricht Treaty on the establishment of Trans-European Networks in the areas of transport, telecommunications, and energy infrastructures. The purpose of the TENs was to make the most of the single market and to further economic and social cohesion by "promoting the interconnection and the interoperability of national networks as well as access to such networks." In other words, the TENs were intended to complete the EU's patchy infrastructural networks, thereby improving competitiveness, creating jobs, and reinforcing cohesion.

It was one thing for national governments to agree on the desirability of the TENs but quite another for them to agree to fund them. Commission president Jacques Delors, a strong supporter of the TENs, pushed for generous funding. In that regard the TENs were a typical Delorsian product: grandiose, ambitious, and expensive. They were completely out of keeping with the political and economic mood in Europe during and after the Maastricht ratification crisis. Politically, the putative EU was unpopular; economically, recession and financial retrenchment were not conducive to massive public spending.

Undaunted, Delors submitted a paper to the European Council in June 1993 in which he stressed the need to develop transport and telecommunications infrastructures, observing almost casually that "an overall total of ECU 30 billion a year [over a ten-year period] seems to be a realistic minimum target for expenditure in this field."[52] A figure of that magnitude would surely have caught the European Council's attention, although it is possible that few of the national leaders read the paper, and Delors may not have mentioned it in his oral presentation.

What followed during the next three years was a classic example of the difference between the rhetoric of European Council conclusions and the political reality of member state behavior. The European Council invited Delors to prepare a White Paper on a medium-term strategy for competitiveness, growth, and employment. In it Delors emphasized the TENs as an important instrument to promote growth and combat unemployment in the EU.[53] Having discussed the White Paper at their summit in December 1993, EU leaders gave "strong political impetus" to completion of the TENs and set up two high-level groups of representatives: one to explore specific transport projects, the other to examine telecommunications infrastructure and the information society.[54]

Meeting in June 1994, the European Council endorsed the transport group's interim report, including a list of eleven priority projects that, despite their size, seemed economically viable and likely to be completed rapidly. Meeting in December 1994, the European Council endorsed the information group's addition of three more projects, making a total of fourteen transport networks and ten telecommunications networks.

Despite continued rhetorical support for the TENs, it was obvious that the European Council's enthusiasm was waning. Undoubtedly the national leaders wanted to accelerate big road, rail, and telecommunications projects for symbolic as well as substantive reasons, but funding—even on a far more manageable scale than Delors's original estimate—was an insurmountable problem. Contributions from the structural funds, the Cohesion Fund, the European Investment Bank, and the recently established European Investment Fund could cover only a small part of the projected cost. National governments were strapped for cash, and there was no question of going above the EU's budget ceiling. EU leaders could agree only to a total TENs budget of €2.3 billion for the period 1995–1999. The Commission and member states were eager to secure additional funding from the private sector, but few investors were interested. Delors's suggestion of raising a huge commercial loan received short shrift from national governments in the grip of budget discipline and debt reduction motivated by their commitment to monetary union.

Jacques Santer, Delors's successor, championed the TENs at subsequent meetings of the European Council, but to little avail. In June 1996 Santer tried to get the European Council to commit €1 billion of surplus funds from the CAP budget, but the national leaders had other ideas for the money, some of which they used to compensate farmers for losses as a result of the BSE (mad cow) crisis. Nevertheless, the European Council reiterated its conviction that "the trans-European networks . . . can make a vital contribution to job creation and competitiveness."[55] Thereafter, TENs receded into the background of European Council deliberations, although they reappeared in November 1997 when EU leaders noted that the European Investment Bank was "prepared to grant a long grace period" for the TENs and to "provide further support for the creation of appropriate public-private partnerships."[56] EU leaders agreed on an appropriation of €4.6 billion for the TENs in the 2000–2006 budget.

The TENs received a new lease on life in 2003 when the EU launched the "European initiative for growth." The idea was to focus funding from a number of sources, notably through loans from the European Investment Bank and the involvement of the private sector, on so-called quick-start programs (about fifty priority projects "of European interest" that could be launched within three years). The much-heralded initiative for growth was more a political priority of the otherwise lackluster Italian presidency of the EU than a serious undertaking by the member states.

Although a number of TENs-related projects have been completed or are still under way (examples include the high-speed train between London, Paris, and Brussels), the scale of the operation has been nowhere near what Delors and others envisioned. Whether this outcome represents a lost opportunity for European competitiveness is debatable. Undoubtedly the EU needs improved infrastructures, but the scale of the original TENs proposal may have been excessive. Certainly its political cost was unacceptable to the European Council, notwithstanding a lot of rhetoric to the contrary. In the event, national investment in infrastructural development continued unabated (depending on the economic circumstances), and the EU itself continued to spend money on transport through the structural funds and telecommunications and energy networks in other ways. These measures may not be adequate to boost growth and employment on the scale imagined by the Commission, but full-fledged TENs are a political impossibility.

▪ Education and Vocational Training

Despite its economic importance for the EU as a whole and its political potential for inculcating a sense of "Europeanness," education remains predominantly the preserve of national governments. Nevertheless, the Maastricht Treaty formally introduced education and youth programs as new areas of EU competence. Accordingly, the EU aims to support and supplement action taken by member states in areas such as cooperation between educational establishments, student and teacher mobility, youth exchanges, and language teaching. To that end, the Council adopts "incentive measures" using the codecision procedure and makes recommendations via qualified majority voting on proposals from the Commission.

Formal involvement in education policy came on the heels of highly successful educational and exchange programs organized by the EU since the late 1980s, including

- European Community Action Scheme for the Mobility of University Students (Erasmus), a program to facilitate student and faculty exchange throughout the EU by offering grants to facilitate exchanges, curriculum development, and a badly needed course credit–transfer system
- Action Program to Promote Foreign Language Competence in the European Community (Lingua), a program to provide financial support to encourage second- and third-language acquisition, thereby helping students and educators to exploit the full potential of Erasmus
- Trans-European Mobility Scheme for University Students (Tempus), a program to link universities throughout Europe and the United States and fund joint research projects in a wide variety of disciplines

Since 1995, these educational programs have been reorganized and funded under the umbrella of the so-called Socrates program. Erasmus is the best known and most popular program in the Socrates stable, having facilitated countless student exchanges (the Commission estimates that by 2007, two million students will have studied in another country thanks to Erasmus).[57] In some cases these exchanges may have reinforced national prejudices and stereotypes, but in the vast majority of cases they have broken down barriers and helped students feel more European (they also spawned innumerable transnational love affairs). Having existed since 1987, Erasmus has generated a large network of former participants who are now in influential positions in government, industry, and the professions.

Other Socrates programs sound like items from an IKEA catalog. They include:

- Grundtvig: a program for adult learners and their instructors to develop EU-friendly teaching materials and networks
- Comenius: a program for secondary school students and teachers
- Minerva: a program to apply new technologies to education, funded in part by the eLearning component of the eEurope Action Plan
- Erasmus Mundus: an extension of the Erasmus program that helps fund master's degree courses offered jointly by at least three universities in at least three European countries

The equivalency (or nonequivalency) of degrees remains one of the most formidable obstacles to the mobility of university graduates in the EU job market. How similar (or different) are master's degrees in Ireland and Estonia? What about bachelor's degrees in Scotland and Slovenia? Inevitably, the Commission wants to promote convergence and comparable qualifications in higher education without trying to impose uniformity in an area that is politically sensitive in most member states. With some reluctance, member states agreed through the so-called Bologna process to bring the requirements for bachelor's and master's degrees approximately into line throughout the EU by 2010. For education ministry officials and university administrators, this is not necessarily a welcome development.[58]

Complementing Socrates, the Leonardo da Vinci program promotes vocational training exchanges throughout Europe, including Switzerland (through Swiss government funding). The program encourages innovation and entrepreneurship by exposing vocational students and trainee workers to different approaches and new ideas in other parts of Europe. It dovetails with the work of the European Center for the Development of Vocational Training in Thessaloniki, Greece, an EU agency that provides information on and analysis of vocational training policy. The Copenhagen process is attempting to do for vocational training what the Bologna process is attempting to do in university education: converge toward a common set of requirements and standards in the EU.

Language is perhaps the biggest practical barrier to realizing the potential of the single market, let alone to developing a European demos, or common political culture. EU citizens may be free to work anywhere in the EU, but unless they are fluent in the language of their host country, they will be restricted to menial labor. EU citizens may be interested in knowing about developments in other member states, but unless they have mastered other languages, their knowledge of other member states is bound to be limited. English may well be the lingua franca of government and business in the EU, and native English speakers therefore have an inherent advantage, but those who speak only English are at a major disadvantage when it comes to exploiting a range of cultural, social, economic, and political opportunities. Apart from the Lingua program, the EU has launched a number of initiatives to promote the acquisition of other languages, especially less used languages. The Commission's goal ("mother tongue plus two") is for EU citizens to know two EU languages in addition to their own. Many young European professionals have already attained that goal. For most Europeans, however, it is unrealistic and unrealizable.

■ Reviewing the Lisbon Strategy

Progress on implementing the economic aspects of the Lisbon strategy, notably on reaching a range of targets in the various policy areas discussed in this chapter, has been mixed. The economic downturn of the early 2000s did not help, but it also took the shine off the economic performance of the United States, on which the Lisbon strategy was largely based. France and Germany have dragged their feet on energy and transportation liberalization, complained about the rigorous enforcement of competition policy, and turned toward old-fashioned industrial policy. Other member states, more comfortable with economic modernization and reform, have become increasingly impatient. Business leaders, grateful for any progress, have tried to maintain the momentum for further reform.

Since the Lisbon summit, nearly every meeting of the European Council—not only the annual spring follow-up meetings—has produced a ritualistic endorsement of either the Lisbon strategy as a whole or one or another of the Lisbon goals. However, the gap between rhetoric and reality is glaring. As outgoing single market commissioner Bolkestein told the Competitiveness Council in July 2004, "[the EU] must kick the habit of declaratory politics. There have been far too many empty statements enshrined in endless pages of Council conclusions."[59]

A High Level Group under the leadership of former Dutch prime minister Wim Kok reported on the Lisbon strategy in November 2004 and painted an unflattering picture. According to the High Level Group, the strategy was "too broad to be understood as an interconnected narrative. Lisbon is about everything and thus about nothing. Everybody is responsible and thus no one." The strategy was in danger of becoming "a synonym for missed objectives and failed promises." The report decried the failure of the member states "to act on the Lisbon strategy with sufficient urgency" and complained about the crowded agenda and poor coordination. It also urged the Commission to "report clearly and precisely on success and failure in each Member State." Noting that "many Member States have not taken the execution and delivery of the agreed measures seriously enough," the report nonetheless did not name and shame the member states concerned.[60]

Given that the EU economy is not a single economy but consists of twenty-five separate but closely connected national economies, the Kok Report concluded that "the task is to develop national policies in each Member State, supported by an appropriate European-wide framework, that address a particular Member State's concerns and then to act in a more concerted and determined way. . . . In the end, much of the Lisbon strategy depends on the progress made in national capitals: no European procedure or method can change this simple truth. Governments and especially their leaders must not duck their crucial responsibilities. Nothing less than the future prosperity of the European model is at stake."[61]

The Kok Report echoed a consensus in the Commission that there are too many targets, that the strategy needs to be streamlined, and that a much smaller set of actions and priorities is in order. Commission president Barroso has taken this message to heart and made the success of the Lisbon strategy the leitmotif of his presidency. Many member states, including a large number of the Central and Eastern European ones, are eager to implement the strategy, although no member state is entirely blameless when it comes to particular proposals. The problem would appear to lie primarily with France and Germany, which, while undertaking some domestic reforms, are politically unwilling or unable to follow through on the Lisbon strategy.

▓ Notes

1. European Council, Presidency Conclusions, March 2000.
2. European Commission, *Growth, Competitiveness, and Employment: The Challenges and Ways Forward into the 21st Century,* COM(93)700.
3. Peter Ludlow, "A View from Brussels," no. 2 (July 2000): 12.
4. Quoted in *Financial Times,* March 24, 2000, p. 4.
5. Frits Bolkestein, speech at the informal meeting of the Competitiveness Council, July 2004, Maastricht, at www.hi.org/news/europe/midex/2004/04-07-02.midex.html.
6. On the development of the single market, see Lord Cockfield, *The European Union: Creating the Single Market* (Chichester, UK: John Wiley, 1994), pp. 37–60; and Michelle Egan, *Constructing a European Market: Standards, Regulation, and Governance* (Oxford: Oxford University Press, 2001).
7. Bulletin EC 5-1992, point 1.1.7.
8. For an assessment of the wider implications of the case, see Karen Alter and Sophie Meunier-Aitsahalia, "Judicial Politics in the European Community: European Integration and the Pathbreaking *Cassis de Dijon* Decision," *Comparative Political Studies* 24, no. 4 (1996): 535–561.
9. Helmut Schmitt Von Sydow, "The Basic Strategies of the Commission's White Paper," in Roland Bieber, Renaud Dehousse, John Pinder, and Joseph Weiler, eds., *1992: One European Market? A Critical Analysis of the Community's Internal Market Strategy* (Baden-Baden, Germany: Nomos Verlagsgesellschaft, 1988), p. 93.
10. See Jacques Pelkmans, "The New Approach to Technical Harmonization and Standardization," *Journal of Common Market Studies* 25, no. 3 (March 1987): 32–55.
11. European Council Resolution, *Official Journal of the European Communities* (OJ) C 10, January 16, 1990.
12. European Commission press release IP(92)546, July 3, 1992.
13. European Commission, *An Energy Policy for the European Community,* COM(95)682.
14. European Commission, *Liberalization of Telecommunications Infrastructure and Cable Television Networks,* COM(94)440 and COM(94)682.
15. SEC(92)2277, December 2, 1992.
16. Quoted in *Eurecom* 9, no. 5 (May 1997): 3.
17. European Commission, *Action Plan for the Single Market,* CSE(97)1, June 4, 1997.
18. See Michael Calingaert, *European Integration Revisited: Progress, Prospects, and U.S. Interests* (Boulder, CO: Westview Press, 1996), pp. 19–38.
19. Leon Brittan, "Competition Law: Its Importance to the European Community and to International Trade," speech at the University of Chicago Law School, April 24, 1992, p. 8.

20. European Council Regulation 17/62, OJ 62, no. 87, special edition (1959): 62/87.

21. Leon Brittan, *European Competition Policy: Keeping the Playing Field Level* (Brussels: CEPS, 1992), p. 18.

22. OJ L 72, March 18, 1992, p. 1.

23. European Council Regulation 4064/89, December 21, 1989, OJ L 395, December 30, 1989, p. 1.

24. Reported in the *Economist*, October 18, 1987, p. 61. The day in question was October 13.

25. Bulletin EC 11-1994, point 1.2.34.

26. Bulletin EC 5-1998, point 1.3.

27. Bulletin EC 7-1992, point 1.3.47.

28. See European Parliament, *Fact Sheets on the European Parliament and the Activities of the European Community* (Luxembourg: Office for Official Publications of the European Communities, 1991), p. 1.

29. See Brittan, *European Competition Policy,* pp. 48–50.

30. *Financial Times*, July 26, 2004, p. 26.

31. Quoted in *Financial Times*, July 26, 2004, p. 26.

32. J. Patrick Raines, "Common Market Competition Policy: The EC-IBM Settlement," *Journal of Common Market Studies* 24, no. 2 (December 1985): 137.

33. Mario Monti, "Convergence in EU-US Antitrust Policy," speech at the UCLS First Annual Institute on US and EU Antitrust Aspects of Mergers and Acquisitions, Los Angeles, CA, February 28, 2004, at http://europe.eu.int/rapid/pressReleases Action.do?References=speech/04/107&format=HTML&aged=0&language=EN&gui Language=EN.

34. See Sherill Brown Wells, *French Industrial Policy: A History, 1945–81* (Washington, DC: Office of the Historian, U.S. Department of State, 1991), pp. 61–80.

35. European Commission, *The European Community's Industrial Strategy* (Luxembourg: Office for Official Publications of the European Communities, 1983), p. 47.

36. Jean-Jacques Servan-Schreiber, *Le Défi Américain* (Paris: Denoel, 1967).

37. Walter Grunsteidl, "An Industrial Policy for Europe," *European Affairs* 3, no. 90 (Fall 1990): 19.

38. See Martin Bangemann, *Meeting the Global Challenge: Establishing a Successful European Industrial Policy* (London: Kogan, Page, Pounds, 1992), p. 8.

39. Quoted in European Commission, *21st Report on Competition Policy* (Luxembourg: Office for Official Publications of the European Communities, 1992), p. 22.

40. European Commission, "Industrial Policy in an Open and Competitive Environment: Guidelines for a Community Approach," COM(90)556 final, November 16, 1990.

41. SEC(91)565, April 3, 1991.

42. European Council Resolution, November 18, 1991.

43. *Economist*, May 22, 2004, p. 45.

44. Frits Bolkestein, "Let the Market Choose Europe's Champions," *Financial Times*, June 14, 2004, p. 19.

45. Barroso, portfolio assignment letter to Verheugen, http://europa.eu.int/comm/commissioners/newcomm_pdf/pf_verheugen_en.pdf.

46. Erkki Liikanen, "An Industrial Policy for an Enlarged Europe," speech at the Industrial Policy Day Press Conference, Brussels, May 27, 2004, at http://europe.eu.int/rapid/pressReleasesAction.do?References=speech/04/268&type=HTML&aged=0&language=EN&guiLanguage=en.

47. Bolkestein, "Let the Market Choose," p. 19.

48. See Bulletin EC 5-1982, point 2.1.152; Bulletin EC 6-1983, points 2.1.268–2.1.269.

49. Grunsteidl, "Industrial Policy," p. 17.

50. See Margaret Sharp, "The Single Market and European Policies for Advanced Technologies," in Colin Crouch and David Marquand, eds., *The Politics of 1992: Beyond the Single European Market* (Oxford: Basil Blackwell, 1990), pp. 100–120.

51. Frits Bolkestein, speech at the Informal Meeting of the Competitiveness Council, Maastricht, July 2, 2004.

52. Copenhagen European Council, "Presidency Conclusions," Annex 1, "Orientations for Economic Renewal in Europe," Bulletin EC 6-1993, point 1.4.

53. European Commission, *Growth, Competitiveness, and Employment.*

54. European Commission, *1994 General Report* (Luxembourg: Office for Official Publications of the European Communities, 1995), point 321, p. 110.

55. Florence European Council, "Presidency Conclusions," Bulletin EC 6-1996, point 1.4.

56. Luxembourg European Council, "Presidency Conclusions," Bulletin EC 11-1997, point 1.6.

57. U. Teichler, "Changes of ERASMUS Under the Umbrella of SOCRATES," *Journal of Studies in International Education* 5, no. 3 (September 2001): 201–228.

58. On the Bologna process, see Thierry Malan, "Implementing the Bologna Process in France," *European Journal of Education* 39, no. 3 (September 2004): 289–298; Wachter Bernd, "The Bologna Process: Developments and Prospects," *European Journal of Education* 39, no. 3 (September 2004): 265–274; and A. Rauhvargers, S. Bergan, and J. Divis, "United We Stand: The Recognition of Joint Degrees," *Journal of Studies in International Education* 7, no. 4 (December 2003): 342–354.

59. Bolkestein speech, Maastricht, July 2, 2004.

60. Wim Kok et al., *Facing the Challenge: The Lisbon Strategy for Growth and Enlargement: Report of the High Level Group* (Brussels: European Commission, 2004), pp. 6, 7, 10.

61. Ibid., pp. 18, 45.

14

Social Policy, Employment, and the Environment

The Lisbon strategy rests on three pillars: economic, social, and environmental. The economic pillar, discussed in Chapter 13, aims to boost productivity and growth in the EU. Economic improvement, in turn, needs to generate more jobs—not simply low-skills, low-wage jobs but high-paying jobs in the new knowledge economy. Otherwise Europe may no longer be able to afford its elaborate and expensive social welfare systems. Nor should a stronger economy and higher employment undermine in any way the EU's lofty environmental standards.

Europe's social model is expensive to maintain. Without economic growth and more employment, it may become unaffordable. As the Kok Report on the Lisbon strategy put it:

> At risk—in the medium to long run—is nothing less than the sustainability of the [European social model]. Europeans have made choices about how to express the values they hold in common: a commitment to the social contract that underwrites the risk of unemployment, ill-health and old age, and provides opportunity to all through high-quality education, a commitment to public institutions, the public realm and the public interest, and that a market economy should be run fairly and with respect for the environment. These values are expressed in systems of welfare, public institutions and regulation that are expensive in a world where low cost and highly efficient producers are challenging the old order. If Europe cannot adapt, cannot modernize its systems and cannot increase its growth and employment fast enough then it will be impossible to sustain these choices. Europe, in short, must focus on growth and employment in order to achieve the Lisbon ambitions.[1]

The European social model stands in marked contrast to the American economic model (there is no American social model), which prizes individual initiative and responsibility, entrepreneurship, and flexibility. The American model is also antithetical to government intervention (but not averse to corporate welfare). High productivity and job creation are its hallmarks, but so

447

are massive income and social inequities. When Europeans talk about ensuring social inclusion and preventing social exclusion, or about promoting social cohesion—terms that have no meaning in the United States—they have America very much in mind. Europeans are both impressed and appalled by the American model: impressed by its economic achievements and appalled by its social callousness. The Lisbon strategy aims to emulate the best of the United States while eschewing the worst of it.

Although every national leader has signed on to the Lisbon strategy, there are noticeable differences in the degree of enthusiasm for it among member states. The main proponents of the Lisbon strategy (Britain, Ireland, the Netherlands, Spain, and many of the new Central and Eastern European member states) have a liberal economic orientation. Having reformed (or begun to reform) their own welfare states and improved (or begun to improve) their own economic performances, they are eager to push a similar agenda at the European level in order to safeguard and capitalize on their achievements at the national level. The member states with a more traditional socioeconomic outlook, by contrast, view the Lisbon strategy with some skepticism. They may understand the logic of economic reform, but they fear its social consequences. France, in particular, is vigilant against the spread of "Anglo-Saxon" capitalism in the guise of the Lisbon strategy.

Nevertheless, even France is moving away from the old-fashioned notion that EU social policy necessitates heavy regulation of working conditions, an approach that may have made it more difficult to increase employment. Like other member states, France acknowledges that social policy must complement, not conflict with, employment policy. Indeed, "social policy and employment" is the official name in the EU for what was once called "social policy."

Despite a consensus within the EU on a new approach to social policy and the overriding importance of job creation, translating economic growth into additional jobs is a tricky process. The EU lacks competence for many of the factors that affect employment. Given that the EU is not a single economy but a collection of twenty-five closely connected economies, and that responsibility for pensions, health care, education, taxation, and other relevant areas rests with national governments, the EU's approach to employment policy depends greatly on the open method of coordination. Since the late 1990s the EU has constructed an elaborate procedure that includes national reporting, multilateral surveillance, peer review, and guidelines for better performance and involves the so-called social partners (workers' and employers' representatives), the Commission, European Parliament, EU advisory bodies, the Council of Ministers, and, at the apex of the system, the European Council. Whether because of that or other developments (or, more likely, a mixture of both), the EU's employment figures are moving in the right direction, though the new jobs are not by any means all high-paying ones in the knowledge economy.

There is less contention among member states over environmental policy. The costs of environmental policy are high, but so are the benefits. Europeans are unwilling to sacrifice environmental standards for greater economic growth or even, it appears, for more employment. Rapid technological advances may ease the presumed trade-off between environmental degradation and economic growth. As a champion of sustainable development, the EU hopes to position itself as a global leader in the burgeoning field of alternative, environment-friendly energy sources and cleaner manufacturing processes. As well as its role in the Lisbon strategy, the environment looms large in the EU's external relations.

◼ Social Policy

The EU's social policy builds on a long history and a strong tradition of social legislation in the member states. Only Britain, during eighteen years of Conservative government (1979–1997), disputed the philosophical underpinnings of the EU's social policy agenda. Thus, Brussels became the battleground for ideological, political, and economic disputes over such issues as women's rights, workers' rights, and, especially, "industrial democracy"—employee participation in company decisionmaking. More than simply trying to improve working and living conditions in the EU, the Commission aggressively advocated social policy as a means of promoting a "people's Europe." Because legislation on social issues potentially affects the everyday lives of almost everybody in the EU, a progressive social policy was a useful means by which the Commission could stress the relevance of European integration.

From the Treaty of Rome to the Single European Act

The Rome Treaty contained a number of social policy provisions pertaining to labor mobility (one of the prerequisites for a fully functioning internal market) and equal pay for equal work performed by men and women. It also called for the establishment of the European Social Fund to help achieve the EU's social policy objectives, which, apart from the treaty's specific provisions, include improved living and working conditions and close cooperation among member states on labor issues.

The EU built the first phase of its social policy in the 1960s almost entirely on the treaty provisions for labor mobility. However, movement of labor and the professions remained restricted for another twenty years until the momentum of the single market program finally made it possible to resolve outstanding issues. In the meantime, broader aspects of social policy got a boost at the Hague summit in 1969, thanks in part to the leadership of Willy Brandt, Germany's Social Democratic chancellor. EU leaders reiterated their commitment to a comprehensive and effective social policy at their next summit, in Paris in 1972.

Given the economic setbacks about to beset the EC, this was a false dawn. Like other EC activities, social policy suffered from the political and economic retrenchment of the 1970s. Yet there was some progress. Buoyed by the Paris summit's endorsement of an active social policy, in 1974 the Commission proposed and the Council accepted the EC's first social action program, which included wide-ranging measures intended to achieve full employment, better living and working conditions, worker participation in industrial decisionmaking, and equal treatment of men and women in the workplace.

A flurry of activity followed, but the legislative output was unimpressive. Successful measures included directives on workers' information and consultation rights and on equal pay and equal treatment for women. The fifth company law directive and the European Company Statute—measures that included provisions for worker participation—became bogged down in disputes among member states and trade unions over which model of industrial democracy to use. Apart from its legislative agenda, the EC established two institutions—the European Foundation for the Improvement of Living and Working Conditions and the European Center for the Development of Vocational Training—to disseminate information and conduct research on social policy issues. Nevertheless, the EC's performance paled in comparison with the promise of the Paris summit and the social action program.

Fresh ideological winds did not bode well for social policy in the EC, with a right-wing reaction against excessive government intervention in economic and social affairs. In the prevailing political climate, few national governments supported as active a social agenda as the Commission proposed. Thus, a combination of renewed economic recession and emerging market forces pushed social policy onto the back burner in the early 1980s, which helps to explain why the single market program initially lacked a social dimension.

The 1985 White Paper touched on social policy only in relation to the free movement of people (workers and professions). The Single European Act went further, affirming in its preamble the need to "improve the [EC's] economic and social situation by extending common policies and pursuing new objectives" and by including a new title on economic and social cohesion. Moreover, the Single European Act introduced qualified majority voting for legislation on "the health and safety of workers," which produced the largest and most important body of social policy legislation in the late 1980s and early 1990s and opened a loophole through which the Commission tried to enact other social policy measures. This effort led to a number of legal challenges, most notably by the British government against the Council's adoption in December 1993 of the "working time" directive, which set a maximum forty-eight-hour workweek (with many exceptions) as a health and safety measure (needing only a qualified majority to pass) rather than a social policy measure (needing unanimity). In its judgment, the Court of Justice rejected Britain's challenge by ruling that the principal aim of the directive was, indeed, to promote the health and safety of workers. (For that reason the Court struck down the directive's provision that the minimum weekly rest day should be a Sunday: why, the Court asked, was Sunday more relevant to the health and safety of workers than any other day of the week?)[2]

The Single European Act also obliged the Commission to endeavor "to develop the dialogue between management and labor at Community level which could, if the two sides consider it desirable, lead to relations based on agreement." This put an additional stamp of approval on the "Val Duchesse process," begun in 1985 when the Commission convened a meeting in Val Duchesse outside Brussels to encourage the social partners to develop a working relationship in order to provide informal input into the EC's legislative process. The Union of Industrial Employers' Confederations of Europe (UNICE) represents employers in the social partnership; the European Trade Union Confederation (ETUC) represents labor. UNICE has always been more coherent, better organized, and generally more influential than ETUC. Indeed, the Commission has consistently bolstered ETUC in order to provide a counterweight on the labor side to UNICE on the management side.[3]

The member states' commitment in the Single European Act to economic and social cohesion led them in 1988 to overhaul and substantially increase the structural funds. By acquiring new missions and more money, the European Social Fund was a beneficiary of that reform. Thus, the European Social Fund became a more effective instrument used to fight long-term unemployment and facilitate the integration of young people into the workforce, largely through vocational training. The role of the European Social Fund in promoting social and economic cohesion is discussed in Chapter 12.

The Social Charter

In an effort to ameliorate the possible adverse effects of economic liberalization and to counter criticism that the single market program would benefit only businesspeople, in 1988 Commission president Jacques Delors—a man of the left and a former trade union official—began what he called a "careful consideration of [the single market's] social consequences." Delors explored the social dimension of the 1992 goal, calling it a "key to the success of the large market."[4] With the obvious exception of British prime minister Margaret Thatcher—a woman of the right and a union buster—most government leaders, whether Social Democrats or Christian Democrats, supported Delors. Some sympathized with the ideological underpinnings of a social dimension and saw an EC initiative as a way to improve social policy at home without losing competitiveness abroad. They also feared "social dumping," the possibility that member states with higher labor costs would lose market share to other member states with lower labor costs or, worse, that firms would relocate from the former to the latter.

With the single market well on track and the economy booming, political support for an active social policy began to gather speed. Meeting in June 1988, the European Council stressed the relevance of the social dimension for the 1992 program. The presidency conclusions noted that as the internal market had to be conceived "in such a manner as to benefit all our people," it was necessary to improve working conditions, living standards, protection of health and safety, access to vocational training, and dialogue between the two sides of industry.[5]

Buoyed by the European Council's support, the Commission attempted to give substance to the social dimension in a working paper released in September 1988.[6] Using a format similar to its famous White Paper on the single market, the Commission outlined the intellectual and economic rationale for a social dimension and listed eighty possible measures (but without a timetable for implementation). Proposals covered the familiar and the new with an emphasis on creating conditions necessary to bring about worker mobility, an essential attribute of an integrated market.

Inspired by similar declarations from the Council of Europe, the International Labour Organization, and the Organization for Economic Cooperation and Development (OECD) and eager to dramatize the single market's social dimension, Delors proposed a charter of basic social rights. The French government made this a priority of its Council presidency in the second half of 1989. Despite more pressing issues, such as monetary union and events in Central and Eastern Europe, eleven of the twelve national leaders adopted the "Community Charter of the Fundamental Social Rights of Workers" (the Social Charter) at the Strasbourg summit in December 1989 (Thatcher was the lone dissenter).[7]

Following a preamble that outlined the development of social policy at the European level, the Social Charter listed twelve categories of fundamental social rights:

- freedom of movement
- employment and remuneration
- improvement of living and working conditions
- social protection
- freedom of association and collective bargaining
- vocational training
- equal treatment for men and women
- information, consultation, and participation for workers
- health protection and safety in the workplace

- protection of children and adolescents
- protection of elderly persons
- protection of disabled persons

According to the social affairs commissioner, the Social Charter formed "a keystone of the social dimension in the construction of Europe, in the spirit of the Treaty of Rome supplemented by the Single European Act."[8] Being entirely hortatory, however, it lacked binding legal force. Nevertheless, the charter implied strong political support for an active social agenda.

The Social Charter never had much popular appeal, perhaps because from the outset it seemed too lofty and remote. Persistently high unemployment contrasted with its rhetoric and threatened to erode popular support for the single market program itself. Potential popular disaffection offered a powerful impetus for member states to focus on the nuts and bolts of social policy in the late 1980s. While endorsing the Social Charter, the European Council therefore stressed that "integration of unemployed young persons into working life and the fight against long-term unemployment . . . [partly through] vocational training . . . constitute decisive aspects of the Community social dimension."[9]

The charter's brief concluding section called on the Commission to submit proposals to implement those rights for which the EC had competence to enact legislation. Sensitive to the subsidiarity principle, the Commission was careful not to encroach upon aspects of social policy that could best be dealt with at the national level. Nor did it want governments to use subsidiarity as a way to prevent the enactment of legislation in Brussels. Accordingly, the Commission's "action program" sought to strike a balance between what was desirable, what was appropriate, and what was feasible at the European level.[10]

Of the action program's forty-seven measures, only seventeen were new. The predominance of preexisting measures testified to the EC's poor record of social policy legislation. Inevitably, familiar proposals dealing with industrial democracy, women's issues, and vocational training resurfaced in the action program; their proponents hoped that the momentum generated by the Social Charter would somehow carry them through. Aware of the huge stumbling block posed by the unanimity requirement for most social legislation, the Commission resorted in many cases to instruments other than legally binding directives or recommendations. The Social Charter also called on the Commission to prepare an annual report on its implementation. Those reports—the first of which appeared in December 1991—are a useful guide to the state of social policy in the EU.

The Council's treatment of the Commission's proposals for legislation at the European level demonstrated the continuing controversy surrounding social policy, notwithstanding the rhetoric of successive summits. By the end of 1992 the Council had adopted only eight directives (including two based on unanimity), concerned primarily with the less contentious question of health and safety at work. As the Commission coyly observed in its second report on the Social Charter, "Discussions on most of the proposals for directives on important matters have not made sufficient progress to enable a final text to be adopted."[11] In other words, at least one member state—usually but not always Britain—had prevented the Council from reaching unanimity on draft directives covering such issues as the length of the workweek, atypical work, European works councils, and transport for the disabled.

The Social Charter and the ensuing action program represented the high point of EU activism in the realm of social policy. Far from being an impartial civil service, the Commission had consistently acted as a lobbyist and pushed a progressive agenda. The Commission in general, and the social affairs directorate-general in particular, had cogent political and bureaucratic reasons to advance EC social policy. For its part, the European Parliament traditionally took a strong stand in support of women's rights, industrial democracy, and other staples of EU social policy. The Parliament's social affairs committee produced numerous reports on social issues, focusing especially on improving the conditions of the most vulnerable groups in society: the disabled, migrant workers, and the poor. The European Economic and Social Committee, an advisory body, had been established under the terms of the Rome Treaty in order to institutionalize discussions between workers' and employers' representatives on a range of social and economic issues. Apart from its involvement in early deliberations on the Social Charter, however, the committee was conspicuous by its absence from the high-level social dialogue launched in 1985 and by its marginal impact on the EC's social legislation.

The Social Protocol

Given Britain's intense opposition to the Social Charter in particular and to social policy in general, it was not surprising that the 1991 intergovernmental conference on political union almost foundered on the social chapter, a package of social policy provisions based on the Social Charter, that other member states wanted to include in the Maastricht Treaty. Prime Minister John Major adamantly opposed the social chapter at the Maastricht summit in December 1991. Realizing the extent of Major's intransigence, Delors suggested removing the social chapter entirely and replacing it with a protocol on social policy attached to the treaty.

All twelve member states subsequently signed the social protocol, which authorized eleven of them (Britain being the exception) to proceed along the lines laid down in the Social Charter and to use the EU's institutions and decisionmaking procedures for that purpose. Britain would not take part in relevant Council deliberations or decisionmaking; in such cases the Council would decide by a qualified majority recalculated to take account of Britain's nonparticipation. Needless to say, any legislation adopted via the social protocol would not apply to Britain. However, Britain remained subject to the social policy provisions of the Rome Treaty as revised by the Single European Act and by the Maastricht Treaty (apart from the social protocol). The three member states that joined the EU in 1995 happily subscribed to the social protocol, and the threshold for a qualified majority in the Council with respect to social policy decisionmaking was recalculated accordingly.

The social protocol included

- revised policy objectives, such as the promotion of employment
- an extension of qualified majority voting procedures to cover proposals on working conditions, consultation of workers, and equality between men and women with regard to labor market opportunities and treatment at work
- unanimous decisionmaking in areas such as social security, termination of employment, and third-country worker protection
- a greater role in the formulation of social policy for the employers' and employees' representatives

The social protocol also reinforced the role of the social partners and provided for collective agreements at the European level. Specifically, if management and labor reached an agreement on certain social policy issues, the Commission could submit that agreement to the Council, which could enact it into Community law by qualified majority vote.

The possible ramifications of the social protocol for European integration were a cause of some concern in the early 1990s. The protocol apparently set a precedent for a two-tier EU, a development inherent as well in the Maastricht Treaty's provisions for monetary union. There were additional fears that Britain's exclusion from certain labor legislation would distort competition and have a negative impact on the single market. Fears of social dumping seemed justified even before ratification of the Maastricht Treaty when Hoover announced its decision to relocate a manufacturing plant from France to Scotland (in fact, a variety of reasons influenced the decision).[12]

Concern about the political and economic implications of Britain's exclusion from the social protocol dampened the Commission's ardor for using it to introduce new social policy legislation. Thus, the Council enacted only two directives under the auspices of the social protocol. The first, on European works councils (mechanisms for worker information and consultation in large companies), followed the social partners' failure to negotiate a collective agreement on the subject. The Commission then submitted a new legislative proposal that sailed through the Council (Britain did not participate in the deliberations). The lesson was not lost on the social partners: the next time they had an opportunity to reach a collective agreement under the social protocol—on establishing a worker's right, regardless of gender, to unpaid parental leave or time off for other important family reasons—they did so within the requisite nine-month period. The Council quickly translated into law its agreement of December 1995 to a minimum three months' unpaid leave in all member states (except Britain, of course).

Because these directives did not apply to Britain, their enactment emphasized both the peculiarity of EU social policy and Britain's increasing isolation in the EU. Other member states wanted to end the anomaly of the social protocol at the 1996–1997 intergovernmental conference on treaty reform but knew that there was no hope of doing so as long as Britain's Conservative Party remained in power. Labour's victory in the May 1997 general election settled the issue. Within days the new government announced its support for bringing the social protocol into the treaty proper, thereby ending both British exceptionalism and differentiated integration with respect to social policy. Incorporation of the social protocol into the Amsterdam Treaty restored the unity and coherence of EU social policy. The government also announced its willingness to abide by the two directives adopted under the social protocol, prompting the Commission to introduce proposals for legislation to extend the European works councils and parental leave directives to Britain.

The Amsterdam Treaty also added equality between men and women to the list of Community objectives. A new provision of the treaty extended the scope of EU involvement beyond the issue of equal pay for equal work to equal treatment more generally and to equal opportunities. Another new provision authorized the Council, acting unanimously, to take "appropriate action" to combat discrimination based not only on sex but also on race, ethnicity, religion, disability, age, or sexual orientation.

The Demise of Traditional Social Policy

The Labour government's embrace of the social protocol implied a sea change in Britain's approach to a hitherto extremely sensitive issue. Yet the new government's position on the substance of social policy was not so different from that of the old government. Whereas the Conservatives opposed social policy on ideological grounds and had painted themselves into a corner politically, Labour took a pragmatic approach. The new government did not like every aspect of social policy but saw no reason to exclude Britain from a long-standing area of EU activity.

Other member states had also grown more pragmatic in their approach to social policy. By the mid-1990s, with unemployment moving to the top of the EU's agenda, there was little support anymore for old-fashioned social policy. The Commission lost much of its zeal even before Delors's departure, emphasizing instead the flexible and employment-enhancing nature of selective social policy measures. The Amsterdam Treaty's section on employment avoided "anything that might smack of a social approach to employment" and was "inserted next to [the title on] economic and monetary union, not social policy."[13] Under the circumstances, the Labour government's acceptance of the social protocol was an easy way to repudiate the previous government's EU policy without endorsing a radical social policy agenda.

A more restrained approach was clearly evident in the Commission's 1994 White Paper on the development of social policy in the period 1995–1999.[14] In keeping with prevailing concerns over employment and competitiveness, the White Paper argued rather defensively that social policy was not an obstacle to economic growth but rather was a key element of it. The White Paper's main themes were job creation, labor mobility, equal opportunity, and the integration of social and economic policies. In its next social action program, the Commission was careful not to propose a lengthy new legislative agenda.[15] By relying less on legal instruments to protect and strengthen workers' rights and more on discussion and conciliation, the program signaled a shift in the direction of EU social policy as well as the Commission's increasing aversion to interventionism. Despite its incorporation of the social protocol and despite also including an explicit reference to fundamental social rights, the Amsterdam Treaty further reflected the toning down of EU social policy. Thus, the social protocol was incorporated into the treaty largely unchanged, and unanimity was still required in certain policy areas.

The last gasp of old-fashioned social policy came in the second half of 2000, during France's presidency of the Council. Despite having a Conservative (although relatively statist) president, France at the time had a socialist government that put social policy at the top of the country's presidency agenda. The Commission had adopted a social policy agenda in June 2000, which it wanted the European Council to endorse at the end of the year, following input from the European Parliament and other interested bodies. France's social affairs minister was none other than Martine Aubrey, Jacques Delors's daughter. Whereas her father had tempered his enthusiasm for traditional social policy, Aubrey remained a true believer. Using language redolent of an earlier time, she set her sights during France's council presidency on "build[ing] a social Europe that works."[16] To that end, she attempted to tweak the Commission's social policy agenda in a more interventionist direction.

That push was too much for Britain, Spain, and some of the other member states, as well as the Commission, which resented the Council presidency's intrusiveness. The British stoutly resisted, for instance, the idea of introducing social criteria into merger applications. In general, the British emphasized the importance of flexible labor markets and disputed the necessity for regulation. The French made predictable noises about the dangers of globalization and the need for social protection but eventually acquiesced in a more moderate document. EU leaders endorsed the Social Policy Agenda at the Nice summit in December 2000, where most of their time was taken up with concluding the intergovernmental conference on treaty reform. The agenda's key objectives illustrated the shift in social policy away from traditional goals toward an explicit emphasis on growth and employment. The key objectives were

- more and better jobs
- achieving a new balance between flexibility and security in a changing work environment
- combating poverty, social exclusion, and discrimination
- modernizing social protection systems
- promoting equality between men and women
- reinforcing the social dimension of enlargement and external relations

▧ Employment Policy

The link between employment and social cohesion is obvious. The Kok Report on the Lisbon strategy put it bluntly: "High levels of employment are essential for achieving greater social cohesion and eradicating poverty within the European Union. Having more people in employment is the best way of safeguarding the social and financial sustainability and further development of European welfare systems."[17] Yet employment is the weakest pillar of the Lisbon strategy and is the EU's Achilles' heel.

In the mid-1990s, even as the EU enjoyed respectable levels of economic growth, unemployment continued to hover around 11 percent of the workforce. Persistently high unemployment was devastating for the EU. A former secretary-general of the Commission estimated that unemployment benefits cost EU member states almost €200 billion a year, requiring high levels of taxation that drained the public purse.[18] Politically, double-digit unemployment undermined the EU's credibility—after all, the single market program and monetary union had promised to deliver economic growth and jobs. Instead, the post-Maastricht drive toward monetary union was widely seen to have exacerbated unemployment.

The Commission has been sensitive to the scourge of unemployment since the late 1980s, when it produced the first of its annual reports on employment in the EC. The European Council took up the cause of unemployment in the early 1990s, issuing ritualistic denunciations of it in successive summit conclusions. Delors's 1993 White Paper, *Growth, Competitiveness, and Employment: The Challenges and Ways Forward into the 21st Century,* dealt explicitly with the challenge of job creation, prompting an EU-wide debate on the issue in the mid-1990s.[19] Germany, in the grip of high unemployment, put the issue at the top of its Council presidency agenda in the second half of 1994. Based on the 1993 White Paper and subsequent discussions, the European Council agreed in Essen in December 1994 on a possible cure to Europe's illness: better vocational training, moderate wage policies, more efficient labor markets, and assistance for specific groups, such as women and the long-term unemployed, to get into the workforce. This was the first in a long series of European Council deliberations and declarations on employment.

The inclusion in the Amsterdam Treaty of a title (section) on employment greatly strengthened the EU's approach to the issue. The treaty modified the EU's objectives to include "a high level of employment" and affirmed the necessity for "coordination between (member state) employment policies . . . with a view to enhancing their effectiveness by developing a coordinated strategy for employment." Competence for employment policy would remain at the national level, but the European Council would develop "common guidelines" based on input from various EU institutions and bodies. The Commission would monitor compliance with these guidelines, leaving it up to the European Council to take additional political steps. The Amsterdam Treaty also included an important institutional innovation: the establishment of the Employment Committee to facilitate a continuous dialogue on employment and other structural policy issues at the EU level and to help prepare Council deliberations on the subject.

Concern about job losses had reached the top of the EU's political agenda by the time of the Amsterdam summit, as unemployment in France and Germany peaked at record levels. Jacques Santer made employment a centerpiece of his Commission presidency, proposing in January 1996 a "confidence pact on employment" to boost jobs by improving the single market, curbing state aids, strengthening education and vocational training, and helping small and medium-sized enterprises. French prime minister Lionel Jospin, a Socialist, won the May 1997 parliamentary elections with a pledge to cut unemployment; French president Jacques Chirac, a Conservative, sought to outdo Jospin in proclaiming the importance of job creation. In Germany, Chancellor Helmut Kohl's attention grew more and more focused on unemployment in the run-up to the September 1998 federal elections.

The EU's high unemployment level disguised the fact that national rates varied greatly, reflecting the diversity of economic policies among member states themselves. Most member states pursued economic policies that guaranteed a high rate of structural unemployment (Britain, which undertook painful economic reforms in the 1980s, reaped the benefit of low unemployment in the mid-1990s). Labor market rigidities included high minimum wages, generous employment benefits that lasted for long periods, weak tests for claiming unemployment benefits, and strong trade union bargaining power. Industrial rigidities included an inability to grow small firms quickly into big ones and, at the other extreme, an inability to downsize quickly (by firing workers).

The cure for high unemployment in the EU might therefore have seemed obvious: lower and shorter-term unemployment benefits, stricter tests for receipt of benefits, lower payroll taxes and other statutory charges, greater wage flexibility, less job protection, and the provision of earned-income tax credits.

Taken together, of course, these recommendations read like a recipe for what many Europeans decried as the callous Anglo-Saxon economic model, which a majority of EU member states were loath to embrace precisely because of its supposed social consequences—growing income inequalities, the emergence of a "working poor" underclass, and the lack of a social safety net. However, the United States had an enviable record of sustained economic growth in the 1990s and low unemployment without inflationary pressure. Millions of working poor may have been an indictment of the U.S. economic system, but the EU's millions of long-term, socially excluded unemployed also reflected poorly on the gentler European model.

Intellectually, most national governments, of whatever ideological stripe, hoped to find a middle way between the U.S. model and the much-vaunted European model. The Netherlands seemed to have found that middle way, but what worked for a small country with a culture of consensus was more difficult for large countries such as France and Germany. Moreover, the French government advocated a thirty-five-hour workweek and public-sector job creation, whereas the conservative German government failed to introduce potentially employment-enhancing tax reforms in 1997 and 1998 because of its weak hold on power (the new Social Democratic–Greens government was not inclined to revisit the issue).

Lack of EU competence for social security and related areas, as well as the diversity of economic systems and the vagaries of political circumstances among member states, precludes the adoption of concerted EU measures to make the reforms necessary to translate economic growth into large-scale job creation. The EU has had to rely instead on soft measures such as multilateral surveillance, benchmarking, and peer pressure. The latter evolved during the late 1990s into a highly choreographed and stylized process called the European Employment Strategy, launched at a special jobs summit in Luxembourg in November 1997, soon after the Amsterdam Treaty was concluded. The strategy involved member states submitting national employment action plans for annual peer review. These would follow common guidelines focusing on employability, entrepreneurship, adaptability of individuals and enterprises, and equal opportunity. Britain also put employment at the top of its presidential agenda in early 1998 but seemed keen to move the process along while stressing a flexible rather than legislative approach. At the concluding summit of Britain's presidency, held in Cardiff in June 1998, the European Council discussed for the first time the member states' annual employment action plans, based on earlier assessments by the Commission and the Council of Ministers. As well as making some general statements about the contents of the existing plans, the European Council adjured the relevant formations of the Council of Ministers—notably the Social Affairs Council and the Economic and Finance Council—"to continue to work together to exchange best practice . . . [and] to develop peer group evaluation" of future plans.[20]

The European Employment Strategy received a huge political boost when the European Council agreed to the Lisbon strategy in March 2000. Member states, especially the economically more liberal ones, saw implementation of the strategy as an essential means of realizing the Lisbon employment objective of raising the overall employment rate in the EU to 70 percent, and the employment rate for women to more than 60 percent, by 2010. The European Council sharpened these targets in March 2001, when it concluded that the overall rate should be increased to 67 percent (57 percent for women) by 2005 and added that the employment rate for older workers should be at least 50 percent by 2010.

Following a recommendation by the European Council in March 2002, the EU streamlined its annual economic and employment policy coordination cycles (the centerpiece of economic coordination being the Broad Economic Policy Guidelines and the centerpiece of employment coordination being the European Employment Strategy, which is subordinate to the Broad Economic Policy Guidelines). The main elements of the employment strategy and the annual sequencing of economic and employment policy coordination (a rolling program of yearly planning, examining, reporting, and monitoring) are as follows:

January: Implementation Package. This contains

- Broad Economic Policy Guidelines Implementation Report
- Internal Market Strategy Implementation Report
- Draft Joint Employment Report (prepared by the Commission and the Council, this is a synthesis of the member states' National Action Plans and comparative analysis of their implementation as well as a progress report on the employment situation in the member states and collectively in the EU)

March: Spring Report. Prepared by the Commission, this report outlines the main agenda items for the spring summit and sets out the Commission's strategic priorities for the EU.

March: Spring Summit. This is the annual meeting of the European Council devoted to reviewing the Lisbon strategy. The European Council conclusions provide general political orientation for the European Employment Strategy.

April: Guidelines Package. Based on general political orientations provided by the European Council, the Commission prepares

- Broad Economic Policy Guidelines
- Employment Guidelines (containing specific policy objectives)
- Employment Recommendations

April–June: Input from the European Parliament and Relevant Council Formations. The Parliament and relevant Council formations provide input into the Guidelines Package.

June: European Council. The European Council reaches political agreement on the guidelines and issues conclusions.

June: Council of Ministers' Action. The relevant Council of Ministers formations adopt (by qualified majority voting)

- Broad Economic Policy Guidelines
- Employment Guidelines
- Employment Recommendations

July–December: National Action Plans and Peer Review. Based on the Broad Economic Policy Guidelines, Employment Guidelines, and Employment Recommendations, member states adopt National Action Plans to implement the Employment Guidelines in specific national circumstances and contexts; this process includes a two-day presentation and critique of member states' National Action Plans.

Impact of the Employment Strategy

The European Employment Strategy is procedurally intricate and impressive, but is it effective? It is tempting to dismiss it as a classic example of EU procedural excess. Yet the point of the strategy is to get member states to coordinate closely in policy areas that have traditionally been off the agenda of European integration but that have a profound effect on the EU's overall economic performance. Given the domestic political stakes, member states are extremely wary of putting issues such as tax incentives, wage policies, and job security on the formal agenda of European integration. Indeed, some of these issues are not even included in the employment strategy.

National suspicions continue to haunt the employment strategy and wider Lisbon strategy. The Kok Report conceded that "the call for more reform is frequently seen as no more than code for more flexibility which in turn is seen as code for weakening workers' rights and protections."[21] The report did not name names but clearly had France in mind. In view of French and others' concerns, it is remarkable that the process is so well established and relatively successful.

According to Commission and other evaluations, the four-pillar structure of the employment strategy (employability, entrepreneurship, adaptability, and equal opportunity) is sound, although progress has been more pronounced on the employability and entrepreneurship pillars. This leads critics to suggest that the strategy favors quantity over quality when it comes to job creation, and that the traditional agenda of EU social policy has been sacrificed on the altar of Anglo-Saxon economic liberalism. In terms of numbers of people in the workforce, the employment situation has improved in Europe since the low point of 1997–1998. Between 1997 and 2004, over ten million new jobs were created in the EU15. This may have had as much to do with the general economic situation, which improved at the turn of the decade, as with the impact of the employment strategy (most likely it was a combination of the two). Many of the new jobs, however, provided only part-time and low-quality employment. The EU is generating new jobs that are qualitatively similar to many of the new jobs generated in the United States, but quantitatively it still lags far behind the United States in job creation.

The Kok Report concluded that the EU's labor markets and employment policies are more efficient and adaptable as a result of the employment strategy, and that the employment situation had improved throughout the EU15. Though the improvement was "by far not enough to achieve the Lisbon targets . . . they prove convincingly that reforms are necessary and that they do pay off."[22] The report stressed the importance of greater labor market flexibility, more investment in human capital (through education and training, and especially lifelong learning), and keeping older people in the workforce or bringing them back into the workforce.

Enlargement changed the employment situation for the worse, despite potentially improving the EU's economic prospects. The average employment rate in the EU dropped as a result of enlargement by almost 1.5 percentage points. The long-term unemployment rate in the EU25 is 4 percent, compared to 3.3 percent in the EU15. Enlargement also encumbers the employment strategy, adding many more member states to the process. Anticipating these difficulties, the Commission began preparing the candidate countries for participation in the employment strategy long before 2004, notably through the production of Joint Assessment Papers on each country's employment situation in the run-up to enlargement.

The solution to Europe's employment problems is not easy. Member states seem finally to be on the right track, with most national governments introducing more wage and labor flexibility, however reluctantly. For members of the eurozone, the old option of increasing public spending is no longer available (and for nonmembers of the eurozone it is in any case not desirable). The Stability and Growth Pact, a key feature of monetary union, imposes a framework within which the employment strategy needs to operate. Ironically, monetary union, which supposedly exacerbated unemployment in the mid- and late 1990s, may be helping to reduce it substantially a decade later by forcing member states to adopt sound macroeconomic policies.[23]

■ Environmental Policy

Sustainable development is a pillar of the Lisbon strategy and, beyond that, a guiding principle for the EU. Far from being seen as a potential drag on economic development, and therefore having been inserted reluctantly or defensively into the Lisbon strategy, sustainable development is widely seen in the EU as environmentally essential and economically advantageous, although some industry sectors complain that environmental regulation decreases their international competitiveness. As climate change becomes ever more apparent, fossil fuels become scarcer and more difficult to extract, and China—the world's most populous and most rapidly developing country—acquires an insatiable appetite for energy and pumps out vast quantities of greenhouse gases, demand for environmentally friendly technologies, manufacturing processes, and products is bound to grow. The EU believes that it is well placed to meet that demand, both at home and abroad.

Europeans have suffered their fair share of environmental catastrophes over the years, ranging from the excesses of industrialization in the nineteenth and twentieth centuries (compounded by the shortsightedness of central planning in Eastern Europe under the communist regimes) to the occasional industrial or transportation disaster, such as the loss of the *Prestige* oil tanker off the coast of Spain in 2002. On a day-to-day basis, the environment in Europe is under enormous stress from the problems associated with affluence and high population density (the continent is relatively small and crowded), notably disposing of billions of tons of waste annually and curbing soaring carbon dioxide emissions from homes and vehicles.

EU environmental policy is therefore rooted in pragmatism. Yet there is also an ideological edge to Europe's attachment to environmentalism. This became acute in 2001 when U.S. president George W. Bush brusquely dismissed the Kyoto Protocol on climate change, which his predecessor had signed. Never mind that the agreement, intended to curb the production of greenhouse gases, had major flaws, or that the U.S. Senate would not have ratified it. The fact and the manner of Bush's rebuff elevated the Kyoto Protocol, in the EU's eyes, to a higher political plane. It also cast environmental policy as a defining issue in the transatlantic relationship. Having already caricatured the United States as a bastion of heartless capitalism, the EU could now caricature it as well as a profligate polluter uninterested in pressing environmental problems, a notion that many Americans would surely find risible.

The Evolution of Environmental Policy

Although not originally mentioned in the Rome Treaty, the environment is now one of the most important and highly regulated areas of EU policy.[24] Growing popular distress about environmental degradation, the impact of a number of heavily publicized environmental disasters, and the politicization of the environmental movement in the 1970s and 1980s account for the EU's increasing involvement in the area. At the same time, fearing that national environmental measures would distort the single market, governments strengthened the EC's environmental policymaking power as a corollary to the 1992 program. A number of global concerns—climate change, depletion of the ozone layer, dwindling natural resources, and excessive pollution—increased the EU's involvement in international environmental affairs. As a result, environmental policy has been at the top of the EU's political and economic agenda since the late 1980s.

Early EC environmental legislation tended to be narrow and technical, justified either as an internal market measure or on the basis of a vague commitment in the preamble of the Rome Treaty to improve "the living and working conditions" of people in the EC. Examples include a 1967 directive on the classification, packaging, and labeling of dangerous substances and 1970 directives on noise levels. As the environmental movement gathered momentum throughout Western Europe, national governments and the Commission developed a keen interest in environmental issues. Accordingly, at their summit in Paris in October 1972, EU leaders called unequivocally for an EC environmental policy.

Within a year the Commission proposed and the Council adopted the first Environmental Action Program (EAP). This and the second program (1977) listed various measures that were essentially corrective in nature; the third (1982), fourth (1987), and fifth (1993) programs emphasized preventive measures. Reflecting the economic malaise of the early 1980s, the third program specifically called for environmental action that would contribute to economic growth and job creation through the development of less-polluting industries. It also advocated a European-level environmental impact assessment procedure and, for the first time, offered some EC financing for environmental projects.

Reflecting the growing importance of environmental policy in the EC, in 1981 the Commission established a separate directorate-general (DG) to deal with environmental issues. Although smaller than other major directorates-general, DG Environment quickly acquired a reputation for activism and as a main channel for environmental groups to pressure the Commission to pursue "greener" policies. This reputation often put DG Environment at odds with its powerful counterparts engaged in economic and internal market activities. Among the member states, the so-called green troika of Denmark, Germany, and the Netherlands pushed hardest for environmental legislation at the European level, and the poorer southern countries put up most resistance at the legislative and implementation stages.[25]

The 1985 intergovernmental conference on treaty reform, held on the eve of the EC's Iberian enlargement, gave national governments an opportunity to incorporate environmental policy into the treaty. Accordingly, the Single European Act devoted an entire section to environmental policy and included in its single market provisions a new article on environmental protection. Whereas the Single European Act apparently gave the EC wide scope for environmental action, in fact its provisions seemed to limit that scope by invoking, for the first time in the EC treaty, the principle of subsidiarity. Moreover, the act's general environmental provisions and specific provision on environmental protection relating to the single market used different decisionmaking procedures to achieve essentially the same result.

Little wonder that, as far as environmental policy was concerned, the Single European Act seemed "confusing, ambiguous, and contradictory."[26] Yet to a great extent it worked. Based on the Single European Act and on the designation of 1987 as the European Year of the Environment, the EC developed new environmental principles and measures in its fourth Environmental Action Program (1987). References to environmental policy in successive European Council conclusions testified to growing political interest in the issue. At the macrolevel, the Commission pursued a new approach, making environmental policy an integral part of all other policies—notably economic, industrial, transport, energy, agricultural, and social—whether at the national or European level. At the microlevel, the Commission worked on priority areas such as atmospheric and marine pollution, waste management, biotechnology, and enforcement of environmental legislation.

The Maastricht Treaty reiterated the importance of taking environmental policy into account when formulating and implementing other EU policies. In addition, the treaty assuaged the concerns of poorer member states by allowing temporary derogations and/or financial support from the Cohesion Fund to compensate them for environmental measures involving disproportionately high costs. However, the treaty's most important environmental provisions tidied up the decisionmaking process and specified three legislative methods: the cooperation procedure (for most environmental measures), unanimity in the Council (for specified measures), and the codecision procedure (for general action programs).

Written with the Maastricht Treaty in mind, the EC's fifth Environmental Action Program, covering the period 1993–2000, noted a "slow but relentless deterioration . . . of the environment" despite two decades of EC action. The report advocated "sustainable development," defined in general terms as that which "meets the needs of the present without compromising the ability of future generations to meet their own needs." More specifically, the report called for waste reduction through reuse and recycling, lower energy use, a change of general consumption patterns, integrated pollution-control measures, environmentally friendly transport, and industrial risk assessment. It identified five target sectors: industry, energy, transport, agriculture, and tourism. One of the report's most striking aspects was a shift in the EU's general approach from purely regulatory measures, such as emissions limits, to an emphasis on economic and fiscal measures, including taxes, incentives, and subsidies through the structural funds.

Earlier, in 1992, the EU had established the Financial Instrument for the Environment (LIFE) to contribute to the development and implementation of EU environmental policy. Under the terms of the program, the EU would cofinance environmental activities in member states and in nonmember states bordering the Mediterranean and the Baltic Sea (except countries with which the EU had Europe agreements, which received other funds for environmental assistance). Updated every few years, LIFE now has an annual budget of more than €700 million for a wide range of environmental projects in EU and neighboring countries.

Due mostly to pressure from the Netherlands and the two new Nordic member states, negotiations on environmental policy at the 1996–1997 intergovernmental conference on treaty reform focused on three main issues: heightening environmental awareness by stressing the need for sustainable development, extending codecision, and introducing higher environmental standards than provided for in the EU's harmonization measures. Accordingly, the Amsterdam Treaty enshrined the principle of sustainable development as one of the EU's aims and included a general stipulation that "environmental protection requirements must be integrated into the definition and implementation of . . . Community policies and activities . . . in particular with a view to promoting sustainable development." It also extended the codecision procedure to environmental policymaking and, in deference to Finland and Sweden, which had higher environmental standards than most other member states, allowed exceptions to EU rules because of environmental considerations as long as proposed national measures were based on new scientific evidence and the problem being addressed was specific to the member state proposing the exceptional measures. Nevertheless, the treaty explicitly gave the Commission the right to reject such measures even if they were not found to be a means of arbitrary discrimination or a disguised restriction on trade.

Even before the Amsterdam Treaty came into effect, the European Council endorsed a Commission paper on integrating the environment into EU policies. Since then the Commission and the relevant Council formations, prodded by the European Council, have developed an environmental dimension for most policy areas, not just the obvious ones such as agriculture and fisheries, through the so-called Cardiff process. The same heightened interest in sustainable development infused the sixth Environmental Action Program, which covers the period 2001–2010. Its priorities are

- tackling climate change and global warming
- protecting the natural habitat and wildlife
- addressing environment and health issues
- preserving natural resources and managing waste

Sweden, a leader in environmental policy within the EU, pushed during its presidency in 2001 for adoption of a strategy for sustainable development with both an intra-EU and an external dimension. Margot Wallström, the forceful commissioner for the environment, was also Swedish. She and the Council presidency worked closely on devising the strategy, which the European Council endorsed in Göteborg in June 2001. As part of the Göteborg strategy, the environment became the third pillar of the Lisbon strategy for economic modernization. At the annual spring summit, a meeting of the European Council dedicated to reviewing the Lisbon strategy, EU leaders devote considerable time and attention to the environmental implications of the economic reforms under discussion.

The environmental aspects of the Lisbon strategy address climate change (ratification of the Kyoto Protocol, progress in reaching the Kyoto targets, and meeting the target of satisfying 12 percent of energy needs and 22 percent of electricity consumption from renewable sources by 2010); seek to decouple economic growth from resource use; and include some regulatory goals. The Kok Report was more sanguine about the environment pillar of the Lisbon strategy than the economic and social pillars, stressing the opportunities that environmental policy provides for innovation and competitiveness through greater resource efficiency and new investment. The report urged the EU to promote the development and diffusion of ecoinnovations and built on its existing leadership in key ecoindustry markets. It also added a precise recommendation: the greening of public procurement, focusing especially on renewable energy technology and new vehicle fuels.[27]

Key Legislation

Environmental legislation enacted at the EU level now exceeds the quantity and generally exceeds the quality of environmental legislation enacted at the national level. EU environmental legislation has developed unevenly, varying from measures on specific problems to directives on catchall issues. In the mid-1990s EU environmental legislation developed along two main lines: (1) the proposal of framework directives such as those on air quality and the ecological quality of water, and (2) the consolidation or revision of existing directives such as those on environmental impact assessments, the prevention of major accidents involving dangerous substances (the so-called Seveso directive), and the quality of bathing water.

General. In 1985 the Council adopted a directive requiring member states to demand environmental impact assessments (EIAs) before approving projects that by virtue of size, nature, or location are likely to have a significant impact on the environment. Assessments are mandatory for certain types of industrial and infrastructural projects, and other types of activity may be subject to EIAs at the discretion of member states.

In December 1996 the Council adopted a directive obliging member states to install regulatory systems that would issue a single permit to enterprises covering all types of emissions (air, water, and soil). The directive obliges regulatory authorities to evaluate the overall effect of a given operation on the environment not only by using criteria based on environmental quality standards but also by comparing emissions levels to those possible with the "best available technology."

Accidents. After much debate following a major industrial disaster in Seveso, Italy, in 1977, the Council adopted a directive aiming to ensure that manufacturers using dangerous materials, as well as local authorities, have adequate contingency plans to limit the environmental impact of accidents. A revised and updated Seveso directive, adopted in December 1996, retained the basic principles of the original directive but added new requirements and measures to achieve more consistent implementation.

Habitats, Ecosystems, and Wildlife. A 1982 directive instituted a system of licensing to implement the 1973 international Convention on Trade in Endangered Species (CITES). In response to the impending elimination of border controls, in 1992 the Commission proposed further measures to improve internal implementation of CITES rules, resulting in a Council regulation of December 1996.

The so-called wild birds directive, updated six times between 1981 and 1994, is designed to protect more than 100 "particularly vulnerable" species of birds and their habitats. The directive also restricts hunting of additional species, but this provision is widely disregarded in certain member states (especially France) because of the strength of hunting lobbies.

In May 1992 the Council adopted a directive establishing a general program for the protection of natural habitats, later called "Natura 2000." This allows the EU to designate sites as special conservation areas even if they have not been proposed by member states.

Responding to steadily increasing volumes of motor vehicle traffic and to public concern, EU standards have become stricter over time; as a result, emissions have been reduced by an astounding 80–90 percent per car since 1980.

A 1970 directive began the process by setting technical standards for emissions of carbon dioxide and unburned hydrocarbons for most gasoline-powered vehicles. The 1970 directive was based on "optional harmonization": member states were not obligated to implement the standards set forth in the directive but had to approve vehicles from other member states that met those standards. In a series of directives designed to ensure that lead-free gasoline was available throughout Europe at competitive prices, the EC also took action to lower emissions of lead by motor vehicles.

Although the Council amended its landmark 1970 motor vehicle emissions directive several times, the standards set by the amendments lagged behind those set in other large markets, notably the United States. The Commission and Council entered into an extended debate over updating EC emission standards in 1988 and 1989, with member states split over whether to introduce stricter standards for small cars (there was strong opposition from France and Italy, whose producers would be most affected). Eventually, bowing to pressure from the European Parliament and the Dutch government, the Council adopted a directive requiring cars marketed in the EU after January 1993 to meet standards equivalent to those prevailing in the United States (in other words, all new cars must be equipped with catalytic converters).

A subsequent directive further tightened standards and called on the Commission to propose even stricter guidelines by mid-1996. The Commission did so, but the Council and the Parliament failed to reach agreement by the end of 1997, as stipulated in the 1991 directive. Apart from setting strict auto standards, the Commission has also concluded that further improvements in vehicle emissions will have to come from sources other than cars themselves (for example, new fuel mixes, better mandatory maintenance and inspection, and reduction in the use of cars).

Other legislation covering air pollution can be divided roughly into two categories: air-quality standards and emissions limits. Following serious damage caused by acid rain to many European forests and the resulting public outcry, in the late 1970s the EC took action to limit emissions of sulfur dioxide and nitrous oxide. Emissions of lead and other pollutants are also restricted, and industrial plants are required to use the best available technology "not entailing excessive costs."

As concern grew over the effect of widely used chlorofluorocarbons (CFCs) on the earth's protective ozone layer, the EC took steps to limit use of CFCs in the early 1980s. The Commission and member states participated in the negotiation of the 1985 Vienna Convention for the Protection of the Ozone Layer, the 1987 Montreal Protocol (which created a mechanism for limiting use of CFCs and other ozone-damaging chemicals), and subsequent protocols tightening these restrictions and accelerating the phaseout of some substances. The EU implemented the Montreal Protocol through regulations in 1991 and 1994 on substances that deplete the ozone layer.

Amid rising public concern about the prospect of global warming and scientific findings that it could cause rising sea levels and other disasters, the EC committed itself in 1990 to stabilizing emissions of carbon dioxide at a 1990 benchmark level by the year 2000. To help achieve that goal, the Commission proposed a combined EU tax on energy and carbon dioxide emissions to be imposed by national governments. The proposed measure, which would have raised energy prices by the equivalent of U.S.$10 per barrel of oil over a ten-year period (a price hike that seemed shocking at the time), inevitably engendered strong opposition in many quarters. Environment ministers cautiously endorsed it, but industry and finance ministers showed less enthusiasm. Aside from industry opposition, the main problems with the proposal were the technical difficulties of designing the tax itself and the political issue of exemptions for poorer member states. Although several member states adopted carbon dioxide taxes, and despite a 1995 Commission amendment to its proposal making adoption of the tax voluntary, the EU tax proposal became a dead letter.

Water. The Commission divides legislation on water into three categories: quality objectives or other requirements, industry or sector regulations, and limits on the discharge of dangerous substances.

Building on a 1976 framework directive, the EC enacted most of its legislation on water quality during the next decade and passed updated legislation in the 1990s. The framework directive identified substances deemed to pose a threat to the environment, dividing them into a "blacklist" (carcinogens and other dangerous substances, such as mercury or cadmium, for which discharges are prohibited) and a "graylist" (certain other metals and substances that affect the taste or smell of water, for which discharges should be restricted).

In addition, major horizontal directives cover the quality of drinking water and bathing water, discharges to groundwater, quality of water containing freshwater fish and shellfish, quality of surface water for drinking, and treatment of urban wastewater. The urban wastewater directive represents a departure from the traditional emphasis on quality standards and discharge limits and embodies a more general approach to confronting water pollution. It requires member states to provide for treatment of all urban wastewaters within a specific time frame (tailored to individual states and regions).

Eager to consolidate various water-quality initiatives, in February 1996 the Commission issued a communication on EU water policy, setting out objectives, principles, and proposed measures. Chief among these was a framework directive for water resources laying down quality standards to be achieved by December 2007. Perhaps because of the far-off target date, the other EU institutions have been slow to act on it.

Waste. The EU began regulating waste disposal (hazardous and nonhazardous) in 1975 with the adoption of a framework directive that defined waste in general terms ("any substance disposed of by the holder") and required member states to designate competent authorities and set up permit systems for waste disposal. A series of directives dealing with specific areas of waste disposal, relating mainly to hazardous wastes, followed the original framework directive.

A directive originally enacted in 1978 requires member states, producers, holders, and disposers of toxic wastes to keep close track of the movement and disposal of those wastes through the use of permits and extensive documentation. A subsequent Council directive defined hazardous waste, established general requirements for facilities that deal with it, tightened documentation requirements to include registration of all wastes discharged at waste sites, established a consignment note system for transfer of such wastes, and restricted mixing hazardous wastes with each other or with nonhazardous wastes.

The EU has a system of compulsory prior notification and authorization for transport of hazardous wastes across national borders, including uniform documentation requirements. A series of directives since the mid-1970s regulates treatment and disposal of specific types of waste, including polychlorinated biphenyls and polychlorinated terphenyls, waste oils, asbestos, batteries and accumulators, and waste arising from the manufacture of titanium dioxide.

The Commission made its first foray into the reduction of nonhazardous waste with a directive in 1985 requiring member states to draw up a four-year program to reduce the contribution of beverage containers to the waste stream. In 1989, with the release of a communication on EC strategy for waste management, the Commission took a broader approach, promising to make a series of proposals covering multiple aspects of waste management, including

- stricter controls on the movement of all waste and ratification of the Basel Convention and OECD decision on transboundary movement of waste
- a directive on civil liability for damage caused by waste
- directives on uniform site design for landfills and standards for incineration of hazardous waste
- a proposal on recycling waste packaging

Among these, a 1993 directive on shipments of waste is probably the most important. Numerous disputes over EU competence and national sovereignty (including whether shipments within member states should be covered and whether a member state could ban imports of waste from another member state) delayed adoption for well over a year. In its final version, the regulation covers only shipments between states, although it obliges governments to establish "an appropriate system" for control of shipments within their own borders and to notify the Commission of that system. In keeping with the "proximity" principle (wastes should be disposed of as near as possible to where they were generated), the Commission conceded that member states should be allowed to ban waste imports systematically except in cases that involve specialized wastes coming from small member states.

Other elements of the Commission's strategy were even harder to enact. For example, a draft directive on civil liability for damage caused by waste made little progress in the Council and was eventually subsumed into a Green Paper on remedying environmental damage, released by the Commission in March 1993. It reemerged in March 1997 in a Commission proposal for a new directive, which then worked its way through the legislative process.

The Commission began to advocate common rules for packaging and packaging waste starting in 1992 after Germany adopted legislation threatening to disrupt the single market by requiring producers to take back, or guarantee recycling of, all packaging waste from consumer products sold in Germany. Initially, the Commission called for recycling 60 percent of each type of packaging waste and energy recovery (incineration) of a further 30 percent in each member state within ten years. The proposal also required extensive tracking of waste generation and disposal trends in the packaging area while leaving precise methods of implementing the targets to individual member states. Initially, the proposal provoked lively controversy, with some member states complaining that the directive was too lax and industry objecting that the targets were technologically unreachable for certain types of materials. The debate grew tenser as it became clear that Germany was meeting its seemingly admirable recycling goals via massive exports of used packaging materials, threatening to destroy national recycling systems by driving prices below cost throughout Europe. After an arduous discussion with the European Parliament and a host of interest groups, in December 1994 the Council finally adopted a much more modest directive requiring member states to reach targets of between 50 percent and 65 percent recovery (a figure covering both recycling and incineration) of packaging waste with a further minimum level of between 25 percent and 45 percent for recycling alone and a minimum of 15 percent for recycling of each type of packaging material by the first target date of 2001, with regularly upgraded targets thereafter. Member states are free to exceed the targets as long as they do not produce "excessive" waste exports (that is, disrupt the status quo elsewhere).

Problems of Enforcement

Enforcement is a critical problem in the search for an effective EU environmental policy. Differing legal regimes, economic concerns, degrees of public interest, and levels of political commitment among member states have contributed to uneven implementation of environmental directives throughout the EU. Until the European Environment Agency became fully operational in 1995, the Commission was hampered by a dearth of reliable data on the state of the environment in Europe. The Commission remains constrained by its reliance on national governments for the information needed to pursue some infringement proceedings.

The Commission generally paints a gloomy picture of enforcement of EU environmental rules by the member states; only Austria and the Nordic countries usually escape criticism. Problems range from egregiously late transposal of EU measures to failure to conform to standards established in EU legislation to nonsubmission of required reports. Calls for better implementation are a staple of Commission reports on environmental policy. Indeed, fuller implementation and better enforcement of environmental policy obligations are priority objectives of the sixth Environmental Action Program (2002–2006).

Economic actors often disregard the Environmental Impact Assessment directive, a key piece of EU environmental legislation. Impact assessments are a fruitful source of conflict between the Commission and the member states, not least because the directive allows environmental organizations to appeal to another, highly visible authority against the action (or inaction) of their own governments regarding local development issues. The Commission has brought infringement proceedings against a majority of member states for failure to implement the directive in full. Even where the procedure laid down by the directive is formally complied with, the Commission complains that impact studies are often of mediocre quality and almost always underestimate harm to the environment.

In areas covered by substantive legislation (air, water, waste, and the like), the Commission considers the situation to be least satisfactory where EU legislation lays down obligations to plan ahead. Water quality is a prime example: many member states simply have not undertaken the massive public investment programs necessary to meet the standards to which they agreed in the Council. This failure is especially evident with respect to the drinking and bathing water directives, where concentrations of certain pollutants routinely exceed EU norms, sometimes with the explicit permission of national authorities. There are a number of flagrant abuses in the area of air quality (Athens comes immediately to mind), although the problem is often lack of information on the real situation in member states.

In addition to the usual plethora of disputes over conformity of implementing legislation, a key problem in the area of waste is violation of control and documentation rules by waste shippers and an increase in uncontrolled or illegal dumps or landfills. The Commission is far from certain that member states are disposing of waste in accordance with EC law. In the area of nature protection, the Commission cites continual problems over member states' failure to designate adequate numbers of special preserves, as well as the persistence of hunting in violation of the directives on protection of birds and other wildlife.

The Environment and Enlargement

Finland and Sweden, which joined the EU in 1995, are famous for their assertive approach to environmental issues regionally and globally. Their accession negotiations on the environment chapter were especially contentious because standards were generally higher in Finland and Sweden than in the EU. Negotiators on both sides therefore strove to reconcile the desire of the applicant states to maintain their higher standards until EU standards reached an equivalent level with the EU's desire to maintain the free movement of goods in the single market. The so-called third-option alternative provided an acceptable compromise. It promised a review of EU environmental directives within four years of enlargement, during which time the new member states could maintain their higher standards.[28] The issue of higher environmental standards in Finland and Sweden then became bound up in negotiations at the 1996–1997 intergovernmental conference, resulting in a treaty revision allowing exceptions to environmental rules in exceptional circumstances.

The problem with the environment dossier in the next round of enlargement negotiations, involving the Central and Eastern European states, was the opposite of what it had been during the negotiations with Finland and Sweden. After decades of Soviet-style economic planning and performance, the environmental situation in Central and Eastern Europe was truly abysmal. Although air and water pollution levels in the region dropped significantly in the 1990s, thanks to the collapse of the heavy-industry and mining sectors, the applicant states had a long way to go to meet EU requirements. Nuclear contamination and the risk of nuclear accidents were particularly worrisome and expensive to rectify.

The Europe agreements between the EU and the Central and Eastern European states, concluded in the early and mid-1990s, stipulated in general terms that the associated countries' economic policies must be guided by the principle of sustainable development and take full account of environmental conditions. Beyond that, the Commission's 1995 White Paper on integrating the applicant states into the internal market covered only a small fraction of the EU's environmental rulebook. In its opinions on the Central and Eastern European states' membership applications, the Commission included an assessment—often bleak—of the environmental situation in each of the applicant countries, whose difficulties with conforming to the EU's environmental standards inevitably complicated the enlargement negotiations.[29]

Bringing the Central and Eastern European states up to Western European environmental standards would require massive investment in everything from wastewater treatment to solid-waste management to air pollution reduction. It would also require a huge improvement in the administrative capacities of the applicant countries. Without efficient regional and local environmental administrations, for instance, the Central and Eastern European states would not be capable of issuing a single permit to enterprises covering all types of emissions, as required by the integrated pollution prevention and control directive, a key piece of EU legislation.

Beginning in the mid-1990s, the EU provided financial assistance under the PHARE program to help bring the prospective new member states up to EU environmental standards. The Central and Eastern European states were also eligible to take part in the LIFE program. Later, in the run-up to enlargement, the EU provided specific preaccession assistance for environmental improvements. This aid was sometimes conditional on the applicants taking certain steps, such as developing waste management plans, although the Commission had less leverage as the date of enlargement approached unless it was willing to block the applicants' accession on environmental grounds. In general, the Commission estimated that bringing Central and Eastern Europe fully up to Western European environmental standards would require an investment of 2–3 percent of the new member states' GDP. Nevertheless, the accession countries did not receive any derogations or exemptions from EU environmental law, only some transitional periods for its implementation. The new member states therefore needed to transpose the EU's voluminous environmental *acquis* into national law.

Just as the 2004 enlargement caused a drop in the average per capita GDP in the EU, it also reduced the average level of environmental well-being in the EU. It will take Central and Eastern Europe a long time to catch up to Western Europe environmentally as well as economically. Indeed, many Central and Eastern Europeans fret that the costs of environmental improvements will hold back their economic development. For that reason the Central and Eastern European member states may be less aggressive in the pursuit of EU environmental policy than their Western European counterparts.

The EU's Role in International Environmental Affairs

Almost from the beginning, EU environmental policy acquired an international dimension. Realizing that pollution knew no bounds and that environmental degradation was a global problem, member states undertook as early as 1973 to coordinate their international positions on environmental issues. On that basis, the EU became increasingly involved in worldwide environmental affairs.

The Single European Act authorized the EC to enter into international agreements on environmental issues "with third countries and with . . . relevant international organizations," and the fourth Environmental Action Program called on member states and the EC to participate actively on the international stage to protect the environment. As a result, the EU is now party to over thirty international conventions and agreements on the environment that are regional or global in scope, covering issues such as acid rain, biodiversity, climate change and greenhouse gases, desertification, and protection of major rivers. The EU also participates in environmental activities with the OECD, the UN Environment Programme, and the Economic Commission for Europe. In addition, environmental criteria are integral to EU assistance to the countries of "wider Europe" and the southern Mediterranean and to EU development policy (for instance, the Cotonou Convention provides for general environmental cooperation and includes a specific ban on exports of hazardous waste to the participating African, Caribbean, and Pacific countries).

The EC and the member states participated in the Rio conference in June 1992, which adopted three basic texts:

- the Rio Declaration on the Environment and Development (general principles relating to the environmental implications of economic development)
- Agenda 21 (a comprehensive work program covering virtually every aspect of environment and development)
- a nonbinding statement on forest principles

The EC and the member states signed the UN Framework Convention on Climate Change and the Convention on Biodiversity at the Rio conference, both of which emerged from negotiations begun long before that.

Of all the issues discussed at Rio, climate change was arguably the most consequential and also the one that became the most controversial internationally. Beginning with a 1990 commitment to stabilizing carbon dioxide emissions, which required richer member states to reduce emissions, the Commission attempted to stake out a position for the EU as a leader in reducing emissions of greenhouse gases and to exert moral pressure on others (mainly the United States) to follow the EU example. In practice, most member states found it impossible to meet their virtuous-sounding targets; the exception, Germany, was able to post impressive reductions after reunification led to the shutdown of most East German soft-coal electricity-generating plants. The Commission's failure to persuade member states to adopt a Community-wide carbon dioxide tax in the early 1990s further widened the gap between rhetoric and results.

Nevertheless, the EU entered into negotiations leading up to the Kyoto Conference on Climate Change in December 1997 with the ambitious proposal that industrial countries reduce emissions by 2010 to 15 percent below 1990 levels of three greenhouse gases; the proposal imposed no targets on developing countries. The EU's biggest trading partners declined to follow this lead. The United States, which had some of the highest per capita emissions, proposed stabilization, and Japan offered a 2.5 percent cut. The United States opposed the exclusion of developing countries; indeed, the U.S. Congress went so far as to threaten rejection of any deal not including developing-country commitments. Another contentious issue was the means by which countries could take credit for gains occurring elsewhere. The EU proposed allowing EU countries, including new member states, to take collective credit for any reductions; the United States pushed for "joint implementation" that would allow it to take credit for reductions achieved through U.S. investment in Russia and other fuel-inefficient countries. In the end, the EU reduced its target to 8 percent reductions below 1990 levels in six greenhouse gases between 2008 and 2012, accompanied by commitments of 7 percent for the United States and 6 percent for Japan and Canada, with provisions allowing for emissions trading and a "clean-development mechanism" to attract private-sector investment to developing countries in return for tradable emissions credits.

The EU's target is shared among the EU15 (the Kyoto Protocol was concluded in 1997), with separate targets for each of the member states under that overall umbrella. Six of the new Central and Eastern European member states have to reduce emissions by 8 percent below 1990 levels; Hungary and Poland, by 6 percent (Cyprus and Malta do not have targets). Individual member state targets are binding under EU law. The protocol would enter into force only when at least fifty-five of the signatories ratified it, including industrialized countries accounting for at least 55 percent of carbon dioxide emissions in 1990. Over 120 countries had ratified the agreement by early 2004, but not enough industrialized countries to meet the 55 percent emissions threshold. Because the United States accounted for 36 percent of greenhouse gas emissions in 1990, its withdrawal from the protocol endangered implementation of the agreement. With 17 percent of carbon dioxide emissions in 1990, Russia held the fate of the protocol in its hands. Russia's belated ratification of the protocol in November 2004 meant that the agreement could finally come into effect. It also meant that Russia would make a lot of money by selling its remaining emissions quota to other parties (Russia's greenhouse gas emissions are about 30 percent below their 1990 levels, thanks to the collapse of heavy industry in the former Soviet Union).

The EU seems well on track to meet the Kyoto goal. In order to help its member states meet their individual targets, and therefore help the EU15 meet its collective target, the EU set up a European Emissions Trading Scheme that became effective in January 2005. It allows all twenty-five member states to trade their remaining quotas with each other. Reductions in the discharge of greenhouse gases in Central and Eastern Europe as countries phased out inefficient coal-generating energy-producing methods in the 1990s made the new member states attractive emissions trading partners. In the longer term, however, accelerating economic growth in Central and Eastern Europe will cause an increase in emissions that may be difficult to control without drastic fiscal measures or unforeseeable technological advances.

In addition to the Kyoto Protocol, the EU has taken a prominent position on a range of global environmental issues. For instance, the EU played a leading part at the world summit on sustainable development in Johannesburg in

August 2002. Being a leader on the environment, a cause of urgent global concern, helps the EU to raise its international profile, especially as the United States has abdicated leadership in that area. Environmental policy is therefore as important internationally as domestically for the EU, at least in terms of identity and image.

▓ Notes

1. Wim Kok et al., *Facing the Challenge: The Lisbon Strategy for Growth and Enlargement: Report of the High Level Group* (Brussels: European Commission, 2004), p. 16.

2. European Council Directive (EC) 93/104, November 13, 1993, concerning certain aspects of the organization of working time.

3. Beverly Springer, *The Social Dimension of 1992* (New York: Praeger, 1992), p. 39.

4. Jacques Delors, speech to the European Parliament outlining the Commission's program for 1988, January 20, 1988. Bulletin EC S/1-1988, p. 12.

5. Bulletin EC 6-1988, "Presidency Conclusions," point 1.1.1.

6. Bulletin EC 9-1988, points 1.1.1–1.1.6.

7. Bulletin EC 12-1989, "Presidency Conclusions," point 1.1.10.

8. European Commission, *Social Europe: First Report on Application of the Social Charter of Fundamental Social Rights for Workers* (Luxembourg: Office for Official Publications of the European Communities, 1992), p. 5.

9. Bulletin EC12-1989, "Presidency Conclusions," point 1.1.10.

10. COM(89)568 final, November 29, 1989.

11. COM(92)562 final, December 23, 1992.

12. See *Financial Times,* February 5, 1993, p. 1.

13. Michel Petite, "The Amsterdam Treaty," Harvard Jean Monnet Chair Working Papers Series (1988), no. 2/98, http://law.hardavd.edu/Programs/JeanMonnet/papers98/98-2-.html, p. 18.

14. COM(94)333.

15. COM(95)134.

16. Quoted in *European Report*, September 27, 2000, p. 6.

17. Kok, *Facing the Challenge*, p. 31.

18. David Williamson, "The European Union: New Money, New Treaty, New Members," *The European Union: Speeches,* www.eurunion.org/news/speeches/971211dw.htm.

19. European Commission, *Growth, Competitiveness, and Employment: The Challenges and Ways Forward into the 21st Century,* COM(93)700.

20. Cardiff European Council, "Presidency Conclusions," Bulletin EC 6-1998, points 1.2–1.4.

21. Kok, *Facing the Challenge,* p. 31.

22. Ibid., p. 32.

23. See D. Ashiagbor, "EMU and the Shift in the European Labour Law Agenda: From 'Social Policy' to 'Employment Policy,'" *European Law Journal* 7, no. 3 (September 2001): 311–331.

24. On environmental policy generally, see John McCormick, *Environmental Policy in the European Union* (Basingstoke, UK: Palgrave, 2001).

25. See Alberta Sbragia, "The Push-Pull of Environmental Policy-Making," in Helen Wallace and William Wallace, eds., *Policy-Making in the European Union*, 3rd ed. (Oxford: Oxford University Press, 1996), pp. 235–256.

26. Ida Johanne Koppen, *The European Community's Environment Policy: From the Summit in Paris, 1972, to the Single European Act, 1986*, EUI working paper no. 88/328 (Florence: EUI, 1988), p. 62.

27. Kok, *Facing the Challenge,* pp. 35–38.

28. Francisco Granell, "The European Union's Enlargement Negotiations with Austria, Finland, Norway, and Sweden," *Journal of Common Market Studies* 33, no. 1 (March 1995): 129.

29. European Commission, *Agenda 2000: For a Stronger and Wider Europe*, Brussels, July 16, 1997, COM(97)2000 final.

15

Economic and Monetary Union

There have been three major monetary policy initiatives in the history of European integration: the Werner Plan to achieve economic and monetary union (EMU) by 1980; the European Monetary System (EMS), launched in 1979; and the 1991 intergovernmental conference on EMU that resulted in the Maastricht Treaty. All were due, in part, to deliberate decisions to "relaunch" European integration. Unlike the third initiative, the two earlier ones were also a response to international currency crises or challenges. In the case of the Werner Plan, international exchange rate fluctuations, culminating in the collapse of the Bretton Woods system, impelled the European Community to act; in the case of the EMS, the destabilizing impact of foreign currency movements, notably the dollar, had the same effect.

By comparison, the 1991 intergovernmental conference took place at a time of stable exchange rates between member state currencies, thanks in part to the relative success of the EMS. Moreover, in marked contrast to the 1970s, the late 1980s was a period of economic buoyancy in the EC as the single market program boosted business confidence and set the stage for deeper integration. The circumstances seemed particularly propitious not only for a new monetary initiative but also for the achievement of economic union, which in the European Union means not a common economic policy for all member states but the existence of a single market plus close coordination of member states' economic policies. A three-stage plan for EMU was the centerpiece of the Treaty on European Union, concluded at the Maastricht summit in December 1991.

The politics of EMU dominated the 1990s. Would a majority of member states meet the convergence criteria in time to launch Stage III of EMU (the single currency) in 1997? If not, which member states would meet the criteria by 1999? Would France and Germany be among them? Would skeptical member state publics accept the kinds of austerity measures necessary in order to qualify for Stage III? Would they endure the high unemployment that seemed an inevitable accompaniment of EMU? Would EMU continue to divide Britain's (then) ruling Conservative Party? Would Britain's (then) opposition Labour Party overcome its differences on EMU and be able to present itself as a credible alternative government? Would mainstream political parties on the continent exploit popular concern about the loss of national currencies and play the anti-EMU card?

Despite a poor economic climate in the mid-1990s and despite having missed the 1997 target date, a majority of member states (including France and Germany) indeed qualified for the 1999 deadline for the launch of Stage III. By that time Helmut Kohl, the architect of EMU, was out of office in Germany, although only indirectly because of EMU. By that time also the Conservatives were out of office in Britain, having been replaced by an EU-friendly Labour government. However, the new government decided to exercise Britain's opt-out from Stage III despite meeting the criteria for participation in it. Denmark had already negotiated an opt-out, Sweden chose not to participate, and Greece did not meet the convergence criteria. As a result, eleven of the fifteen member states participated in monetary union at the outset, in January 1999, accepting a common monetary policy and irrevocably fixing their exchange rates. Greece joined them in January 2001, in time to participate in the launch of the euro as a real currency (in people's pockets) in January 2002.

Monetary union marks a highly advanced stage of European integration. The transition to Stage III of EMU was wrenching for most member states, although the introduction of the euro itself went remarkably smoothly. Managing monetary union without a complete economic union is a daunting task. In the heady days of the mid-1990s, as national economies finally picked up after a disappointing start to the decade, member states agreed to abide by the so-called Stability and Growth Pact once they entered Stage III of EMU. A decade later, with most national economies again performing poorly, it is difficult for some member states to keep their budget deficits under 3 percent of GDP, as stipulated by the pact. France and Germany's disregard of the pact in 2003 provoked a minor political crisis and raised serious questions about the credibility and long-term viability of EMU. In the meantime, Britain, Denmark, and Sweden show no signs of wanting to adopt the euro, although the new Central and Eastern European member states are likely to do so before the end of the decade. Managing EMU (on the fiscal as well as the monetary side) while coping with enlargement is one of the biggest challenges facing the EU today.

■ The New Impetus for EMU

In October 1990 an exuberant Jacques Delors, president of the Commission, declared emphatically that "we need a single currency before the year 2000."[1] The necessity of EMU was debatable on economic grounds, but Delors's remark demonstrated his personal drive and political ambition. As finance minister in 1983, Delors had convinced French president François Mitterrand to reverse his socialist economic policy and commit France uncompromisingly to the exchange rate mechanism of the EMS, arguably saving both the French government and the EMS in the process. The Single European Act and the successful launch of the single market program in the late 1980s greatly enhanced Delors's standing and provided a powerful new impetus for EMU. It was no coincidence that Delors chaired the committee charged by the European Council with plotting a path to EMU or that the committee's influential report unofficially bore his name.

Market Integration and Monetary Union

By advocating EMU, Delors championed a long-standing objective of European integration. The Rome Treaty's goal of market integration and espousal of "ever closer union" implicitly endorsed EMU. Yet the treaty contained few provisions for economic and monetary coordination, partly because of the political constraints on European integration in the late 1950s in the aftermath of the failed European Defense Community initiative. In addition, the fixed exchange rates of the Bretton Woods system, to which the member states belonged, made monetary union unnecessary.

Predictably, the EC's first overt espousal of EMU came at a time of international financial upheaval in the late 1960s, culminating in the breakdown of the Bretton Woods system. A call by EC leaders in 1972 for EMU by 1980 nevertheless proved unrealistic. More than a decade later, in the preamble of the Single European Act, member states reaffirmed their commitment to "the progressive realization of economic and monetary union." The Single European Act's modest provisions for an EC monetary capacity and pointed reference to "the experience acquired in cooperation within the framework of the European Monetary System" provided a modest political push toward EMU.

The single market program, which took off with the Single European Act, greatly advanced the goal of EMU.[2] Exchange rate fluctuations seemed inconsistent with and contradictory to the objectives of the single market. In the early 1980s, before the launch of the single market program, a group of influential academics had argued that "a common market with common policies can be viable in the long run only within a coherent framework of macro-economic and monetary policies."[3] With the 1992 program off to a strong start, the symbiotic relationship between it and EMU became a new orthodoxy. In his influential report on the single market program's implications for the European economy, Tomaso Padoa-Schioppa strongly endorsed the link between completing the single market and embarking on EMU.[4]

By the end of the 1980s, market integration as a rationale for EMU was almost unquestioned. A communication by the Commission in August 1990 developed the link: "A single currency is the natural complement of a single market. The full potential of the latter will not be achieved without the former. Going further, there is a need for economic and monetary union in part to consolidate the potential gains from completing the internal market, without which there would be risks of weakening the present momentum of the 1992 process."[5] The Commission's much-quoted cost-benefit analysis of EMU appeared two months later. Its title, *One Market, One Money,* reinforced the 1992-EMU connection and became a mantra for advocates of a single currency.[6] A Commission publication, prepared by the information directorate-general, maintained that "the creation of a single currency is a natural and necessary attribute of a smoothly functioning single market."[7]

The EMS, which had helped to make the single market possible, provided another impetus toward EMU in the late 1980s. Padoa-Schioppa pointed out that with complete capital mobility (a feature of the single market), the exchange rate mechanism and the existing degree of monetary policy coordination would be insufficient to promote price stability and ensure orderly trade relations among member states. "In a quite fundamental way," Padoa-Schioppa concluded, "capital mobility [1992] and exchange rate fixity [the EMS] together leave no room for independent monetary policies."[8] Put another way, a unified market with a free flow of capital could put the EMS under unbearable pressure.

Member states would discover the extent of that pressure during the currency crisis of 1992. In the meantime, the perceived success of the EMS in the late 1980s increased the momentum for EMU. Given the stability of the exchange rate mechanism since early 1987, when the last general alignment had occurred, the EMS tended to be seen as a forerunner of EMU. Further economic convergence, it seemed, would reinforce exchange rate stability and turn the EMS into a quasi–monetary union. Therefore, moving from the EMS to EMU seemed logical and relatively effortless. As commissioner Leon Brittan remarked in October 1990, "The ERM [exchange rate mechanism] is the kernel of the future single European currency."[9]

Brittan's audience of businesspeople was predisposed to the idea of monetary union thanks to the success of both the EMS and the single market program. In 1990 management consultants Ernst and Young conducted a survey for the Commission that showed widespread optimism in business circles about the economic impact of monetary union combined with completion of the single market.[10] The experience of working together in the exchange rate mechanism also reconciled many government officials and politicians to the prospect of EMU. Twenty years earlier Leo Tindemans had reported regretfully that there was not enough trust between member states to transfer responsibility for EMU to a central authority.[11] Without doubt, participation in the EMS had helped member states to overcome such distrust.

The Delors Report

The decisive Delors Report did not take an explicit stand on whether monetary union was necessary to ensure the success of the single market, nor did it develop a cost-benefit analysis of EMU. Instead, the committee of central bank governors of the (then twelve) member states, two commissioners, and three independent experts outlined what EMU would look like and devised specific steps that could result in its achievement. Taking a lead from the Werner Report, the Delors Report defined monetary union as "the assurance of total and irreversible convertibility of currencies; the complete liberalization of capital transactions and full integration of banking and other financial markets; and the elimination of margins of fluctuation and the irrevocable locking of exchange rate parities."[12] Although the committee did not explicitly endorse a single currency, its definition of monetary union necessarily involved a centralized monetary policy for the Community.

The report identified four basic elements of economic union:

1. a single market, within which persons, goods, services, and capital can move freely
2. competition policy and other measures aimed at strengthening market mechanisms
3. common policies aimed at structural change and regional development
4. macroeconomic policy coordination, including binding rules for budgetary policies

Three of these were already being put in place:

1. The single market program was in full swing.
2. The importance of an effective competition policy to create a "level playing field" in the single market was uncontested.
3. Member states had agreed in February 1988 that a huge increase in regional development assistance was necessary to make a success of the single market. A decade earlier the EC had offered financial assistance to poorer countries participating in the exchange rate mechanism and, for the same reason, would establish a sizable Cohesion Fund in 1992 for disadvantaged member states hoping to embark on EMU.

Only macroeconomic coordination would represent a noticeable new departure. Although economic union would not necessitate a common economic policy, the Delors Report stressed the need for centralized control over national fiscal policies in order to operate EMU successfully. Specifically, the report advocated effective upper limits on the budget deficits of individual member states, no recourse to direct central bank credit and other forms of monetary financing, and limited recourse to borrowing in non-EC currencies.[13]

The Delors Report proposed a federal European System of Central Banks (ESCB) made up of a central institution (a "Eurofed") and constituent national central banks to formulate and implement a common monetary policy. Reflecting both the influence of Karl-Otto Pöhl, president of the Bundesbank (German central bank) and a member of the committee, and a high degree of satisfaction with the existing EMS, the report emphatically identified price stability as the ESCB's primary objective. Like the Bundesbank's directorate, the ESCB's council would be rigidly independent of government influence or control.

The Delors Report is best known for proposing a three-stage approach to EMU:

- Stage I: free capital movement in the EC and closer monetary and macroeconomic cooperation between member states and their central banks
- Stage II: launch of the ESCB to monitor and coordinate national monetary policies; stronger supervisory powers for EC institutions, notably the European Parliament and the Council; and a progressive narrowing of margins of fluctuation within the exchange rate mechanism
- Stage III: establishment of "irrevocably fixed" exchange rate parities; granting of full authority for monetary policy to EC institutions

A phased approach was inevitable. Nor were the contents of each stage surprising. Mindful of the embarrassment caused by the EC's commitment in 1972 to achieve EMU by the end of the decade, the Delors Report did not adopt a timetable for a renewed effort to achieve EMU. Instead, the report merely recommended that Stage I start no later than July 1990, when capital movements were due to be liberalized anyway as part of the single market program.

Toward Monetary Union

The Delors Report sparked a lively debate. The most explosive political point, inherent in any discussion of EMU, centered on the question of national sovereignty. Most participants in the exchange rate mechanism had already lost control over national monetary policy. By the late 1980s their currencies were pegged to the German mark, the system's unofficial anchor. The Bundesbank formulated monetary policy in the EMS, and member states reaped the political and economic rewards of low inflation and stable exchange rates. In effect, Germany's partners in the EMS gave up using interest rates and nominal exchange rates as instruments of national policy. In any case, prevailing opinion in the 1980s held that using devaluations to tackle such problems as declining demand for a country's products was both ineffective and likely to fuel inflation.

As far as monetary union was concerned, most participants in the exchange rate mechanism stood to regain sovereignty rather than lose it. By joining a federal monetary system, they would wrest some power back from the Bundesbank. This was the reasoning behind French finance minister Edouard Balladur's influential advocacy of EMU in early 1988. By the same token, Germany should have been the least happy about monetary union. Indeed, the Bundesbank had serious concerns about surrendering its virtual monopoly on decisionmaking, at least until it could be sure that an alternative arrangement offered as good a prospect of price stability as did the existing mechanism.[14] But the German government, which in any event supported monetary union for political reasons, could hardly argue in favor of maintaining a monopoly over monetary policy in the EC.

Economic union would involve less centralization of power than would monetary union because a single economic policy did not seem essential. Sensitive to the political climate of the late 1980s, the Commission claimed that "the Community's involvement in economic decision-making should be based on a balance between subsidiarity and parallelism [between the economic and monetary parts of EMU]."[15] Whereas economic policy could be formulated at different levels of government, responsibility for monetary policy would rest squarely with a new EC institution, the European Central Bank (ECB).

The debate over national sovereignty was loudest in Britain, where the economic benefits of EMU were also least apparent. In a speech to the House of Commons in January 1991, the chancellor of the exchequer (finance minister) explained that safeguarding the "sovereign right of Parliament" would be one of his priorities in the forthcoming intergovernmental conference on EMU.[16] Even before the intergovernmental conference began, Prime Minister Margaret Thatcher complained in July 1991 that the exchange rate mechanism, into which she had reluctantly brought Britain the previous October, was "tearing the heart out of parliamentary sovereignty." As for EMU, handing over responsibility for monetary policy to the putative ECB would reduce "national finance ministers to the status of innocent bystanders at the scene of an accident."[17]

The question of sovereignty also hinged on powerful political symbols. Money was both a means of transacting business and a badge of national identity or, in the event of a single currency, a symbol of European unity. As a compromise, Leon Brittan suggested keeping existing coins and banknotes and simply denominating their European currency unit (ECU) value on one side.[18] A number of countries designed new currency along those lines. As the

Maastricht ratification crisis would show, attachment to the national symbolism of money ran deep throughout the EC, especially in Germany, where the mark epitomized postwar prosperity and stability.

The Commission did not try to calculate the political costs or benefits of EMU apart from an oblique reference to possible "psychological" problems.[19] Member states would have to reach their own conclusions, but for most it was clear that the anticipated benefits of EMU outweighed the intangible political costs. Not only had most countries already sacrificed national sovereignty by participating in the exchange rate mechanism but some—notably Italy—saw future EC curbs on national fiscal policy as the only way to cut their exorbitant budget deficits.

Instead, the Commission focused on economic losses and gains, identifying the elimination of transaction costs and exchange rate vulnerability, resulting in greater trade and investment, as a major advantage. The Commission estimated that EC-wide savings on transaction costs could amount to as much as 0.3 to 0.4 percent of GDP.[20] Yet the Commission conceded that the EC was not an "optimum currency area" in which labor would move freely in order to offset country-specific shocks; nor would Brussels have a fiscal system capable of making income-stabilizing transfers. Given that economic shocks would continue to affect each member state differently, that labor would remain relatively immobile because of cultural and linguistic barriers, and that the EC would not acquire a sizable fiscal system, the advantages of EMU seemed far from obvious. Based on additional analysis applied to the EC's actual structure and situation, however, the Commission not surprisingly concluded that "the case [for EMU] can stand powerfully on economic criteria alone."[21]

The Commission's arguments failed to impress some influential economists on both sides of the EMU debate. Peter Kenen, professor of economics and international finance at Princeton University and a supporter of monetary integration, regretted that *One Market, One Money* did not prove conclusively "that the benefits would exceed the costs," its title being "as close as the study came to making a case for EMU."[22] Martin Feldstein, professor of economics at Harvard University and an opponent of EMU, refuted the assertion that a single market needed a single currency, let alone monetary union. Feldstein argued that monetary union would not necessarily increase trade and that the success of the EMS weakened the anti-inflationary argument for EMU.[23] Perhaps the Commission should have produced an aggregate estimate of the impact of EMU, along the lines of the Cecchini Report on the single market. The Commission explained in August 1990, however, that the nature of EMU, conditional as it was on "the responses of governments as well as private economic agents," made such an approach infeasible.[24]

In the event, as Feldstein noted disapprovingly, the main push for EMU was political, not economic. It emanated mainly from Paris, Brussels, and

Bonn. Indeed, the conclusions of successive European summits in the late 1980s chronicled the seemingly unstoppable political pressure that had developed for EMU:

- It was striking that in June 1988 the European Council charged the Delors Committee not with exploring the rationale for EMU but with suggesting concrete steps for achieving it.[25]
- Twelve months later, in Madrid in June 1989, the European Council reiterated its "determination progressively to achieve economic and monetary union," endorsed the Delors Report as a basic blueprint for EMU, and decided to launch Stage I of EMU on July 1, 1990.[26]
- At the Strasbourg summit in December 1989, Mitterrand noted that the necessary majority existed to convene an intergovernmental conference on EMU.[27]
- The European Council decided in June 1990 to begin the intergovernmental conference six months later in Rome, with a view to concluding and ratifying a treaty before the end of 1992.[28]
- Finally, at an extraordinary summit in Rome in October 1990, two months before the launch of the conference, eleven of the twelve heads of state and government—Thatcher was the odd one out—agreed to begin Stage II of EMU on January 1, 1994.[29]

The Maastricht Treaty

The ensuing Maastricht Treaty duly adopted a three-stage process for the completion of EMU but differed from the Delors Report in a number of important respects, not least by affirming a single currency (and not simply fixed exchange rates) as EMU's ultimate goal. The single currency would be launched at the beginning of Stage III, for which the Maastricht Treaty set a deadline of January 1999. A European Monetary Institute would be established at the beginning of Stage II to make technical preparations for Stage III and monitor member state compliance with the requirements for participation in it. The council of the European Monetary Institute would consist of national central bank governors, although the council president would be "selected from among persons of recognized standing and professional experience in monetary or banking matters" from outside the governors' circle.

According to the treaty, member states wishing to participate in Stage III would have to meet a number of criteria intended to ensure "a high degree of sustainable [economic] convergence" (Article 121 TEC). There were four so-called convergence criteria:

- *Price stability:* an average inflation rate not exceeding by more than 1.5 percent that of the three best-performing member states

- *Budgetary discipline:* a government financial position that does not include an excessive deficit (a protocol attached to the treaty provided two reference values: a budget deficit of less than 3 percent of GDP and a public debt ratio not exceeding 60 percent of GDP)
- *Currency stability:* observance of normal fluctuation margins of the exchange rate mechanism for at least two years with no devaluations
- *Interest rate convergence:* an average nominal long-term interest rate not exceeding by more than 2 percent that of the three best-performing member states

Before the end of 1996 the Council—meeting at the level of heads of state and government—would assess the degree of economic convergence among member states. If they decided that a majority of member states met the convergence criteria, EU leaders could set a date in 1997 or 1998 for the launch of Stage III. If they decided by the end of 1996 that a majority of member states failed to meet the criteria, EU leaders would make another assessment before July 1998. Member states meeting the criteria at that time, regardless of whether they constituted a majority, would go ahead and launch Stage III in January 1999.

From the beginning of Stage III (whether in 1997, 1998, or 1999), exchange rates between participating countries would be irrevocably fixed and a single currency (later named the euro) introduced. The European System of Central Banks, consisting of the ECB and national central banks, would replace the European Monetary Institute on the eve of Stage III and formulate the participating states' single monetary policy. National central banks would thus become branches of the ECB and carry out operations necessary to implement a single monetary policy.

According to the treaty, the primary objective of the ESCB is to maintain price stability (in other words, to fight inflation). In the tradition of the Bundesbank, it is independent of member state governments and other EU institutions. The ESCB's governing council, consisting of the ECB's executive board (selected by the European Council) and governors of the national central banks, is the ESCB's highest decisionmaking body, responsible for monetary policy, foreign exchange operations, management of the official foreign reserves of member states, and smooth operation of a payments system. The executive board manages monetary policy on a day-to-day basis in accordance with decisions and guidelines laid down by the governing council.

Clearly, the treaty's provisions for EMU were comprehensive and complicated. But would they work? In a reply to Feldstein's criticism of EMU, a number of eminent European economists described the endeavor as "full of calculated risk [but] a risk worth taking."[30] The authors of the treaty had tried to minimize the risk by elaborating what they considered to be sound institutional and procedural prerequisites, although the convergence criteria seemed arbitrary and not necessarily related to the conduct of sound monetary policy. Given the politics of European integration and the unpredictability of global economics, the treaty's provisions for EMU could hardly have been flawless. Inevitably, the following few years put the treaty and its framers to the test.

■ Getting to Stage III

Although Stage I had begun without fanfare in July 1990, the post-Maastricht path to EMU got off to the worst possible start. Not only did the Danish referendum result of June 1992 and the ensuing ratification crisis put the future of the Maastricht Treaty in doubt, but a related crisis in the exchange rate mechanism that erupted in September 1992 and crested in July 1993 shattered public confidence in the possibility that EMU could ever be achieved. Throughout 1992 the mark rose steadily as high German interest rates attracted funds from the United States, where interest rates were low and the dollar continued to depreciate. As the mark climbed in value, weaker EC currencies fell to the floor of their exchange rate mechanism bands. Certain currencies—notably the Italian lira and the British pound—were inherently weak and ripe for devaluation. Dealers sensed that a realignment of the exchange rate mechanism was imminent. The Maastricht Treaty had itself encouraged speculation about an inevitable realignment or series of realignments before the advent of fixed exchange rates. Such speculation, in turn, tended further to strengthen strong currencies and weaken weak ones.

Of more immediate concern, the Bundesbank was less and less inclined to prop up weak currencies. In July and August, the Bundesbank spent a small fortune trying to keep the lira above its exchange rate mechanism floor. Convinced of the Bundesbank's unwillingness or inability to support the lira indefinitely, dealers moved large amounts of money out of the Italian currency and into the mark. Similar concerns about sterling led to massive sales of the pound and purchases of the mark. Ironically, the removal of exchange controls as part of the single market program contributed to the imminent crisis by making it possible to move money freely around the EC.

The evolution of the EMS into what looked like a fixed-rate regime exacerbated tension. The frequency of realignments before 1987 (thirteen altogether) and absence of them afterward gave the impression that the EMS had turned into a quasi–currency union. Except in Germany and some other "core" currency countries, "realignment" became a dirty word, synonymous with political indecision and economic frailty. The pound had joined the exchange rate mechanism in October 1990 at a high benchmark central rate (2.95) against the mark, but it was politically impossible for the British government to contemplate realignment, especially with a general election in the offing.

Although the Maastricht Treaty prompted speculation about the inevitability of realignments before Stage III of EMU, most governments feared that a parity change would affect their credibility, undermine confidence in the convergence criteria, fuel inflation, and thereby make Stage III harder to achieve. Realignments appeared to be incompatible with the treaty's convergence strategy and with the goal of EMU; as a tool of macroeconomic management, they seemed anachronistic at a time when the EC was moving toward a single monetary policy. For all of those reasons, governments unwisely but understandably endured mounting pressure in the exchange rate mechanism, often at a cost of high interest rates and declining competitiveness.

The Currency Crisis

Matters came to a head in September 1992, partly because of the negative result of the Danish referendum and the unpredictability of the upcoming French referendum. First the Finnish markka, unofficially linked to the exchange rate mechanism, collapsed under the strain of huge speculative attacks. The Swedish krone, also unofficially linked to the exchange rate mechanism, was next. In the EMS, the Italian and British governments desperately shored up their ailing currencies with noticeably unenthusiastic German support.

An informal meeting of finance ministers at the beginning of the month presented an opportunity to defuse the looming crisis and avert imminent disaster. Instead, the meeting ended in acrimony as Britain blamed the Bundesbank for the EC's high interest rates, economic ills, and currency turbulence. Helmut Schlesinger, the Bundesbank president, promised only that Germany would not raise interest rates further. As for a possible realignment, Schlesinger neither proposed a devaluation of sterling nor suggested a new parity for the pound. Even had he done so, it is doubtful whether Britain would have gone along with it.

The surprise realignment of September 13, involving a 7 percent devaluation of the lira, did not affect the pound's parity in the exchange rate mechanism. More money flowed out of sterling as dealers sought a safer haven and speculators renewed their attacks. Two days later the pound closed just above its floor in the exchange rate mechanism. Reports of Schlesinger's support for a broader realignment made the pound's position untenable. Having spent billions trying to prop up the pound, the British government pulled sterling out of the exchange rate mechanism on "Black Wednesday," September 16. Unable to stanch further speculative flows despite the Bundesbank's decision to cut interest rates, Italy followed suit.[31] In a preemptive move, Spain devalued the peseta by 5 percent against the remaining currencies in the exchange rate mechanism.

Opinion polls showing a possible French rejection of the Maastricht Treaty increased attacks against the franc, which were already acute. The French "yes," regardless of the margin, failed to stem the outward flow of funds. Only concerted efforts by the French and German governments and central banks averted a disaster in late September and prevented a French devaluation. Currency turbulence continued in late 1992 and early 1993, with the franc again under pressure, Spain and Portugal devaluing by 6 percent on November 23, and Ireland devaluing by 10 percent two months later.

The currency crisis contributed to the contemporaneous Maastricht ratification debacle by undermining public confidence in the EMS and, by extension, in deeper European integration. With the pound outside the exchange rate mechanism and the Danish krone still inside but under growing pressure, public opinion in Britain and Denmark—already bitterly divided over Maastricht—hardened against ratification. Although the treaty survived, the EMS crisis had other consequences for EMU. Britain's and Italy's abrupt departure from the exchange rate mechanism made it seem highly unlikely that either country would rejoin in time to participate in Stage III of EMU. Of course, Britain's participation was already doubtful for political reasons, Italy's for economic reasons. The embarrassing events of September 1992 had diametrically opposite consequences for both countries. Whereas the exchange rate mechanism crisis indeed strengthened British antipathy to EMU, it convinced many Italians that the solution ultimately lay in EMU itself. As a result, Italy's humiliating exit from the exchange rate mechanism in 1992 strengthened the country's resolve to meet the convergence criteria and join the single currency in 1999.

Elsewhere in the EC, the crisis shook confidence in the EMS but did not undermine the foundations of the system or seriously weaken intellectual and political support for EMU. Government officials pointed out that the crisis merely restored the EMS to its original state: a system of fixed but adjustable exchange rates. Wim Duisenberg, president of the Dutch central bank and later president of the ECB, put the situation in perspective: "What crisis?" he asked in January 1993. "The problem was that we had forgotten how to realign."[32]

Duisenberg spoke too soon. Currency turmoil peaked in summer 1993. On July 29, when the Bundesbank decided not to make an eagerly awaited cut in interest rates, other EMS currencies—notably the franc—came under huge pressure. Angered by French criticism of German monetary policy, the Bundesbank conspicuously failed to provide the massive assistance necessary to prop up the franc. After an emergency meeting in August 1993, EC finance ministers announced that apart from the Dutch guilder, which would stick to its original 2.5 percent band, EMS currencies would float within a 15 percent band around their parity with the mark.

Staying the Course

Most government officials and politicians defended the EMS tenaciously during the protracted crisis. After a meeting in September 1992, finance ministers issued a joint communiqué describing the EMS as a "key factor of economic stability and prosperity in Europe."[33] Not surprisingly, the Commission claimed at the height of the crisis that "only a single currency will put an end to [the] waves of speculation which we have witnessed over the last weeks."[34] The Organization for Economic Cooperation and Development concurred, suggesting that "rather than casting doubt on the prospect for monetary unification, recent events should strengthen the EC members' resolve to conclude EMU as quickly as possible."[35]

Currency turmoil may have strengthened the rationale for EMU, but it widened the already growing gap between political and public opinion in most member states. Ordinary mortals could comprehend neither the complexities of the exchange rate mechanism nor the reasons for its existence. To most people, the currency crisis had shown the impracticability, if not the impossibility, of currency union. The Maastricht ratification and currency crises had damaged public confidence in EMU, and deep recession and growing economic divergence made it unlikely that member states would satisfy the prerequisites for EMU within the stipulated period.

Most striking, Germany's high interest rates forced other participants in the exchange rate mechanism to pursue equally tight monetary policies, which exacerbated the EU's economic downturn and made the convergence criteria harder to meet. The Bundesbank's decision less than a week after the Maastricht summit to raise interest rates by 0.5 percent was widely denounced as an affront to the spirit of EMU and an egregious example of the bank's blatant "Germany first" approach. Of course, the Bundesbank's duty was solely to Germany and not at all to the wider Community. Nevertheless, the persistence of high German interest rates in the mid-1990s suggested that the Bundesbank would continue to subordinate wider European interests to German policy interests, possibly to the detriment of convergence among member states. Inasmuch as the Bundesbank wanted to warn the EU, the message was that high inflation could not be tolerated and that a form of monetary Darwinism would weed out the noncharter members of EMU.

Germans like to point out that their experience of hyperinflation in the early 1920s forged an anti-inflationary consensus that accounted for the Bundesbank's preoccupation with price stability and determination to make it the primary objective of the ECB. The Bundesbank always argued that there was no trade-off between inflation and employment. As Karl-Otto Pöhl insisted in 1977, well before becoming Bundesbank president, "Inflation does not reduce unemployment. On the contrary, it is one of its major causes."[36] Economic theory and empirical evidence bear out the Bundesbank's point, except in the short term. And in the short term of the mid-1990s, as the Bundesbank pursued a tight monetary policy at a time of deep economic recession, unemployment rose alarmingly in most member states. This outcome further eroded support for EMU by creating the impression that a future ECB, like the present Bundesbank, would pursue price stability regardless of the EU's unemployment level.

High interest rates exacerbated the economic situation by increasing the cost of borrowing money, thereby reducing investment. With unemployment rising and consumer spending declining, governments took in less revenue through direct and indirect taxation and paid out more money in unemployment and other benefits. This situation made it impossible for governments to bring down deficits and debts toward the Maastricht-stipulated reference points. In many cases, not least in postunification Germany, public-sector borrowing rose at a time when, according to the EMU timetable, governments should have been exercising strict budget discipline.

Thus, in the mid-1990s, EMU seemed an unlikely prospect. Few member states could satisfy the government finance criterion; most member states' inflation rates ranged outside the targeted band of not more than 1.5 percent of the EU's three best performers; and although interest rates had converged, they had done so at an unacceptably high level. Ironically, only the currency stability criterion was unproblematic, but it was not uncontroversial. The Maastricht Treaty stipulated that participants in the exchange rate mechanism should stay within "normal" fluctuation margins. In 1991, when the treaty was drafted, the prevailing 2.5 percent margin was presumed to be normal. But in August 1993, in the aftermath of the currency crisis, finance ministers widened the band to 15 percent. By claiming that "normal" now meant 15 rather than 2.5 percent, finance ministers fudged one of the conversion criteria and in effect removed exchange rates as a factor in the EMU equation.

It was little wonder, under the circumstances, that a single currency seemed unlikely to be introduced before the end of the century. The first edition of this book, written in 1994, concluded that "with Europe in the grip of recession and the exchange rate mechanism in disarray, it is difficult to see EMU coming into being within the Maastricht Treaty time frame."[37] Meeting in Madrid in December 1995, the European Council abandoned the goal of launching Stage III in 1997. Despite the European Council's earlier-than-expected decision, both the European Monetary Institute and the Commission had statutory obligations to produce reports in 1996 on progress toward convergence. Whereas the Commission's report stressed the positive progress that had already been made toward meeting the criteria, the European Monetary Institute emphasized the distance that member states still had to travel.[38] Together with the European Council's decision that Stage III could not be launched in 1997, the reports fed prevailing skepticism about the feasibility of EMU at any time in the foreseeable future.

Technical Preparations

Although the European Council abandoned 1997 as a starting date for Stage III of EMU, it nevertheless affirmed its commitment to starting Stage III in January 1999. At the time, the European Council's steadfastness seemed unrealistic. Yet in retrospect, the Madrid summit of December 1995 was a turning point in the EMU's fortunes. The summit's significance lies not only in the affirmation of the 1999 deadline—after all, European Councils are notorious for their optimistic announcements—or in the decision to name the new currency the euro but in the adoption of a technically detailed post-1999 scenario for switching to the single currency. EMU could come about only by political will and administrative fiat. The Madrid summit showed that despite popular indifference or even opposition to EMU, political will existed in abundance. Moreover, deep administrative foundations were being laid regardless of rising Europessimism.

The abundance of political will was all the more surprising in view of otherwise weak leadership. Apart from prevailing public skepticism about further integration, few governments enjoyed large parliamentary majorities. This was especially true of Germany, where Kohl had narrowly won the October 1994 election and was hampered not only by a small majority in the lower house of parliament but also by a Social Democratic majority in the upper house. Yet Kohl pursued EMU with a passion, staking his political future and his place in history on its achievement. Kohl's obsession with EMU was partly emotional and partly rational—emotional in that despite his equivocation in the late 1980s, he had advocated EMU unhesitatingly during and after the intergovernmental conference, and rational in that he strongly believed EMU was essential for Germany's and Europe's political and economic welfare.

Mitterrand shared Kohl's conviction, but his presidency ended in May 1995. Jacques Chirac, Mitterrand's successor, had been ambivalent about EMU during the presidential election campaign, having earlier called for a referendum in France to endorse the single currency. As a neo-Gaullist, Chirac was not well disposed toward deeper European integration. Once in office, however, Chirac realized that France had no choice but to press ahead with EMU. Chirac's relationship with Kohl would never be close, and Chirac's stubbornness over the selection of the ECB president would later cast a shadow over the launch of Stage III. But on EMU itself Chirac proved resolute. Although Franco-German relations lost their coziness after Mitterrand's departure, the Franco-German tandem continued to advocate EMU and take the unpopular steps necessary to achieve it.

While Kohl, Chirac, and other EU leaders used European Councils as media-saturated opportunities to press ahead with EMU, administrative work proceeded apace in national central banks, the Commission, and the new European Monetary Institute. Although EMU threatened to turn them into branch offices of the European System of Central Banks, national central banks—including the Bundesbank—relished the intellectual and analytical challenges of preparing for Stage III. The Commission had a more obvious bureaucratic incentive to lay the groundwork for EMU. Indeed, at the height of EMU skepticism in early 1995, the Commission issued a detailed Green Paper on technical aspects of launching the single currency.[39]

As stipulated in the treaty, the European Monetary Institute bore the brunt of the administrative work necessary to ensure EMU's success. The institute had been set up at the beginning of Stage II, in July 1994. Its location, a highly political decision, provoked a row between France and Germany. At Kohl's insistence, the European Council decided at a special summit in October 1993 to locate the institute in Frankfurt, seat of the Bundesbank and a symbol for Germans of sound monetary policy. Alexandre Lamfalussy, former president of the Bank of International Settlements in Basel, was appointed the institute's first president.

The European Monetary Institute was neither an extension of the Committee of Central Bank Governors, which it replaced, nor a synonym for the ECB, which it preceded. Instead, it had two main tasks: to make technical preparations for Stage III of EMU and to help coordinate member states' monetary policies. The foremost technical preparation was to specify, by the end of 1996, the regulatory, organizational, and logistical framework for the European System of Central Banks (including the ECB), which would come into existence on the eve of Stage III. Thus, the institute drafted the "changeover scenario" that the European Council adopted in December 1995, developed monetary policy instruments and procedures, prepared the TARGET cross-border payment system, and compiled EU-wide statistics (see Table 15.1). In addition, the institute had to strengthen cooperation among national central banks in an effort to coordinate national monetary policies. Here it was powerless to make decisions, as member states remained responsible for their monetary policies until the beginning of Stage III. Nevertheless, the monthly debates of the board of the institute and its regular reports on monetary policy and economic performance in the EU helped nudge member states toward compliance with the convergence criteria.

Between the technical level of the national central banks, the Commission's services, and the European Monetary Institute on the one hand and the highest political level of the European Council on the other, the Economic and Financial Affairs Council (Ecofin) and its preparatory monetary committee played a key role in bringing about Stage III. Ecofin had an obvious vested interest in ensuring the venture's success. In a post-EMU world, the coordination of national economic policies would assume greater political importance. As a result, Ecofin's stature would rise, especially vis-à-vis that of its main rival in the EU pecking order, the General Affairs Council (foreign ministers).

The European Council asked Ecofin in December 1995 to study two issues central to EMU's success. One was the problem posed by the fact that some member states would not participate initially (if ever) in Stage III. The other, at Germany's insistence, was to ensure the sustainability of EMU

Table 15.1   Key EMU Decisions and the Changeover to the Euro, 1995–2002

Date	Events and Developments
December 1995	The European Council decides on the changeover timetable and the name "euro."
June 1997	The European Council agrees on the Stability and Growth Pact and on ERM II.
May 1998	The European Council selects the participating member states for Stage III of EMU, fixes bilateral conversion rates, and selects the president and executive board of the European Central Bank.
June 1, 1998	The European Central Bank is set up in Frankfurt, replacing the European Monetary Institute, under the presidency of Wim Duisenberg; the European System of Central Banks is also set up.
January 1, 1999	The start of Stage III—irrevocable fixing of exchange rates and entry into force of relevant legislation; launch of the single monetary policy; the beginning of foreign exchange operations in euros; the inauguration of the TARGET payment system; new public debt is issued in euros.
January 1, 1999–December 31, 2001	Currencies with irrevocably fixed exchange rates are exchanged at par value.
January 1, 2002	Euro banknotes and coins begin to circulate.
July 1, 2002	The legal tender status of national banknotes and coins is canceled.

through the continuation of budgetary discipline *after* the launch of Stage III. Based on contributions from the Commission and the European Monetary Institute, Ecofin proposed a revised exchange rate mechanism (dubbed ERM II) to regulate relations between the euro and nonparticipating member state currencies and a stability pact to ensure budgetary discipline after the launch of the euro.

The ERM II proposal was relatively straightforward and uncontroversial. The European Council adopted an ERM II framework in December 1996 and a resolution setting out the mechanism's principles and fundamentals in June 1997. Modeled on the existing exchange rate mechanism, ERM II would allow relatively large fluctuation margins (15 percent) for noneuro currencies in relation to the euro. The European System of Central Banks and the central banks of noneuro member states would intervene if necessary to maintain currency parities within the fluctuation limits.

Sustainability, Employment, and Oversight

By contrast with ERM II, the proposed stability pact caused a political storm. Bearing an obvious German imprint, the draft agreement threatened automatic penalties for eurozone countries running excessive budget deficits. Like the budget deficit criterion for participation in Stage III stipulated in the Maastricht Treaty, the proposed stability pact defined "excessive" as above 3 percent of GDP. By 1996, when the proposal was being drafted and debated, member states were cutting budgets in order to bring deficits below the 3 percent ceiling. As budget cuts resulted in less government hiring, fewer and smaller business subsidies, and lower expenditure on public works, unemployment inevitably increased. As budget cuts also resulted in less generous social welfare programs, unemployment became less congenial for many Europeans. These developments reinforced a popular perception that EMU itself caused unemployment and worsened the plight of the unemployed.

Nowhere was this perception stronger, and nowhere was a government more sensitive to its political repercussions, than in France. Chirac's ambivalence about EMU was due largely to the domestic political risk of embracing it enthusiastically. Once elected, Chirac would take the credit for EMU if and when it succeeded. In the meantime, Alain Juppé, his prime minister, took the blame for unpopular austerity measures. Already French workers had rioted in Paris in December 1995, protesting proposed changes in the social security system. In deference to French sensitivity, Germany watered down the terms of the proposed stability pact, making fines not automatic but subject to approval by governments. Also in deference to the perception that EMU was imposing a fiscal straitjacket that destroyed jobs, Ecofin renamed the proposed agreement, which the European Council adopted in Dublin in December 1996, the Stability and Growth Pact.

Eager to have a government whose term would coincide with the remainder of his seven-year presidency, the latter part of which would include the launch of Stage III and the changeover to the euro, Chirac brought forward the date of parliamentary elections from March 1998 to March 1997. He miscalculated badly: Juppé paid for his unpopularity in the polls, and Lionel Jospin, Chirac's Socialist opponent in the earlier presidential election, formed a new government. France now entered a new period of cohabitation (the presidency and government were held by opposing political parties), and Jospin was outspoken in his criticism of EMU.

One of Jospin's first steps as prime minister, at the Amsterdam summit in June 1997, was to demand a renegotiation of the Stability and Growth Pact. This irked the Germans and delayed discussion of the summit's most pressing business: the Amsterdam Treaty. Jospin succeeded only in having the European Council adopt a separate resolution on growth and employment that stressed member states' determination to keep employment firmly at the top of the political agenda. The European Council also decided to hold an extraordinary summit in Luxembourg in November 1997 to discuss job creation.[40]

A call by Jospin for an "economic government" to watch over the supposedly independent ECB caused even greater alarm in Frankfurt and Berlin. Germany and like-minded member states had no intention of undermining the ECB's independence or commitment to price stability, but they were willing to establish a forum for discussions among eurozone countries about such key issues as maintaining fiscal discipline, coordinating taxation policy, and setting the euro's exchange rate. Accordingly, the European Council agreed in December 1997 to form a "Euro-X" council of finance ministers ("Euro" referring to the single currency, "X" to the variable number of participating member states). It later became known as the Eurogroup.

The EMU Juggernaut

The controversy surrounding the Stability and Growth Pact and the Eurogroup demonstrated both the increasing politicization of EMU and the increasing likelihood that it would be launched on time. As late as 1996 most political pundits argued that Stage III would have to be deferred beyond 1999; by mid-1997 the prevailing opinion was that Stage III would begin on time but with a minority or at most a small majority of member states. By late 1997 this view had given way to the conviction that Stage III would begin on time with eleven member states, that is, with all the member states that wished to participate minus Greece (Britain, Denmark, and Sweden opted out for political reasons).

The growing conviction that EMU would be launched on time was due to several factors:

- the manifest determination of France and Germany to meet the convergence criteria by hook or by crook
- the impact of economic recovery
- the acquiescence of public opinion
- detailed and credible technical preparations by the European Monetary Institute and other bodies
- the seriousness with which large banks and businesses treated the EMU venture

French and German efforts to meet the convergence criteria by engaging in what some critics derided as "creative accounting" reinforced the impression that Stage III would be launched in 1999 at all costs. France's creative accounting was successful; Germany's was a failure. The Commission allowed France to apply a huge onetime payment from France Telecom in 1997 against the country's deficit. However, the Bundesbank rejected the German finance minister's effort to revalue Germany's gold reserves in May 1997 and apply the proceeds against the country's deficit. These stratagems demonstrated both countries' determination to meet the most difficult convergence criterion, if necessary by subterfuge. Given that the decision as to which countries met the criteria would be a political one and that the political establishments of most member states had set their sights on the starting date of January 1, 1999, it became increasingly obvious that Stage III would be launched on time. Unless certain of EMU's punctual launch, France and Germany would not have argued so hard over the terms of the Stability and Growth Pact or the proposed Eurogroup.

The Maastricht Treaty's criteria for the measurement of "excessive deficit" gave member states ample wiggle room. The 60 percent reference point for national debt could be exceeded if "the ratio [of debt to GDP] is sufficiently diminishing and approaching [60 percent] at a satisfactory pace." Similarly, the 3 percent reference point for budget deficit could be relaxed if the ratio (of deficit to GDP) declined "substantially and continuously and reached a level that comes close to [3 percent]," or if the excess "is only exceptional and temporary and the ratio remains close [to 3 percent]."

Yet the budget deficit criterion of 3 percent became a rigid yardstick for measuring member states' eligibility for EMU. That was not only because the 3 percent figure had been bandied about more than any other in the EMU debate but also because opponents of EMU, especially in Germany, had seized on it as the absolute limit for the budget deficit of an aspiring Stage III participant—hence the French and German governments' extraordinary measures to get their deficits below the 3 percent ceiling.

Even with recourse to such measures as privatization and gold-reserves revaluation, neither France nor Germany looked likely in early 1997 to come under the 3 percent ceiling. If one or both of them proved unable to participate in EMU, the entire project would collapse. By mid-1997, however, Europe's economic recovery began to have an impact on the member states' budget deficits. It seemed that France, Germany, and most other member states would confound the skeptics and meet the 3 percent standard. The Commission's fall 1997 economic forecast bore out this rosy scenario and strengthened the growing conviction that EMU would start with a large majority of member states.[41]

Most surprising of all was the likelihood that Portugal, Spain, and Italy, countries with a tradition of lax monetary policy and financial profligacy, would make the first cut. Even strong supporters of EMU derided the possibility of the Mediterranean countries' participation in it. Snide comments by German officials about Italy's ineligibility for EMU strained relations between the two countries. Yet whereas the German government had sneakily tried to revalue the Bundesbank's gold reserves in order to meet the convergence criteria, Italy's center-left Olive Tree coalition government had taken such politically courageous steps as introducing tough austerity measures and levying a special tax to help cut the budget deficit. For Italy, then in the throes of post–Cold War political upheaval, failure to make the EMU grade came to be seen as a potential national disaster.

Germany's concerns about Italy, shared by most northern countries, pertained especially to sustainability. Even if Italy met the convergence criteria, would it sustain the 3 percent budget deficit ceiling after 1999? Opponents of Italy's participation may have had legitimate concerns, but attempting to keep Italy out of Stage III on grounds of nonsustainability would have implicitly acknowledged the worthlessness of the Stability and Growth Pact, which the European Council had already adopted to deal with this issue.

A technical announcement by Ecofin in September 1997 that finance ministers would fix conversion rates between single-currency countries several months earlier than stipulated in the treaty reinforced the impression that EMU was firmly on track. Instead of waiting until the end of 1998, Ecofin would agree on the conversion rates in early May 1998, when the heads of state and government were due to select countries for participation in Stage III. Although intended to deter speculative attacks on prospective participants' currencies in the run-up to January 1999, the announcement inevitably boosted political confidence in EMU's prospects.

One of the most surprising aspects of the EMU juggernaut was the extent to which the public went along with it. The Maastricht ratification crisis had exposed a high degree of public opposition to deeper integration, which many observers expected to crystallize around EMU. Moreover, the popular equation of EMU with austerity and unemployment seemed destined to spark protests at the polling booth and in the streets. Yet apart from demonstrations in France in December 1995 and the French government's defeat in May 1997, public concern about EMU failed to manifest itself. Clearly, the degree of public opposition to EMU and the extent to which ordinary Europeans would demonstrate such opposition had been exaggerated.

In reality, the pain of EMU was unevenly spread, and reaction to it differed widely among aspiring participants. Luxembourg was already a model of fiscal rectitude. Belgium considered that EMU membership was its birthright and so did not bother to tackle seriously its bloated public debt. Alone among the Nordic member states, Finland was highly motivated to participate in EMU. The criteria caused little pain in Ireland and the Netherlands, which had already embarked on economic restructuring and were enjoying strong economic growth. The convergence criteria caused a lot of pain in Italy, Portugal, Spain, and Greece, but these countries badly needed a pretext to put their public finances in order and at the same time feared the humiliation of not coming up to EMU standards.

Only in France and Germany, the EU's core countries, might hostile public opinion have jeopardized EMU. France seemed especially vulnerable because of its tradition of government surrender in the face of violent political protest. Nor did the appointment as prime minister of Lionel Jospin, who had made lavish campaign promises, seem auspicious. In the event, economic recovery made it possible for Jospin to square the circle of EMU-inspired austerity and traditional Socialist extravagance. Anti-EMU protests never materialized, and the government did not have to put its EMU commitment to the ultimate political test of facing down demonstrators.

In contrast to France, Germany's political tradition is one of public obedience to authority. That helps to explain why, despite numerous polls showing how unhappy the majority of Germans were to give up the mark, a powerful anti-EMU movement failed to materialize during the 1998 federal election campaign. Germans confined their protests to writing letters to the editor and bringing a case before the Constitutional Court. Most Germans reckoned that the political consequences of abandoning EMU were potentially more destabilizing than the economic consequences of staying the course. The opposition Social Democratic Party learned that lesson in local elections in 1997, when anti-EMU Social Democratic candidates lost decisively. Gerhard Schröder, who emerged in early 1998 as the Social Democratic contender for the chancellorship (and who beat Kohl in the September 1998 election), took the lesson to heart by abandoning his earlier equivocation about EMU.

With the realization by late 1997 that opposition to EMU was muted and that most member states would meet the convergence criteria, the procedure for selecting Stage III participants in 1998 lost its political edge. In February 1998, member states released data showing a high degree of nominal convergence (Table 15.2).

Based on these figures, of the twelve countries hoping to participate in Stage III, only Greece would fail to qualify because its budget deficit was a full percentage point above the reference point. (By devaluing its currency and joining the exchange rate mechanism in March 1998, Greece signaled its determination to join Stage III perhaps as early as January 2001, subject to continued deficit and inflation reduction.) Britain, Denmark, and Sweden, which had decided not to adopt the single currency, came in well under the 3 percent ceiling. By contrast, France reported a deficit of 3.02 percent, sufficiently close to the reference point to assuage critics and opponents of EMU. The member states' figures on national debt were less impressive, with Belgium, Italy, and Greece coming in well above 100 percent (the reference point being 60 percent).

In their respective convergence reports, published in March 1998, the European Monetary Institute and the Commission drew attention to these large debts and adjured member states to accelerate economic reform and restructuring. In particular, the institute warned that "decisive and sustained corrective policies of a structural nature" were necessary in most countries. Nevertheless, both reports recommended that eleven member states begin Stage III

Table 15.2   Member State Finances in February 1998

Member State	Public Deficit (% of GDP)	Public Debt (% of GDP)	Participation in EMU Stage 3?
Belgium	2.1	122.2	yes
Denmark	−0.7[a]	64.1	no[b]
Germany	2.7	61.3	yes
Greece	4.0	108.7	no[c]
Spain	2.6	68.3	yes
France	3.0	58.0	yes
Ireland	−0.9	67.0	yes
Italy	2.7	121.6	yes
Luxembourg	−1.7	6.7	yes
The Netherlands	1.4	72.1	yes
Austria	2.5	66.1	yes
Portugal	2.5	62.0	yes
Finland	0.9	55.8	yes
Sweden	0.4	76.6	no[b]
Britain	1.9	53.4	no[b]
Maastricht limits	3.0	60.0	

Source: Agence Europe, February 28, 1998.
Notes: a. Negative denotes a budget surplus.
b. Country has chosen not to participate for domestic political reasons.
c. Country failed to meet convergence criteria.

in January 1999.[42] At the same time, the Commission's spring economic fore-cast predicted strong economic growth throughout the EU despite the possible impact of the Asian economic crisis.[43]

The Commission and institute recommendations, obligatory under the terms of the Maastricht Treaty, made it inevitable that the European Council, meeting in Brussels in May 1998, would formally select the same eleven member states for participation in Stage III. Only twelve months earlier, the Brussels summit had been expected to be contentious because of the possibility that the participants would have to decide on the composition of the eurozone by qualified majority vote. By early 1998, however, consensus on the composition of the eurozone threatened to rob the summit of all drama. In the event, the Brussels summit was highly memorable because of a drama of a different kind: a bitter row between Chirac and Kohl over the presidency of the ECB that overshadowed the formal selection of the single currency countries.

The Duisenberg Row

The row originated in a decision by central bank governors in May 1996 to appoint Wim Duisenberg to succeed Lamfalussy as head of the European Monetary Institute on the understanding that Duisenberg would then become president of the ECB. Although the ECB was to be independent of national influence, the choice of its president was nonetheless a political decision. The Maastricht Treaty acknowledged that fact by giving the European Council responsibility for selecting the ECB president. Realizing that the European Council would formally appoint the ECB president several months before the launch of Stage III, in May 1996 the central bank governors got their national leaders' approval of Duisenberg's eventual succession to the ECB presidency.

Chirac was unhappy about Duisenberg's selection both because Duisenberg was clearly the German government's candidate (having won the battle to locate the ECB in Frankfurt, Germany could not also have pushed one of its own nationals to head the new bank; Duisenberg was the next best thing) and because the selection procedure smacked of unelected central bankers usurping the prerogative of elected government leaders. Chirac grumbled at the time but objected publicly to Duisenberg's otherwise uncontested nomination only in November 1997, when he nominated Jean-Claude Trichet, governor of the Bank of France, for the job.

Thereafter the issue was Chirac's insistence on a Franco-German trade-off: a German location for the ECB (already decided) and a French president for the ECB (not yet decided). Ironically, Chirac did not much like Trichet, who as head of the Bank of France had pursued an independent monetary policy. As far as Chirac was concerned, Trichet's strengths were that he was a member of the central bankers' club and, more important, that he was French.

To everyone's surprise, Chirac pursued this nakedly nationalistic position to the end, compromising only to the extent that Duisenberg could begin the ECB presidency's first eight-year term but would have to step down for Trichet halfway through. Chirac held out for a written commitment by Duisenberg to resign no later than January 2002. After ten hours of bitter negotiation, which Kohl described as among the most difficult in his lengthy EU experience, Chirac accepted a decision by Duisenberg, supposedly reached "of my own free will . . . and not under pressure from anyone," to step down sometime after mid-2002.[44] As part of the compromise, the European Council agreed that another Frenchman would become Duisenberg's vice president and that Trichet would succeed Duisenberg for a full eight-year term.[45] (Duisenberg eventually resigned in November 2003, and Trichet duly took over.)

The outcome of the Brussels summit suggested that the ECB's independence was compromised even before the bank came into being and that the French government would attempt to interfere in European monetary policymaking. Such concerns were largely assuaged by Duisenberg's robust performance at a hearing in the European Parliament the following week and by the composition of the ECB's governing board; all of its members are experienced, independent-minded central bankers. The significance of Chirac's behavior was what it portended not for EMU but for Chirac's relations with his EU partners. Apart from insulting his fellow EU leaders, Chirac further undermined

Kohl's chances of reelection in September 1998. Nor should Chirac's conduct
be dismissed as "typically French." Although the French are generally not self-
conscious about advocating national interests, Chirac's definition of the national interest was unusually narrow and his behavior clearly idiosyncratic.

■ Managing Monetary Union

Stage III of EMU began for eleven member states in January 1999, when the
ECB assumed responsibility for their common monetary policy and their national currencies became, in effect, denominations of the euro (still a virtual
currency). Greece applied to join in March 2000, when it submitted data
showing that it met the convergence criteria to the Commission and the Council of Ministers. It later came to light that the Greeks had cooked the books
and submitted false figures. Unaware of that problem at the time, the European Council gave Greece the green light to join Stage III. In January 2001
Greece therefore became the twelfth member state to participate in monetary
union.

Would EMU work? The short answer is yes, it *would* work because a majority of Europeans decided that it *had to* work. During the transition stages,
member states displayed a determination to make it happen, new and existing
administrative bodies demonstrated the necessary expertise to bring it about,
and public opinion showed surprising compliance with it. Having concluded
during the transition stages not only that EMU was feasible but also that the
political and economic costs of failure were greater than the costs of success,
politicians, technocrats, and ordinary Europeans alike were bound to conclude
after the launch of Stage III that the costs of maintaining the single currency
were considerably lower than the costs of its collapse.

Nevertheless, the challenges of managing monetary union were considerable. The first and most obvious one was to launch the euro itself, as a real
currency, in January 2002. The challenge was mostly logistical and informa-
tional. It involved printing euro notes (some €15 billion worth) and minting
euro coins, distributing the new currency, withdrawing the old currencies, adjusting coin-operated machines and ATMs, preventing possible counterfeiting
(the final designs of the euro banknotes were revealed only at the end of August 2001), and alerting businesses and consumers to the changes about to
take place. To prepare people for what lay ahead, retailers displayed prices in
euros as well as in national currencies for at least two years before the
changeover. In the meantime, the Commission launched a huge public information campaign ("Euro 2002"), and governments conducted similar campaigns nationally.

The transition to the new currency went remarkably smoothly. As one
commentator noted, "vending machines did not jam, ATMs did not melt, the

plague of allergic reaction to the new coins' alloy did not stalk the land, and no great inflationary pyre lit the euro area's winter sky."[46] People seemed to enjoy the novelty of the notes and coins, although for years afterward all except those who were very young at the time of the changeover would mentally convert the euro into what soon came to be called "old money." Participating countries had six months during which they could allow transactions in either the new or old currencies. Most people switched immediately to the euro, and most governments concluded that the six-month transitional period was both unnecessary and undesirable.

Perhaps more than any other event in the history of the EU, the introduction of the euro brought home to ordinary Europeans the extent and impact of European integration. Public acceptance of the new currency proved surprisingly easy. Few people mourned their national currencies: as long as the euro was sound and not eroded by inflation, the public was more than willing to come to terms with it. There were some allegations of price rises as a result of the changeover, many businesses having conveniently rounded prices up or taken the opportunity to charge substantially more in euro for their products and services. There was keen competition in cross-border sales in participating countries as shoppers in border regions reaped the reward of price transparency and the convenience (and savings) of not having to change money, everything being denominated and paid for in euros. Millions of eurozone residents who went on holidays in each other's countries immediately enjoyed the benefit and ease of being able to use the same currency while vacationing abroad.

Even before the launch of the euro, more residents of the eurozone may have taken their holidays in other eurozone countries because the external value of the virtual euro dropped markedly in the first three years of its existence. The late 1990s was therefore a great time for Americans, for example, to vacation in the eurozone but an expensive time for eurozone residents to travel to the United States. The big drop in the external value of the euro was due partly to the strength of the U.S. economy and partly to uncertainty about the intentions of the new ECB and the teething troubles of the new European central bankers. Many European politicians and officials, who wrongly viewed the value of the euro as an indicator of the EU's virility, were understandably disappointed with its early performance in foreign exchanges. Businesspeople, who had a more pragmatic outlook, appreciated the advantage of a weaker euro for foreign sales. Exports from the eurozone enjoyed a considerable boost from 1999 until 2002 as a result of the euro's depreciation, especially vis-à-vis the U.S. dollar.

The situation reversed itself in the mid-2000s as the euro appreciated rapidly and the dollar declined precipitously on foreign exchanges. The same European politicians and officials who had lamented the weakness of the euro only a few years previously now complained bitterly about the impact of the strong euro on the competitiveness of eurozone exports. The same European businesspeople who had enjoyed the export advantages of a weak euro now paid the price (fewer foreign sales) of a strong euro. Once again, the value of the euro reflected the weakness of the U.S. economy more than the strength or inherent attractiveness of the eurozone economy. Moreover, U.S. politicians and officials talked down the value of the dollar in 2003 and 2004 in an effort to gain a competitive advantage for U.S. exports, thereby introducing another bone of contention into the transatlantic relationship. For residents of the eurozone, at least, the reversal in the euro's fortunes had a silver lining: vacations in the United States became extremely affordable. Given the exchange rate between the euro and the dollar in the winter of 2004–2005, it would not have been substantially more expensive for Dutch skiers to go to the slopes in Colorado or Utah than in Austria or France. By contrast, U.S. visitors to the eurozone experienced severe sticker shock.

Regardless of the fluctuating value of the euro, the ECB operated quietly and successfully in Frankfurt, pursuing an independent monetary policy aimed primarily at maintaining price stability. In fact, there was little inflationary pressure throughout the eurozone, apart from some hot spots such as Ireland, which had huge economic growth and high price increases. The disparity in economic performance and inflationary pressures between Ireland and Germany, the weightiest economy in the eurozone, highlights a concern about EMU: the suitability of a one-size-fits-all monetary policy to a collection of national economies that in many respects seem to be diverging rather than converging.

Given such diversity, monetary tightening or loosening would obviously affect member states in different ways at different times. Managing the single currency, like preparing for it, imposes costs that are unevenly spread among member states. In extreme cases, an economic shock in one member state could prompt a response from the ECB that would disadvantage another member state; alternatively, the ECB's refusal to respond to a regional economic shock could undermine support for the ECB and therefore the EU in that part of the eurozone. Without financial transfers to compensate those parts of the eurozone in recession and with relatively little cross-border labor mobility and strong constraints on the use of national fiscal instruments, the ECB's likely response to asymmetrical shocks has assumed great political importance.

Apart from such extreme cases, precisely because of the difference in size between the Irish and German economies (to return to that example), the ECB is bound to pay much more attention to developments in Germany than in Ireland when formulating its monetary policy, inevitably giving rise to accusations of a pro-German bias. With the sluggish performance of the German economy and the lively performance of the Irish economy, Germany could have benefited in the late 1990s and early 2000s from lower interest rates and

Ireland from higher ones. Ironically, the ECB kept interest rates at a relatively high level not because of Ireland's circumstances (Ireland could have done with much higher interest rates) but because of its treaty-mandated obsession with fighting inflation. If anything, the ECB seemed divorced from the reality of economic circumstances in Germany, the country in which it was located. Poor economic performance and high unemployment in Germany cried out for fiscal and monetary policy incentives as well as domestic structural reforms. Ideology and party politics limited the possibility of domestic reforms, the Stability and Growth Pact constrained the government's fiscal policy options, and the ECB's independence and obsession with price stability meant that a loose monetary policy was unlikely to happen.

Frustration boiled over in Germany in 1999 when Oskar Lafontaine, a populist Social Democrat and finance minister in the new Green–Social Democratic coalition government of Gerhard Schröder, publicly attacked the ECB for its tight monetary policy, which, he claimed, exacerbated unemployment. An old-fashioned Socialist who was inexperienced in government, Lafontaine broke the golden rule by publicly criticizing an independent institution, especially such a hallowed institution as the new ECB. The ensuing scandal caused Lafontaine to resign in a huff (Schröder was happy in any case to see him go) and strengthened the credibility of the ECB, which had refused to cave in to political pressure. Reflecting the credibility and maturity of both EMU and the ECB, governments and financial markets have become less sensitive over the years to public criticism of the bank. Thus, when Hans Eichel, Lafontaine's successor, criticized the bank in 2003 (although not as stridently), there was no political fallout.

Apart from making public statements, governments could try (and may well have tried) to pressure individual members of the ECB to support particular policies or positions. However, the likely loss of credibility resulting from public knowledge of a board member's susceptibility to such pressure serves as a strong deterrent. There is no guarantee that board members would not succumb privately to national pressure, although obvious nationalistic behavior would be unlikely to escape their colleagues' notice and opprobrium. Moreover, the ECB's board members are highly reputable and experienced former national bankers who are adept at keeping national governments at arm's length.

Those who are disadvantaged by or unhappy with prevailing monetary policy tend to direct their anger at "Brussels" as well as "Frankfurt," thereby fueling Euroskepticism and calling the legitimacy of the ECB into question. This relates to a wider, long-standing problem of democratic accountability and representation in the EU. Nevertheless, the legitimacy of the ECB is especially touchy because of the necessity to maintain its political independence and also because its decisions have a profound impact on economic activity throughout the eurozone.

Concerns about the bank's legitimacy and policy responses have made it imperative for ECB board members to give frequent speeches, interviews, and press conferences about the bank's policy goals and instruments, within the bounds of confidentiality. The European Parliament is the ECB's obvious official interlocutor at the European level. Regular meetings with the Parliament's Committee on Economic and Monetary Affairs have helped to personalize the ECB and build public support for its actions. Nevertheless, it is difficult to build the legitimacy of the ECB on that of the Parliament, which, despite being directly elected, is neither well liked nor well understood throughout the EU.

Stage III of EMU has been an obvious success in the narrow sense of the euro's acceptance and survival. Beyond that, EMU had the potential to succeed by prompting economic restructuring, boosting employment, and propelling growth in the eurozone. As Commission president Jacques Santer commented during the selection of the eleven euro countries in early 1998, the euro was "not an end in itself but an instrument to spur and sustain economic growth into the next century."[47]

A small degree of economic growth indeed followed the launch of Stage III, due to the abolition of currency conversions between participating countries and (after the launch of the euro) to greater price transparency. The eradication of bank charges and commissions, as well as of personnel and other costs relating to currency management and hedging, saved exporters money and, together with the initial drop in the external value of the euro, greatly increased their profits. Similarly, the removal of currency barriers stimulated some additional cross-border shopping. Nevertheless, proponents of EMU greatly exaggerated the cost of currency conversions and the prospect that their abolition would spur cross-border trade. Business and consumer spending did not increase appreciably, despite a fall in some prices in some member states due to price transparency across borders. In any event, prices did not converge in the eurozone, not least because of vastly different tax rates among member states.

A more significant issue was whether EMU would spur sustained economic growth and make a serious dent in unemployment. That would depend not only on global economic circumstances but also on whether EMU would trigger major economic and financial restructuring in participating states. The Lisbon strategy, an EU-wide initiative, sought to incorporate the potential of EMU for economic modernization and reform in the eurozone and beyond. The fact that the EU launched the Lisbon strategy, however, implied a realization among member states that major economic reform was not following automatically in the wake of EMU.

National responses to the opportunities of EMU and the challenge of the Lisbon strategy depend to a great extent on political and cultural considerations. For example, the debate about a possible overhaul of taxation, subsidies, and labor market policies touches a raw nerve in France, where the kinds of economic reforms associated with achieving the full potential of EMU are generally seen as incompatible with the much-vaunted European model of society and as providing a foothold for the much-derided Anglo-Saxon model. Apart from its potential for economic reform, however, EMU is also seen in France and elsewhere as limiting opportunities for economic growth and even contributing to economic stagnation because it requires national governments to maintain fiscal discipline. Whereas most countries would see this as a good thing, some EMU participants, notably France and Germany, complain that the Stability and Growth Pact unduly restricts their Broad Economic Policy Guidelines and promotes monetary stability at the expense of economic growth.

Economic Coordination and the Stability and Growth Pact

The "E" in EMU implies a common economic policy. In fact, member states are treaty-bound only to coordinate their economic policies within Ecofin (the council of finance ministers) in order to help ensure the success of monetary union. They do so through the Broad Economic Policy Guidelines, which Ecofin draws up and the European Council approves on the basis of Commission recommendations. The Broad Economic Policy Guidelines used to be drawn up annually; since 2003 they cover a three-year period (for example, from 2003 to 2005). The guidelines are both general (for the EU as a whole) and specific (for each member state). Ecofin and the Commission monitor member states' implementation of the guidelines, sometimes recommending corrective action if member states appear to be disregarding them.

The Broad Economic Policy Guidelines are a key aspect of the process of multilateral surveillance for the conduct of economic policy in the EU. They complement the European Employment Strategy and are published at the same time as the employment guidelines (see Chapter 14). The Broad Economic Policy Guidelines typically call for labor market reforms, implementation and enforcement of single market measures, and greater scope for enterprise and entrepreneurship (the kinds of thing incorporated since March 2000 into the Lisbon strategy). They also advise sound economic management and budgetary discipline in keeping with the Stability and Growth Pact. The pact both complements and constrains the Broad Economic Policy Guidelines by setting the "medium-term objective of budgetary positions close to balance or in surplus . . . [which] will allow all Member States to deal with normal cyclical fluctuations while keeping the government deficit within the reference point of 3 percent of GDP."

The pact imposes a political and legal obligation on member states. Politically, member states agree to participate in peer review (and therefore to accept peer pressure) through a budget surveillance process to help ensure that they do not exceed the 3 percent reference value in the event of a deficit. To that end, member states submit annual stability programs (noneurozone countries submit convergence programs), which the Council examines. The Council may trigger an "early warning mechanism" if it is concerned about a member state's budgetary situation. In the event that a member state exceeds a 3 percent budget deficit, the Council may invoke the "excessive deficit procedure," which includes the possibility of fining errant member states.

When they agreed to the pact in 1997, member states presumed that their economic circumstances would improve after the launch of the euro. Having struggled to achieve the 3 percent budget deficit reference point in order to make the grade for Stage III of EMU, it never really occurred to them that their public finances might be parlous again. Most member states were in reasonably good shape in the late 1990s, but the economic downturn early in the new decade had a negative impact on public finances. As with their general economic performance, member states differed widely in the states of their public finances. As the economic downturn intensified, France and Germany (architect of the pact) approached and soon exceeded the 3 percent limit.

Ireland, by contrast, had a budget surplus. Yet the Commission publicly rebuked Ireland in February 2001 for having loosened its fiscal policy, in contravention of the Broad Economic Policy Guidelines. It seemed bizarre for the Commission to take the EU's best economic performer to task, especially as Ireland had a budget surplus at the time of 4.6 percent of GDP. The incident suggested that the Commission would police the Stability and Growth Pact vigilantly. Indeed, in July 2002 the Commission launched the excessive deficit procedure against Portugal for having run up a deficit of 4.2 percent the previous year. Portugal and Ireland were small, relatively uninfluential member states. Would the Commission act so aggressively against large member states? All eyes turned to France and Germany, whose deficits for 2002 were projected to exceed 3 percent of GDP.

As their budgetary situation deteriorated, France and Germany, traditionally in the vanguard of European integration, complained bitterly about the futility and illogicality of the pact. They may have had a point: sticking rigidly to an arbitrarily chosen reference point for fiscal management ignored prevailing economic circumstances and could, at times, be counterproductive (the Bush administration would certainly agree with that notion). The Germans also pointed out that if their contribution to the EU budget were discounted, they would comfortably come under the 3 percent limit. Other member states, especially those struggling to meet the limit, were unsympathetic. So was the ECB, which argued that the credibility of EMU rested on member states respecting the provisions of the pact. The Commission as a whole was equally adamant, although a typically maladroit statement by Romano Prodi, its president, caused considerable embarrassment: he called the pact "stupid."[48]

Because of his reputation for making silly statements, Prodi's dismissal of the pact was less damaging than it could have been. If anything, it strengthened the determination of the Commission (especially the commissioner for economic and financial affairs) to impose the pact's rules. Matters came to a head in November 2003, the second successive year in which France and Germany exceeded the 3 percent limit, when the Commission tried to censure them at a meeting of Ecofin. France and Germany promptly marshaled the requisite number of Council votes to reject the Commission's proposal, whereupon the Commission brought the Council to Court for exceeding its authority.

The Court ruled against the Council in July 2004. But it was a Pyrrhic victory for the Commission. With France and Germany unapologetic, although eager to restore their public finances to good health, in effect the pact remained in abeyance. Revelations in November 2004 that Greece had misled the EU about the state of its public finances in 2000, when it had applied to participate in Stage III of EMU, cast further discredit on the eurozone's fiscal framework. The Commission resolved to reform the pact, taking account of the need for member states to make credible commitments and the reality of the political and economic pressures that they face. The reforms eventually agreed to by the European Council in March 2005 kept the 3 percent reference point for budget deficits but gave members of the eurozone ample room for maneuver. The entire episode was a stark reminder of the fragile foundations on which EMU rests.

Enlarging the Eurozone

Notwithstanding the shenanigans over the Stability and Growth Pact, the eurozone seems more likely to expand than to contract in the near future. Britain, Denmark, and Sweden could join, but that seems unlikely. Denmark held a referendum in September 2000 on whether to adopt the euro. The result was a resounding rejection (with a turnout of 88 percent, 53 percent voted against). As usual in such cases, the result reflected general dissatisfaction with the EU rather than specific concerns about EMU. The national debate before the referendum had as much to do with sovereignty, identity, the role of Germany, and possible cuts in social welfare as with the economic advantages or disadvantages of adopting the euro. Nevertheless the result clearly showed that a majority of Danes simply did not want to give up their own currency.

Undaunted, Sweden held a referendum on the same issue in September 2003. The debate in Sweden was similar to that in Denmark. So was the result: 56 percent against. The murder of Sweden's strongly proeuro foreign minister in a seemingly random attack in Stockholm only days before the referendum had no appreciable impact on the result (there was talk of a sympathy vote in favor of the proposal). As in Denmark, there was a marked difference between urban (mostly favorable) and rural (mostly unfavorable) voters, just as there were concerns about further loss of sovereignty and identity.

Tony Blair, the British prime minister, has made no secret of his preference for participation in Stage III of EMU, but Gordon Brown, his political rival and chancellor of the exchequer, has made no secret of his skepticism on the issue. In order to put the question of Britain's eurozone membership on as objective a footing as possible, the government set five economic tests for adopting the euro. Blair also promised that Britain would not join without first holding a referendum. The five tests are:

1. *Convergence:* Are British and eurozone business cycles and economic structures compatible so that Britain could live comfortably with euro interest rates on a permanent basis?
2. *Flexibility:* If problems arose, would Britain be able to make quick economic adjustments to deal with them?
3. *Investment:* Would joining the eurozone improve conditions for firms deciding to invest in Britain?
4. *Financial services:* Would joining the eurozone improve the competitive position of Britain's financial services industry, particularly the City's wholesale markets?
5. *Employment and general economic performance:* Would joining the eurozone promote higher growth and more employment?

The government occasionally publishes its assessment of the tests, using the opportunity to launch various economic reforms. The government's main concern has been about meeting its own criteria for sustainable convergence and flexibility. Regardless of the tests, however, opinion in Britain is generally running against adoption of the euro. A populist "Save the Pound" campaign both feeds and feeds off a virulent Euroskeptical movement, undermining prospects of bringing Britain into the eurozone.

Despite the unlikelihood that Britain, Denmark, and Sweden would adopt the euro anytime soon, many of the new member states were eager to do so. All of them are obliged to join the eurozone (there are no opt-outs), but they first have to meet the convergence criteria (covering price stability, budgetary discipline, currency stability, and interest rate convergence). Although there are marked variations among the new member states, meeting the criteria is unlikely to pose insuperable obstacles: inflation is generally low, public finances are by and large sound, the margins of the ERM II are generous (15 percent), and interest rates are converging. Familiarity with the euro in the new member states will undoubtedly help in making the transition to it, but not everyone necessarily wants to give up their own currency. As is the case in Britain, Denmark, and Sweden, many people in the new member states are concerned about the implications of EMU for national sovereignty and identity. Nevertheless, almost all of the member states that joined the EU in 2004 are expected to adopt the euro by 2010 at the latest.

The possible expansion of the eurozone necessitated changes in the governing structure of the ECB.[49] Thanks to a provision in the Nice Treaty, these could be made without recourse to an intergovernmental conference. At issue was the anticipated increase in the size of the Governing Council (consisting of the ECB's six-member executive board and the governors of the national central banks, with each member having a right to vote). If all ten of the new member states joined the eurozone, the Governing Council would increase from eighteen to twenty-eight members, possibly impairing its decisionmaking capacity. Accordingly, in December 2002 the ECB proposed limiting the number of voting members of national central bank governors to fifteen in the new Governing Council and instituting a complicated rota for those fifteen seats at the decisionmaking table.[50] The rota would be based on the economic, not demographic, size of each member state, thereby privileging little Luxembourg over populous Poland, for example. The European Council adopted the new rules in March 2003, despite complaints from the prospective new member states of bias against them.

■ Notes

1. Interview in *Wall Street Journal,* October 29, 1990, p. 1.
2. On the development of EMU, see Kenneth Dyson, *Elusive Union: The Process of Economic and Monetary Union in Europe* (London: Longman, 1994); Daniel Gros and Niels Thygesen, *European Monetary Integration: From the European Monetary System Towards Monetary Union* (New York: St. Martin's Press, 1991); and Kathleen McNamara, *The Currency of Ideas: Monetary Politics in the European Union* (Ithaca, NY: Cornell University Press, 1997).
3. Karl Kaiser et al., *The European Community: Progress or Decline?* (London: RIIA, 1983), p. 13.
4. Tomaso Padoa-Schioppa, ed., *Efficiency, Stability and Equity: A Strategy for the Evolution of the Economic System of the EC* (Luxembourg: Office for Official Publications of the European Communities, 1987), p. 8.
5. European Commission, *Economic and Monetary Union* (Luxembourg: Office for Official Publications of the European Communities, 1990), p. 11.
6. European Commission, *One Market, One Money: An Evaluation of the Potential Benefits and Costs of Forming an Economic and Monetary Union* (Luxembourg: Office for Official Publications of the European Communities, 1990), p. 9.
7. European Commission, *From Single Market to European Union* (Luxembourg: Office for Official Publications of the European Communities, 1992).
8. Padoa-Schioppa, *Efficiency,* pp. 3, 13.
9. Leon Brittan, speech to the British Chamber of Commerce in Germany, October 31, 1990.
10. See Commission, *One Market,* p. 10.
11. Bulletin EC S/1-1976, p. 20.
12. Committee for the Study of Economic and Monetary Union, *Report on Economic and Monetary Union in the European Community* (Delors Report) (Luxem-

bourg: Office for Official Publications of the European Communities, 1989), pp. 18–19.

13. Delors Report, p. 24.

14. See Dorothee Heisenberg, *The Mark of the Bundesbank: Germany's Role in European Monetary Cooperation* (Boulder, CO: Lynne Rienner, 1999).

15. Commission, *Economic and Monetary Union,* p. 21.

16. *Hansard,* 184/41, Cols. 470–479, January 24, 1991.

17. Quoted in *Manchester Guardian Weekly,* July 7, 1991, p. 6.

18. Leon Brittan, speech to the British Chamber of Commerce in Germany, October 31, 1990.

19. Commission, *Economic and Monetary Union,* p. 17.

20. Commission, *One Market,* p. 251.

21. Ibid., pp. 28–29.

22. Peter Kenen, "Speaking Up for EMU," *Financial Times,* July 28, 1992, p. 15.

23. Martin Feldstein, "Europe's Monetary Union: The Case Against EMU," *Economist,* June 13, 1992, pp. 19–22.

24. Commission, *Economic and Monetary Union,* p. 11.

25. Bulletin EC 6-1988, "Presidency Conclusions," points 1.1.1–1.1.4 and 3.4.1.

26. Bulletin EC 6-1989, "Presidency Conclusions," point 1.1.11.

27. Bulletin EC 12-1989, "Presidency Conclusions," point 1.1.11.

28. Bulletin EC 6-1990, "Presidency Conclusions," point 1.10.

29. Bulletin EC 10-1990, "Presidency Conclusions," points 1.2–1.6.

30. Paule de Grauwe, Daniel Gros, Alfred Steinherr, and Niels Thygesen, "Reply to Feldstein," *Economist,* July 4, 1992, p. 67.

31. See "The ERM Crisis," *Financial Times,* December 12–13, 1992, p. 2.

32. Quoted in *Financial Times,* January 15, 1993, p. 2.

33. Council press release 8854/92, September 28, 1992, 1604th Council Meeting.

34. Henning Christopherson, speech to the European Institute, Washington, DC, September 21, 1992.

35. OECD, *Financial Market Trends,* October 1992, p. 16.

36. Quoted in *Financial Times,* May 17, 1991, p. 18; Pöhl inserted this phrase into the final communiqué of the 1977 G7 summit.

37. Desmond Dinan, *Ever Closer Union? An Introduction to the European Community* (Boulder: Lynne Rienner, 1994), p. 435.

38. European Commission, *Report on Convergence in the European Union in 1996,* COM(96)560, November 6, 1996; European Monetary Institute, *Progress Towards Convergence* (Frankfurt: European Monetary Institute, November 1996).

39. European Commission, "Green Paper on Technical Preparations for the Single European Currency," COM(95)333.

40. Amsterdam European Council, "Presidency Conclusions," Bulletin EC 6-1997, point 1.1.10.

41. European Commission, *European Economy,* Supplement A, no. 10 (October 1997).

42. European Commission, *Euro 1999: Progress Towards Convergence* (Luxembourg: Office for Official Publications of the European Communities, 1999); and European Monetary Institute, *Convergence Report* (Frankfurt: European Monetary Institute, 1998).

43. Commission, *European Economy,* Supplement A, nos. 3/4 (March–April 1998).

44. The statement is reproduced in http://ue.eu.int/ueDocs/cms_Data/docs/pressData/en/ecofin/08170-R1.EN8.htm.

45. See Lionel Barber, "The Euro: Single Currency, Multiple Injuries," in *Financial Times,* June 10, 1999, p. 10.

46. Massimo Beber, "'One Careful Driver from New': Earning the European Central Bank's No-Claims Bonus," *Journal of Common Market Studies Annual Review* 40 (2002): 75.

47. Quoted in *International Herald Tribune*, March 26, 1998, p. 4.

48. Quoted in *Financial Times*, November 2, 2002. On the trials and tribulations of the Stability and Growth Pact, see Marco Buti and Gabriele Giudice, "Maastricht's Fiscal Rules at Ten: An Assessment," *Journal of Common Market Studies* 40, no. 5 (December 2002): 823–848; Paul De Grauwe, "Challenges for Monetary Policy in Euroland," *Journal of Common Market Studies* 40, no. 4 (November 2002): 693–718.

49. See Manfred J. M. Neumann, "The Impact of EU Enlargement on Voting Procedures of the ECB Governing Council," *Atlantic Economic Journal* 31, no. 4 (December 2003): 309–312; and Helge Berger and Jakob De Haan, "Are Small Countries Too Powerful Within the ECB?" *Atlantic Economic Journal* 30, no. 3 (September 2002): 263–283.

50. See Dorothee Heisenberg, "Cutting the Bank Down to Size: Efficient and Legitimate Decision-making in the European Central Bank After Enlargement," *Journal of Common Market Studies* 41, no. 3 (September 2003): 397–420.

16

External Relations

By virtue of its economic size, policy scope, and political profile, the European Union is a leading global actor. Most third countries (nonmember states) have diplomatic missions in Brussels accredited to the EU. The Commission conducts trade policy and negotiates on member states' behalf in the World Trade Organization (WTO); participates in the work of the Organization for Economic Cooperation and Development (OECD) and the Group of Seven/Eight (G7/8) industrialized countries; organizes extensive development assistance to a large group of African, Caribbean, and Pacific states; coordinates humanitarian aid all over the world; and has over 150 diplomatic missions and offices in every corner of the globe. The Commission president and the president-in-office of the Council meet regularly with the leaders of China, Russia, the United States, and other favored interlocutors, while commissioners and EU officials frequently visit and receive government ministers from nonmember states to discuss trade, investment, environmental, labor, and related socioeconomic issues.

Like its constituent member states and other countries in the international system, the EU aims through its external relations to enhance prosperity and security. The EU and its member states attempt to coordinate their external relations, although sometimes their objectives and initiatives seem to compete with rather than complement each other. Unlike most nation-states, the EU does not have an army. Nevertheless, it has a vast array of "soft power" instruments at its disposal, such as trade concessions, development assistance, and European Investment Bank preferential lending, which it may use to try to alter the behavior of nonmember states and shape the international system to its liking.

The primary objective of EU trade policy is to get the best bargain for European manufacturers and consumers by gaining access to third-country markets while occasionally protecting the EU market (although EU policymakers would never admit to being protectionist). The primary objective of EU development policy is to help poor countries, especially those with historical ties to the EU's member states, grow economically, but not at the risk of exposing politically sensitive EU sectors to greater competition. Most of the EU's agreements with developing countries include conditionality clauses linking trade concessions to improvements in human rights and standards of governance.

In pursuit of its external relations objectives, the EU has developed an intricate web of interregional and bilateral contacts covering commercial and political relations with almost every country in the world. Most of these relationships are highly institutionalized, sometimes involving annual summit meetings, ministerial meetings, meetings of high-level officials, and meetings of interparliamentary bodies. Referring to the EU's relations with the Association of Southeast Asian Nations, external relations commissioner Chris Patten remarked in September 2002 that he was "keen to avoid heavy new institutional obligations for either side. We all attend too many meetings, and need, if anything, to streamline what already exists."[1] Patten's observation is true of most of the EU's relations with third countries and other regional groups. As with European integration itself, procedure sometimes seems more important than substance in the conduct of EU foreign policy.

▧ Trade Policy

Under the terms of the Rome Treaty (incorporated into the Constitutional Treaty), the Common Commercial Policy gives the EU exclusive competence for external trade relations, which aim "to contribute, in the common interest, to the harmonious development of world trade, the progressive abolition of restrictions on international trade, and the lowering of customs barriers." The original treaty authorized the Commission to conduct the EU's external trade relations subject to direction from the Council (using qualified majority voting), an arrangement that remained essentially unchanged through successive treaty reforms. The treaty also gave the EU the authority to conclude international agreements (with the Council also acting by qualified majority vote). The European Parliament plays a relatively minor role in the Common Commercial Policy.

The Political and Policymaking Context

Member states have different trade policy preferences and orientations. Historically, the French are notoriously protectionist, whereas the British and Dutch champion free trade. Most member states are somewhere in between. On certain issues the French are more liberal than the British and Dutch; on other issues the British and the Dutch are surprisingly protectionist. Having been locked for most of the post–World War II period into a mercantilist system constructed by and for the benefit of the Soviet Union, the new Central and Eastern European member states generally favor an open international system and are more inclined than some of the older member states to reach agreement with the United States on contentious transatlantic trade issues. As in other policy areas, only more so, the Council of Ministers (and occasionally the European Council) attempts to reconcile strong national interests and preferences.

Apart from sector- and case-specific disputes among member states, two interinstitutional controversies have dominated the conduct of EU trade policy. One pertains to day-to-day Commission-Council relations, the other to the question of competence for trade policy given the emergence of new issues and the rapidly changing international trade agenda. Both are classic examples of the struggle between intergovernmentalism and supranationality in the EU system.

Commission-Council Relations. Article 133 TEC states that the Council must approve Commission proposals to implement the Common Commercial Policy and must also approve Commission recommendations to open negotiations for agreements with third countries (in both cases acting by a qualified majority). In addition, Article 133 provides for "a special committee appointed by the Council to assist the Commission" with its negotiations "within the framework of such directives as the Council may issue to it." This is the famous 133 Committee of member state civil servants that meets regularly with Commission officials to approve the Commission's negotiating strategy and proposals. Similarly, Article 300 TEC authorizes the Commission to negotiate international agreements subject to the Council's oversight.

The Commission has a love-hate relationship with the 133 Committee, whose presence behind the scenes ensures that Commission negotiators stick to the agreed-upon Council position. The committee's existence inherently strengthens the Commission's negotiating position because third countries know that the Commission has the committee's—and therefore the Council's—support. On the other hand, the committee's existence reduces the Commission's room for maneuver. Either way, the Article 133 regime means that the Commission is always involved in parallel sets of negotiations: with member states to agree upon and (when necessary) adjust a negotiation position and with third countries to conclude a trade accord.

Inevitably the Commission tries to maximize its influence and input and frequently exceeds its negotiating brief. Sometimes the 133 Committee is too intrusive; at other times it is surprisingly lax and can be "captured" by the Commission. How much the Commission gets away with usually depends first and foremost on the political and economic importance of the negotiations. Other factors that determine the Commission's degree of flexibility in the conduct of external trade negotiations include

- the complexity of the issues under discussion (the Commission has a long institutional memory and a high level of expertise)
- the stature of the trade policy commissioner and of the country currently holding the Council presidency
- the Commission's willingness and ability to take initiatives, build coalitions of member states, and mobilize interest groups
- the timing of the negotiations and the pressure (or nonpressure) for agreement; the involvement of various sectoral councils as well as the General Affairs Council (which has overall authority for trade policy)
- the busyness of the Commission's own political agenda

The Question of Competence.   Member states started to dispute the extent of Community competence for trade relations once trade began to account for a larger share of GDP and as the international economic system grew more complex. When the original version of Article 133 was drafted, trade barriers consisted mostly of tariffs and quotas. Subsequently, regulatory barriers such as standards, conformity testing, certification, and product approval assumed paramount importance. At the same time, trade in goods lost its primacy to trade in services, and issues such as investment and the environment impinged more and more on the international trade agenda. The acceleration of technological change introduced new products (such as genetically modified organisms) and new processes (such as electronic commerce). Sometimes new products necessitated a reconfiguration of existing services (such as the impact of cell phones on the provision of telephone service).

The Commission consistently interpreted the treaty's commercial policy clauses flexibly, arguing that the EC retained exclusive competence for trade relations regardless of these developments. Partly because of institutional rivalry, but mostly because the economic stakes were so much higher, member states (through the Council) took a more rigid view of Article 133. There were frequent spats between the Council and the Commission in the 1980s, but matters came to a head during the final stages of the Uruguay Round of the General Agreement on Tariffs and Trade (GATT) in the early 1990s. When member states questioned the Commission's competence to conclude agreements on trade in services and trade-related aspects of intellectual property rights, the Commission responded by requesting a ruling from the Court of Justice. Much to the Commission's surprise, the Court interpreted Article 133 conservatively and ruled against the Commission.[2]

The Commission unsuccessfully attempted during the 1996–1997 intergovernmental conference on treaty reform to extend the scope of Article 133 to cover trade in services and intellectual property rights. By stipulating in the revised article that the Council could decide in future *by means of unanimity* to extend Article 133, national governments effectively maintained the status quo. Nor did they accede to a request from the European Parliament to change Article 133 in order to give the Parliament a formal role in commercial policy decisionmaking. Although the Parliament has an influential Committee on International Trade and frequently passes resolutions and sends delegations to major trade negotiations, the treaty still limits the conduct of the Common Commercial Policy to the Commission and the Council.

The Commission had long complained to the Council that the 133 regime made the EU a difficult and complicated trade partner for third countries to negotiate with. In the Commission's view, mixed or joint EU–member state competence for new trade issues compounds the problem. The Commission is not usually solicitous of third countries, but it has a point about the complexity of their dealings with the EU. For instance, in the WTO committee on trade in goods, the Commission alone represents the EU. In the services and intellectual property committees, the Commission and member states negotiate jointly on behalf of the EU. Third countries may find this strange, but they have managed to come to terms with it. Similarly, third countries have reconciled themselves for a long time to the 133 regime and have learned to exploit it on occasion by lobbying the 133 Committee before key negotiating sessions.

Perhaps a more serious problem for third countries, but one to which the Commission does not draw attention, is the proliferation of trade-related directorates-general and portfolios within the Commission itself due to the oversupply of commissioners in an EU of twenty-five member states, each of which sends a commissioner to Brussels. Although there is only one portfolio for trade policy, a number of commissioners have responsibility for trade-related issues. The likelihood of further enlargement makes it equally likely that the division of responsibility for external economic relations among a number of directorates-general and commissioners will continue for some time.[3]

Key Developments and Issues

The Common Commercial Policy is the external manifestation of the customs union, itself the foundation upon which the single market and monetary union were built. The common external tariff, established in July 1968 upon completion of the customs union, is a key regulatory instrument of the Common Commercial Policy. Technically the Common Commercial Policy was not complete until the single market program put an end (in 1992) to long-standing quota restrictions and other controls that individual member states had imposed against certain imports (mostly textiles, cars, and consumer electronics) from third countries. According to the Commission, the single market program meant, among other things, "putting in place the final elements of the Common Commercial Policy."[4]

Fortress Europe or Partner Europe? The single market program was a crucial event in the development of EU trade policy for another reason as well. To the Commission's dismay, external reaction to the 1992 agenda was far from favorable. "Fortress Europe" became a catchphrase in the United States and elsewhere to signal concern about the implications for nonmember states of greater market integration. The EU had given little thought to the external perception of the internal market and responded to international criticism by emphasizing its commitment to free trade and open markets. In an effort to allay growing concern beyond the EC's borders, the European Council proclaimed in December 1988 that "the single market will be of benefit to Community and non-Community countries alike, by ensuring continuing economic growth. The internal market will not close in on itself. 1992 Europe will be a partner and not a fortress Europe."[5]

The phrase "partner Europe" lacked the resonance and appeal of "fortress Europe." Moreover, the EC's trading partners were unconvinced that the post-1992 European market would be as accessible as the European Council promised. The contemporaneous Uruguay Round of the GATT seemed a fortuitous opportunity to test the EC's resolve to maintain a liberal international trading system and for the EC to leverage concessions from its trading partners based on the single market's expected benefits. The tortuous course of the Uruguay Round, however, sent mixed signals about the EC's commitment to global trade liberalization (negotiations almost collapsed because of the EC's agricultural protectionism). In the event, market integration and external trade liberalization became mutually reinforcing for the EC (and later the EU), resulting in improved market access for external suppliers and increased exposure of the EU economy to global competition.

The EU's trade policy is reasonably open, with the exception of the agricultural and (for cultural reasons) audiovisual sectors. Apart from films and farm products, third countries complain most about limited market access for items such as textiles, clothing, and cars. The EU's average industrial tariff is about 10 percent (the EU's main trading partners generally have a lower rate) but is declining to about 3 percent as a result of Uruguay Round commitments. Other trade-related concerns of third countries include

- the impact of EU enlargement (concerns about trade diversion have been a feature of every EU enlargement)
- the impact of the EU's growing network of preferential and regional agreements on the multilateral system
- the frequency and severity of EU antidumping actions in sensitive sectors such as electronics, steel, and textiles
- the trade-restricting impact of EU health, safety, and environmental directives

For its part, the EU

- has always been willing to negotiate compensation for countries that encounter new or higher trade barriers in their dealings with the enlarged EU (although the Commission has not always conducted such negotiations with alacrity)
- argues that there is no inconsistency between progressive multilateral liberalization and the conclusion of preferential trade agreements
- doggedly defends its recourse to antidumping measures under agreed-upon WTO rules
- claims that its health and safety legislation is not politically inspired but is based on sound scientific advice or, more weakly, "consumer preference"

In December 1996 the EU signaled a tough approach to third-country trade barriers by launching a "Market Access Strategy."[6] This approach involves identifying persistent barriers to European exports and deciding how best to combat them using existing instruments. The initiative included establishing a new database with information on all trade barriers faced by EU firms in foreign markets, broken down by sector and country. Although largely a domestic public relations exercise, the strategy provides a useful overview of the conduct of EU trade policy.

The World Trade Organization.   The WTO came into being in January 1995, nearly fifty years late. Toward the end of World War II, the United States had proposed setting up the International Trade Organization (ITO) as the third pillar of a new liberal international economic system—the other two were the World Bank and the International Monetary Fund. The proposed ITO was stillborn because the U.S. Senate failed to ratify its founding treaty (the Havana Charter of 1950). Thus, the GATT, which had been launched in January 1948 as an interim measure until negotiation and ratification of the ITO, became by default the key forum for international trade liberalization. Only at the end of the Uruguay Round—the longest, most complicated, and most contentious "round" of multilateral trade liberalization negotiations held under the auspices of the GATT—did the GATT's "contracting parties" (or members) establish a successor organization. In deference to the United States, the new organization was called the WTO instead of the ITO.

The WTO is much weightier than the interim (although long-lived) GATT ever was. Regular ministerial meetings give the WTO a political prominence that the GATT conspicuously lacked. Substantively, the WTO encompasses not only the old GATT but also the General Agreement on Trade in Services (GATS) and the Trade-Related Aspects of Intellectual Property Rights (TRIPs) agreements, both of which were negotiated as part of the Uruguay Round and came into effect when the WTO became operational. One of the WTO's most important innovations is the Dispute Settlement Body and Appellate Body to resolve disputes between contracting parties. This is a major improvement on the GATT system of dispute resolution, which, because it operated on the basis of unanimity, was weak and generally ineffective. The EU strongly supported establishing a Dispute Settlement Body and an Appellate Body not only because their rulings would be binding but also because they could be used to check unilateral action by the United States.

The EU is one of the WTO's two heavyweight boxers; the other is the United States. Paradoxically, the EU is not a WTO contracting party (nor was it ever a contracting party to the GATT). Only by virtue of its member states' treaty obligations to act as one in the international trade arena (an obligation that yields solid political and economic advantages) is the EU a de facto WTO member. Japan is less weighty but nonetheless influential within the WTO. The EU, United States, Japan, and Canada form the Quad, an informal group of the WTO's most powerful players. The G20 plus, a group of rapidly developing countries led informally by Brazil and South Africa, is challenging the preeminence of the United States and the EU in the WTO and setting the pace for a global agreement in the Doha Development Round.

The EU sought to put its stamp on the new WTO by taking an aggressive approach to procedural and institutional issues. For instance, the EU successfully insisted that "its candidate" become the WTO's first secretary-general and unsuccessfully insisted on two "EU seats" on the supposedly nonpartisan Appellate Body (the EU agreed to only one seat when the United States did likewise). In both cases, the EU thought of itself as acting not only in the EU's interests but also against U.S. interests.

The EU has adopted a three-part approach to the WTO. One is simply to carry out its commitments under the Uruguay Round and related agreements. These included implementing the Agreement on Textiles and Clothing (ATC), which entered into force with the WTO agreement and applies GATT rules to a sector undergoing considerable restructuring in the EU (notably Portugal); reducing tariffs on industrial goods on a year-by-year basis; phasing out remaining quantitative restrictions on imports; and cutting levies and price supports for agricultural products.

Another part of the EU's approach to the WTO is to use the dispute-resolution mechanism as a major trade policy instrument (the EU is the complainant far more often than it is the defendant). The EU has won some high-profile cases and lost a few as well. For instance, the EU lost a big case against its banana-import regime, which discriminates against larger, cheaper Latin American bananas in favor of more expensive, poorer-quality bananas from countries that were party to the EU's Lomé Convention (an aid and preferential trade program for former European colonies in Africa, the Caribbean, and the Pacific that is now covered by the Cotonou agreement). The EU also lost a case brought by the United States against its ban on hormone-treated beef because the ban was not based on scientific evidence (and therefore contravened international trade rules). Both cases caused considerable political upset in the EU. Despite the advice of then trade commissioner Leon Brittan that "it is vital for Europe to be able to take the rough with the smooth," the EU (like the United States) tends to abide selectively by WTO rulings, preferring to pay the price of sanctions rather than incur the political pain of reform.[7]

Participation in the WTO's Work Program. Involvement in the WTO's work program for further multilateral liberalization, which includes unfinished GATT business as well as new initiatives, is the third, most far-reaching aspect of the EU's WTO policy. Highlights include:

Telecommunications. The EU was in the forefront of efforts to reach a WTO agreement on the liberalization of global telecommunications markets. When the United States pulled out of the talks—largely for domestic political reasons—shortly before the initial deadline of April 1996, it and the EU agreed to prolong negotiations for almost another year. Although discussion went down to the wire, sixty-nine countries (including the EU15) signed the agreement at WTO headquarters in Geneva before the deadline expired. The agreement opened voice telephony, electronic data transmissions, telex, and fax services to global competition and covered all means of service (cable, fiber optics, radio, and satellite). For the first time in a global accord, the agreement also included a commitment to basic competition policy principles. Implementation of the agreement, and the granting of temporary derogations for some countries, mirrored the calendar for the EU's own liberalization of telecommunications.

Information technology. The EU and the United States sought the Information Technology Agreement (ITA) in order to eliminate tariffs on a host of nonconsumer electronic products, including telecommunications equipment, computers, computer chips, and software. The EU pushed for the agreement partly to counter what it perceived as the discriminatory aspects of the U.S.-Japan semiconductor accord. In late 1996 the U.S. trade representative accepted a Commission proposal to postpone a meeting of the U.S.-Japan semiconductor industry council until March 1997, by which time the EU hoped to conclude the ITA. After hectic negotiations, the EU15 and twelve other countries (including the United States) concluded the agreement by the end of 1996. Together, the countries concerned accounted for over 80 percent of global information technology trade.

Financial services. The EU was instrumental in achieving an interim multi-lateral agreement on financial services in July 1995, covering the period until December 1997, despite U.S. withdrawal from the talks because of dissatis-faction with the market-opening offers on the table, especially from emerging economies. The agreement promised foreign access (in varying degrees) to the banking, insurance, and securities sectors in more than ninety countries (covering 90 percent of all international financial business). The EU trum-peted its ability to lead the talks to a successful conclusion, regardless of the U.S. walkout, as a major international achievement. The EU then sought to translate the interim agreement into a permanent arrangement that included the United States. Although prospects for doing so seemed to fade in the clos-ing stages of the talks as the Asian economic crisis distracted some of the Asian countries' attention and dimmed their enthusiasm for market liberaliza-tion, a permanent agreement was secured at the last moment (in December 1997) with the full participation of the United States.

Foreign direct investment. The EU has long taken the lead in calling for bind-ing multilateral rules to cover foreign direct investment (FDI), the means by which businesspeople establish new firms or buy existing ones in other coun-tries. The Commission sees FDI as "the second pillar of the international econ-omy" (trade being the first).[8] Although the GATS and the trade-related invest-ment measures (TRIMs) have a bearing on FDI and are under the WTO umbrella, the EU has been keen to negotiate a comprehensive multilateral agree-ment that would range from investment rules to environmental protection and sustainable development. However, the complexity and political sensitivity of many FDI-related issues have thwarted the Commission's initiatives to promote a global regime. The most ambitious effort to date took place not in the WTO but in the OECD, where negotiation of the proposed Multilateral Agreement on Investment (MAI) ended in deadlock. Growing controversy over the provisions of the MAI, which many private pressure groups and some government officials perceived as a threat to national sovereignty; the environment; and sundry other entities forced OECD members to shelve negotiations in May 1998.

China and Russia in the WTO. Conditional support for China's and Russia's WTO membership was a separate issue on which the EU took a lead. By con-trast with the United States, which rejected China's candidacy outright until China lifted some well-documented trade barriers, the EU supported China's accession to the WTO as a means of encouraging economic reform by lock-ing China into a rule-based organization. Critics contended that the EU also had selfish motives, that perhaps it hoped China would look more favorably on European exporters and investors. Nevertheless, the EU's support for China was not unconditional. Only when the EU and China concluded a bi-lateral agreement on WTO accession, allaying European concerns about financial services, public procurement, intellectual property rights, and other sensitive issues, did the EU rally wholeheartedly behind China's candidacy. The EU-China deal complemented a separate U.S.-China agreement that finally paved the way for China's membership in the world trade body.

The question of Russia's WTO membership also divided the United States and the EU, although not as sharply and not with ideological overtones. Whereas the EU is sympathetic to Russia's application, the United States holds that Russia has a long way to go before it develops a market economy with a trade regime that complies with rigorous WTO rules. Without agreement between the United States and the EU, Russia is unlikely to be admitted to the WTO.

The Doha Development Round. The Uruguay Round agreement committed the WTO to opening two new sets of negotiations, on agriculture and on services, no later than the year 2000. The EU—more specifically Leon Brittan—wanted instead to have a single, broader, more inclusive round, similar to the Uruguay Round but shorter and less acrimonious. Knowing that it would be pressed to make concessions on agriculture, the EU wanted in turn to be able to leverage concessions in other areas by conducting the agricultural negotiations in the context of a multifaceted trade round. As Brittan put it, "the more horses there are to trade, the more logical it becomes to trade them within the same market."[9]

Few other WTO players, including some EU member states, shared the Commission's enthusiasm for a grand new round of trade liberalization talks. Post–Uruguay Round fatigue was still prevalent, and the WTO already had plenty on its plate. Denied congressional authorization for "fast-track" trade talks, the U.S. administration had little appetite for a new round either, as a commitment to begin such a round was not likely to win votes in the 2000 U.S. presidential election.

The antiglobalization demonstrations at the WTO ministerial meeting in Seattle in early December 1999 dampened whatever enthusiasm remained for a new round of negotiations, although the terrorist attacks on the United States in September 2001 galvanized governments to demonstrate a common commitment to economic globalization. Hence the launch of a new round of negotiations in Doha in November 2001, for which the U.S. president received fast-track authority. In deference to the antiglobalization movement and the demands of the poorer countries, the new round of talks was officially called the Doha Development Round.

The EU has been criticized for using the Doha Round to push the so-called Singapore issues (investment, competition, transparency in government procurement, and trade facilitation), which many poor countries see as potential barriers to their development. Not surprisingly, however, agriculture has become the biggest sticking point in the negotiations, with the EU tenaciously defending the Common Agricultural Policy (see Chapter 12). The Cancun ministerial meeting, held in September 2003 approximately halfway between the launch and the expected end of the Doha Round, broke down in acrimony over agriculture and the Singapore issues. Nor did the negotiators meet the deadline of January 2005 for completion of the Doha Round. The EU is by no means the only or the worst culprit, but its positions on agriculture and the Singapore issues (however laudable) are an obstacle to moving the negotiations along.[10]

■ Regional Perspectives

The EU has a thick network of relationships with countries and groups of countries all over the world. These range from narrow bilateral agreements involving minimal commitments on either side to intensive bilateral and interregional agreements covering a range of economic and political issues. The EU offers an unofficial hierarchy of agreements to third countries. In ascending order, these are

- Free Trade Agreements
- Partnership and Cooperation Agreements
- Customs Unions
- Association Agreements
- Europe Agreements

A Europe Agreement, the highest form of agreement with the EU, is usually a prelude to EU membership. In addition, the EU offers strategic partnerships, a political designation, to certain countries.

This section provides an overview of the EU's external relations with third countries and other regional organizations, beginning with the EU's immediate neighbors. The African, Caribbean, and Pacific states, with which the EU has a special trade and development assistance agreement, are discussed in the next section.

The European Economic Area

The European Economic Area (EEA) extends the EU's single market to three of the four members of the European Free Trade Association (EFTA): Iceland, Liechtenstein, and Norway. Switzerland, the fourth member of the European Free Trade Association, chose not to join the EEA after a referendum on the issue in December 1992. When the EEA came into being in January 1994, Austria, Finland, and Sweden were also European Free Trade Association members; their accession to the EU in January 1995 therefore robbed the EEA of much of its significance. Despite the huge imbalance between its EU and European Free

Trade Association members, the EEA is nevertheless the most highly institutionalized and integrated external economic arrangement involving the EU. Substantively, the EEA covers the single market, competition, and some other core economic policy areas. Institutionally, the EEA includes

- a council composed of government ministers and commissioners (meets twice a year)
- a joint committee composed of high-level representatives of the Commission and the EEA member states (meets at least monthly)
- a joint parliamentary committee composed of members of the European Parliament and the national parliaments of the EFTA states (meets twice a year)
- a consultative committee composed of representatives of employers' and workers' groups (meets twice a year)

The EEA was to have included a supranational court, but the Court of Justice ruled in December 1991 that the establishment of such an institution would have contravened EC law by undermining the supremacy of the Court of Justice, the EU's highest judicial body. At EU insistence, the EFTA members scrapped the proposed EEA court and agreed that disputes between the two sides in the EEA (the EU and non-EU members) would have to be settled politically in the EEA council. The EEA acquired ten new members—on the EU side—when the Central and Eastern European countries, plus Cyprus and Malta, joined the EU in May 2004, making it easily the world's largest commercial bloc.

Switzerland

Located in the middle of the EU but having decided not to join the EEA, Switzerland is in a category all its own. Although the Swiss people chose, by virtue of rejecting the EEA, not to pursue EU membership, successive Swiss governments, with strong backing from Swiss business leaders, have pursued a policy of de facto European integration. As a result, no other country has as many agreements with the EU. The current, highly developed relationship between the EU and Switzerland rests on two sets of bilateral agreements:

- seven agreements concluded in June 1999 and implemented in June 2002 (before the referendum on EEA membership)
- nine agreements concluded in October 2004, whose implementation is subject to ratification on both sides

The existing and yet-to-be-ratified agreements cover everything from free trade in goods and services to Switzerland's participation in the Schengen regime for the free movement of people throughout the EU. In view of Swiss people's concerns about being swallowed up by the EU behemoth, Switzerland and the EU have a touchy political relationship. Accordingly, the first EU-Switzerland summit did not take place until May 2004.

Southeastern Europe

Southeastern Europe, or the Western Balkans, is a troubled region consisting of Albania, Bosnia and Herzegovina, Croatia, Serbia and Montenegro, and Macedonia. Albania was a highly repressed, almost completely isolated doctrinaire communist country during the Cold War. More than fifteen years after the end of the Cold War, it is deeply impoverished and highly dysfunctional. It is also home to violent criminal gangs that have spread their operations throughout much of Europe. The EU is doing its best to help through various humanitarian and development programs and through generous trade preferences (not that Albania has much to export). Albania's prospects for EU membership are slim for a long time to come.

The other four countries in the region were constituent republics of Yugoslavia before that country's violent breakup in the early 1990s. Despite Serbian leader Slobodan Milošević's efforts to establish a greater Serbia in the region, the rump state of Serbia and Montenegro is all that is left of the old Yugoslav federation. First Croatia, then Bosnia and Herzegovina, fought bitter wars of secession from Yugoslavia and also fought against each other during several years of vicious ethnic strife. Macedonia has a volatile ethnic mix but has so far escaped the kind of violence that tore through Bosnia and Herzegovina a decade ago. In deference to Greek sensitivities (Greece has a province called Macedonia), the EU refers to Macedonia as the "former Yugoslav Republic of Macedonia." The United States dropped the pretense in November 2004 and decided to call the country Macedonia. The region contains another territorial entity that, in principle, is part of Serbia but, in practice, is a United Nations protectorate: Kosovo.

Making up for its failure to prevent or stop the fighting in the former Yugoslavia in the 1990s, the EU is now extremely active in the region. The EU is the largest donor of development assistance in the the Western Balkans as a whole, largely through the Community Assistance for Reconstruction, Development, and Stabilization program, which provided about €5 billion in assistance during the period 2000–2006. The European Agency for Reconstruction manages the main EU assistance programs in Serbia, Kosovo, Montenegro, and Macedonia.

The EU sees the situation in Southeastern Europe after the recent wars as being similar to the situation in Europe as a whole after World War II. Not surprisingly, the EU advocates the same solution: economic and political integration as the best means of promoting peace, stability, and prosperity. The

Stabilization and Association Process (SAP) is the integrative framework for the EU's approach to Southeastern Europe. Under its auspices, the EU encourages economic, political, judicial, and administrative reform through the provision of financial aid, trade preferences, and technical advice. The next step in the process is the conclusion of tailor-made stabilization and association agreements, which two countries, Croatia and Macedonia, have so far signed with the EU. The stabilization and association agreements are analogous to Europe Agreements and hold out the prospect of EU membership.

Croatia is well on its way to joining the EU, having applied in February 2003 and received a positive Commission opinion about a year later. The European Council endorsed Croatia's application in June 2004, giving the country candidate status. Because of Croatia's relatively strong economy and solid democratic structures, the accession process should be reasonably smooth. The most difficult issue remains the question of Croatia's relations with the International Criminal Tribunal for the former Yugoslavia. Croatia allegedly is sheltering a number of indicted war criminals, although, under intense U.S. and European pressure, it continues to improve its cooperation with the court.

The European Council affirmed in March 2003 that the countries of the Western Balkans have a future in the EU. Indeed, the lure of possible EU membership has had a marked effect on the conduct of the countries concerned. Arguably the situation will not be normal until Serbia, historically the regional power and still a cultural beacon in Southeastern Europe, joins the EU. Before hoping to do so, however, Serbia will have to come to terms with its recent past and pursue a policy of reconciliation toward its neighbors, an important element of the integration process.

Wider Europe

The phrase "wider Europe," coined by the Commission, covers the EU's neighbors to the south and east, running in an arc from Morocco in the far west to Russia in the far north, including everything in between (the Maghreb, parts of the Middle East, Turkey and the Balkans, and much of the former Soviet Union). The name and the so-called European Neighborhood Policy associated with it seek to reassure countries in the region that the 2004 enlargement does not mean the emergence of a new dividing line in and around Europe. To emphasize the point, the EU invited leaders of fourteen neighboring countries to discuss enlargement on the occasion of the signing ceremony for the accession treaties for the new member states in April 2003 in Athens.

Although the countries of the Western Balkans as well as Russia and Turkey are in the wider Europe, they have special relationships with the EU and therefore are not part of the neighborhood policy. By contrast, the EU-Mediterranean (Euro-Med) partnership, an association of EU and southern Mediterranean states, is a pillar of the neighborhood policy. Participation in the neighborhood policy does not qualify a nonmember state for eventual EU membership on the grounds of being "European." Nevertheless, some of the countries of the wider Europe aspire to joining the EU.

The countries of the "wider Europe" are extremely diverse culturally, historically, economically, and politically. Many have little in common with each other apart from geographical propinquity to the EU. Some are a cause of acute concern to the EU, being vulnerable to economic collapse, political extremism, and religious fundamentalism and being sources (or potential sources) of illegal immigration and smuggling of people and drugs. Above all, the EU wants to try to stabilize the region around itself.

Inevitably, the European Neighborhood Policy speaks of promoting good governance, economic liberalism, respect for human rights, sustainable development, and social cohesion—sincere and admirable goals that are hardly realistic in all cases. The EU already has agreements of some kind with most of the countries in the region. The new policy provides an overarching framework for these agreements, sets policy priorities, and promises a series of action plans for each participant. The European Neighborhood Instrument, a fund to help implement the action plans, would become active in 2007 as part of the EU's new financial perspective. Yet there is no guarantee that member states will allocate much money to the fund or that the new policy will improve the quality or effectiveness of existing EU initiatives in the vast "pan-European and Mediterranean region."

Just as the EU has difficulty determining, for purposes of enlargement, where Europe ends, it has difficulty determining, for purposes of the neighborhood policy, where wider Europe ends. The Commission left the Southern Caucasus outside its original formulation of wider Europe, yet the three countries in the region—Georgia, Armenia, and Azerbaijan—are members of the Council of Europe and are in dire need of EU assistance with economic development and conflict resolution. Accordingly, the Commission later included these countries in its neighborhood policy. In the Middle East, Iran and Iraq border Turkey, a candidate for EU membership. Should they be included in the neighborhood policy? And what about the Gulf Cooperation Council, with which the EU is negotiating a free trade area? The EU now has to grapple with those questions.

Russia. Political and economic factors are impossible to disentangle in the case of the EU's dealings with Russia, a strategically important country on the EU's eastern flank. Politically, a stable Russia is essential for European security and for the success of the EU's neighborhood policy. Economically, the EU is Russia's main Western partner, and Russia provides a growing amount of the EU's energy needs. Without more trade and investment, Russia could stagnate politically and economically. Without stability and structural reform in Russia, however, EU trade and investment there cannot reach their full potential.

In 1989 the EC concluded a trade and cooperation agreement with the Soviet Union, a "modest and prudent first step" in developing an economic and political relationship.[11] By that time the Soviet Union was on its last legs. As the situation there deteriorated, the European Council approved emergency food aid and an ambitious technical assistance program.[12] Nevertheless, the EC's relations with the declining Soviet Union were tense as officials in Brussels protested against Soviet repression in the Baltic States in early 1991 and fretted about the apparent ascendancy of conservative Communists in the Kremlin. Yet the Commission opened an office in Moscow later in 1991, just in time to observe at close quarters the failed military coup in August, Boris Yeltsin's triumph over Mikhail Gorbachev, and the rapid dissolution of the Soviet Union.

The collapse of the Soviet Union in December 1991—coincidentally, during the second day of the Maastricht summit—presented the EC with a major political and economic challenge. As a grudging host to several hundred thousand former Soviet troops in the eastern part of the country, Germany urged the EU to pursue a positive, constructive policy toward Russia, the main successor state of the former Soviet Union. The EU duly reorganized its aid to Russia and other former Soviet republics in a program called Technical Assistance for the Commonwealth of Independent States (TACIS) and laid the foundations for a longer-term, more substantive relationship. This approach bore fruit in a political declaration issued in Brussels in December 1993 and a partnership and cooperation agreement signed by Russia and the EU in June 1994. The EU's overall objectives were to bolster political and economic reform in Russia and win Russian support for—or at least acceptance of—EU enlargement in Central and Eastern Europe. However, a succession of trade disputes, coupled with Russia's brutality during Chechnya's secessionist war in 1995, held up ratification of the partnership and cooperation agreement, delayed conclusion of an interim agreement, and caused considerable tension in EU-Russia relations.

For Russia, struggling to come to terms with the Soviet Union's demise, resentful of the United States as the world's sole remaining superpower, and on the verge of economic collapse in 1998, relations with the EU assumed special importance. Only the EU could give Russia the political respect and, more important, the economic assistance and market access that were indispensable for putting the country back on its feet. EU-Russia relations improved in the late 1990s, especially in terms of trade and aid. In return, Russia did not attempt to block EU enlargement. Moreover, without the EU's considerable economic assistance and political support, it is doubtful that Russia would have dropped its resistance to North Atlantic Treaty Organization enlargement.

Since then, EU-Russia relations have cooled considerably. The new Central and Eastern European member states are understandably wary of Russia and irritated by the Western European member states' benign attitude and approach toward their old nemesis. President Vladimir Putin's resumption and conduct of the war with Chechnya, without even the pretense of respect for human rights, is a major thorn in the side of EU-Russia relations. Putin, who personifies brooding resentment of Russia's loss of power and influence, resents his country's dependence on EU support and assistance. Hence the inherent tension in the biannual EU-Russia summits. Putin postponed the summit scheduled for November 2004 in The Hague, ostensibly because the Barroso Commission was not yet in office but more likely because of irritation with the Dutch presidency for criticizing Russia's handling of a hostage crisis in Ossetia the previous September and with continuing complaints in the EU about Russian human rights abuses in Chechnya. Postponement of the summit, and underlying tensions in EU-Russia relations, delayed the conclusion of agreements between the two sides on a number of important issues, such as foreign and security policy cooperation and collaboration on research and development.

Although leading Russian politicians occasionally remark that Russia might one day apply for EU membership, neither Russia nor the EU seriously considers that Russia will ever do so, or would ever be admitted. Were it to include Russia, the French prime minister observed in November 1994, the EU "would become unbalanced, doomed to paralysis and ineffectiveness."[13] A key Commission report on relations with Russia, published in 1995, envisioned an emerging Europe based on the EU in the West and Russia in the East, with most of the former Soviet republics gravitating toward "Russian" Europe.[14] Nothing in the intervening period has changed that assessment, although Russia's continued weakness raises doubts about the attractiveness of the Russian "pole" in Eastern Europe.

Ukraine. Strategic considerations also account for the high degree of EU interest in Ukraine, which borders three EU member states and is a country larger and more populous than France. Ukraine's continuing independence helps prevent the reemergence of a Russian empire in Eastern Europe, as distinct from a Russian zone of influence. The EU has provided considerable economic assistance to Ukraine, largely through the TACIS program. The EU had a particular interest in closing down the Chernobyl nuclear power station, which was the site of a major disaster in 1986 and was considered unsafe for many years thereafter. The EU signed a partnership and cooperation agreement with Ukraine in June 1994, only days before signing a similar agreement with Russia. The EU-Ukraine agreement became operational in March 1998, after extensive ratification delays on both sides. Apart from mixed EU-Ukraine political relations, Ukraine's failure to restructure its economy stymies Western investment in the country and threatens the political independence that Ukraine and the EU want, above all, to maintain. The situation in Ukraine became critical in November 2004 when mass demonstrations paralyzed the capital city following a disputed presidential election. Acting as a counterpoint to Russia, the EU helped to broker the agreement to hold new elections at the end of the following month, which Viktor Yushchenko, the pro-Western candidate, won by a convincing margin.

The Mediterranean and Middle East. For historical, strategic, and economic reasons, the EU has always had a close relationship with neighboring Mediterranean countries. To emphasize the importance of that relationship, EC leaders adopted the Global Mediterranean Policy as long ago as 1972. Although the EC had already concluded a variety of trade agreements with a number of Mediterranean countries, the Global Mediterranean Policy promised to deepen and broaden its involvement in the region. Yet the grandiloquently named policy sounded more impressive than it really was. Economic recession later in the 1970s diminished the EC's ambitious plans for the Mediterranean basin. The accession of Greece, Spain, and Portugal in the 1980s strengthened the EC's Mediterranean orientation but strained its economic relations with non-member Mediterranean countries, whose products faced high barriers to enter the larger EC marketplace.

In the late 1980s, southern Mediterranean countries worried about the economic consequences of the single market program and feared that massive financial transfers to Greece, Spain, and Portugal as part of the single market initiative (and later as part of the monetary union initiative) would further widen the economic divide between member and nonmember Mediterranean states. The EU's growing preoccupation with developments in Central and Eastern Europe in the early 1990s almost blinded officials in Brussels to developments in the Mediterranean region, where economic and political instability threatened the EU's well-being. Anxiety about a possible influx of immigrants from the east finally drew the EU's attention to the reality of mass migration from the south.

Despite the launch more than two decades earlier of the Global Mediterranean Policy, the EU's relations with most Mediterranean countries remained precarious. The situation in the western Mediterranean was especially sensitive. In October 1987 the Council rejected Morocco's application for EC membership on the self-evident grounds that Morocco was not a European country. Relations with Morocco deteriorated further in the early 1990s after the European Parliament voted down a large assistance package under a cooperation agreement because of Morocco's poor human rights record. Morocco responded by freezing its agreement with the EC and jeopardizing a four-year fishing accord vital to Spain's large fleet. The crisis ended only after the Council agreed to explore a wide-ranging free trade agreement with Morocco, possibly also including Algeria and Tunisia.

At the other end of the Mediterranean, political problems also overshadowed the EC's economic relations with Israel, which are based on a 1975 free trade agreement that became fully operational in 1989. Israel wanted to upgrade its economic relations with the EU, its main trading partner, but until the September 1993 Israel–Palestine Liberation Organization Accords, political obstacles proved insurmountable. The EU was extremely critical of Israel's hard line in the Occupied Territories, and Israel objected to full EU participation in the Middle East peace process. Neighboring countries with which the EU had trade agreements dating from the 1970s—Syria, Egypt, Jordan, and Lebanon—also sought closer economic relations with the EU but objected to further EU trade concessions to Israel.

These and other worrisome regional developments were the backdrop against which the Commission worked in the mid-1990s to devise a new Mediterranean strategy. The Commission eventually came up with a typically ambitious proposal to establish a huge free trade area stretching from Morocco in the west to Turkey in the east; altogether it would embrace twelve Mediterranean countries. Negotiations between the EU and the so-called Mediterranean 12 (MED 12) (Algeria, Cyprus, Egypt, Israel, Jordan, Lebanon, Malta, Morocco, Syria, Tunisia, Turkey, and the autonomous Palestinian territories) culminated in a declaration issued at an EU–MED 12 summit in Barcelona in November 1995. The Barcelona Declaration—the cornerstone of the EU's new Mediterranean policy—covered a wide range of issues beyond commercial relations. Chief among these were steps to enhance regional security and to strengthen EU–MED 12 cultural and educational ties.[15]

Nevertheless, economic and financial affairs were at the heart of the new Euro-Mediterranean partnership, and the success of the Barcelona Declaration depended on the EU's ability to promote regional development. The main vehicle for this was the proposed free trade area, due to be completed by 2010, which necessitated negotiating separate Association Agreements between the EU and the MED 12 countries and negotiating similar agreements among the MED 12 countries themselves. The EU-Syria Association Agreement, concluded in October 2004, completed the network of Association Agreements with the EU's partners in the Barcelona process (Syria was the EU's most difficult and elusive partner). In the meantime, two of the original MED 12 states (Cyprus and Malta) became EU members, and another (Turkey) became a candidate for membership.

Given the political volatility of the region and the degree of animosity between some of the now MED 10 countries (Israel and Syria are officially at war with each other), it is hard to see how the free trade area will come into being. Nor are relations between each of the MED 10 countries and the EU on an equal footing. For instance, whereas Turkey is a candidate for EU membership, the EU's relations with Israel deteriorated further following the resumption of hostilities between Israel and the Palestinians in the Occupied Territories. Thus, the apparent symmetry of EU–MED 10 relations disguises a series of bilateral relations that range in their conduct from friendly to frosty and cast in doubt the possible achievement of a large free trade area by 2010.

Although its ultimate goal may seem unattainable, the Barcelona process serves a useful purpose by keeping the EU focused on the Mediterranean region, especially in the context of the European Neighborhood Policy. Frequent follow-up meetings, including biennial summits, monitor the state of EU-Mediterranean relations and sustain the momentum for closer political and economic cooperation. Nevertheless, as far as the EU is concerned, commercial considerations are secondary to political and security ones. EU trade concessions to neighboring Mediterranean countries are worth the potential benefit of enhanced regional stability, despite the reluctance of some of the EU's own Mediterranean member states to pay the price.

The Americas

Relations with the United States dominate the EU's dealings not only with the Americas but also, to a considerable extent, with the world as a whole. Given the economic and political importance of the United States for the EU, U.S.-EU relations are examined separately in Chapter 18. Partly to try to alleviate the overwhelming economic influence of the United States on its immediate neighbors, the EU cultivates especially close relations with Canada and Mexico, partners of the United States in the North American Free Trade Association (an organization launched in 1994 as a counterweight to accelerating regionalization in Europe). For the same reason, only more so, Canada and Mexico are delighted to oblige, although both know that economic and geopolitical realities bind them inexorably to the United States.

Canada. Although greatly overshadowed by the United States, Canada is a pillar of the wider transatlantic relationship. The EU and Canada discuss a range of economic, political, and security issues under the auspices of their "Partnership Agenda," announced at a bilateral summit in March 2004. In a thinly veiled dig at the United States, the two sides like to emphasize their commitment to multilateralism in the global system. Nevertheless, the EU-Canada relationship is not without friction, notably on agricultural trade and the use of artificial hormones in beef (the EU bans Canadian as well as American beef imports). Canada likes to think of itself as being markedly different from the United States and to some extent as a "European" country, especially in view of its progressive social policies (moreover, the Queen of England is the head of state, and Quebec and other provinces are French-speaking). Of course, there are obvious limits to how close Canada and the EU can become.

Latin America. The EU's relations with Latin America date from the early 1960s and were originally based in part on close cultural, historical, and social ties between the two regions. For that reason, relations with Latin America should have received a boost when Spain and Portugal joined the EC in

1986. For example, Spain's bridge-building across the Atlantic helped restore diplomatic relations between Argentina and the EC, broken off in 1982 during the Falklands/Malvinas War. A gradual rapprochement in EC-Argentina relations led to a cooperation agreement in April 1990; three months later Argentina further improved its standing with the EC by restoring diplomatic relations with Britain.

Nevertheless, the EC's dealings with Latin America generally languished in the 1980s and early 1990s because of the region's economic stagnation, high indebtedness, and political instability. It was only later in the 1990s, when democracy took hold throughout most of Latin America, that relations improved. Latin America began to attract European investment and trade missions. Once again Spain took the lead within the EU, especially during its Council presidency in late 1995. As a result, in December 1995 the Council approved a Commission communication on ways to strengthen EU–Latin America relations, which the European Council also endorsed at its meeting later that month.[16] It was in December 1995 as well that the EU and Mercosur, a common market embracing several Latin American countries, signed an agreement, the first ever between two customs unions.[17] Spain again reinvigorated EU–Latin America relations during its Council presidency in early 2002, providing a welcome political boost to an important but sometimes neglected area of the EU's external relations.

Ironically, although EU trade with Latin America has risen since the mid-1990s, Latin America's proportion of total EU trade has continued to decline. Nevertheless, Latin America is important economically as well as politically to the EU, whose relations with the region are part of a broader strategy to raise its profile as a global actor. Latin America's traditionally close (although rocky) relationship with the United States adds an extra dimension to the EU's involvement in the region. Many Latin American countries see the EU as a potential counterweight to the United States, and the EU sees its involvement in Latin America as a way to assert itself politically vis-à-vis the United States.

The EU has a political relationship with the Rio Group, a loose association of all the countries of Latin America as well as some Caribbean countries. The EU and the Rio Group hold occasional ministerial meetings and less frequent summits, such as in Rio de Janeiro in 1999 and Madrid in 2002. On a day-to-day basis, however, the EU's relations with Latin America are based on a close association with the Central American countries, Mercosur, and the Andean Community and two countries that do not fall within any of these groupings: Mexico and Chile.

The EU has steadily intensified and institutionalized its relations in Latin America, despite deep-rooted differences over EU agricultural protectionism and the EU's preferential trade agreements with some Caribbean countries (a cause of discrimination against Latin American bananas). Notwithstanding the seemingly harmonious development of EU–Latin American relations, the

EU and Latin American nations are often at loggerheads in the Doha Development Round of negotiations for further global trade liberalization.

Mexico. Mexico is one of the EU's most important trading partners in Latin America, and the EU is Mexico's second trading partner after the United States. The EU also views Mexico as a key political interlocutor in the region. The EU and Mexico signed a partnership and cooperation agreement in December 1997, which came into effect in October 2000. The agreement established a regular political dialogue at the highest level (including occasional summits) and called for the establishment of a free trade area, the opening of government procurement markets, the liberalization of capital movement, and better cooperation in the areas of competition policy and intellectual property rights. The newly established EU-Mexico (Ministerial) Council duly agreed on a free trade area in goods (effective July 2000) and services (effective March 2001). Trade between the EU and Mexico immediately grew by 26 percent but soon fell back again as part of the global economic downturn. The EU-Mexico dialogue, held under the auspices of the partnership and cooperation agreement, covers a variety of social and political issues, including poverty, terrorism, human rights, democracy, migration, and regional affairs. The EU allocates about €15 million annually to development projects in Mexico.

Central America. The EU and Central America have an unusually close relationship, a legacy of EU efforts through the so-called San José Dialogue to bring peace to the region in the mid-1980s, when many countries there were wracked by civil war. The EU has progressively strengthened its formal ties to the region, beginning in 1993 with a cooperation agreement and continuing ten years later with a farther-reaching political and cooperation agreement. The EU aims not only to promote economic development but also to encourage regional integration among the countries of Central America (Costa Rica, El Salvador, Guatemala, Honduras, Nicaragua, and Panama). In 2004, the EU and the Central American countries agreed to start the process of elevating their relationship to the level of an Association Agreement.

The Andean Community. The EU has long supported the process of Andean regional integration, which dates from the Andean Pact of 1969. The EU holds regular meetings with the Andean Community (Bolivia, Colombia, Ecuador, Peru, and Venezuela) on topics such as economic development, democracy and human rights, and the all-important fight against drugs. The EU and the Andean Community first concluded a formal agreement in 1983. It was upgraded in 1993 and again in December 2003, when the EU and the Andean Community signed a new political and cooperation agreement. They have since begun negotiations to conclude an Association Agreement, which would include a free trade area.

Mercosur. Established in 1991, Mercado Común del Cono Sur (Mercosur), the Common Market of the Southern Cone, is a customs union whose members are Argentina, Brazil, Paraguay, and Uruguay. The European Union has supported Mercosur from the outset. The two sides signed an interregional cooperation agreement in 1995 as the basis for a free trade agreement, which has proved elusive due to protectionist proclivities in both the EU and Mercosur. Much depends on Brazil, a regional giant that is also emerging as a global power in the WTO, especially through its leadership of the G20 plus (a group of rapidly developing countries that also includes China and India). Whereas the EU sees its relationship with Mercosur primarily in strategic terms (as a potential lever in its relations with the United States), Brazil sees Mercosur, and Mercosur's relationship with the EU, in a broader hemispheric and global context. The strategic games that the two sides are playing may militate against the development of mutually beneficial EU-Mercosur economic relations.

Chile. Until the late 1980s, Chile was cut off from the international community because of its authoritarian, military regime. Since the restoration of democracy there, the EU has developed an unusually close relationship with Chile, culminating in an Association Agreement signed in November 2002 (it came into effect in February 2003). The Association Agreement covers three main areas: political relations, trade enhancement, and development cooperation.

Asia

The wider Asia-Pacific region is a vast area that accounts for 56 percent of the world's population, 25 percent of the world's GDP, and 22 percent of global trade. It includes four distinct subregions:

- South Asia (Bangladesh, India, Nepal, Pakistan, and Sri Lanka)
- Southeast Asia (Indonesia, Malaysia, the Philippines, Singapore, Thailand, and Vietnam)
- Northeast Asia (China, Japan, Korea)
- Australasia (Australia, New Zealand, and neighboring islands)

As former external relations commissioner Chris Patten, the last British governor of Hong Kong and someone with a keen interest in the region, noted, "Given the sprawling variety of Asia, it is absurd to think of a monolithic EU-Asia relationship, a single policy or approach, equally valid across the whole region."[18] Nevertheless, the EU pursues the same general objectives in Asia as it does elsewhere in its external relations: peace and security; human rights, democracy, good governance, and the rule of law; freer trade and investment; and international development. A particular challenge for the EU in much of the region is the different values and political ideas embodied in the so-called Asian model of modernization and development, which are at odds with those of Western liberal democracy. Those differences, and the legacy of European colonialism in a large number of Asia countries, complicate the EU's dealings with the region.

For a long time the EU's involvement in Asia meant essentially the EU's dealings with Japan. To be more specific, it meant EU efforts to open Japan's market and stem the flood of Japanese products into Western Europe. Nevertheless, the EU had long-standing relations with the Association of Southeast Asian Nations (ASEAN), which now includes ten countries in the subregion. The EU's interest in those countries was also primarily economic, especially in the 1980s, when fear of international competition from the so-called Asian Tigers swept across Western Europe. More recently, EU-China relations have come to dominate the EU's interest in Asia. Like the United States, the EU appreciates China's enormous economic and political potential, regionally and globally. Also like the United States, the EU hopes to shape China's emergence as a great power in a mutually agreeable way. Finally, the EU is increasing its engagement with another emerging power in Asia, a country with which it has had diplomatic relations since the early 1960s: India.

The EU's growing interest in Asia dates from the mid-1990s and was partly a reaction to renewed U.S. economic interest in the region, notably through Washington's rejuvenation of the Asia Pacific Economic Cooperation group, a loose association that spans the Pacific from Canada to Korea and includes the ASEAN countries. The EU's new approach manifested itself most obviously in an intensification of contacts with China and in the launch of a new, biennial summit attended by leaders of the EU and all its member states, the ASEAN countries, China, Japan, and Korea. The purpose of the so-called Asia-Europe Meeting (ASEM) is to have a relatively free and informal exchange of ideas on a range of issues. However, the large number of participants, the attendant linguistic muddle, and the sensitivity of some topics inevitably inhibit progress. For instance, a dispute between the EU and ASEAN over the participation of Burma/Myanmar, a country with an atrocious human rights record and against which the EU has imposed sanctions, overshadowed the fifth ASEM, held in Hanoi in October 2004.

The Burma/Myanmar dispute illustrates one of the difficulties for the EU of dealing with the region. Indeed, the EU's Asia strategy is beset with disagreements with a number of countries over social policy, environmental issues, and human rights concerns. To compound matters in the late 1990s, the onset of the Asian financial crisis dampened the EU's newfound enthusiasm for Asia and prompted complaints from countries in the region that the EU was more concerned with safeguarding its fledgling monetary union than with helping Asia to recover. Although overshadowed by many such recriminations, the second ASEM, in April 1998, at least provided an opportunity to involve the EU in the Asian crisis and exchange ideas on restoring financial health to the region.

In the mid-2000s, ten years after intensifying its interest in the region, the EU made a renewed effort to engage the countries of Asia in a deeper political and economic relationship. A Commission strategy paper, published in June 2004, sought to provide an overall context and greater coherence for EU policy in the region. The Commission urged deeper EU involvement in Asia through closer bilateral and multilateral relations and suggested a framework for programs covering more than one Asian country, especially in the fields of trade, investment, education, and the environment. Publication of the Commission paper highlighted both the extent of EU involvement throughout Asia and the political and administrative challenges of dealing with such a fluid, dynamic, and distant part of the world.

Japan. Despite having suffered a serious economic slowdown in the late 1990s and early 2000s, Japan remains an economic giant. The United States, the EU, and Japan together still dominate the global economy. Yet the EU-Japan relationship is the weakest side of the trilateral U.S.-EU-Japan relationship. Until recently, relations between the EU and Japan were almost exclusively economic, whereas both have had robust political and economic relations with the United States for a long time. Japan's weak political relationship with the EU is due not simply to its geographical distance from Europe but primarily to disputes over Japan's protected domestic market and huge trade surplus with the EU.

In 1990 the Japanese ambassador to the EC complained pointedly that during the previous year the Commission president had met the U.S. president five times but had met the Japanese prime minister only once. After the United States and the EC concluded the Transatlantic Declaration in November 1990, Japan pressed the EC for a similar accord. The epilogue and prologue to the EC-Japan Declaration, eventually concluded in July 1991, illustrated the extent of the EU's concern about Japanese trade practices. French insistence on references to reciprocity and "balance," at a time when Japan's trade surplus with the EC had grown sharply, delayed the declaration. Eventually, France accepted a Commission compromise calling for the EC and Japan to have "equitable access to their respective markets and to remove obstacles, whether structural or other, impeding the expansion of trade, on the basis of comparable opportunities."[19]

The declaration established an institutional framework for annual meetings among the Japanese prime minister, the Commission president, and the Council president as well as regular meetings between Japanese ministers and EC commissioners. But those provisions, and the declaration's lofty rhetoric about "a deeper partnership based on the common ideals of freedom, democracy, and the rule of law," could not alter the reality of an unhealthy trade imbalance. Japan's expanding trade surplus, especially in electronics and cars, continued to alarm the EU. Shortly after publicly issuing the joint declaration, the Commission and the Japanese government announced that they had concluded an export-restraint agreement—euphemistically called "Elements of Consensus"—to limit the number of Japanese cars entering the European market until the year 2000.[20]

The auto agreement, which followed two years of arduous negotiations within the Commission, among member states, and between the Community and Japan, was a classic example of a voluntary export restraint imposed by the EU on a country with a strong competitive advantage in a politically sensitive sector.[21] It was controversial not only because of its protectionism but also because of uncertainty about its impact on cars produced by Japanese "transplants" in the EU. Located chiefly in Britain, these Japanese-owned factories have revolutionized car manufacturing in Europe and captured a substantial share of the market. The British government claimed that the car agreement did not impose a ceiling on transplant production in the EU, strongly protectionist French and Italian car manufacturers reached the opposite conclusion, and the Commission sat on the fence by citing vague "working assumptions" for transplant output. Largely because of the growth of transplant production, Japanese quotas under the auto agreement were rarely filled and the agreement did not have to be renewed.

The fledgling political relationship between Japan and the EU continued to suffer from mutual misunderstanding and distrust. Japanese investment in the EU remained far in excess of EU investment in Japan, and the trade surplus widened further in Japan's favor. This situation led to calls from European industry for retaliatory measures against alleged dumping of Japanese products and for EU efforts to break down supposed structural impediments to member states' entry into the Japanese market. As a result, the EU intensified its market-opening efforts.

Bilateral economic relations indeed warmed up as Japan's trade surplus with the EU fell sharply and as the EU made inroads into the Japanese marketplace. The resolution of two long-standing trade disputes between the EU and Japan in the late 1990s—one on Japan's insufficient music copyright protection, the other on Japan's discriminatory liquor taxes—improved relations further. In both cases the WTO had ruled in the EU's favor, but Japan had not fully implemented the required changes. Tension rose again during the Asian economic crisis when Japan resumed its export-led growth strategy with the assistance of a greatly depreciated yen. Hopes that the Asian crisis and the continuing deterioration of the Japanese economy would impel Japan to undertake fundamental structural reforms, upon which a more satisfactory relationship with the EU and its other trading partners could be built, were unavailing.

Nevertheless, Japan's protracted economic recession, an intensification of the EU-Japan dialogue over touchy trade and regulatory issues, and the widespread acceptance of Japanese transplants as legitimate EU enterprises contributed to a marked improvement in EU-Japan relations. Compared to the late 1980s, when Europeans feared the encroachment of a seemingly unstoppable Japanese economic juggernaut, EU-Japan relations are serene twenty years later. Rarely has such a difficult political problem (in this case, how to defend against the Japanese economic onslaught) in effect melted away.

China. Given its spectacular, export-led economic growth, China could replace Japan as the EU's bogeyman in the next ten years. The EU has had a long and variable relationship with China going back to the mid-1970s, when the two signed a trade and economic cooperation agreement (Communist China never shared the Soviet Union's squeamishness about dealing with the capitalist EC). So vigorous was their economic relationship that in 1985 China and the EC signed a new agreement to provide for more comprehensive cooperation. Three years later the Commission opened a delegation (embassy) in Beijing.

The EC's cozy relationship with China came to an abrupt end in June 1989, when the Chinese government ruthlessly suppressed the prodemocracy student demonstrations in Tiananmen Square. The European Council condemned China's repression, suspended high-level bilateral meetings, postponed new cooperation projects, and cut existing programs.[22] Over a year later, pragmatism triumphed over principle and the EC decided gradually to normalize relations with China, although the dilemma between upholding human rights and enhancing bilateral trade continued to trouble some member states, especially over the issue of the arms embargo (a legacy of Tiananmen Square), which China has been pressing the EU to lift.

As a key component of its new strategy toward Asia, in 1995 the EU developed a "comprehensive, independent, and consistent long-term strategy" for relations with China, by that time an emerging economic and political powerhouse and the EU's fourth-largest export market and fourth-largest supplier.[23] Eager to maximize trade and investment opportunities for Europeans in China, and eager also to raise the EU's international profile, the EU intensified its "constructive engagement" with China. The ASEM process further demonstrated the EU's and China's interest in each other and in broader Asian affairs. In 1998 the Commission launched yet another initiative, covering a range of political and economic issues, to strengthen and deepen relations with China.[24]

Despite the progressive intensification of contacts, EU-China relations remained touchy throughout the 1990s. Negotiations to reduce quotas and other barriers to trade were difficult and prolonged. Although the EU was one of the earliest major trading partners to grant China fully unconditional most-favored-nation status (nondiscriminatory tariff access for China's goods and services), the EU resented what it saw as continuing barriers to European exports. For their part, the Chinese resented the frequent use by the EU of antidumping measures. China's disregard for intellectual property rights was another major irritant in EU-China relations. Although China finally put intellectual property laws in place (thanks largely to U.S. pressure), problems of enforcement remain. A long-standing dispute over maritime transport was eventually resolved to the EU's satisfaction and, as the EU likes to point out, to the benefit of China's other trading partners as well.

In order to alleviate bilateral disputes, promote regional stability, and increase prospects for global prosperity, the EU was keen to integrate China fully into the world economy, notably through membership in the WTO. A bilateral EU-China deal on WTO accession was a key stepping-stone for China's eventual membership in the world trade body. The agreement satisfied EU concerns about restrictive Chinese practices in a number of areas, notably financial services, public procurement, and access to the burgeoning domestic Chinese market. The EU-China agreement complemented a similar U.S.-China agreement, which removed the last obstacles to China's entry into the WTO.

The EU's interest in China still encompasses humanitarian and, more recently, environmental concerns. The EU wants to help China feed its huge population, make better use of its natural resources, reduce environmental damage (due especially to China's huge coal consumption), and alleviate rural poverty. The EU promotes these objectives through direct financial and technical assistance, support for nongovernmental organizations (NGOs) working in China, and humanitarian aid through the European Community Humanitarian Office (ECHO).

Overall, the EU's policy toward China is ambitious and maybe somewhat unrealistic. The Commission and the member states are trying to achieve greater coordination of EU activities and national policies relating to China and a higher political profile for the EU in China and throughout Asia. Despite the EU's economic preponderance, there is a political asymmetry in China's favor. Whereas the EU views China as an emerging regional and possibly global power, China views the EU as an important economic entity but not necessarily as a political power. China's strategic focus is across the Pacific toward the United States, not across Central Asia toward the EU. Together with the country's renowned prickliness and opacity, that focus makes the EU's ambitious objectives toward China difficult to attain.

India. India was one of the first countries to establish diplomatic relations with the EC. Bilateral agreements for economic cooperation followed in 1973 and 1981. Relations were upgraded in December 1993, when the EU and India signed a wide-ranging cooperation agreement. This took the predictable form of calling for an intensification of trade and investment, better market access on both sides, and a political dialogue on issues of common concern. It also established an institutional structure along expected lines but went beyond the usual apparatus by including annual summit meetings (they usually take place in October or November each year). As India liberalized its economy, developed its high-technology sector, and became a major player regionally and globally, relations with the EU flourished. Trade and investment grew constantly in the late 1990s and early 2000s, with the EU becoming India's main trading partner and biggest investor. The EU and its member states also became the biggest contributors to India's development programs and biggest provider of humanitarian assistance. Little wonder that in June 2004 the Commission recommended upgrading the EU-India relationship to a strategic partnership, an impressive-sounding designation that would provide an added impetus for cooperation on a range of economic, development, and political issues. India's rapid economic development, strong democratic values (despite religious and social impediments to pluralism), and de-escalation of tension with Pakistan make the country a favored EU interlocutor in the region.

■ Development Policy

What do Burkina Faso (a landlocked African state), Belize (a small Central American country), and Vanuatu (a tiny and possibly soon-to-be-submerged Pacific island) have in common? Or South Africa, Cuba, and Papua New Guinea? All belong to a group of African, Caribbean, and Pacific (ACP) states that forms the core of the EU's development policy. Not coincidentally, all are former colonies of EU member states. Since 2000, EU-ACP relations have been organized under the Cotonou Partnership Agreement (named after the capital city of Benin, where the agreement was signed). Cotonou is the successor agreement to the Lomé Convention, which existed in various forms for twenty-five years. Before that, the EC concluded the first Yaoundé Convention with the ACP states in 1963 and a second Yaoundé Convention in 1969. From the time of the first Yaoundé Convention to the current Cotonou Agreement, the EU enlarged from six to twenty-five member states and the ACP countries covered by the conventions and agreement increased from forty-six to seventy-seven. The nature and scope of the agreements also changed, from a basic development assistance program, to a program combining development assistance and preferential access to the EU market, to a program that now emphasizes trade liberalization, political conditionality, and regional differentiation among the ACP states.

The EU's dealings with the ACP states were originally based on a provision of the Rome Treaty allowing non-European countries and territories that had a "special relationship" with member states to become associated with the

EC. "Special relationship" was a euphemism for being a current or former colony. Initially most such countries or territories were French-African (France had insisted during the negotiation of the Rome Treaty on special treatment for its former colonies). Indeed, all three ACP agreements (Lomé, Yaoundé, and Cotonou) were signed in the capitals of former French African colonies.

In addition to the Yaoundé and Lomé Conventions, the EC became a major provider of international development assistance, ranging from food aid to technical support to financial assistance. Member states incorporated the goal of "development cooperation" into the Maastricht Treaty. Accordingly, the EU's objectives in this area were to foster sustainable economic and social development in the world's poorer countries; encourage the poor countries' smooth and gradual integration into the global economy; campaign against global poverty; and promote democracy, the rule of law, and respect for human rights.

Among other things, the relevant treaty articles adjure member states to coordinate their own development policies with those of the EU. Indeed, the persistence of separate member state development policies (some member states contribute more development assistance than the EU itself, and EU development assistance amounts to only about 20 percent of what the member states contribute altogether) is a reminder of member states' unwillingness to surrender policy instruments in the international sphere. Most member states want to maximize their own international influence while also benefiting from a collective effort. In the case of development assistance in particular, most member states have specific preferences and agendas that are best pursued individually rather than collectively.

The fact that the European Development Fund (EDF), used to finance the Cotonou Agreement, is not part of the EU budget is another peculiarity of EU development policy. Because the member states are also signatories of the agreement in their own right (Cotonou is a "mixed" agreement) and want to control spending as much as possible, the EDF is not included in the development cooperation section of the EU's general budget, much to the chagrin of the European Parliament. Yet this does not result in greater efficiency: intergovernmental negotiations to renew the EDF can be contentious and extend beyond the stipulated deadline, and lengthy national ratification procedures often delay implementation of the new financial arrangements. Apart from the EDF, European Investment Bank loans to countries in the Mediterranean region, Asia, and Latin America that have concluded cooperation agreements with the EU are an integral part of the EU's development policy.

Institutionally, the Commission's role in development policy is complicated by the fact that its staff is too small to manage such a large policy area, responsibility for which is spread among a number of commissioners and directorates-general (the most important commission portfolios in that regard are external relations and development). The Parliament's influence over development cooperation has increased over time, partly because of many parliamentarians' personal interest and expertise in the area and partly for institutional reasons. Although the EDF is not part of the EU budget, the Parliament has a degree of control over parts of the development budget; the assent procedure covers development-related international agreements (such as Cotonou); and under the Amsterdam Treaty development policy decisionmaking is subject to the codecision procedure.

From Lomé to Cotonou

Britain's impending accession to the EC in the early 1970s, together with Dutch and German pressure for a new Community approach to the Third World, led to a revision of the original principles underlying the Yaoundé Conventions. Instead of a traditional donor-recipient relationship, the EC strove for a novel partnership with an increasingly heterogeneous group of countries—including numerous British former colonies—in Africa, the Caribbean, and the Pacific. EC-ACP negotiations began in July 1973 and ended in February 1975 when both sides signed a new convention in Lomé, the capital of Togo.

The Lomé Convention was inspired as much by the prevailing vogue for a New International Economic Order as by the member states' desire to favor former colonies. The convention included the following main elements:

- a development assistance package
- a system of generalized preferences in trade (practically all products originating in the ACP countries were given free access to the EC, in return for which the ACP states had to give the EC only most-favored-nation status)
- the System for the Stabilization of Export Earnings from Products to guarantee ACP export prices regardless of fluctuations in world commodity prices
- a host of innovative aid and technical assistance programs

Lomé also established an elaborate institutional framework, which now includes an ACP-EC council (composed of members of the Council of Ministers, the Commission, and a government minister from each of the ACP countries) and an ACP–European Parliament joint assembly.

The EU and the ACP states renegotiated the Lomé Convention every five years and redesignated it accordingly (see Table 16.1). Lomé IV, negotiated in December 1989, covered a ten-year period, although its midterm review in 1995 was tantamount to an extensive renegotiation (hence, after 1995 Lomé IV became known as Lomé IVb).

Table 16.1   EU-ACP Agreements

Yaoundé I	1964–1970
Yaoundé II	1970–1975
Lomé I	1975–1979
Lomé II	1980–1984
Lomé III	1985–1989
Lomé IVa	1990–1994
Lomé IVb	1995–1999
Cotonou	2000–2020

A Difficult Relationship. The EU's dealings with the heterogeneous and eco-nomically diverse ACP states have never been easy. Despite the much larger number of countries on the ACP side, the EU's immensely greater wealth and international influence, together with the inherent tension between former colonial powers and their former colonies, made for a difficult relationship. The EU complains that the ACP countries demand too much, and the ACP countries complain that the EU offers too little. Negotiations for successive Lomé Conventions in the recessionary 1970s and economically uncertain 1980s grew more and more edgy. In the late 1980s the ACP states feared that the EU's preoccupation with the single market program, obduracy in the Uruguay Round, and increasing involvement in Central and Eastern Europe meant that Brussels had lost interest in the Third World.

Following arduous negotiations in 1989, Lomé IV included a number of important innovations apart from its ten-year time frame. While retaining its predecessors' relatively complex structure and comprehensive provisions, Lomé IV included greater emphasis on human rights (and especially on women's rights); environmental protection; regional economic integration; and the need for overall, self-reliant, and self-sustained development. Provisions to help ACP countries manage their existing debt and avoid additional debt were another novelty in Lomé IV (ACP debt had more than doubled in the 1980s).

Changes in the international political and economic system in the early 1990s, together with awareness on the EU's part that Lomé had not succeeded in restructuring the economies of the ACP states, led to a difficult midterm review of the fourth convention. With the Cold War well and truly over, member states began to demand democratization and good governance in Third World countries instead of merely using such rhetoric to disguise support for authoritarian, anticommunist regimes. Economically, the process of liberalization and globalization rendered traditional trade-and-aid assistance even less effective than in the past, and in some cases incompatible with the Uruguay Round agreement and WTO rules (the banana regime was an obvious example).

The 1995 review reflected some of these changes. For instance, Article 5 in the convention declared that "respect for human rights and democratic principles and the rule of law, which underpins relations between the ACP states and the Community and all the provisions of the Convention, and governs the domestic and international policies of the Contracting Parties, shall constitute an essential element [of Lomé IVb]." At the same time, a general climate of fiscal restraint induced by the convergence criteria for monetary union made it more difficult for member states to renegotiate the terms of the EDF to pay for the revised convention. A last-minute French concession— made primarily to save the concluding summit of the French Council presidency in June 1995—facilitated agreement on a new EDF, thereby bringing the Lomé review to an end.

The Cotonou Agreement. Continuing concern about Lomé's suitability and effectiveness overshadowed the run-up to the convention's renegotiation in 1999. Following an intensive internal debate in the preceding two years, the Commission suggested moving away from an all-embracing Lomé agreement toward separate economic cooperation and partnership agreements with groups of African, Caribbean, and Pacific countries. As it was, most Lomé recipients had little in common with each other. The Commission argued that geographical differentiation would improve the effectiveness of EU assistance and accelerate the integration of recipient countries into the global economy. Whether genuinely unconvinced by the Commission's arguments or simply afraid of the future, many ACP countries clung to the Lomé framework and opposed what they saw as EU efforts to sunder supposed ACP solidarity.

More controversial than the possible regionalization of the ACP states was the Commission's increasing emphasis on political conditionality for future EU assistance. In the Commission's view, the EU should support only countries that—apart from being economically needy—respected democracy, governed themselves well, and attempted to eradicate corruption. In effect, the Commission wanted to establish a political climate conducive to a successful development policy. Just as they opposed the regionalization of Lomé assistance, however, many ACP countries resented the Commission's efforts to impose political conditions, pointing out that Lomé IVb already contained commitments to democracy and better governance.

In the meantime, the deteriorating economic situation throughout the developed world put the Lomé Convention under further pressure. Looking beyond Commission statements about sound management and good governance, many ACP countries saw an EU that was preoccupied with monetary union and enlargement and whose international interests appeared limited to maximizing trade with developed countries. On the EU side, there was a reluctant acknowledgment that Lomé was a worthy but failed experiment in development assistance. Over the years, the ACP states had made little progress: their trade with Western Europe had declined and consisted of a relatively small number of primary products, just as it had in colonial days.

A successor to Lomé eventually emerged from lengthy negotiations within the Commission, among the Commission and the member states, among the ACP countries, and between the EU and the ACP countries. The ensuing Cotonou Agreement differed significantly from its predecessor. Whereas the Lomé Conventions were essentially preferential trade-and-aid programs uniformly applied to all ACP states, Cotonou included three key innovations:

- *Trade liberalization:* The agreement aims to integrate the ACP states into the global economy by promoting free trade as the cornerstone of economic growth; the convention therefore includes deadlines for the progressive reduction of trade barriers and conformity with WTO rules and norms. It also emphasizes the importance of competition policy, protection of intellectual property rights, standardization, consumer protection, environmental protection, and the like.
- *Political conditionality:* Respect for human rights, democratic principles, and the rule of law are essential elements of the agreement. In deference to the sensitivities of the ACP states, good governance is a fundamental rather than an essential element (but it is important nonetheless); the agreement provides for possible sanctions against countries that fail to meet the political conditions, culminating in possible suspension from the agreement.
- *Regional and economic differentiation:* In a major break from past conventions, the agreement differentiates not only among regions but also among countries on the basis of their level of development and ability to withstand global competition; the agreement therefore calls for the negotiation by 2008 of several Regional Economic Partnership Agreements under the ACP umbrella. The six regional partners within the ACP are Central Africa, Western Africa, Eastern and Southern Africa and the Indian Ocean, the Southern African Development Community, the Pacific Region, and the Caribbean Region.

In keeping with the new policy of differentiation, the agreement stipulated that the least developed countries (LDCs) would remain subject to the old Lomé regime of preferential access to the EU market and large-scale assistance from the EU. "LDC" is a United Nations category for countries that are particularly badly off (there are forty-nine LDCs altogether). Almost all of the LDCs covered by the Cotonou Agreement are in Africa (only one is in the Caribbean, and six are in the Pacific).

For the rest of the ACP states, the EU will continue to offer help with debt reduction, balance-of-payments problems, structural reforms, and institutional development as well as assistance for stabilization of export earnings, especially in the agricultural and mining sectors, subject to the recipient countries' commitment to trade liberalization and adherence to the political conditions of the agreement. In addition, the agreement stresses the importance of the private sector for economic growth and development and of involving civil society in the governance process.[25]

Negotiations on the new regional economic partnership agreements began in 2002 and are expected to continue until 2008. The Cotonou Agreement itself lasts until 2020, when, ideally, it will not need to be renewed. Inevitably, many of the ACP states will still need assistance, especially the least developed. Some of the more economically advanced ACP states, however, may be able to stand on their own feet by then.

South Africa

South Africa is a special case for the EU in a number of respects. Member states were embarrassingly divided on the question of sanctions against South Africa during the apartheid years, especially after the escalation of violence there in the mid-1980s. After the collapse of apartheid and the democratization of the country, South Africa became one of the few positive case studies for the EU's Common Foreign and Security Policy as member states rallied in support of the new regime. Economic relations with the new South Africa were problematical because of the country's size and its peculiar status as both a developed and a developing country (depending on the sector). South Africa wanted to join the Lomé Convention, but the existing Lomé countries feared being crushed by South African competition, and the EU feared a WTO challenge from non-Lomé trading partners. Accordingly, in 1997 South Africa became a "qualified member" of Lomé under a special protocol attached to the convention. Whereas South Africa enjoyed some benefits of Lomé membership, it was excluded from the convention's special trade regime. Similarly, South Africa is a qualified member of the Cotonou Agreement. EU–South Africa trade relations are governed instead by a trade, development, and cooperation agreement that was signed in Pretoria in October 1999 and entered into force in January 2000.

Everything But Arms

In February 2001 the EU launched a new development initiative when the Council adopted the so-called Everything But Arms (EBA) regulation, granting duty-free access to imports of all products from the LDCs without any quantitative restrictions except for arms and munitions. Only imports of bananas, rice, and sugar—highly sensitive products in the EU—were not fully liberalized immediately. The EU plans to keep the EBA regulation in place indefinitely rather than subjecting it to periodic renewal under the Generalized

System of Preferences (see the next section). This is the first time that the EU used a country's level of development as a criterion for a particular development program (as opposed to historical ties to the EU, as in the case of the Cotonou Agreement). The initiative offers the LDC participants in the Cotonou Agreement, which includes the vast majority of the world's LDCs, a better preferential trade arrangement than does Cotonou, suggesting that Cotonou and the EBA are somewhat at cross-purposes with each other. For the first time also, non-ACP countries—the LDCs that are not party to the Cotonou Agreement—receive better treatment from the EU than do the ACP countries.

The Generalized System of Preferences

Under the Generalized System of Preferences (GSP), the EU grants duty-free access for industrial goods and some agricultural produce from a number of developing countries. The EU introduced a new dimension to its GSP regime in the late 1990s by providing additional trade benefits to countries that meet core labor and environmental standards (such as International Labor Organization standards for the protection of workers' rights and International Tropical Timber Organization standards for tropical wood products). Some GSP beneficiaries, such as Brazil, Pakistan, and Indonesia, have expressed concern about EU intrusion into their internal affairs and about EU conditionality regarding their continued eligibility for preferences. The EU argued that it is not limiting the GSP regime but is instead offering special incentives for developing countries to comply with internationally set social and environmental standards. However, a WTO ruling in 2004 upheld an Indian challenge to the EU's drugs scheme (which benefited textile exports from Pakistan, among others, in an effort to combat illegal drug production), saying that it was not based on clear, transparent, and nondiscriminatory criteria. In October 2004 the Commission adopted a new system, in effect for the three years starting in June 2005. The new scheme replaces the drugs, social, and environmental incentive schemes with a "GSP-plus" system, which offers additional benefits to "vulnerable" countries that accept various international conventions.

■ Humanitarian Assistance

Apart from contractual development assistance agreements such as Cotonou, the EU dispenses large amounts of aid unilaterally. In 1992 the EU established the European Community Humanitarian Office to provide emergency humanitarian and food aid wherever needed around the world. ECHO now funds nearly 2,000 projects in over eighty countries on four continents. ECHO operates through a wide range of partners, including NGOs, which administer nearly 60 percent of ECHO funding, and UN agencies, which administer over

25 percent. ECHO's high dependence on NGOs reflects both a dearth of Commission officials on the ground and the Commission's frequent need to try to circumvent corrupt recipient governments. Ironically, the EU itself stands accused of major fraud and mismanagement in the conduct of ECHO affairs.

▨ Notes

1. Chris Patten, speech at Chatham House, September 2, 2002.

2. European Commission, *1994 General Report* (Luxembourg: Office for Official Publications of the European Communities, 1995), point 989.

3. On the question of trade policy competence, see Alasdair R. Young, *Extending European Cooperation: The European Union and the "New" International Trade Agenda* (Manchester, UK: Manchester University Press, 2002).

4. European Commission, *Europe: World Partner* (Luxembourg: Office for Official Publications of the European Communities, 1991), p. 11.

5. Bulletin EC 12-1988, "Presidency Conclusions," point 1.1.10.

6. European Commission, *1995 General Report* (Luxembourg: Office for Official Publications of the European Communities, 1996).

7. Leon Brittan, "Everybody Free Up, Please," in *The World in 1998* (London: The Economist, 1998), p. 55.

8. See European Commission, "Investment as an Engine of Growth: A Need for Better Rules of the Game," in *European Union: World Trade* (Brussels: European Commission, 1998).

9. Brittan, "Everybody Free Up," p. 55.

10. On the EU and the Doha Round, see Alasdair R. Young, "The EU and World Trade: Doha and Beyond," in Maria Green Cowles and Desmond Dinan, eds., *Developments in the European Union 2* (Basingstoke, UK: Palgrave Macmillan, 2004), pp. 200–220.

11. John Pinder, *The European Community and Eastern Europe* (London: RIIA, 1991), p. 75.

12. Rome European Council, "Presidency Conclusions," Bulletin EC 12-1990, point 1.31.

13. Quoted in *Le Monde*, November 30, 1994, p. 2.

14. European Commission, *The European Union and Russia: The Future Relationship*, COM(95)223.

15. Bulletin EC 11-1998, point 2.2.12.

16. Madrid European Council, "Presidency Conclusions," Bulletin EC 6-1989, point 1.2.25.

17. Commission, *1995 General Report*, point 926.

18. Patten, speech at Chatham House, September 2, 2002.

19. Bulletin EC 7/8-1991, point 1.3.33.

20. The agreement is secret, but the *Financial Times* published details of it on September 23, 1991, p. 4, and September 26, 1991, p. 7.

21. See Dick K. Nanto, "The U.S.-EC-Japan Trade Triangle," in U.S. Congress, House Committee on Foreign Affairs, *Europe and the United States* (Washington, DC: Government Printing Office), p. 361.

22. Madrid European Council, "Presidency Conclusions," Bulletin EC 6-1989, point 1.2.24.

23. COM(95)279.

24. European Commission, *Building a Comprehensive Partnership with China,* COM(98)181 final.

25. On the Cotonou Agreement, see Martin Holland, "Development Policy: Paradigm Shifts and the 'Normalization' of a Privileged Partnership?" in Maria Green Cowles and Desmond Dinan, eds., *Developments in the European Union 2* (Basingstoke, UK: Palgrave Macmillan, 2004), pp. 275–295.

17

Internal and External Security

The internal and external economic policies of the European Union aim to enhance the member states' general welfare, including overall security. Well-off, democratic countries, locked into a supranational association of states, are unlikely to go to war against each other. European integration has helped to resolve the German question; consolidate democracy in Greece, Portugal, and Spain; and ease the transformation of the countries of Central and Eastern Europe into stable and secure liberal democracies. European integration has also helped to ameliorate and manage conflict within the EU, notably in Cyprus, in Northern Ireland, and between Britain and Spain over Gibraltar. Similarly, the possibility of eventual EU membership helps to promote reform and better interstate relations in the Western Balkans, a notoriously volatile region on Europe's periphery.

As the EU became a leading international economic actor, its relatively weak political presence on the world stage appeared increasingly anomalous. For reasons of symmetry, if nothing else, a common EU foreign policy seemed to make sense. Just as member states could maximize their commercial clout in a common trade policy, so too might they be able to leverage their international influence in a common foreign policy. Another motive for a common foreign policy is the ideology of European integration. Many advocates of deeper integration believe that the EU's destiny is to become a major global power and that the member states must "speak with one voice" internationally (this is the metaphor most frequently used by academics and officials to describe the rationale for a common foreign policy in the EU). Finally, the importance of counterbalancing the United States, the world's sole superpower, is another possible reason for a common EU foreign policy. Arguably, a unipolar world is inherently unstable, especially if the hegemon uses its power irresponsibly. Best to balance that power against an equally powerful entity: the EU.

Of course, the EU could never become a superpower without developing a common defense policy and military capability comparable to those of the

United States, which is unlikely ever to happen. National sovereignty remains a formidable barrier to the development of a truly common foreign policy, let alone a common defense policy or a common army. So do different national foreign policy interests, orientations, and traditions. Moreover, small member states are instinctively wary of the big member states' motives and tendencies when it comes to foreign and defense policy cooperation, notwithstanding Germany's reluctance since the end of World War II to assume an international political profile commensurate with its economic weight.

The possibility of a single EU seat in the United Nations Security Council illustrates the challenge of developing a common foreign policy. If the EU wants to speak with one voice internationally, logically it should have a single seat in the Security Council. But Britain and France, permanent Security Council members, are opposed to that idea. Nor do most other EU member states want to give up the prospect of occasionally sitting in the Security Council as nonpermanent members. Germany, less reticent recently about asserting itself internationally, is pressing for a seat of its own in the Security Council, to which Italy objects. In addition, Britain and France disagree strongly on international issues (the war in Iraq is an obvious example), despite a call in the Maastricht Treaty for member states that are permanent members of the Security Council (in other words, Britain and France) to "ensure the defense of the positions and the interests of the Union."

Nevertheless, the EU has what it calls the Common Foreign and Security Policy (CFSP) and is developing a common defense policy with a military capability. Clearly, the CFSP is not a common policy like the Common Commercial Policy. In other words, the member states have not pooled responsibility for foreign and security policy, let alone defense policy, in the EU. Notwithstanding the misleading nomenclature, the CFSP undoubtedly helps the EU to raise its international profile and to apply additional pressure to promote stability and help resolve conflicts beyond the EU's borders. Tentative though it still is, the common defense policy gives the EU a limited military capacity to intervene in trouble spots, especially close to home.

Developing the CFSP and the common defense policy has been a protracted process. Although member states accept that closer foreign and defense policy cooperation is in their interests, the political obstacles remain high. Perhaps the greatest spur to developing the CFSP and, especially, a common defense policy came from the EU's inability to prevent the Balkan wars of the 1990s triggered by the disintegration of Yugoslavia. It was humiliating for the EU to have to depend on the United States to halt Serbia's aggression first in Bosnia, then in Kosovo, and shameful for the EU to have done so little to avert the slaughter of thousands of Europeans in a far corner of the continent. Chris Patten, external relations commissioner from 1999 to 2004, remarked, "The people of the Western Balkans are our fellow Europeans. We cannot wash our hands of them. Let us remember the consequences of our refusal to get involved. The shattered ruins of Vukovar. The ghastly siege of Sarajevo. The charnel house of Srebrenica. The smoking villages of Kosovo. The European Union did not commit these crimes. But 200,000 or more fellow Europeans died in Bosnia and Herzegovina alone. As Europeans we cannot avoid a heavy share of responsibility for what happened."[1]

Instability on Europe's fringes could cause instability in the EU not least because of the possible influx of thousands of refugees and asylum seekers. Lack of economic opportunities in the "wider Europe" inevitably triggers mass migration into the EU, mostly by illegal immigrants. Free movement of people among member states, a belated benefit of the single market program, necessitates the development of common asylum and immigration policies. The opportunity for criminals (including terrorists) to exploit free movement within the EU necessitates close police and judicial cooperation among member states. Hence the decision by EU leaders, enshrined in the Amsterdam Treaty, to establish an area of "freedom, security and justice." Putting that concept into practice has proved every bit as difficult as developing a common foreign and security policy for many of the same reasons, notably concerns about sovereignty and discordant national philosophies and practices in the area of justice and home affairs.

It is easy to caricature the EU's plodding progress in the areas of internal and external security. Given the political and historical constraints, however, the EU's record is not unimpressive. Advocates of deeper integration may wish otherwise, but the EU is not a state (let alone a superstate in the making) and cannot behave accordingly. Even the Constitutional Treaty, which sharpens the EU's political profile and strengthens its policymaking capacity in the fields of internal and external security, does not endow the EU with the means necessary to become a statelike unitary actor in such politically sensitive policy areas.

▪ Internal Security: Justice and Home Affairs

Cooperation among member states on justice and home affairs—a range of activities pertaining to internal security—began in the mid-1970s in response to a wave of terrorism in Western Europe. Based on their experience of foreign policy cooperation, member states decided to set up a committee of senior officials from national ministries to share information on terrorist organizations and activities. Given its mission and the secrecy inherent in security cooperation, the so-called Trevi group worked unobtrusively on the margins of the EC.

It is impossible to assess the contribution of the Trevi group to antiterrorism. But procedurally at least it brought justice and interior ministries into the fold of European integration, albeit on an informal and intergovernmental basis. There was something of a spillover effect as the Trevi group extended its scope from terrorism to other transnational security threats, including organized crime and soccer hooliganism. Nevertheless, the group remained peripheral to the EC's main activities and methods of operation.

That began to change in the mid-1980s with the launch of the single market program. The Single European Act of 1986 called for completion of the single market—"an area without internal frontiers, in which the free movement of goods, persons, services and capital is ensured"—by the end of 1992. Of these "four freedoms," free movement of people was particularly problematic because it implied the introduction of a host of difficult accompanying measures dealing with political asylum, immigration, and visas for nonmember state nationals entering the EC and moving freely among its member states, as well as better police networks and external border measures directed against terrorism, drug smuggling, and other criminal activity. Such measures—unlike those necessary to implement the free movement of goods, services, and capital—were mostly a new departure for the EC. Government ministers asked the Trevi group to consider the broader security implications of a frontier-free Europe. However, the large and equally contentious area of immigration and asylum had yet to be addressed comprehensively.

Schengen

Buoyed by general enthusiasm in the mid-1980s for deeper integration, the EC's geographically core countries (France, Germany, Belgium, the Netherlands, and Luxembourg) took the first steps toward abolishing all frontier formalities among them. First France and Germany signed an agreement in July 1984 to reduce border checks; then the five countries signed a more far-reaching agreement in June 1985, in the town of Schengen in Luxembourg. The Schengen agreement launched a lengthy series of meetings and negotiations to identify and implement the numerous measures necessary to abolish internal frontiers and establish a common external border around the signatory states. Major challenges included setting visa requirements, dealing with asylum applications, combating illegal immigration, improving police cooperation in order to counter terrorism and other crime, and physically reconfiguring airports in order to segregate passengers traveling within the so-called Schengen area from those on other flights.[2]

The Single European Act should have made Schengen redundant. Indeed, the EC established an Ad Hoc Group on Immigration (under the Trevi framework) at the end of 1986 to plan the abolition of internal border controls. But three member states—Britain (for reasons of history and national sovereignty), Ireland (because it wanted to keep a common travel area with Britain), and Denmark (because of the possible impact of free movement in the EC on free movement among Nordic countries)—did not subscribe fully to the call in the Single European Act for unrestricted travel. To be precise, they subscribed to the free movement of member state nationals, but not nationals of third countries. As it would have been impossible to distinguish between member state and non–member state nationals without checks at intra-EC borders, Britain, Ireland, and Denmark insisted on keeping some frontier controls even after completion of the single market. As a result, the Schengen states continued their preparations to establish an area inside the EC in which people could move freely. Here was a striking example of differentiated integration within the EC.

The other member states—those neither in the Schengen group nor opposed to free movement—wanted to join Schengen and resented their exclusion from it. Italy, the only original EC member state not in the group, was especially miffed. The Schengen countries held out the prospect of expanded membership, hoping that Schengen would eventually be incorporated into the EC itself. Yet they were reluctant to allow Italy, Greece, Portugal, and Spain into the fold until confident of those countries' willingness and ability to impose rigorous border checks.

It took nearly five years for the Schengen countries to conclude a convention (called Schengen II) to implement the measures necessary to ensure that "internal borders may be crossed at any point without any checks on persons being carried out." Key issues and features included

- *Visas:* The convention aimed at harmonizing immigration law in order to devise a common list of third countries whose nationals needed a visa to enter the Schengen area and common rules for granting or denying visas, as well as agreement on a common visa stamp or sticker.
- *Illegal immigration:* Given the size and nature of the Schengen area's external borders, combating illegal entry posed a large and potentially expensive challenge. Moreover, the expense of securing external borders would have to be shared by those countries (such as Belgium and the Netherlands) whose borders diminished or disappeared because they were subsumed into a large free-travel area. The issue of illegal immigration grew increasingly sensitive in the late 1980s after the collapse of communism in Central and Eastern Europe, when a tide of illegal immigrants was expected to inundate the West.
- *Asylum:* For historical reasons (memories of Jews fleeing Germany and being denied refuge in other European countries were still vivid), asylum was a particularly sensitive issue on the Schengen agenda. There was little controversy about the definition of asylum or about how asylum seekers should be treated (EC member states had signed the relevant international agreements on the subject—the Geneva Convention and the New York Protocol). The main challenge was to prevent an individual from submitting more than one asylum request

in more than one country, either serially or simultaneously. Accordingly, the Schengen Convention included criteria to determine which state should deal with which asylum application. It also outlined a system for tracking asylum seekers within the Schengen area.

- *Police cooperation:* There was already a high degree of cooperation among Schengen police forces, although mostly on a bilateral and informal basis. Media coverage of the Schengen negotiations occasionally raised the specter of a common European police force snuffing out national sovereignty and disregarding individuals' rights. No national government contemplated a supranational police authority, although cooperation would have to include an EC-wide system for exchanging information and intelligence (this was the genesis of Europol, the European police agency). Given the sensitivity surrounding police cooperation, especially at the operational level, provisions dealing with issues such as cross-border surveillance and "hot pursuit" were hedged with limitations and qualifications.

- *Judicial cooperation:* Negotiations about judicial cooperation contained the same pitfalls as those about police cooperation, although the convention contained a number of provisions to increase contacts and strengthen cooperation among judicial authorities, especially on the sensitive issue of extradition.

- *Schengen Information System (SIS):* The Schengen Convention included provision for the Schengen Information System, headquartered in Strasbourg and linking relevant databases in participating states. Access to the SIS at border posts and other locations would allow officials to retrieve information quickly on missing persons, arrest warrants, false passports, stolen vehicles, and so on. Without the SIS, Schengen simply could not function. Yet the development of the SIS further alarmed the sovereignty-conscious as well as civil libertarians. Inevitably, strict privacy and confidentiality laws were put in place to govern the system's content and use. Apart from political and legal problems, the technical difficulty of linking so many different national systems delayed completion of the SIS and contributed to the delay in implementing the Schengen Convention.

- *Institutional structure:* The Convention established an institutional structure (outside the EC framework) to manage its operation and future development, including an executive committee at the ministerial level, a central negotiating group of senior officials, and numerous working groups.

The Schengen Convention was to have come into effect in January 1990, three years before completion of the single market program. However, growing fears of mass immigration from Central and Eastern Europe prompted second thoughts about the abolition of member state controls. France announced that it would continue border checks on non-EC nationals (which, by implication, meant some control of all individuals entering the country). Much to the relief of its Schengen partners, in December 1989 Germany postponed signing the convention because of uncertainty about the rights of East Germans to travel in the Schengen zone. After renewed negotiations the convention was eventually signed in June 1990, although its implementation was delayed for several years, partly for political reasons and partly because of the difficulty of organizing the information system.

Thus, by the time the single market was to have been fully implemented, at the end of December 1992, free movement of people was still a chimera even among the Schengen states. Despite successive European Council statements about the need for free movement of people, the Commission's efforts to achieve that goal within the EC itself merely elicited a suggestion that member states allow EC nationals to show, but not hand over, their passports at intra-EC borders. Seeing no point in hauling disobedient member states before the Court of Justice, the Commission shifted to a lame emphasis on the need for "confidence building" to occur before passport checks could be eliminated throughout the EC and once again urged the European Council "to ensure that the goals of [the EC treaty] in the area of the free movement of persons are realized."[3]

Using the Schengen process as a precursor to EC-wide action on the free movement of people, the Ad Hoc Group on Immigration drafted some of the provisions of the Schengen Convention into two separate international conventions that all member states signed in 1990: the Dublin Convention on Asylum and the External Borders Convention. The fact that these international conventions were drafted intergovernmentally without reference to the EC's supranational institutions demonstrated the continuing sensitivity for member states of justice and home affairs issues. In the event, problems of sovereignty and a territorial dispute between Britain and Spain over Gibraltar long delayed ratification of the Dublin Convention and the External Borders Convention.

Continuing concern about uncontrolled immigration and a variety of country-specific concerns—ranging from widespread criticism of Luxembourg's bank secrecy laws to French criticism of the Netherlands' policy on soft drugs—demonstrated the degree of disarray in the area of justice and home affairs even among Schengen states. Nevertheless, work continued on implementing the Schengen Convention, to which Italy acceded in November 1990, Portugal and Spain in June 1991, and Greece in November 1992. By that time the process of European integration had accelerated due to the success of the single market program and the unification of Germany. Indeed, many of Schengen's objectives were incorporated into the Maastricht Treaty, although Schengen continued to exist independently of the EU.

The Maastricht Treaty

Given the topicality of justice and home affairs in the late 1980s and the desire of some member states, notably Germany, to strengthen the EC's competence in that regard (ultimately by bringing Schengen into the treaty), justice and home affairs was a major item on the agenda of the 1991 intergovernmental conference on treaty reform. Yet doubts about free movement of people and difficulties surrounding the Schengen Convention did not bode well for the negotiations on justice and home affairs. In the event, proponents of supranationalism, including the Commission, spent most of their political capital on issues such as monetary union and institutional reform rather than on the thorny area of justice and home affairs, which became a separate intergovernmental pillar (the so-called third pillar, next to the first pillar of supranational integration and the second pillar of intergovernmental cooperation on foreign and security policy).

Nevertheless, justice and home affairs issues were not rigidly segregated from the EC proper. Indeed, the establishment of Union citizenship reinforced the salience of justice and home affairs for the development of the EU as a whole (a new article asserted that "every citizen of the Union shall have the right to move and reside freely within the territory of the member states"). Accordingly, another new article gave the Council, acting unanimously on a proposal from the Commission, power to determine those countries whose nationals needed a visa in order to enter the territory of the EU, and to adopt measures for a uniform visa format. A new provision for action to prevent drug dependence, in an article on public health, brought another justice and home affairs issue into the first pillar. And in the third pillar itself, member states agreed to act intergovernmentally "without prejudice to the powers of the European Community."

The bulk of the Maastricht Treaty's provisions for justice and home affairs was located in a new title at the end of the treaty, the first article of which listed nine areas of "common interest" subject to intergovernmental cooperation:

- asylum
- the crossing of external borders
- immigration
- combating drug addiction
- combating fraud on an international scale
- judicial cooperation in civil matters
- judicial cooperation in criminal matters

- customs cooperation
- police cooperation

Being closer to the core of national sovereignty, the last three areas were qualitatively different from the rest. Accordingly, they were not included in the *passerelle* (gateway) provision that allowed for the transfer of third-pillar issues to the first pillar. Although the *passerelle* provision was not used during the brief lifetime of the Maastricht Treaty before the Amsterdam Treaty reforms, the exclusion from it of police, customs, and most judicial cooperation suggested that member states would keep these areas in the intergovernmental third pillar, whatever the outcome of the 1996–1997 intergovernmental conference.

The Maastricht Treaty established three instruments for the implementation of justice and home affairs policy: joint positions, joint actions, and conventions. Joint positions and joint actions resembled similar instruments established in the treaty's second pillar (foreign and security policy cooperation) but were even less precisely defined. Conventions were already a familiar though unproductive feature of cooperation among member states on justice and home affairs (witness the Dublin Asylum Convention and the External Borders Convention). Not surprisingly in an intergovernmental pillar, the justice and home affairs ministers would have to act unanimously in the Council of Ministers except on procedural matters and when deciding on measures to implement joint actions.

The Maastricht Treaty established a coordinating committee (later known as the Article 36 committee after implementation of the Amsterdam Treaty) of senior member state officials to work on justice and home affairs issues and prepare Council meetings (in collaboration with the Committee of Permanent Representatives). The Maastricht Treaty stipulated that the Commission would be "fully associated" with the work of the third pillar. In fact, the Commission received a nonexclusive right of initiative in the first six policies of common interest to member states and no right of initiative in the remaining three areas. As for the European Parliament, the treaty used weak verbs such as "inform" and "consult" to describe its limited involvement in the third pillar. Paradoxically, the Parliament's almost nonexistent role opened a democratic deficit in an important policy sphere at precisely the time when member states were moving toward greater parliamentary accountability in EU affairs. The absence of the Court of Justice from the third pillar caused a similar "judicial deficit," although the treaty gave the Court authority to interpret the provisions of justice and home affairs conventions, subject to member state approval, on a case-by-case basis.

A final article in the original third pillar stipulated that "the provisions of this Title shall not prevent the establishment or development of closer cooperation between two or more Member States in so far as such cooperation does not conflict with, or impede, that provided for in this Title." In other words, national governments acknowledged that differentiated integration would continue to be a feature of cooperation on justice and home affairs among member states.

From Maastricht to Amsterdam

According to a senior Commission official, the third pillar got off to "a misleadingly good start."[4] Officials and ministers busied themselves preparing a work program and an action plan, which the European Council endorsed in December 1993. But the sudden flurry of activity could not disguise the fact that the work program consisted mostly of old, repackaged items and that the action plan was condemned to inactivity as long as unanimity remained the norm. The Parliament immediately denounced the third pillar as an insult to the Community method and pressured the Commission to involve itself as aggressively as possible in justice and home affairs issues. Already reeling from the Maastricht ratification crisis, the Commission initially preferred a less confrontational approach. In an effort to move things along and establish its own credibility in a hostile intergovernmental environment, the Commission sent the Council general communications rather than proposals for legislation on third-pillar issues. Nevertheless, the Commission did not hesitate to take some legislative initiatives, which resulted, for example, in a regulation on a uniform format for visas (May 1995) and a regulation establishing a legally binding list of countries whose nationals needed a visa to enter the EU (September 1995).

Given the history of cooperation on justice and home affairs, the cloak of confidentiality that shrouded the new Council formation and preparatory committee, the imprecision of the new instruments, and the ability of member states to veto decisions, it was inevitable that there was little or no headway on most issues covered by the third pillar. Yet public support for EU-wide measures to combat illegal immigration and organized crime was remarkably high despite widespread hostility during and after the Maastricht ratification crisis toward the EU and its institutions. Within the Schengen framework at least, despite differences of opinion and occasional political grandstanding, ministers and officials made some progress. In March 1995, the Schengen Convention finally became operational for seven of its signatory states (Italy and Greece needed to make additional adjustments; new member state Austria, which signed up in April 1995, also needed a lengthy transition period).

The fate of Europol, which occupied more time and got more attention than any other third-pillar issue in the mid-1990s, demonstrated the continuing difficulty of making progress within the EU in the field of justice and home affairs. Although ministers reached political agreement in June 1993 to establish Europol, the necessary implementing convention became a major battleground in the war between intergovernmentalists and supranationalists.

Germany and the Benelux countries insisted on a role for the Court of Justice; Britain, supported to some extent by Denmark and (after January 1995) Sweden, fiercely resisted. In the meantime, in deference to public anxiety about transnational drug dealing, EU member states launched the Europol Drugs Unit (EDU) in January 1994 in a renovated police barracks in The Hague. The EDU did not undertake any operations itself but supported operations involving two or more member states by facilitating access to information, intelligence, and analysis. The EDU's strengths were its highly sophisticated computer links and the discretion and personal contacts of its national liaison officers.

As the dispute over the Europol Convention dragged on, member states progressively broadened the EDU's scope to cover trafficking in stolen vehicles, illegal immigration, trafficking in human beings, and money laundering. In effect, the EDU was Europol under a modified name (it lacked competence only for terrorism and other serious crimes such as kidnapping and arms trafficking). France wanted to resolve the Europol row during its Council presidency in early 1995 but failed to overcome British opposition to the Court's involvement in Europol's affairs. The dispute then became bound up politically in an equally embittered row over bovine spongiform encephalopathy (mad cow disease), of all things. EU leaders finally reached a settlement in June 1996, when they agreed to allow the Court to give preliminary rulings on the interpretation of the Europol Convention.[5]

Public support for EU efforts to enhance internal security, together with disappointing progress to date on the third pillar, emboldened the Commission and like-minded member states in the run-up to the 1996–1997 intergovernmental conference. Nevertheless, preparations for the conference revealed deep divisions over how to strengthen and reorganize the EU's involvement in justice and home affairs. Not all member states favored extending Community competence over part of the third pillar or incorporating Schengen into the EU, albeit "by means of flexible arrangements."[6]

Given its political and procedural complexity, justice and home affairs was therefore one of the most thoroughly discussed issues at the conference itself. Germany and the Benelux countries (supported by the Commission and the Parliament) advocated moving the first six areas of common interest listed in the third pillar into the supranational first pillar and bringing the more than 3,000 pages of rules and regulations that had accrued since the launch of the Schengen process in 1985 into the *acquis communautaire*. Having joined Schengen in 1996, the Scandinavian member states did not demur (non-EU member states Iceland and Norway became associate members of Schengen), although Denmark insisted on an opt-out from those justice and home affairs provisions that were moved to the first pillar. Only Britain continued to object to a radical restructuring in the Amsterdam Treaty of justice and home affairs provisions, an objection that ended when the Labour Party formed a new government in May 1997. Nevertheless, like the Danish government, even the new British government insisted on an opt-out from the provisions that were moved to the first pillar.

The Amsterdam Treaty

Thanks in large part to the change of government in Britain and to aggressive Dutch chairmanship of the concluding stages of the intergovernmental conference, the Amsterdam Treaty included radical changes in the realm of justice and home affairs. The most striking innovation was the wholesale transfer into the first pillar of responsibility for visas, asylum, immigration, and other policies related to the free movement of people. Largely in deference to Germany, however, which absorbs the bulk of asylum seekers and refugees in the EU and where the state governments share responsibility for the matter, the new first-pillar provisions on immigration and asylum were hedged with intergovernmental and other qualifications. Provisions for police cooperation and judicial cooperation on criminal matters remained within a truncated third pillar. Whether taken under the auspices of the first or third pillars, justice and home affairs measures would help realize a new objective of the EU: "to develop . . . an area of freedom, security, and justice." Moreover, member states agreed to implement such measures during a specific time frame, "within a period of five years after the entry into force of the Treaty of Amsterdam" (which meant, in effect, May 2004).

New First-Pillar Provisions. New decisionmaking procedures outlined in the Amsterdam Treaty severely mitigated the impact of moving the areas of border controls and visas, asylum, refugees, immigration, and judicial cooperation in civil matters into the first pillar. During the five years leading up to the establishment of an area of freedom, security, and justice, the Council would continue to act by unanimity, with the Commission having only a shared right of initiative and the European Parliament being consulted only on proposed legislation. In other words, decisionmaking on the free movement of people remained essentially intergovernmental rather than supranational. After the transitional period, the Commission would acquire an exclusive right of initiative and the Council would decide whether to use the codecision procedure to enact legislation on the free movement of people—but the Council would make that decision unanimously. Finally, the role of the Court was still heavily restricted.

Determined to maintain control over its own borders, Britain won an opt-out from the treaty's new provisions on the free movement of people. Willing in principle to accept those provisions but constrained in practice by a desire to maintain a Common Travel Area with Britain, Ireland also opted out. Although both countries could decide on a case-by-case basis to adopt legislation on justice and home affairs issues in the first pillar—in effect, they could selectively opt back in—they would not be able to prevent other member states from adopting such legislation. Because its hands were tied politically by earlier Maastricht Treaty opt-outs, the Danish government reluctantly opted out also from the justice and home affairs provisions of the Amsterdam Treaty, but could also opt back in on a case-by-case basis.

The Truncated Third Pillar. According to the Amsterdam Treaty, the purpose of the third pillar—now confined to police cooperation and judicial cooperation on criminal matters—was to give EU citizens "a high level of safety" within the putative area of freedom, security, and justice. The treaty also mentioned the importance of preventing racism and xenophobia, but only in passing. As the third pillar is an intergovernmental one, the roles of the Commission, Parliament, and Court remain limited. Nevertheless, the Commission gained the right of initiative (shared with member states) in all areas, and the Parliament gained the right to be consulted on most issues.

The Amsterdam Treaty included a range of new and revised third-pillar instruments:

- *Common positions* would define the approach of the EU to a particular matter.
- *Framework decisions,* used to approximate laws and regulations on third-pillar issues, would bind member states as to the results to be achieved, but member states themselves could decide how to implement them. The more "progressive" member states hoped that framework decisions would replace conventions—often negotiated but rarely implemented—as the main third-pillar instrument.
- *Decisions* (as opposed to framework decisions) could be used to achieve objectives other than by harmonizing member state laws and regulations.
- *Conventions* remained an option in the third pillar but, once adopted by at least half of the member states, could enter into force for those member states.

Closer Cooperation. The Amsterdam Treaty included a flexibility clause allowing member states wanting to cooperate more closely to do so using EU institutions, procedures, and mechanisms. Thus, the Council could authorize closer cooperation, acting by a qualified majority at the request of the member states concerned. As in similar flexibility provisions covering cooperation on foreign and security policy, the provisions for justice and home affairs included an "emergency brake": by invoking "important and stated reasons of national policy," a member state could prevent the Council from voting to authorize closer cooperation. Although the Council could then vote to refer the matter to the European Council for a decision by unanimity, it seemed unlikely that a member state that pulled the emergency brake in the first place would release it because the issue had been pushed up to the level of the heads of state and government.

Schengen. In view of the Amsterdam Treaty's provisions for an area of freedom, security, and justice, including a flexibility clause for closer collaboration on justice and home affairs issues, there was no need to continue the Schengen Convention's separate existence. Accordingly, a protocol attached to the treaty provided for Schengen's incorporation into the EU framework with special provision (in a separate protocol) for non–Schengen members Britain and Ireland to accept some or all of the Schengen *acquis*. Having recently joined Schengen, Denmark was in the peculiar position of opting out of the justice and home affairs provisions into which Schengen was about to be folded. Denmark's situation was further complicated by the fact that non–EU members but fellow Nordic Union members Iceland and Norway remained fully associated with the Schengen *acquis* following its incorporation into the EU. The inelegant solution to Denmark's dilemma was a clause in the "Danish protocol" stipulating that within six months of the Council taking a decision that built on the Schengen *acquis,* Denmark would decide whether to incorporate that decision into national law.

Establishing an Area of Freedom, Security, and Justice

EU leaders devoted their meeting in October 1999 in Tampere, Finland, to identifying the steps necessary for establishing an area of freedom, security, and justice, as called for in the Amsterdam Treaty. This was the first meeting of the European Council ever devoted exclusively to justice and home affairs issues. It symbolized the growing importance of justice and home affairs in the EU and signaled the member states' political commitment to achieving real progress in the areas of asylum and immigration policy, border controls, and police and judicial cooperation. The Tampere summit set out the principles and objectives of EU cooperation on justice and home affairs and focused on the development of a common asylum and immigration policy, the establishment of a European area of justice, and the fight against organized and transnational crime.

The entry into force of the Amsterdam Treaty brought to an end the separate existence of the Schengen system outside the EU. The incorporation of Schengen into the EU saw the launch of a new formation of the Council of Ministers: the Justice and Home Affairs Council. As a result of the "communitarization" of many aspects of justice and home affairs, the so-called Article 36 Committee restricted its Council preparatory work to the reconfigured third pillar (covering police and judicial cooperation on criminal matters).

Rather than allowing the Committee of Permanent Representatives (Coreper) to coordinate the Council's work on the other aspects of justice and home affairs, however, a number of member states pressed successfully for the establishment of the Strategic Committee on Immigration, Frontiers and Asylum, separate from Coreper. This reflected the political sensitivity of immigration, asylum, and border control for most member states and the exceptional nature of these policy areas notwithstanding their incorporation into the first pillar of the EU.

The Commission was also restructured as a result of the Amsterdam Treaty's provisions for justice and home affairs. The old Task Force for Justice and Home Affairs became a full-fledged directorate-general with two directorates (for the communitarized and intergovernmental parts of the portfolio). In view of the growing importance of the portfolio and the vigor of the first commissioner with responsibility for it (Antonio Vitorino of Portugal), justice and home affairs became an important directorate-general. Because of the vagaries of Commission staffing, however, the justice and home affairs directorate-general was chronically understaffed. The Commission itself became a more prominent player within the EU in the area of justice and home affairs, making good use of its new powers in the communitarized part of the portfolio. The European Parliament continued to complain about the democratic deficit with regard to justice and home affairs and used every opportunity that it had to muscle into the increasingly important policy area.

Differing national perspectives on justice and home affairs became more pronounced as the policy area became more prominent as a result of the changes in the Amsterdam Treaty and the political push provided by the Tampere summit. As "frontline" states on the eastern edge of the EU, Germany, Austria, and Italy wanted a single asylum and immigration policy, hoping perhaps for a tougher European-level regime than would be politically possible at the national level (this was especially true of Germany, where memories of the Nazi past made it difficult for any government to tighten domestic asylum and immigration laws). Countries such as Britain, Denmark, and Ireland, more distant geographically from the EU's eastern border, were less interested in a common policy, preferring closer cooperation. France was primarily interested in establishing an EU-wide judicial area in which citizens would have equal access to agreed-upon standards of justice. France favored the harmonization of national laws for that purpose, whereas Britain and some other member states argued that mutual recognition was more practical and politically feasible.

In general, EU member states took a restrictive position on justice and home affairs. Despite rhetoric to the contrary, their emphasis in the putative area of freedom, security, and justice was squarely on "security." Europeans fretted more and more about illegal immigrants crossing the Mediterranean or coming from Central and Eastern Europe. Serbian aggression in Kosovo in early 1999 triggered another exodus of Balkan refugees. Albania and Bosnia were becoming notorious as staging areas for the trafficking of drugs, people, and stolen property in the EU. The EU's citizens wanted more cooperation among national governments on justice and home affairs, but mostly to keep out undesirable illegal immigrants, asylum seekers, and refugees; to catch drug dealers and other criminals who exploited free movement across member states' borders; and to seal the EU's external borders as tightly as possible.

Legal immigration was another issue. The Lisbon strategy drew attention to the EU's chronic demographic and economic problems. As some member states (such as Germany) appreciated more than others, the EU needed an influx of highly skilled workers to fuel the knowledge economy. Yet there was widespread popular resistance to the idea of large-scale legal immigration, despite (or possibly because of) the fact that the EU had already become a multicultural immigrant society. Nor was it easy to make the case for large-scale legal immigration at a time when right-wing political parties were winning votes on anti-immigration platforms.

The terrorist attacks on the United States in September 2001 increased the political salience of justice and home affairs but focused attention further on the security aspect of it. The fact that some of the planning for the attacks had taken place in Europe was an obvious cause of concern. The terrorist attacks in Madrid in March 2004, every bit as traumatic for Spain as the New York and Washington attacks of September 2001 had been for the United States, caused Europeans to fret even more about internal security. Antiterrorism became a major focus of EU cooperation on justice and home affairs, with some attention being given also to the importance of integrating immigrants into their new countries rather than having them live apart in social and cultural (and sometimes actual) ghettoes. Concerns about internal security, assimilation, and integration came uppermost in the Netherlands (and elsewhere in Europe) after the murder of a prominent film director by a Muslim extremist in October 2004 (the assailant held dual Dutch and Moroccan citizenship).

EU enlargement in Central and Eastern Europe had a profound impact on justice and home affairs. Many of the measures that member states adopted in the late 1990s and early 2000s with regard to asylum and immigration were intended to keep Central and Eastern Europeans out of the EU. With enlargement, the Central and Eastern Europeans would no longer be at the gates but would instead be inside the EU. Germany and other member states responded by pressing successfully for restrictions on the free movement of Central and Eastern Europeans even after their countries had acceded to the EU, a move that undercut one of the key principles of the EU and cast the Central and Eastern Europeans as second-class EU citizens.

Bulgaria and Romania were widely seen as problem countries with respect to the origin and transit of illegal immigrants into the EU. Yet, given their status as candidate countries, member states had little option but to include them in the "white list" of countries whose citizens did not need a visa to enter the EU. Moreover, Romania was of special interest to Hungary because of the large Hungarian minority there (the Hungarian government did not want ethnic Hungarians in Romania to have to get a visa to visit their ancestral homeland once Hungary entered the EU).

The prospect of Central and Eastern European enlargement focused EU attention especially on the control of external borders. Existing member states, especially those adjoining the prospective new member states, wanted to ensure that the candidate countries had the means to secure their eastern borders, even at the expense of severing long-standing connections between the candidate countries and their eastern neighbors (Poland and Ukraine are a good example). Thus, looming Central and Eastern European enlargement provided the main impetus for a proposed common European border force. Apart from that, the applicant countries struggled before enlargement to incorporate the Schengen *acquis* as part of their preaccession strategies. Most lacked the administrative capacities and financial resources to do so. As a result, it looked at one point as if enlargement could delay the establishment of an area of freedom, security, and justice or as if the establishment of an area of freedom, security, and justice could delay enlargement. In the event, the EU provided considerable financial and technical assistance to the candidate countries to help them meet the requirements of membership in the area of justice and home affairs.

Asylum, Immigration, and External Borders. Up to 400,000 people apply for asylum in the EU each year.[7] The number of illegal immigrants is, by definition, much harder to estimate. Illegal immigrants come mostly from countries whose nationals require visas to enter the EU (the Council drew up a list of those countries—the "black list"—in December 2000). They either enter the territory of the EU without a visa or enter with a visa but stay illegally after it has expired. Boatloads of prospective illegal immigrants are regularly intercepted at sea; others wash up on Europe's shores. As part of the Tampere objectives, the EU is attempting to develop common policies on asylum and immigration while strengthening external border security to block asylum seekers and illegal immigration. The EU tries to balance economic, humanitarian, and security concerns in its approach to asylum and immigration, although widespread public irritation with asylum seekers and illegal immigrants has pushed the EU toward adopting a restrictive approach.[8]

Policy toward asylum and immigration involves a myriad of politically sensitive issues. It also involves efforts to prevent asylum seekers and illegal immigrants from leaving their countries of origin or passing through countries that border the EU, to stop them at the border, and to deal with them inside the EU's borders. National policies and approaches toward asylum seekers and illegal immigrants vary enormously, making it difficult to adopt common policies. Unanimity in Council decisionmaking is a practical impediment to progress.

Preventive measures include working with the main countries of origin and transit to try to stop the flow of asylum seekers and illegal immigrants into the EU. In 1999 the EU identified Afghanistan, Iraq, Somalia, Morocco, and Sri Lanka as the key countries in question. A year later it adopted an action plan for Albania, a chaotic country on the EU's southeastern border. Later the EU raised the problem of illegal immigration with China, many of whose citizens reside illegally in EU member states. The best way to stop illegal immigration is to promote stability and economic development in the countries of origin. This is a key objective of EU foreign policy and especially of EU development policy. Popular concerns about the impact on the EU of massive illegal immigration strengthen the member states' interest in having an effective common foreign and security policy and in being able to provide considerable development and humanitarian assistance.

A much less ambitious strategy toward countries of origin and transit involves getting their approval to take back illegal immigrants and asylum seekers whose applications have been rejected. The EU offers economic or other inducements to win those countries' agreement. Yet another possibility is to ask transit countries to provide refuge and even to help process EU asylum seekers. The British government made such a suggestion in June 2003, as did the German government in October 2004. Civil libertarians and other opponents of a restrictive EU immigration policy easily misconstrued those suggestions, which predictably went nowhere.

As for dealing with asylum seekers and illegal immigrants within the EU, the Tampere conclusions called for a common European asylum system that would include common standards for the examination of asylum applications; minimum reception conditions for asylum seekers; the approximation of rules on refugee status; and an improvement in the functioning of the Dublin Convention, which had finally come into effect in 1997, on the allocations of responsibility among member states for the examination of asylum applications.

The EU made slow progress on all these issues. Some member states continued to legislate in the area of asylum and immigration at the national level despite efforts to coordinate policy at the European level. Member states differed among themselves over the right of asylum and the rights of asylum seekers. Those member states that were inundated with asylum seekers and illegal immigrants, such as Austria, Germany, and Italy, wanted to institute a burden-sharing arrangement within the EU; others were content to let the matter rest.

Political developments in France in early 2002 provided a reminder of the extreme sensitivity of immigration issues and the need for progress at the European level. Much to everyone's surprise, the candidate of the anti-immigration National Front, an extreme right-wing party, beat the candidate of the mainstream Socialist Party in the first round of the presidential elections and faced Jacques Chirac in the runoff. Although Chirac easily won, the fact that the National Front had done so well sent shock waves throughout France and the EU and convinced many national leaders to push ahead with a common asylum and immigration policy. As a result, Spain put immigration at the top of its Council presidency agenda and devoted considerable time to discussing the issue at the Seville summit in June 2002.

The Council finally reached agreement in January 2003 on the reception of asylum seekers and refugees. After a long delay due to differences among member states on a range of issues, including the status of unmarried partners, the Council approved a directive on the right of family reunification in September 2003, albeit with plenty of exceptions and reservations. The Council also enacted a regulation in February 2003 to overhaul and replace the Dublin Convention. The new regulation assigned responsibility for processing an asylum application to the member state in which the asylum seeker had a legally resident family member. As most asylum seekers did not meet that criterion, they became the responsibility instead of the member states whose territory they first entered illegally. In order to help process asylum applications, the Commission proposed in 2000 the so-called Eurodac system to compare the fingerprints of asylum seekers. It eventually became operational in January 2003.

Other aspects of asylum and immigration policy made little progress at the European level. Indeed, progress was slow generally on asylum and immigration within the purview of justice and home affairs, but slower on immigration than on asylum. Frustrated by the difficulty of getting the Council to adopt legislation on immigration, in July 2001 the Commission proposed using the open method of cooperation in immigration policy, in much the same way that it was being used in employment policy. Member states would exchange information, agree on best practices, set benchmarks, and adopt national action plans on issues such as the management of migration flows and cooperation with third countries, with the Commission acting as a monitor and scold. Yet the open method of coordination never became as popular or pervasive with asylum and immigration policy as it was with employment policy.

Tightening the EU's external borders is another factor in the equation of asylum and immigration policy. Fearing that the new Central and Eastern European member states lacked the means to secure what would become their external EU borders, it is also an area in which the EU15 collaborated closely in the run-up to enlargement. In November 2001, in a communication on illegal immigration, the Commission first floated the idea of a common European border force. Some member states were receptive; indeed, they were already cooperating closely with each other in that regard.

Based on preparatory work by the Commission and subsidiary Council committees, in June 2002 the Council of Ministers approved an ambitious plan for managing the EU's external borders. It called for a phased approach, beginning with the establishment of networks among member states, moving on to the conduct of joint operations, then setting up joint training programs and a common syllabus for border guards, and culminating in establishment of a European Corps of Border Guards, possibly within five years.

Police and Judicial Cooperation in Crime Fighting. Europol, the most visible manifestation of cooperation among member states in the fight against crime, finally became fully operational in July 1999.[9] Yet Europol was hobbled by entrenched national reservations about sharing confidential information, let alone conducting joint police operations across national boundaries, which was well beyond Europol's remit in any case. A Belgian presidency report on justice and home affairs in December 2001 complained about Europol's inadequacies and called for more information exchange among member states and better management and analysis within Europol. The list of crimes that Europol could cover grew longer as member states added issues such as forgery (a major concern before the launch of the euro) and money laundering.

The terrorist attacks in the United States in September 2001 gave Europol a new lease on life as counterterrorism became a major European as well as global preoccupation.[10] Reflecting the importance of transnational cooperation in the fight against terrorism, member states agreed to increase Europol's budget by 50 percent in 2002. In November 2003 the Council of Ministers adopted a protocol amending Europol's convention, following lengthy negotiations over the course of the previous two years. Subject to ratification by each member state (a requirement that vividly demonstrates Europol's intergovernmental nature), the new protocol increased the scope and flexibility of Europol's activities, not least in view of the urgency of closer European cooperation in the fight against international terrorism.

Terrorism had long been a cause of concern in the EU, especially for Germany and Italy, which endured domestic terrorist attacks in the 1970s, and Britain, Ireland, and Spain, which were combating terrorist campaigns by extreme nationalist and separatist groups (notably the Irish Republican Army and ETA, the militant Basque movement). The attacks of September 2001 heralded a new, transnational terrorist threat that reverberated throughout Europe. Member states responded in two ways: by intensifying judicial, police, and intelligence cooperation with the United States and by pushing through antiterrorist measures at the EU level that had been contemplated for some time but had not yet been acted on.

Chief among these were a framework decision on combating terrorism and a framework decision on the European arrest warrant.[11] The decision on combating terrorism, reached by the council of justice and home affairs ministers in December 2001, included a common definition of terrorism (not an easy thing to get) and agreement on penalties for directing terrorist groups. The decision on the arrest warrant, which cut to the core of national sovereignty, was more controversial and difficult to arrive at. It also upset Italian prime minister Silvio Berlusconi, who was embroiled at home in allegations of corruption. The issue became quite heated in the European Council in December 2001 and required deft handling by the Belgian presidency. Italy finally agreed to include corruption and money laundering in the list of crimes covered by the warrant, subject to the amendment of certain provisions in the Italian constitution.

EU leaders had agreed at Tampere in October 1999 to establish Eurojust, a body consisting of one representative per member state, with support staff, to promote judicial cooperation among prosecutors in the EU. Member states conceived of Eurojust as the flip side of Europol. Indeed, after the usual row over the location of new EU agencies, they agreed to locate Eurojust close to Europol, in The Hague. There was uncertainty about Eurojust's precise role and functions, however, which reflected some member states' extreme reluctance to institutionalize cooperation in the judicial sphere.

EU leaders also agreed in Tampere to strengthen cooperation among national police chiefs and to set up a European Police College. Neither initiative reached its full potential, at least not immediately. Member states fussed especially over the location, activities, and status of the police college, which opened its doors in temporary accommodations in December 2000. The police college eventually established itself outside London, where it developed a curriculum drawn from best national practices and offered courses to officers drawn from all member states. European police chiefs began to meet in their new EU guise (the EU Police Chiefs Operational Task Force) in 2000, exchanging ideas, building trust, and developing a strong network. Their work at home and collaboratively in the EU increasingly focused on terrorism.

Judicial Cooperation in Civil Affairs. Judicial cooperation in civil affairs, such as ensuring equal access for EU citizens to justice, regardless of where they reside or happen to be in the EU, was much less newsworthy but no less important than other aspects of justice and home affairs. Mutual recognition became the most important means of developing an "area of justice" in the EU, as called for by the European Council in Tampere in October 1999. Member states increasingly granted mutual recognition to judgments and other legal decisions. Nevertheless, legislation remained an essential ingredient of developing judicial cooperation on civil affairs. For example, a Council directive of January 2003 on access to legal aid in cross-border disputes provided an important building block for the European area of justice.

Efforts to promote the integration of asylum seekers and immigrants into their new societies were also important. Hence the emphasis on fighting racism and xenophobia, which resulted in measures to ensure equal treatment of people regardless of their race or ethnic origin. The European Monitoring Center for Racism and Xenophobia, opened in Vienna in April 2000, promotes the integration of racial minorities into the EU, an aspect of justice and home affairs that received enormous attention following an uncharacteristic outbreak of intolerance in the Netherlands in October 2004.

Beyond Amsterdam and Tampere

The Commission launched a scoreboard in 2000 to monitor progress in the area of justice and home affairs. Updated twice a year, the scoreboard shadows Commission proposals through the Council's decisionmaking machinery and outlines Commission plans for new legislative proposals or other initiatives. The scoreboard and other monitoring devices show mixed progress, especially on asylum and immigration policy, over the years. In December 2001, in a midterm review of the Tampere program (halfway between implementation of the Amsterdam Treaty and the deadline of May 2004 for the achievement of a number of objectives in the field of justice and home affairs), the Belgian presidency delivered an unusually hard-hitting report, criticizing member states for not doing enough to achieve a common asylum and immigration policy or to cooperate more closely to combat transnational crime. Nevertheless, the Commission presented a positive appraisal of the Tampere work program in June 2004.

Following up on the still incomplete Tampere program, EU leaders agreed on a new program for justice and home affairs at their summit in The Hague in November 2004. Based on input from the Commission, European Parliament, relevant Council bodies, and the twenty-five member states, the so-called Hague program set objectives in all areas of justice and home affairs for the next five years. For instance, it called for a common asylum system by 2010. To facilitate decisionmaking and increase democratic accountability, member states agreed to use qualified majority voting and the codecision procedure in the areas of asylum and immigration (apart from legal immigration) as of January 2005.

Heightened popular concern about asylum, immigration, and transnational crime, together with institutional and political impediments to effective decisionmaking in these areas, brought justice and home affairs to the top of the agenda of the Convention on the Future of Europe. The Convention's working party on justice and home affairs presented a report to the Convention's leadership in December 2002 advocating far-reaching reforms. These included the abolition of the pillar structure, thereby bringing justice and home affairs under the umbrella of a unitary EU, and greater use of qualified majority voting in order to end legislative logjams. Nevertheless, the working group, as well as the Convention as a whole, appreciated that unanimity would have to remain in use for decisionmaking in the most politically sensitive areas of police and judicial cooperation on criminal matters. The Convention included most of these proposals in its draft Constitutional Treaty of June 2003.

The intergovernmental conference of 2003–2004 incorporated most of the Convention's proposals with respect to justice and home affairs into the Constitutional Treaty, although it made a number of significant changes as well. The most striking innovation in the Constitutional Treaty is indeed the abolition of the third pillar. As a result, the array of acts currently used (common positions, decisions, framework decisions, conventions) would be replaced by laws and framework laws adopted using the ordinary legislative procedure (in other words, by codecision), except for the proposed European Public Prosecutor's Office. The Council could establish this office out of Eurojust, acting unanimously and after obtaining the consent of the European Parliament, but only to combat crimes affecting the financial interests of the EU. However, the Constitutional Treaty provides for the possibility of the European Council extending the powers of the European Public Prosecutor's Office to include serious crime with a cross-border dimension. The Constitutional Treaty extends and clarifies the operational powers of Eurojust, allowing it to initiate criminal investigations, propose to national authorities that prosecutions be initiated, and coordinate investigations and prosecutions being conducted by national authorities.

In the field of judicial cooperation in criminal matters and criminal law, the Commission and the member states continue to share the right of initiative. Nevertheless, member states may no longer act alone but only in a group of not less than one-quarter of the EU's membership, thereby reducing the number of member state initiatives taken under the old system. The Convention proposed the use of qualified majority voting for decisions on judicial cooperation in criminal matters and criminal law, but the intergovernmental conference added an "emergency brake": a member state could refer a proposal that it strongly opposed to the European Council, thereby suspending the ordinary legislative procedure. After some time, the European Council could restart the ordinary procedure or ask either the Commission or the group of member states that had drafted the proposal to submit a new one. If the European Council did not act, after a certain time one-third of the member states could act through enhanced cooperation.

The Constitutional Treaty provides a limited role for national parliaments in monitoring the implementation of justice and home affairs policy and enables the Court to review member state compliance. It also retains the special arrangements for Britain and Ireland in the area of justice and home affairs and the Danish government's opt-outs. On a minor but noteworthy point, under the terms of the Constitutional Treaty, the Article 36 Committee, which coordinates the work of the justice and home affairs ministers, would become the internal security committee.

Clearly, cooperation on justice and home affairs will continue to be a vital area of EU activity. Europeans generally want "more Europe," not less, in that policy area. Nevertheless, some civil libertarians are concerned about the impact on people's rights of European-level cooperation on justice and home affairs, especially with regard to antiterrorist measures. Even as provided for under the Constitutional Treaty, justice and home affairs in the EU appears to lack transparency and full democratic scrutiny. Of course, the challenge of democratic accountability in the area of justice and home affairs is not peculiar to the EU. It is always hard to strike the right balance between secrecy and transparency in the pursuit of greater security. It is harder still in an era of global terrorism.

■ External Security: Foreign and Defense Policy

Meeting in The Hague in 1969, EU leaders called for member states to cooperate on foreign policy in a procedure known as European Political Cooperation. They did so at a time of imminent enlargement lest a "wider" EC become politically "weaker." The launch of *Ostpolitik* (Germany's policy of establishing relations with the countries of the Soviet bloc) at about the same time provided a strong impetus for member states to exchange information on international issues and to attempt to coordinate their policies toward Central and Eastern Europe and the Soviet Union. The 1973 Middle East war and subsequent Euro-Arab dialogue had a similar impact on the development of European Political Cooperation. Indeed, the Venice Declaration of June 1980, in which member states publicly recognized the special position of Palestine in the Arab-Israeli conflict, showed how closely member states coordinated their Middle East policies and how radical their joint position could be.[12]

The Conference on Security and Cooperation in Europe (CSCE), which began in the early 1970s and culminated in August 1975 in the so-called Helsinki Final Act, helped greatly to forge an international identity for the EC and to promote European Political Cooperation. Member states indicated at an early stage of the CSCE process that they would act as a group and abide collectively by CSCE commitments. Member states fared best in negotiations on "Basket Two" (economic cooperation) and "Basket Three" (human rights) of the CSCE's agenda. There was never an EC delegation in the CSCE, and the Community itself could not make proposals, but Commission officials, attached to the national delegation of the Council presidency, participated fully in the negotiations.

European Political Cooperation procedures were based on the Luxembourg Report of 1970 and the Copenhagen Report of 1973, which identified four levels for conducting the process:

- meetings of the *heads of state and government* (later institutionalized as the European Council) to provide overall direction
- meetings of *foreign ministers* "in European Political Cooperation" as opposed to the Council of Ministers (an artificial distinction that was later dropped) to prepare and follow up on summit meetings and to deal with foreign policy issues on a regular (monthly) basis
- meetings of the *Political Committee* (foreign ministries' political directors) to prepare and follow up on foreign ministers' meetings
- meetings of *working groups* (midlevel foreign ministry officials) to exchange views and prepare reports on a variety of geographical and functional issues, and of the group of European correspondents (junior foreign ministry officials) to liaise between foreign ministries and prepare meetings of the Political Committee

National foreign ministries set up Coreu, a secure communications system, exclusively for the conduct of European Political Cooperation business.

The Council presidency chaired European Political Cooperation meetings at all levels. There was no voting; instead, lengthy negotiations in a search for consensus created informal pressures to agree. Consensus became one of the procedure's fundamental rules. As in other policy areas, although no one wanted to be outvoted, no one wanted to be isolated either. A strong tendency to follow the opinion of the majority therefore developed. Unofficial and subtle linkages between European Political Cooperation and other policy areas reinforced this tendency despite obvious exceptions (for most of the 1980s, for instance, the socialist Greek government had scant regard for foreign policy consensus building).

In the early 1980s, when the EC's external relations were every bit as problematic as its internal development, the procedural limits of European Political Cooperation became obvious. The onset of the "second Cold War"—the sudden heightening of East-West tension in the late 1970s after a decade of relatively benign relations—tested the EC's ability to act internationally. European Political Cooperation proved an inadequate mechanism, especially in response to sudden crises such as the Soviet invasion of Afghanistan in December 1979. Two years later, following the imposition of martial law in Poland in response to the success of the anticommunist Solidarity movement, member states met more promptly in European Political Cooperation to try to coordinate their response. Yet it was not until March 1982 that the EC imposed limited sanctions against the Soviet Union.

A worsening East-West climate and member states' slow response to international crises led to a number of initiatives in the early 1980s to improve European Political Cooperation and broaden its agenda to encompass security and even defense issues. The 1981 London Report introduced minor procedural reforms but limited discussions within European Political Cooperation to "the political aspects of security." The German and Italian foreign ministers launched a joint initiative in November 1981 to strengthen the EC's institutional structure and to extend EC competence in external relations. The so-called Genscher-Colombo proposals sought to end the distinction between European Political Cooperation and EC external economic policy and make it possible for member states "to act in concert in world affairs so that Europe will increasingly be able to assume the international role incumbent upon it."[13]

Foreign ministers acting at the behest of the European Council failed to find a way forward and could not concur on the relatively mild foreign and security policy proposals contained in the Genscher-Colombo proposals. Some member states (such as Britain and the Netherlands) were wary of developing an EC-based security structure that might upset Washington; others (such as Ireland, Denmark, and Greece) faced domestic political constraints. Consequently, the foreign ministers' report, presented at the Stuttgart summit in June 1983, was a classic compromise. It resulted only in the "Solemn Declaration on European Union," a vague proclamation of the EC's international identity.[14]

The Single European Act

Member states soon had a better opportunity, during the 1985 intergovernmental conference on treaty reform, to revamp European Political Cooperation. Once again emphasizing the distinctiveness of European Political Cooperation from other EC activities, the Political Committee considered foreign and security policy in a separate conference working party. The evolution of European Political Cooperation since the early 1970s, together with a number of member state proposals, formed the basis of its discussions. All member states agreed on the need to make the EC's external economic policy and the member states' foreign policies more consistent with each other. Other ideas included formalizing European Political Cooperation in the Rome Treaty, strengthening cooperation procedures, providing a special secretariat for the process, and incorporating military and defense issues. Neutral Ireland shied away from going too far down the defense road, as did pacifist (though NATO member) Denmark and idiosyncratic (though also NATO member) Greece.

These discussions led to a separate section on European Political Cooperation being included in the Single European Act. Procedural improvements included associating the Commission fully with European Political Cooperation, ensuring that the European Parliament was "closely associated" with it, creating a mechanism for convening the Political Committee or the General Affairs Council on short notice at the request of at least three member states, and establishing a special secretariat in Brussels. The Single European Act also stipulated that "the external policies of the EC and the policies agreed in Political Cooperation must be consistent" and charged the presidency and the Commission with ensuring such consistency. However, European Political Cooperation remained largely intergovernmental—in effect in a pillar separate from the EC—and was not subject to judicial review by the Court of Justice.

Revolution in Central and Eastern Europe and the abrupt end of the Cold War brought security concerns to the top of the EC's agenda. Simultaneously, the Commission's leadership of the international aid effort in Central and Eastern Europe helped to narrow the conspicuous gap between foreign policy cooperation and the EC's external economic relations. A paper on Central and Eastern Europe prepared collectively by the Council presidency, the Commission, and the foreign policy secretariat for the European Council in June 1989 set an important precedent in joint EC–European Political Cooperation policymaking. Thereafter, "the Community and its member states" became standard usage in European Political Cooperation documentation.

The Maastricht Treaty

With the imminence of German unification in 1990, there was near unanimity among member states on the need to reform European Political Cooperation. Indeed, member states decided to convene an intergovernmental conference on political union largely for that reason. By transforming European Political Cooperation into the Common Foreign and Security Policy, which became an intergovernmental pillar of the EU, member states and the Commission hoped to strengthen European security at a potentially destabilizing time, boost the new EU's international standing, and bind external economic and political policymaking more closely together.[15]

Member states optimistically called in the Maastricht Treaty for consistency between the EC and the CFSP pillars of the EU and charged the Commission and the Council with achieving that goal. The treaty's CFSP provisions were contained in a new series of articles, the first of which set out the policy's objectives:

- to safeguard the common values, fundamental interests, and independence of the EU
- to strengthen the security of the EU and its member states in all ways
- to preserve peace and strengthen international security in accordance with the principles of the UN charter and the Conference on Security and Cooperation in Europe
- to promote international cooperation
- to develop and consolidate democracy and the rule of law and respect human rights and fundamental freedoms

The Maastricht Treaty introduced two novel instruments to implement the CFSP:

- common positions to establish systematic cooperation on a day-to-day basis
- joint actions to allow member states to act together in concrete ways based on a Council decision as to the specific scope of such actions, the EU's objectives in carrying them out, and (if necessary) the duration, means, and procedures for their implementation

The success of the CFSP would depend in part on how these instruments were adopted. Some member states advocated the use of qualified majority voting; others insisted on unanimity for anything having to do with foreign and security policy. The treaty struck a clumsy compromise by providing for qualified majority voting for the implementation of joint actions, which the Council first had to adopt on the basis of unanimity.

The treaty stipulated that the Commission would be fully associated with the work of the CFSP, although it would not have an exclusive right to submit proposals. The treaty contained a weaker commitment to involve the European Parliament with the CFSP. Given that the CFSP occupied an intergovernmental pillar, from which the Court of Justice was excluded, there was no way of enforcing member state compliance with these or any other CFSP provisions.

The Western European Union

Iraq's invasion of Kuwait in August 1990 coincided with preparations for the intergovernmental conference on political union. Despite having reacted promptly and forcefully within the limits of its ability to news of the Iraqi invasion, the EC soon came in for criticism, especially in the United States, for its inability to do more. To some extent the EC was a victim of its own success. Prevailing Europhoria and pervasive discussion of a putative CFSP had raised unrealizable expectations about the EC's capacity to take concerted international action, especially involving the use of force. Accordingly, the inadequacy of the EC's overall performance in the crisis revealed more than merely the limits of European Political Cooperation. A marked divergence of opinion among member states on the advisability of using force against Iraq demonstrated the difficulty of their ever developing a common security policy with a defense component. Reactions varied from Britain's instinctive following of the U.S. line, to Spain's strong support for military action, to France's unilateral diplomatic démarche, to Germany's hiding behind a supposed constitutional ban on sending troops outside the NATO area, to Ireland's whining about the limits of "neutrality."[16]

To the extent that they wanted to cooperate militarily during the Gulf crisis, the Western European Union (WEU) provided a ready-made mechanism for member states to do so. The WEU also had considerable potential for long-term EC defense cooperation, not least because the United States was not a member. In 1984, during the height of renewed U.S.-Soviet tension, the then seven members of the WEU—Britain, France, Germany, Italy, Belgium, the Netherlands, and Luxembourg—had revived the moribund organization in order to assert their security and defense identity. With member states striving in 1991 for a common foreign and security policy as an element of political union and some of them eager to cooperate militarily in the Gulf, the WEU (which Portugal and Spain had subsequently joined) inevitably returned to the forefront of the debate.

As expected, negotiations about security and defense proved especially arduous during the intergovernmental conference. The outbreak of war in Yugoslavia in June 1991 highlighted the difficulty of reconciling member states' notoriously discordant positions. Few member states supported establishing a full-fledged EU defense policy (neutral Ireland and pacifist Denmark especially bristled at the "D-word"). Nevertheless, there was near unanimity about at least establishing an EU defense identity and about using the WEU to do so. This suggestion led to difficult negotiations about the precise relationship among the EU, the WEU, and NATO. "Atlanticist" countries such as Britain, the Netherlands, and Portugal—staunch NATO supporters—traditionally shied away from initiatives that might weaken, or appear to weaken, the Atlantic Alliance.

The end of the Cold War, doubts about NATO's future, and uncertainty about the role of the United States in Europe complicated the issue and increased the Atlanticists' reluctance to forge too close a link between the EU and the WEU. "Europeanist" countries—notably France—argued the contrary case, making the old point that a stronger European pillar would bolster the alliance and the new point that with the end of the Cold War, Europe needed to develop its own defense organization because the United States was bound to reduce its military involvement on the continent. Germany sided instinctively with the Europeanists but, at least as long as Soviet troops remained in the eastern part of the country, opted pragmatically for the Atlanticists.

Member states struck a compromise in the Maastricht Treaty between the Europeanists and the Atlanticists, allowing for "the eventual framing of a common defense policy, which might in time lead to a common defense." The unequivocal use of the D-word represented a new departure by the member states. The treaty also recognized the WEU as "an integral part of the development of the European Union" and authorized the Council, acting on the basis of unanimity, to ask the WEU "to elaborate and implement [the EU's] decisions and actions . . . which have defense implications."

A declaration attached to the treaty explained the member states' intention to "build up [the] WEU in stages as the defense component of the Union." However, the declaration also spelled out the WEU's relationship to NATO, citing the WEU's future development "as a means to strengthen the European pillar of the Atlantic Alliance." The treaty's language allowed both sides in the defense debate to claim victory. Yet a commitment in the treaty to review defense arrangements within five years hinted that the EU's defense identity would increasingly assume a Europeanist rather than an Atlanticist appearance.

From Maastricht to Amsterdam

The CFSP got off to a shaky start. Even before EU leaders put the finishing touches on the treaty at the Maastricht summit, there was a feeling among negotiators and observers that the treaty's provisions for foreign and security policy were flawed. Accordingly, the treaty included specific provisions for a review of the CFSP in an intergovernmental conference that would take place in 1996. Some optimistic officials may have hoped that such a review would give the CFSP a supranational character; most simply wanted to be able to iron out the CFSP's institutional and procedural wrinkles within a few years of the treaty becoming operational.

Even though implementation of the CFSP was delayed by the Maastricht ratification crisis, member states and EU institutions lost little time preparing to put the treaty into effect. Meeting in Lisbon in June 1992, the European Council outlined EU policy toward certain countries or groups of countries and "domains within the security dimension" that could be subject to joint action. These included the Organization for Security and Cooperation in Europe (formerly the Conference on Security and Cooperation in Europe) process; disarmament and arms control, including confidence-building measures; nuclear nonproliferation issues; and economic aspects of security, in particular control of the transfer of military technology to third countries and control of arms exports.[17] Once the time came to adopt common positions and joint actions, however, there was considerable confusion among member states, the Council secretariat, and the Commission about the difference between the two instruments and the advisability of choosing one rather than the other in any given situation. In the meantime, member states seemed wedded to high-sounding but harmless declarations, which had been a feature of European Political Cooperation but were not provided for in the CFSP.

Eventually the Council settled on a formula whereby common positions would be used to set out an agreed-upon approach to an issue and joint actions to make concrete commitments or undertake specific initiatives. The European Stability Pact, proposed by the French prime minister as a means of resolving long-standing disputes among the countries of Central and Eastern

Europe, became one of the EU's first joint actions in 1994. Another joint action (in 1995) involved an EU reconstruction and reconciliation effort in Mostar, a city in Bosnia bitterly divided between Croats and Muslims. This was the only time that the EU called upon the WEU to help implement a CFSP decision, although the operation was a civilian rather than a military one (the WEU provided a small police force).

Despite these successful joint actions (Mostar was successful only in the procedural sense; the EU's involvement was a dismal failure), most other joint actions and common positions were less clear-cut and less impressive. Even more striking were the joint actions and common positions that the EU should have taken but never did. The problem was both procedural and political. Despite possible recourse to qualified majority voting to implement joint actions, member states stuck doggedly to unanimity. Thus, the consensus principle of European Political Cooperation permeated the CFSP, thwarting effective decisionmaking and in some cases keeping worthy foreign and security policy issues off the EU's agenda.

Other challenges confronting the new CFSP ranged from the difficulty of setting up the CFSP unit in the Council secretariat to the nature of the Council presidency to the tendency of member states to go it alone on issues of particular national interest. The problem with the CFSP unit was not administrative but cultural: officials seconded to the unit from member state foreign ministries had a completely different outlook than their colleagues drawn from the Council secretariat itself. Whereas the former had a national perspective, the latter had a European (although not necessarily a supranational) one. It took at least two years for the new unit to establish itself bureaucratically in the Council secretariat and for its mixed group of officials to begin to work harmoniously together.

The problem with the presidency was multifaceted: some presidencies threw themselves wholeheartedly behind the CFSP; others had different priorities. The Greek presidency in early 1994 distinguished itself by pursuing foreign policy interests that ran counter to the EU's own interests (notably by refusing to recognize the former Yugoslav Republic of Macedonia and imposing sanctions against it, in response to which the Commission took Greece—the Council presidency—before the Court of Justice). Lack of continuity due to the biannual presidential rotation inevitably affected the implementation of the CFSP and weakened the EU's external representation.

The Yugoslav Debacle. Unprecedented challenges confronting the EU in the early 1990s exacerbated the CFSP's procedural problems. The greatest challenge came from Yugoslavia, where Europe's first post–Cold War conflict erupted in June 1991. Initially the Yugoslav army fought a short, unsuccessful war against secessionist Slovenia. Later that summer Serbia (Yugoslavia's dominant republic) launched a war against Croatia, which had also seceded from the Yugoslav federation. The new round of fighting unleashed a ferocity last seen in Europe during World War II. In April 1992 fighting spread to Bosnia, where both Serbia and Croatia wanted to expand but where mutual hatred of Serbia turned Bosnian Muslims and Croatian nationalists into temporary allies. Although all sides committed atrocities, Serbia's ruthless siege of Sarajevo, Bosnia's capital, seemed especially callous. Nightly news film of maimed and murdered Bosnians, victims of Serb sniper and artillery attacks, sickened the outside world. Evidence of Serb "ethnic cleansing" in Bosnia recalled Europe's nightmare of World War II and made an even more compelling humanitarian case for EC intercession in the conflict.

Coincidentally, a meeting of the European Council had opened in Luxembourg on the same day that fighting first broke out in Yugoslavia. The troika of foreign ministers (from the current, immediately preceding, and immediately succeeding presidencies) left Luxembourg on a dramatic overnight peace mission to Belgrade, returning to report to EC leaders before the summit's end. A remark by the Dutch foreign minister (a member of the troika) showed how confident the EC was of brokering a cease-fire: "When we went on this mission to Yugoslavia, I really had the feeling that the Yugoslav authorities thought that they were talking to Europe, not just to a country incidentally coming by but to an entity whose voice counts."[18]

The instruments available to the embryonic EU included arbitration, inspection, diplomatic recognition or nonrecognition of the warring parties, and economic sanctions and inducements. The EU could neither take nor threaten to take military action, although individual member states and the WEU could. In practice, deep divisions among its member states hampered the EU. Although many of them instinctively sympathized with Croatia and especially with Bosnia, both victims of Serb aggression, Greece sympathized with Serbia, with which it had close cultural and religious ties. Greece also blocked EC recognition of neighboring Macedonia unless the former Yugoslav republic, having stolen "a historically Greek name and feeding long-nourished appetites for Greek territory," changed its name.[19]

The most divisive row within the EC, however, centered on Croatia as Germany (responding to mounting domestic pressure) began to press for EC recognition of the breakaway republic in the fall of 1991. A majority of member states doubted that fragmentation of the Yugoslav federation would ultimately resolve the conflict and feared that diplomatic recognition would encourage, not discourage, Croatian and Serbian irredentism. Matters came to a head at a meeting of the Council of Ministers in December. After ten hours of fierce debate, the foreign ministers drew up criteria for the recognition of new states in Yugoslavia and the former Soviet Union and agreed in effect to recognize Croatia's independence early in the new year.[20]

The EC's high hopes of intercession in the former Yugoslavia were an early victim of these and other disputes among member states over how best to respond to the conflict. Serbia's intransigence at the conference table and belligerence on the battlefield undermined the EC's mediation efforts, which fared badly following the escalation of hostilities in Croatia and Bosnia. A strong public reaction against Serbian atrocities in Bosnia redoubled the EC's diplomatic offensive, culminating in a joint UN-EC conference in London in August 1992 and follow-on negotiations in Geneva, which produced a comprehensive peace plan for Bosnia in 1993.

This was the high point (or possibly the low point) of EC (and later EU) mediation in the conflict. Bosnian Muslims' unwillingness to accept a proposal that seemed to reward Serbian aggression, Bosnian Serbs' reluctance to cede control over any part of their recently acquired enclaves, and Croatia's determination to grab more territory in Bosnia doomed the painstakingly prepared peace plan. With its mediation effort in tatters, the EU's involvement in the Bosnian conflict was reduced to providing humanitarian assistance, although individual member states also sent troops under UN auspices to protect so-called safe areas.

The failure of the CFSP with regard to the Yugoslav wars became even more evident in April 1994 with the establishment of the Contact Group, consisting of Britain, France, Germany, Russia, and the United States, to "manage" the Yugoslav situation. Although the three EU member states in the group (later joined by Italy) supposedly represented the EU, in fact they were included because of their size and influence and represented only themselves. The establishment of the Contact Group and the lack of formal EU membership in it harked back to the old days of great-power politics and caused considerable resentment among other member states, especially those (such as the Dutch) with sizable contingents of troops in Bosnia.

The Bosnian war reached its denouement in the summer and fall of 1995, when Serbian atrocities in Sarajevo and Srebrenica finally compelled the United States to act militarily. Heavy NATO bombardment of Serbian positions in August 1995 brought the Serbs to their senses. The United States followed up diplomatically by convening a peace conference in Dayton, Ohio, at which a settlement was hammered out. In order to emphasize the transatlantic nature of the peace initiative, the so-called Dayton Accords were formally signed in Paris in November 1995. Yet this move could not disguise the predominantly U.S. stamp on the peace process and the failure of EU efforts to end the fighting in the former Yugoslavia during the preceding four years.

Lessons for the EU. Although unique in many respects, the Yugoslav war provided a lesson in the limits of EU involvement in post–Cold War conflict resolution. The Balkans' history of instability, which had dragged the great powers into World War I and which, as German unification reminded every-one, cast a long shadow over twentieth-century Europe, complicated the EU's response to the fragmentation of Yugoslavia. Yet it is an exaggeration to claim that "unlike the situations in 1914 and 1939 . . . Europe [has been spared] a wider conflagration as a result of the policies of the EU and other key princi-pal actors."[21] Undoubtedly, Germany's support for Croatian independence in 1991 jogged memories of Nazi support for fascist Croatia fifty years previ-ously and sparked an ugly media reaction in France. Similarly, France's in-stinctive sympathy for Serbia in 1991 echoed its support for Serbia during World War I. But the democratization of Germany (and Italy) since 1945, the demise of aggressive nationalism in Western Europe, and Western European solidarity during the Cold War—to which the EC certainly contributed—en-sured that the Yugoslav war did not risk pitting EU member states against each other (although, as a Balkan country, Greece almost became embroiled in the conflict).

The impossibility of sending large numbers of German troops to Yu-goslavia was a more pertinent legacy for the EU of recent Balkan and Euro-pean history. Britain's "Northern Ireland syndrome" made the government in London extremely cautious about intervening militarily in Yugoslavia apart from providing limited humanitarian assistance under UN auspices. Of the EU's three "great powers," only France appeared willing to take some form of military action, but not alone. The member states' reluctance to use force not only limited their policy options but also hindered the development of an EU "defense identity" during the early years of the CFSP's existence.

Developments in Yugoslavia had exposed deep foreign policy differences among member states and shown the limits of EU international action.[22] They also illustrated the extent to which "the dominant foreign policy reflex in Western Europe [continued to be] national, not communitarian."[23] The EU's ineffectual involvement in the conflict sapped popular support for European integration and for the fledgling CFSP. The EU's performance had a similarly debilitating effect on opinion in the United States. A rash boast in early July 1991 by the foreign minister of Luxembourg, then in the Council presidency, that "this is the hour of Europe, not the hour of the Americans," gave explo-sive ammunition to critics of the EU, especially those in the U.S. Congress.[24]

Its initial intervention in Yugoslavia may have given the embryonic EU a sense of identity and self-importance, but the EU's subsequent failures there seriously undermined its international standing and foreign policy effective-ness. Nor would the EU have performed better had the CFSP been in place earlier. The problem lay not simply in a lack of mechanism or structure but rather in profound historical differences compounded by a radical contextual change caused by the end of the Cold War. The Yugoslav crisis was a salutary lesson in the limits of European integration, specifically in the difficulty of sharing sovereignty in the sensitive areas of security and defense.

Foreign and Security Policy Reform:
The Amsterdam Treaty

Planning for the 1996–1997 intergovernmental conference on treaty reform took place in the shadow of the Yugoslav debacle. Painfully aware of the weakness of the CFSP, member states now had an opportunity to make procedural and institutional changes. As the preparatory work for the conference showed, however, the precise nature of those reforms was highly contested. The lessons of Yugoslavia were not sufficient to weaken the ramparts of national sovereignty in the foreign policy field, nor did member states interpret them uniformly. Accordingly, at the outset of the conference there was consensus among national governments only on what the CFSP-related negotiations should cover: instruments; decisionmaking, representation, planning and analysis, the budget, and the ever-present issue of EU-WEU relations. The ensuing reforms were far from ideal, but nonetheless strengthened the CFSP appreciably.

Instruments. In an effort to clarify and improve the means available to make a success of the CFSP, the Amsterdam Treaty identified four policy instruments:

- *Principles and guidelines* (adopted by the European Council) to provide general political direction.
- *Common strategies* (adopted by the European Council) to provide an umbrella under which the Council could adopt joint actions and common positions by qualified majority voting (except those with military and defense implications). Common strategies would set out "the objectives, duration, and the means to be made available by the Union and the Member States" in areas of mutual interest.
- *Joint actions* (adopted by the Council) were refined to address specific situations requiring "operational action," including a revised list of their possible contents. The Council could request that the Commission submit proposals to ensure the proper implementation of joint actions.
- *Common positions* (adopted by the Council) were also refined to "define the approach of the Union to a particular matter of a geographical or thematic nature."

In effect, joint actions and common positions became tools to implement common strategies, which the architects of the Amsterdam Treaty envisioned as the key CFSP device.

Decisionmaking. As in the past, the clarity and effectiveness of these instruments would depend on the quality and capacity of the decisionmaking process. Also as in the past, few member states were willing to give up unanimity in all areas of the CFSP. Nevertheless, there was widespread acknowledgment during the conference of the need to provide greater scope for qualified majority voting and to allow a majority of member states to act on sensitive international issues even if a minority did not want to participate in such action. As a result, the treaty incorporated two new decisionmaking formulas:

- *Constructive abstention:* As long as they did not constitute more than one-third of weighted votes in the Council, member states could abstain from a decision taken unanimously by the other member states.
- *Emergency brake:* Where decisions could be taken by qualified majority voting, such as the adoption of joint actions, a member state could declare "for important and stated reasons of national policy" its opposition to a vote being taken on such a decision. In that case, the Council could decide, by qualified majority vote, to refer the matter to the European Council, which could in turn decide the matter unanimously. The presumption seemed to be that a reluctant member state would succumb to peer pressure in the European Council and go along with the otherwise contested decision. In reality, if a member state felt strongly enough about an issue to pull the emergency brake in the first place, other member states would be unlikely to vote the matter up to the European Council. Even if they did, the European Council would hardly be able to reach a unanimous decision.

These reformed decisionmaking procedures were more complicated than the original ones without necessarily being an improvement on them. Not only was the emergency brake a throwback to the Luxembourg Compromise but also the codification of abstentionism and the introduction of various restrictions and qualifications seemed likely to reduce rather than enhance the effectiveness of the CFSP. The emergence of such an outcome reflected strong national sensitivities about foreign and security policy cooperation in the EU.

Representation. As a solution to the problem of external representation, especially the problem of the rotating presidency, member states agreed to the establishment of the position of high representative for the CFSP, who would also be head of the Council secretariat. The treaty called on the high representative to "contribute" to the formulation and implementation of policy and to "assist" the work of the Council, all the while acting at the "request" of the Council presidency. These weak verbs suggested that the high representative would be no more and no less than a particular presidency wanted him or her to be and that the presidency would remain central to CFSP representation and to other aspects of the CFSP's operation. Indeed, the high representative formed part of a new troika, along with the Council presidency and the Commission, to represent the EU in dealings with nonmember states.

Planning and Analysis. Lack of planning and analysis was generally seen as one of the main weaknesses of the CFSP. Accordingly, a declaration attached to the Amsterdam Treaty established the Policy Planning and Early Warning Unit in the Council secretariat, under the authority of the high representative. The success of the policy unit (as it soon came to be called) would depend on the seniority and ability of the officials appointed to it from the Commission, the WEU, the member states, and the Council secretariat itself. Member states were obliged to provide the unit with all relevant information, even of a confidential nature, and the presidency could authorize the unit to present policy papers for the Council's deliberation. As in the case of CFSP representation, therefore, the effectiveness of the unit would depend in part on the presidency's interests and orientations.

Budget. Under the Maastricht Treaty, member states could charge CFSP operations either to their own budgets or to the EU's budget. Not surprisingly, member states preferred to draw on the EU budget but were unwilling to pay the political price of scrutiny of CFSP operational expenses by the European Parliament. For the Parliament, effectively shut out of the EU's intergovernmental pillars, such scrutiny provided a way to exert some influence over CFSP activities. Member states resolved the issue in the Amsterdam Treaty by agreeing that most CFSP operational expenditures were to be charged to the EU budget (the major exceptions were those with military implications), thereby acknowledging a role for the Parliament. This treaty reform complemented an interinstitutional agreement on CFSP funding negotiated among the Council, Commission, and Parliament while the intergovernmental conference was still in progress.

What to Do with the WEU? Collaboration between the EU and WEU, as envisioned in the Maastricht Treaty, proceeded slowly and unspectacularly in the mid-1990s. In 1993 the WEU moved its headquarters from London to Brussels in order to be close to NATO and EU headquarters. The WEU established a closer working relationship with NATO than with the EU, where it was rarely represented at relevant meetings of the Council of Ministers. Nor, with the exception of the Mostar operation, did the EU call upon the WEU for assistance. Instead the WEU occasionally assisted NATO, for instance in Operation Sharp Guard (to enforce sanctions against Serbia in the Adriatic).

Reflecting the nature of post–Cold War security challenges, in 1992 the WEU adopted the so-called Petersberg Declaration (named after the town outside Bonn where the declaration was adopted), which, among other things, included peacekeeping, humanitarian, and rescue missions in the organization's mandate. The WEU also established a planning cell to prepare troop deployments for Petersberg and other tasks and to act as an operation headquarters in the event of a crisis.

The asymmetry between EU and WEU membership became more marked in 1995 when three neutral states—Austria, Finland, and Sweden—joined the EU. The WEU responded to this and another asymmetry of the European security architecture, whereby not every European member of NATO was also a member of the WEU, by bringing everybody under the same roof through different kinds of affiliations, such as associate membership and observer status.

NATO's close collaboration with the WEU, together with general support for NATO's continued primacy in security affairs (after Bosnia not even die-hard Gaullists wanted a NATO-free Europe), took the edge off the old division between those member states with a more independent or a more Atlanticist preface for EU security policy. Just as ardent Europeanists came to terms with NATO's post–Cold War role, the United States swung in the early 1990s from concern about the emergence of a CFSP to genuine support for a European security and defense identity. Indeed, in January 1994 NATO (and therefore the United States) endorsed the establishment of Combined Joint Task Forces with NATO capabilities available to the organization's European members for operations outside the NATO area in which the United States chose not to participate.

Defense-related negotiations at the 1996–1997 intergovernmental conference centered once again on whether to merge the EU and the WEU. This time the implications for transatlantic relations were not as serious as during the 1991 conference, when the United States had launched a diplomatic offensive to prevent an EU-WEU merger from taking place. By 1996 there was still a discernible difference between Atlanticists and Europeanists (those who wanted to keep the EU and WEU apart and those who wanted to bring them together), but the political ramifications of their positions were less profound for NATO's future.

The presence of the three new neutral member states added a new factor to the equation. In order to give greater substance and effectiveness to the EU's security and defense identity and strengthen the European pillar of the Atlantic Alliance, a majority of member states wanted the EU and WEU to merge. Faced with strong opposition from Britain and Denmark, which opposed the militarization of the EU, and from the neutral countries, which remained opposed to participation in a military alliance, the member states agreed only to "the possibility of the integration of the WEU into the EU, should the European Council so decide."

The Amsterdam Treaty nevertheless included an important step with military implications: inclusion in the treaty of so-called Petersberg tasks in the EU (with the full support of the neutral member states), therefore raising the possibility of future EU peacekeeping operations. The NATO summit in Madrid in July 1997, held only a month after the EU summit in Amsterdam, where the intergovernmental conference came to an end, not only took a key decision about NATO enlargement (the admission of the Czech Republic, Hungary, and Poland) but also blessed the EU's efforts to develop a security and defense identity.

Foreign and Security Policy After Amsterdam

In June 1999, shortly after the Amsterdam Treaty came into effect, EU leaders selected Javier Solana to be the first high representative for the CFSP (he took up the position in October 1999). It was an inspired choice. As secretary-general of NATO, Solana knew and was trusted by U.S. military and foreign policy leaders; as a former foreign minister of Spain, he had considerable diplomatic experience. Perhaps more than any other factor, Solana's dynamism, judgment, and skill account for the acceleration of foreign and defense policy cooperation in the EU since the late 1990s. Solana was adept at working with successive presidencies and with the commissioner for external relations, a potential institutional rival (Solana had excellent relations with Chris Patten, who held the job from November 1999 until November 2004, and Benita Ferrero-Waldner, who succeeded Patten). Within a short time, Solana personified the EU's emerging security and defense policy. In that sense he truly became "Mr. CFSP."

The EU adopted its first two common strategies under the CFSP in 1999 (on Russia and Ukraine). It also adopted twelve joint actions and twenty-two common positions. Nine of the joint actions and five of the common positions were on the Western Balkans, reflecting the EU's overriding interest in the region. Thereafter the EU adopted few common strategies, which never became an important CFSP instrument (both Solana and Patten complained that common strategies were too general to be effective). The EU adopts about fifteen joint actions and twenty common positions every year, on a range of regional and thematic issues, and produces scores of declarations and statements annually. Examples of CFSP activities include the dispatch of election monitors all over the world, visits by the troika to international trouble spots, and mediation by Solana in a number of disputes in the "wider Europe," notably in Macedonia in 2003 and Ukraine in 2004. The Council occasionally appoints special representatives to spearhead EU involvement in particular issues or regions, such as the Middle East peace process or the Great Lakes region in Africa. The EU also regularly imposes sanctions such as arms embargoes, trade restrictions, or visa and travel bans under the auspices of the CFSP. The most striking CFSP development since the late 1990s, however, has been in the area of defense policy and military capability.

The European Security and Defense Policy. In December 1998, at an Anglo-French summit in St. Malo, Prime Minister Tony Blair proposed developing an EU military capability. This was music to Chirac's ears, given that the

French had always wanted that to happen. Blair's initiative was a way to demonstrate the prime minister's pro-EU credentials, especially as Britain would not be participating in the common monetary policy, then the most important item on the EU's agenda. More to the point, Blair appreciated the importance for the EU of being able to tackle "future Bosnias." Although U.S. diplomats expressed surprise at Blair's new approach, the prime minister would not have done anything to impair his relations with Washington. Nor, in view of the outcome of the NATO summit the previous year, did Blair's proposal seem in any way antithetical to U.S. interests.[25]

The necessity of tackling future Bosnias became only too apparent in early 1999, when Serbian president Slobodan Milošević got up to his old tricks, this time in Kosovo. The EU did not yet have the military means to act against him but seemed finally to have the political will to do so. Having watched Milošević start one Balkan war after another, and having been lied to repeatedly by him, EU leaders had little doubt about the need to stop the Serbian leader from causing yet another humanitarian disaster. In NATO's name, the United States conducted an eleven-week air war against Serbian forces in Kosovo and military and government targets in Serbia itself. Once again the EU was sidelined. Milošević's capitulation and ouster soon afterward removed the immediate possibility of another Balkan conflict. Nevertheless, the Kosovo crisis and NATO campaign strengthened Blair, Chirac, and other EU leaders in their determination to develop an EU military capability. The sophistication and power of the U.S. military operation also showed how far the EU would have to go before having an effective joint force.

Only the European Council had the political authority to take the decisions necessary to establish within the CFSP what came to be called the Common European Security and Defense Policy (known as the European Security and Defense Policy, or ESDP). Meeting in Cologne in June 1999, the European Council declared that in order to be able to carry out the so-called Petersberg tasks (conflict prevention and crisis management), the EU "must have the capacity for autonomous action, backed up by credible military forces [and] the means to decide to use them, and a readiness to do so." Meeting in Helsinki six months later, the European Council set a "headline goal" for the ESDP: by 2003 member states should be able "to deploy in full [up to 60,000 troops] within 60 days . . . [and] sustain such a deployment for at least one year. . . . These forces should be militarily self-sustaining with the necessary command, control and intelligence capabilities, logistics, other combat support services, and additionally, as appropriate, air and naval elements."[26]

The European Council called on the Council of Ministers to establish by March 2000 a number of interim committees and bodies to get the ESDP up and running. These included

- the *Political and Security Committee* (replacing the existing Political Committee), consisting of senior national representatives, to prepare meetings of foreign and defense ministers on CFSP and ESDP issues
- the *Military Committee,* consisting of senior military officers, to advise and make recommendations to the Political and Security Committee on military matters and to direct the Military Staff
- the *Military Staff,* national military officials based in the secretariat of the Council of Ministers, to provide military expertise and support especially for the conduct of EU-led military crisis management operations

Building on the momentum generated principally by Britain and France, progress on the ESDP continued apace in 2000, especially under the French presidency of the Council in the second half of the year. Member states held a Capabilities Commitment Conference in Brussels in November at which they pledged forces to meet the Helsinki headline goal. A French presidency paper, presented to the European Council in Nice in December 2000, addressed some of the remaining political challenges confronting the ESDP, notably the precise operational relationship between the EU and NATO (covering EU access to NATO assets and permanent consultation arrangements) and the role of Turkey (a large NATO European country being kept at arm's length by the EU). As part of the package of treaty reforms agreed to in Nice, EU leaders decided to make permanent the CFSP/ESDP interim committees that were already operational and, in effect, to incorporate the WEU into the EU.

Member states strove in 2001 to develop the civilian component of international crisis management. This became a priority of the Swedish presidency in the first half of the year. Accordingly, at the Göteborg summit in June 2001, the European Council agreed that the EU should make the following resources available for civilian crisis management: a police force of up to 5,000 officers, including 1,000 deployable within thirty days; a team of judges, prosecutors, and other legal experts; a group of civilian administrators; and rapid-response teams to assess emergency situations. EU leaders established a civilian crisis management committee to oversee the development and possible deployment of these resources.

The Impact of September 11. The terrorist attacks in the United States of September 11, 2001, gave a tremendous boost to the CFSP and the ESDP. Europe had long been wracked by terrorism, but of the homegrown variety. European governments realized that the September 2001 attacks typified a new kind of global security challenge to which they were not immune. The EU immediately issued a declaration under the CFSP condemning the attacks and held an extraordinary meeting of the European Council on September 21 to express solidarity with the United States. The EU troika undertook several visits at ministerial level to countries in Central Asia and the Middle East, firming up support for the fight against terrorism. According to an authoritative commentary on the EU's response to September 11, "There can be little doubt that the UN-backed agreement on political transition in Afghanistan signed in Bonn [in December 2001] would not have been possible in its final form without EU efforts in the CFSP context."[27]

Militarily, by contrast, the EU was sidelined in the aftermath of September 11. The most significant collective European response came from NATO, not the EU, which in any case was still underequipped to play a military role. Not that the United States wanted or needed military assistance for the campaign against the Taliban in Afghanistan, which ended swiftly in November 2001. Like the Americans, however, the Europeans appreciated that the war against international terrorism would be a protracted affair. The attacks of September 2001 therefore gave added impetus to the ongoing effort to operationalize the ESDP.

Two developments ensuing directly from the events of September 11 were both helpful and potentially harmful to the emergence of the ESDP. The helpful development was Germany's willingness finally to act militarily as a leading European power. Germany was constrained in that regard not only by history but also by politics: the governing coalition of Chancellor Gerhard Schröder included the pacifist Green Party. In view of recent events in the Balkans and the terrorist attacks in the United States, only the most extreme pacifists could argue that military action was never justifiable or warranted. Germany may still have lacked the means to undertake major military operations around the world, but it no longer lacked the will to do so.

The potentially harmful development with respect to the ESDP was exposure of the rift within the EU between big and small member states, or more specifically between the "big three" (Britain, France, and Germany) and the rest, that lurked beneath the surface of security and defense cooperation. Traditionally, the smaller member states have brooded about the propensity of the big member states to dominate cooperation on security and defense policy. Their fears seemed justified in October 2001 when Blair, Chirac, and Schröder held informal talks on Afghanistan on the margins of a European Council meeting. The Belgian presidency and the Commission were particularly perturbed by this and by an invitation that Blair extended to Chirac and Schröder to continue their discussions some days later at a dinner in Downing Street, the prime minister's residence in London. The Belgians, Dutch, Italians, and Spanish kicked up such a fuss that Blair eventually invited them as well, along with Solana.

Though amusing, the diplomatic row over who was coming to dinner demonstrated the other member states' suspicion of the intentions of the big three. Far from undermining the ESDP, however, the incident may have helped each side to see the other's point of view. The majority of member states concluded that they had probably overreacted. After all, Britain, France, and Germany have considerable international political clout and the preponderance of military force in the EU. They did not propose acting alone, without regard to the other member states. Indeed, by clearing the air about the intentions of the big three, the incident may have helped pave the way for the diplomatic effort undertaken by Britain, France, and Germany on behalf of the EU two years later to mediate the dispute with Iran over that country's nuclear capability.

Despite the tiff between the big three and the other member states at the end of 2001, the ESDP continued to thrive. The Political and Security Committee began to hold regular meetings with the North Atlantic Council (the political arm of NATO), and the EU and NATO military committees began to cooperate closely. A Capabilities Improvement Conference took place in November 2001 to try to rectify the deficiencies in the EU's "Force Catalogue." The meeting of the European Council in Laeken, Belgium, later in December represented another milestone in the organization of the ESDP, although a Belgian presidency announcement that the Rapid Reaction Force was operational proved premature. The EU took over most of the functions and bodies of the WEU in 2002, including the Satellite Center and the old WEU think tank, located in Paris, which became an autonomous EU agency under the CFSP. The renamed European Union Institute for Security Studies promotes research and debate on ESDP-related issues and acts as a forward studies unit for the CFSP high representative. EU defense ministers also began to meet regularly in 2002 on the margins of the General Affairs Council.

By the time that the Convention on the Future of Europe opened in February 2002, the CFSP and ESDP were high on the EU's agenda. The Convention and the ensuing intergovernmental conference presented a good opportunity to make further progress in these fields. There was little surprise or objection when France and Germany submitted a proposal to the Convention at the end of 2002 to merge the positions of the high representative for the CFSP and the commissioner for external relations in a new position, that of EU foreign minister. The Convention endorsed the idea, and the intergovernmental conference wrote it into the Constitutional Treaty. The EU foreign minister would chair the proposed External Relations Council while also being vice president of the Commission with responsibility for external relations. This would be a considerable institutional improvement for the CFSP.

The Impact of Iraq. Between the launch of the Convention on the Future of Europe in early 2002 and the end of the intergovernmental conference in mid-2004, the situation in Iraq dominated international affairs and convulsed the EU. Influential elements within the U.S. administration appear to have decided soon after the terrorist attacks of September 2001 to depose Saddam

Hussein. Their intentions became clear in the latter part of 2002. Thereafter, a U.S. invasion of Iraq seemed only a matter of time. Blair backed the United States unreservedly; Chirac and Schröder, who exploited the issue for electoral gain in September 2002, opposed it wholeheartedly. That situation set the stage for a bitter altercation among member (and soon-to-be-member) states that appeared to destroy recent progress on security and defense policy cooperation.

The extent of the disarray within the EU was plain for all to see when the leaders of five member states (Britain, Denmark, Italy, Portugal, and Spain) and three candidate countries (the Czech Republic, Hungary, and Poland) signed an open letter at the end of January 2003 expressing strong support for the United States. Chirac and Schröder were furious; Solana was embarrassed (he heard about the letter while listening to the radio). The following week, ten other Central and Eastern European countries (the other candidates plus Albania, Croatia, and Macedonia) issued a similar declaration of support for the United States, further infuriating Chirac and Schröder, who at least enjoyed the support of Belgium and Luxembourg.

Although a majority of governments may have supported the United States in the run-up to the war, a majority of Europeans seemed resolutely opposed to the venture. Massive public protests in London and Madrid in mid-February showed that Blair and José Maria Aznar, the Spanish prime minister, did not represent popular opinion in their views on the war. The divisions over Iraq were therefore deeply personal, with EU leaders holding entrenched positions for or against the imminent invasion.

Having a small country like Greece in the presidency in early 2003, when the war eventually took place, epitomized one of the representational and organizational problems of the CFSP. Under the circumstances, however, it was better to have had a small country in the presidency rather than one of the big member states, each of which had taken a rigid position for or against the war. Greece also opposed the war but made a valiant attempt to maintain EU unity on the issue, even going so far as to convene a special meeting of the European Council in mid-February 2003, as war appeared imminent. The European Council managed to produce an anodyne statement condemning Saddam Hussein and hoping for a peaceful resolution to the conflict.

Chirac soon shattered any pretense of EU unity when, at a press conference after the summit, he castigated the Central and Eastern European countries for daring to take a position on Iraq contrary to his own. "Frankly, I believe that they behaved childishly," Chirac thundered, "as membership in the EU involves a measure of consideration for others, a degree of consultation . . . with the Union one proposes to enter. . . . Without beating about the bush, these countries have been badly brought up."[28] Chirac's outburst was somewhat ironic because he presumed to speak on behalf of the EU without bothering to consult the other member states or the candidate countries. Clearly, Chirac was worried about the prospect of enlargement as well as frustrated by the refusal of other member states and the candidate countries to follow his lead. Leaders of the candidate countries, who met the following day with the leaders of the EU troika, signed up to the European Council's position on Iraq but made no secret of their exasperation with Chirac.

The Panglossian statements of Commission president Romano Prodi could not disguise the extent of the EU's disarray. After the special summit in mid-February, for example, Prodi declared that the EU now had "a message [to send] to the world: Europe is united and its voice must be heard."[29] Solana was more realistic, observing that "the EU still does not have a genuine common external policy, it has several. One day there is an agreement and the next day this is torn to shreds."[30]

The low point for the EU came in April 2003, about a month after the U.S. invasion of Iraq, when Belgium, France, Germany, and Luxembourg held a summit to press ahead with their own plans for defense cooperation and announced afterward that they intended to establish a military headquarters in the Brussels suburb of Tervuren. It was as if the ESDP, put together so painstakingly over the previous five years, did not exist. Within a short time, however, the four countries realized that they had overreacted. A European military initiative without Britain, Europe's leading military power, simply did not make sense. For better or for worse, the EU would have to act together in the defense realm.

Despite having generated considerable bitterness among EU leaders, the crisis over Iraq did not derail the ESDP. Blair and Chirac even managed to overcome their differences at a bilateral summit in February 2003, in the run-up to the war, in order to emphasize the importance of the ESDP and to commit more resources to it. The two leaders looked forward to the EU's first military operation the following month (taking over from NATO in Macedonia), and to operations as well in Bosnia and possibly in Africa later in the year. The relevant ESDP committees continued to plan these military missions regardless of the very visible rows among EU leaders over Iraq. Indeed, "Iraq . . . proved to be something of a cathartic experience for the Union as far as ESDP was concerned. Far from undermining it, the crisis effectively served to kick-start [it by] breaking the log-jam created by underlying tensions and discord over the nature of incipient EU defense policies."[31]

Evidence that Iraq did not mean the end of the ESDP was readily apparent. For example, the EU began a police mission in Bosnia in January that year. Greek and Turkish nitpicking, which had prevented an agreement from being reached until December 2002 between the EU and NATO on the so-called Berlin-Plus arrangements for EU access to NATO assets, delayed the start of the EU military operation in Macedonia until the end of March 2003. This became an EU police mission in December. In June 2003 the EU deployed a French-led peacekeeping mission, authorized by the UN Security Council, for three months to Bunia in the Democratic Republic of Congo. This was the first EU military mission undertaken without recourse to NATO, and the first mission outside Europe. In December 2003, the European Council announced that the EU would consider fielding an EU military mission in Bosnia to replace the NATO Stabilization Force there. The EU eventually took over in November 2004, launching its biggest military operation to date, with over 7,000 troops. All of these operations took place despite highly visible sniping among national political leaders over the war in Iraq and its aftermath.

One of the most striking examples of the development of the ESDP after the war in Iraq was the presentation by Javier Solana of a European Security Strategy to EU leaders in June 2003. He called for an assertive EU foreign and security policy, including the possible use of military force, and identified three key threats to European security: terrorism, the proliferation of weapons of mass destruction, and failed states. In contrast to the position of the United States, the EU security strategy, which EU leaders endorsed in December 2003, identified the UN Charter as the "fundamental framework" for international relations. Strengthening the charter was an EU priority.

Relations among the EU's member states may have survived the fallout from Iraq, but relations between the EU and the United States suffered greater damage. After the war, Tony Blair became increasingly isolated within the EU, within Britain, and within the ruling Labour Party for his unconditional support of the United States. Although Britain continued to support the ESDP, the United States came to view it as a French invention, or at least as a policy inspired by French anti-Americanism and anti-NATO sentiment. France had always wanted to develop a European military capability independent of NATO and the United States. It was hard for France not to gloat over U.S. difficulties in postwar Iraq or not to hint that the ESDP was, in fact, contrary to American interests.

Distrust between the United States and France did not stand in the way of an agreement being reached in December 2003 on the establishment of an EU planning capability within NATO's military headquarters outside Brussels. The French had initially wanted a full-fledged EU military headquarters, but having overplayed their hand when they held a summit with Belgium, Germany, and Luxembourg in April 2003 to develop a completely autonomous European defense force, they accepted the compromise pushed by Britain and acceptable to the United States.

A Stronger CFSP and ESDP

The CFSP and the ESDP have come a long way in a short time. Considering the member states' traditional reluctance to cooperate on security and defense policy in the framework of European integration, progress has been remarkable. Yet considering also the combined military potential of the member states, the EU's military capability seems underwhelming. The objective of the ESDP was never to establish a European army, however, but to make an EU force available on a relatively limited scale for crisis management in international hot spots. The EU's military capability is modest but increasingly effective. Thus, in November 2004 defense ministers pledged up to 165,000 troops to make up a series of EU "battle groups," each consisting of about 1,500 troops from one or more member states, deployable within ten days to help quell or contain international conflicts.

European publics generally applaud the idea of military intervention beyond the EU's borders, under UN auspices, to combat clear-cut cases of aggression. Nevertheless, the same publics are generally unenthusiastic about spending more money on defense. Command and control, intelligence, strategic transport, training, logistics, and weapons are extremely expensive prerequisites for successful military intervention. Member states could save a lot of money by eradicating duplication among national forces. Yet precisely because each member state has its own forces, such duplication is inevitable and unavoidable. The EU is not a state; therefore, it does not have (or aspire to have) statelike military forces. The EU is not even a mutual defense organization (neutral member states are unwilling to make a collective defense commitment, leaving that responsibility to what remains of the WEU and, of course, to NATO).

■ Notes

1. Chris Patten, "The Western Balkans: The Road to Europe," speech to European Affairs Committee of the Bundestag, Berlin, April 28, 2004, http://www.ear.eu.int/agency/main/agency-a1a2g3.htm.

2. On Schengen generally, see Monica den Boer, ed., *Schengen: Judicial Cooperation and Policy Coordination* (Maastricht, the Netherlands: EIPA, 1997).

3. Copenhagen European Council, "Presidency Conclusions," Bulletin EC 6-1993, point 1.4.

4. John Adrian Fortescue, "First Experiences with the Implementation of the Third Pillar," in R. Bieber and J. Monar, eds., *Justice and Home Affairs in the European Union* (Brussels: European Interuniversity Press, 1995), p. 23.

5. Florence European Council, "Presidency Conclusions," Bulletin EC 6-1996, point 1.6.

6. The Reflection Group Report is published in European Parliament, *White Paper on the 1996 IGC*, vol. 1: *Official Texts of the EU Institutions* (Luxembourg: European Parliament, 1996), pp. 149–212.

7. See *European Report*, January 15, 2003, p. IV.8.

8. On the development of asylum and immigration policy in the EU, see Mohamed Elewa Badar, "Asylum Seekers and the European Union: Past, Present and Future," *International Journal of Human Rights* 8, no. 2 (Summer 2004): 159–176; Rosemary Byrne, Gregor Noll, and Jens Vedsted-Hansen, eds., *New Asylum Countries? Migration Control and Refugee Protection in an Enlarged European Union* (The

Hague: Kluwer Law International, 2002); R. Byrne, G. Noll, and J. Vedsted-Hansen, "Understanding Refugee Law in an Enlarged European Union," *European Journal of International Law* 15, no. 2 (April 2004): 355–380; Stephen Gallagher, "Towards a Common European Asylum System: Fortress Europe Redesigns the Ramparts," *International Journal* 57, no. 3 (Summer 2002): 375–394; Virginie Guiraudon, "Immigration and Asylum: A High Politics Agenda," in Maria Green Cowles and Desmond Dinan, eds., *Developments in the European Union 3* (Basingstoke, UK: Palgrave Macmillan, 2004), pp. 160–180; T. J. Hatton, "Seeking Asylum in Europe," *Economic Policy* 19, no. 38 (April 2004): 5–63; J. Huysmans, "The European Union and the Securitization of Migration," *Journal of Common Market Studies* 38, no. 5 (December 2000): 751–778; S. Lavenex, "The Europeanization of Refugee Policies: Normative Challenges and Institutional Legacies," *Journal of Common Market Studies* 39, no. 5 (December 2001): 851–875.

9. On the development of police and judicial cooperation in criminal matters, see John Occhipinti, *The Politics of EU Police Cooperation: Toward a European FBI?* (Boulder, CO: Lynne Rienner, 2003); and M. Jimeno-Bulnes, "European Judicial Cooperation in Criminal Matters," *International Journal of Human Rights* 8, no. 2 (Summer 2004): 159–176.

10. On the impact of the events of September 2001 on justice and home affairs, see Monica den Boer and Jurg Monar, "Keynote Article: 11 September and the Challenge of Global Terrorism to the EU as a Security Actor," *Journal of Common Market Studies, Annual Review of the EU 2001/2002* 40: 11–28; and Jorg Monar, "The EU as an International Actor in the Domain of Justice and Home Affairs," *European Foreign Affairs Review* 9, no. 3 (Autumn 2004): 395–416.

11. See Susie Alegre and Marisa Leaf, "Mutual Recognition in European Judicial Cooperation: A Step Too Far Too Soon? Case Study—The European Arrest Warrant," *European Law Journal* 10, no. 2 (March 2004): 200–218.

12. See David Allen and Alfred Pijpers, *European Foreign Policy-Making and the Arab-Israeli Conflict* (The Hague: Martinus Nijhoff, 1984).

13. "Draft European Act," Bulletin EC 11-1981, point 3.4.1. For an academic appraisal of Genscher-Colombo, see Joseph Weiler, "The Genscher-Colombo Draft European Act: The Politics of Indecision," *Journal of European Integration* 4, nos. 2 and 3 (1983): 129–153.

14. Bulletin EC 6-1983, point 1.6.1.

15. On the development of the CFSP and, later, the ESDP, see Roy Ginsberg, *The European Union in International Politics: Baptism by Fire* (Lanham, MD: Rowman and Littlefield, 2001); Jolyon Howorth and John T. S. Keeler, *Defending Europe: The EU, NATO and the Quest for European Autonomy* (Basingstoke, UK: Palgrave Macmillan, 2003); Simon J. Nuttall, *European Foreign Policy* (Oxford: Oxford University Press, 2000); Martin Holland, *Common Foreign and Security Policy: The Record and Reforms* (London: Pinter, 1997); Elfride Regelsberger, Philippe de Schoutheete, and Wolfgang Wessels, eds., *Foreign Policy of the European Union: From EPC to CFSP and Beyond* (Boulder, CO: Lynne Rienner, 1997); Karen E. Smith, *The Making of European Union Foreign Policy* (New York: St. Martin's Press, 1998); and Karen E. Smith, *European Foreign Policy in a Changing World* (Cambridge, UK: Polity Press, 2003).

16. See Pia Christina Wood, "EPC: Lessons from the Gulf War and Yugoslavia," in Alan Cafruny and Glenda Rosenthal, eds., *The State of the European Community: The Maastricht Debates and Beyond* (Boulder, CO: Lynne Rienner, 1993), pp. 227–244.

17. Lisbon European Council, "Presidency Conclusions," Bulletin EC 6-1992, point 1.2.4.

18. Interview in the *International Herald Tribune*, July 1, 1992, p. 2.

19. Embassy of Greece, *News from Greece,* 16/92, November 10, 1992, p. 1.

20. EPC press release P129/91, December 16, 1991.

21. Roy Ginsberg, "The EU's Common Foreign and Security Policy: An Outsider's Retrospective on the First Year," *ECSA Review* (Fall 1994): 14.

22. For an insider's account of the EC's failure in Yugoslavia, see Henry Wynaents, *L'Engrenage* (Paris: Denoel, 1993). Wynaents was a senior Dutch diplomat involved in the EC's peace efforts.

23. Reinhardt Rummel, ed., *Toward Political Union: Planning a Common Foreign and Security Policy in the European Community* (Boulder, CO: Westview Press, 1992), p. 298.

24. Quoted in *Financial Times*, July 1, 1991, p. 1.

25. On the St. Malo initiative and its consequences, see John Roper, "Keynote Article: Two Cheers for Mr. Blair? The Political Realities of European Defence Cooperation," *Journal of Common Market Studies, Annual Review of the EU 1999/2000* 38: 7–24.

26. Cologne European Council, "Presidency Conclusions," June 1999, Bulletin EC 6-1999; Helsinki European Council, "Presidency Conclusions," Bulletin EC 12-1999.

27. Den Boer and Monar, "11 September and the Challenge of Global Terrorism," p. 15.

28. Quoted in *European Report,* February 19, 2003, p. V.15.

29. Quoted in ibid., p. V.14.

30. Quoted in *European Report,* February 26, 2003, p. V.12.

31. Anand Menon, "From Crisis to Catharsis: ESDP After Iraq," *International Affairs* 80, no. 4 (2004): 631–649.

18

U.S.-EU Relations

It is easy to forget in the current climate of transatlantic relations that, throughout the latter part of the twentieth century, the United States consistently (and genuinely) supported European integration largely for strategic reasons. It saw the European Community as an essential element of the post–World War II peace settlement and as an important contributor to the security of Western Europe during the Cold War. Thereafter it saw the European Union as indispensable for the security and stability of post–Cold War Europe. Throughout that time, the United States and the EU developed the world's largest and deepest economic relationship.

In many respects the relationship remains healthy and stable. By contrast with the structural problems inherent in EU (and U.S.) relations with Asia, the U.S.-EU trade balance reliably reflects growth rates and macroeconomic developments on both sides of the Atlantic. Yet friction between the world's two largest trading blocs often obscures the underlying soundness of transatlantic economic relations. Persistent trade disputes, spillover from domestic controversies, and rivalry on the world economic stage have dogged the economic dialogue between the United States and the EU.

Despite U.S. support for it, the process of European integration inevitably contained the seeds of transatlantic political discord. Not surprisingly, mutual frustration and occasional unproductive rivalry have marked political relations between the United States and the EU. Deep cultural, philosophical, and foreign policy differences between Europe and the United States have become acute under the administrations of President George W. Bush. Many Europeans deplored the resurgence of the religious right in the United States, the profound conservatism of much of American society, and the administration's apparent international adventurism and disdain for old allies and partners. Of course many Americans were equally shocked by those developments. It is therefore difficult to gauge whether recent political changes in the United States are transient or permanent. Even if the United States were to swing

609

back toward a more moderate position, strains in the relationship would most likely endure.

The United States is (and will remain for the foreseeable future) the world's sole superpower. As a result, American leaders, regardless of their political persuasion, are bound to view the world differently from their European counterparts, especially since the terrorist attacks of September 2001. The United States appreciates the EU's economic importance and weight but recognizes that the EU has only a limited foreign policy capacity. The United States wishes the EU well but has little patience for the procedural complexity of European integration, which even to many Europeans seems to have become an end in itself. Especially in view of the urgent challenges that it faces around the world, the United States unashamedly judges the EU by its actions, not its rhetoric.

For its part, the EU is frustrated by its own relative impotence and resents not being taken as seriously by Washington as it takes itself (and is taken by others). Apart from having a legitimate complaint about America's international behavior, the EU tends to overreact to perceived (or real) American slights. Rampant anti-Americanism in Europe, although corrosive for the transatlantic relationship, is a powerful force in EU identity building. It is often easier for Europeans to articulate what they *are not* than what they *are*. Thus, they are not moralistic, self-righteous, uncaring capitalists who devour the world's scarce resources and act unilaterally in their own selfish interests. In other words, according to this widespread caricature, they are not Americans.

Yet Europe and the United States are bound together by more than commercial ties. For all the undoubted difficulties between them, they share fundamental political values, now under threat from Islamic fundamentalism. Europe and the United States have a common interest in bolstering democracy and stability in a deeply troubled world. Their global economic outlook is similarly aligned, even to the point of protecting their own agricultural interests at the risk of jeopardizing a new international trade agreement. Indeed, the current state of transatlantic relations disguises a great degree of quiet cooperation between the EU and the United States on a range of issues of bilateral and global interest.

■ Underlying Difficulties

Well before the recent deterioration in U.S.-EU relations, it was popular in Europe to ascribe sour notes in the transatlantic relationship to American resentment of the emergence of a strong and united Europe and to the resulting decline in U.S. influence on the continent. The truth is more complicated. The uneasy relationship between the United States and the EU is a result of a number of inherent asymmetries in their structure and outlook. Whereas the

United States and the EU undoubtedly have far more in common with each other than with any other world region, the devil, as always, is in the details.

From the U.S. perspective, the initial difficulties lay in the incremental, often untidy nature of European integration, which caused constant changes in the scope of the EU's agenda and in the character of its policy-formulating process. By contrast, bilateral, country-to-country relations were easier to comprehend and manage: both sides had a well-understood governmental structure and a readily identifiable set of issues. But in the case of the EU as it evolved over the years, who exactly had decisionmaking power, and where precisely was the boundary between Community and member state competence?

Understandably, the tenuous connection between the trade and commercial policies conducted by the EU and the geopolitical concerns of its member states made it difficult for the United States, a traditional nation-state, to achieve the normal trade-offs between political and economic goals. Despite early U.S. support for European integration, the frustrations of dealing with this unnatural compartmentalization of political and economic policy soured many U.S. policymakers on the EC and its institutional machinery. Increasing pressure on world agricultural markets as a result of subsidized exports from the EU and the steady erosion of U.S. agricultural exports to EU member states exacerbated the problems. Typically, disputes over European restrictions on agricultural imports—long the most visible element of the EU's international mandate—have been the biggest source of bilateral friction.

Other asymmetries have added to the difficulties of both sides in multilateral negotiations. The Commission's need to develop trade policy by negotiating with member states, a feature of the Common Commercial Policy, often results in lowest-common-denominator mandates that leave the Commission little room for maneuver in the multilateral sphere. By the same token, the U.S. administration's need to persuade Congress to accept the final package can leave an entire multilateral agreement in agonizing suspense for months or can lead to peculiar negotiating positions designed to placate a handful of powerful senators. Shifting boundaries between EU and member state competencies have led to conflicting signals in areas such as aviation policy.

Finally, although the United States and the EU dominate the world trading system, their international and regional priorities are different. The United States has formidable trading interests to protect around the Pacific Rim, and its troubled relationship with Japan was for a long time at the center of its trade policy. The EU, by contrast, is primarily a regional power: the bulk of its trade is with its neighbors, and its links with Asia, especially Japan and China, are substantially weaker than those of the United States. Furthermore, successive enlargements have steadily brought the EU's most important regional trading partners into the fold and sapped the EU's energy for broader external relations, notwithstanding the EU's claims to the contrary.

The growing role of the EU as a political actor has undoubtedly added desirable depth to the relationship at a time when the simple verities of the Cold War were replaced by messy and nearly unmanageable regional breakdowns. However, this role brought with it new difficulties generated by incompatible expectations and capabilities on each side. For U.S. policymakers, it was always easier to work with those European countries whose outlook and approach were similar to theirs and to rely on firm alliances with Britain, Germany, and others such as the Netherlands, ignoring opposition elsewhere in Europe. Although great-power groupings such as the G7/8 and the Contact Group continue to play a role in international management, the Common Foreign and Security Policy (CFSP) has made this traditional U.S. strategy harder to pursue.

Inevitably, in moments of crisis, the United States tends to go back to its old friends and bypass the EU decisionmaking structures so painstakingly developed. This tendency is exacerbated by the fact that EU political clout does not extend much beyond the power of the purse. EU aid disbursements to the Western Balkans and, beyond that, the wider Europe, for example, dwarf those of the United States, yet the big decisions, such as on military intervention in trouble spots, remain the province of the nation-states. Although U.S. development assistance has steadily declined in real terms during the postwar era, the United States remains the military power of last resort.

While a gross generalization, it also seems reasonable to observe that many Europeans are resentful of the United States because of its economic and military power and its cultural influence. EU officials are not entirely free of such prejudice, operating as they do with a vision of Europe that is always slightly ahead of reality. Many of them complain that Americans are only dimly aware of the EU. Certainly the great American public knows little about the EU, just as the great European public knows little about how the U.S. government works. However, academic study of the EU is as advanced in the United States as it is in Europe. As for U.S. officials and businesspeople, those who deal with the EU regularly know well how it works and what it does; the U.S. Mission to the EU and the EU Committee of the American Chamber of Commerce are among the most effective lobbyists in Brussels.

EU officials are especially irritated by what they see as the refusal of Americans who deal regularly with them to acknowledge the EU as a serious political actor. In their view, U.S. officials are either unwilling to see the EU as a political equal or unable to comprehend the complexities of the CFSP. Indeed, many U.S. officials are frustrated with the EU politically not because of the opacity of EU foreign policymaking but because more often than not, EU action fails to match EU rhetoric. Although Europeans may retort that Americans do not appreciate the difficulty of reaching a common EU position, Americans believe with some justification that the EU cannot expect to be taken seriously as a political entity as long as the results of its foreign policy coordination efforts are so meager. The problem is not that U.S. officials are unfamiliar with the intricacies of the CFSP but that they are only too well aware of its procedural and political weaknesses.

To some extent, these problems and resentments have been tempered (or at any rate muffled) by the growing mutual engagement that has resulted from the EU's increasing powers and mandate. Since the beginning of the 1990s, leaders on both sides have tried to speed this process by a series of ever more ambitious initiatives intended to increase U.S.-EU cooperation and engagement across the board and to raise the profile of the relationship. These have been only partly successful. Through innumerable high-level meetings and rising piles of communiqués, they have created an aura of dynamism and progress and have provided political cover for some quiet compromises on especially touchy issues. They have been less successful in resolving either the persistent irritants in the trade field or the fundamental differences in political priorities and social outlook that will continue to produce friction, especially in transatlantic trade, which is increasingly affected more by regulatory policy than by "traditional" protectionism.

The Development of U.S.-EU Relations

Despite early U.S. support for European unity, the development of European integration was bound to bring with it a degree of transatlantic discord. An economically strong EC caused a decline in U.S. market share within the EC itself and in some third countries. Since the early 1960s, the United States and the EU have been embroiled in disputes over alleged Europrotectionism and unfair EU practices in the international marketplace. Beginning with the so-called chicken and pasta wars, continuing with tit-for-tat restrictions on steel trade generated by domestic pressure to protect tottering industries, and culminating in a seemingly never-ending dispute over hormones in beef, the history of U.S.-EU relations has been replete with issue-specific disputes even as transatlantic trade and investment flourished.

Politically, an assertive EC might have challenged U.S. hegemony in Europe and the superpower's global preeminence. Certainly French president Charles de Gaulle saw such a challenge as the EC's main raison d'être. But the EC's member states never displayed a willingness, let alone ability, to form a political and military bloc that could rival the United States. During the Cold War, when Western Europe depended on U.S. military protection, it would have been foolhardy for Western European countries to risk antagonizing the United States by challenging its ascendancy in NATO (de Gaulle could afford to do so precisely because no other country would follow his lead). In the early 1970s EC member states launched a process of foreign policy cooperation; a decade later, during a resurgence of Cold War tension, some sought to extend that process into the security domain. But the frosty U.S. response, or some member states' anticipation of a frosty response, helped restrict foreign policy cooperation among the member states to the "political and economic aspects" of security.

Ultimately, the changes that swept across Europe in the wake of the Single European Act offered the chance to breathe new life into transatlantic relations. Initially, however, American reactions baffled and annoyed EC policymakers caught up in a vision of a Europe without borders. Businesspeople and some policymakers in the United States, their opinions of the EC shaped by the Common Agricultural Policy as well as by limitless European subsidies for "national champion" and "Eurochampion" industries such as Airbus, were unimpressed by the stated aims of the single market. They charged that the single market would bring about a "fortress Europe" in which the fruits of economic integration would be reserved for Europeans. Commission officials, perceiving themselves as the vanguard of a liberalizing force, were hurt and angry at this charge, which they unwittingly abetted at the outset through a crude effort to use market integration as a bargaining chip in the banking sector. This move raised such an outcry, supported by U.S. policymakers, among U.S. banks long established in Europe that the Commission was forced to rewrite much of its initial draft directive.

Despite their resentment of U.S. pressure, Commission officials were ultimately forced to address the international consequences of their internal decisions. As a practical matter, the structure of the single market program would have made it difficult to deny its benefits to foreign economic actors, but U.S. pressure made it necessary for the Commission to resist the temptation to try. Although rightly rejecting U.S. demands for "a seat at the table," the Commission agreed to beef up consultations with and develop greater institutional ties between U.S. and European standards-setting bodies and to develop mutual recognition agreements that would allow manufacturers to sell in both EC and foreign markets without the need for additional certification. Simultaneously, a second look at the internal market program itself persuaded many U.S. firms, especially those already established in Europe, that the single market presented more opportunity than threat. Ever eager to jump on the bandwagon, U.S. business became a cheerleader for European deregulation and elimination of internal barriers, and seminars on "1992" became a cottage industry for U.S. consulting firms.

At the same time, institutional developments in the EC as a result of the Single European Act complicated U.S.-EU relations politically and procedurally. These institutional developments, notably the increasing assertiveness and growing authority of the Commission and the emergence of the European Parliament as a potent political actor, were somewhat perturbing for the United States, where the name of the Commission itself evoked an unfavorable (and wholly unfair) image of all that was iniquitous about the EC: a bloated bureaucracy, an opaque administration, and an unaccountable authority. Who drafted proposals in the Commission? When were they circulated outside Commission headquarters? How could third countries express their points of view? The answers to those questions seemed to differ from one directorate-general to another. And the European Parliament, notorious for its occasional off-the-wall motions and resolution, reveled in taking the United States to task for real or imagined wrongdoing.

Post–Cold War Transitions

The context of U.S.-EU relations changed dramatically with the end of the Cold War.[1] The United States responded to the events in Central and Eastern Europe with a fundamental review of policy toward the continent. The essence of the "New Atlanticism" for the United States was a determination to preserve NATO regardless of the changes ahead, an appreciation of the role of what later came to be called the Organization for Security and Cooperation in Europe, and recognition of the EC's importance as a political and economic anchor in post–Cold War Europe. At the G7 summit in July 1989, the first President Bush manifested U.S. confidence in the EC by asking the Commission to coordinate Western aid to Hungary and Poland.[2] The acceleration of reform in Central and Eastern Europe, and the EC's ability to mobilize massive amounts of aid to help the process, further convinced the United States of the EC's political significance, especially as a crucial underpinning for a united Germany, which the United States strongly supported.

Changing U.S. policy toward the EC and a continuing surge in the EC's political importance in the late 1980s provided the background to the Transatlantic Declaration. The United States therefore accepted with alacrity a proposal by the Council presidency in early 1990 to formalize U.S.-EC relations. The appeal for the United States of such an arrangement grew throughout the year as the EC responded to the complete collapse of communism in Central and Eastern Europe and the sudden inevitability of German reunification by calling for an intergovernmental conference on political union in addition to the previously scheduled conference on monetary union.

The Declaration on US-EC Relations (known as the Transatlantic Declaration), signed in Washington in November 1990 by the U.S. president and the presidents of the Council and Commission, seemed long on rhetoric and short on substance. Among the reasons for a solid U.S.-EC relationship, the declaration included a new factor: "the accelerating process by which the European Community is acquiring its own identity in economic and monetary matters, in foreign policy and in the domain of security." Yet apart from its general significance, the declaration's only tangible contribution to U.S.-EC relations was a strengthened framework for regular consultations to enable both sides to "inform and consult each other on important matters of common interest, both political and economic, with a view to bringing their positions as close as possible, without prejudice to their respective independence."[3]

Changes in the political atmosphere, however, had little effect on the long-standing problems and tensions in the economic relationship. Soon after the Transatlantic Declaration was signed in Washington, the Uruguay Round negotiations of the General Agreement on Tariffs and Trade (GATT) collapsed in Brussels over deep-seated transatlantic differences, with the United States and the EC accusing each other of never having been serious about a successful conclusion.[4] The EC especially objected to what seemed like excessive and high-handed U.S. demands for reform of the Common Agricultural Policy at a time when the Commission had not completed its own internal negotiations on this supremely touchy issue. Some in Europe interpreted the EC's stance as evidence of a newfound willingness to "stand up" to the United States. In fact, there was more of the old than the new in the EC's position, which resulted from a French veto of a last-minute compromise. For its part, the United States saw the failure of the Brussels talks as evidence of the EC's continuing intransigence and introversion. The EC seemed neither able nor willing to face up to its international responsibilities.

What was less evident in the strife surrounding the final stages of the Uruguay Round negotiations was the extent to which it illustrated the duality of the economic relationship between the United States and the emerging EU: a continuing pattern of intractable disputes obscuring a far larger set of common interests vis-à-vis the rest of the world. Apart from agriculture, well-publicized spats between U.S. and European negotiators over the nuances of issues such as trade in services, intellectual property protection, and antidumping and subsidy rules suggested that the Uruguay Round was a struggle between titans with the rest of the world looking on. In fact, much of the force driving the talks came from the joint determination of the United States and the EU to restore the credibility of the GATT and drag the rest of the world into a liberalized trading system (developing countries, including several of the Asian "Tigers," were by no means eager to open their domestic markets). A more muscular world trading regime would not only secure better market access for U.S. and European exporters but could also contain transatlantic trade disputes that threatened to poison the broader economic and political relationship.

The emergence in May 1992 of a CAP reform package made possible the so-called Blair House agreement between the United States and the EU, which provided for gradual reduction and limitation of agricultural subsidies. This agreement paved the way for the belated conclusion of the Uruguay Round and the birth of the WTO in 1995, which led to a respite in many long-running U.S.-EU skirmishes. Some issues, such as U.S. complaints about EU oilseed subsidies, were subsumed into WTO commitments under the Blair House agreement; others, such as disputes over beef hormones and bananas, went temporarily on hold until they could be revived as WTO cases under more stringent dispute-settlement rules.

New Transatlantic Initiatives

The Transatlantic Declaration appeared little more than a transitional measure pending the results of the intergovernmental conferences in December 1991 and the development of U.S.-EU relations in the post-Maastricht period. The already well-known Delors Plan had set the agenda for the conference on monetary union, the outcome of which was unlikely to cause much surprise in Washington. But the negotiations on political union held out an entirely different prospect, including a possibility that the EC might finally extend its agenda to include "hard" security and defense.

As it was, the transition to a new political relationship with the emerging EU proved difficult for the United States, which sometimes seemed alarmed, or at least discomfited, by the EU's rising political profile. On top of this, security and defense issues initially brought a new edge to transatlantic relations. Efforts by some member states during the intergovernmental conference to give the EU a security dimension and, ultimately, a military capability provoked an intemperate U.S. response, with warnings from Washington about the dangers of undermining NATO. Rather than being representative of U.S. policy toward European security in the post–Cold War period, however, this infamous outburst was a throwback to earlier Cold War ways.

The Europeans' apparent responsiveness to U.S. demands in 1991 not to risk undermining NATO by developing an EU defense identity suggested that the United States continued to wield considerable diplomatic clout and that member states took seriously the implied threat of U.S. military withdrawal from Europe. Indeed, member states drew back in the Maastricht Treaty from acquiring an independent defense capability for themselves or the EU and opted instead to use the Western European Union (WEU) as a bridge between NATO and the EU. But their reasons for doing so were more diverse than simply succumbing to a U.S. démarche. Regardless of Washington's position, member states could not agree among themselves so soon after the end of the Cold War about the form or content of an EU defense identity. Moreover, few were willing to surrender sovereignty in this area.[5]

From the U.S. perspective, the outcome of the 1991 intergovernmental conferences was satisfactory. As expected, the negotiations on monetary union led to a general endorsement of the Delors Plan and a decision to establish a common monetary policy and single currency by 1999 at the latest. To the annoyance of EU politicians and officials, in the mid- and late 1990s their U.S. counterparts seemed indifferent or even hostile to monetary union. In fact, the United States was reasonably sanguine about it. Far from trying to thwart monetary union and abort the euro, most Americans who thought about the issue seemed more enthusiastic about the idea of a single currency than the fabled European man in the street. At the same time, U.S. officials appreciated that the launch of the euro would have important repercussions for transatlantic relations, although probably in the long term.

As for political union, the Maastricht Treaty formally altered the EU's competence and institutional framework in ways that were not uncongenial to the United States. The extension of Community competence in a variety of policy areas for the most part formalized the status quo (the treaty's industrial policy provisions were not as damaging to the United States as they might have been had certain member states, notably France, had their way). Institutional changes introduced in the treaty, together with a vogue for transparency, promised to make the decisionmaking process more open and amenable to outside influence, a prospect welcomed by the United States. At the very least, the institutional provisions of the treaty did not require a radical reappraisal of the U.S. foreign policy apparatus for dealing with EC affairs.

The arrival of the Clinton administration in 1993, headed by the first U.S. president from the postwar generation, appeared initially to increase European ambivalence over relations with the United States. In fact, there was little in the early months of the Clinton administration to suggest a turn away from Europe. Clinton's trade representative steered the United States through the final months of the Uruguay Round, and Clinton himself spearheaded a vigorous push to get congressional ratification of the results. However, Clinton's abrupt shift of attention to the North American Free Trade Agreement, and to the Pacific, with growing emphasis on the fledgling Asia Pacific Economic Cooperation dialogue, rattled European leaders. The curious result of their anxiety was the sudden emergence in 1994 and 1995 of European calls for negotiation of the Transatlantic Free Trade Agreement. Its earliest advocates were not trade negotiators, who were exhausted after the Uruguay Round, but some of Europe's leading foreign ministers and defense ministers.[6]

The idea of a transatlantic free trade agreement was illusory. Under GATT rules, any free trade agreement would have to cover "substantially all trade." Negotiation of a transatlantic free trade agreement would therefore require reopening of all the agricultural and other disputes that had plagued the Uruguay Round talks. This was hardly a recipe for greater transatlantic unity. The idea also raised worries among other WTO members that the United States and the EU would retreat to their own cozy condominium, creating the world's largest trading bloc and relegating the WTO to irrelevancy. However, the notion of a transatlantic free trade agreement served its purpose by putting the ball in the U.S. court. America's failure to respond would be interpreted as a signal that the transatlantic relationship was deteriorating. U.S. officials made suitably encouraging, though vague, statements about the need for closer economic and political cooperation.

In the event, then EU trade commissioner Leon Brittan proposed something at once less and more than a free trade agreement. The "transatlantic economic zone" was a highly flexible concept that would liberalize trade in certain areas while skipping over others. Its relation to existing WTO rules was ambiguous. U.S. policymakers, more legalistic in their outlook, were uneasy about the haziness of the concept and reluctant to be dragged into transatlantic free trade negotiations through the back door. Nevertheless, the United States signaled its willingness to go along with negotiation of a "transatlantic economic area" in the context of a broader bilateral effort to expand the Transatlantic Declaration of 1990 to include substantive cooperation under the existing consultation mechanisms.

The New Transatlantic Agenda. Thus, the second grand bilateral initiative, the New Transatlantic Agenda, was born. Following short but intensive negotiations, President Clinton and the presidents of the Council and the Commission signed the New Transatlantic Agenda in Madrid in December 1995.[7]

The new agenda was much more concrete than the old declaration. To the usual rhetoric about common values, it added broad areas in which the United States and the EU were to make joint efforts to

- promote peace, stability, democracy, and development
- respond to global challenges relating to issues such as the environment, terrorism, and international crime
- expand world trade and promote closer economic relations
- build "bridges" across the Atlantic in the cultural and educational domain

The New Transatlantic Agenda further beefed up the schedule of mandatory meetings established under the Transatlantic Declaration to include those of a "Senior-Level Group" charged with the task of adding substance to the twice-yearly, and increasingly perfunctory, U.S.-EU summits instituted under the declaration.

An accompanying action plan listed a number of short- and medium-term goals to achieve the agenda's objectives, ranging from the conclusion of issue-specific trade negotiations to closer educational cooperation. For the most part, the political game plan was heavily weighted with words such as "cooperate," "reinforce," and "pursue," reflecting the intractable nature and resistance to schematization of problems such as Bosnia, Cyprus, the Middle East, and the recurring crises in Africa. The few specifics involved referred mostly to participation in negotiations or conferences and implementation of various agreements already negotiated. Economic commitments were slightly more specific, covering both the multilateral issues of the day and continuing bilateral efforts.

Neither the New Transatlantic Agenda nor the action plan contained any reference to a free trade area. Instead, in addition to a host of promises to fulfill WTO commitments and strengthen the international system, the agenda and action plan called for a "new transatlantic marketplace" to be achieved by progressive reduction or elimination of bilateral trade barriers, stronger regulatory cooperation, and commitments to complete various negotiations then in progress. In short, the new transatlantic marketplace was less a radical departure from the past than an effort to breathe new life into a continuing process.

The New Transatlantic Agenda included one real innovation on the economic front: the Transatlantic Business Dialogue (TABD), which brought together senior corporate officials to help set an agenda for government negotiators. The TABD—the first truly transatlantic lobby—quickly showed its value in focusing the attention of trade negotiators on the bread-and-butter issues most important to those actually doing the trading; it placed a heavy emphasis on unglamorous but important tariff problems and standards, testing, and certification concerns. Successive U.S.-EU summits called for transatlantic environmental, consumer, and labor dialogues, but these have had only mixed success. Indeed, the fortunes of the TABD fluctuated in the following years; the dialogue almost ceased in the early 2000s before coming back to life in 2004, partly to try to offset the political problems then besetting the transatlantic relationship.

Beyond formalizing and making obligatory meetings among senior officials that had already been taking place on an ad hoc basis, the New Transatlantic Agenda cannot be said to have substantially improved transatlantic cooperation. Although later U.S.-EU summits helped create pressure for progress on issues such as U.S. sanctions that affected European firms (a major bone of contention between the EU and the United States in the late 1990s), the increasingly frantic meeting schedule did not necessarily facilitate lasting progress on otherwise intractable issues. Even the combined pressure of regular U.S.-EU summits, since scaled back to one a year, and the persistent nagging of the Transatlantic Business Dialogue could not spur negotiators to complete the initial round of talks on mutual recognition agreements in less than six years, let alone come to a real meeting of the minds on the correct approach to a problem country such as Iran.

Old Wine in New Bottles? The temptation to put old wine in new bottles—that is, to repackage the relationship—returns periodically to U.S. and EU officials, especially when the relationship appears to be moribund. In the late 1990s, tensions over U.S. sanctions and new agricultural trade irritants were again on the rise. Growing congressional skepticism of multilateral trade initiatives and corresponding U.S. ambivalence about European proposals for a broad new Millennium Round increased European misgivings. In early 1998, therefore, Leon Brittan proposed to cap a long and brilliant career in the Commission with yet another bilateral initiative. This one, initially known as the New Transatlantic Marketplace (which had figured as one of the elements of the New Transatlantic Agenda of 1995) was carefully composed of elements, such as free trade in services, that both sides (particularly the EU) could presumably accept. It conspicuously did not include any proposals in the traditionally touchy areas of agriculture and culture.

The U.S. response to Brittan's swan song was cautiously receptive; the proposal met a much frostier reception in Europe. The French openly rejected the initiative on the grounds that it had not been vetted first by the member states. Others expressed concern about the advisability of some of the elements, especially efforts to achieve bilateral free trade in services at the expense of the multilateral process. As the Commission worked to finesse all these objections, the proposed New Transatlantic Marketplace was transmogrified and watered down into the Transatlantic Economic Partnership. Publicly unveiled at the May 1998 U.S.-EU summit, the Transatlantic Economic Partnership was worthy but anodyne. Its stated objective was the "intensification and extension of multilateral and bilateral cooperation." On the multilateral side, it affirmed that the two sides would cooperate to pursue a list of initiatives that for the most part were already under way in the WTO. On the bilateral side, the highlight was a promise to concentrate on "those barriers that really matter," especially regulatory barriers, with a nod to the efforts of the Transatlantic Business Dialogue. Following the New Transatlantic Agenda model, this rather general declaration was to be followed as soon as possible by a common action plan.

The idea of a transatlantic free trade area was again mooted in 2004, when a new European Commission was being put in place. Pascal Lamy, Leon Brittan's successor as trade commissioner, fretted that Peter Mandelson, his own successor in the job, would try to resurrect the proposal for the New Transatlantic Marketplace. The idea of a transatlantic free trade area was something "backed by Britain's economic policy-makers and hated by the French establishment in equal measure."[8] Not coincidentally, Lamy is French and Mandelson British.

Monetary Union: A New Dimension in U.S.-EU Relations

The launch of the euro entailed a major shift in the substance of the U.S.-EU dialogue. A relationship forged in the slow-moving and compartmentalized world of trade disputes would have to evolve substantially to cope with fast-breaking exchange rate fluctuations and international capital movements. The traditionally close relationship among G7 finance ministers and central bankers, particularly between the United States and Britain, would also have to give way to a more complex and possibly less collegial interplay among the eurogroup finance ministers, other EU finance ministers, members of the European Central

Bank and noneurogroup central banks, and their U.S. counterparts. EU efforts to solve the conundrum of eurogroup representation in G7 summits suggested that for the short term, decisionmaking on the EU side would be cumbersome and plagued by disputes over who was to speak for whom. The risk was that European internal problems would irritate U.S. policymakers and confirm them in their tendency to act alone rather than coordinate with the EU in finding solutions to future financial crises. The continuing role of member state finance ministries in providing International Monetary Fund (IMF) resources and emergency financial assistance during crises, despite the existence of a monetary union among twelve of the member states, further complicated U.S.-EU relations. As in the case of the Common Foreign and Security Policy, in times of crisis the United States was inclined to go back to its old friends for help rather than wait for the EU process to produce a response, much to the irritation of the smaller member states (both in and out of the eurogroup) and the Commission.

In the long term, however, the two sides must and will engage as equal partners. The euro has more weight on the world scene than any of its European predecessors, even the mighty German mark. The advent of monetary union already had a calming effect on EU investor expectations in the wake of the 1997 Asian financial crisis. Over time the euro will inevitably grow into a primary reserve currency, and the makers of EU currency policy will be key players in addressing any global financial problem. The obvious solution would be to realign international institutions, especially the G7, to correspond with this new reality. However, European G7 members have shown little inclination to do so. The G7 is an awkward and illogical grouping, a historical artifact made even more ungainly by the partial grafting onto it of Russia in the 1990s (hence the designation G7/8). Full membership in the G7 carries a certain glamour that members are reluctant to relinquish; proposals to make it more representative or more compact have fallen on deaf ears. Perhaps it will gradually become marginalized, replaced by informal contacts between the U.S. Federal Reserve and the European Central Bank, on the one hand, and the Federal Reserve and a shifting group of EU finance ministries, on the other. New ad hoc groups may spring up. In the meantime, the United States and the EU will have to draw upon fifty years of experience and adjust again to the shifting nature of the relationship.

Reconciling the Security Dilemma

In the early 1990s, the United States and its European allies resolved only temporarily the post–Cold War security dilemma of trying to maximize Europe's collective security identity and capability (the "Europeanist" position) and trying to maintain the status quo of U.S. preeminence in NATO (the "Atlanticist" position). Member states' differing and at times contradictory responses to the two major international crises during the course of the 1991 in-

tergovernmental conference on political union—the Gulf War and the outbreak of hostilities in Yugoslavia—made it even more difficult for them to
agree on an EU-based security structure independent of the United States,
which the United States in any case did not want to emerge. The EU's performance in both crises fueled doubts in Washington about the EU's ability ever
to fashion a coherent foreign and security policy.

The Maastricht Treaty formula whereby the WEU became both the proto-
typical defense arm of the EU and a vehicle through which the European pillar
of NATO could be strengthened was up for grabs at the 1996–1997 intergovernmental conference. By that time, Clinton's political and military advisers
had abandoned much of the previous administration's prickly resistance to the
emergence of closer European cooperation within NATO and had obligingly
stepped back to allow the EU's nascent Common Foreign and Security Policy
to try to deal with the Yugoslav wars, a morass from which senior U.S. diplomats instinctively recoiled. Paradoxically, by 1996 the EU was therefore almost
uniformly Atlanticist, whereas the United States had become somewhat Europeanist. In other words, based especially on the lessons of Bosnia and the Dayton peace settlement, erstwhile Europeanists (including the French) saw the necessity for a strong U.S. military presence in Europe, whereas the United States
pressed its European allies to strengthen their own capability to confront security threats in Europe's backyard.

As seen in Chapter 17, agreement within NATO in January 1994 on the
concept of Combined Joint Task Forces—an arrangement that would make
NATO assets available to NATO's European members for operations outside
the NATO area in which the United States did not want to participate—demonstrated a new transatlantic consensus on European security and the U.S. role in
it. Of greater political importance in the aftermath of the Bosnian debacle was
the outcome of the July 1997 NATO summit in Madrid, which endorsed the
EU's development of a security and defense identity but asserted NATO's primacy. Only a month before, when they had concluded the intergovernmental
conference at the Amsterdam summit, member states had agreed to incorporate
WEU peacekeeping tasks into the Common Foreign and Security Policy,
thereby raising the possibility of future EU peacekeeping operations. Unlike in
1991 (during the previous intergovernmental conference), there was no U.S.
diplomatic intervention during the 1996–1997 intergovernmental conference
to try to prevent a WEU-EU merger.

The Madrid NATO summit also endorsed the NATO membership applications of the Czech Republic, Poland, and Hungary. Yet the debate about
NATO enlargement had angered many Europeans because of the U.S. administration's apparently high-handed approach to one of the most important security issues in post–Cold War Europe. Essentially, the United States alone decided which Central and Eastern European countries would joint NATO first
and when they would do so. Related suggestions in the U.S. Congress that EU

membership was either a substitute for NATO membership or a consolation for those Central and Eastern European countries not initially admitted to NATO, together with criticism of the EU's slow enlargement process and arm's-length attitude toward Turkey, demonstrated serious misunderstanding in American political circles of the EU's nature and procedures. Although intensely irritating for Europeans, U.S. conduct of NATO enlargement and critical or erroneous comments about EU enlargement did not unravel the solid transatlantic consensus on the post–Cold War European security structure that seemed to exist at the end of the 1990s. That consensus seemed to fray only after the change of administration in the United States, especially in the aftermath of the war in Iraq.

George W. Bush, September 11, and Iraq

The inauguration of George W. Bush as president of the United States in January 2001 ushered in a period of great difficulty in the transatlantic relationship. Bush knew little and cared less about the EU; those around him who knew anything about the EU were generally disdainful of it. The so-called neoconservatives, who provided the intellectual rationale for Bush's foreign policy, tended to dismiss the process of European integration as deeply flawed (after all, they valued national sovereignty above all else) and the outcome of European integration as derisory. They scoffed at the EU's economic sluggishness and foreign policy failings, especially in the Balkans in the late 1990s. In other words, they were ardent Euroskeptics.

Robert Kagan, a prominent neoconservative, touched a raw nerve in the EU with his book *Of Paradise and Power,* a stinging critique of the nature of European integration and what followed logically from it, the EU's multilateralist worldview.[9] According to Kagan, the EU engaged in endless negotiation in search of artful compromise because its member states, many of them former great powers, lacked the ability and had lost the will to do anything else. The United States, by contrast, was bound to act decisively and unilaterally in defense of its interests because it had the means and the determination to do so. In his view, the differences between the United States and the EU were historical, philosophical, and structural. They were also unbridgeable. As Kagan put it so pithily, America is from Mars, Europe from Venus.

Bush's abrupt dismissal of major international initiatives such as the Kyoto Protocol and International Criminal Court was consistent with a profoundly conservative outlook on the sanctity of national sovereignty as well as a socioeconomic philosophy that elevated narrowly perceived corporate interests above all else. The apparently selfish and sanctimonious outlook of Bush and those around him was bad enough for the Europeans; what made it extremely damaging for transatlantic relations and dangerous for the world as a whole was the administration's reaction to the terrorist attacks on the United States of September 2001. The EU rallied in support of the United States in the aftermath of the attacks. Only die-hard anti-Americans and fervent pacifists (sometimes one and the same thing) opposed the U.S. war in Afghanistan and regretted the overthrow of the Taliban. If anything, many European governments regretted that the United States had not accepted their offers of military assistance.

The successful efforts of key members of the U.S. administration to exploit the terrorist attacks to press for an invasion of Iraq greatly exacerbated the deepening rift in transatlantic relations. Initially, it divided Europeans among themselves. Member states differed in their responses to America's march to war, which began in the summer of 2002 and became unstoppable by early 2003. Britain and France had long been at loggerheads over policy toward Iraq, with Britain participating alongside the United States, since the end of the Gulf War, in occasional attacks against Iraqi antiaircraft batteries, and France unswervingly opposed to any military intervention. Britain and France now took diametrically opposite positions on the looming war. Britain (more precisely, Prime Minister Tony Blair) wholeheartedly supported the United States, while France refused to back a UN resolution intended to bless the imminent invasion. German chancellor Gerhard Schröder adamantly opposed the American war effort, which may have ensured his reelection in October 2002. Italy and Spain were the only two other member states to strongly support the American position, whereas almost all of the Central and Eastern European candidate countries did so. That split prompted U.S. defense secretary Donald Rumsfeld's infamous quip about the division between "old Europe" (France and Germany) and "new Europe" (the prospective member states).

For Rumsfeld and his ilk, the divisions in Europe over Iraq merely reinforced a tendency to dismiss the EU as irrelevant. Some Europeans fretted that the United States was attempting to set member states against each other and weaken the EU politically. In fact, the administration did not care enough about the EU to adopt such a strategy. Moreover, the EU seemed perfectly capable of tearing itself apart without U.S. prompting or assistance. What really irritated EU officials and politicians was precisely that the Bush administration was so dismissive of them.

The nonexistence of weapons of mass destruction in Iraq (the ostensible justification for the war), U.S. mishandling of the occupation after the invasion, and apparent U.S. indifference to the simmering Israeli-Palestinian conflict soon united Europeans in their condemnation of the United States. Most Europeans could not resist indulging in schadenfreude, taking malicious pleasure in America's military misfortunes despite the suffering of the Iraqi people. Blair became more isolated in his own country and in the EU, Chirac grew more openly anti-American, and Schröder had little incentive to mend fences with Washington (not that he received any encouragement from the U.S. administration to do so).

The fallout from Iraq also shattered the fragile transatlantic consensus on the emerging European Security and Defense Policy. Whereas the Clinton administration had accepted that an independent European military capability was compatible with NATO and ultimately in America's interest, the Bush administration was extremely skeptical, seeing it instead as a Gaullist plot to undermine NATO and weaken the United States. Washington's distrust of European defense initiatives was tempered only by the administration's certainty that they were bound to fail. In the aftermath of the Iraq war, the French played into the administration's hands by reverting (unofficially) to an anti-American and anti-NATO rationale for European Security and Defense Policy. Far from permanently dividing the EU, however, the war in Iraq may have emboldened member states to accelerate their plans for a common defense policy, although not necessarily for the reasons espoused by France.

Most Europeans were shocked by the news of Bush's election victory in November 2004. They were incredulous: how could Americans reward a president whose economic policies were so wrong and military adventures so dangerous with another four years in office? For their part, many Americans wondered how Spanish voters could have caved in to terrorism and voted the Conservatives out of office after the Madrid bombings in March 2004. Clearly, there were gross misperceptions on both sides of the Atlantic: whereas many Europeans decried the American electorate's stupidity, many Americans decried the Spanish electorate's spinelessness. Such was the sorry state of transatlantic relations in the middle of the decade.

Nevertheless, the two sides could at least agree on the perils confronting them in an increasingly unstable world, if not on how best to respond internationally. The EU security strategy, endorsed by the European Council in June 2003 in the aftermath of the war in Iraq, identified the proliferation of weapons of mass destruction, the menace of failed states, and the spread of terrorism as the main threats confronting Europe (and the West). Acting on behalf of the EU and in the interest of the Unites States as well, Britain, France, and Germany—the three most influential member states—attempted in 2004 and 2005, by applying diplomatic pressure and offering economic inducement, to convince Iran not to develop a nuclear weapons capability. The United States was skeptical of the Europeans' prospects but had little to offer when it came to dealing with Iran except the threat of war, a prospect uncongenial to most Americans, especially after the Iraq imbroglio.

One of the few bright spots in an otherwise gloomy U.S.-EU relationship during the Bush presidency was the extent of cooperation between the two sides on measures to combat terrorism, ranging from visas to border controls to sharing intelligence. Although the U.S. authorities have occasionally been high-handed in their pursuit of "homeland security," and despite the negative consequences for trade and citizens' rights of the U.S. Patriot Act, EU officials have generally been understanding and cooperative in their approach to these issues. For example, the EU agreed to comply with U.S. demands for information on passengers traveling to the United States, much to the chagrin of the European Parliament, which took the Commission to task for its apparent violation of the EU data privacy directive (discussed later in this chapter). Europeans' horror at the attacks on the United States in September 2001 and the bombings in Spain in March 2004 generated broad transatlantic agreement on specific measures to combat terrorism.

■ Enduring Differences

The severe tension in transatlantic political relations had some economic fallout, notably a drop in European sales of brand-name products closely associated with the United States. Beyond that, the transatlantic economic relationship remained surprisingly buoyant in the aftermath of the Iraq war, as both sides made every effort to insulate huge trade and investment flows from negative political feelings.[10] Nevertheless, U.S.-EU trade disputes persisted, as they had throughout the history of the relationship. Concrete progress in some areas in the late 1990s—such as the conclusion of multilateral trade agreements on telecommunications and financial services and bilateral mutual recognition agreements in the area of standards, testing, and certification—remains overshadowed by new and daunting problems such as regulation of genetically modified organisms and privacy-related restrictions on electronic data transmission. At one extreme, political-economic issues such as trade sanctions have generated serious tensions. At the other extreme, disputes related to product regulation for both safety and environmental reasons are proliferating. Far from being primarily technical in nature, many of these issues evoke emotional public responses that make them difficult for the EU to manage.[11] Moreover, traditional trade barriers such as quotas, tariffs, and other forms of trade protection remain a periodic irritant in the relationship.

Traditional Issues: Tariffs, Quotas, and Subsidies

Traditional disputes over tariffs, quotas, and subsidies continue to bedevil the transatlantic relationship. The EU and the United States have scrapped for decades over U.S. complaints about European subsidization of Airbus and European complaints about indirect U.S. subsidization of Boeing through military procurement contracts. The two sides seemed on the verge of an agreement in January 2005 when they called a ninety-day truce, but hostilities erupted again in April because of lack of progress in the interim. This was especially jarring because it came at a time when Bush had just completed a trip to Europe to mend fences with some of his harshest critics and to acknowledge the political importance of the EU. The flare-up was a salutary reminder that economic disputes are a staple of transatlantic relations regardless of prevailing political circumstances. The dispute will most likely be brought before the WTO, which does not necessarily guarantee a permanent resolution of it (the EU and the United States have a history of finessing WTO findings to suit themselves).

The most prominent traditional dispute is the continuing row over bananas.[12] Quotas on banana imports from countries not party to the Lomé Convention (the EU's preferential trade and aid agreement with a large group of African, Caribbean, and Pacific countries), long imposed by certain member states in order to favor former colonial banana growers, were extended in 1993 to the entire EU as part of the single market program, thus denying access by so-called dollar banana growers in Central America. Although the United States grows few bananas itself, U.S. corporations are among the major banana brokers; thus, U.S. trade officials vigorously opposed the EU measures.

A WTO case led to a judgment in May 1997, later confirmed by an appellate body, that the EU quotas were indeed illegal under WTO rules. Mindful of the vehement opposition from the old colonial powers to eliminating the preferential quotas, however, the Commission chose a legalistic response that adjusted the regime to meet some of the technical objections raised by the WTO panel over administration of the quotas while skirting the larger issue of the legality of the quotas themselves. To no one's surprise, the United States and a number of Central American countries promptly objected again. Weary of the ensuing debate over whether another dispute panel was required to decide if the new plan was also WTO-illegal (as seemed likely), the United States announced its intention to take retaliatory measures by January 1999 if the EU did not comply to its satisfaction with the initial judgment. Following lengthy negotiations, in April 2001 the United States and the EU reached an understanding in an effort to resolve the ongoing dispute whereby the United States agreed to the EU imposing a temporary tariff-rate quota through the end of 2005, under which a duty of €75 per metric ton (the prevailing most-favored-nation rate) would apply to all other bananas while African, Caribbean, and Pacific (ACP) bananas could be imported into the EU duty-free.

The United States agreed to this lengthy transition period in order to afford the Lomé countries (now covered by the follow-on Cotonou agreement) and the EU sufficient opportunity to adjust to a final tariff-only regime. To the dismay of the United States, the EU announced in October 2004 that as of January 2006 its tariff on banana imports that do not originate in the ACP countries would be €230 per metric ton. This would effectively shut out bananas originating elsewhere. To make matters worse for the United States and the Central American producers, the EU market from which non-Cotonou bananas were effectively being shut out became considerably larger after the accession of ten new member states in May 2004.

EU enlargement tends to exacerbate U.S.-EU disputes or risk introducing new ones. For instance, in the mid-1980s, U.S. objections to the loss of agricultural export markets in Spain and Portugal as a result of their accession to the EC were eventually satisfied by the establishment of special quotas for U.S. exports to Spain and Portugal outside Common Agricultural Policy limits. The application of EU tariffs to U.S. electronic components that had hitherto entered Austria, Finland, and Sweden duty-free became a source of transatlantic friction at the time of the 1995 enlargement before being resolved under the WTO Information Technology Agreement of 1997.

The 2004 enlargement generated similar problems. Having refrained on political grounds from challenging the more dubious trade provisions of the EU's Europe Agreements (preaccession association agreements) with the countries of Central and Eastern Europe, the United States appeared much less lenient when it came to the terms of the accession agreements. Thus, the United States was determined to negotiate, within the framework of WTO provisions on the expansion of customs unions, generous compensatory arrangements to offset the extension to the new member states of EU tariff and nontariff barriers to U.S. trade.

In March 2002 President Bush announced that the United States was imposing temporary higher duties on steel imports under Section 201 of U.S. law, in order to protect against a surge in steel imports and falling steel prices and give the U.S. steel industry breathing room to restructure (the WTO allows such temporary safeguard duties to protect an industry from a surge of fairly traded imports but sets restrictions). The president's action was politically rather than economically inspired: it sought to curry favor and win votes in steel-producing states, which were considered pivotal in the next presidential election. The EU cried foul and brought the matter before the WTO, which ruled in July 2003 that the U.S. action was not WTO-compliant. The EU promptly announced that it would impose retaliatory duties on a range of imports from the United States. Bush backed down in December 2003, claiming that the original measures had served their purpose of allowing the U.S. steel industry to become more competitive (there had indeed been a rash of restructuring in the U.S. steel sector in late 2002 and 2003, including several mergers and acquisitions). Bush reaped the domestic political reward in November 2004 when he handily won in the so-called swing states, but at the cost of considerable international opprobrium. The episode confirmed many international observers' negative impression of the Bush administration and gave the EU another stick with which to beat the United States.

On another front, U.S. and EU antidumping actions, which impose tariffs on foreign producers supposedly selling below cost, continue to generate predictable complaints from the targets of those actions on both sides of the Atlantic. Antidumping actions and ensuing complaints tend to increase in intensity in times of economic downturn.

Regulatory Issues: Standards, Science, and Consumer Anxiety

Contentious though traditional tariffs and quota issues remain, they pose less of a threat to transatlantic trade than do complex issues emerging from the regulatory arena. During implementation of the single market program, the United States and the EU haggled over procedures for the development of product standards, as well as procedures for testing and certifying those products, in various industrial sectors. The difficulty surrounding standards, testing, and certification was evident from the protracted negotiations of bilateral mutual recognition agreements in a limited number of sectors; the negotiations finally concluded in 1997, years after their scheduled dates of completion.

Yet disputes over product standards are far less intractable than issues in which scientific results and popular attitudes have proved almost impossible to reconcile. Nowhere do U.S. and EU policymakers face greater challenges than in the area of food regulation, where questions of science, popular emotion, social judgments about acceptable level of risk, and regulatory responsibility have become hopelessly entangled. Regulatory issues ranging from the use of hormones in meat production to control of BSE (mad cow disease) to the role of genetic engineering in grains have seemingly transcended their technical origins to become symbolic of larger anxieties over the pace of change and the role of science in modern life. In the process they have generated increasingly stubborn trade disputes.

Some observers have seen in the rising tensions over food regulation a reflection of deep differences between the U.S. and European publics—for instance, in their conception of nature. A more modest explanation is that they reflect differences in public confidence in the efficacy of government regulation. Here, as in other areas, the structural asymmetry between the United States and the EU is an underlying cause of the tension. For example, despite complaints from business about its slowness and inefficiency, the U.S. Food and Drug Administration, in existence for the better part of a century, enjoys a broad degree of confidence among the American public. By contrast, until recently the EU lacked a single politically independent and effective regulatory body that could play the role of public guardian (the European Food Safety Authority is new and will take some time to become fully operational and effective).

Commission officials have long argued that the system of mutual recognition and member state consultation (via various scientific advisory committees) is effective, but in practice Commission officials have limited control over the behavior of member-state regulatory agencies. The BSE scandal of the mid-1990s—which erupted when British scientists found a link between beef consumption and Creutzfeld-Jacob disease, a degenerative brain disease in humans—exposed the weakness of EU institutions and EU-level regulatory oversight in the face of political pressure, seriously eroding public confidence in the process. Lacking credibility as impartial authorities in this area, EU and member state officials instinctively bow before every expression of public alarm over new processes or substances. As U.S. agriculture transforms itself with the aid of genetic-engineering techniques, the EU's reflexive response is bound to lead to serious disruptions in trade flows.

In retrospect, the U.S.-EC dispute in the 1980s over the use of hormones in beef was an indicator of problems to come. The dispute arose out of a public scandal in Italy, where farmers were found to have been dosing cattle with large amounts of certain hormones known to be dangerous and banned in both the EC and the United States. In an effort to respond to public indignation over a case involving egregious failure to enforce existing laws, EU policymakers decided to ban all use of any hormones in the production of beef (with an exception for "therapeutic" use), including a number of hormones that scientific studies had shown to be benign. Arguments based on scientific evidence were brushed aside with responses about "consumer preference" and the impossibility of proving that the use of any hormone was completely safe. After the GATT's weak dispute-settlement mechanism proved unable to resolve the quarrel, the United States retaliated against the EC for lost beef exports. When more stringent WTO rules took effect after 1995, the United States promptly hauled the EU back into dispute settlement. A WTO panel predictably concluded that the hormone ban was scientifically unfounded and thus inconsistent with WTO obligations. In response, the EU announced that it would gather scientific evidence to justify the ban, which had already been in effect for ten years. In effect, the EU had little political room for maneuver: after years of official denunciation of "hormone beef," public attitudes were firmly set; efforts to relax the ban would have been politically suicidal in many member states.

In the event, the Commission changed its regulation from a permanent ban on six hormones to a provisional ban of indefinite duration on five hormones and continuation of the permanent ban on the sixth. The Commission claimed that it was now in compliance with its WTO obligations, although it kept the EU's ban on hormone-treated beef in place. To add insult to injury, the EU instituted proceedings in the WTO against the United States (and Canada) for not lifting sanctions against the EU's original ban on beef imports. U.S. senator Charles E. Grassley, chairman of the powerful Senate Committee on Finance, complained in a letter to outgoing trade commissioner Pascal Lamy in November 2004 that this new version of the ban isn't backed by sound science any more than the old ban that was ruled illegal by the WTO. Instead, the new ban appears to be backed by "political" science. This exercise in smoke and mirrors sets a poor example. By replacing one scientifically unfounded ban with another and claiming compliance, the EU significantly discredits the DSU [dispute settlement understanding of the WTO]. And in the meantime, beef producers in my home state of Iowa and across the United States will continue to be injured, while consumers in Europe will continue to be denied access to high-quality beef. That is hardly a thoughtful and effective way to resolve a dispute that has been left outstanding for far too long.[13]

When another dispute arose in the 1990s with the United States over the use of BST, a hormone used to improve milk yields in cows, the Commission proposed to add a political escape clause to all scientific reviews of new substances. This new hurdle would have required that after passing the tests of safety, quality, and efficacy, new substances would be judged on socioeconomic grounds. (In the case of BST, the socioeconomic argument advanced was that its use would unfairly benefit large farmers and would add to already rampant overproduction in the dairy sector.) Policymakers and businesspeople in the United States, including the developer of BST, denounced this idea as a perversion of the role of regulators and a form of hidden protectionism.

Although the agricultural and veterinary provisions of the Uruguay Round agreement ruled out the use of an additional hurdle and raised the burden of proof required for banning products on health grounds, regulatory issues in the agriculture area continued to play a growing role in U.S.-EU tensions. In particular, under intense pressure to respond forcefully to the BSE crisis, the EU hastily passed a broad-based ban in July 1997 on all products containing beef derivatives from any source. Only later did it emerge that the ban encompassed approximately $20 billion in transatlantic trade, much of it in the pharmaceuticals sector. A brief delay in implementation of the ban averted major disruptions in trading patterns and enabled the United States and the EU to settle down to an extended argument over who could qualify as "BSE-free" and which standards were to be used in making that decision.

In addition, the rapid entry of genetically modified crop varieties into U.S. agriculture set the scene for long-running disputes over the pace of approval of genetically modified organisms (GMOs) in Europe and gave rise to a contentious dispute over the appropriateness of requiring labels for all foods containing any trace of a genetically modified ingredient. The fundamental problem was a significant difference in public attitude. Americans for the most part seemed reconciled to genetic engineering as a more modern form of plant breeding and accepted scientific judgments on the safety of these products. Europeans for the most part were deeply suspicious of such "unnatural" products and either disbelieved the scientists or argued that it could not be known for sure that GMOs are absolutely safe in every respect (this is a reflection of the well-known difficulty of proving a negative).

Much to the irritation of the United States, the EU responded to these pressures by periodically adding extra steps to the already arduous approval process for GMOs laid out under a 1990 directive on the subject, updated in 2001. In effect, beginning in 1998 the EU imposed a moratorium on the approval of new genetically modified products, thereby sharply curtailing U.S. exports of corn and soybeans to EU member states. The United States initiated a WTO case in May 2003 against the de facto EU ban, although strong consumer opposition in Europe to GMO products has probably done more damage to U.S. market share than deliberate EU foot dragging. In the meantime, new genetically modified crop varieties are being approved and planted in the United States, which does not require genetically modified soybeans, for instance, to be separated from other varieties. A combination of dilatory EU approvals and fierce consumer resistance therefore bedevils the impact of biotechnology on transatlantic trade.

The Information Revolution: A New World of Disputes?

The rapid evolution of the Internet in the mid- and late 1990s, both as a business tool and as a commercial environment, presented new dilemmas and new potential sources of friction to U.S. and EU regulators. Perhaps the most serious was the problem posed for transatlantic data flows by the EU data privacy directive, which set up a regulatory structure to ensure that personal data were properly protected both by government authorities and by the private sector. As a corollary, it prohibited transmission of personal data on EU citizens to countries in which adequate protection of data (by EU standards) did not prevail. The United States has no centralized regulatory structure protecting data privacy comparable to that set forth in the directive; it has traditionally relied on self-regulation by companies.

Thus, the directive caused consternation among major firms both in the United States and in the EU, which feared that the law would prevent routine intracorporate transfer of data such as personnel and payroll records and could well hamper transactions such as airline reservations or electronic commerce. Efforts to come to a resolution whereby the EU would accept voluntary commitments by U.S. firms as adequate for the purposes of the directive had not made much progress by the time the directive entered into force in October 1998. Fortunately, the low level of implementation in the EU and member state reluctance to cut off data flows without a greater effort to find a solution helped avoid a major meltdown in transatlantic relations over the issue.

Eventually, in July 2000, the United States and the Commission concluded the so-called Safe Harbor arrangement to help bridge the differences between the EU and U.S. approaches to privacy protection and ensure that data flows were not interrupted. Under the arrangement, U.S. companies falling under the regulatory authority of the Federal Trade Commission or the Department of Transportation could voluntarily participate in Safe Harbor by self-certifying to the Department of Commerce. The arrangement has worked well, although the impact of the directive on other U.S. entities, such as those engaged in financial services, remains uncertain and a potential source of U.S.-EU discord.

In other Internet-related areas, such as electronic commerce (involving the sale of products and services entirely via the Internet), prospects for true regulatory cooperation appear better. Relatively speaking, regulation of the Internet is a blank page, making it easier to avoid conflicts emerging from the clash of established regulatory structures and to come to a meeting of minds before positions are set. In December 1997, for example, the United States and the EU issued a joint declaration on electronic commerce, which helped set the agenda for WTO examination of the issue (with the United States and the EU starting out on the same side for a change). This fairly general document stated certain common principles, among them the need to keep regulation to a minimum and to avoid new taxes on Internet transactions.

However, electronic commerce entails difficult and potentially divisive legal issues such as the validity and authentication of electronic signatures. As another example of possible points of conflict, the "no new taxes" pledge does not solve the problem of collecting existing taxes such as VAT on electronic commerce. Governments are worried not only about loss of revenue but also about the inequities between electronic and nonelectronic traders of the same products that would result from an entirely tax-free Internet. A Council directive of May 2002 on the collection of VAT on electronically supplied services, regardless of the source of such sales, led to complaints that U.S. businesses were being treated unfairly. For example, unless a U.S. business established a permanent base in the EU it would have to collect and remit VAT at 25 different rates depending on the consumer's country of residence. By contrast, EU suppliers would have to collect and remit VAT at the rate of the member state in which that supplier is registered. As this case shows, regimes set up to address the challenges of electronic commerce have the potential to cause trade problems if not carefully coordinated. It also shows that such coordination is not always a given.

The inherent bias toward or against government involvement in new economic areas differs on each side of the Atlantic, as it does among member states; for example, a number of U.S. firms reacted with alarm to a Commission proposal in the late 1990s to develop a "charter" for electronic commerce. Another tricky issue has been data encryption. Technology that allows private users to encrypt data transmissions over the Internet offers greater privacy and security to businesses and citizens but also presents serious problems for law-enforcement agencies. U.S. efforts to control export of encryption technology and ensure that "keys" that allow law officers to break codes would remain accessible to U.S. authorities have caused friction with EU member states that resent the implication that ultimate control of all these technologies should remain in U.S. hands. A decision by the United States in late 1998 to ease these rules appeared to address most of these concerns, until the terrorist attacks of September 2001 renewed the U.S. government's interest in the issue.

◼ Conclusion

In looking at the long, complicated, and fractious relationship between the world's two greatest economic powers, it is clear that permanent harmony is neither achievable nor, perhaps, desirable. In most important respects, the relationship remains sound. The overwhelming importance of the economic ties and the slow but definite growth of a strong institutional framework make it difficult to conceive of a major breakdown in U.S.-EU relations, notwithstanding the political differences over Iraq and other American initiatives. However, many of the most visible disputes between the two arise from real differences in social and political outlook, ranging from the role of foreign policy in economics to the role of governments in ensuring public safety and managing scientific risk. These are unlikely to yield to any grand initiatives; convergence, if it occurs, will happen incrementally and over time.

A recurring theme in U.S.-EU economic dialogue has been the importance of regulatory cooperation, whereby the two sides try to find a common approach to thorny issues, thus eliminating disputes in advance. This is clearly a rational approach that has particular promise in areas where both sides are not already burdened with long-standing institutional differences. It would be a mistake to imagine, however, that true convergence is possible in regulating the economies of two societies with vastly different histories, geographies, demographics, and social philosophies.[14]

One could argue that such an outcome is not even necessarily ideal. A single market is one of the guiding tenets of the EU, faced as it is with the challenge of fostering integration in the face of intractable linguistic and historical barriers. The United States, with a single language, a single currency covering its entire territory, and a singularly mobile population, has been much more willing to tolerate certain residual regulatory barriers. And in areas where it chooses to regulate, as a nation-state the U.S. has a federal regulatory apparatus far more powerful than anything sovereign European nation-states would be prepared to accept. Under the circumstances, it is hard to argue that the benefits of eliminating remaining trade barriers from a relationship in which the overwhelming majority of trade already flows unhindered would be greater than the costs of trying to impose a one-size-fits-all economic regime, even if such a regime could be devised.

Thus, persistent efforts to make incremental progress on hard issues (such as agricultural trade), coupled with a willingness to live through occasional acrimonious rows in the WTO without paralyzing other important areas of cooperation, are likely to remain the preferred formula for managing the U.S.-EU relationship. Periodic announcements of grand new initiatives are part of the picture and occasionally aid in achieving breakthroughs on particular issues. The risk, of course, is that an unending line of such initiatives will lead to meeting fatigue among policymakers and perhaps strain institutional resources with increasingly trivial processes such as "dialogues" among various social groups or redundant efforts to increase social and cultural exchanges. On balance, nevertheless, such initiatives appear to serve the important purpose of reaffirming that both sides still care about each other and that what they have in common far outweighs the remaining differences, irritating though they may be. As seen in the WTO, despite their differences the United States and EU are doomed to remain close collaborators, not only because of the importance of their bilateral relationship but also because of the need to defend their common interests and approaches in a world where democratic values and functioning market economies remain largely ideals rather than realities.

■ Notes

1. For an overview of U.S.-EU relations in the post–single market and post–Cold War period, see Michael Calingaert, *European Integration Revisited: Progress, Prospects, and U.S. Interests* (Boulder, CO: Westview Press, 1996), pp. 151–206; Kevin Featherstone and Roy H. Ginsberg, *The United States and the European Union in the 1990s: Partners in Transition* (New York: St. Martin's Press, 1996); and John Peterson, *Europe and America in the 1990s: The Prospects for Partnership*, 2nd ed. (London: Edward Elgar, 1993).

2. Bulletin EC 7/8-1989, points 1.1.1–1.1.5.

3. "Declaration on US-EC Relations," U.S. Department of State, November 11, 1990.

4. Bulletin EC 12-1990, point 1.4.94.

5. On the U.S. démarche, see John Newhouse, "The Diplomatic Round: A Collective Nervous Breakdown," *New Yorker,* September 7, 1991, p. 92.

6. On the Transatlantic Free Trade Agreement and related proposals, see Ernest H. Preeg et al., "Policy Forum: Transatlantic Free Trade," *Washington Quarterly* 19, no. 2 (Spring 1996): 105–133.

7. Bureau of Public Affairs, "The New Transatlantic Agenda and Joint EU-U.S. Action Plan," Department of State Dispatch 6, 49 (December 3, 1995).

8. *Economist*, August 21, 2004, p. 46.

9. Robert Kagan, *Of Paradise and Power: America and Europe in the New World Order* (New York: Alfred A. Knopf, 2003).

10. For an upbeat account of the state of transatlantic economic relations, see Joseph P. Quinlan, *Drifting Apart or Growing Together? The Primacy of the Transatlantic Economy* (Washington, DC: Center for Transatlantic Relations, 2003).

232

12. For the background to the dispute, see Christopher Stevens, "EU Policy for the Banana Market," in Helen Wallace and William Wallace, eds., *Policy-Making in the European Union*, 3rd ed. (Oxford: Oxford University Press, 1996), pp. 325–352.

13. Letter from Charles E. Grassley, chairman of the U.S. Senate Committee on Finance, to Pascal Lamy, November 18, 2004, reprinted in http://usinfo.state.gov/eur/Archive/2004/Nov/19-727564.html.

14. See David Vogel, *Barriers or Benefits: Regulation in Transatlantic Trade* (Washington, DC: Brookings Institution, 1997).

Abbreviations and Acronyms

ACP	African, Caribbean, and Pacific
ALA	Asia and Latin America
APEC	Asia Pacific Economic Cooperation
ASEAN	Association of Southeast Asian Nations
ASEM	Asia-Europe Meeting
Benelux	Belgium, the Netherlands, and Luxembourg
BSE	bovine spongiform encephalopathy
BST	bovine somatotropin
CAP	Common Agricultural Policy
CCP	Common Commercial Policy
CE	European conformity
CEAC	Conference of European Affairs Committees
CEDEFOP	European Center for the Development of Vocational Training
CEEP	European Center of Public Enterprises
CEN	European Standardization Committee
CENELEC	European Electrotechnical Standardization Committee
CET	common external tariff
CFCs	chlorofluorocarbons
CFI	Court of First Instance
CFSP	Common Foreign and Security Policy
CITES	Convention on Trade in Endangered Species
COPA	Committee of Professional Agricultural Organizations of the European Community
COR	Committee of the Regions
Coreper	Committee of Permanent Representatives
COST	European Cooperation in the Field of Scientific and Technological Research
CSCE	Conference on Security and Cooperation in Europe
CSFs	Community Support Frameworks
CTMO	Community Trademark Office

DG	directorate-general
EAGGF	European Agricultural Guidance and Guarantee Fund
EAP	Environmental Action Program
EBA	Everything But Arms
EBRD	European Bank for Reconstruction and Development
EC	European Community
ECB	European Central Bank
ECHO	European Community Humanitarian Office
ECHR	European Convention for the Protection of Human Rights and Fundamental Freedoms
ECJ	European Court of Justice
Ecofin	Council of Economic and Finance Ministers
ECSC	European Coal and Steel Community
ECU	European currency unit
EDC	European Defense Community
EDF	European Development Fund
EDU	European Democratic Union
EDU	Europol Drugs Unit
EEA	European Economic Area
EEA	European Environment Agency
EEC	European Economic Community
EEIG	European Economic Interest Grouping
EESC	European Economic and Social Committee
EFTA	European Free Trade Association
EIA	environmental impact assessment
EIB	European Investment Bank
EIF	European Investment Fund
ELDR	European Liberal, Democratic, and Reformist Party
EMCDDA	European Monitoring Center for Drugs and Drug Addiction
EMEA	European Medicines Agency
EMS	European Monetary System
EMU	economic and monetary union
ENs	European Norms
EP	European Parliament
EPC	European Political Cooperation
EPP	European People's Party
EPP-ED	European People's Party and European Democrats
EPU	European Payments Union
EPU	European Political Union
Erasmus	European Community Action Scheme for the Mobility of University Students
ERDF	European Regional Development Fund
ERM	exchange rate mechanism
ERT	European Round Table of Industrialists
ESCB	European System of Central Banks
ESDP	European Security and Defense Policy

ESF	European Social Fund
ESPRIT	European Strategic Program for Research and Development in Information Technology
ETSI	European Telecommunications Standards Institute
ETUC	European Trade Union Confederation
EU	European Union
Euratom	European Atomic Energy Community
Euro-Med	EU-Mediterranean
Europol	European police agency
FDI	foreign direct investment
FP	Framework Program
G7	Group of Seven Most Industrialized Countries
G8	Group of Seven Most Industrialized Countries plus Russia
G20 plus	Group of Rapidly Developing Countries
G24	Group of Twenty-Four Most Industrialized Countries
GAC	General Affairs Council
GATS	General Agreement on Trade in Services
GATT	General Agreement on Tariffs and Trade
GDP	gross domestic product
GMO	genetically modified organism
GMP	Global Mediterranean Policy
GNI	gross national income
GNP	gross national product
GSP	Generalized System of Preferences
IGC	intergovernmental conference
IMF	International Monetary Fund
IMP	Integrated Mediterranean Program
ITA	Information Technology Agreement
ITO	International Trade Organization
JRC	Joint Research Center
LDC	least developed countries
LIFE	Financial Instrument for the Environment
Lingua	Action Program to Promote Foreign Language Competence in the European Community
MAI	Multilateral Agreement on Investment
MCAs	monetary compensatory amounts
MED	Mediterranean
Mercosur	Mercado Común del Cono Sur (Southern Cone Common Market)
MFA	Multifiber Arrangement
MFN	most favored nation
MFP	multiannual framework program
MRA	mutual recognition agreement
NAFTA	North American Free Trade Agreement
NATO	North Atlantic Treaty Organization
NGO	nongovernmental organization
NTA	New Transatlantic Agenda

NTB	nontariff barrier
OECD	Organization for Economic Cooperation and Development
OEEC	Organization for European Economic Cooperation
OLAF	European Anti-Fraud Office
ONP	Open Network Provisions
OSCE	Organization for Security and Cooperation in Europe
PCA	partnership and cooperation agreement
PCBs	polychlorinated biphenyls
PCTs	polychlorinated terphenyls
PES	Party of the European Socialists
PHARE	Poland-Hungary: Actions for Economic Reconstruction
PLO	Palestine Liberation Organization
R&D	research and development
SAP	Stabilization and Association Process
SEA	Single European Act
SIS	Schengen Information System
SMEs	small and medium-sized enterprises
STABEX	System for the Stabilization of Export Earnings from Products
TABD	Transatlantic Business Dialogue
TACIS	Technical Assistance for the Commonwealth of Independent States
TAD	Transatlantic Declaration
TEA	Transatlantic Economic Area
TEC	Treaty Establishing the European Community
Tempus	Trans-European Mobility Scheme for University Students
TENs	Trans-European Networks
TEP	Transatlantic Economic Partnership
TEU	Treaty on European Union
TRIMs	trade-related investment measures
TRIPs	Trade-Related Aspects of Intellectual Property Rights
UFE	Union for Europe
UNICE	Union of Industrial Employers' Confederations of Europe
USSR	Union of Soviet Socialist Republics
VAT	value-added tax
WEU	Western European Union
WTO	World Trade Organization

Bibliography

Acheson, Dean. *Present at the Creation: My Years in the State Department*. New York: W. W. Norton, 1969.

Adenauer, Konrad. *Memoirs, 1945–1966*. Chicago: Henry Regnery, 1966.

Anderson, Jeffrey J. *German Unification and European Union*. Cambridge: Cambridge University Press, 1999.

Archer, Clive, and Fiona Butler. *The European Union: Structure and Process*. 3rd ed. New York: St. Martin's Press, 2000.

Armstrong, Kenneth, and Simon Bulmer. *The Governance of the Single European Market*. New York: St. Martin's Press, 1998.

Artis, Michael, and Norman Lee. *The Economics of European Union: Policy and Analysis*. Oxford: Oxford University Press, 1997.

Avery, Graham, and Fraser Cameron. *The Enlargement of the European Union*. Sheffield, UK: Sheffield Academic Press, 1998.

Bache, Ian. *The Regional and Structural Policies of the European Union*. Sheffield, UK: Sheffield Academic Press, 1998.

Bangemann, Martin. *Meeting the Global Challenge: Establishing a Successful European Industrial Policy*. London: Kogan Page, 1992.

Barnes, Ian, and Pamela Barnes. *The Enlarged European Union*. London: Longman, 1995.

Baun, Michael. *An Imperfect Union: The Maastricht Treaty and the New Politics of European Integration*. Boulder, CO: Westview Press, 1996.

———. *A Wider Europe: The Politics of European Union Enlargement*. Lanham, MD: Rowman and Littlefield, 1999.

Begg, Iain, and Nigel Grimwade. *European Union Own Resources*. Sheffield, UK: Sheffield Academic Press, 1998.

Bianchi, Patrizio. *Industrial Policies and Economic Integration: Learning from European Experiences*. London: Routledge, 1998.

Bieber, Roland, and Jörg Monar, eds. *Justice and Home Affairs in the European Union*. Brussels: European Interuniversity Press, 1995.

Bieber, Roland, Jean-Paul Jacqué, and Joseph Wieler, eds. *An Ever Closer Union: A Critical Analysis of the Draft Treaty on European Union*. Luxembourg: Office for Official Publications of the European Communities, 1985.

Blondel, Jean, Richard Sinnott, and Palle Svensson. *People and Parliament in the European Union: Participation, Democracy, and Legitimacy.* Oxford: Oxford University Press, 1998.

Bomberg, Elizabeth. *Green Parties and Politics in the European Union.* London: Routledge, 1999.

Bond, Martyn, and Kim Feus, eds. *The Treaty of Nice Explained.* London: Federal Trust for Education and Research, 2001.

Bulmer, Simon, and Andrew Scott, eds. *Economic and Political Integration in Europe: Internal Dynamics and Global Context.* Oxford: Blackwell, 1995.

Bulmer, Simon, and Wolfgang Wessels. *The European Council: Decision-Making in European Politics.* London: Macmillan, 1987.

Burgess, Michael. *Federalism and European Union: Political Ideas, Influences, and Strategies in the European Community, 1972–1987.* London: Routledge, 1987.

Byrne, Rosemary, Gregor Noll, and Jens Vedsted-Hansen, eds. *New Asylum Countries? Migration Control and Refugee Protection in an Enlarged European Union.* The Hague: Kluwer Law International, 2002.

Cafruny, Alan, and Carl Lankowski, eds. *Europe's Ambiguous Unity: Conflict and Consensus in the Post-Maastricht Era.* Boulder, CO: Lynne Rienner, 1997.

Cafruny, Alan, and Patrick Peters, eds. *The Union and the World: The Political Economy of a Common European Foreign Policy.* The Hague: Kluwer, 1998.

Cafruny, Alan, and Glenda Rosenthal, eds. *The State of the European Community: The Maastricht Debates and Beyond.* Boulder, CO: Lynne Rienner, 1993.

Calingaert, Michael. *European Integration Revisited: Progress, Prospects, and U.S. Interests.* Boulder, CO: Westview Press, 1996.

Calleo, David, and Eric Staal, eds. *Europe's Franco-German Engine.* Washington, DC: Brookings Institution, 1998.

Cecchini, Paolo. *The European Challenge 1992: The Benefits of a Single Market.* Aldershot, UK: Wildwood House, 1988.

Chryssochoou, Dimitris. *Democracy in the European Union.* New York: St. Martin's Press, 1998.

Cini, Michelle. *The European Commission: Leadership, Organization, and Culture in the EU Administration.* Manchester, UK: Manchester University Press, 1996.

Cockfield, Arthur. *The European Union: Creating the Single Market.* Chichester, UK: John Wiley, 1994.

Coffey, Peter. *The Future of Europe.* Aldershot, UK: Edward Elgar, 1995.

Connolly, Bernard. *The Rotten Heart of Europe: The Dirty War for Europe's Money.* London: Faber and Faber, 1995.

Coombes, David. *Politics and Bureaucracy in the European Communities.* London: Allen and Unwin, 1977.

Corbett, Richard. *The European Parliament's Role in Closer European Integration.* Basingstoke, UK: Macmillan, 2001.

Corbett, Richard, Francis Jacobs, and Michael Shackleton. *The European Parliament.* 4th ed. London: John Harper, 2000.

Corcelle, Guy, and Stanley Johnson. *The Environmental Policy of the European Communities.* London: Kluwer, 1995.

Cram, Laura. *Policy-Making in the European Union: Conceptual Lenses and the Integration Process.* London: Routledge, 1997.

Cremona, Marise, ed., *The Enlargement of the European Union.* Oxford: Oxford University Press, 2003.

de Bassompierre, Guy. *Changing the Guard in Brussels: An Insider's View of the EC Presidency.* New York: Praeger, 1988.

de Gaulle, Charles. *Memoirs of Hope: Renewal and Endeavor*. New York: Simon and Schuster, 1971.

De Grauwe, Paul. *The Economics of Monetary Union*. 5th ed. Oxford: Oxford University Press, 2003.

Dehousse, Renaud. *The European Court of Justice: The Politics of Judicial Integration*. New York: St. Martin's Press, 1998.

———, ed. *Europe After Maastricht: An Ever Closer Union?* Munich: LBE, 1994.

Deissenberg, Christophe, et al., eds. *European Economic Integration*. Oxford: Blackwell, 1998.

Delors, Jacques. *Le Nouveau Concert Européen*. Paris: Editions Odile Jacob, 1992.

———. *Mémoires*. Paris: Plon, 2004.

———. *Our Europe: The Community and National Development*. London: Verso, 1992.

Den Boer, Monica, ed. *Schengen: Judicial Cooperation and Policy Coordination*. Maastricht: European Institute of Public Administration, 1997.

De Porte, Anton. *Europe Between the Superpowers: The Enduring Balance*. New Haven, CT: Yale University Press, 1979.

De Ruyt, Jean. *L'Acte Unique Européen: Commentaire*. Brussels: Editions de l'Université de Bruxelles, 1987.

Dimitrakopoulos, Dionyssis G., ed. *The Changing European Commission*. Manchester, UK: Manchester University Press, 2004.

Dinan, Desmond. *Europe Recast: A History of European Union*. Boulder, CO: Lynne Rienner, and Basingstoke, UK: Palgrave Macmillan, 2004.

———, ed. *Encyclopedia of the European Union*. Boulder, CO: Lynne Rienner, and Basingstoke, UK: Macmillan, 1998.

Drake, Helen. *Jacques Delors: Perspectives on a European Leader*. London: Routledge, 2000.

Duchêne, François. *Jean Monnet: The First Statesman of Interdependence*. New York: W. W. Norton, 1994.

Duff, Andrew, John Pinder, and Roy Price, eds. *Maastricht and Beyond: Building the European Union*. London: Routledge, 1994.

Dyson, Kenneth. *Elusive Union: The Process of Economic and Monetary Union in Europe*. London: Longman, 1994.

Dyson, K., and Kevin Featherstone. *The Road to Maastricht: Negotiating Economic and Monetary Union*. Oxford: Oxford University Press, 1998.

Edwards, Geoffrey, and Alfred Pijpers, eds. *The Politics of European Treaty Reform: The 1996 Intergovernmental Conference and Beyond*. London: Pinter, 1997.

Edwards, Geoffrey, and David Spence, eds. *The European Commission*. London: Catermill, 1994.

Edwards, Geoffrey, and Helen Wallace. *The Council of Ministers of the EC and the President in Office*. London: Federal Trust, 1977.

Eeckhout, P. *The European Internal Market and International Trade: A Legal Analysis*. Oxford: Oxford University Press, 1994.

Egan, Michelle. *Constructing a European Market: Standards, Regulation, and Governance*. Oxford: Oxford University Press, 2001.

Eichengreen, Barry. *European Monetary Unification: Theory, Practice, and Analysis*. Boston: MIT Press, 1997.

Eichengreen, Barry, and Jeffry Frieden, eds. *Forging an Integrated Europe*. Ann Arbor: University of Michigan Press, 1998.

Eichengreen, B., J. Frieden, and J. von Hagen. *Politics and Institutions in an Integrated Europe*. Heidelberg: Springer, 1995.

Emerson, Michael. *The Economics of 1992*. Oxford: Oxford University Press, 1988.

Emiliou, Nicholas, and David O'Keeffe, eds. *European and World Trade Law After the GATT Uruguay Round*. Chichester, UK: John Wiley, 1996.

Endo, Ken. *The Presidency of the European Commission Under Jacques Delors: The Politics of Shared Leadership*. New York: St. Martin's Press, 1999.

Eriksen, Erik Oddvar, John Erik Fossum, and Agustín José Meníndez, eds. *Developing a Constitution for Europe*. London: Routledge, 2004.

Estrin, Saul, and Peter Holmes, eds. *Competition and Economic Integration in Europe*. London: Edward Elgar, 1998.

Featherstone, Kevin, and Roy H. Ginsberg. *The United States and the European Union in the 1990s: Partners in Transition*. 2nd ed. New York: St. Martin's Press, 1996.

Fennell, Rosemary. *The Common Agricultural Policy: Continuity and Change*. Oxford: Clarendon Press, 1997.

Flessdal, Andreas, ed. *Democracy and the European Union*. Berlin: Springer Verlag, 1997.

Fountas, S., and B. Kennelly. *European Integration and Regional Policy*. Galway, Ireland: Center for Development Studies, 1994.

Frellesen, Thomas, and Roy H. Ginsberg. *EU-U.S. Foreign Policy Cooperation in the 1990s: Elements of Partnership*. Brussels: CEPS, 1994.

Frieden, Jeffry, Daniel Gros, and Erik Jones. *The New Political Economy of EMU*. Lanham, MD: Rowman and Littlefield, 1998.

Fukuda, Koji, and Hiroya Akiba, eds., *European Governance After Nice*. London: RoutledgeCurzon, 2003.

Furlong, Paul, and Andrew Cox. *The European Union at the Crossroads: Problems in Implementing the Single Market Project*. Boston: Earlsgate Press, 1995.

Fursdon, Edward. *The European Defense Community: A History*. New York: St. Martin's Press, 1980.

Galloway, D. *The Treaty of Nice and Beyond: Reality and Illusions of Power in the EU*. Sheffield: Sheffield Academic Press, 2001.

Galtung, J. *Europe in the Making*. New York: Crane Russak, 1989.

Gardner, Brian. *European Agriculture: Policies, Production and Trade*. London: Routledge, 1996.

Gaynor, K. B., and E. Karakitsos. *Economic Convergence in a Multispeed Europe*. New York: St. Martin's Press, 1997.

Geddes, Andrew. *Immigration and European Integration: Towards Fortress Europe?* Manchester, UK: Manchester University Press, 2000.

Genscher, Hans-Dietrich. *Erinnerungen*. Berlin: Siedler Verlag, 1995.

George, Stephen. *An Awkward Partner: Britain in the European Community*. 3rd ed. Oxford: Oxford University Press, 1998.

———. *Politics and Policy in the European Union*. 3rd ed. Oxford: Oxford University Press, 1996.

George, Stephen, and Ian Bache. *Politics in the European Union*. Oxford: Oxford University Press, 2001.

Gillingham, John. *European Integration, 1950–2002: Superstate or New Market Economy?* Cambridge: Cambridge University Press, 2003.

———. *Coal, Steel and the Rebirth of Europe, 1945–1955: The Germans and French from Ruhr Conflict to Economic Community*. Cambridge: Cambridge University Press, 1991.

Ginsberg, Roy H. *The European Union in International Politics: Baptism by Fire*. Lanham, MD: Rowman and Littlefield, 2001.

————. *Foreign Policy Actions of the European Community: The Politics of Scale.* Boulder, CO: Lynne Rienner, 1989.

Goldsmith, M. J. F., and K. K. Klausen, eds. *European Integration and Local Government.* London: Edward Elgar, 1997.

Grant, Wynn. *The Common Agricultural Policy.* Basingstoke, UK: Macmillan, 1997.

Greenwood, Justin, and Mark Aspinwall, eds. *Collective Action in the European Union: Interests and the New Politics of Associability.* London: Routledge, 1998.

Gros, Daniel, and Niels Thygesen. *European Monetary Integration: From the European Monetary System Towards Monetary Union.* London: St. Martin's Press, 1991.

Grosser, Alfred. *The Western Alliance: European-American Relations Since 1945.* New York: Vantage, 1982.

Gstöhl, Sieglinde. *Reluctant Europeans: Norway, Sweden, and Switzerland in the Process of Integration.* Boulder, CO: Lynne Rienner, 2002.

Hackett, Clifford. *Cautious Revolution: The European Community Arrives.* 2nd ed. New York: Praeger, 1995.

Hall, S. *Nationality, Migration Rights and Citizenship of the Union.* Dordrecht: Nijhoff, 1995.

Hallstein, Walter. *Europe in the Making.* London: Allen and Unwin, 1972.

Hanrieder, Wolfram. *Germany, America, Europe: Forty Years of German Foreign Policy.* New Haven, CT: Yale University Press, 1989.

Harrop, Jeffrey. *Structural Funding and Employment in the European Union: Financing the Path to Integration.* London: Edward Elgar, 1996.

Hauf, K., and B. Soetendorp, eds. *Adapting to European Integration: Small States and the European Union.* London: Addison-Wesley, 1998.

Hayes-Renshaw, Fiona, and Helen Wallace. *The Council of Ministers.* New York: St. Martin's Press, 1996.

Heinelt, Hubert, and Randall Smith, eds. *Policy Networks and European Structural Funds.* Brookfield, VT: Avebury, 1996.

Hix, S., and C. Lord. *Political Parties in the European Union.* Basingstoke, UK: Macmillan, 1997.

Hogan, Michael. *The Marshall Plan: America, Britain and the Reconstruction of Western Europe, 1947–1952.* Cambridge: Cambridge University Press, 1987.

Holland, Martin. *Common Foreign and Security Policy: The Record and Reforms.* London: Pinter, 1997.

Hooghe, Liesbet, ed. *Cohesion Policy and European Integration: Building Multi-Level Governance.* Oxford: Oxford University Press, 1996.

————. *The European Commission and the Integration of Europe: Images of Governance.* Cambridge: Cambridge University Press, 2001.

Hooghe, Liesbet, and Gary Marks. *Multi-Level Governance and European Integration.* Lanham, MD: Rowman and Littlefield, 2001.

Howorth, Jolyon, and John T. S. Keeler. *Defending Europe: The EU, NATO and the Quest for European Autonomy.* Basingstoke, UK: Palgrave Macmillan 2003.

Hurwitz, Leon, and Christian Lequesne. *The State of the European Community: Policies, Institutions and Debates in the Transition Years.* Boulder, CO: Lynne Rienner, 1991.

Ingersent, K. A., A. J. Rayner, and R. C. Hine. *The Reform of the Common Agricultural Policy.* Basingstoke, UK: Macmillan, 1998.

Isaacson, Walter. *The Wise Men: Six Friends and the World They Made.* New York: Simon and Schuster, 1986.

Jacquemin, Alexis, and Lucio Pench. *Europe Competing in the Global Economy*. London: Edward Elgar, 1997.

Jans, Jan. *European Environmental Law*. London: Kluwer, 1995.

Jansen, Thomas. *The European People's Party: Origins and Development*. New York: St. Martin's Press, 1998.

Jenkins, Roy. *European Diary, 1977–1981*. London: Collins, 1989.

———. *A Life at the Centre*. London: Macmillan, 1991.

Jones, Erik. *The Politics and Economics of Monetary Union*. Lanham, MD: Rowman and Littlefield, 1999.

Jones, Robert A. *The Politics and Economics of the European Union: An Introductory Text*. London: Edward Elgar, 1996.

Jovanovic, Miroslav N. *European Economic Integration: Limits and Prospects*. London: Routledge, 1997.

Judge, David, and David Earnshaw. *The European Parliament*. Basingstoke, UK: Palgrave Macmillan, 2003.

Kaiser, Karl, et al. *The European Community: Progress or Decline?* London: Royal Institute of International Affairs, 1983.

Katz, Richard S., and Bernhard Wessels, eds. *The European Parliament, the National Parliaments, and European Integration*. Oxford: Oxford University Press, 1999.

Keating, Michael. *The New Regionalism in Western Europe: Territorial Restructuring and Regional Change*. London: Edward Elgar, 1998.

Kenen, Peter B. *Economic and Monetary Union in Europe: Moving Beyond Maastricht*. Cambridge: Cambridge University Press, 1995.

Keohane, Robert, and Stanley Hoffmann, eds. *The European Community: Decision-making and Institutional Change*. Boulder, CO: Westview Press, 1991.

Kolodziej, Edward. *French International Policy Under de Gaulle and Pompidou: The Politics of Grandeur*. Ithaca, NY: Cornell University Press, 1974.

Kreppel, Amie. *The European Parliament and Supranational Party System: A Study in Institutional Development*. Cambridge: Cambridge University Press, 2002.

Laffan, Brigid. *The Finances of the European Union*. Basingstoke, UK: Macmillan, 1997.

Lankowski, Carl, ed. *Germany and the European Community: Beyond Hegemony and Containment?* New York: St. Martin's Press, 1993.

Laurent, Pierre-Henri, and Marc Maresceau, eds. *The State of the European Union: Deepening and Widening*. Boulder, CO: Lynne Rienner, 1998.

Laursen, Finn. *The Ratification of the Maastricht Treaty: Issues, Debates, and Future Implications*. Maastricht: European Institute of Public Administration, 1994.

———, ed. *The Amsterdam Treaty: National Preference Formation, Interstate Bargaining, and Outcome*. Odense, Denmark: Odense University Press, 2002.

———, ed. *The Political Economy of European Integration*. The Hague: Kluwer, 1995.

Laursen, Finn, and Sophie Vanhoonacker, eds. *The Intergovernmental Conference on Political Union*. Maastricht: European Institute of Public Administration, 1992.

Lindberg, Leon. *The Political Dynamics of European Integration*. Palo Alto, CA: Stanford University Press, 1963.

Lindberg, Leon, and Stuart Scheingold. *Europe's Would-Be Polity*. Englewood Cliffs, NJ: Prentice-Hall, 1970.

Lipgens, Walter. *History of European Integration*. 2 vols. Oxford: Oxford University Press, 1981 and 1986.

Lodge, Juliet, ed. *The European Community and the Challenge of the Future*. London: Pinter, 1989.

Lord, Christopher. *Democracy in the European Union*. Sheffield, UK: Sheffield Academic Press, 1998.

Ludlow, Peter. *The Making of the European Monetary System: A Case Study in the Politics of the European Community*. London: Butterworths Scientific, 1982.

Luif, P. *On the Road to Brussels: The Political Dimension of Austria's, Finland's, and Sweden's Road to Accession to the European Union*. Vienna: Austrian Institute for International Affairs, 1995.

Majone, Giandomenico. *Regulating Europe*. London: Routledge, 1996.

Maresceau, Marc, ed. *Enlargement and the European Union: Relations Between the European Union and Central and Eastern Europe*. London: Longman, 1997.

Marjolin, Robert. *Architect of European Unity: Memoirs, 1911–1986*. London: Weidenfeld and Nicolson, 1989.

Marks, Gary, Fritz W. Scharpf, Philippe C. Schmitter, and Wolfgang Streeck. *Governance in the European Union*. Thousand Oaks, CA: Sage, 1996.

Maurer, Andreas, and Wolfgang Wessels, eds. *National Parliaments on Their Ways to Europe: Losers or Latecomers?* Baden-Baden, Germany: Nomos Verlag, 2001.

Mayes, David G., ed. *The Evolution of the Single European Market*. London: Edward Elgar, 1997.

Mayhew, Alan. *Recreating Europe: The European Union's Policy Towards Central and Eastern Europe*. 2nd ed. Cambridge: Cambridge University Press, 2002.

Mazey, S., and C. Rhodes. *The State of the European Union: Building a European Policy*. Boulder, CO: Lynne Rienner, 1996.

Mazzuchelli, Colette. *France and Germany at Maastricht: Politics and Negotiations to Create the European Union*. New York: Garland, 1997.

McCormick, John. *Environmental Policy in the European Union*. Basingstoke, UK: Palgrave Macmillan, 2001.

———. *The European Union: Politics and Policies*. Boulder, CO: Westview Press, 1996.

McDonagh, Bobby. *Original Sin in a Brave New World: The Paradox of Europe: An Account of the Negotiation of the Treaty of Amsterdam*. Dublin: Institute for European Affairs, 1998.

McGoldrick, Dominic. *International Relations Law of the European Union*. London: Longman, 1997.

McLeod, I., I. D. Hendry, and Stephen Hyett. *The External Relations of the European Communities*. Oxford: Oxford University Press, 1996.

McNamara, Kathleen R. *The Currency of Ideas: Monetary Policy in the European Union*. Ithaca, NY: Cornell University Press, 1998.

Meny, Yves, Pierre Muller, and Jean-Louis Quermone. *Adjusting to Europe: The Impact of the European Union on National Institutions and Policies*. London: Routledge, 1996.

Miall, Hugh, ed. *Redefining Europe: New Patterns of Conflict and Cooperation*. London: Pinter, 1994.

Miles, Lee, ed. *The European Union and the Nordic Countries*. New York: Routledge, 1996.

Milward, Alan. *The European Rescue of the Nation-State*. Berkeley: University of California Press, 1992.

———. *The Reconstruction of Western Europe*. London: Methuen, 1984.

Milward, Alan, F. Lynch, and R. Ranieri. *The Frontier of National Sovereignty: History and Theory, 1945–1992*. London: Routledge, 1993.

Monar, J., and Roger Morgan, eds. *The Third Pillar of the European Union: Cooperation in the Fields of Justice and Home Affairs*. Brussels: Interuniversity Press, 1994.

Monar, J., and W. Wessels, eds. *The European Union After the Treaty of Amsterdam.* London: Continuum, 2001.

Monnet, Jean. *Memoirs.* Garden City, NY: Doubleday, 1978.

Moravcsik, Andrew. *The Choice for Europe: Social Progress and State Power from Messina to Maastricht.* Ithaca, NY: Cornell University Press, 1998.

Mullard, Maurice, and Simon Lee, eds. *The Politics of Social Policy in Europe.* London: Edward Elgar, 1997.

Neal, Larry, and Daniel Barbezat. *The Economics of the European Union and the Economies of Europe.* Oxford: Oxford University Press, 1998.

Neill, Patrick. *The European Court of Justice: A Case Study in Judicial Activism.* London: European Policy Forum, 1995.

Nelsen, Brent F., and Alexander C.-G. Stubb, eds. *The European Union: Readings on the Theory and Practice of European Integration.* 3rd ed. Boulder, CO: Lynne Rienner, and Basingstoke, UK: Palgrave Macmillan, 2003.

Newhouse, John. *Europe Adrift.* New York: Pantheon, 1997.

Newman, Michael. *Democracy, Sovereignty, and the European Union.* New York: St. Martin's Press, 1996.

Nicholson, Frances, and Roger East. *From the Six to the Twelve: The Enlargement of the European Communities.* Chicago: St. James Press, 1987.

Nicolaides, Phedon, ed. *Industrial Policy in the European Community: A Necessary Response to European Integration?* Maastricht: European Institute of Public Administration, 1993.

Nicoll, William, and Trevor C. Salmon. *Building European Union: A Documentary History and Analysis.* Manchester, UK: Manchester University Press, 1997.

Norton, Philip, ed. *National Parliaments and the European Union.* London: Frank Cass, 1996.

Nugent, Neill. *The European Commission.* Basingstoke, UK: Palgrave Macmillan, 2001.

———. *European Union Enlargement.* Basingstoke, UK: Palgrave Macmillan, 2004.

———. *The Government and Politics of the European Union.* 5th ed. Basingstoke, UK: Palgrave Macmillan, and Raleigh, NC: Duke University Press, 2003.

———, ed. *At the Heart of the Union: Studies of the European Commission.* 2nd ed. Basingstoke, UK: Palgrave Macmillan, 2001.

Nuttall, Simon J. *European Foreign Policy.* Oxford: Oxford University Press, 2000.

Occhipinti, John. *The Politics of EU Police Cooperation: Toward a European FBI?* Boulder, CO: Lynne Rienner, 2003.

Ovendale, Richard. *Foreign Policy of the British Labour Government, 1945–1951.* London: Pinter, 1984.

Overturf, Stephen F. *Money and European Union.* New York: St. Martin's Press, 1997.

Pappas, Spyros, and Sophie Vanhoonacker, eds. *The European Union's Common Foreign and Security Policy: The Challenges of the Future.* Maastricht: European Institute of Public Administration, 1996.

Paraskevopoulos, Christos C. *European Union at the Crossroads: A Critical Analysis of Monetary Union and Enlargement.* London: Edward Elgar, 1998.

Paraskevopoulos, Christos C., Ricardo Grinspun, and Theodore Georgakopoulos, eds. *Economic Integration and Public Policy in the European Union.* London: Edward Elgar, 1996.

Pelkmans, Jacques. *European Integration: Methods and Economic Analysis.* London: Longman, 1997.

Peterson, John, and Helen Sjursen. *Common Foreign Policy for Europe? Competing Visions of the CFSP.* London: Routledge, 1998.

Piening, Christopher. *Global Europe: The European Union in World Affairs*. Boulder, CO: Lynne Rienner, 1997.

Pinder, John. *European Community: The Building of a Union*. Oxford: Oxford University Press, 1991.

———. *The European Community and Eastern Europe*. London: Royal Institute of International Affairs, 1991.

Pitchford, Ruth, and Adam Cox, eds. *EMU Explained: Markets and Monetary Union*. London: Reuters, 1997.

Poidevin, Raymond. *Robert Schuman: Homme d'Etat, 1866–1963*. Paris: Imprimerie Nationale, 1986.

Preston, Christopher. *Enlargement and Integration in the European Union*. London: Routledge, 1997.

Pryce, Roy, ed. *The Dynamics of European Union*. London: Croom Helm, 1987.

Redmond, John, ed. *The 1995 Enlargement of the European Union*. Aldershot, UK: Ashgate, 1997.

Redmond, John, and Glenda G. Rosenthal, eds. *The Expanding European Union: Past, Present, and Future*. Boulder, CO: Lynne Rienner, 1997.

Regelsberger, Elfride, Philippe de Schoutheete, and Wolfgang Wessels. *Foreign Policy of the European Union: From EPC to CFSP and Beyond*. Boulder, CO: Lynne Rienner, 1997.

Rhodes, Carolyn, ed. *The European Union in the World Community*. Boulder, CO: Lynne Rienner, 1998.

Richardson, Jeremy, ed. *European Union: Power and Policy-Making*. London: Routledge, 1996.

Rosamond, Ben. *Theories of European Integration*. Basingstoke, Palgrave, 2000.

Roseman, Mark. *Recasting the Ruhr, 1945–1958: Manpower, Economic Recovery, and Labor Relations*. New York: Berg, 1992.

Ross, George. *Jacques Delors and European Integration*. Oxford: Oxford University Press, 1995.

Rudden, Bernard. *Basic Community Law*. Oxford: Clarendon Press, 1996.

Sauter, Wolf. *Competition Law and Industrial Policy in the European Union*. Oxford: Clarendon Press, 1998.

Sbragia, Alberta M., ed. *Europolitics: Institutions and Policymaking in the "New" European Community*. Washington, DC: Brookings Institution, 1992.

Schmidtchen, Dieter, and Robert Cooter, eds. *Constitutional Law and Economics of the European Union*. London: Edward Elgar, 1997.

Schmitt, Herman, and Jacques Thomassen, eds. *Political Representation and Legitimacy in the European Union*. Oxford: Oxford University Press, 1998.

Scobie, H. M., and Homa Motamen-Scobie, eds. *European Monetary Union: The Way Forward*. London: Routledge, 1998.

Serfary, Simon, ed. *The Finality Debate and Its National Dimensions*. Washington, DC: CSIS Press, 2002.

Simonian, Haig. *The Privileged Partnership: Franco-German Relations in the European Community, 1969–1984*. Oxford: Clarendon Press, 1985.

Smith, Brendan P. G. *Constitution Building in the European Union: The Process of Treaty Reform*. The Hague: Kluwer Law International, 2002.

Smith, Karen Elizabeth. *The Making of European Union Foreign Policy*. New York: St. Martin's Press, 1998.

Smith, Michael, and Brian Hocking. *Beyond Foreign Economic Policy: The United States, the Single European Market, and the Changing World Economy*. London: Pinter, 1997.

Soveroski, Marie, ed. *Agenda 2000: An Appraisal of the Commission's Blueprint for Enlargement*. Maastricht: European Institute of Public Administration, 1997.

Springer, Beverly. *The Social Dimension of 1992*. New York: Praeger, 1992.

Stavridis, Stelios, and Roger Morgan. *New Challenges to the European Union: Policies and Policy Making*. Brookfield, VT: Ashgate, 1997.

Stevens, A., with H. Stevens. *Brussels Bureaucrats? The Administration of the European Union*. Basingstoke, UK: Palgrave Macmillan, 2001.

Stirk, Peter. *European Unity in Context: The Interwar Period*. London: Pinter, 1989.

Svensson, Anna-Carin. *In the Service of the European Union: The Role of the Presidency in Negotiating the Amsterdam Treaty, 1995–1997*. Uppsala, Sweden: Acta Universitatis, 2000.

Swann, Dennis. *European Economic Integration: The Common Market, European Union, and Beyond*. London: Edward Elgar, 1996.

Symes, Valerie, Carl Levy, and Jane Littlewood. *The Future of Europe: Problems and Issues for the Twenty-First Century*. Basingstoke, UK: Macmillan, 1997.

Taylor, Paul. *The European Union in the 1990s*. Oxford: Oxford University Press, 1996.

———. *The Limits of European Integration*. London: Croom Helm, 1983.

Temperton, Paul, ed. *The Euro*. New York: John Wiley, 1997.

Thatcher, Margaret. *The Downing Street Years*. New York: HarperCollins, 1993.

Thody, Philip. *An Historical Introduction to the European Union*. London: Routledge, 1998.

Tiersky, Ronald. *Europe Today: National Politics, European Integration, and European Security*. Lanham, MD: Rowman and Littlefield, 1999.

Tsoukalis, Loukas. *The New European Economy Revisited: The Politics and Economics of Integration*. 3rd ed. Oxford: Oxford University Press, 1977.

———. *The Politics and Economics of European Monetary Integration*. London: Allen and Unwin, 1977.

———. *What Kind of Europe?* Updated ed. Oxford: Oxford University Press, 2005.

Ungerer, Horst. *A Concise History of European Monetary Integration: From EPU to EMU*. Westport, CT: Greenwood Press, 1997.

Van der Eijk, Cees, and Mark N. Franklin, eds. *Choosing Europe? The European Electorate and National Politics in the Face of Union*. Ann Arbor: University of Michigan Press, 1996.

Van Dijck, Pitou, and Gerrit Faber, eds. *The External Economic Dimension of the European Union*. The Hague: Kluwer, 1998.

Van Oudenaren, John. *Uniting Europe: European Integration and the Post–Cold War World*. 2nd ed. Lanham, MD: Rowman and Littlefield, 2005.

Van Tartwijk-Novey, Louise B., and Christopher Mark. *The European House of Cards: Towards a United States of Europe?* New York: St. Martin's Press, 1995.

von der Groeben, Hans. *The European Community: The Formative Years: The Struggle to Establish the Common Market and the Political Union (1958–66)*. European Perspectives Series. Luxembourg: Office for Official Publications of the European Communities, 1985.

Wallace, Helen, and William Wallace, eds. *Policy-Making in the European Union*. 5th ed. Oxford: Oxford University Press, 2005.

Wallace, William. *The Transformation of Western Europe*. London: Royal Institute of International Affairs, 1990.

Watson, Alison. *Aspects of European Integration: The Politics of Convergence*. New York: St. Martin's Press, 1998.

Weidenfeld, Werner, and Wolfgang Wessels. *Europe from A to Z: Guide to European Integration*. Luxembourg: Office for Official Publications of the European Communities, 1997.

Weiler, J. H. H., Iain Begg, and John Peterson, eds. *Integration in an Expanding European Union: Reassessing the Fundamentals*. Oxford: Blackwell, 2003.

Welsh, Michael. *Europe United? The European Union and the Retreat from Federalism*. New York: St. Martin's Press, 1996.

Werts, Jan. *The European Council*. Amsterdam: North-Holland, 1992.

Westlake, Martin. *The Commission and the Parliament: Partners and Rivals in the European Policy-Making System*. London: Butterworth, 1994.

———. *The Council of the European Union*. London: Catermill, 1995.

———. *A Modern Guide to the European Parliament*. London: Pinter, 1994.

Wexler, Imanuel. *The Marshall Plan Revisited: The European Recovery Program in Economic Perspective*. Westport, CT: Greenwood Press, 1983.

Whitman, Richard G. *From Civilian Power to Superpower? The International Identity of the European Union*. New York: St. Martin's Press, 1998.

Williams, Allan M. *The European Community: The Contradictions of Integration*. 2nd ed. Oxford: Blackwell, 1994.

Wood, David M., and Birol Yesilada. *The Emerging European Union*. White Plains, NY: Longman, 1996.

Wyllie, James H. *European Security in the New Political Environment*. London: Longman, 1997.

Index

About the Book

Accessible, engaging, and completely up-to-date, *Ever Closer Union* clearly explains the complexities of European integration from the 1950s to the present.

This new edition retains the familiar three-part structure—history, institutions, and policies—but incorporates expanded coverage of both enlargement issues and constitutional change. New policy and institutional developments are thoroughly explored, and an entirely new chapter examines the decisionmaking dynamics among the Commission, Council, and Parliament.

The completely revised chapter on the complicated EU-U.S. relationship includes discussions of the Bush administration's worldview, the broad repercussions of the terrorist attacks in the United States and Spain, and the ongoing fallout from the war in Iraq.

Desmond Dinan is Jean Monnet Professor of Public Policy at George Mason University.